Jim abt
10-5-13

Get threshhold of Hell
Albert B

Hellious y the Deep
Robert Grannon

They Never Surrendered
Jesus Vallamor

Critique
Australian Lt Stant Holland

The Japanese Merchant Marine in WW-2
Mark Parillo

U.S. Submarine Attacks y WWII
Com. John D Alden

Find 'Em, Chase 'Em, Sink 'Em

• • • • • •

Find 'Em, Chase 'Em, Sink 'Em

The Mysterious Loss
of the WWII Submarine
USS *Gudgeon*

■ ■ ■ ■ ■ ■

Mike Ostlund

THE LYONS PRESS
Guilford, Connecticut
An imprint of The Globe Pequot Press

To buy books in quantity for corporate use
or incentives, call **(800) 962–0973, ext. 4551,**
or e-mail **premiums@GlobePequot.com.**

The Lyons Press is an imprint of The Globe Pequot Press.

10 9 8 7 6 5 4 3 2 1

Printed in the United States of America

ISBN-13: 978-1-59228-862-5
ISBN-10: 1-59228-862-6

Library of Congress Cataloging-in-Publication Data is available on file.

To the men who fought on *Gudgeon*

For Bill

"Find 'Em, Chase 'Em, Sink 'Em"

USS *Gudgeon* motto

▪ Contents ▪

▪ Foreword ▪

When Mike Ostlund contacted me about two years ago inquiring about my experiences aboard the *Gudgeon*, SS-211, during the six war patrols I made aboard her, I was a little dubious as to his intent. I had read so many self-aggrandizing books by submarine "heroes" that one chapter told me all about the gist, the meat, the subject matter, of the story and I knew it was a duplication of the many books that had preceded it. There would be reams written about one individual, 99 percent of the time the captain, and hardly a word about the motor machinist mates, the electrician mates, the quartermasters, without whom the boat would never have got to her patrol area. Then there was the torpedomen whose responsibility was the weapon, without which there would be no reason to even be on the patrol, and many more rates, all imperative for the success of the mission.

I was also near nausea every time I saw a submarine movie, becoming a firm believer that whomever had been the advisor on the movie filming most assuredly didn't know the intelligence level of the enlisted personnel, nor had he made a war patrol, particularly aboard the *Gudgeon*. We also had junior officers who when designated as heads of different departments had to learn the job from the people they were going to supervise. Once in awhile the gunnery officer, or the engineering officer, would be recognized for the performance of his department, but it was rare indeed that the men who had taught them the job, and did the performing, ever received any accolades. Somehow in the endeavor to make heroes, those that concocted the hero forgot the details of the people who made it all possible. Submarine operation was entirely teamwork, and everyone was essential for the operation to be a success. As the reader progresses into the factual operation of the *Gudgeon*, he will understand why a defeated Japanese admiral in Yokohama told me personally, "The greatest mistake of our attack on Pearl Harbor was not sinking your submarines. They killed us."

While attending a reunion of World War II sub vets accompanied by two shipmates, Irvin "Moose" Hornkohl and Ray "Guts" Foster, I had the distinct pleasure of meeting the aspiring author Mike Ostlund. We found that he had lost an uncle, Lt. Jr. Grade Bill Ostlund when the *Gudgeon* met her demise in 1944. Mike had gone to great length in his search for information, any information, pictures, documents, letters, and personal interviews to get a true picture of the type of people that served with, and are entombed with, his Uncle Bill. He had read the now-unclassified patrol reports, as we had, that were submitted by the captain to the squadron commander, thence to ComSubPac after every patrol for evaluation. The reports do not tell the real story. Their reports were often self-serving and lacked key details about others aboard the *Gudgeon* who participated in the success or failure of the patrol. Mike pointed out something that we had been aware of since we graduated from boot camp, but it was amusing that he, a civilian, could see the debasement of those who made the submarine a fighting machine. "How is it that one man can be classified as a hero when 74–80 men participated in the incident that is classified as heroic?" Mike wanted to know.

HE WANTED AUTHENTICITY, and the only credible source was the men who had been there, knew exactly what happened, and were ready to affirm what was not in the reports submitted by the commanding officer. There were instances where either an enlisted man or a junior officer was instrumental in saving the boat and the lives of all aboard, but whose actions went unreported. To refute the patrol report would be like cutting one's throat. They had no recourse, neither had the enlisted personnel. And if the powers that be decided that the patrol deserved a Navy Cross, one would think the captain would thank the crew for their assistance in his getting the award. This rarely happened. "Guts" Foster would put it succinctly, "We got them one hell of a lot of Navy Crosses."

Another sore spot was in how medals were distributed. These honors were rarely awarded to the lackeys who deserved it. Ron Schooley, for example, a gunner's mate striker, once spotted the largest troop transport in the Japanese merchant marine while on lookout one night, reported it to the officer-of-the-deck, who in turn reported it to the captain. We sank the transport and the officer-of-the-deck got the Navy and Marine Corp medal, while Ron got promoted to third class torpedoman, a rate for which he had already passed the exam. During another run where we sank two transports, a cook got the Navy and Marine Corp medal because he baked the captain's favorite cookies. So much for heroes and medals.

What I felt when I entered Pearl Harbor, aboard the SS-210, the new submarine *Grenadier*, a short time after the attack, and viewed the still smoking remnants of our fleet was not defeat, but an unadulterated hatred for the people who had perpetrated this vile deed. I am pretty certain this feeling was shared 100% among the crew, for we were practically all prewar submariners. Our job was to hold the line until our ships were repaired, replaced, and replenished. I didn't get the opportunity aboard the *Grenadier*. But, fortunately I became a member of the *Gudgeon*, the first submarine to make a patrol off Japan, sink a man-of-war, and go on to achieve an incredible number of sinkings. There are many men who have raised a family and lived a long life because of the thousands of Japanese troops that we killed before they could get a chance to kill our men on the beaches. *Gudgeon* and many others did the job and more. We called her "The Queen" because she was definitely majestic.

I was sold on helping Mike Ostlund write this historical narrative. His desire for authenticity had led him to search tirelessly through the Japanese archives of ships sunk by all military sources and to discover where *Gudgeon* was lost, facts that had remained mysterious to the military until now. He was also able to almost pinpoint the position where it occurred. This information has been given to a sea-searching company that may use it in the near future to find *Gudgeon*.

Mike's desire was to be thorough, making countless interviews and sifting through thousands of pages of documentary evidence. Those of us who offered our stories as part of this historical epitaph to the *Gudgeon* and the real heroes who were lost on her seek nothing but the opportunity to have the truth known and recorded in history. Our sole reward is to see the real story of submariners told in its entirety. We feel society owes us this much.

Quentin Russell "George" Seiler
Torpedoman USS *Gudgeon*
Mesa, Arizona – August 2003

"We shall never forget that it was our submarines that held the lines against the enemy while our fleets replaced losses and repaired wounds."

Fleet Admiral Chester Nimitz, USN

▪ Preface ▪

The USS *Gudgeon*'s story during World War II is one of unclaimed gallantry, historic achievement, professional excellence, tremendous sacrifice, and a key component to Allied victory against the Japanese. And yet, *Gudgeon*'s legacy is marred by her mysterious disappearance and her present state of obscurity.

Those who study the great U.S. submarines of World War II's Pacific fleet are familiar with the epic combat exploits of *Tang*, *Wahoo*, *Trigger*, and many others, yet no book has been written about the USS *Gudgeon* (pronounced "*guj'n*"), one of the war's most formidable undersea warriors.

An article carried by the Associated Press in January 1944, after *Gudgeon* was awarded a prestigious Presidential Unit Citation (PUC) for her "remarkable record," said that *Gudgeon* "has written a sensational record— a story of ship sinkings and damagings so large the navy is keeping the figures secret. . . . When the navy eventually lifts the veil surrounding the exploits of the sub one of the war's most astounding stories will be released." With this book, *Gudgeon* is getting her due—sixty years after the fact.

This is *Gudgeon*'s story, from her prewar voyages to her enigmatic disappearance in April 1944. It is the story of the valiant sailors who manned her and officers who commanded her. *Gudgeon*'s eleven war patrol reports, signed by her first four skippers, have been indispensable in the writing of this book. These reports were typed on an old manual typewriter by the boat's yeoman in a tiny compartment on *Gudgeon*, then approved and signed by the skipper. Because *Gudgeon* disappeared without a trace in early 1944, there is no twelfth war patrol report to tell of *Gudgeon*'s final days. I have also drawn from material contained in books on submarine warfare and other histories, interviews with family members of former submariners and from seven surviving submariners, long forgotten personal logs and diaries, and the official wartime records of the Imperial Japanese

Navy. Included is a collection of historic *Gudgeon* photos. These have been culled from the private family collections of the many relatives of *Gudgeon* sailors who died, and from those surviving submariners who allowed their precious photos to be used.

This is also the story of my paternal uncle, Lieutenant (jg) William C. Ostlund, who perished along with 78 other men on *Gudgeon*'s twelfth war patrol. For over half a century, the submarine's epitaph, "Overdue and presumed lost," was all that was known with any certainty about the death of the men on *Gudgeon*. Chapter 12 details original research into the loss of *Gudgeon*, shedding considerable light on the circumstances of *Gudgeon*'s demise.

Since I did not fight the war aboard *Gudgeon*, much effort has been made to cross-check the written source material in the text with the interview material and other sources in order to make as certain as possible that the only book written about the uss *Gudgeon,* and the men who sailed her, is accurate. In so doing, the rare account offered by a *Gudgeon* submariner that might seem inconsistent with other documents or the eyewitness statements of others was not used. Some interesting but ambiguous material has been left aside in order to improve the accuracy of the book.

The author acknowledges the possibility of errors in this account. Four former *Gudgeon* submariners, men who lived through these harrowing events, have completed technical reviews of the book so that *Find 'Em, Chase 'Em, Sink 'Em* is as true to the events and to World War II submarining as possible. Any errors which remain are sincerely regretted.

Interviews with surviving members of the *Gudgeon* have proved an invaluable asset in the writing of this book. It is my firm belief that these tough old veterans, these honorable men, understood that this book is likely going to be the only testament of their service to the United States during the war.

Despite the horrors of the war, most of them pinpoint their time on *Gudgeon* as the greatest days of their life. These men went through it all. They continually saw each other at their rawest, their most vulnerable, and their worst, when even the slightest noise, such as a dropped wrench during silent running, could have meant the end of their lives. At the same time, they saw each other at their best, each acting with extreme courage and selflessness under fire. To the sailors, they were just doing their duty. "Courage" is a word that they eschew just as they reject the words "hero" and "bravery" to describe their actions during the war. They know that because other men "just did their duty" under fire that they owe their very lives to those comrades, living and dead, who accompanied them on those most critical days, the days that the USS *Gudgeon* and other submarines patrolled the waters in and around Japan in search of prey.

My family, the Ostlund family of Webster City, Iowa, had no idea what had happened to Bill Ostlund, oldest brother of John and my father Bob. Not until my twin brother Chris stumbled across a notation in a book on World War II submarines at a garage sale in 1996 was it even conceivable that *Gudgeon*'s true fate could be determined. The book said that it might have been *Gudgeon* that was sunk 166 miles off "Yuoh" Island. The sinking was still a mystery because, as the Navy concluded, there is no island in the Pacific named Yuoh Island, nor one that even *sounds* like Yuoh Island. *Gudgeon*'s loss remained unexplained. But Chris's discovery of this garage sale kid's book was the beginning of my quest for the truth about the uncle I never knew: Uncle Bill.

And, that is where the story begins.

▪ Introduction ▪

The stories of the men who sailed and fought on *Gudgeon* were not altogether unlike the stories of other Depression-era submariners who comprised "The Greatest Generation." Yet *Gudgeon*'s story is full of unique challenges and first-time heroics that set it apart from the others. At one time, the USS *Gudgeon* (SS-211) was the only United States submarine to have undertaken a trans-Pacific war patrol, finally settling off the southeast tip of Japan, surrounded on all sides, and above, by the Imperial Japanese Navy.

The enlisted men who served aboard the pre-World War II ships had their own stories of why they chose to serve in the Navy. The *Gudgeon* submariners, who contributed their memories so that this book would be a complete story of *Gudgeon*'s wartime experiences, had one quality in common with other Navy regulars: they chose to be in the Navy. They were not drafted. They did not join because of a desire to kill the Japanese, nor did anti-Japanese sentiment necessarily play a role. They did not join because they wanted to use the G.I. bill to build their careers after their service; the G.I. bill did not even exist when these sailors enlisted. These sailors were not, as a whole, very well-educated or well-to-do. Yet, these young men were able to look beyond the desolate economic times and personal family circumstances to a career in the Navy for which they were well-suited, a career to which they brought determination and courage.

These men were children of the Great Depression. They came from working-class families and were often destitute. They were men who were desperate for a path in life and a way to traverse that path. They were searching for a way to relieve their families of the burdens that their needs presented; a means to take care of themselves and to be men. The early war submariners were highly trained professionals. They were specialists, yet capable of performing all of the jobs on a submarine. The submarines of the day were engineering marvels, though many of the functions required manual operation. Knowing all of the systems and being able to operate them in combat was an exacting challenge.

Although they shared the experiences of the Depression, *Gudgeon*'s skippers tended to be more privileged socially and economically, and many of the early war officers were Naval Academy graduates. Some of the *Gudgeon* skippers had been raised in families with long military backgrounds and traditions. Their family histories are replete with wartime exploits of heroism, including one Congressional Medal of Honor winner, and involvement in historic events from the early days of the American Revolution through World War I. On occasion, the histories created overwhelming pressure to seek military careers and, if war beckoned, to perform in the manner of their illustrious forbears. Those men did not disappoint. All five were heavily decorated wartime officers. Three would become admirals; a fourth would become a signatory on the Japanese surrender papers. The fifth, Lieutenant Commander Robert Alexander Bonin, was lost on *Gudgeon*'s fateful twelfth patrol before he would have the opportunity to carve out a distinguished military career as a submarine commander.

The officers and crew alike were members of the Navy's elite submarine service, all of whom were commonly regarded as the "cream of the crop" in the United States Navy. They were teachers, farmers, industrial workers, merchants, lawyers, laborers, miners, or in the case of Bill Ostlund, the operator of a farm implements business in sleepy, fertile Webster City, Iowa.

All of these men, whether they were regular Navy forces or reserves, were capable of performing their wartime specialties under the most trying circumstances, circumstances which many are only now coming to understand and appreciate. They were profoundly brave men who could, after fifty days trapped in the tiny confines of a submarine, endure a ten-hour barrage of depth charges, keep their wits, and perform their duties, day after day, patrol after patrol. For two and a half years, *Gudgeon* fought with unrelenting valor, tenaciously seeking the enemy despite the perils. *Gudgeon*'s men steadfastly and faithfully performed their duty. In doing so, they made Japan pay dearly for her aggression at Pearl Harbor in December 1941.

Until now, accounts of the fate of *Gudgeon* on her final patrol have been by necessity largely guesswork because the facts of the sinking went down with the boat. No one knew anything for certain, though as it would turn out, there were a few theories floating around. What was known was that *Gudgeon* failed to return from patrol and was never heard from again.

Part I

· · · · · ·

Gudgeon at War

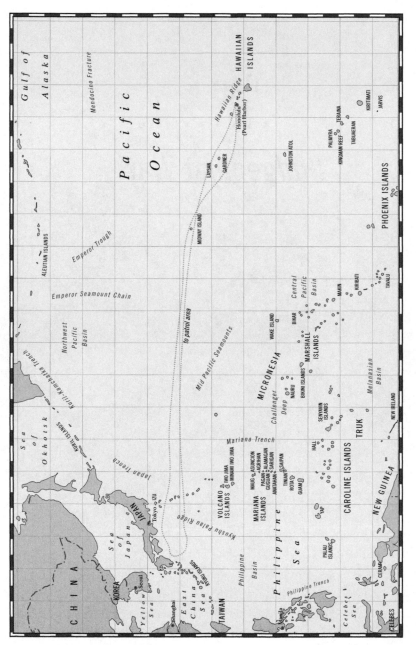

First War Patrol • Approximate Course • Dec. 11, 1941–Jan. 31, 1942

▪ 1 ▪
Lone Wolf

The merit belongs to the beginner
should his successor do even better.

Egyptian proverb

Early in the morning of December 7, 1941, on one of those dazzlingly beautiful days in Hawaii, a hung-over Irvin W. Hornkohl of the battleship USS *Oklahoma** rolled out of his bunk in the submarine base barracks. He was not on his ship much these days because he had been sent to mine school ashore. The training seemed to be taking on added importance as the Japanese made increasingly menacing diplomatic and military moves. There had been a sense of tension on the base for some time.

On this sunny morning, nursing the ills of the prior night and eating a little breakfast was front and center for Seaman Hornkohl. He was lucky and he knew it. Where else on the planet could you work off a hangover more easily than in this place, Pearl Harbor? In a sense, it was difficult to feel bad at all on this lovely tropical island. By the time he reached the mess hall located behind the submarine base's swimming pool, it was nearly 8 A.M. As he was sitting down, the usual banter between the men was interrupted by "ratatattat ratatattat" sounds outside the barrack windows.[1] He hurried outside to see what the ruckus was all about and saw two menacing big red balls on the undersides of the wings of four Japanese fighters soaring not even

---

* Unless otherwise noted it may be assumed that all American vessels are submarines.

fifty feet overhead. As he watched in uncomprehending astonishment, the fighters chewed their way past the barracks and worked toward the submarine base. Before reaching battleship alley the invaders turned quickly, nose down, and began strafing Hornkohl and the other sailors looking on in stunned amazement.

After a moment of frozen disbelief, the men realized that war had come to Pearl Harbor. It was time to fight. No more training. The men raced toward the armory to get their hands on a weapon—a machine gun, pistol, any weapon—before the bombers made it to Battleship Row. If they made it, it would be a catastrophe. As Hornkohl raced to the fight, he was witnessing the progression of a war that had involved many countries on several continents but had now developed into what would become the most destructive war in the history of mankind.

Within a few seconds, torpedo bombers joined the Zeros and were strafing anything that moved in and around the big ships. From his location near the armory Hornkohl said he could have "thrown a rock and hit Ford Island" where the battleships were gently rocking, passive and bloated.[2] A sailor quickly knocked off the lock on the armory. Hornkohl, still dressed in his Navy whites, grabbed a Springfield rifle and two bandoleers of ammunition and sprinted frantically toward the submarine base. He opened fire in a futile attempt to deflect the violent attack on what had been a peaceful, quiet Sunday. Some of the men around him were shooting Lewis machine guns. The men on board *Tautog* were manning the water-cooled machine guns on the moored submarine. The noise and chaos overpowered paradise and turned it into hell.

Irvin Hornkohl recalled the incident vividly: "I was squeezing them off, trying to knock the suckers out of the air." Hornkohl watched as a Japanese pilot roared toward him in his plane. "He was really intent on what he was doing. He did not look left or right. I could almost see his eyeballs." The attacking planes were so close to each other "it's a wonder they weren't knocking each other's wings off. That's how close they were flying to each other." From his vantage point, Hornkohl watched as a bomb dropped through one of *Arizona*'s stacks. "It seemed like it was minutes, but all of a sudden this big rumbling and big sheet of flames came out of the *Arizona* and she went to the bottom with all those guys aboard." When the *Oklahoma* went under he lost "four or five hundred" shipmates, including many of his good friends from the Third Division.[3] In fact, the Third Division was virtually wiped out when the massive ship exploded and rolled over on her side, trapping those who survived the bombs. This would be the first time while in uniform that the truly fortunate Seaman Second Class Irvin W. Hornkohl would survive solely on the luck of the draw. If he had been slated to receive his mine training later, he would almost certainly have died on December 7, 1941. By 10 A.M., Hornkohl was a sailor very sorely in need of a ship.

Not far from where Hornkohl was firing at the overwhelming Japanese forces, Signalman Arthur C. Barlow was atop the signal tower at the submarine base. It had been a strange day for the now wide-awake Barlow, who had his sleep interrupted when the first bomb fell. At first, Barlow thought that a work crew had gotten an unusually early start blasting to install underground oil tanks. Barlow rolled over for more rest, telling the sailor in the next bunk, "They ought to knock that off, one of these days that will really happen," meaning of course, that the workers, with their continual dynamiting had created an atmosphere of indifference to such explosions around the island.[4] Before he could close his eyes again, he heard more bombs *and* planes, and then he knew. With this realization, he threw on his uniform and scurried to the tower to communicate with the ships in the harbor. He did not fire a weapon at the invaders, commenting, "You don't need a gun to signal," so signal away he did.[5] Barlow and the other signalmen were crammed into the ten-by-ten signal tower high above the carnage below. The signalmen could only watch as the men on *Tautog* lit up the skies like a Roman candle. A few feet away, Irvin Hornkohl continued to fire frenetically at the Japanese.

With each pass of the planes streaking by, the bombs, the chaos, sailors and civilians running to and fro, much of the Pacific Fleet was being destroyed. The entire catastrophe was displayed in panoramic view at the feet of Arthur C. Barlow as he and the other signalmen frantically flashed codes with a light and ran the signal flags up and down a mast. The scene was awesome and appalling at the same time. Although the attack itself lasted a couple of hours, it seemed to Barlow as though it was over in five minutes. From his perch, he was hardly safe. When the attack was over, the signalmen picked up five buckets of shrapnel from the roof. Miraculously the shells fell all around them but did not kill or injure any of the men. Barlow would soon realize that the only good thing that had happened all day was that the Japanese military planners had withdrawn without a final attack to finish the job. Barlow said of the now very poorly defended island, "They really dropped the ball. They would have really clobbered us."[6]

That night Art Barlow and one of the chiefs set up a couple of bunks at the signal tower to run a "two man on, two man off" shift.[7] Barlow and his new roommate went to get some rest, but neither man was able to fall asleep, so they returned to the top of the tower to relieve the two men who had drawn duty. Before long, the other men returned from the makeshift barracks, also unable to fall asleep, and the four men sat there all night on duty, searching for the Japanese and signaling as needed. No doubt their thoughts were on everything important to them that night—their families, their lovers, the men they had known who had likely died in the carnage that still burned below them. But thoughts about the now-hated Japanese were foremost. Could they be defeated? Would they be defeated? They probably wondered where they would be in the upcoming years. Would they survive, or would they too soon be lying dead, just another corpse in what would surely be a long bitter fight with a determined and ruthless enemy?

Throughout the entire air raid, throughout the devastation that played out below him, Barlow had not gotten a shot off, yet this was not his role. He could take solace, knowing that he had performed his duty under fire. Like a maestro leading a huge orchestra of mayhem from high atop his perch, he had signaled with his flags, desperately trying to communicate with the fleet. The fires in the harbor continued to blaze. Men worked frantically to try to save those trapped in the ships. The smell of burned flesh filled the air.

On the morning of the attack at Pearl Harbor, a little further south and east off the island of Maui at Lahaina Roads, a weary submarine crew and Navy planes were practicing for war. The USS *Gudgeon*'s shakedown cruise progressed toward the day's next drill, being the all-important dive. At 8:05 A.M., December 7, 1941, *Gudgeon* was cruising on the surface waiting for the Catalina-type seaplanes to practice communications. At that same moment Radioman First Class John Sheridan Jr. received a "Very Urgent" plain language message: AIR RAIDS ON PEARL HARBOR, THIS IS NOT DRILL. Sheridan, a former bellhop from Providence, Rhode Island, hurriedly handed the message to the communications officer, Ensign Sigmund A. Bobczynski, who in turn gave it to Lieutenant Commander Elton W. "Joe" Grenfell, *Gudgeon*'s skipper. Grenfell read the note. He found it impossible to believe until he heard the boat's radio from Hawaii describing the attack. He had been fully aware that war was becoming more and more likely as 1942 approached. But now *Gudgeon*, his boat, was at war. It was sobering to realize that he was now responsible for the lives of more than sixty men on board. Grenfell ordered that *Gudgeon* dive and remain submerged while awaiting orders. Before long *Gudgeon* was ordered to stay below and remain far away from Pearl Harbor. Grenfell realized that if the ship surfaced, the chances of being attacked by a spooked U.S. flyer were about equal to being attacked by a Japanese bomber.

War had arrived and everybody on *Gudgeon* knew it. These were highly trained Navy men who underwent rigorous physical and psychological evaluation in order to even *attend* the demanding instruction at New London, Connecticut, home of the Navy's submarine school. Passing was even tougher. The United States submariner was the best of the best as far as the Navy was concerned. Torpedoman First Class, Raymond F. Foster of Ukiah, California, a small city nestled between Mendocino National Forest and the Pacific Ocean said years later that after notification of the attack, there was not a sign or hint of nervousness or apprehension among any of the men. The after torpedo room workbook for December 7 reflected this toughness and professionalism. A *Gudgeon* torpedoman wrote: "got all 8 torps fully ready for war shots (War Declared)."[8]

A few hours later in Vallejo, California, an excited and expectant Eleanor King Loughlin Farrell was whiling the time away, wishing desperately that she could just snap her fingers and make it be December 13. That was the day that the newly commissioned USS *Gudgeon* would return and she would be reunited with her beloved husband, Lieutenant Richard M. "Dixie" Farrell, *Gudgeon*'s engineering officer. Mrs. Farrell was listening to the radio, while tending to her nine-month-old daughter, Jo Ann, when an "absurd" radio report came across the waves.[9] She could not believe that someone was putting out all this "false stuff" about a Japanese attack at Pearl Harbor.[10] That was ridiculous. That was where Dixie and *Gudgeon* were. It could not be. It could not be.

In order to put the rumors to rest, she called her best friend, Joan Nimitz. "Joanie" was married to Chester Nimitz Jr., a naval officer and submariner, and had not heard of the events in Hawaii. When informed, she too was in disbelief. Eleanor pleaded with her friend to call her father-in-law Admiral Chester Nimitz, chief of the bureau of navigation in Washington, D.C., to confirm that the radio broadcast was false, as she had surmised. Admiral Nimitz, relatively unknown in these prewar days, was not yet the man of note that he would become. Joan "refused to get upset" and promised she would call Washington immediately.[11] But, before long, the awful truth was confirmed; Eleanor Farrell was overwhelmed stating, "I phoned everyone I knew" that day, frantic for support.[12] She, too, found that there was no point in going to bed that night. She wasn't tired. Her idyllic life as the wife of a dashing submarine officer had disintegrated into a pile of rubble, not unlike the twisted, smoking hulks that lay along Battleship Row at Pearl Harbor. Overwhelmed with the barrage of nightmarish news emanating from Hawaii, she decided to cope the only way she knew how. After the phone calls to loved ones, after Jo Ann had been safely nestled in bed, Eleanor Farrell drank. She drank a lot. Still, even after the liquor had worked its way into and then out of her anxious mind, the situation was unchanged. Japan had attacked Pearl Harbor, and much of the naval fleet was in ruins. The stark reality facing her was that her husband, the father of her beautiful daughter, was going to be fighting in a war, a war he might not survive. A few weeks later, that reality slapped her across the face when she opened a letter from Dixie containing a life insurance policy. Eleanor Farrell took one look at it and flung it across the room where it lay for several days.

Just when it seemed that things could not get worse, they did. The next day her dear friend Joanie, equally devastated at the news and its implications for her submarine officer husband, miscarried. Eleanor Farrell's only brother was a submariner in the Navy, so this added to her anxiety. Like so many people now, Eleanor Farrell did not know what to do. She could go to Washington, D.C., and live in her brother's home while he was away, but she hoped that *Gudgeon* would return to Mare Island, the naval facility at Vallejo, and she wanted to be there when *Gudgeon* arrived. There was no way for her to know it at the time, but the reunion with Dixie, which would have occurred in a few days, would take place after fourteen months of fear and loneliness.

In far away Webster City, Iowa, surrounded by the fertile fields of this little north central Iowa town, twenty-three-year-old William Conrad Ostlund, his youngest brother John, and a host of friends were just leaving the Granada movie theatre when they heard about the attack at Pearl. It had cost them thirty cents to watch the day's feature, Frederic March's *One Foot in Heaven*. News had spread quickly throughout the city. Bill, John, and the others at the theater agreed that the Japanese were stupid for having attacked the United States Navy, and predicted loudly "They will really get it now."[13] With the assurance of youth, they were certain that the war would be over very quickly. What they did not appreciate was that while they had been chasing girls, playing sports, and pursuing young men's amusements in this quiet little city, their counterparts in Japan were practicing military drills and dreaming of a glorious fight for their beloved god-like Emperor Hirohito.

Before long, Bill, the oldest brother, and Bob, middle brother, who were both Butler University graduates, would enlist along with John. Each brother joined a different branch of the armed forces. They were just three of the astonishing number of around twelve-hundred men from Webster City, a city of 6,736, who would serve in one of the branches of the armed forces during World War II. Late in 1943, Bill would report aboard *Gudgeon*.[14] Despite all of his dreams and the hard work that it took for him to get there, it would be a meeting with a terribly tragic outcome.

In Hawaii, as the shocking events of December 7 unfolded, Lieutenant Commander Elton W. Grenfell kept *Gudgeon* lying silently below the surface. Grenfell knew that everybody on *Gudgeon* was tired. She had departed the San Francisco area for an extended shakedown cruise, arriving in Sitka, Alaska, on September 25. The cruise continued with stops at Kodiak and Dutch Harbor. On October 4, 1941, she headed south for Pearl Harbor. At sea near Hawaii, the testing continued until the attack of December 7. The work had ground down everyone. Twenty pressure-packed hours a day, for forty straight days, the men on *Gudgeon* prepared the submarine for Acceptance to the Fleet Inspection. She had passed with flying colors. But even having passed the test, when the attack at Pearl Harbor took place, the crew had not yet been able to repair and test all of the systems that the submarine needed to be ready to go to war.

Upon *Gudgeon*'s arrival in Pearl Harbor, the international situation was so tense that the Navy cancelled plans for her to complete her construction and make needed modifications at Mare Island. When *Gudgeon* left Mare Island for her shakedown cruise, she still lacked twenty or thirty items which had been called for and which were to be installed on the submarine's return. In early November, *Gudgeon* was ordered out of Pearl Harbor for "intensive and extensive" advanced training around the island chain, to simulate a war patrol. During these training sessions, *Gudgeon* had fired thirty-three torpedoes and had scored an amazing thirty-two "hits," though none of the practice torpedoes had been loaded with explosives. Grenfell now knew that he had a fine torpedo crew and one of the finest torpedo officers in the service in Robert E. "Dusty" Dornin.

Shortly before the Japanese began their attack at Pearl Harbor, on December 7, Joe Grenfell had received a message from the submarine force commander saying that *Gudgeon* would no longer have to delay her return to Mare Island to receive the much-needed work. Following the exercises with seaplanes later in the day, she could head home to Vallejo. The crew on the boat cheered heartily after Grenfell made the announcement. The men had been away from their families for four months. However, as Grenfell noted later, "the morrow was to bring an entirely different story."[15] Some time later many would realize that there was one fortunate outcome of the submarine-to-plane exercises when the news of the attack arrived. Since so many of the men were involved in various aspects of the training exercises, nobody was manning the radio room. As a result, *Gudgeon* didn't relay the message to the planes above, and the planes arrived back at base about three minutes after the last Japanese plane had left. Fifteen minutes earlier, they would have been mauled by the Japanese Zeros.

At sea off Lahaina about seventy miles away from Pearl Harbor, Joe Grenfell decided that he would have *Gudgeon* surface only at night to freshen the air supply and charge the batteries that powered the electric motors. While lying there on the seventh, the sonar man picked up the sound of a submarine. Japanese submarines I-71, I-72, and I-73, part of

Admiral Shigeyoshi Miwa's Third Submarine Group, had been sent to the Lahaina Roads area to make certain there were no American ships present, to attack any U.S. vessels fleeing Pearl Harbor, and to pick up downed Japanese aviators. In a stroke of coincidence, there was the very real possibility that the unidentified submarine that *Gudgeon* had heard was none other than the hulking I-73, a boat with which *Gudgeon* would have a historic encounter later on the first patrol.

In a declassified interview released after the war, Dusty Dornin recalled that *Gudgeon*'s first contact was definitely on December 7 with a Japanese submarine in the area of Lahaina. At the time, the soundmen aboard *Gudgeon* could not definitely identify the submarine as to national origin. Later, however, after checking the positions of the U.S. submarines in the area, the underwater invader was determined to be of Japanese origin. Dornin could tell that it was not a Japanese midget submarine; the screws on a smaller submarine are quite easily discerned from a larger fleet submarine. He said, " . . . he didn't attack and we didn't attack, it was just a question of both submarines being scared of the other one, I think."[16] *Gudgeon* and the Japanese submarine—whether she was the I-73 or one of her sister ships—would remain warily unengaged.

The tension aboard *Gudgeon* was hardly allayed by the radioman's report that the Japanese were invading Hawaii. Electrician's Mate First Class Jack Camp had enough on his mind already. Camp recorded his experiences on the submarine's first two war patrols in a personal log. Unfortunately, nothing is known about Camp's background, other than his service number and date of enlistment, March 9, 1940. At the time, he was married and quite worried about his pregnant wife Mildred and his yet-to-be-born child, who would be named Gail, regardless of sex. He knew that she would be worried about him.

On the seventh, he wrote that when the crew heard the radioman's report that Pearl Harbor was under attack, they all laughed and said, "Can't be."[17] By the eighth Camp and the rest of the crew were aware that the reports were true, but also that the "boys on shore" had repulsed the Japanese. Finally on December 9, after two long days spent mostly on the bottom, *Gudgeon* and four other submarines, *Thresher*, *Plunger*, *Pompano*, and *Pollack*, sailed into Pearl Harbor with an escort. Seeing Pearl Harbor, Camp proclaimed in the "gee whiz" jargon typical of 1941 that the sight he saw that day was one that he would never forget, and that he "wanted to turn around and go after those damn rats."[18]

After *Gudgeon* had docked, her energetic skipper hurried over to headquarters. Admiral Thomas Withers was then the Commander of Submarines of the Pacific Fleet (ComSubPac). When asked what shape his submarine was in, Grenfell replied that *Gudgeon* was in "good shape and ready to go" as soon as she could be loaded up.[19]

A world away, on December 10, 1941, Philippine Air Force Captain Jesus A. Villamor of the almost-nonexistent Philippine flying corps had received word that the Japanese were once again attacking Zablan Field near Manila. On the eighth, an overwhelming force of fifty-four Mitsubishi bombers and seventy-nine Zeros had wiped out the entire Air Force contingent stationed there. Now it was Villamor's turn to defend Manila. With the city's church bells ringing in alarm, he raced on foot to the airfield. Before long, Zeros were everywhere. Finally, he made it to his obsolete plane, a P-26 built in 1932 and one of the six planes that had been given to the Filipinos by the United States. Compared to the attacking Zeros, it was woefully inferior in speed, maneuverability, and firepower. Having to fight a numerically and technologically superior Japanese air force in a plane nicknamed the "Peashooter" could not have instilled much confidence in the Filipino pilots. Nevertheless, Villamor had much courage and more than a little luck. Somehow, he was able to zig and zag, dodging in and out of the Zeros, which were headed at him despite being outgunned and outmanned. He was able to shoot down one of the attacking Zeros, much to the delight of the throngs of Filipinos below, watching the man who is widely considered to be the first Philippine war hero of World War II. Before long, Villamor would eventually be involved in similar defensive actions against the invading Japanese. Outnumbered and outclassed each time, Villamor somehow found a way to survive. A year or so later, Villamor would team up with *Gudgeon*, the battle-tested trailblazer of the United States submarine force. *Gudgeon* would put Villamor and five other men ashore on the Japanese controlled island of Timor. However, that meeting, which would occur on *Gudgeon*'s sixth war patrol, was a long way off.

Grenfell met with his superiors for his assignment. When told that *Gudgeon* was assigned to the Bungo Suido, a strait of Japan, Grenfell said he could "hardly believe [his] ears"—no American submarine in history had ever been assigned a wartime cruise of that duration and range.[20] The patrol was between the northeast coast of Kyushu and Shikoku, mainly south and east of the Japanese main island, Honshu, about thirty-seven hundred nautical miles from Pearl Harbor. What made the situation even more daunting was that there would be no stop along the way at Midway Island because the new submarine base there was not yet ready to receive them. Later in the war, a stopover at Midway, however brief, was a much-welcomed respite from the stresses of war patrolling.

Grenfell was ordered to proceed on one engine in order to preserve fuel, so *Gudgeon*'s invasion of Imperial waters would proceed at a turtle's pace. The fact that *Gudgeon* would soon be in Japanese waters was of little concern to Japanese foreign minister Baron Kijuro Shidehara, who had once declared, "the number of submarines possessed by the United States is of no concern to the Japanese inasmuch as Japan can never be attacked by American submarines."[21] This was a remarkably stupid thing to say in light of the fact that the island nation of Japan was critically deficient in raw materials. In his *History of the Second World War*, B. H. Liddell Hart pointed out that Japan was even *more* dependent upon overseas materials than Great Britain. Hart explained, "[Japan's] war making capacity depended on large seaborne imports of oil, iron ore, bauxite, coking coal, nickel, manganese, aluminum, tin, cobalt, lead phosphate, graphite and potash, cotton, salt and rubber."[22] In fact, petroleum, an absolute necessity, was available *only* from foreign lands. At the war's onset, Japan possessed just over six million tons of shipping, which sounds adequate until one considers that at the same time, Great Britain had ninety-five-hundred ships and twenty-one million tons of shipping at her disposal. In order to maintain a merchant fleet to meet her needs at war, Japan would have to have in place sufficient merchant shipping, shipmaking capacity, and the means to defend a merchant fleet. The Japanese ministers failed to plan for an adequate system to protect their valuable merchant ships, or *maru*, as they were known. Without the maru available to replenish the factories with the raw materials for the Japanese war-making machine, Japan would be brought to her knees as surely as if the Silent Service had dropped off hundreds of thousands of marines in an invasion of the Japanese mainland.

The maru were also made more vulnerable in light of the fact that within six hours of the attack at Pearl Harbor, the chief of naval operations ordered "unrestricted submarine warfare" against the Japanese. This order represented a significant departure from past policy. The United States had been a signatory at the London Naval Conference of 1940, which prohibited unrestricted sinking of merchant shipping. The rules of the day seem archaic now, as if they were created by chivalrous knights sitting at a round table. Protocol called for an attacking submarine skipper to send a message to the merchant ship, giving the people on board a chance to get off the endangered vessel into lifeboats. Then, and only then, could the submarine sink the enemy ship. But with this new order arriving so quickly after the Japanese treachery, the long-standing policy was, as far as the United States was concerned, no longer in force. The effect was to protect Joe Grenfell and the other World War II submariners from the ancient laws of the high seas and possible execution as pirates. In reality, that would not be the case; the Japanese would be particularly barbaric to American submariners.

Shortly after *Gudgeon* had returned to the devastated Pearl Harbor, the first of two false air raid alarms sounded, rattling everyone. Jack Camp, on shore, found himself at the "butt end of a 30-30" ready for another Japanese attack, still seething from what he had beheld as *Gudgeon* had maneuvered through the sunken hulks and devastation; he told his mates that if he could not hit the Japanese with a bullet he would "throw the damn thing at them."[23]

On the tenth, the crew loaded fresh water, battery water, ammunition, food, clothes, extra shoes, matches, candy, electric razors, spare parts, and huge quantities of diesel fuel. Camp even decided to take his portable Victrola along to combat the anticipated tedium of the upcoming patrol and to calm the nerves. Then the torpedoes were loaded. The routine was to load the six torpedo tubes in the forward torpedo room at the bow of the submarine, and then the four torpedo tubes in the after torpedo room at the stern. For the first patrol, the submarine would get a full load of twenty-four fish. Ten additional torpedoes were placed carefully on the racks in the forward room, four in the after-torpedo-room racks. To make certain that the torpedoes would hit their marks, the men in the forward room placed a brass Buddha lucky piece between the tubes. Finally, December 11 arrived. Rumor had it that *Gudgeon* would patrol what Camp called a "hot spot" off the southern end of Japan.[24] Never having been at war, he admitted to himself that he felt "a little funny," but by now he was able to rationalize the prospect of death by writing, "what the hell is 54 men when all have died in P.H."[25]

With the order to execute unrestricted air and submarine warfare against Japan, Lieutenant Commander Elton W. Grenfell weaved *Gudgeon* through the graveyard of the once mighty United States Navy at 9 A.M., December 11, 1941. Ray Foster, torpedoman first class, had anchor duty on deck and remembered the occasion well:

> It was the most sickening thing I ever saw in my life. The smell was horrible with fuel oil and burned flesh and ships turned over. The *Arizona*'s masts were sticking out and burning when we came in. I think the flames had finally gone out. And, then the *West Virginia* had rolled over. They had depleted our whole battleship group right there. There was two destroyers sunk in dry dock, and the *Nevada* tried to get under way when she got hit. Instead of sinking she went aground there, trying to get out.[26]

Foster had no thoughts of his place in history as *Gudgeon* got underway to undertake the first submarine war patrol of World War II. As she moved slowly past the Navy Yard, and the devastated hangars at Hickam Field, Ford Island, and what was left of Battleship Row—grotesque and twisted and still smoking to the starboard side of *Gudgeon*—he tried to fight off thoughts about the carnage and lost lives. The hardly noted event would be the first trans-Pacific war patrol in the history of the United States Navy, the first of *Gudgeon*'s pioneering achievements. Foster watched in silence as *Gudgeon* crept slowly toward the submarine nets protecting Pearl Harbor. Just as progress was being made, a message was received that Pearl Harbor was once again in an alert situation. Turning a three-hundred foot submarine around in a small body of water is very difficult, especially with the waves and breeze pushing the *Gudgeon* in an undesirable direction. By the time Grenfell had turned *Gudgeon* around, the alarm was cancelled, and *Gudgeon* was once again headed to sea.

■ ■ ■

A frustrated Grenfell sent orders below to padlock the "damned radio room door."[27] Grenfell was determined to get *Gudgeon* out of port before some other panicky alert hindered his departure. *Gudgeon* passed the final buoy, dropped in behind escort destroyer USS *Litchfield*, and made ready for dive. There is confusion about this historic event. Some accounts report that *Gudgeon* left by herself, others with *Plunger* and *Pollack*, and still others with only *Plunger*. Grenfell's wartime diary stated that *Litchfield* and only *Plunger* accompanied *Gudgeon* out of port. After the war he wrote that "*Gudgeon* was accompanied by *Plunger*, who, however, after getting outside the channel, had to turn around and go back for minor repairs and did not leave until several days later."[28] It is clear from the first war patrol reports of the two submarines that *Pollack* left Pearl Harbor for her first war patrol on December 13, followed by *Plunger* on the fourteenth. No mention is made in either report of an abortive attempt to leave Pearl Harbor on the eleventh.

Grenfell said that the crew was very pleased to leave Pearl Harbor because they had received very little sleep due to the many false alerts and the need to get *Gudgeon* ready for patrol. Later, on the very day that *Gudgeon* started the American submarine offensive against Japan, Joe Grenfell would learn that Germany had declared war on the United States. Grenfell took comfort in the knowledge that he had not only the best submarine crew in the Navy but also one of the most experienced. Neither Grenfell nor anyone on the crew could have anticipated that this undersea warrior would perform wartime firsts unmatched in United States naval history, or know that *Gudgeon* herself would be lost after having inflicted tremendous damage to the Japanese war effort.

Gudgeon was the twelfth and final *Tambor* class submarine to be built. The others were the "T" boats, *Tambor, Tautog, Thresher, Triton, Trout,* and *Tuna*, assigned hull numbers 198–203 and the "G" boats from *Gar* with hull number 206, through *Grampus, Grayback, Grayling, Grenadier* and finally *Gudgeon*, SS-211. *Tambor* class submarines as a group were very similar to each other, and the G boats were almost identical. But because the G boats were built in three different shipyards, each had slight variations on the theme developed by their engineers.

Gudgeon was commissioned into the Navy a mere fourteen months after her keel was laid. She was a little longer than a football field at 307 feet, was 27.3 feet on beam, and displaced 1,475 tons of water on the surface, 2,370 underwater. She was powered by four Fairbanks-Morse 5,400 horsepower diesel engines for surface running and 252 battery cells for running submerged. Her listed surface speed of 20.8 knots represented a slight improvement over her predecessors. Underwater, the submarine could make 8.75 knots, roughly equivalent to 10 mph on land, but in most situations the submarine would make six or seven knots. In addition to her ten torpedo tubes, *Gudgeon*'s deck was mounted with a three-inch gun and two .50 caliber machine guns. *Gudgeon* was huge compared to the vaunted German Type VII ocean-going attack submarines, which were only 220 feet in length and a little over twenty feet on beam. The German vessel was rated at seventeen knots on the surface, and 7.4 submerged. *Gudgeon*'s actual foe, the Imperial Japanese Navy, boasted the huge Kadai class I boats, which at 331 feet were longer than *Gudgeon*. But, of utmost importance to the men who rode *Gudgeon* were the prewar improvements in armament. *Gudgeon*'s armor was much superior to the older S boats in the fleet. Advances in metallurgy and welding allowed the early war fleet boats to leave port with safety-tested depths of around 300 feet. Their predecessors, the S boats, were only tested safe at 200 feet. The general rule was that a submarine could go one-and-a-half times deeper than the tested depth.

The USS *Gudgeon* was the two-hundred-eleventh boat built since John Holland was able to persuade a skeptical Congress and Navy Department to commission his fifty-four foot submarine, the *Holland VI* in late 1900. Already persuaded was Theodore Roosevelt, the Secretary of the Navy, who foresaw the potential of underwater combat vessels. Later, on March 25, 1905, Roosevelt would be the first American president to board a submarine and make a dive. At the moment of her christening, *Gudgeon* was the queen of the force, and the men who would ride her into Japanese-controlled waters would lovingly refer to her as the *Queen Gudgeon*, a testament to her perceived majesty.

The "SS" before her hull number stands for submarine, not "submersible ship." Most, but not all, of the submarines in the fleet were named after fish. Submarines had been named after their inventor (Holland), as well as mammals and spiders, but starting with *Pike* in 1935 through World War II, all but a few submarines were named after fish. A *Gudgeon* is a small, European freshwater fish that is easily caught and used for bait. *Gudgeon* was one of twelve submarines in Allan R. McCann's Submarine Squadron Six, composed of Division Sixty-One commanded by Charles "Shorty" Dixon, made up of the six aforementioned T submarines, and Division Sixty-Two commanded by Forrest Marmaduke O'Leary, made up of the G boats.

On board as officers for the first patrol in addition to Grenfell were: Lieutenant Hylan B. Lyon, Naval Academy Class of '31, Executive Officer and Navigator; Lieutenant (jg) Robert E. "Dusty" Dornin, Class of '35, Torpedo Officer and Gunnery Officer; Lieutenant (jg) Richard M. "Dixie" Farrell, Class of '35, Engineering and Electrical Officer; and Ensign Sigmund A. Bobczynski, Class of '39, Communications Officer. Ensigns V. F. Sorensen, out of the University of Washington, and W. R. Robinson, a recent graduate of the University of California ROTC program, handled the minor duties as low men on the totem pole.

The "Old Man," the skipper of the boat, Elton Watters Grenfell, was only 5'6"—or 5'6½" if he stood "correctly." [29] Grenfell had by this time already amazed the crew that had been on board since commissioning day in April. Despite having not met many of the crew that day, Grenfell moved through the boat greeting every sailor by name. Almost sixty years later, the feat was still deemed remarkable by Ray Foster. This savant-like ability to memorize names was not some sideshow act; it was of real importance. Admiral Thomas Withers recounted a story about a movie director who was convinced that a submarine was the worst ship that anyone could get stuck on during a war. The director, talking to a group of World War II submariners, asked them why in the world they wanted to serve on a submarine and not on *any* other class of ships in the Navy. One sailor responded, "Well, on a submarine your skipper knows you. He knows all about you. Hell, he could even give my wife some pointers." [30]

Grenfell was typical of submarine commanders at the outset of the war. He was thirty-eight years old, older than most or all of the others on board, a Navy regular, and a Naval Academy graduate with a strong engineering background. In the submarine command, it was a general consensus that since the diesel engines were having so many problems at the time, the commanding officer should be an engineer. Grenfell was born and raised in Fall River, Massachusetts, and entered the Academy in 1922 where he ran track, became an expert rifleman, and sang in the choir. His bio in the Navy's *Lucky Bag*, the Naval Academy yearbook, took jabs at him for his strong East coast accent (it is not Harvard, it's "Haavad"). He was described as a mix of mild Puritanism with liberal portions of worldiness, which yielded a "manmetal of grim tensile strength."[31] It was predicted that his life would be a "fast, happy one."[32] And it would. While at the Academy, he ran the mile like his idol, Joey Ray, a well-known miler of the day. In fact, Grenfell so adored Joey Ray that his nickname became "Joey" or "Joe," which stuck his whole life. Acquiring the nickname was a break for Grenfell because he despised his name, "Elton." Grenfell was a good student, graduating ninety-third in a class of 456 in 1926, at which time he was commissioned an Ensign. He served on several ships before attending sub school in 1928. His first submarine was the R-4, where he remained until 1933. He then returned to Annapolis for postgraduate instruction in Mechanical Engineering before being assigned duty at Cal-Berkeley where he received his Masters degree in 1936. He took part in the commissioning of the submarine *Pickerel* and served on her until 1939. *Pickerel*'s shakedown cruise was a four-thousand mile trip up the Amazon River. Then he served in the Navy's Bureau of Engineering in Washington, D.C. His Naval biography indicates that in this role, he was "primarily responsible" for the "procurement and development" of the first Landing Craft Personnel Vehicles (LCVP) and Higgins boats by the Higgins Company.[33] The LCVP was a small craft that transported troops to invasion sites, the large metal door dropping so that thirty-six soldiers could hit the beach. Grenfell's work here was of profound importance. Dwight D. Eisenhower once stated that it was Andrew Higgins and the development of the LCVP that won the war for the United States. Grenfell then reported to Mare Island Navy Yard to assist in fitting out *Gudgeon*. Among friends, Joe Grenfell was an energetic, wisecracking character, who was fully capable of swearing like a sailor.

The weapons officer on *Gudgeon*, Robert Edson "Dusty" Dornin, would become one of the great World War II submarine commanders. Dusty, though younger than Joe Grenfell, had a similar background. Dornin was born in 1912 in Berkeley and entered the Academy in 1931. At the

Academy Dornin was a standout on the basketball and lacrosse teams, but it was as a speedy wide receiver that he achieved All-American status. His photographs appeared in the *Lucky Bag* in write-ups about the basketball and football teams. While at the Academy, Dornin earned a reputation for "dragging a new girl each term," "bull sessions," "purloining Misery Hall equipment," and for having a short fuse, a trait he would take with him to war.[34] Despite his commitments to sports and girls, Dornin was an excellent student, graduating forty-eighth out of 442 in the class of 1935.

He served aboard some surface ships and the submarine *Cuttlefish* before returning to the Naval Academy for temporary duty as an assistant football coach. He completed submarine school in New London and then served on *Plunger*. In March 1941, he left *Plunger* and joined Grenfell to prepare *Gudgeon* for service in the fleet. As the torpedo data (TDC) operator aboard *Gudgeon*, Dornin became well known among submariners when he sank thirty-two of thirty-three targets in practice. Torpedoes, which cost around $10,000 each, were considered too expensive to be blown up in drills. Rather, torpedoes were set to go under the target, thus testing the marksmanship of the firing party but not, unfortunately, whether the torpedo would actually explode when it hit an enemy vessel. As a result of this false economy, entire generations of post–World War I submariners had never seen or heard a torpedo explode, and defects in the torpedoes would, indeed, cost the United States dearly in lives lost, ships not sunk, and a longer, costlier war.

Long before the war, while at the Naval Academy, another of *Gudgeon*'s officers, Sigmund Bobczynski, had been nicknamed "Bobo" or Czar," both easier to pronounce than Bobczynski's real last name, which is pronounced "Bob chin'ski." The likeable Detroit native was "free and easy," and as the war would reveal, Bobczynski was a little more "cultured" than the average *Gudgeon* submariner.[35] While at the Academy, Bobo was known as a lover of classical music as well as a member of the Academy's "B" football team.

The crew consisted of fifty-six men, including the all-important chief of the boat, James C. "Gunner" Ogden, who had authority over all the crew on board. Low men on the submarine were the five unrated seamen. Rounding out the crew were the pharmacist's mate (who acted as doctor, nurse, and pharmacist), electricians, cooks, a yeoman, a host of machinist's mates, gunner's mates, quartermasters, radio operators, many firemen, and seven torpedomen. This was a rather small crew by standards developed later in the war.

As *Gudgeon* headed toward Japan, some of the crew used the time to fix air leaks. When duty time was over, playing cards, listening to music, talking with shipmates, smoking, drinking coffee, and sleeping helped make the time on board the submarine less tedious. Those who had not earned the coveted dolphin insignia kept busy sketching the submarine's various systems, attempting to learn how to operate all of the machinery and other equipment on the boat. When a submariner qualified on submarines, he had the right to wear a small dolphin on his dress sleeve that signified that he knew how to perform all of the systems on board, a necessity in the event of the death or incapacitation of the man assigned to a given post.

Grenfell, who had been sternly warned to be careful lest his boat become another casualty in a Navy that had lost far too many ships in the last several days, proceeded at a snail's pace. One *Gudgeon* submariner reported that when the submarine was submerged, the boat was usually only able to make about six knots, about the same as seven miles per hour on land. On a good day, with the engines at top efficiency and the ocean pushing the craft, the boat could make perhaps eight knots. *Gudgeon* would surface at night to charge the batteries and travel at a faster rate, and then dive at daylight to continue her very slow approach to the enemy's home waters.

Because *Gudgeon* was hurried out to war before her completion, there was inadequate water-making capacity on board. As a result, water was strictly rationed. In order to make certain that the water was not wasted; Grenfell ordered that provisions be loaded into the three showers, making it impossible for the men to shower. The showers were thus occupied for the first half of the patrol; Grenfell said that out of necessity "French baths" were "the vogue."[36] But, in truth, even French baths would not do much to remove the stench from the hard-working submariners.

On December 12, 1942, at 0920, still in what was assumed to be friendly waters, *Gudgeon* had to dive to avoid being mistaken for an enemy submarine. Later on the same day two trigger-happy U.S. Army Air Force bombers approached the submarine, and *Gudgeon* had to dive again. Indeed,

Gudgeon was in great danger. She could be attacked and sunk by any bomber flying from any country. Grenfell found that the American bomber pilots were so eager for action that they would not wait for identification—choosing to attack first, ask questions later. The next day the submarine dove again to avoid "friendly" bombardment.

The submarine had proceeded beyond Midway Island by the seventeenth. Grenfell ordered that *Gudgeon* make a trim dive in the morning and noted that the wind and sea had been blowing in his face the entire cruise. At 1540 *Gudgeon* passed the 180th meridian. At night the men on watch were horrified by the presence of a phosphorescent wake that outlined the entire hull of the boat. A phosphorescent wake is caused by the billions of tiny plankton that luminesce when disturbed. For submariners, they present a significant danger, because they represent a large arrow pointing out a juicy target to any enemy bombers in the area. It would not be the last time that the tiny plankton would irritate the men on board and endanger their lives. As one *Gudgeon* sailor said later, "It used to bother the hell out of us, because it was just like a lamp."[37] Despite the danger, the sight must have been something to behold on a beautiful, balmy starlit Pacific night. The waves bending off the submarine's bow were described as virtual sheets of light.

West of Midway, there would be no ships to assist *Gudgeon*. Every vessel sighted was assumed to be the enemy, an enemy doing its best to destroy *Gudgeon* and every man aboard. This enemy was clearly superior in numbers to the United States fleet. As of January 1941, the Japanese had 10 aircraft carriers, 10 battleships, 35 heavy cruisers, and 111 destroyers, as well as 60 submarines.

By Christmas Eve day the waves were an enormous twenty-five feet high. The wind and rain were extremely heavy. Jack Camp, still quite worried about his wife and his soon-to-be-born child, wrote in his log that *Gudgeon* was passing some islands near the anticipated "HOT SPOT."[38] Lookouts saw several fishing boats after dark and were confused as to why they would be running with lights on at night. The fishermen surely had no idea that an American submarine had penetrated Japanese waters. The men on board sang Christmas carols in the mess room to the tunes offered by Eli Masse on the accordion. Grenfell made and circulated a Christmas card for the crew and told them he wished that next Christmas would be better than the present one. It wouldn't. But it would be a more exciting time than this patrol had been. So far.

The men on board were slowly working into a routine. Grenfell described life on *Gudgeon*: "We breakfast at seven on good, wholesome food, for we are far from home and health is one of our important assets. The watch changes at 8 am and some of the men fall into their bunks for eight hours of sleep. We maintain a four hours on and eight off watch and it is up to the man himself whether he sleeps during the day or night. It's all the same on a submarine. We eat again at 12 noon and change watch. There is a relaxation period following for off-watch standers. We have sun lamp booths for men who can't get topside at any time. The phonograph is grinding out 'Give me My Boots and Saddle.' Cowboy songs and cowboy magazines are favorites with the crew. We eat again at 5:30 and at dark we surface with a rush, white water pouring through out superstructure. The officers in heavy weather clothing man the bridge and begin night surface patrol. Over us is the limitless sky and around us the limitless ocean. It is lonely and invigorating at the same time. The submarine pulses on under a million stars."[39]

The anxious and glum Camp, not surprisingly perhaps, chose to keep his feelings to himself and uncharacteristically did not make an entry for December 25. Grenfell wrote in his log, "Merry Christmas," and then continued on as if it were any other day.[40] The submarine was ordered to assume Condition I. *Gudgeon* would be more prepared than ever for battle. Dusty Dornin and Joe Grenfell decided that while in Japanese waters they would sleep in the conning tower in order to be available immediately in the event a ship was sighted.

Using stars for navigation, *Gudgeon* proceeded. Grenfell and the officers decided to modify their system for diving. From now on, if the bridge watch sighted anything of interest, the Officer of the Deck (OOD) would verify any claim made by one of the four men on watch, each of whom was assigned to cover a quarter of the boat and beyond. If a threat was confirmed, the OOD would give the order to "clear the bridge." Word was then telephoned to the control room, where the helmsman would move the annunciator up one notch, causing the diesel engines to be shut down in preparation for a dive so that *Gudgeon* could make way on her batteries under water. The control room personnel would close the main induction and rig out the bow planes. The torpedomen would, in the meantime, be getting their torpedo tubes ready for firing. Finally the fire control party would man the Torpedo Data Computer (TDC). Grenfell noted with confidence that the boat would thus be sealed and ready for either a surface or submerged approach.

On December 27, the sixteenth day of the tedious patrol, the men manning the sound gear reported some very unusual hammering noises. The sounds were almost rhythmic and could be heard on the surface. Nobody had any idea what was causing the racket. It did not sound like screws, sonar, or any other device known to exist at the time. It is understandable that Grenfell's imagination ran wild. He feared that it was a Japanese listening device. By the twenty-eighth the hammering continued. One almost wants to suggest that the bizarre noises were the sounds of battle on nearby Wake Island, which *Gudgeon* had recently passed. In his book *Silent Victory*, wartime submariner Clay Blair was severely critical of Admiral Thomas Withers for not sending *Gudgeon*—by this time being followed by *Pollack* and *Plunger*—to bolster the tiny garrison of 350 defenders being pounded on Wake Island. Blair said that the three United States submarines, if joined by *Triton*, *Tambor*, *Trout*, and *Argonaut*, which were in the area, might have turned back the invasion or at least rescued the marines who were fighting so valiantly on Wake.

However, it was not to be. *Gudgeon* proceeded toward Bungo Suido. By this time Grenfell had concluded that the odd noises must be due to volcanic quakes. At times, now deep in Japanese waters, lookouts mistook glass fishing balls on top of the waves for periscopes. High-flying birds and planets seen during daylight looked like Japanese planes. As the lookouts gained experience, they made such errors less frequently. The next several days were a disappointment. No targets presented themselves aside from small fishing craft lit at night despite *Gudgeon*'s ideal position. On December 31, mast tops popped up directly east of Bungo Suido. Grenfell tried to approach a large freighter but gave up the hunt because the approach angle was excessive, the target too distant.

Three and a half months before Lieutenant Colonel Jimmy Doolittle's valiant bomber strike on Tokyo, Joe Grenfell's *Gudgeon* arrived alone off the Japanese mainland. On New Year's Day 1942, the underwater hunter lay in wait off the southeast tip of Kyushu for anything big enough to put a torpedo into. *Gudgeon* torpedomen had been meticulously working their load of torpedoes all the way from Pearl Harbor, making sure they were ready for the battle. None of the men had any idea that extra attention to the torpedoes was necessary at that time of the war. They did it because it was their job. And since their lives depended upon how well those torpedoes worked, it made sense to keep them tuned up and clean.

One of the challenges *Gudgeon* faced was that she had to rely on the relatively primitive sonar technology on this first patrol. Admiral Thomas Withers would say later that *Gudgeon* was not equipped with SD radar, useful for detecting airplanes. In addition, *Gudgeon* had night periscope problems and racks of torpedoes that were potential duds. As yet undiscovered, torpedoes could have any one, or all, of three distinct flaws. Those defects would not become fully corrected until late in 1943. For the fleet as a whole, there was also a critical shortage of torpedoes. Grenfell was under strict orders to use only one torpedo, two maximum, on merchant ships, a restriction that wouldn't exist later in the war. *Gudgeon* was also slowed by instructions from headquarters. When *Gudgeon* was within a (500 mile) radius of enemy islands, it would generally be advisable to remain submerged during daylight, proceeding on the surface during dark. This, of course, would slow *Gudgeon* down, giving her less hunting time in the area.

On the first day of 1942, *Gudgeon* finally sighted a potential target at an estimated 8,000 yards. However, the moon was very bright behind the submarine. In order to avoid appearing as a 307-foot, fully silhouetted target, Joe Grenfell ordered a submerged and very slow sound-and-periscope approach. Before long, Grenfell realized that the target ship's course made it almost impossible to attack. At this time in the war, sinking an enemy ship was quite difficult at best. Maneuvering a very slow submarine under water into a proper firing position on a faster-moving surface ship was at times impossible. But at that time an underwater approach was irrefutable doctrine.

Once sighted, the enemy's range, speed, and "angle on the bow"—the angle of the target's course in relation to the submarine's line of sight—were estimated, all based upon observations through the periscope. At the same time the skipper would constantly scan the horizon for the enemy.

Then various estimates and calculations needed to be made based upon the skipper's estimate of the actual length of the target ship's mast. When the Japanese were especially wary of submarines, they would drop into a zig-zag pattern. The ships would move back and forth at very sharp angles so their course would be very difficult to predict. In an attack, the submarine skipper had to factor in the speed and spread of the torpedoes. Before long, it would become apparent that the torpedoes were the real wild card. Would the torpedo explode? Would it burst prematurely? Or, as would soon be learned, would the torpedo travel at the depth it was set or drive harmlessly under the target vessel? The answer was that they would fail as often as not.

The *Gudgeon* also had a Torpedo Data Computer (TDC)—which when compared to today's computers, can hardly be called a computer. But for its purpose and in its time the TDC was a remarkable technological achievement that was quite effective. Once all the data was fed into it, the TDC would quickly kick out a "solution," including precise torpedo settings for the targets.

A surface approach from a distance sufficient to prevent sighting by the enemy would have allowed far greater speed and would have been preferable. The standard practice for a surface attack during the war would become an "end run," which refers to the practice of the submarine running parallel to the target on the surface and moving ahead of the vessel. Once sufficiently ahead of the enemy ship, the submarine would turn toward the vessel and sit a few thousand yards away, waiting at periscope depth.

In addition to the technical difficulties of performing a successful attack, there was also a misconception held by submariners as a consequence of the prewar training they had received. One *Gudgeon* submariner noted that in war exercises with the fleet, if the surface ship sighted the periscope, the submarine was considered sunk. This would prove to be far from realistic. Eventually the typical World War II submarine skipper would learn to adjust for the training bias toward caution and become very skilled at evading depth charge and depth bomb attacks. However, on this first war patrol adjustments to this mindset had yet to be made. But at least *Gudgeon* was on station. Surely there would be plenty more opportunities, and anticipating success, the men in the torpedo room had decorated the fish with appropriate seasonal sentiments like "Merry X-Mass," "Happy New Year," or "So Sorry."[41] *Gudgeon* continued to search the seas off the Bungo Suido for a target worthy of such holiday greetings.

Gudgeon continued to operate submerged most of the time, which caused Camp to wonder what fresh air and daylight were like. On January 4, 1942, the masts and stack of a small coastal freighter were sighted. The submerged *Gudgeon* tried to close at full speed. When the Japanese ship was at about twenty-six hundred yards, Grenfell fired two torpedoes. This was *Gudgeon*'s maiden attack and one of the submarine service's first in World War II. The target was rather small and distant for *Gudgeon* to have much of a chance for success. High seas made periscope observation difficult, and sound could not get a bearing. Both shots missed. *Gudgeon* moved on.

Now lying off Bungo Suido, Grenfell decided to wait for whatever might come his way. There was no source of information for him to consult in order to counter whatever antisubmarine threats the Japanese would present. No one knew for certain whether the enemy's radar was effective, what technologies the Japanese had developed, or even whether or not the Japanese had a systematic antisubmarine program. There was no report from a war-experienced United States submariner to describe how to survive in Japanese home waters. This was all new; caution seemed to make a lot of sense.

Joe Grenfell chose to play it the way he had been taught, with *Gudgeon* lying below the surface around one-hundred feet, occasionally rising to take a daytime observation through the periscope before once again dropping down to the safer depths below. *Gudgeon*'s stouthearted skipper would write later:

Although targets were almost nonexistent, our time in area was not wasted for we were learning how to conduct a war patrol. Since the introduction of submarines into our Fleet they had never had any experience in wartime patrolling; in World War I our submarines were not capable of conducting war patrols—indeed they had no targets for the German Fleet and merchant marine were bottled up. There was not a single officer or man on any submarine who had ever heard a torpedo explode or had even heard a depth charge. We were learning lots of things about how to conduct war patrols such as how to conserve water and fuel, how to protect our eyes at night so that one could see quickly when called to the bridge—we had no red lights installed in those early days. As a result the fire control officer and I slept in the dark in the conning tower every night while in area. We learned about the many and various sonar noises which also caused many alerts—noises of fish which sounded like Motor Torpedo Boat propellors [sic]—explosive noises from subterranean earthquakes and many other peculiar fish noises. We learned how to take star sights at predawn and shortly after dark to position ourselves when out of range of land. We learned how to get rid of garbage and trash without leaving any traces. We learned lots of things which were to be of great benefit to our successors. We were the pioneers of submarine war patrolling.[42]

Commenting on the dangers of the patrol, Dusty Dornin said, "Yeah, we were anxious all right. Pearl Harbor made us angry, it made us mad. But, don't let anyone kid you, we were frightened as hell. We didn't even know how to fight a war."[43]

For the next four days, the few target ships found remained too distant to approach. Torpedoman Ray Foster remembered the first patrol well. Even when there were no ships present to attack or evade, danger was always present. During the first run, Foster had the sobering experience of moving slowly under water and hearing a metallic object scraping the side of *Gudgeon*. Foster, who had been to mine school, knew full well that the sound was caused by chains that were attached to enemy mines protecting the entrance to Bungo Suido. He would recall that the experience did not scare him, but acknowledged that it made him "think" a lot.[44] Whenever *Gudgeon* would come across such mines, Foster refrained from commenting about the hideous scraping sound, certain that the officers knew what the sounds were and not wanting to scare any sailors emboldened by their own naïveté. It was not only every ship or plane above the surface that threatened them; the enemy had also peppered the ocean's depths with mines. No spot in the ocean off Japan was truly safe.

The dearth of good targets continued, but that was only part of the problem. Once they sighted a target, the mandated and accepted doctrine of the day to carry out slow, submerged approaches invariably let the targets track beyond range, and the submarine could not close in time to attack.

By this time, Joe Grenfell and the men on board were becoming discouraged. Occasionally a far-off patrol plane would come into view or there was a fishing boat to break the monotony, however slightly. But all in all, it was becoming very clear; this "hot spot" was as cold as ice. Finally, late on January 9 and into the morning hours of the tenth, things changed. *Gudgeon* sighted a darkened freighter of an estimated five-thousand tons. This time lighting was to *Gudgeon*'s advantage because the rising moon silhouetted the target. With *Gudgeon* having successfully closed on the surface, the target a mile and a half away, at 0015 Grenfell and Dornin fired three torpedoes from the stern torpedo tubes. Ray Foster remembered this particular attack very well. The exterior doors on the torpedo tubes had to be opened by hand which took about thirty seconds. After the tubes were ready for firing, Grenfell ordered, "FIRE SEVEN. FIRE EIGHT. FIRE NINE." One large boom was heard, and Grenfell ordered "Foster to the bridge." Grenfell said, "You had a premature explosion, what happened?" At about that time, Foster said the ship started burning "from one end to the other."[45] Foster was dismissed. Grenfell reported in his post action report that he believed at least one torpedo hit the freighter because he felt a "distinct shock."[46] He added that personnel in the after torpedo room felt two thuds and believed that two torpedoes had hit their mark. The men in the sound room reported hearing explosive reverberations over their sound gear. There was no mention in the war patrol report that the ship had been seen burning as Ray Foster stated, but Ray Foster's memory, like that of other *Gudgeon* sailors interviewed long after the war, invariably proved to be correct. This time was no exception.

Grenfell's handwritten personal log, set down at the time of the first patrol, confirms Ray Foster's recollection that the ship was burning: "At 0010 fired 3 torpedoes from stern tubes. Sank him-watched him sink in moonlight after feeling 2 thuds & seeing heavy clouds of smoke. Sound heard explosive reverberations. OOD [Officer of the Deck] and CO [Commanding Officer] watched ship sink bow first with stern high in air. Position of sinking L 31-57 N, L 132-15 E."[47] Just why Grenfell did not put all of this convincing information in the official war patrol report is not known. One would think that he would have done so in order to establish that the ship had been sunk. The existing war patrol report prepared by Joe Grenfell is quite nonstandard and leaves out a lot of information that would be customarily included in every war patrol report thereafter.

When interviewed by the Navy in 1943, Dusty Dornin said that they fired three torpedoes at the seven-thousand ton ship while on the surface. Dornin, like Grenfell in his personal log and Foster when interviewed many years after the war, said that two hits were observed on the very dark night. He continued, stating that the stricken vessel "seemed" to sink in five minutes.[48] *Gudgeon* would receive wartime credit for having sunk a five-thousand ton merchant ship, only to have the sinking disallowed in the report released shortly after the war by JANAC, The Joint Army Navy Assessment Committee. JANAC's findings would come to be known as the official record on matters related to destruction of Japanese vessels, though they are widely considered inaccurate by countless former wartime submariners.

An ecstatic Jack Camp and crew were sure that they had hit the freighter with three torpedoes and that the fat freighter had gone down in four minutes. He said he was "happy as hell." The post-Pearl fury of the submariner was evident with Camp concluding that "nothing was too good for those yellow B— after P.H."[49] Surprisingly, the fury was not so strong that the straitlaced father-to-be could allow himself to overcome his personal distaste for swearing to actually write the word "Bastards." He noted that the three fish that had sunk the freighter had been fired out of his battle station in the after torpedo room. Following the attack, Grenfell noted that the Japanese were now turning off their running lights at night. Indeed, the Japanese had finally learned that a United States fleet submarine could travel all the way from Pearl Harbor to Imperial Japanese waters and mount an attack on Japanese shipping.

After the triumphant celebration ended on the tenth, things quieted down, and *Gudgeon* sighted no more ships in the area. Camp was sure that the Japanese "probably know the ole *Gudgeon* is around by now"[50] and were avoiding them. Joe Grenfell looked at it differently. *Gudgeon* had attacked only two ships since arriving in the patrol area and had sunk only one of them. On the fourteenth, a reluctant Lieutenant Commander Joe Grenfell turned *Gudgeon* toward the submarine base at Pearl Harbor.

Dusty Dornin would say later that the reason for the lack of targets on the patrol was that the bulk of Japanese shipping had been sent south to the Philippines. *Gudgeon* had tried to get between Japanese ships and the coast. It was easier to sink them that way. If *Gudgeon* were hugging the coast, the Japanese merchant ships could not scurry into a port and leave the submarine behind in waters too distant for an attack. *Gudgeon* had gotten as close to the shore as one thousand yards, hoping the merchant vessels would steam toward them in search of a protective place to dock. However, the shallower the water, the more dangerous it was for the submarine. Submarines cannot effectively maneuver to avoid a depth charging in shallow water.

Like the rest of the crew, Ray Foster was disappointed by so few targets. He brought exceptional competence to his work aboard *Gudgeon*. He referred to himself as the leading torpedoman aboard *Gudgeon* at that time, and for good reason. He was the only member of the torpedo gang who had worked in a torpedo shop overhauling torpedoes before he came aboard. And Foster was not entirely devoid of wartime experiences. After graduating from high school in 1936, he decided that there would be very few job opportunities for him locally, so he enlisted in the Navy. He found his way to torpedo school after his recruit training and was assigned to a light cruiser, the USS *Milwaukee*, which was soon on her way to Sydney, Australia.

On December 12, 1937, the Japanese bombed the United States gunboat *Panay* on the Yangtze River near Hankow, China. Before long the *Milwaukee* and Ray Foster found themselves in China, a result of the bombing of the small gunboat. Foster was assigned to the American consulate on Kulangsu, a small island off the southern coast of China, located near Amoy, a mainland town directly across the strait from Formosa (or Taiwan, as it is now known). Foster was one of forty-two Americans, forty-two British, and forty-two French soldiers assigned to protect the staff and families of each nation's consulate. While there, the American military contingent lived in tents and had little to do except play tennis and roam around the island. With the Japanese at war with the Chinese, the European powers had pulled their troops out but left 126 token soldiers stationed on the island. Eventually, as Foster explained, the Japanese landed 300 marines, posing great peril to the smaller force of men and the various nationals still on the island.

Intense negotiations led to a Japanese withdrawal; Foster and the others quickly evacuated.

He was then assigned to a gunboat, which did not prepare him particularly well for his torpedo specialty on the *Gudgeon* because it had no torpedoes. At one stop along the Chinese waters, Foster and some friends found a bar in Swatow and were just beginning to enjoy their drinks when Japanese bombers attacked. With air raid sirens shrieking, civilians scurrying to find cover, and the sounds of bombs and machine gun fire all around them, the sailors knew that they would be expected to hurry back to their ship. But they remained seated, drinking as if, since they were foreigners, they were somehow immune to the advances of the Japanese.

The Japanese dove down on the city in their single engine bombers. Foster recalled clearly that the planes were so close he could see the pilots looking back and forth as they sought a suitable target to bomb. No wonder Ray Foster would acquire the nickname "Guts." Some say he was called Guts because of the cocksure way he went through life saying whatever he liked to his superior officers and anyone else and for the bravery he showed at war. Others said it had more to do with the small pot gut that he carried throughout the war. No doubt each was accurate.

He eventually transferred to the *Blackhawk*, an old auxiliary destroyer that had been sent to China at the end of World War I. By this time, Foster had already achieved torpedoman third class and desired to move up to second class. There was nothing else to do but work and study, so Foster literally lived in *Blackhawk*'s torpedo shop. In fact, he bathed and ate there also. Before long, he tested for second class, passed, and was informed that he had the highest score in the Asiatic fleet. Surprised at how well he had done on the exam, he eventually learned that many of those he was competing with were illiterate. They had joined the Navy to flee the Depression and had dropped out of school much earlier than Foster, who was a high school graduate. He was then transferred to the old four piper destroyer USS *Marker*. After eight months, the squadron yeoman pulled him aside and told him that he was due to transfer and asked him if he was a "luetic." Foster, ever the sharp-tongued young man, shot back, "You tell me what a luetic is, and I'll tell you whether I am one or not."[51] After learning that he was being asked whether or not he had syphilis, he responded in the negative and was transferred to the United States Naval Base at Cavite, Philippine Islands.

After he got to Cavite, a chief told the new arrivals that they were to return Monday, sober, with their bags packed. He said, "You're going to sea, but I can't tell you where, it's classified."[52] On Monday morning, the sailors were loaded onto a bus where they sat until 4:00 P.M. when they were hurried onto a waiting ship, the USS *Washington*. Once aboard, the men were ordered to stay below deck until *Washington* got under way and out of port. They learned later that the United States was evacuating all of the Navy, Army, and Marines along with their families because the Japanese were making menacing moves in the area. Luckily for Foster and the others on *Washington*, three bombs that had been planted on board were located before they were all blown sky high.

After his tour was up, Foster arrived in San Francisco and was discharged. Desiring to get on submarines, he wrote the Navy a letter and requested admission to submarine school. His request was approved, so with ten cents' travel money in his pocket, he hitched a bus to Kansas City. In Kansas City, Foster and seven others bound for submarine school took their physicals. Unfortunately, Foster had tied one on the night before and flunked the physical because of high blood pressure. When the physician questioned him about the medical finding, Foster was open about his excessive drinking the night before. The physician must have faced this problem a thousand times and was sympathetic, telling Foster to lie on a bench and sleep. When his blood pressure went down, the results were within acceptable limits. Ray Foster was on his way to Submarine School in New London, Connecticut in January 1941.

After completing the demanding program, Foster was transferred to *Gudgeon* about the time she was commissioned in April 1941. In short order *Gudgeon*, Foster, and the rest of the crew on board were heading first to Alaska and then to Pearl Harbor where the fleet was soon to endure the fateful attack. Foster, a feisty, short, but wiry man had a history that was not unusual for sailors at the time. Before the war, the regulars oftentimes had years of experience on a variety of ships, in many different ports. Later in the war, with huge manpower demands, the enlistees were quickly trained in their area of specialty and hurried about their assigned ship. The

Ninety-Day Wonders, as they were sarcastically called, would receive far less training than the prewar sailors.

On January 15, 1942 Foster and the other men found themselves on *Gudgeon* inching their way home. The seas were very rough and caused problems on board. One time a huge wave sent a flood of water down the air induction vent and one of the hatches. At sixty feet, periscope depth, the seas were so strong that it was difficult to make an observation. At ninety feet, the sea was still so unruly that the submarine rolled five to ten degrees from side to side.

Until January 25, *Gudgeon's* homeward bound voyage to Pearl Harbor had been without incident. The next day as *Gudgeon* approached Midway Island, Joseph Rochefort's code breakers at Pearl Harbor sent a secret radio communication that three Japanese submarines would soon be approaching *Gudgeon*. Grenfell and the men on board swung into action. The Japanese submarine I-73, a Kaidi Type 6a fleet submarine, was much larger than *Gudgeon*. The I-73 displaced around 1,785 tons on the surface, she was 331 feet long, and her speed on the surface was supposed to be greater than *Gudgeon's* despite her greater size. The Japanese said that the I-73 could make twenty-three knots on the surface, 8.5 knots submerged, with a whopping cruising range of 14,000 nautical miles.

Luckily for *Gudgeon* the I-73 took steps that betrayed her position. After the I-73's unfruitful involvement off Pearl Harbor, perhaps a few miles from *Gudgeon* off Lahaina, she took a cruise along the west coast of the United States and announced her presence by shelling a refinery near Los Angeles. This allowed American code breakers to track the I-73, as well as the I-71 and I-72 that accompanied her. At the same time, the trio of submarines carried on long-winded radio conversations with their base, which allowed their location to be roughly placed through direction-finding (DF) techniques used during the day. After announcing their presence by radio and hostile action, the submarines headed back to Japanese waters and their base in Kwajalein. On January 25, they passed Midway Island heading west and once again imprudently announced their whereabouts by firing a few shells at the island, while at the same time sealing their fate.

At 2320 on the twenty-sixth Grenfell received a direct message from ComSubPac (Commander Submarines Pacific Ocean) giving a firm indication that one of the submarines was on a course that would intersect with *Gudgeon*. Fortunately, there were enough torpedoes left for the chore. *Gudgeon* submerged and lay silently in wait for the careless trio of submarines to arrive. Grenfell wrote in his war patrol report that at latitude 28°-24' North, longitude 178°-35' East, at 0900 hours, at a location about 214 nautical miles west of Midway Island, on January 27, 1942, while submerged, the sound operator reported hearing "fast screws" on the port bow. Lieutenant Hylan B. Lyon, the OOD (Officer of the Deck) made periscope observations, hoping to find at least one of the submarines close enough for an attack. Lyon was the first to see a submarine on the surface at 5,000 yards. Grenfell described the action, "I went into the control room, took one look, and determined he wasn't one of ours. He was a Japanese all right. They were going home and coming right toward us."[53]

Because of the forward position of the deck gun, the shape of the conning tower, and other characteristics typical of Japanese submarines, silhouettes of which had been studied by every man on board, Joe Grenfell correctly surmised that this was one of Hirohito's I-boats and gave the command: "All hands General Quarters. Make ready all forward tubes. Down periscope."[54] With Lieutenant Dusty Dornin at the TDC, the firing party of *Gudgeon* was now ready to attack.

As Foster and the others in the forward torpedo room swung into action, Grenfell hurried over to the periscope that had just dropped into position. Grenfell observed six men on the bridge of the I-73, and then bellowed, "FIRE ONE. FIRE TWO. FIRE THREE." He would say later, "The phonograph is playing 'Look for the Silver Lining.' The tenor squawks to a stop on, 'When the Dark Clouds Come Your Way.' The Jap is boiling along, unsuspecting on the surface."[55] At 0907, the first of three torpedoes swished as it left *Gudgeon*. The range of the unidentified submarine 1,800. Grenfell would note in his personal memoir that Japan's successful attack at Pearl Harbor had "gone to their heads" and made them "very cocky."[56] As he said, "The Japs felt that they ruled the waves and controlled the whole ocean."[57] This submarine was exhibiting the same sense of invulnerability as the rest of the Fleet. Grenfell continued, "He had bombarded Midway a night or two before and they were riding along, high, wide, and handsome.

It was a nice day, their hatches were open, and the deck was crowded with Japanese sailors sitting around on deck laughing and enjoying themselves. It was a nice set-up." [58]

Though Joe Grenfell had seen six men on the bridge and a deck full of Japanese sailors, there was no hesitation in his voice as he ordered the attack. Once again, Captain Grenfell took action to end the lives of other human beings. However, as far as Grenfell and the men on board were concerned, the Japanese were much deserving of the furious revenge from *Gudgeon*'s forward torpedo tubes that day. Grenfell stared intently through the periscope and could see that the torpedoes had made their turn and were looking good. Just then, the heavy seas destabilized the submarine, causing her to lose proper depth control for about a minute, and Grenfell lost sight of the target.

Gudgeon personnel were convinced that two torpedoes had hit their mark because of the two "thuds" they heard, followed by explosions. Unfortunately, at the time of contact, the periscope was still under water. Within thirty seconds of the thuds, Grenfell was able to look for the I-73. It was nowhere to be seen. Propeller noises stopped entirely after explosive reverberations ceased at about one minute and forty-five seconds after firing. Grenfell, in his post-action patrol report stated that two of three torpedoes had hit this submarine of the I-68 class. Knowing that there were two other Japanese submarines in the area, he noted that he resisted the temptation to surface and search for wreckage.

For a boat with the aggressive motto, "Find 'Em Chase 'Em Sink 'Em," it is ironic that *Gudgeon*'s first big kill was neither found, nor chased.

Ray Foster, knowing full well that it could have been *Gudgeon* that had been caught on the surface and that they had sunk a ship full of submariners, was still rather subdued more than fifty years later, while describing the attack: "We were submerged and they were on the surface, and it was just one of those things. It was lucky for us and unlucky for them. We fired three torpedoes and all we saw was the smoke and they were gone. It was an untimely death for those folks." [59] After the attack, there was nothing subdued about the reaction of the *Gudgeon* crew. The men erupted with cheers and oaths in an explosion of pent-up frustration and anger. The men on *Gudgeon* deserved to celebrate. They had just become the first United States submarine in history to sink a warship from another country.

Most books on World War II naval warfare incorrectly credit *Gudgeon* with having sunk the I-173, not the I-73. In May 1942 after the I-73 had been sunk, the Japanese renumbered their submarines. The I-73 would have become the I-173 had she survived until that time, but she did not. No submarine named the I-173 *ever* served Japan during the war.

The victorious *Gudgeon* and her tired but proud crew continued toward Pearl Harbor. *Gudgeon* continued to dive during daylight hours to avoid being bombed by American planes patrolling in the area or being attacked by Japanese submarines reported to be in the area west of Pearl Harbor. By this time a system had been developed that was supposed to make the return trip for submarines a little safer than *Gudgeon*'s voyage to the Bungo Suido. When a submarine sent in her course and speed, the information was shared with the air forces around Pearl Harbor. This system would allow *Gudgeon* to travel on the surface, at least for the last leg of the long patrol. *Gudgeon* met the destroyer escort *Litchfield* outside Pearl Harbor and was escorted in. Jack Camp was surprised to see that the cleanup of the devastation of Pearl Harbor had been very thorough, but he surely exaggerated when he said that it "looked like nothing had happened." [60]

On January 31, 1942, *Gudgeon* tied up alongside the submarine tender *Pelias*. A patriotic crowd of onlookers was there to greet her. Much of the Navy's brass at Pearl Harbor excitedly boarded *Gudgeon*, including Admiral Chester Nimitz. There were many congratulations and questions. The crew was happy to be home and proud that they had made inroads against the Japanese Navy. It must have been quite a sight to behold when a doctor came aboard and had the men of *Gudgeon* drop their trousers while they were standing on the deck, so that a medical inspection could be done. It seems concern about that "luetic" thing prompted the impromptu inspection.

Gudgeon's men must have found the clean Hawaiian air intoxicating. That is, once they got used to fresh air again. At first, after a long patrol, fresh air seems to smell very bad. They had been deprived of clean oxygen for most of their fifty-two day patrol; having spent so much time submerged breathing air filled with cigarette smoke, diesel fuel fumes, and the expelled carbon dioxide from the lungs of their shipmates, to say nothing of the myriad body odors that abounded aboard the submarine. Fresh fruit was brought aboard and passed to the men waiting on the deck. The officers and crew devoured it. But that was not all. *Gudgeon*'s Executive Officer, Lieutenant Hylan B. "Pop" Lyon, announced that the crew would receive regal treatment at the plush Royal Hawaiian Hotel, which had been set aside for the Navy's underwater crews.

Grenfell submitted his war patrol report to Forrest O'Leary, commander of Submarine Division Sixty-Two. Divisions Sixty-One and Sixty-Two combined to make Submarine Squadron Six, commanded by Allan McCann. McCann was widely known as the man most responsible for the development of the diving rescue chamber. The bond between one Squadron Six submariner and another is more than just administrative. To this day, surviving former *Gudgeon* submariners talk with pride about Submarine Squadron Six and their place in it. During the war, submariners in a given squadron or division tended to go to war together, hang out ashore together, fight one another on occasion, and even switch from one boat to another.

After Joe Grenfell arrived in Pearl, he hurried to see Admiral Thomas Withers. As a former Naval Academy miler, Grenfell had only one speed: full throttle. His hope of course was that the patrol would be well received, the criticisms few, and that constructive suggestions would be made for the next patrol.

Grenfell submitted his patrol report for review. The comments at each level—division, squadron, and force—were made in what were called endorsements, which gave Grenfell feedback, both positive and negative, along with advice and directives. Grenfell reported that they had sighted only four freighters in *Gudgeon*'s assigned patrol area, along with nine sampans and two Japanese planes flying down the coast of Kyushu. The area of ocean outside the assigned patrol area had almost as many potential targets as had the operating area; they had observed a large freighter, a second vessel believed to be a freighter, a submarine, and twelve sampans there. Grenfell reported that he had made approaches on all seven ships worthy of attack. Using the underwater approach common in the early days of the war, *Gudgeon* had only been able to close within firing range on three of the ships. At the time, Grenfell thought he had sunk a freighter and possibly a submarine, along with the sure miss on January 4. All in all this was an impressive record considering the factors that were working against *Gudgeon* at the time.

Grenfell felt that the morale of the personnel was good throughout the patrol despite the fact that the men on board had been planning to head to the west coast for some R & R, the very day of the Japanese attack at Pearl Harbor. The patrol followed an extended shakedown cruise, and the crew had every right to be worn out. Even before the Japanese attack, *Gudgeon's* schedule had been exhausting. The men were due for a break, but they had to return to sea and fight a war.

The crew's performance was not entirely exemplary. When interviewed in 1943, Dusty Dornin discussed the difficulties that one sailor had on the first patrol. Dornin said that the sailor, Eugene J. Butts, mess attendant third class, was a "negro mess boy." [61] Every time *Gudgeon's* diving alarm sounded, Butts would scurry off with a Momsen Lung. The Momsen Lung was invented by Swede Momsen as a breathing device to be worn by individual submariners so that they could leave a sunken submarine and safely make their way to the surface. Apparently Butts would panic and head for the after part of the boat, which was closest to the surface on a dive. As he hurriedly moved through the submarine, he would cause such disruption that a few of the chiefs threatened to bang him over the head with a monkey wrench. Dornin said that Butts was "temperamentally unfit" for submarines, and he was transferred off *Gudgeon* after the first patrol. [62]

The submarine service of the day seemed to be a little more enlightened than the other branches of the segregated military, or perhaps it was that segregation of blacks from whites was impossible in the packed confines of a fleet submarine. The minority sailor was usually restricted to servant-like roles such as mess attendant, but at times served in more crucial roles, such as lookout.

When interviewed recently, Ray Foster said that one sailor had "acted up" on *Gudgeon's* maiden patrol and been kicked off *Gudgeon*. Foster said that the sailor, who seems certain to be Butts, had not had submarine training. Foster refused to give the man's name. Whatever problems Butts may have had—and anybody who has never experienced what Butts experienced would be highly foolish to be critical of him—overall the crew performed remarkably well. Indeed, the psychological and physical challenges to the men on board the submarine for the first patrol seem daunting.

After the attack, *Gudgeon* returned to Pearl Harbor, past the still smoldering wreckage of the Pacific fleet. Then she headed out to sea to face the dangers of the Allied bombers as well as the Imperial Japanese Navy. Finally, weeks later, the men aboard *Gudgeon* were within sight of the Japanese main islands, undersea in cramped stuffy quarters, unbathed and uncertain, all the while thinking of brothers and lifelong friends in uniform. They came to realize that all of those prewar plans for the big job, education, or marriage were remotely possible and meaningless. All of this, then having to hold your breath as the thin-shelled *Gudgeon* rubbed dangerously, metal-on-metal, against the chains attached to the mines which could blow a gaping hole in the boat, insuring a ghastly death for every man on board. A death that would mean an anonymous grave deep in enemy waters, far from home.

From December 25, 1941 until January 20, 1942, surfacing after sundown and diving before dawn, the men on board had not seen the sun, not even once. *Gudgeon* had left port with her full complement of twenty-four torpedoes but had only fired eight by the time she returned to Hawaiian waters. Of the two torpedoes fired at the first ship, both were set to run at a depth of twenty-five feet. Grenfell believed they both passed in front of the intended target. The three torpedoes fired at the second freighter were set at twenty feet. He said that he thought the warhead of the second and perhaps the third torpedo exploded on impact, and that two of the three torpedoes fired at the submarine had exploded. He wrote that all torpedoes ran hot, straight, and normal.

This conclusion was made at a time in the war when torpedo problems were only the stuff of nightmares. Indeed, *Gudgeon*'s torpedo crews prided themselves on the diligent practice of "working the torpedoes" while on patrol so that they would function properly. Despite the problems that would plague the submarines that fought the war early on, the torpedoes used on *Gudgeon*'s first patrol *seemed* to work well.

The torpedoes of the day were as ingenious as the submarines themselves. Most likely *Gudgeon* had been supplied with a load of Mark 14 torpedoes although the available records do not clarify this issue. The Mark 14 was the most advanced torpedo available at that time. It was twenty-one inches in diameter and could travel as fast as 46 knots for 4,500 yards. They could be shot farther and slower though the skippers of the fleet much preferred the faster speed. The Mark 14 torpedoes were a whopping 24 feet in length, weighed over 2,200 pounds, and contained a 500 pound warhead that was set to explode on contact or by magnetic induction when passing through the naturally-occurring magnetic field under and around any ship made of steel or iron.

A problem with the Mark 14 torpedo that would eventually be discovered was that it ran 10 feet deeper than it was set. Problems with the magnetic exploder mechanism were also present and often caused premature explosions about 50 yards in front of the submarines, right after the screws on the torpedo had spun enough to arm it. Peering through the periscopes, the skippers would see the premature explosion between them and the target ship and oftentimes think that they had hit the vessel. The enemy ship, however, remained undamaged and was now alerted to the presence of an enemy submarine. The third problem with the torpedo was that when using the contact detonator (as opposed to the magnetic detonator) the torpedo would not explode unless it struck the target at an oblique angle. A right angle at impact, which was preferred by the skippers and Navy doctrine, would often result in the torpedo hitting the side of the ship, flying into the air, or bouncing off. More importantly, it crushed the detonation pin before the warhead could explode. The submarine skipper would, of course, be disappointed and frustrated to see a perfectly aimed torpedo hit the side of an enemy ship and then fly into the air like a javelin, especially since the ship could then follow the torpedo wakes and attack the submarine. The torpedoes of the day were equipped with a Mark 6 magnetic exploding mechanism, which was supposed to blow up when the torpedo was 15–20 feet below the waterline of a target vessel. Early in the war, it was thought that a torpedo exploding under a ship was three times more effective than a torpedo that struck the side of a ship, particularly warships because they are more heavily armored there. This would be disproved later in the war, but early on, submarine skippers were usually aiming for a hit under the target, which was another factor which made sinking Japanese ships more difficult than it needed to be.

The three torpedo flaws that dogged the submarine fleet were supposed to have been completely resolved by October–November 1943. *Gudgeon* and her sister submarines were forced to fight the war with faulty torpedoes for almost two years. Stated another way, this meant that *Gudgeon* had imperfectly operating torpedoes for about twenty-two of her twenty-eight months of *wartime* service.

In Joe Grenfell's first post-patrol report, he said that one or two of the torpedoes exploded when the I-73 had been attacked. When interviewed in 1943 by the Navy, Dusty Dornin indicated that "two hits were obtained" and that this was verified by the fact that the torpedo exploded at the right time, and because wreckage had been sighted.[63] Yet Joe Grenfell did not claim a sinking when he returned to Pearl Harbor. The sinking was confirmed by the code breakers who determined that after the attack on January 27, 1942, the always-active radio of the I-73 was silenced forever.

Oddly, when interviewed by Clay Blair Jr. for *Silent Victory* many years after the war, Dornin contradicted claims made during the war. He said that neither he nor Dixie Farrell thought that the torpedoes had exploded. He said they thought that the Japanese had seen the approaching torpedo wakes and the torpedoes had dudded against the side of the submarine and sunk harmlessly to the bottom or that the torpedoes had suffered a premature explosion. Either way, he thought this caused the submarine's skipper to panic and dive with the hatches open, flooding and sinking the boat. One fact is incontrovertible; the I-73 was never heard from again, and one way or another *Gudgeon* sank her. However, there were many questions about both the performance of the torpedoes and whether or not *Gudgeon* had even hit the I-73 with torpedoes. The wartime statements contrasting with those that came later.

Executive Officer Hylan B. Lyon commented upon *Gudgeon*'s good fortune. "The entire thing came about purely by accident. If you had two ships from two different locations over one-thousand miles apart, and tried to make their courses coincide, it would be nearly impossible to do. We practically didn't have to change course or change speed. We just got the torpedoes ready and fired."[64]

F. M. O'Leary, the Division Commander, weighed in first, praising Grenfell in particular for the "extremely satisfactory" manner in which he had conducted the patrol.[65] Because Joe Grenfell had successfully downed the I-73, he recommended him for a Navy Cross. A. R. McCann, at the squadron level, called the patrol "excellent" and was careful to point out that he was not being critical of Grenfell for having been submerged so long in transit, as had O'Leary, but he did advise the skipper that the time spent under water could have been "materially" decreased, which would have allowed for more patrol time in the assigned area than the twelve days that *Gudgeon* achieved.[66] This criticism must have been very perplexing to Lieutenant Commander Grenfell, who had patrolled and traveled to his patrol area exactly as he had been told to do.

Admiral Thomas Withers, Commander Submarines Pacific Ocean, did criticize Grenfell for being on station on only twelve of the fifty-two days *Gudgeon* was at sea. He said that he realized *Gudgeon* did not have radar for plane detection, but with more efficient lookouts, more surface cruising could have been done to increase the time on station. He noted that only two aircraft had been seen in the operating area, then said that *Gudgeon* could have surfaced as night fell to increase speed en route. Grenfell usually surfaced around 2100 hours, several hours after dark. If he had surfaced earlier in the night, it would have allowed for the battery-powered engines to be recharged earlier in the night. Admiral Withers may not have noted that the area outside the assigned patrol area had been just as bountiful as the area to which *Gudgeon* had been sent. Then again, perhaps that misses the Admiral's point.

Lieutenant Commander Grenfell fired only one-third of his torpedoes on the patrol. This fact did not stop Withers from criticizing him for having fired five torpedoes at the two freighters *Gudgeon* attacked on the patrol, citing concern about the shortage of torpedoes available. This shortage would continue until mid-1943 when it was alleviated by increased rates of manufacture. By this time, word had been passed to Grenfell's superior that the I-68 class submarine had disappeared from radio traffic since the moment of the attack on January 27. *Gudgeon* got credit for the sinking. Grenfell received much praise by all three of his superiors for having sunk the boat. Withers promised to install a vapor compression still so that water rationing would come to an end. The *Gudgeon* crew had been restricted to 1.8 gallons of water per day per man. Withers addressed the crew's desire to keep up with the war news by furnishing listings of all of the commercial radio stations which could be copied in the Pacific Ocean area. Finally,

Gudgeon was credited for having sunk a 5,000 ton merchant vessel and a 1,400 ton submarine.

When Grenfell returned to Pearl Harbor, he was also criticized by the Office of the Chief of Naval Operations for not having submitted his latest fitness reports in a timely manner. This criticism was easily deflected by Grenfell when he reminded the land dwellers at the bureau that he had not responded earlier because he had been a little busy, fighting a war off Japan.

During the course of the war submariners of the day commonly overestimated the size of ships sunk. When they sighted a ship, the men on board would look in the Japanese Merchant Ship Recognition Manual, a book that showed silhouettes of known merchant ships. The men would compare the outline of their target with one in the book and decide which vessel their target most resembled. It was the natural tendency of the skippers to choose the larger of two silhouettes when they were similar. This resulted in frequent overestimation of the target's size.

The freighter attacked on January 9, 1942, by *Gudgeon* was said by Ray Foster to have been "burning from one end to the other."[67] Joe Grenfell wrote at the time that he and the OOD saw it sink. Dusty Dornin said that they saw two hits and that it "seemed" to sink in five minutes. In this situation, the men were not apparently misled by tall plumes of water or thuds on the side of the vessel. Yet, the freighter's sinking was ultimately disallowed by JANAC. When Grenfell and the OOD said they saw it sink, one can conclude that either the two officers were incomprehensibly mistaken or that the men on the JANAC commission erred.

Withers did not give Lieutenant Commander Grenfell a "well done." He did him one better, pinning a Navy Cross on him for having sunk a five thousand ton freighter and for having severely damaged a submarine. Credit for the sinking of the I-73 would come after the ceremony. Not acknowledged by Grenfell's superiors was the fact that *Gudgeon* had just completed the war's first patrol, one lasting fifty-two days. It would seem that the praise that had been heaped on *Pollack*, which left Pearl Harbor a few days after *Gudgeon*, is appropriate for the SS-211. Submarine Division Forty-Three Commander, N.S. Ives, commenting upon *Pollack*'s patrol to Japan wrote that such a successful patrol "not long ago was thought to be impracticable if not impossible. The extraordinary achievement in conducting a successful war patrol thirty-five-hundred miles from home in close and patrolled enemy waters involving over eight-thousand miles of surface and submerged cruising without suffering damage from the enemy or loss of any personnel through sickness or enemy action is worthy of consideration in itself which is further amplified by losses to and harassing effect upon the enemy."[68]

Dixie Farrell, Dusty Dornin, and Joe Grenfell would eventually each receive a Silver Star, in part because of what *Gudgeon* had accomplished on her first patrol. As ace torpedoman Ray Foster, speaking for the entire crew, said sarcastically of the officers' decorations, "And we all got a pat on the head."[69] Once ashore, lovesick Jack Camp found out that his first daughter, Gail, had arrived on Christmas day, and that Mildred and Gail were doing very well.

The men of *Gudgeon* had rendered valiant service to their country and advanced the craft of undersea warfare in the Pacific. But even more importantly, the ships of the Imperial Japanese Navy were now in danger. No matter where they were, at sea or in port, the Silent Service of the United States could get them. In fewer than four years virtually every Japanese-owned ship that was able to float would be sunk. And, it was the men of the USS *Gudgeon* and those who followed that would do most of the damage.

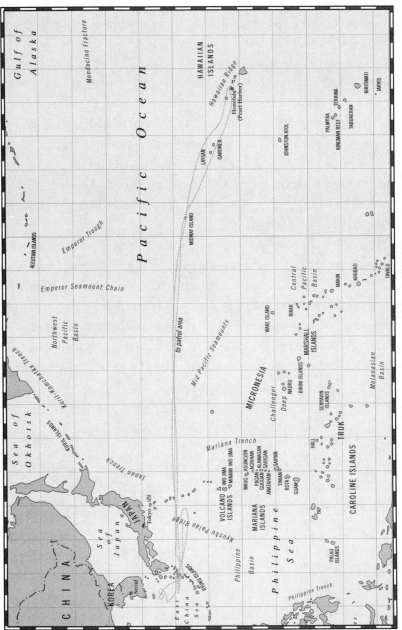

Second War Patrol • Approximate Course • Feb. 22–April 15, 1942

▪ 2 ▪

Escape from the East China Sea

SECOND WAR PATROL: February 22, 1942–April 15, 1942

We are never so easily deceived as when
we imagine we are deceiving others.

La Rochefoucauld

*G*udgeon was the first to leave Pearl Harbor but not the first to return. *Pollack*, having completed a successful but shorter thirty-nine day patrol outside Tokyo Bay, returned on January 21 having expended sixteen torpedoes in six attacks. *Pollack* had sighted fifteen ships of sufficient size to attack, more than twice as many targets as *Gudgeon* had sighted in a much longer patrol. Lieutenant Commander Stanley Mosely of *Pollack* and Joe Grenfell were each credited with two sinkings.

Joe Grenfell, Dusty Dornin, and the rest of the *Gudgeon* crew were allowed three weeks of R & R between patrols. Though the crew on the *Gudgeon* was not the first group of submariners to return, they were still regarded as the "big men on shore." The war was so fresh that military and civilian personnel alike were just itching to hear about their adventures. However, the men were under very strict orders to say nothing about what had transpired and, indeed, said nothing. The lack of bragging opportunities did not dampen the thrill of the new digs at the plush Royal Hawaiian Hotel. While the men relaxed, all of the responsibilities for *Gudgeon* were turned over to a relief crew assigned to the submarine tender, the matronly USS *Pelias*. To make the time as restful as possible, the weary submarine crew of *Gudgeon* found that it almost took an act of Congress for one of them to be allowed back on the submarine base during leave, not that any of them wanted to get back on board the *Gudgeon* very badly. The Navy wanted the men to do their relaxing as far away from *Gudgeon* as possible.

Between the first and second patrols, on February 2, 1942, in faraway Des Moines, Iowa, William C. Ostlund a recent Butler University graduate with a degree in Business Administration enlisted into the Navy. It would be some time however, before the twenty-three year old would board a submarine at war.

Once ashore, at Pearl Harbor, the men were not very astonished to find that Honolulu had become an armed camp. The authorities had grounded private planes. There was news and mail censorship, blackouts at night, curfews, and gas rationing. Every civilian on Oahu over the age of six had gone to have their fingerprints taken. Even the beautiful sands at Waikiki had been stricken by war: Barbed wire twisted down the beach as far as the eye could see.

Except for one difficulty, Jack Camp had a very nice time on shore: He found himself unable to drop off to sleep. The 4 to 8 watches he had been doing had decimated his sleep cycle. Camp, ever the loyal husband, spent much of his time swimming at the Royal Hawaiian. According to his diary, there were no late night shenanigans with the other *Gudgeon* sailors. He sent Mildred and his new baby daughter, Gail, who were stateside, flowers and money, eventually receiving a letter from Millie, which made him feel "swell."[1] Of course, Camp was not the only *Gudgeon* submariner to spend his time at the hotel that cost $75 a night before the war.

The Royal Hawaiian, known as the Pink Palace of the Pacific, was a huge pink stucco, Spanish-Moorish style resort with around four-hundred rooms. It had been opened shortly before the start of the Depression and was a favorite of the stars of the day including Douglas Fairbanks Jr., Al Jolson, and Mary Pickford, as well as super-rich industrialists such as the Fords and the Rockefellers. An enlisted man could stay at the swank Hawaiian, which the Navy leased throughout the entire war, for twenty-five cents a night. It was too good an offer for a battle-weary sailor to turn down. On occasion, aviators and individuals from other branches were allowed to recuperate at the hotel, but in general, the Royal Hawaiian was specifically designated for submarine crew and officers. Navy planners believed that submarine duty was the toughest duty of all because of the restrictive nature of submarines. Many men on *Gudgeon* had not made it out of the confines of the submarine on even one occasion during the two-month patrol. Submariners were supposed to be given two weeks' minimum rest between patrols. The relief crews preparing the submarine for the next patrol would usually need a week or so to get everything ready. Then the submarine crew would come aboard and take the boat out to sea for several days to test the equipment.

Unfortunately, rather than the fine cuisine that had been served prior to the war at the Royal Hawaiian, the food was All Navy. The Royal Hawaiian fit the bill in other ways though. There was no reveille and the submariners were allowed much more freedom than was otherwise customary. The bar was open in the afternoon and served beer and soft drinks, but hard liquor was verboten. According to some of the *Gudgeon* submariners, none of the hard liquor that was available was even minimally tolerable anyway. The "Five Islands Gin" that *was* served on the island was distilled in a bathtub on Tuesday and available for drinking on Wednesday.

Unknown to the submariners the hotel's expensive champagne, liquors, and vintage wines were stored deep in the bowels of the building. It was a good thing the submariners didn't know this because the thirsty and clever men who served *Gudgeon* likely would have tried to get their hands on it, though it was a job that almost certainly would have been too much for them. After the war, the Royal Hawaiian's chief engineer would accompany the head of security and many guards into the confines of the deep dark basement to an ordinary-looking wall piled high with dirt and then spend two days jack-hammering through a two-foot-thick wall in order to free the rich stocks.

The fact is, that the lack of good booze available in Hawaii was not much of a problem for the men of *Gudgeon* or the other submarines in the fleet. As will be seen, there was a very potent alcohol available for the submariners to drink on every one of the submarines in the fleet, if the men were shrewd enough to get it off the boat, then patient enough to prepare it.

The pale submariners would sleep four to a room, hanging their skivvies in the windows to dry in the soft breezes of the island paradise, which now looked more like an armed camp. Card games, oftentimes very expensive games of poker or acey-deucey, occurred anywhere at the Pink Palace—the hallways, the stairs, or any other convenient place for a group of men with their hazardous duty pay and a deck of cards. Before the war, an apprentice seaman was paid $21 per month. This was raised to $50 during the war. Chiefs received around $120. Submariners got an additional 50 percent for submarine duty and then 20 percent more when they were at sea. At only twenty-five cents a night for room and board, the *Gudgeon* sailors had a lot of extra money to spend on their leaves. Sometimes, such as after *Gudgeon*'s first patrol, about two months' worth of pay had been accumulated, thus making the card games high stakes affairs.

Best of all, perhaps, the submariners at the Royal Hawaiian would soon learn that women, who were so greatly outnumbered by lonely young men on the island, regularly attended the dances at the ballroom of the hotel. If the submariners were lucky, the hottest big bands of the day headed by Benny Goodman or Tommy Dorsey would be filling the halls of the plush, heretofore far-too-expensive hotel with their frenetic, high-energy music. There were also other, clandestine ways of meeting women. It didn't take long for Hotel Street in downtown Honolulu to become well known for its many prostitutes, tattoo parlors, and cheap bars.

Just when things were really getting to be swell ashore, the relief crew of the submarine tender *Pelias* finished their repairs and turned the boat back over to Lieutenant Commander Grenfell on February 12. Just where the SS-211 would be going next was a matter of rumor. Jack Camp wrote in his log that there was "no dope yet as to where our next trip is to be but all have a good idea."[2]

Once the men were on board, Lieutenant Hylan B. "Pop" Lyon called them to quarters and told the crew where they were going. They would be heading back toward Japan, a little further south and west of the Bungo Suido, where they had first patrolled. Lyon said it was going to be a good area. Camp was by now very skeptical of such claims, writing that the assigned area was "supposed to be a good one" or "so everyone says."[3] Gene Butts and eight other crew members were transferred off *Gudgeon*. Irvin Hornkohl, formerly of the *Oklahoma*, would join *Gudgeon* on her second patrol. A little more than two months earlier, his breakfast had been interrupted by the Japanese attack and, standing exposed and vulnerable on the dock of the Pearl Harbor submarine base, he had bravely fired at the marauding Japanese Zeros. In addition, William Russell Hofer from the sunken *Nevada* and fourteen other new submariners arrived for their first patrol on *Gudgeon*.

After spending the early morning hours of December 7 on the dock, Hornkohl joined a work party attempting to cut through the bottom of the capsized *Oklahoma* to free his shipmates who were trapped inside, pounding on the hull, hoping to be saved. Hornkohl handled the air hoses, while men at the other end cut through the bottom of the ship. Hornkohl never forgot the tapping his shipmates made from the wrong side of the hull of the massive battleship. He watched as the saws finally made it through the thick skin of the *Oklahoma*, the air rushed out, and the water surged in to stifle the screams of the trapped men, their hands protruding from the vessel then slowly slipping back into their watery grave as the compartment became fully engorged.

Hornkohl, Hofer, and the rest of the new crew relished the opportunity for revenge against the Japanese, who had devastated their ships and killed so many buddies. A few weeks after the attack, Hornkohl and a group of the men who had been attending mine school volunteered for submarines. Hornkohl volunteered and went to the submarine relief tender USS *Pelias*, and when *Gudgeon* returned from her first patrol, the volunteers replaced those who had been transferred. When asked whether he would like to serve on *Gudgeon*, Hornkohl, with thoughts about the lost *Oklahoma* constantly on his mind and a fury like he had never known, realized that this would be his chance and responded simply, "I'm your man." He would say later that he was so determined that if he had to, he would have gone after the Japanese on a "rowboat with a machine gun."[4]

Hornkohl was in awe of submariners, yet confident. He knew that he had never had any problems with claustrophobia, so he felt that he would do well aboard a submarine. He remembered seeing *Gudgeon* after her first patrol. The white "211" on the side of the conning tower was still faintly visible. The numbers had been removed for intelligence purposes once the war started. He thought, "That's the one I want," and considered himself lucky to be assigned to *Gudgeon*. He found the submarine's graceful lines and lethality an alluring combination.[5]

Hornkohl said that the Chief of the Boat, James C. "Gunner" Ogden, nicknamed all the new crew as they came aboard. For some reason, learning that Hornkohl had Native American ancestry, he named him "Moose," a nickname that has stuck to this day. William Russell Hofer, the *Nevada* orphan, inexplicably became "Jake."[6] "Moose" Hornkohl had been raised in a rural area west of Denver, Colorado. He was born in 1923 to a family that scrimped and scraped and got along by raising cows and other means as opportunities arose. The area was rural and poor. After attending school through the seventh grade, he told his folks that he did not want to go anymore. His parents obliged and at the age of twelve he started working in Denver at a sheet metal company. He rode into the city with his father, worked all day, and then rode home. Demands upon young Irvin and his father to make money were great, opportunities few. At the time, his father was a "car knocker," a railcar inspector, for the Burlington Railroad. Not seeing much opportunity in Denver, when he turned eighteen, Hornkohl enlisted in the Navy and was eventually assigned to the *Oklahoma*. It was very difficult to get off battleships. Being an unrated seaman, he was not a hot commodity, so he put in for mine school to increase his skills and improve his future in the Navy. Then the attack on Pearl Harbor came and Moose Hornkohl joined *Gudgeon* for her second war patrol, a prospect which pleased the young man.

Al McCann, Commander Submarine Squadron Six, must have felt relieved by February 1942 when all six of his twelve submarines, the ones that had gone out on patrol, returned intact. However, *Tautog, Trout, Tambor,* and *Triton* did not have any sinkings. *Gudgeon* had bagged a couple of ships for sixty-five-hundred tons, and *Thresher* an additional vessel for forty-five-hundred tons. Of the six Squadron Six submarines, only *Gudgeon* had gone to Empire waters off the mainland. *Tautog* and *Thresher* had patrolled the Marshall Islands; *Trout* was based off Midway Island; *Tambor* and *Triton* patrolled Wake.

In February, McCann sent out five "G" submarines from Division Sixty-Two. *Gar* and *Grenadier* went to Empire waters, *Grampus* to the Marshalls, *Grayback* the Marianas, and the USS *Gudgeon* patrolled the East China Sea. With the *Grayling* already in the Carolines, *Tuna* off Japan, *Trout* on a special mission off Corregidor and *Triton* patrolling the East

China Sea, each Squadron Six submarine was or had been in action. They would have much more success than on the first patrols after the attack at Pearl Harbor. All but *Grenadier* and *Grayling* would receive credit for at least one sinking this time out. Lessons learned on the first patrols were paying dividends. Perhaps of the most importance was that they learned where most of the Japanese merchant marine was heading: south of Japan.

Gudgeon left Hawaiian waters on February 22, 1942, with a large crowd of patriotic civilians in attendance to shout encouragement. A Navy band jauntily played "Anchors Aweigh." Moose Hornkohl remembered clearly that he had felt "very alone" heading out for war the first time.[7] The destroyer *Litchfield* once again escorted *Gudgeon* on her way toward Japan. The next day, before *Litchfield* left *Gudgeon*, she dropped a depth charge well off *Gudgeon*'s port beam for training purposes. The hope was that having heard and felt the real thing, a Japanese depth charging would not be such a jolt to the crew. It was training that would turn out to be aptly timed because this time out the men on board *Gudgeon* would take a brutal pounding from Japanese "shit cans," as they were spitefully called during the war.

Gudgeon arrived at Midway Island on the twenty-sixth. While she was being topped off with fuel, the crew had a chance to go ashore and see the marines stationed there. Jack Camp concluded that the leathernecks had a tough life on the primitive island but that it was not as tough a life as that of a submariner. He got a kick out of the countless white Layson Albatross birds ashore, known widely by their nickname, "gooney birds." The albatross is very graceful in the air but quite awkward on land.

By dusk, *Gudgeon* was full of diesel fuel and departed for her area south and west of the Japanese mainland. Grenfell once again played it safe, diving during the day and surfacing after sundown. By March 1, however, Joe Grenfell feeling more confident and still outside Japanese-dominated waters had the ship cruising boldly on the surface during daylight hours on two of her diesel engines. It would have been faster to plow forward on all four diesels, but the expenditure in fuel would have been too costly. Compared to the first patrol, *Gudgeon* was making good time and would have more time on station to search for Japanese shipping, which would satisfy Admiral Withers and the other critics of Grenfell's performance on his first patrol.

At 0645 on March 2, *Gudgeon* had to dive to avoid the menacing actions of United States aircraft. Ray Foster recalled vividly what happened: "We used to get permission to go up and relieve the lookout for fresh air and sun and so forth when we were off of Midway Island. The Captain was on the bridge, and I was one of the lookouts. I was there about half an hour when I said, 'Aircraft, aircraft,' and the OOD [Officer of the Deck] said, 'Clear the bridge, dive, dive, dive.' The Captain said, 'Where? Where?' I pointed back and went down the hatch. I was rigging out the bow planes and the Captain said, 'Send Foster to the conning tower.' When I got there, the Skipper asked, 'Are you sure you saw a plane?' 'What kind was it?'" Knowing that it would have been foolish for him to have stood around to identify the type of plane and its national origin the wisecracking Foster replied, "The kind whose wings don't flap."[8] Joe Grenfell did not appreciate the smart attitude of the torpedoman, and Foster was curtly dismissed.

The plane Foster had sighted turned out to be an SBD Dauntless dive bomber off the carrier *Enterprise* and mistook *Gudgeon* for a Japanese submarine. The *Gudgeon* crew had made a crash dive in forty-six seconds, and as Jack Camp reported, "By golly [we] got down just in time because we got a depth charge off our stbd. quarter."[9] Camp was apparently in his bunk when the depth charge exploded and must have been more than a little shook up by the blast because Dusty Dornin ribbed him about his reaction. Luckily, *Gudgeon* sustained no damage, but Grenfell decided to stay down the rest of the day.

When interviewed in 1943, Dusty Dornin said the U.S. plane got in so close because *Gudgeon*'s radar was turned off at the time. As *Gudgeon* reached eighty feet submerged, a five-hundred pound bomb rocked *Gudgeon*'s underwater haven. Camp wrote proudly, "Ole *Gudgeon* goes through first attack with flying colors."[10] Camp seems not to have been aware that it was an American pilot who had attempted to sink the submarine. He concluded incorrectly that since the SD radar was on all night after the bombing and the Japanese had not sent other ships or planes to continue the attack, the Japanese must have figured they sank the *Gudgeon*. Grenfell was infuriated when he later learned the truth. The first attack on the USS *Gudgeon* had been made by a careless American bomber.

Things were uneventful after the bombing. Numerous small, lighted sampans were seen quite frequently, but they were not deemed to be of military significance by Joe Grenfell and *Gudgeon* ignored them. On the tenth, *Gudgeon* arrived on station after a fourteen-day passage, with the submarine entering her area through the Colnett Straits. Grenfell decided to patrol at a place that would surely be loaded with prey—the confluence of the three steamer lanes: Nagasaki–Indo-China, Nagasaki–Manila, and Shanghai–Yokohama. Three days later, on March 13, 1942, off the southwest tip of Kyushu, the lookouts sighted a small, armed merchant ship, or as Grenfell would refer to it later, a "broken down tramp steamer."[11] Grenfell fired two torpedoes. The wake of the first torpedo was seen passing under the vessel. When both the torpedoes missed, Grenfell said that his able torpedo officer, Dusty Dornin, "just about broke down and wept over the negative results."[12] Though Dornin was upset at the time, he could not have known then that the failure in this attack very possibly had nothing to do with his performance. The torpedoes probably ran deeper than they were set to run, or as would be learned later, other factors might have accounted for the vessel's survival. Leaving the tramp off in the distance, *Gudgeon* moved on in search of greater prey.

The attack procedure was similar to that on other fleet submarines and was described by Moose Hornkohl. "There was a torpedoman on watch all the time. I mean they could sit down and do anything they wanted, but he was the first one to make a move when they made a sighting or something. He started everything within a matter of minutes. If the Officer of the Deck sighted a ship or sighted something suspicious, the first thing the OOD would do was be to call down to the Old Man. He'd send a messenger down if it was at night, and he'd go to the state room and get the skipper out of his bunk. The skipper would come out even if he was in his underwear and he'd run up on the bridge and get the information and make the decision about whether to go to battle stations, to put four main engines on the line and chase the guy. There were a lot of decisions to be made."[13]

On the fifteenth, with the United States Navy in desperate straits following the Pearl Harbor debacle and the Battle of Midway still months away, Camp wrote excitedly that there were supposed to be three Japanese carriers in the area. He looked forward to sighting this "big meat." One of the carriers was eventually identified as *Kaga*. Grenfell maneuvered the submarine into the lane that intelligence considered to be the most likely one for the carriers to take, *Gudgeon* would make no sightings, and none of the submarines in the area were able to intercept these prized Japanese warships.

Camp, fighting back the boredom and tedium of *Gudgeon*'s eighteenth straight all-day dive, kept his morale high by reminding himself that he and the crew were fighting the war to help keep his family safe. The dives would start around 5 A.M. and end after dark, around 7:30 P.M. The patriotic and angry Camp wrote that if need be "by heck I'll stay out here forever." [14] By 3:00 P.M. each day, Camp found that the air on board was getting foul. Inexplicably, the skipper had decided not to use anything to absorb the excessive carbon dioxide although devices were available on board to do so. The men's anxiety was heightened by numerous uncharted islands, which presented grounding dangers. Camp figured that those who had been on *Gudgeon* since the prewar days had been on land nineteen days in the last five months and wrote, "Christopher Columbus hasn't a thing on us. War is 'h'." [15] In the next nine days, the lookouts sighted twenty-nine sampans, small flat-bottomed boats of Chinese origin with the oars in front, all too small to be a fit target.

On March 26, 1942, *Gudgeon* did find a worthwhile target. Jack Camp had just fallen asleep when he was awakened around 0200 by Grenfell ordering the crew to get the stern torpedo tubes ready for firing. Grenfell had sighted a darkened freighter making nine knots. When the torpedomen in the forward torpedo room placed the brass Buddha lucky piece between the torpedo tubes, they had performed the ultimate insult to the Japanese, calling upon Buddha, the Japanese religious symbol for good luck and fortune to help them kill the Japanese sailors. Before an attack, regardless of which tubes were being used, stern or bow, the torpedomen and anyone else who could get close to the little brass piece would walk by and rub the Buddha's fat belly. Like all superstitions, as soon as *Gudgeon* had good fortune, the Buddha's capacity to bring the submarine luck was firmly established. The little Buddha would carry the *Gudgeon* through the war, or so the men hoped. For good measure, when *Gudgeon* found herself in a pinch— whether during a depth charge attack or while engaged in a deck gun battle—the fat little Buddha's belly would get a good working over.

Just south of Korea and West of Kyushu, Joe Grenfell and his men maneuvered *Gudgeon* into a good attack angle and fired three torpedoes. Two torpedoes found the mark. Grenfell watched the ship go down by the stern and turn over but had great difficulty explaining what had happened in the attack. The visibility was extremely poor, and the problem of prematurely exploding torpedoes was not known by this time in the war. *Gudgeon* would eventually be given credit for having sunk a five-thousand ton cargo vessel, reduced to 4,000 tons by JANAC.

A groggy Jack Camp said he was "thrilled" to hear the ship blowing sky high.[16] Camp wrote in his log that after the attack, lights on the water had been observed and that some of the crew had probably made it into lifeboats. Grenfell did not pick up survivors nor execute those still living. Camp said he felt a little sorry for the "B's" but "after Pearl Harbor there's nothing too good for the whole lot of the Japs."[17] Camp had noticed that many in the crew were ill on this patrol. One of the new crew members had passed out the night before, the stresses and strains of an underwater war patrol no doubt taking its toll upon at least one rookie submariner.

The next day, a little further north, also at 0200, *Gudgeon* sighted a ten-thousand ton cargo-passenger ship making twelve knots. *Gudgeon* approached the ship and fired three torpedoes. There was no doubt that two torpedoes hit their mark. Grenfell and Officer of the Deck Dusty Dornin watched the Japanese scurry around the stricken ship, now aflame, men dying and screaming, plumes of smoke and fire lapping high into the night sky. It was a horror show for the *Gudgeon*'s officers. The Japanese sailors, who were able to, threw lifeboats in the water. Jack Camp noted that the water temperature was right around 32°. Once again, Grenfell ignored the lifeboats and men climbing aboard them and moved on. Jack Camp was a polite, kind-hearted soul who had been thrust involuntarily into the savagery of war, however much it went against his nature. Once again, he felt sorry for the "Poor B's," who would very likely die from hypothermia, shock, or wounds before long. Then, perhaps remembering the carnage at Pearl Harbor, yet clearly conflicted with the whole affair, he wrote, "Ole *Gudgeon* is doing some nice work now," and added that the "silly little Japs" would probably stop sending ships her way after these sinkings.[18]

As *Gudgeon* moved on, the crew erupted in celebration. The post-sinking jubilation had become a routine on board *Gudgeon* in times of great success. The stress, strains, and frustrations of battling an enemy from the confines of a submarine were unleashed in a cascade of emotions and pride for a job well done. Moose Hornkohl recalled what it was like after a "victory." "You didn't see a wet eye when them torpedoes went off. We were hollering and yelling, 'kill the bastards,' there was no gallantry whatsoever. You didn't want to let them have the first punch. I never seen a crew so intent as when we were going in under for the attack and trying to sink those suckers. And I tell you we would go to any means to get them. I've seen many times when they would have rammed them. No one really wanted you to know, because you'd lose the boat. But no, we didn't give them any quarters, we hated them. A lot of us like myself saw our buddies floating around."[19]

Hornkohl was trying to acclimate to submarines. He found it easier said than done. By the time the submarine had made it to the refueling point at Midway Island, he was very ill. He had chronic indigestion and carried a bucket under his arm to catch the vomit, which seemed never ending. As one of the lowest rated men on the boat, Hornkohl found himself designated as the submarine's only mess cook, Gene Butts having been transferred after the first patrol.

During his hours on duty, he found himself peeling an unending number of potatoes, cleaning tables, scrubbing the crew's mess deck, and the like, all under the direction of the older, affable Ship's Cook First Class, Emerson Brock. However, with mine training under his belt Hornkohl was planning to strike for third class torpedoman at the first opportunity. He liked Brock, but working as a mess cook was not for him. Hornkohl wanted to fight this war, and to Hornkohl that meant more than cooking and cleaning up after the crew.

By this time, Moose Hornkohl and the other new men on board had received extensive drilling so they would know how to respond quickly in actual wartime situations. One of the more critical skills they learned was how to get below deck from various lookout positions topside in the quickest possible time. Eventually the *Gudgeon* crew would be able to get the four lookouts off the bridge and the officer of the deck below with the hatch sealed and the submarine shears below the surface in forty to forty-five seconds. Last man down was responsible for making sure no one was left on deck. The men would dive—not walk—down the hatch with their hands preceding them, one on either rail support as they guided themselves down. While on lookout or smoking on the cigarette deck aft of the bridge, Hornkohl said, "You would always listen; you would always get one ear out for a 'Clear the Bridge' and another listening for the sighting of a target. When you would be heading up for the watch, the crew would always give you a little encouragement, especially in a war zone, reminding you to do a good job. They were depending upon you." [20] Indeed, when the men went up on top for watch, they were the most important people on the submarine. They literally held the lives of the other seventy or so men in the palms of their hands. If they succumbed to fatigue or excessive daydreaming, an enemy vessel or bomber could get in on *Gudgeon* in no time.

Surprisingly, years later Hornkohl reported that the worst thing about his first patrol was not the eventual pounding that he would receive from depth charges or his chronic seasickness. It was the long daytime dives followed by short nighttime surfaces only to be followed again by another extended dive, with the pattern repeated week after week. This went on from "the time you left Pearl Harbor to the time you got to Japan." [21] By the end of the dives, "you had run out of oxygen and the air was foul and stagnant," and to make matters worse, Hornkohl recalled that everybody on board the submarine smoked.[22] Eventually, the boat was so depleted of oxygen that not even matches would light.

As it turned out, the sinking of the Japanese freighter on March 27, 1942, would be the last for Jumping Joe Grenfell. After one complete patrol and part of a second, he had four ships to his credit, in waters that were teeming with sampans but few worthy targets. However, the date of his final Japanese kill was not the end of the action on the patrol by any means. The next day at around 0730 an old friend, or perhaps more accurately a "scoundrel" as Grenfell called her, returned to *Gudgeon*'s world.[23] The return of this nemesis would result in one of the most controversial incidents in *Gudgeon*'s history. The most enigmatic, of course, would be *Gudgeon*'s eventual loss. With *Gudgeon* patrolling in the East China Sea, east of Shanghai, a small, armed merchantman came within 2,000 yards. She was the same tramp steamer that *Gudgeon* had missed on the thirteenth, when a torpedo passed harmlessly under the vessel. In Grenfell's post-action war patrol report, he referred to this ship as a Q-ship, but, at the time, he did not know that he was attacking one of those disguised little assassins. *Gudgeon* moved in for the kill. The Q-ship waited expectantly, hiding all but her three-inch guns. It was time for the lesson that the Q-ship skipper was all too ready to deliver.

The TDC bearings generated by Dornin jived with the periscope and sound bearings and there was plenty of time to make a satisfactory approach. All looked good for *Gudgeon* this time around. This ship was going down. There would be no tears from Dusty Dornin. With *Gudgeon* submerged, heading toward the target ship, Lieutenant Commander Joe Grenfell firmly ordered, "FIRE ONE. FIRE TWO."[24] and then watched in grim surprise as the second torpedo, which seemed to be right on target, once again passed harmlessly under the ship. The maneuvering vessel avoided a third torpedo. At first, Grenfell could not understand why the ship was still afloat. Watching intently through his periscope, he believed he saw Japanese merchant sailors running back and forth on the deck pointing at *Gudgeon*'s periscope which by now was around 750 yards away. This did not bother Grenfell because all he could see were three-inch guns both fore and aft.

As *Gudgeon* was swinging to port to bring the stern torpedo tubes to bear, Grenfell and the men on board received a big surprise, one they would never forget. The aftereffects probably affected the men at some level for the rest of their lives. It was then that they spotted the expected flashes fore and aft, but were shocked to see flashes amidships. Presumably, the ship did not have anything located amidships that could harm *Gudgeon*. After all, she was just a beat-up old steamer, hardly worth attacking. One of the shots from the middle of the steamer landed very close, knocking the periscope from Grenfell's hands and severely jolting him in the eye. Grenfell thought that the scoundrel had been lucky and rocked the *Gudgeon* with a shell from one of the deck guns. It was at that time that Joe Grenfell realized *Gudgeon* was under attack and in grave danger because this was not an armed merchantman, but a Japanese man-of-war, a submarine-hunting Q-ship.

The term "Q-ship" was coined by the British in World War I to describe German merchant ships, which quickly transformed into submarine hunters. This Japanese Q-ship threw off fabricated smoke, which was designed to be sighted by far-off submarines, to make the ship appear to be an attractive target such as a heavy freighter. The ship would actually have no cargo aboard. Deck guns or depth charge throwers hid underneath tarps. The ships were characteristically very light and difficult to destroy with torpedoes, or they were made of wood, which made the magnetic detonators on the torpedoes useless. Having attracted the unsuspecting submarine to them and being almost invulnerable to torpedoes, they were then free to counterattack with depth charges. Dusty Dornin, explaining how *Gudgeon* was lured into the attack, would say later that by not zigzagging, the Q-ship was like a hooker in a bar, a "direct come-on for any submarine in the area." [25]

Joe Grenfell stared intently at the ship as three more depth charges flipped high into the air heading directly toward *Gudgeon*. Grenfell gave the order to rig for depth charges and frantically began evasive tactics. This Q-ship was dangerously close, less than a half mile from *Gudgeon*.

Gudgeon was in mortal danger and might just go down. Jack Camp wrote in his log that the twenty minute attack resulted in twenty-two depth charges being thrown *Gudgeon*'s way, and said it was "just plain hell" but added proudly of his shipmates, "All hands stand up under fire very well." Camp continued, "We went ahead emergency and reached the depth of three-hundred-fifty feet. Deepest depth ole *Gudgeon* has ever been." With the deafening explosions surrounding the submarine and *Gudgeon* dropping deep, Camp wrote anxiously that "sound keeps picking up screws from Q-ships. They are still looking for us." Camp continued, "Oh! is it 'h' when the sound man says the screws sound as though they are getting closer." [26] The terror that the sailors felt at the time is hardly imaginable, but, once again the mortal danger did not push Camp over the edge, "hell" was still only "h."

A few hours later a destroyer from the Japanese Navy Yard at Nagasaki, some thirty miles away, joined the hunt. Jack Camp wrote in his log that if they had been good ASW (antisubmarine warfare) vessels they would have sunk the *Gudgeon* because they were actually pinging *Gudgeon* with their sonar. When enemy sonar pinged a submarine with a sound wave, it was just about like painting a bull's-eye on the side of the underwater craft. Under those circumstances, all the Japanese had to do was hit the bull's-eye, and that would have been the end of *Gudgeon*.

A half-century later during an interview for this book, Ray Foster described how Grenfell told Lieutenant Dixie Farrell, *Gudgeon*'s diving officer, to "give me 62 feet, and Farrell mistakenly stuck the conning tower out of the water." "So," Foster continued, "the Old Man was screaming, 'get her down, get her down,' and Farrell—who must have been flustered or something—had *Gudgeon* passing 350 feet going down at a fifteen degree angle." [27] One *Gudgeon* sailor explained that a dive at such an angle was greater than routine but not excessive considering that *Gudgeon* was in an emergency dive. Foster added that Executive Officer Pop Lyon relieved the flustered Farrell, and said that *Gudgeon* leveled off at 513 feet, far deeper than test depth. Apparently the diving gauges had been turned off or ignored by the person manning them, then not noticed by Farrell, the diving officer, in the confusion and profound stress of the moment as *Gudgeon* dove for her life.

The air blowers and every other nonessential device were turned off so that the submarine could run silently and remain undetected. At about that time, the Japanese started a depth charge attack. Foster added, "If you don't have anything to do in a depth charge attack, you're supposed to lie down and be very quiet. I was lying there in the forward torpedo room, and the boat had a squeeze on it and rivets kept popping off hitting me on the back, which I'll never forget." [28]

When a submarine is being squeezed and distorted like an empty plastic quart of pop, devices and instruments shear off and drop, hitting the deck or any sailors that happen to be lying on it. When essential pieces of equipment fall off the boat, it means that the submarine is under extreme pressure, a sign that water at a pressure any higher could collapse the pressure hull, instantly killing everybody in the collapsed area. Too much depth can be more dangerous than the depth charges that are being dropped.

Foster remembered what Joe Grenfell did next. Grenfell, quite fearful that *Gudgeon* was going to be sunk, instructed a runner to hurry and, "Tell all of the men in the forward torpedo room that believe in God that it's time to start talking to Him." [29] It was a morbidly quiet and somber group of submariners who dropped their heads in prayer, sweat flowing in streams off their bodies, surges of adrenaline making their hearts pump so hard it felt as if they would be pushed through their rib cages, depth charges exploded around them, the next one worse than the prior charge due to their cumulative effects on the boat and the waning spirits of the exhausted men.

Moose Hornkohl said that he thought the boat had plunged 300–400 feet and offered some insight into what he was experiencing during such an attack. "If anyone made a noise of any kind, they were in danger of getting their eyes ripped out. The crew would treat them very badly if someone messed up and dropped something." [30] Hornkohl recalls thinking about his death, which he thought was very near that day. "What am I going to do when that bulkhead comes in? What is my last two minutes going to be like?" [31]

For six dreadful hours, the Q-ship and the destroyer passed back and forth, pinging all the while, then stopping, then starting again, searching for the deathly quiet submarine. The men continued praying and hoping that the Japanese would somehow miss them. Twice the Q-ship passed overhead. Finally, the pinging died out. The men, exhausted and weak from the heat and the stress, slowly gathered themselves. *Gudgeon* moved along in the opposite direction of the two Japanese antisubmarine vessels, thankfully now very far away.

Camp wrote that "good ole Captain Grenfell" eventually outmaneuvered the hunters and that by 2 P.M. all was well.[32] *Gudgeon* stayed deep all day until they surfaced at 10:30 P.M. when Grenfell put the boat on four diesel engines and sped away from the hornet's nest. Camp said that Grenfell decided to head home because the crew was "pretty shaky." [33] When describing the incident after the war, Grenfell considered that the Japanese had given *Gudgeon* a real pounding and that eighteen to twenty depth charges had been tossed at his submarine.

Foster, who experienced several disagreements with Lieutenant Commander Grenfell during the war, said that after the attack they found out that there were some plates missing from the conning tower and that several planks on the deck had been ripped off. Grenfell sent a message back to base that *Gudgeon* was badly damaged and that he was heading home to Pearl Harbor. A half-century later Ray Foster insisted, "There was nothing wrong with the boat at all. It was seaworthy, and we had ten to twelve torpedoes left." [34] He thought that Grenfell was having family trouble, going through a divorce, and wanted to get back, and concluded the patrol before it was necessary. He added that the reason the patrol report did not state that the boat had gone down to 513 feet was because it was "illegal" to go that deep.[35] However, other submarine skippers would have liked to have known that a Tambor class submarine had descended to 513 feet and survived. Would Grenfell have withheld that information to avoid criticism? Why did Grenfell not mention all of the details of the near-fatal attack? Perhaps he was protecting his diving officer, or himself, as Farrell's superior, though it seems inconceivable that anyone would be criticized for having saved the boat. Foster said that Farrell's mistake during the incident resulted in his being more or less "kicked off the ship."[36] However, Lieutenant Farrell would not leave the *Gudgeon* until after the next patrol, *Gudgeon*'s third. The following day *Gudgeon* spent the day patrolling the southern part of her assigned area looking for submarines, then on the thirtieth she headed for home with, as Foster said, many racks full of torpedoes.

Grenfell described the damage from the depth charge attack as "light" in his war patrol report, yet in addition to the structural damage noted by Foster there was damage to the starboard reduction gear and loss of oil in fuel tanks one and two, because about five-hundred gallons was missing in each tank. There was much loose gear floating around and many broken bulbs and gauge glasses. He added that many instruments on the submarine did not work properly because of excessive wear and that the very critical diving and collision alarms were unreliable and sometimes failed to work, and to make things worse, when *Gudgeon* finally surfaced, Grenfell learned that *Gudgeon* faced a "terrific storm" from the Southeast.[37]

The usually robust Electrician's Mate First Class Jack Camp, like a surprisingly high number of the crew on this patrol, had problems with illness, requiring some recuperation time in his bunk. In fact, Camp noted that on April 4, 1942, with *Gudgeon* on her way back to friendly waters, he had felt sick to his stomach and almost passed out on a four to eight watch. Luckily, for Camp, he was able to talk fellow electrician's mates Bernard Jochim and Bonner Jones into taking over for him. The exhausted Camp, now cramping, was attended by the pharmacist's mate, the "Doc" as Thomas B. Britt was called. Britt found that Camp's temperature was normal. Camp rested in the sick bay for the rest of the day before returning to his normal duties. It sounds as if young Camp had a bad case of "the nerves."

The weather was especially rough on the way back. On the tenth of April a shaky *Gudgeon* crew pulled into Midway. *Gudgeon* loaded up with fuel, water, eggs, apples, and oranges. The men were so tired that even the straitlaced Jack Camp was looking forward to a beer once the boat reached Honolulu. *Gudgeon* continued to inch her way toward Pearl Harbor in a very unfriendly sea, then rendezvoused with the *Pompano* and the dependable old *Litchfield* on April 15, 1942. Everyone was ready for a long break. *Gudgeon* had experienced another very successful, although trying, patrol. She had been all but sunk when attacked by the Japanese Q-ship and destroyer, and she had been at sea for most of the past twelve months.

When *Gudgeon* reached Pearl Harbor, Camp noted that the "Admiral and staff were pleased at *Gudgeon*'s success. Have Ice Cream etc. waiting for us—Go to tender for physical check up, pay (I drew $128.00) and before we leave they feed us one hell of a good chow. Steak & Eggs. One of the best meals I've ever eaten." Jack Camp refrained from the beer after all, then "turned in early." [38]

By this time in the war *Gudgeon* had received credit for four sinkings in two patrols, a noteworthy achievement. Four ships in two patrols with one of the sinkings being a historic naval first was quite an accomplishment considering the difficulty that the submarine service was having at this time sinking *any* ships. If Grenfell had continued at this rate for six or seven patrols, he would have ended up with totals that would have ranked him within the top tier of World War II submarine commanders.

Lieutenant Commander Grenfell was also able to pass on what would prove to be vital information about the performance of the torpedoes, although until enough similar reports had accumulated it would go unheeded by Navy brass, much to the detriment of the Allied war effort. Grenfell stated that in the first attack on the Q-ship he firmly believed that his first torpedo did pass under the ship but had failed to explode. On the second attack, he surmised, probably correctly, that a premature explosion occurred. He concluded that in both attacks on the Q-ship the torpedoes failed to hit the targets were because "a) his draft less than 10' and torpedo ran at 19' instead of 15', b) Magnetic head failed to work at all, c) Ship may have had anti-magnetic device."[39] The ship could have been made of wood, which would have accounted for the magnetic exploder not working, or being a shallow draft vessel, the torpedoes may not have exploded because the ship was too high in the water. Nevertheless, if Grenfell's report, along with those of the other commanding officers who would make similar claims later, had been taken more seriously some of the major flaws of the Mark 14 torpedo and the Mark 6 exploder might have been pinpointed and corrected far earlier than would happen. Grenfell discussed the major flaws in American torpedoes in this, the second war patrol report of *Gudgeon*. They would not be corrected for another year and a half.

When Dusty Dornin was interviewed in 1943, he said when *Gudgeon* was attacked by the Q-ship for the second time they were planning to go as deep as possible, but that "poor depth control caused us to go to 405 feet before we were able to stop it. This vessel then made another run at us and so to speak 'grooved us.' In other words, he dropped the depth charges right over us but apparently too shallow. In my estimation, the depth charges went off at approximately 250 feet and we were at 400 feet. They were, however, directly above us and would force us down as much as ten feet in the water."[40] It seems certain that had *Gudgeon* leveled off at a more customary depth she may have been more severely damaged or sunk. Dornin concluded, as had Ray Foster, that the damage was not great, but disagreed with Foster about ending the patrol early, stating that the damage was sufficient to warrant a return to Pearl Harbor.

When interviewed separately from the other *Gudgeon* submariners, and not having any knowledge of their statements, Radioman John J. Sheridan Jr. said that the deep dive had indeed occurred, but that *Gudgeon* went 640 feet before she leveled off. In his war patrol report, Grenfell had estimated that *Gudgeon* dove 310 feet, Camp and Hornkohl about 350, Dornin 405, Foster 513, and finally Sheridan, who said the dive was a whopping 640 feet. Long after the war, Joe Grenfell relented, stating that the diving error took the submarine to 425 feet.

Making the situation more confusing was Joe Grenfell's response to the error that Dixie Farrell's man had made. After the patrol, Grenfell recommended that Dixie Farrell be awarded a Silver Star, which Farrell received in part for his performance during the Q-ship attack. One supposes that

Grenfell was protecting a well-liked, well-respected officer, and thus said in his patrol report that the dive was 310 feet. Yet it is puzzling that he would praise Farrell so strongly for his control of the submarine and recommend him for the Silver Star in light of the error. The Silver Star Farrell received shortly thereafter would be the first of three Silver Stars that Dixie Farrell would earn during the war. The citation stated that it was given, "For conspicuous gallantry and intrepidity as diving officer of the USS *Gudgeon* during the first two war patrols in enemy Japanese controlled waters. Maintaining excellent trim control of his submarine during several depth charge attacks, Lieutenant Farrell, through his calm, fearless, and efficient performance of duty assisted materially in bringing the *Gudgeon* safely through the engagement."[41]

Perhaps that's it. Perhaps the answer to this seeming contradiction is that Farrell, by taking the submarine so deep, had actually saved the boat and for that reason, Grenfell gratefully overlooked the error and recommended him for the Silver Star, his performance having otherwise been so exemplary. In his war patrol report, Grenfell surmised that it was possible that the deep dive diverted the pings and helped the men avoid disaster. Why did each man say that the dive was at a different depth? Any error made on the dive as well as the different depth estimations offered by those who were on board resulted because the gauges were no longer working, and the men were forced to estimate how deep they felt the submarine had gone. It seems obvious that in spite of the error, Joe Grenfell greatly admired and appreciated Dixie Farrell's service.

Joe Grenfell also praised Lieutenant Hylan B. Lyon for his navigational skill under adverse conditions and for keeping the morale high during the strenuous depth charge attack. In fact, Lyon also received a Silver Star for gallantry and intrepidity in action during the first two war patrols. Finally, sharpshooter Dusty Dornin received a Silver Star for his performance on the TDC during the first and second patrols.

Joe Grenfell wrote that when *Gudgeon* arrived at Midway Island for refueling on April 10, 1942, she had only fifty-five-hundred gallons of diesel fuel left. *Gudgeon* was dangerously low. At the time, for an entire patrol it was taking about twelve to thirteen gallons of fuel for *Gudgeon* to travel a mile. In area, when the submarine was patrolling and fighting, the mileage was about half what it was for the patrol as a whole. It is easy to see that *Gudgeon* had no more than a few days' worth of fuel left when she reached Midway Island. Had the men gotten into situations requiring use of all four of the diesel-guzzling engines, the diesel fuel would have been depleted much more quickly, and *Gudgeon* would have been in real trouble.

Joe Grenfell acknowledged that *Gudgeon* was not damaged seriously and had fired only eleven of the twenty-four torpedoes on board. He did not think that the loss of diesel fuel was anything more than a minor problem, but he was pretty certain *Gudgeon* had been leaking fuel. If so, *Gudgeon* was probably trailing a line of oil pointing like an arrow at the submarine's stern for any Japanese plane in the area to see. A leak such as this led to the loss of *Wahoo* and other submarines.

What is likely is that Foster, the top-notch torpedoman, never heard the main reason Grenfell returned to Hawaiian waters. Grenfell wrote in his patrol report that he terminated the patrol because of "fatigue and sickness among officers and personnel, low fuel, and possible loss of fuel from depth charging."[42] He added that this patrol seemed to be more tiring for everyone. He reported that the men on *Gudgeon* had been worked to their maximum efficiency and endurance since the boat's commissioning in April. He noted that key men were making mistakes that they would not normally make on a patrol, likely in reference to those involved in the overly deep dive to evade the Q-ship.

F. M. O'Leary, Commander of Submarine Division Sixty-Two, was pleased with the patrol. He gave Grenfell and the men a "Well Done" in his patrol endorsement.[43] Grenfell was praised for having successfully evaded the Japanese Q-ship, twice. O'Leary heartily agreed with Joe Grenfell that the commendations for the three officers were well deserved, as was an extended overhaul at Navy Yard, Pearl Harbor. Next up the rung was Allan McCann of Squadron Six. In his endorsement of the patrol, he wrote that twenty days were spent in assigned areas, which represented an improvement (over the twelve days of the first patrol) but that time spent on station remained "extremely low."[44] He noted that some damage was incurred in the depth charge attack by the Q-ship, and that a four-week overhaul at Pearl Harbor should commence immediately. He agreed that the personnel must be tired because so many had been ill. He said that he considered that this patrol was "well conducted," that the crew aggressively developed contacts and that they verified sinkings. Not acknowledging the possibility that the torpedoes ran deep, he incorrectly concluded that the Q-ship must have had a nonmagnetic hull "as the failure of torpedoes to explode when passing under her cannot be explained in any other way."[45] He credited *Gudgeon* with two ships for 15,000 tons. JANAC would later trim the award to two ships for 8,000 tons. *Gudgeon* was awarded a second battle star for her performance on the just completed patrol.

Admiral Withers later concurred with others that more time should have been spent on station, though he did not want the commanding officer to take the remarks as criticism, but as constructive comments for other skippers who would read the endorsements. Withers noted that it was possible that the Q-ship was not hit because the Mark 14 torpedoes of the day may have been running deeper than set. Nobody will ever know how many thousands of men ashore and at sea would die because Withers and others at his level paid no heed to the flawed torpedoes that Joe Grenfell pointed out. Withers agreed that *Gudgeon* should be credited with 15,000 tons and two ships and that the personnel should plan on four to six weeks of recovery time while *Gudgeon* was being overhauled.

Joe Grenfell, having already been awarded a Navy Cross, received a slightly less shiny Silver Star and then scurried around the base trying to tie up loose ends so he could get back to Vallejo to attend to the marital problems that awaited him. For the crew it was off to the Pink Palace and a month of R & R.

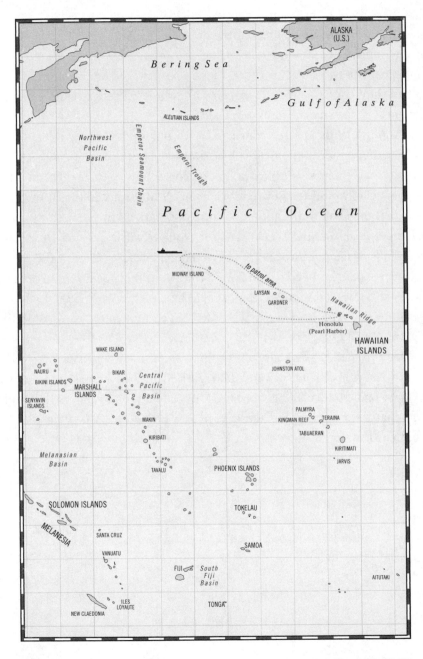

Third War Patrol • Approximate Course • May 26–June 14, 1942

▪ 3 ▪
The Tide Turns

THIRD WAR PATROL: May 26, 1942–June 14, 1942

*Tact in audacity is knowing how far you can go
without going too far.*

Jean Cocteau, 1926

After two successful war patrols, a harrowing encounter with a Japanese Q-ship, three weeks handling administrative matters, and R & R at Pearl Harbor, it was now time for Joe Grenfell to attend to the really gut-wrenching matter: Cookie. On May 6, 1942, he hitched a ride on an Army Air Force flight to California and his mountain of troubles. Shortly after takeoff, as he was helping an older Marine Colonel to be seated, his plane, a PB2Y-2, jerked, throwing him sharply. Engine number three had lost power when a foreign substance became lodged in a carburetor discharge nozzle. The emergency landing went well until a wing tip struck the top of a channel marker, landed, and surged forward striking the corner of a dock opposite the submarine base. Grenfell had survived two war patrols against a vastly superior foe. It seemed that United States aviators were determined to get him one way or the other.

As the plane sliced into the bay, striking a channel marker and sinking in twenty-five feet of water, Grenfell was able to locate a pocket of air and swim to it. He could not move his right leg; his severed tendon throbbed with intense pain. Swimming was nearly impossible. Grenfell lay there for awhile trapped in a plane at the bottom of Pearl Harbor. Miraculously he found a very small hole in the fuselage. For once, Joe Grenfell must have been thankful for his lack of physical stature; he was able to squeeze through this opening and, still in great pain, float to the surface. One wing protruded out of the water, and he held on until rescue came. As it would turn out, of the twenty-two passengers and crew, half were injured, and two Navy officers drowned.

Grenfell's leg injury required surgery and hospitalization until the fall of 1942. Before traveling to the States by ship for treatment, he relinquished command of the *Gudgeon* to his able executive officer Hylan Benton Lyon. After the war, Admiral Joe Grenfell told Clay Blair, "And that's how I lost command of the good ship *Gudgeon.*" [1]

As surprising as it may have been for *Gudgeon* to be handed to him under such circumstances, Lyon could take comfort in knowing that *Gudgeon* was due for some extensive work, which would mean a lot of R & R time to prepare for command. At the time of the attack at Pearl Harbor, *Gudgeon* had not yet completed her shakedown cruise. After two patrols, *Gudgeon* would acquire the items missing during sea trials as well as during two war patrols. In addition, the long overdue overhaul would be completed before *Gudgeon* left port. All of this would take a month or a month and a half.

Lieutenant Commander Lyon arose from a colorful and historic group of military predecessors. His great-great-grandfather was Matthew Lyon, born in 1750 in Ireland. When Matthew was a small boy, his father engaged in a conspiracy against the British and was executed. His widow remarried. Matthew's stepfather was cruel to the young lad, and Lyon sought safe haven in the New World. In 1764, he boarded a ship bound for the British colonies in America. Upon arriving in New York, he was sold as an indentured servant to pay for his passage, despite having been told that by serving the captain, his voyage would be paid for. Lyon eventually married the niece of future famed American revolutionary war officer Ethan Allen and fought as one of Allen's legendary Green Mountain Boys.

The former servant became a colonel and then a member of Congress. In 1798 between sessions of Congress, Lyon was made the butt of jokes by congressional representatives from the opposing Federalist Party. The not-so-friendly Connecticut Congressman, Roger Griswold, chose to poke fun at Lyon for an incident that had occurred during the Revolutionary War. At one time, Lyon and others had rebelled against their officers, with Lyon temporarily being drummed out of the service by General Horatio Gates. This act was referred to jokingly at the time, as General Gates having given Lyon a "wooden sword."[2]

On January 30, 1798, during a lull in congressional proceedings, Lyon loudly criticized the representatives from Connecticut for not truly representing the wishes of their constituents. Lyon spoke loud enough for Griswold to hear him say he could go to Connecticut, start printing newspapers explaining his political stances, and within six months he could have the incumbent representatives thrown out of office. An angry Griswold overhearing the claim, called, "If you go into Connecticut, you had better wear your wooden sword."[3] The exchange became more heated, and Lyon spat in Griswold's face—bedlam erupted. For fourteen days, the House debated whether to expel "Spitting Matt," as he was now known for "riotous and disorderly behavior."[4] Lyon's defense was that the congressional proceedings were at a standstill when he spat on Griswold. Since there was no formal business going on, less decent behaviors were acceptable. However weak his argument may have been, none other than Thomas Jefferson rose to defend him, claiming that the only objective in the squabble was to rid the Republicans of one member of the House (i.e., Lyon). The vote for expulsion failed.

Later, Lyon fought with the President of the United States himself. Under terms of the recently enacted Sedition Act, it was made unlawful to criticize the Congress, the government, or the President of the United States. He openly opposed passage of the seemingly unconstitutional act as well as the foreign policy of President John Adams. Lyon was tried, found guilty of sedition, fined one-thousand dollars, sentenced to four months in jail, and imprisoned. Once behind bars, he became a martyred hero. While languishing in a cold dungeon that formerly housed runaway slaves, he was reelected to Congress, much to the chagrin of First Lady Abigail Adams, who described him as "the Beast of Vermont."[5]

The first Hylan Benton Lyon, grandson of the fiery patriot Matthew Lyon, was a member of the West Point class of 1852. After graduation, he found himself fighting American Indians out West. When Civil War broke out, Lyon, a Kentuckian, resigned his commission in the United States

Army and raised an artillery company for the Confederates. As the war dragged on, Lyon became a general and proved to be a most determined and resourceful leader. Late in the war, General Lyon commanded a ragtag group of men whose best training for the war was hunting rabbits. None of General Lyon's troops had been in service more than four months. Half the men were fellow Kentuckians he had conscripted a few days earlier. One hundred of the cavalrymen had no horses, and many had no blankets, overcoats, or shoes. Nonetheless, on December 9, 1864, General Lyon would have a day that would have made any submarine skipper in World War II proud. After taking Cumberland City, Lyon captured a large steamer loaded with forage and provisions. He went on to secure two other Union steamers and four barges. Lyon seized and destroyed what he estimated to be around one million dollars of Union resources. It was for escapades like this one and for what was to come that General Lyon was regarded by his enemy in none too flattering terms, once being called the "degenerate son of a noble sire."[6]

The Confederate general's son, Frank B. Lyon would become an admiral in the United States Navy, the same navy that his father had fought so intensely. Admiral Lyon would travel to the Far East as part of President Theodore Roosevelt's Great White Fleet. Frank B. Lyon was the father of *Gudgeon* skipper Hylan B. Lyon, who was born in Annapolis, Maryland, in February 1910. Lyon was involved in athletics in his native Virginia, where he played football, boxed, and ran track. He maintained his involvement in athletics at the Academy. He was a member of the Navy football team his final year, as well as participating in swimming and crew. His bio in the Navy yearbook described him as a good-natured "Don Juan" who was popular with his classmates as well as the women. He graduated in 1931 and was commissioned an ensign.[7]

After a variety of assignments, including service on the battleships *Pennsylvania* and *Colorado*, he attended submarine school in New London, graduating and being assigned to his first submarine, the old USS *R-4*, as engineer. He then attended postgraduate engineering school at the Academy and was assigned to *Gudgeon* as the engineering officer and then promoted to executive officer to serve second to Joe Grenfell. He acquired the nickname "Pop" in his days at the Naval Academy because his peers thought he was much more mature than they were. Now at Pearl Harbor awaiting completion of the work on the *Gudgeon*, things changed quickly. Just as the orderly planning for *Gudgeon* had fallen apart when Japan attacked Pearl Harbor, impending developments near Midway Island necessitated that *Gudgeon* be ordered out of the Navy Yard "as soon as possible with the highest military effectiveness possible" before all its repairs could be completed.[8] On May 26, 1942, *Gudgeon* departed from the submarine base at Pearl Harbor three weeks ahead of schedule. On board were twenty-two new crew members. However, many of the new sailors had transferred to *Gudgeon* from submarine tenders or other submarines and were experienced submariners.

One of those men was Torpedoman Third Class Quentin Russell Seiler. By today's standards, Quent Seiler had virtually no childhood. Combined with a little luck, Seiler's tough background would help him survive the war and the many battles that would follow. Seiler's background is typical of those that made up the prewar crews throughout the U.S. Navy. He was named Quentin after the son of Theodore Roosevelt, a World War I pilot killed in a dogfight over France in July 1918.

Quent spent his boyhood in tiny Connellsville, Pennsylvania, in the heart of bituminous coal country, which at the time was "the coke center of the world." Like the rest of the nation mired in the swampy quagmire of the Great Depression, people like Quent had to work at anything he could to help feed his family. Seiler's father, George Seiler, was "half German and half Cherokee," a sometimes coal miner, stonemason, and carpenter who did his best to eke out an existence for his family.[9] The elder Seiler left the family when Quent was eight, leaving poor Mrs. Seiler to raise Quentin, his brother George, and three other children.

It was expected that anybody in the remaining family of six who could contribute anything in the way of work and money would do so. Quent Seiler's oldest brother, George, worked in a foundry. His other brother was hard at work full time by the age of sixteen. At the age of twelve, Quent Seiler found himself shoveling coal in a mine as an assistant to a journeyman miner who lived on the same street as the Seilers. Seiler spent four summer vacations in this manner earning six dollars a week for sixty hours of work. His mother would give him a quarter of his hard-earned money every Saturday night so that he could go to a movie. Unfortunately, the exhausting work always did young Quent in. He never was able to stay awake and go to the movie theater. Not once.

Finally, the summer vacation of 1935 arrived, and Seiler was determined to never set foot in a coal mine again. He told his mother that he was going to hitch a train to California and find work. His mother asked him if he had any idea how far California was from Connellsville. He replied, "About three-thousand miles." [10] The accurate response sold his mom. She consented and the adolescent Seiler was on his way, grabbing a ride on a B & O freight train heading for Chicago. He met a friendly old hobo in Connellsville who taught him the ropes. The first lesson was the most important: how to stay alive, or rather how to get enough food to stay alive. Seiler's mentor told him, "There is always someone who will give you a meal if you give them something in return. And work is all we have to give." [11] It took Seiler about ten days to reach Sacramento, having left his mentor in Chicago, but less than an hour to climb aboard a truck that was carrying laborers to a sugar beet farm outside Lodi to hoe beets at $2.50 an acre. After Seiler's first day, there were only two men left in the field: the determined Quentin Seiler and an old black man named Dean Goslash. Goslash explained to Quent that the farmer was weeding out the workers who were the hardest working from those that only wanted "an easy meal." [12] Thus, the men off the truck had been assigned the worst field the farmer had to offer.

Dean Goslash proved to be a prophet, because, as Seiler reported, chuckling, a half century later, "You could actually see beets in the acreage we were in the next day." [13] The field would require much less work to complete. Still, it was incredibly demanding. Seiler described it this way: "I don't know if you have ever hoed an acre of potatoes, tomatoes, or beets, but I can tell you from experience, it is one hell of a lot of work. However, if one gets up in the morning, around four o'clock, when it is still dark, eats a hearty breakfast, takes his lunch with him, gets to the field before daylight, and starts to hoe as soon as one can distinguish a weed from a beet, it is possible to hoe an acre if you work until it is too dark to see the plant." [14] Then the pot of gold was there for the taking. The $2.50 was all yours.

When it came time to return to Connellsville, Seiler managed to ride the whole way from Lodi, California, to his home without spending a penny. Seiler, deeply suntanned for the first time in his life, reached his home one hot sultry summer evening at 2 A.M. and knocked on the door. His stepfather answered and took one look at his stepson, whom he no longer recognized. The hard-working young man proudly handed his mom $150, an incredible sum.

Because of his experiences away from the coal mines, an adventuresome spirit was now firmly embedded in Quentin Seiler. Connellsville, Pennsylvania, had little to offer the young man after a summer in California. Off he went to the nearest Navy recruiting office in Uniontown. The Navy, it seemed to Seiler, was the ideal place because it offered food, money, shelter, and travel opportunities. Young Seiler was sure he would soon be far away in some exotic place aboard some huge Navy ship. However, Quent Seiler was only sixteen-and-a-half years old, too young to enlist, and returned home crestfallen.

The following week the recruiter visited the Seiler home in Connellsville. Having been told by Quent of his California adventures, the recruiter was able to persuade Mrs. Seiler that Quent needed more adventure in his life and that he could handle it. He finally convinced her by asking, "Wouldn't you feel more comfortable knowing where he is, that he is well fed, that he will be learning something beneficial to his life, than running all over the country on freight trains and perhaps getting killed in the process?"[15] The appeal was persuasive. Seiler would be allowed to enlist when he turned seventeen. On August 4, 1936, Quentin Russell Seiler enlisted in the United States Navy at Pittsburgh, Pennsylvania. The Depression-toughened Seiler and the others of his generation who joined the Navy would have the adventures they were seeking. And more.

After completing boot camp at Newport Training Station in Newport, Rhode Island, Seiler was assigned to the heavy cruiser *Salt Lake City*, which was berthed at Long Beach. After learning that submarine service offered additional money and food, he volunteered for transfer but heard nothing. Quent Seiler, who had grown up in the claustrophobic coal mines of Pennsylvania, knew that he would have no difficulty dealing with the tight spaces of a prewar submarine.

In the summer of 1937, the *Salt Lake City* cruised up and down the North American west coast, passing under the Golden Gate Bridge for its opening ceremony in May 1937. She later traveled to tiny Ketchikan, Alaska. While there, Quent Seiler had the opportunity to become a Good Samaritan, and the consequences of his good work changed his life forever. After spending a night ashore to see the sights, meet ladies, and no doubt imbibe the best whiskey available, Seiler was standing on a dock waiting for a motor launch to take him back to the cruiser. Lo and behold, wobbling down the pier was dear old Chaplain McManus of the *Salt Lake City*. He had drunk too much and proceeded to teeter back-and-forth before walking off the end of the pier into the bay. Seiler quickly came to the priest's assistance, jumped into the water, and led the grateful father to a ladder. Seiler thought nothing more of his act of kindness.

A short while later the Japanese sank the U.S. gunboat *Panay* on the Yangtze River in China. As a result, Seiler and a few of his buddies were quickly slated for Far East service in anticipation of more difficulty with Japan. Seiler felt that because of the relative luxuries and other amenities of the submarine service, he would try to avoid Far East duty aboard a cruiser. He got nowhere with the personnel officer, so Quent Seiler sought the assistance of his old friend Chaplain McManus. Sure enough, with the help of the chaplain, the personnel officer relented, and Seiler was sent to submarine school in New London, Connecticut. After sub school, he was assigned to the ancient submarine *R-14*.

With a lot of hard work, Seiler qualified in submarines in 1938. This meant that he had successfully learned all of the systems on all the compartments of the *R-14* and could prove mastery by demonstrating his expertise to the chief of the boat and an officer. Quent Seiler could now handle virtually any function on a submarine should the need arise. Qualifying in submarines was a major accomplishment for submariners and meant they could wear the coveted dolphin insignia. Seiler said it took six months of hard work for those who were fast learners.

Life was good for Quent Seiler. He was single, handsome, strong as an ox, had some coins in his pocket, and played on a very fine base basketball team. He had also been approached about boxing semiprofessionally. It was a violation of Navy regulations to do so, but Quent Seiler decided to give it a try, using the alias "George." While in the Navy, from that time forward, Quent Seiler would be known as George to his pals. Seiler proved to be a rough customer in the ring. He was feeling good about his newfound profession and enjoyed the extra money he made when he won, which was most of the time. That is, until he found himself staring eye-to-eye with the skipper of his boat, the *R-14*, while warming up for a fight.

When Seiler first started boxing, he had a lazy left hand, meaning that he tended to leave it very low, and thus allowed his opponent to freely jab the left side of his face. Seiler quickly acquired scar tissue over the eye, which tore very easily. Since he always fought on Friday or Saturday nights, he would usually return to the *R-14* to teach classes on Monday with a clip keeping his skin tight so it would heal faster.

Eventually the captain asked Seiler about the clip; George Seiler lied to avoid the trouble that would surely follow should the skipper find out the truth. He told the skipper that he had bumped his eye and cut it open. After several such "accidents," which always occurred over the weekend, the skipper became highly suspicious. The captain's suspicions were buoyed when he noticed that there was a guy named "George" Seiler whose name always appeared on the sports pages over the weekends.

A few weeks later, Seiler found himself fighting the main event in a large arena in Hartford, Connecticut. Seiler climbed into the ring feeling confident and ready to fight. As the ring announcer introduced him, Seiler looked down and saw his skipper accompanied by his wife, standing at ringside. Catching Seiler's eye the skipper stood up and yelled to Seiler, "When the hell did you become 'George' Seiler?" [16] Seiler now very flustered and wanting to get away from "the scene of the crime," made very quick work of his opponent and hurried to the locker room. All weekend his mind ran wild imagining what the *R-14*'s skipper would do to him on Monday. When Monday arrived, Seiler reported for duty. The captain looked him over and said, "You didn't bump your eye this weekend, did you George?" [17] And luckily that was the end of it.

After a year or so of submarine service on the *R-14*, Seaman Seiler and another sailor, Robert Weld, found themselves flipping a coin to see which of two new submarines they would be assigned. The *Stingray* was reputed to be a boat to avoid because of poor morale. The alternative was the much more attractive, sparkling new and clean USS *Squalus*. Seiler, who wanted desperately to go to the *Squalus*, lost the flip. As a result, for the first of many times in his life, Quent Seiler got a break that ensured his continued survival. The *Squalus* went down a short while later on one of her sea trials, and the winner of the flip of the coin, Fireman Second Class Bob Weld, was lost forever.

Compared to what could have happened to him on *Squalus*, his service on *Stingray* went quite well. Yet, before long, Seiler's stint in the Navy was over. When he saw that war was approaching, he reenlisted and was assigned to another ancient pigboat, the *R-13*, then to the submarine *Grenadier* as part of the commissioning crew. While *Grenadier* was en route to Pearl Harbor, the Japanese attack occurred. After arriving at the catastrophic scene, he was assigned to serve on a relief crew of the submarine tender USS *Pelias*. One of the submarines alongside *Pelias* was the USS *Gudgeon*. Seiler asked for transfer to *Gudgeon*. When she returned to port after the second patrol, his transfer came through.

By May 1942, Japan had committed a large portion of her fleet in support of an invasion of tiny Midway Island. At first, there was disagreement between Japanese Admiral Yamamoto and other factions of the military hierarchy within the Army and Imperial General Staff about the wisdom of venturing that far from Japan. The conflict concerned whether or not Midway could be adequately resupplied once taken. Because of their early successes, the Japanese were very confident and decided to invade Midway Island for use as a forward base.

Japan's miscalculations in this battle were to doom her imperial designs, and *Gudgeon* was to play a role, however slight. *Gudgeon*'s trip to her designated position was not dull. Within forty-five minutes of leaving Pearl Harbor, the men on watch sighted a large U.S. task force consisting of two aircraft carriers and their escorts, and several destroyers and cruisers heading for Midway Island. It must have been reassuring to know that for once, it would not be *Gudgeon* acting as a lone wolf against every Japanese ship in the area. Running on the surface *Gudgeon* repeatedly sighted United States patrol planes, the second of which, a PBY, turned to attack despite the submarine's best efforts to exchange identification signals with the pilot. He persisted in his desire to sink *Gudgeon*, necessitating Lyon to order a hurried dive to 100 feet.

Along the route, Lieutenant Commander Lyon ordered gunnery practice with the three-inch deck gun and the 50-caliber machine guns. The crew was only allowed to fire five of the three-inch shells, Lyon saving the rest of the ammo for more important targets. For this patrol marksman Dusty Dornin served as executive officer in addition to his routine duties on the TDC. It was not long before Lieutenant Commander Lyon realized that a longtime problem with his vision was getting worse at the worst of times, when he was in command of a submarine at war.

Gudgeon was on station as ordered for the start of hostilities on June 4. She was one of three clusters of submarines ordered to screen Midway Island for the oncoming Japanese assault force. *Gudgeon*'s group was designated Task Force 7.1 and was under the command of Rear Admiral Robert H. English. Being positioned from southwest to northwest of Midway, the cluster of submarines was to fan out from Midway Island and watch for the approaching attack. Included in this large screen were the submarines *Nautilus*, *Dolphin*, *Cachalot*, *Flying Fish*, *Grouper*, *Grenadier*, *Grayling*, *Gato*, *Trout*, *Dolphin*, *Tambor*, and *Cuttlefish*. Based upon their location toward the northern edge of the formation, *Gudgeon*, *Nautilus*, and *Grouper* were in the most favorable position to come in contact with the Japanese task force. *Plunger*, *Narwhal*, and *Trigger* hovered behind the main screen.

At 0700, *Cuttlefish* sighted a Japanese tanker west of Midway Island. Soon, more of the invasion force was observed, driving *Cuttlefish* below. United States PBY's also observed and reported the strike force's whereabouts which resulted in the few Navy, Army, and Marine fighters on the island coming to life hurriedly preparing for battle. The submarines headed for the oncoming Japanese task force.

At 0715, Lyon received word indicating that contact had been made with an approaching enemy aircraft carrier. *Gudgeon* surfaced. With all four diesel engines running full bore, Lyon set *Gudgeon* on a course to attack the Japanese flat top. The skies filled quickly with American planes, a situation that created a vexing problem for Lieutenant Commander Lyon. Every time *Gudgeon* dove, it slowed her progress toward the big carrier somewhere in the distance. Yet, if he did not dive, the bombers fully loaded and primed to attack might go after his ship. Every time the bombers got within six miles, Lyon ordered *Gudgeon* below. The bombers, very possibly those sent from the island, would soon be annihilated by the superior firepower of the Japanese. The mission of the bombers on that historic day, undertaken with the realization that they would not be returning, was a testament to their selfless valor.

With *Gudgeon* still moving forward, first on the surface, and then submerged, then on the surface again, Lyon finally came upon two Japanese battleships similar to *Haruna. Gudgeon* dove to attack. When Lyon was finally able to make a periscope sighting, he saw that a group of dive bombers had beat him to the punch. He described the battleships as appearing, "hull down, with one heavy tower forward with stack close behind and a stick mast aft."[18] While the half-blind Lyon stared intently through the periscope, he was not able to see the antiaircraft fire of the Japanese gunners. *Gudgeon* approached on a normal course for forty-five minutes. When Lyon looked again, he saw a large formation of Japanese planes heading toward the area. When they arrived, they turned and headed west. Before long the target vessels disappeared. He was uncertain what to do. After talking it over, Lyon concluded that his present location must be a rendezvous point for returning planes and carriers. He dove and patrolled the area, just hanging around, traveling at a very slow two knots, like a shark trolling for prey near a coral reef.

By 1130, a discouraged Hylan B. Lyon while lying in wait, aware now that the Japanese aircraft carriers were not going to come to him, decided to go after the carriers. He had no idea where they were, because in all the excitement, *Gudgeon* had missed several scheduled messages. By 1600, having sighted many Japanese dive bombers overhead heading west, *Gudgeon* still lay below the surface awaiting instructions as to where she should go to get into the action. Most of the Japanese planes sighted were Type 99 black aircraft carrier dive bombers with red balls on the side of the fuselage. Explosions were heard at a great distance through the submarine's hull. Somebody was being pounded. At 1925, Lyon decided to surface. Just before surfacing he picked up a plane on radar and noted that it was closing fast. Because it was dark, Lieutenant Commander Lyon decided that the plane could not see the submarine, so he left his antenna out to get the rest of a long inbound message. This was the type of mistake that can get a ship sunk. Three minutes later the plane dropped a bomb close to *Gudgeon*. Lyon said the bomb "sounded like a Japanese bomb."[20] Hylan B. Lyon, now wiser, dove to one-hundred feet. Lieutenant Albert "Albie" Strow, writing in his personal log and on board for his maiden patrol, would say later that during the attack Dusty Dornin tried to calm him by telling him that it was not a bomb that they had heard, just something loose in the submarine's superstructure.

Though *Gudgeon* had not been able to develop an attack on either the battleships or the carriers, all was not lost. To say the least, all was not lost. In engagements in the area, Japan had lost carriers *Akagi*, *Kaga*, *Hiryu* and *Soryu*, 2,500 men, a heavy cruiser, and over 300 aircraft. The United States and her Allies were back in the game, and now the hunted would become the hunters. The nation breathed a sigh of relief, knowing that the west coast of the United States and Hawaii were safe and would likely remain free from Japanese invasion for the rest of the war.

Six of the nineteen submarines deployed around Midway Island for the battle were from Submarine Squadron Six, *Gudgeon*'s group. Because of indecisiveness, confusion, and poor communication, *Nautilus* was the only submarine that had been able to score a hit on a ship. The "hit" was a dud torpedo that bounced off the already-damaged carrier *Kaga*. In a rare case of successful one-upmanship, the Japanese submarine force, which would prove to be mostly ineffective throughout the war, was able to sink a destroyer escort of the damaged United States aircraft carrier, USS *Yorktown*, then the *Yorktown* herself. There was one thing the Japanese had that the Americans did not: powerful torpedoes that went where they were supposed to go and blew up.

The next day *Gudgeon* was once again threatened by air, this time by six U.S. dive bombers, which, flying with the sun at their back, mistakenly dove at the submarine. The attack was a perfect one; the planes could not be discerned from the sun. *Gudgeon* did not have time to dive. The men on *Gudgeon* were lucky this time. The frantic efforts of the signalmen on deck worked; a flare was fired, and the bombers acknowledged the signal by pulling up and heading west. At 1030 on the fifth, *Gudgeon* sighted a large U.S. force of two carriers, five heavy cruisers, and several destroyers and exchanged identification with one of the carriers as they proceeded westward.

Once again at 2145 a large U.S. bomber on its way to Midway Island was sighted heading right toward *Gudgeon*. When the plane turned on his landing lights, Lyon feared that the submarine might have been spotted. *Gudgeon* fired a very star of the proper color, and the plane headed off. *Gudgeon* patrolled for several days but was unable to sight any worthwhile targets, and finally headed back to base at Pearl Harbor, found the escort, and docked at 0530, June 14, 1942. Though *Gudgeon* played no significant role in the battle, while she was at sea chasing the battleships, the tables had been turned. The men celebrated heartily. Pop Lyon had completed his one, and what would prove to be his only, patrol as a submarine skipper in World War II. He was regarded as a likeable man, an excellent navigator, and a competent skipper though the book on him in this regard was concluded prematurely. Ray Foster, who had served about as long as anyone with Lyon on *Gudgeon* recalled the skipper's savant-like skills with mathematics, "You could show him a line of figures ten across and twenty long, and he would look at it and give you the answer. He was a brilliant mathematician."[20] Foster was also impressed when on *Gudgeon*'s first patrol, using figures supplied by Lyon and based solely on the undependable method of travel known as celestial navigation, *Gudgeon* surfaced hoping to see an island called Lots Wife and found it right before them.

Unfortunately for Lyon, he had a long history of vision problems which had affected his performance during the patrol. Joe Grenfell had previously noted that Lyon had a history of defective vision for the past ten years, and that his night vision was below average. The report was apparently written early in 1942. In retrospect, many years after the Battle of Midway, it is surprising that Lyon was given command. Perhaps because of the exigencies of war, the Navy overlooked his questionable vision. Indeed his vision may have been considered barely adequate before Midway and then got much worse during the patrol as Lyon later stated.

Lyon reported in his post-patrol write-up: "The commanding officer has had a long history of defective vision which has grown progressively worse with each patrol until now he has difficulty recognizing his friends beyond thirty paces. He therefore views with suspicion anything he sees himself which is not verified by the Officer of the Deck or one of the better lookouts."[21] Ray Foster said it was much worse than that: "During the

Battle of Midway his eyes went bad on him, and he couldn't see forms even six feet away."[22]

The events surrounding the sighting of the battleships are rather confusing. Dusty Dornin said later that he had been the first to see the pagoda masts of the battleships, peering through the periscope while on the surface, which he reported to Lyon who ordered an approach at flank speed and immediately closed to within 5,000 yards of the main Japanese task force. Dornin was quoted later as saying; Lyon was "blind as a bat."[23] Dornin continued, discussing the pursuit of the Japanese battleships, the first ships that *Gudgeon* had sighted in the affair, "We were running on the surface at around 7 o'clock in the morning when we received the orders that they were coming in our direction. We then saw the masts—pagoda shaped masts, of the Japanese battleships and turned into close in for an attack on the surface."[24] Lieutenant Dornin did not think that Lyon ever saw the pagoda masts. Indeed, if he was as impaired as Foster and Dornin say, there was no way he could have seen the masts. Confounding everybody and belying Dusty Dornin's statements, Lyon claimed in his post-action patrol report that he was the only person who had seen the battleships. Dornin was amazed that in Lyon's war patrol report he did not satisfactorily bring the fact out that he [Lyon] had done everything in his power to attack the Japanese ships.

Perhaps Lyon was trying to kill two birds with one stone when he claimed that he was the only one to have seen the battleships and then later that he was badly impaired. On the one hand, maybe he wanted to protect those under his command by taking full responsibility for having seen the battleships and having not successfully closed on them. Similarly, by voicing so emphatically that he was visually impaired, he knew that he would be relieved of command. The claim that he was the only person on board to have seen the battleships and that he was at the same time virtually blind is incompatible. Perhaps declaring that he was the person who had seen the battleships was made to fend off potential criticism for assuming command in the first place.

Dornin was sure that Lyon was a brave submariner and that he dove upon Dornin's urging because the battleships were being swarmed by U.S. bombers. Dornin felt that Lyon had done the correct thing, that it would have been foolhardy to be more aggressive. Hylan B. Lyon had not led *Gudgeon* to disaster. He did his job, but his chance to continue to lead was cut short because of the condition of his eyes. One can only imagine how tortured Lyon must have been knowing that he was almost functionally blind when his opportunity to take command of *Gudgeon* came about. Here he was, peering almost blindly through the periscope, responsible for the boat and all of her men in the midst of what would become known as the most important naval conflict of the world's most murderous war. Hylan Benton Lyon was a young man who had put in many years working toward his goal of commanding a submarine. One could surmise that after the attack on Pearl Harbor, after seeing friends die, his family and nation threatened, he had trouble tempering his enthusiasm for command even though his vision problems begged that he do so.

Commander O'Leary of Division Sixty-Two commended *Gudgeon* for getting ready for war so quickly and Lyon for placing the submarine in the proper position to carry out her mission. He expressed regrets that Skipper Lyon had been physically disqualified for submarine duty. It is almost certain that this deeply disappointed Lieutenant Commander Lyon as well. Yet he would find other important roles and serve the Navy ably throughout the war.

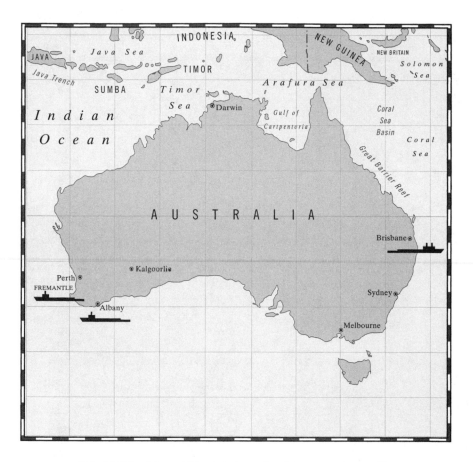

World War II • Allied Submarine Bases • Australia

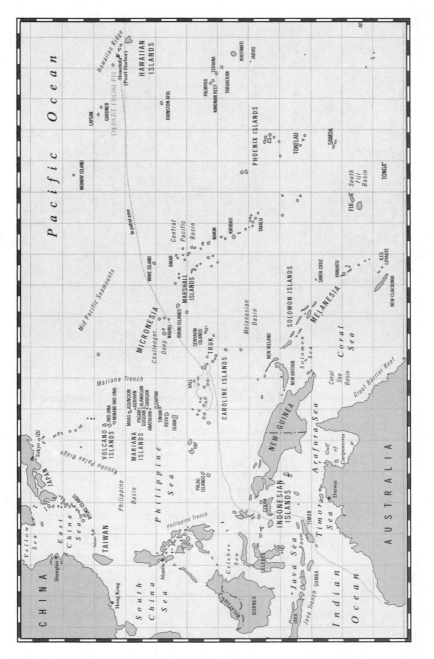

Fourth War Patrol • Approximate Course • July 11–Sept. 2, 1942

▪ 4 ▪
Fortress Truk

Public calamity is a mighty leveler.

Edmund Burke, 1775

As *Gudgeon* prepared for her fourth war patrol, she welcomed three new crew members and a new skipper, Lieutenant Commander William Shirley Stovall Jr. Also departing was the diving officer, Lieutenant Richard M. Farrell.

During a two-month war patrol, seventy or so men on a submarine are crammed together into the severely limited confines of a submarine. Each and every man on board the boat is weaved into a web of interdependence upon the others; each man must do his job or they all die. Yet, George Seiler recalled that when working in the forward torpedo room of *Gudgeon* he would rarely go further aft than the after battery room which was a little over half way toward the stern of the submarine. Once ashore, the submariners on *Gudgeon* rarely socialized with those outside their own compartment. Torpedomen partied with torpedomen, motor machinists tended to hang around together, and so on. One notable exception to the custom was the occasional boat's parties held ashore, which brought the crew and officers together.

There were many items in short supply on the home front during the war—rubber, metals, and gasoline—but, there was another, in Hawaii at least, which seemed just as important, and that was good booze. Of all things considered critical to the well-being of a serviceman on leave during war, good booze was surely one of the top two, and Hawaii's bathtub gin just didn't cut it. There is one thing about the submariner's solution to this vexing and serious problem that is not contained in most of the more well-known books about World War II submarine warfare, and that is that submariners converted "torpedo juice," the actual fuel used in the internal workings of the early war torpedoes into 180-proof alcohol. Unlike the wood alcohol that blinded so many desperate servicemen during the war, this stuff was actually good pure grade grain alcohol, the kind that would put hair on a young seaman's chest, or even knock a sailor on his stern in no time. The men who ran the Navy of the day were not naive. They knew very well that left to their own devices, the men on board a submarine, after it had docked, could do a lot of damage to the stores of torpedo alcohol on board. Therefore, the Navy added a substance that would make it impossible for the sailors to access the torpedo juice, or so they thought. One has to acknowledge the ingenuity of the Navy for their efforts. However, the ingenuity of the men on *Gudgeon* and the other submarines who countered the Navy's efforts to keep the men from drinking the torpedo fuel was even greater.

The Navy added an explosively powerful purgative to the alcohol, known as croton oil, to keep the sailors from drinking the fuel. Croton oil is derived from the shrub, *Croton tiglium*. A single drop of the stuff is usually enough to impart the most severe of symptoms, including intense burning in the mouth, throat, and abdomen, excessive salivation, vomiting, and diarrhea with tenseness and the passage of blood. At its worst, it will kill you. In short, if a person ingested it, his bowels would be clean, lickety split. The stuff is so potent that one of its antidotes is morphine. However, to the men who had withstood depth charges and the frightful experience of lying in coastal waters all alone off Japan, obtaining the alcohol was not a problem. All the submariners had to do was divide the wheat from the chaff. This was easily but tediously done. As George Seiler explained it, "The torpedo had a combustion engine, an injection valve that sprayed the alcohol, and another that sprayed water on top of it. And, of course, the heat in this combustion pot formed steam. The steam turned the turbines which turned the screw," which propelled the torpedo on its way toward the target ship. Seiler continued, "That's where you get the propulsion. Remember seeing those movies where you see the bubbles [from a fired torpedo] come to the top? That's the steam that's creating the trail behind the torpedo."[1]

The torpedo fuel was brought aboard the submarine in five gallon cans and poured into an alcohol tank that contained forty or fifty gallons, too large to be hauled off the boat. Fortunately for the men on board *Gudgeon*, the Navy had entrusted wolves to guard the henhouse. Guts Foster was one of those wolves. He had been charged with the responsibility of holding a key to the area on board boat where the alcohol was locked up. It does not seem that these sailors were in any particular jeopardy for the thievery that was bound to occur; the officers were hardly pristine in this regard. They got their alcohol from the medical supplier on the tender assigned to take care of *Gudgeon*. Furthermore, the interviewed *Gudgeon* submariners made it clear that before the war was over many of the submarine's officers were well aware of what distilled torpedo juice tasted like.

Once the men got the croton-tinged alcohol off the submarine, they would go back to the hotel, the dock, or wherever they could set up a still, and separate the purgative from the clear pure grain alcohol by using homemade stills. These stills varied in design but were usually very simple and much smaller than those seen in movies about southern backwoods moonshiners. They were known as "Gilly stills" for reasons nobody seems to be able to recall though one would like to believe that some time in the past there was a sailor on a submarine by the name of Gilly who devised the first one. It seems more likely that the name derived from the term "gill" which is a measure equal to four fluid ounces.

All a determined submariner had to do was slowly heat the alcohol to the temperature at which alcohol evaporates. The vapor would then rise, hit something cold, oftentimes a plate with ice on it, which was sitting atop a one-gallon pot, heated by a hot plate, and would then condense. The condensation was then drained off into a cup. Within an hour or two, the submariner would have a cup or more of the precious drink without even a trace of the offensive oil. George, Moose, Ray, and their mates would then mix the booze with apple juice or any kind of juice they could find, though grapefruit was preferred. Hornkohl chuckled as he recalled the myriad of unusual and creative types of stills that were in operation ashore after the Battle of Midway. Bathtub gin be damned.

Moose Hornkohl also remembered the near tragic events that occurred after the third war patrol. The men ashore had set up a still in one of the hotels in the area. The thing exploded, causing extensive damage to the room the submariners slept in. Stills were usually placed in bathtubs to protect for just such an occurrence. Luckily, the fire did not spread beyond the sailors' sleeping quarters. None of the sailors involved stepped forward to take responsibility, but all involved pooled their hard-earned money to pay for the damages. The damage caused by the explosion in the hotel room was hardly a rare occurrence. According to some accounts, the heavy-drinking World War II submariners almost demolished the interior of the Royal Hawaiian Hotel during the war. This time there were no prosecutions. A few months earlier, George Seiler had met a woman who would become his first wife. Since she did not drink or smoke Seiler was not with the men when the still exploded. He did recall pitching in to take care of the damage, realizing that it could just as easily been his still, his burden.

The torpedo juice, drunk in sufficient quantities while the men were ashore after Midway, had contributed nicely to the submariners' time off. The men were in a celebrating mood. After a few weeks of hard partying, the sailors would climb back on board *Gudgeon*. George Seiler recalled that some of *Gudgeon*'s sailors were all "spit and polish" when they went ashore, but often looked like "something dumped out of a garbage truck" by the time they boarded the submarine for patrol because of their intense drinking and carousing.[2] Seiler said that on *Gudgeon* only a minority of the men on board *actually* got rest and "beneficial" relaxation.[3]

Now it was time for war. The wild times had by so many of the crew and officers would have to be put behind them. There would be no more hangovers or late nights, no more visits to the whorehouses along Hotel Street. The drinking did not continue once the men boarded the submarine. Men on the USS *Gudgeon* never drank booze once they returned to the boat because it would have been extremely hazardous. Besides, the crew would not be fond of anyone who was impaired and not able to perform his duty. The truth was that anybody who could not do his job was off *Gudgeon* the very second the submarine hit the dock. Thus, one way to determine an outstanding crew member was to look at how many patrols a man did on a submarine. If a man made many patrols, he was surely doing a commendable job. Such men, experts at their craft and generally competent at *all* the roles on board, were allowed to stay. This would not have happened if the skipper thought they were not good submariners. After all, to an extent, each man on board had the life of the skipper in their hands, too. Having outstanding submariners on board, able to perform their duty under wartime conditions without hesitating was the best insurance the commanding officer had that the submarine would return after a patrol.

In retrospect, it seems curious that Dusty Dornin—who at the time was widely considered to be one of the best, if not *the* best Torpedo Data Computer operator in the submarine service, who had served aboard *Gudgeon* since her commissioning and thus knew her like the back of his hand—had not been selected to command the boat for the fourth patrol. On *Gudgeon*'s third patrol, Dusty Dornin had served as second in command, as executive officer. Historians have speculated that Admiral Robert Henry English, the newly appointed replacement for Thomas Withers as the Commander Submarines of the Pacific Force (ComSubPac), thought Dornin was too young and inexperienced, having graduated from the Naval Academy in 1935. Of course, he did not have the hindsight of those living after the war to know what kind of submariner Dornin would become once he was given command.

Fortunately, for the men on *Gudgeon*, William Shirley Stovall Jr., the new commander, was no slouch. Stovall had attended a military institute in preparation for admission to the Naval Academy. At the Academy he acquired nicknames such as "Niddy Noddy" and "Satchel," perhaps because he was known to have been raised in Picayune, Mississippi. But the name that he would be known by throughout his Academy and later years was his middle name, "Shirley." While at the Academy, he played intramural football. According to his *Lucky Bag* bio, Stovall was a popular student because of his "unfailing good nature" and "ready sympathy" as well as his being able to endure the taunts of smaller men because due to his "manly proportions" he was made the butt of many jokes. Stovall graduated from the Academy in 1929 in the top half of his class at the age of twenty-one.[4]

Over the next five years, he served on two surface ships, the *California*, which would be severely damaged on December 7, 1941, but later rebuilt, and the *Wasmuth* as gunnery and engineering officer. Sandwiched between his services on the two vessels was a six-month stint for flight training. He attended sub school at New London in 1934 and was immediately assigned to serve on the submarine uss *S-1*. After two years at code breaking school and a promotion to lieutenant, Stovall was assigned to the *S-18*, again as gunnery and engineering officer. In May 1939, he received his first command, the *S-27*, and served as skipper for three years, a position he held prior to assuming command of *Gudgeon*, which came with promotion to lieutenant commander. Perhaps it was by design that as commanding officer on the *S-27*, he was not sent on war patrols because of his intimate knowledge of American progress in breaking Japanese ciphers. It seems very foolish to have assigned Stovall to *Gudgeon* and sent him to the Pacific theater. If he were taken prisoner, he would have been brutally tortured and possibly given away vital secrets to the Japanese. However, that is what the authorities decided to do. Good skippers were hard to find.

Boarding *Gudgeon* at the same time as the new skipper was Arthur C. Barlow, the man who had signalled during the attack at Pearl Harbor. Barlow found himself aboard a ship for the first time in his career under wartime conditions. Before the war, Barlow had developed an interest in ham radios. In 1940, he volunteered for signal school. The nineteen-year-old high school graduate was sent to the Naval Pier at Chicago for training, then on to San Diego and Pearl Harbor. Technically, Barlow was not a rookie submariner because he had spent some time on the *S-18*, one of those ancient, leaky bucket submarines used for training before the war. Barlow got off the pigboat just in time to avoid being sent to the Aleutians. Art Barlow much preferred Honolulu to Alaska and felt that he was very lucky in other ways as well. The *S-18* was, as he says, built in the early 1920s and was still in the early stages of submarine development. Barlow said that there was as much difference between the *S-18* and the fleet boat *Gudgeon* as there was between *Gudgeon* and the nuclear submarines that would come after the war.

On July 11, 1942, another beautiful sunny day in paradise, *Gudgeon* departed Pearl Harbor for her fourth war patrol. This time she would have her third commanding officer of the war. The men on board would find that William Shirley Stovall Jr. would have the same intensity for battle as Pop Lyon and Joe Grenfell. By this time, Hitler was moving east toward Stalingrad. In the Pacific Theater, Corregidor had fallen; the soldiers at Bataan had walked their cruel death march and the unfortunate Battle of Coral Sea was history. Mercifully for the Allies, the Battle of Midway had turned the tide. As *Gudgeon* pulled away, she enjoyed the protective escort of the destroyer USS *Breese*. With *Gudgeon* now traveling on the surface during day-light hours, the crew received additional practice with their machine guns and the three-inch deck guns, as well as repeated dives and surfaces.

Another of the new crew members for the patrol was Albert J. Rupp, who had decided to join the Navy on December 8, in the dark shadow of the disaster at Pearl Harbor. There was a catch, however, and that was that Rupp, living in Philadelphia, was only fifteen years old, far too young to join the Navy. The bold and angry Rupp had a plan. In one of two books he wrote describing his wartime experiences, *Threshold of Hell*, Rupp said that he went to the township where he was born and acquired a copy of his birth certificate. By means of some clever erasing and ink work, he was able to add a few years to his age. After a couple of days of intense lobbying, he talked his mother into signing the enlistment papers.

On March 9, 1942, the gung-ho Rupp was ordered to report. He was assigned to the Naval Training Station at Newport, Rhode Island. He then volunteered for submarines. Before long he was assigned to *Gudgeon*. Not yet old enough to drive a car, Rupp found himself riding a submarine to war. Although Rupp would only make a few runs on submarines, the war would be a horror beyond understanding. Early in the patrol, he had learned that he had drawn the four-to-eight lookouts. This meant that he would be on watch twice a day, during those hours. At first, he thought that he would have all of his time off between watches. That would not be the case. Chief of the Boat, James C. "Gunner" Ogden told Rupp that he would also be assigned to be the "captain" of the head. Rupp was thrilled, yet his delight at his promotion was misplaced. As he said later, "From seaman to captain in just one day." The green sailor, Albert J. Rupp was soon to learn that "head" meant toilet, and that the term "captain" was a misleading one, which meant he was assigned to keep the crew's tiny toilet area clean.[5]

Rupp was young, though, and full of energy. He went about his duties with vigor, and proudly set about insuring that his head was the most sterile and spotless one in the entire squadron. The whole area, the walls, the toilet, and the deck below, was made of steel. Rupp shined the area down until the toilet area shone brightly. He used a creosote and water solution on the steel deck to make certain that nobody would catch athlete's foot. Rupp was so thorough that he even poured a little of the mixture into the toilet bowl for good measure. After all, wasn't it just as important to make sure that the toilet bowl shone as brightly as everything else?

A few days later Shirley Stovall called Rupp up to the conning tower. Rupp was no doubt feeling proud of his efforts and reported as ordered, expecting heavy praise for his compulsive attention to the crew's toilet. Oddly enough, it was soon clear that Lieutenant Commander Stovall called Rupp up not to praise him, but to bury him. Stovall told Rupp to look through the periscope and tell him what he saw. Uncertain why he was being asked to do so, Rupp looked and reported that he could not see the "emerald green sea" only a football field-sized area of ocean covered by what appeared to be a milky substance.[6]

For the next thirty minutes, Shirley Stovall chewed Rupp out for the error of his ways. By adding creosote to the toilet, he had in effect painted a huge white sign on the ocean surface that read, "Submarine below, deposit depth charges here." The creosote stained water, collecting on the surface of the ocean, formed a white pool above the submarine. It was a rookie mistake that could have cost every man on board his life. Finally, after threats of court martial, Rupp was dismissed. Downcast, the energetic young submariner retreated to the safety of the confines below. It was the kind of mistake a kid would make, and Rupp was after all just a kid.

Early in *Gudgeon*'s fourth patrol, the new skipper designated George Seiler to be the boat's official barber. Though a young man, Seiler had done many things in his life, but cutting hair was not one of them. Flabbergasted, George Seiler took the job. What else could he do? After all, he had been ordered to do so. To the dismay of all aboard, Stovall then ordered that all crew and officers were to get their hair cut every three weeks, and they were ordered to pay Seiler for his services. Appointing George Seiler as boat's barber would come back to haunt Stovall. In order to set an example to the crew, Stovall announced that he would be the torpedoman's first customer. Seiler hurriedly set up his barbershop in the forward torpedo room. Before long, Shirley Stovall took off his officer's hat and settled back into the makeshift barber chair. Stovall had a head full of dark black hair. Soon, the dark waves would take on a look very much unlike they ever had before. Seiler would report years later that once he figured out how to work the barber's shears he dutifully went to work on the new skipper. By the time Seiler had finished with Shirley Stovall, the always-serious captain Stovall looked like a cat who had gone a few rounds with a rabid raccoon. It was a real hatchet job. The crew members who had witnessed the butchery shuddered, by their facial expressions telling Seiler that they wanted nothing to do with him or his clip job. Dusty Dornin, who was present for the scalping of the skipper, made the second biggest mistake of the day. He laughed. Dornin would learn that it was not wise to laugh at Shirley Stovall. As he slowly moved out of the makeshift barber chair, Stovall gruffly ordered Dornin to take his place. It was an order which Dornin would regret but, like Seiler, could not avoid. After sitting down sheepishly in the chair, Dornin said to Seiler, "George, if you make me look as bad as the captain, we're going to shoot you out one of those tubes on our next attack."[7] The men in the forward torpedo room were now very sober-faced, not wishing to say or do anything that would cause them to be designated as Seiler's next customer. As the haircut progressed however, the sailors watching Dornin took great enjoyment describing the ham-handed job that Seiler was doing on *Gudgeon's* number two man. One of them said to Dornin, "Christ, Mr. Dornin, it's going to take the rest of the patrol for that spot to grow out."[8] Dornin, the former All American football player, looked in a mirror, then at Seiler with murder on his face. Seiler, a survivor, a tough man who always seemed to land with his feet on the ground, reached out and asked for the fifty cents that Dornin owed him for the privilege of having been temporarily disfigured. It was at that exact moment that the former boxer knew he would take a rather morbid pleasure from his new job as *Gudgeon's* barber. He could butcher the men or not, but each time, they would pay him for his work. Dornin walked away fuming. As he entered the wardroom where many of the other officers were, the place erupted in laughter. The officers—Lieutenants Harmon B. Sherry, Sigmund "Bobo" Bobczynski, Albie Strow, and the others—were not laughing for long, however. Dornin ordered them to be next in line for the boat's new barber, the Pennsylvania Butcher, George Seiler.

Seiler was on a hot streak. He had avoided death on *Squalus* and then had managed to get himself on one of the top submarines in the Pacific Fleet. Shortly thereafter, he had been appointed boat's barber, which would prove to be a highly profitable affair. In addition, to make matters even better an old friend from the *Stingray*, Ship's Cook Cecil "Carl" Finks, had boarded

Gudgeon with Seiler. George Seiler has never forgotten a fateful encounter Finks had with the father of "Mary," a girlfriend of his. The angry gentleman made an offer that Finks found impossible to turn down. George Seiler picked up the story: "We were in San Diego. I was over the side scraping rust spots and painting the side of a ship in dry-dock when a civilian came walking towards me. He saw me on a stage hanging over the side and asked me if we had a man by the name of Finks aboard. I replied that we did, and he asked if he could speak with him. The gangway watch called down the hatch for Finks to come topside. They were standing above me, and I heard the conversation quite clearly. It went something like this: 'Young man, I think you are acquainted with a young lady by the name of Mary, aren't you?'

"Finks, 'Yes.'

"Mary's father continued. 'Son, Mary is my daughter, she is pregnant, and I came down here to have you make a decision.'

"Finks asked, 'What is the decision I have to make?'

" 'You are going to make a decision whether you want to be a husband or a corpse,' the man responded.

"Finks replied, 'When do you want me to marry her?'

" 'Right now,' said Finks' future father-in-law." [9]

Finks realized that he needed special liberty to leave the boat and get married, so he talked with the boat's captain, Leon N. Blair, who understood the man's plight, the mores of the day being so adamantly opposed to unwed motherhood. Finks was sent on his way, was married, and returned a couple of hours later, as Seiler said, "a husband and expectant father." [10] Seiler was pleased to have Finks on board, because although he was a little crazy, he was also "funnier than hell" and a good buddy. [11]

At 0620 on Thursday, July 23, 1942, *Gudgeon* was patrolling the approaches to Truk Island. *Gudgeon* was accompanied by a host of other submarines, including *Trout*, *Tambor*, *Grenadier*, and *Grayling* from Squadron Six. *Gudgeon* was now far south of her earlier patrol areas. Truk was a strategically located naval fortress, which had been held by the Germans and mandated to Japan by the League of Nations following Germany's defeat in World War I. Japan built it up to the point that it was considered virtually impregnable. A blockade of Truk was critically important so that the base could not be used to build up Japanese troop strength around the Solomon

Islands, an area where a new campaign was being planned by the Allies. Truk, however, did have one weakness. Her waters were vulnerable to submarine assaults. Consequently, for the next several months Truk would be blockaded by United States submarines. Of the submarines sent to Truk from Pearl Harbor, *Gudgeon* would get the first kill.

Early that morning of the twenty-third, *Gudgeon* sighted the first ship off Truk around 18 miles away and headed in *Gudgeon*'s direction. As the target vessel approached slowly at 5 knots, she was acting in a very odd manner. She would approach, come to a stop, and then move forward once again. Lieutenant Commander Stovall was suspicious and concluded that the ship must be a patrol vessel of some kind and, from the ship's behavior, more than likely one of those damned Japanese Q-ships. Stovall suspected that the ship was leading more valuable targets behind it, but when the horizon was scanned, no greater prize was sighted. Stovall, who would become known to his crew for being an aggressive, hard-nosed commander, decided that this ship was deserving of a few torpedoes. Moose Hornkohl said of Stovall, "He was aggressive. He didn't give a crap for anything. He would get out there and kick ass." [12]

Stovall described the ship as about 225 feet long, with two wooden stick masts about 60 feet high. He noted that because no guns could be seen and the well was covered with a low awning of some kind, which might be concealing guns, it may very well have been a Q-ship. The stern of the little vessel contained a few nondescript items which could have been concealed guns. The crew, still smarting from their two battles with a Q-ship on the second patrol, had mixed feelings. They were delighted at the opportunity for battle but knew that these Q-ships packed a punch. Three hours after first sighting the vessel Stovall started firing, sending three torpedo shots, at ten second intervals toward the Japanese ship. The torpedoes were set to run 1,250 yards at a depth of eight feet. One of the torpedoes appeared to run under the target, one just ahead, and another fifty to sixty yards ahead of the vessel.

The Japanese ship then turned away and started echo ranging [sonar] in an attempt to find the attacking submarine. Depth control of *Gudgeon* was lost after firing. *Gudgeon* submerged beyond periscope depth, to 80 feet. Not being able to observe the target's movements, Stovall wisely decided to go very deep, start evasive tactics, and rig for depth charge. The enemy ship threw seven depth charges vaguely in *Gudgeon*'s direction, missing by around 1,200 yards. Stovall was unsure whether the Japanese skipper was confused and launched the explosives the wrong way, or whether he was running scared and fired the ashcans in a weak-hearted gesture to cover his escape. Arthur C. Barlow, on board for his first patrol, was sure the ship was a Q-ship and remembered the episode clearly. The men on board were uncertain what type of vessel the ship had been prior to conversion, but Barlow felt it was probably an old destroyer made to look like a small freighter. At 1030, *Gudgeon* rose to periscope depth for an observation. The Japanese vessel was gone. Stovall was puzzled how the ship could have gotten away so fast. It was not in view, the ship's top speed was estimated at around 10 knots. If the ship had stayed to look for *Gudgeon*, it should still be there. The Q-ship's hasty departure, present absence, and the lack of decisiveness in attack were felt to be evidence of the ship's reluctance to engage *Gudgeon*. This Q-ship, in contrast to those encountered earlier as well as those that would be engaged in battle later in the war, was a pussycat.

In a perfect world, Stovall would have surfaced and found debris from the vessel after it had been sent to the bottom. However, being a submarine skipper in the first years of the war was hardly an ideal situation. One of the torpedoes had been dead on, and set at only eight feet; yet, Lieutenant Commander Stovall watched it drive under and beyond the ship. Dusty Dornin and Shirley Stovall had done all they could do, but torpedoes set at eight feet likely ran at a too-deep eighteen feet. Perhaps even if the torpedoes had run at eight feet, they would have run under and beyond the shallow draft vessel since the hull of Q-ships were made of wood. The wooden hull neutralized the effectiveness of the torpedo's magnetic detonator, which was designed to explode when the torpedo came within the magnetic field of a ship's hull.

Still, as far as Lieutenant Albert "Albie" Strow was concerned, history had taken place, for he had just taken part in his first torpedo attack of the war. He had been on board since the third patrol, but the Lyon patrol of only about three weeks' duration had not resulted in an actual attack being made. Even though the charges exploded far from the submarine, the experience left the green Strow "limp as a rag."[13] With *Gudgeon* deep and in silent running, he wrote in his log that the men on board were "stewing in their juices."[14] All the fans were off, as was the air conditioner and about every other electrical device on board, at least those that made noise. He exaggerated somewhat when he said it was about "150 in the shade." [15] Strow was lucky—when the attack was over, he had watch and could allow the recuperative powers of fresh Pacific air to fill his lungs, the fresh ocean breeze fanning his body, still weak from the stress of the attack. After completion of his watch, he went below and had a lunch consisting of three glasses of water, salt, and vitamin pills, then retired to his tiny bunk, "smelling like a week-dead goat." [16]

Strow was anticipating that once the ship reached their station on the twenty-fourth things were really going to get tough. He already understood that the war the men fought and the war that the folks back home envisioned were completely different. He wrote: "I think that if the Great American Public could see us on one of these patrols, the Navy would lose at least 90% of its glamour. It has been so hot that we have been running around in a pair of shorts and our shoes and that's all. Everybody needs a shave and a haircut and has either gotten up or is just going to bed and as a result we look like tramps. Someone with a shirt and tie on would look as strange as a morning coat and striped trousers would look at home." [17]

The next day, July 24, 1942, *Gudgeon* traveled west. Late in the evening the submarine would have a harrowing encounter that Moose Hornkohl, Ray Foster, and George Seiler would never forget. As Stovall reported, *Gudgeon* traveled to an area somewhat west of Truk Island. *Gudgeon* sighted a merchant vessel accompanied by a destroyer. The two Japanese ships were about 3,500 yards away. The moon was overhead but because of the clouds it was not light enough for a periscope approach. Stovall called for a surface and sonar approach since visibility was limited. About twelve minutes after surfacing, a second destroyer a couple of miles away quickly changed course and headed directly toward *Gudgeon*. Stovall, realizing that danger was near, dove and rigged for another depth charge attack. The destroyer initiated a brutal attack tossing twelve depth charges at *Gudgeon*, each timed a few seconds apart. These depth charges seemed to be larger than the ones dropped by the timid Q-ship the day before, but they did no damage. Immediately after the unsuccessful but sobering attack, the destroyer slowed down and started searching for *Gudgeon* with her sonar. Soon, a second destroyer joined in the search, the two making a coordinated effort to find *Gudgeon*, which was by this time at two-thirds speed, changing directions frequently, and heading north as fast as possible. Stovall wrote later that at 2201 hours, "The Chief Torpedoman reported that he, and other personnel in the torpedo room, heard what sounded like the high speed screws of a torpedo pass above torpedo room, as we passed 150 feet going down on this dive."[18] *Gudgeon* had been narrowly missed by, of all things, a torpedo. Had the fish been slightly deeper it would have hit *Gudgeon* broadside, breaking the 307-foot underwater warrior into pieces and killing every man on board. The whole affair, from the sighting of the destroyer to the time the torpedo slid past *Gudgeon* was only sixteen minutes.

At any rate, that is what Stovall's report said. Moose Hornkohl, Guts Foster, and George Seiler remember the hair-raising details a whole lot differently, illustrating just how thin the line between life and death was for the average World War II submariner. Hornkohl said that he was on watch with several other men, one of whom was Seaman First Class Hershel Kiser. Throughout the war, Shirley Stovall always had three lookouts from the crew as a whole and a fourth, who was always a quartermaster. Each one would be assigned to keep an ever-watchful eye on an imaginary ninety-degree area of sea and air into infinity. A fifth man, one of the officers serving as Officer of the Deck, would conduct an overall search in all directions. Stovall would say later that he preferred to have the men on lookout for one hour. The men on top would rotate with men in the control room who were assigned to the stern and bow planes. This allowed the men on watch to give their eyes a rest. At night the men would wear the special red-lensed goggles which accustomed their eyes for nighttime watches, so that the second they hit the deck, their eyes were attuned to the darkness. Unfortunately, the red goggles had done nothing to stimulate the tired brain of Hershel Kiser, who had apparently fallen into a trance. Kiser had the stern aft lookout area behind Hornkohl who was, of course, stern forward. The occurrence of a sailor on watch falling into a trance was uncommon and could result in the deaths of all the men on board.

In the meantime one of the destroyers off in the murky black distance had changed course and headed directly for *Gudgeon*. Hershel Kiser slept, or he might just as well have been asleep, because a destroyer, then a second started an approach on *Gudgeon* from the area of sea that he was supposed to be guarding. Shirley Stovall was on the bridge with the target-bearing transmitter giving ranges and bearings for the merchant vessel that *Gudgeon* was pursuing. Dusty Dornin was topside and sighted two destroyers bearing down on the submarine. He said, "Captain, there's two destroyers on our starboard beam." [19] Stovall continued to eye the merchantman. Dornin, becoming more alarmed, raised his voice, "Captain, there's two destroyers on our starboard beam, and they're on a collision course." [20] Again, Stovall said nothing, concentrating even more intently on his target. Now thoroughly agitated, Dornin shouted, "Captain, there's two destroyers on our starboard beam making thirty-five knots on a collision course." [21] He hurried over to Stovall, grabbed him by the shoulder, and shook him into action. Stovall, his intense concentration on the attack broken, ordered, "DIVE." [22] The men on top scurried down the ladder and secured the hatch.

Gudgeon went into an emergency dive just ahead of the fire-breathing destroyers now on a dead charge. Ray Foster in the forward torpedo room remembers *two* torpedoes with their fast screws extremely close racing past the forward torpedo room. Seiler, stationed with Foster also reported hearing two torpedoes close by and added, "They must have been within about ten feet of the ship. They were so loud they sounded like trucks going over." [23] Ray Foster continued, "So that night I was up in the torpedo room, and the Old Man run everybody out of the ward room and he had Dusty in there and he said, 'Dornin, I don't ever want you to put your hands on me again.' Well, Dusty Dornin saved the submarine." [24] This was a perfect example of what some sailors would say about Shirley Stovall's demeanor as *Gudgeon*'s commanding officer. He was proper, by the book, and therefore, despite the circumstances, was angry that a subordinate officer had put his hands on him, a superior officer.

Hershel Kiser might just as well have changed his name to Mudd, because that is what he was for the rest of the patrol. As Moose Hornkohl said, "Poor old Kiser was a dirty word for a while. He let those destroyers get in. The guys down below relied on us to the extreme, and when those destroyers got in on us, we could have all been gone in just a few short minutes. They'd have rammed us because of one guy's mistake." [25]

In contrast to the three torpedomen (Seiler, Foster, Hornkohl) who adamantly insist that it was Dusty Dornin that shook Shirley Stovall to attention, Albie Strow wrote in his log that it was Lieutenant Harmon B. Sherry who had done so. In fairness to Shirley Stovall, it was not just Dusty Dornin (or Sherry) who saved *Gudgeon*. Shirley Stovall's work eluding the

Japanese destroyers was nothing short of genius. The two destroyers storming toward the slower submarine at thirty-five knots knew exactly where *Gudgeon* was. All Stovall could do was dive and begin evasive tactics, which he performed masterfully, *Gudgeon* making her escape three hours after the whole affair had started.

Strow recalled later that he had seen Lieutenant George Harvey Penland hurrying down the ladder during the emergency dive and chuckled to himself. Several of the men said Penland had passed them in such a hurry that he was stepping on their toes. Strow wrote in his log that when the Japanese were trying to ping *Gudgeon* their gear put out a very strange wail, like an animal in pain. Strow reflected upon the depth charge attack, writing that he had not done a "life review" though he had been in grave danger of losing his life.[26] He said that the men tended to take the awful depth charging in stride. Stovall had made a very positive impression on Strow, who wrote in his log that he "was glad the Captain had all that training in evasion tactics, for he is *good* at the game."[27]

When interviewed later during the war, Lieutenant Commander Stovall told an anecdote about two of the crew members during a depth charge attack. He said. "The two mess attendants were sitting in the forward torpedo room, one was reading the Bible, the other was doing nothing, and, at this particular moment, propellers were heard to pass overhead. One mess attendant turned and looked at the other and says, 'Mose is them our screw.' [speaking to Mess Attendant Second Class, Eugene Mosley Jr.] And about that time they let go with a couple of depth charges that were very close and shook us pretty badly, so the other looked back at Mose immediately and said, 'No, Mose, them was his'n'."[28]

Moose Hornkohl said that under attack, Shirley Stovall was loose; he "was not afraid."[29] He was a tactician. Seiler added, "He thought that to show any emotion would undermine the old tradition of the military."[30] Consequently, added Seiler, Stovall was not particularly popular with the crew. "With him," Seiler continued, "he was up here, and everybody else was down there,"[31] moving his hand from above his head down to about the level of his chin. Of course, military leaders have been carrying themselves like William Shirley Stovall Jr. throughout history. George Patton was not exactly "one of the boys," yet Patton wasn't trapped in a 307 foot submarine with his boys where it was more difficult to be standoffish. Lieutenant Commander Stovall wasn't there to make friends. That was obvious. His intention was to take the war to the enemy. His demeanor and practices aboard the submarine were what he felt was best suited to achieve this end.

Stovall was the type of commander who was "into himself." He was not personable. He did not socialize with the crew. Moose Hornkohl remembers that, "He never wandered through the boat. He wouldn't go forward. The farthest he would go was to the head, which was right beside the torpedo room."[32] Seiler agreed with this statement, saying that he never saw Stovall in the forward torpedo room other than to take a shower. Ray Foster commented upon *Gudgeon*'s commanding officer, "William Shirley Stovall was an excellent torpedo shot, but in the ward room he sat at the head of the table and the only thing they could discuss was in the line of duty. No jokes, no small talk."[33] Stovall, this tough by-the-book skipper, an emotional island unto himself, was heading for trouble. He refused to practice even the most basic psychological coping mechanisms. There would be no banter, no humor, and as a result, little support and friendship from his subordinates. There was just Shirley Stovall with an overload of responsibility on his shoulders in his high place and everyone else on board, down a little lower.

After watching some Japanese seaplanes with caution above *Gudgeon*'s patrol area on the thirtieth, Stovall finally sighted a target on the thirty-first. As *Gudgeon* moved along on the surface, Albie Strow sighted a ship and called the captain. Lieutenant Commander Stovall was pleased. At around 0245 *Gudgeon* started maneuvering for position on a decent-sized merchant vessel. A destroyer was escorting the ship but fortunately was on the other side. The destroyer's captain would win no medals this day. Stovall estimated that the ship was about 8,500 tons and was approximately 2,500 yards away. Stovall, ever the wiser as time went on, set the torpedoes to run at 21 feet so they would actually hit at around 31 feet. They would be fired from the forward torpedo room.

When interviewed later during the war, Stovall said, "We fired three torpedoes at this target and didn't realize he had an escort until just before we fired. Two torpedoes hit; the third one passed ahead. The escort, which just a moment before had become visible, followed the one miss on down the range and dropped his depth charges at the end of the torpedo run, while we turned around and went went [*sic*] back out on the surface and escaped that way. That was very amusing to us, to see him go in the opposite direction from us and waste his depth charges."[34] It is difficult to conceive of any ship's commander being that incompetent. The six depth charges exploded harmlessly where one of *Gudgeon*'s torpedoes had ended its run, perhaps miles from *Gudgeon*, not even close to the point from which *Gudgeon* had fired. The USS *Gudgeon* sped away on the surface. The target ship and destroyer were temporarily lost from sight because of smoke from the escaping submarine's diesel engines. Stovall assumed that the merchant vessel had gone down; two timed hits having been heard, the target eventually disappearing from sight. The destroyer was now in pursuit, but Stovall found it rather easy to escape.

Dusty Dornin reported later that the merchant ship was observed to sink slowly. When interviewed soon after the incident, Stovall agreed, " . . . we had the pleasure of seeing our target sink as we went away and seeing the escort waste his depth charges."[35] *Gudgeon* would eventually be given wartime credit for the sinking. Despite the statements of *Gudgeon*'s top officers, the JANAC evaluators did not credit *Gudgeon* with a sinking.

Later in the day, *Gudgeon* lookouts sighted a huge 15,000 ton passenger liner. Unfortunately, this big fat target could not be closed upon. Stovall quickly reported the sighting to ComTaskForSeven, hoping someone else would get a shot or two at the monster. Then followed a boring couple of days on the *Gudgeon*. Nothing was sighted, not even a fishing boat. The crew slept, gambled for each other's money, read, wrote letters home, drank weak coffee, shot the breeze about anything and everything—including the usual boasts about past conquests of the shore-bound variety—and just waited. Many of the men who had not yet earned their dolphins studied quietly. When not manning their stations, the crew was supposed to take it easy, in part because doing so would demand less oxygen. Oftentimes the men would listen quietly to records that had been provided by the USO in the crew's mess in the after battery room. A submarine could stay submerged about a day before it was necessary to surface for air and to charge the batteries that powered the electric motors. Once she reached her patrol area, *Gudgeon* would often cruise on one diesel engine, known as "the Dinky," to conserve fuel for matters like battle or running like crazy to avoid being sunk. *Gudgeon* continued to troll back and forth in the assigned patrol area, not really desiring to get any place very quickly.

On August 3, 1942, at 0440, another merchant vessel was sighted, making about 10 knots. Stovall surfaced and attempted an end around. The end around was the commonly used maneuver of the day. The submarine, out of sight because of her lower profile in the water, would run parallel to the target ship on the surface and then move in toward it. Ideally the target would maintain its course and reach a point roughly perpendicular to the submarine. This was most easily done at nighttime because the submarine was even less likely to be seen.

The attack was the only time Lieutenant Commander William S. Stovall Jr. did battle with an unescorted merchant ship as commander of *Gudgeon*. At 0523 the cargo ship, eventually identified as the *Naniwa Maru*, was deemed close enough. Stovall set the torpedoes to run at twenty feet depth for two miles. The men in the forward torpedo room hurried over to their lucky Buddha piece, each man rubbing it in exactly the same way as they had on prior attacks. The submariners thought that their Buddha brought them luck, when in reality, like all such superstitions, it brought them self-confidence, a strength that was reinforced after each successful torpedo attack. Stovall roared, "FIRE ONE. FIRE TWO. FIRE THREE." [36] Each time *Gudgeon* rocked slightly in the water. Stovall saw the second and third torpedoes hit, the ship listing twenty degrees by the bow. After about five minutes, as the ship was ready to sink, a third and unusually loud explosion occurred. Despite the blast the vessel's crew was able to throw some small boats in the water, though it was unclear if anyone made it to them or not. *Gudgeon* sped off. This time *Gudgeon* would receive war and JANAC credit for her work. The stricken vessel weighed 4,858 tons. The attack struck Albie Strow as "brutal." But the men on board were "in the best of spirits and are all ready for a couple more." [37]

After *Gudgeon* left the horrible sight of dead bodies, floating wreckage, and the hopeless and shell-shocked survivors floating in the water, things on board once again became uneventful. The officers goaded the crew into a "we vs. they" acey-deucey tournament. [38] After all the ribbing from the cocky officer contingent on board, the crew was after blood. As champion of the ward room, Lieutenant Albie Strow would play the crew champ. Dusty Dornin told him prior to the championship game that if he lost, he would get duty the first week after *Gudgeon* hit shore. Strow said that the game was "very legal" and that "I got the pants whipped off of me." [39] Then, just to make the day's humiliation complete, Strow did a two hour watch that night and found that it was the most miserable two hours he had ever experienced. There was such a downpour on the 0200–0400 watch that he could not tell whether *Gudgeon* was on the surface. Strow's bad luck continued. An encounter with a Japanese merchant vessel did not pan out, and the boat's air conditioner went out.

The crew became accustomed to the challenge of patrolling below the surface, with little oxygen and less as the day proceeded, clouds of cigarette smoke, the close quarters, the boredom, the necessary tension of patrolling in a deadly enemy's home waters. Now, the crew was heading into the second month of the patrol and had to accept the fact that there would be no air conditioner to filter and cool the air. The sweat ran down the bare backs of the unshaven submariners in rivers. The engine rooms aft of the bridge were by now 120°F. The Navy had learned from the old pigboats, which did not have any air conditioning, that even the toughest of submariners could tolerate oppressive temperatures for only a few days. Therefore, the lack of air conditioning was far more than an issue of comfort. But, the men would keep up with their duties. Everybody on board was depending upon them, and they in turn, on their shipmates. *Gudgeon* moved on in search of their foe.

On August 17, 1942, all hell broke loose from the alluring backdrop of a beautiful sunny day. At about 6 A.M. off Minami Pass, the crew heard systematic depth charging every seven minutes for about three hours. Stovall correctly concluded that there must be a valuable convoy in the area and surmised that the Japanese were throwing depth charges willy-nilly to sober up any submarine skipper who may have had designs on the prized Japanese merchant ships. The result of the depth charging was quite the opposite; *Gudgeon* headed for the convoy. Still west of Truk Island, at 1022 masts were observed. Two eastbound transport/freighter-type ships escorted by two destroyers were making a radical zigzag southerly course. *Gudgeon* submerged and approached by periscope.

Stovall commented, "It was about eleven o'clock in the day, so, of course, we had to make a periscope approach."[40] Stovall and Dornin, along with the crack torpedo crews, formed a lethal team. George Seiler and Guts Foster and the rest of the men manning the forward torpedo room must have been on cloud nine. The little Buddha lucky piece got a real working over. Six torpedoes were fired, three at each transport. Foster described the attack this way: "There were a couple of apples headed our way, and the Old Man said, 'Make six tubes ready. FIRE ONE. FIRE TWO. FIRE THREE. FIRE FOUR. FIRE FIVE. FIRE SIX.'"[41]

The targets were about a mile away. Such an attack was a very complicated undertaking. Shirley Stovall described it this way in his war patrol report: "Fired three torpedoes (a total of six, all bow tubes) at each of the transports which were in column following the screening destroyers. Leading target—3 torpedoes, 118 port track, gyro angle 10 L, torpedo run 2600 yards; second target—3 torpedoes, 108 port track, gyro angle 0, torpedo run 2500 yards. Target course 197, speed 15 knots. Used a two degree spread and ten second firing interval in each salvo. Actual setting on torpedoes 20 feet to make them run at 30 feet. Estimated draft of targets 28 feet."[42]

The men on *Gudgeon*, listening intently, already with two kills under their belts this patrol, were certain that they had hit the first target with all three fish, the second with two. The torpedoes had arrived at their targets and exploded at just the time they should have. That is, the torpedoes exploded at the time they should have made contact with each ship. Two hits on the first target were seen through the periscope, one on the second. The first target was observed to be going down fast, taking a very heavy list to port. No more propeller noises were heard from either ship. Stovall believed that both targets had been sunk.

⤓ Shirley Stovall had a choice. He could keep an eye on the damaged ships to confirm their sinking or take immediate action to avoid the two destroyers that were furiously heading for *Gudgeon*'s visible periscope. Stovall ordered, "DIVE."[43] Stovall and the other officers knew that eluding escorts in the Truk area would be especially difficult. The sound conditions were favorable for the hunter because of the slight water temperature variation and the deep ocean depths; there were no thermal screens to hide under. Five minutes after Guts and George and the others in the forward torpedo room had sent their six-torpedo salvo at the Japanese transports and the triumphant shouts of "Take that, you bastards"[44] had subsided, *Gudgeon*, at around 180 feet depth, underwent the first explosion of a torrent of huge depth charges. The destroyers took turns dropping barrages of ten depth charges apiece, hoping to send *Gudgeon* in a thousand pieces to the bottom. BOOM. BOOM. BOOM. BOOM. BOOM. BOOM. BOOM. BOOM.

BOOM. BOOM. *Gudgeon*'s hull, $^{11}/_{16}$ths of an inch thick and made of a high tensile metal, was under severe strain. The attack continued. BOOM. BOOM. BOOM. BOOM. BOOM. BOOM. BOOM. BOOM. BOOM. BOOM. It would not take long for one of *Gudgeon*'s compartments to fill with water if one of them was broached. The sweat continued to roll off the stark-white faces of the men, lying or sitting silently in their compartments. BOOM. BOOM. BOOM. BOOM. BOOM. BOOM. BOOM. BOOM. BOOM. BOOM. The submariners were thrown around wildly with each detonation, then the water swished loudly past *Gudgeon* in aftershock. The roar of the garbage-barrel-like explosives was almost deafening.

Compared to the few pounds of gunpowder and the loud report of a Fourth of July explosive, the thundering power of an underwater depth charge weighing as much as 500 pounds is nearly inconceivable. Nothing could put the fear of God into a man more surely than a depth charge attack. The furious barrage continued: BOOM. BOOM. BOOM. BOOM. BOOM. BOOM. BOOM. BOOM. BOOM. BOOM. All the men could do was sit there and wait. The sailors wondered if this would be the end, or would *Gudgeon* somehow make her escape. Some of the bombs were so close that when they exploded, the very heavy and large *Gudgeon* was concussively tossed ten feet deeper into the water. When a boat the size of a submarine is pushed ten feet deeper by the violent surge of ocean following the explosion of a depth charge, the men on board the submarine are being thrown like flimsy ragdolls against the hull, the torpedo racks, the deck, and anything else that protrudes and is made of metal. The unending assault continued. BOOM. BOOM. BOOM. BOOM. BOOM. BOOM. BOOM. BOOM. BOOM. BOOM.

Stovall, weighed down already with the burden of command, now had to struggle with the thunderous depth charges as they continually challenged his concentration by throwing him around the conning tower as he tried to guide *Gudgeon* away from the attacking destroyers. The small contingent of men in the conning tower with him worked feverishly to maneuver *Gudgeon* to safety, each explosion increasing the tension among the group. The angry Japanese destroyers moved back and forth dropping one depth charge after another on the ocean surface. One would throw ten depth charges, as the other stopped to listen. Then the second would move in and throw ten more explosives *Gudgeon*'s way, while the first destroyer waited to try to pick up *Gudgeon*'s location. BOOM. BOOM. BOOM. BOOM. BOOM. BOOM. BOOM. BOOM. BOOM. BOOM. Sixty depth charges in one hour. The charges weaved their way down deeper and deeper into the darkness of the ocean below to explode at their preset depth. The destroyers continued to plow through the sea looking for the enemy submarine, and smashing into the helpless Japanese seamen afloat in the waters who had been lucky enough to survive *Gudgeon*'s attack. Each depth charge cascaded white foaming ocean above the surface, sometimes lifting the forlorn men and debris ever higher. The scene was a ghastly horror. Yet, the terror felt by the Japanese paddling frantically in the water must have been far worse than that felt by the men on *Gudgeon*. Atop the ocean, totally exposed, the Japanese survivors could not get out of the way of the depth charges or the destroyers as they came charging by in search of the American submarine.

Albert Rupp described the thunderous attack in *Threshold of Hell*. Once again the young submariner paid for his inexperience. During the attack he had positioned himself under the vulnerable escape hatch above the after torpedo room. He said that the battle caused a "sickening, shuddering and shaking feeling."[45] With the air blowers and most everything else that made noise turned off, Rupp felt a drop of water on his shoulder, then another and another. Fearing the worst, he stared at the hatch, fully expecting to be drowned by the ocean rushing into the submarine. One of the first class torpedomen assured him that he would be OK, telling the youngster, "Don't worry kid, it's just condensed water."[46] The barely pubescent submariner was overwhelmed with relief.

Finally, the destroyers were out of depth charges, or they had developed concern about the fate of their fellow countrymen floating in the water. Shirley Stovall thought the Japanese called off the attack to pick up survivors. Whatever the reason, the men on *Gudgeon* had heard their last depth charge and would live to fight another day.

Irvin Hornkohl described what it was like to undergo a depth charge attack deep in the Pacific Ocean. "Silent running was brutal. They would shut down the air conditioning and turn everything off. Everything went to control by hand. We used minimal lights to save the batteries and keep the heat down. The heat would shoot up to 120°F. It would get up to 120°F in that boat, especially if you were working. You had to pump like you was on the helm. You operated a hydraulic pump that turned the rudder. If you were on the bow planes, you were operating a hand pump to maintain your depth. Bow planes and stern planes. These guys would be sitting right next to one another. Somebody would have to relieve you to give you a good breather, and then you relieved them again. It may take three or four guys to get the trim on. They didn't use the trim pump because they were noisy and the enemy would pick up the sound with the sound gear. It was cat and mouse, and it really worked on your nerves." [47]

Hornkohl continued, "There wasn't a coward on the boat. Nobody was really scared. But, if you dropped a wrench or something, oh God, people would want to kill you. It was terrible." The depth charges "would shake the hell out of you, you're listening and you're hearing these screws, like they're in your ears, sqooish, sqooish sqooish. When they start picking up speed, you knew they were making a run on you, and you sit back and wait for those suckers. Down they would come, and click, whummp. It shakes the damn boat like a dog shaking a cat." [48]

The attack over, Albie Strow would write that William Shirley Stovall Jr. was "really something." [49] He was so impressed with Stovall's performance during attack that he wrote, "If the skipper were to ask any of us to go with him to the gates of hell, he would have seventy-odd men to go with him." [50] In fact, Strow claimed that the attack was so masterful that no American submarine had ever accomplished such a feat before. He said that the submarine was all set to fire on the first transport, which they did, then while those torpedoes were enroute, pivoted and fired three more at the second one. Strow said, the first boat all but evaporated, then the second one was hit and "took a nosedive." [51] Strow was so excited about the sinkings that he yelled over the submarine's speaker system that "we had just sunk two transports and down we went to 350 feet." [52] Strow referred to the attack as "history in the making" and added, "Everything was against us—the sea was like glass and those destroyers were the newest and best they have." [53] Everyone on board was "so proud of themselves that we are just plain silly." [54] He said that Stovall's attack was submarining at its best and that he was proud to have been there. He took a swipe at the Army, stating that they had done nothing to equal the achievements of *Gudgeon* and estimated that *Gudgeon* had, by this time in the war, sunk about sixty-thousand tons which was "as much or more than any other sub. Brag, brag—and damn it—we rate bragging."[55]

Surprisingly enough, after sixty depth charges, some of them close enough and potent enough to throw *Gudgeon* violently deeper with each explosion, Lieutenant Commander Stovall described the *Gudgeon*'s damage from the attack as relatively minor, though he acknowledged the depth charges were very close. Some electrical cables had been pushed around as much as two inches from where they once were. There were no serious leaks. Stovall also said that some cork was knocked from the overhead, a high pressure air leak on a safety tank already in existence before the attack worsened it. *Gudgeon*'s antenna trunk was flooded, and there was a rattle in the superstructure over the engine room. A rattle in the superstructure is a noise that could betray *Gudgeon*'s position to the Japanese.

It was obvious that the antisubmarine warfare skills of the Japanese skippers varied considerably. The better-trained units tended to cluster around important ships or naval sites like the one at Truk Island. After the war, Pop Lyon, *Gudgeon*'s second skipper, recalled that several submarine commanders were trying to get United States aviators to fly over a specific Japanese ship stationed near Truk and drop a Navy Cross on the deck; the skipper was so skilled that the submariners actually developed a deep respect for him.

About five hours later, a jarred *Gudgeon* and crew came to periscope depth at a position six and a half miles west of where the attack had occurred. By this time it was raining. *Gudgeon* fled to avoid being found by Japanese aircraft that would certainly be sent to search the area. The men on board would eventually be given wartime credit for having sunk two more ships though JANAC would disallow credit for the sinkings. This time, it is easy to see why JANAC did so. *Gudgeon* had fled before the men operating the periscope could confirm that either of the ships had actually sunk. The two logs written the day of the attack made it clear that Shirley Stovall and the others on board had not seen the ships go under. Apparently, JANAC could not find evidence that sinkings had occurred from the records that would be evaluated later. In the absence of such documentation, JANAC did not give credit, regardless of what may have been witnessed by those that were present at the time. The JANAC report does not list damage done to enemy vessels, just sinkings. In so doing the official record of the United States

Navy in World War II would in essence just plain ignore *Gudgeon*'s frightful encounter with the Japanese on August 17, 1942.

The still-green Lieutenant Albert Strow would never forget the encounter, though. Strow was born and raised in Benton, a tiny town in western Kentucky, which was said to be known best for its moonshine and mules. Even as a youngster, Albie Strow aspired to be a naval officer. The small rural school he attended did not offer the requisite science curriculum for him to gain admission to the Naval Academy. A bright and determined Strow journeyed to nearby Paducah and moved in with one of his relatives. Albie Strow must have been an impressive young lad, because before long, Senator Alben Barkley appointed him to the Naval Academy. Given Strow's background, the appointment seems to be a bit surprising until one considers that Barkley had been raised on a poor Kentucky tobacco farm, so he knew a little about pulling yourself up by your bootstraps, and he was all too willing to give young Strow a boost. Strow would head off to the Naval Academy, and Barkley would eventually become Harry Truman's vice president after the war. While at the Academy, Strow was not particularly active, but did serve as the manager of the Navy football team his final year. Albie Strow was always proud of his roots, bragging that Paducah was "the biggest little city in the South."[56] He was known as a friendly sort at the Academy, the *Lucky Bag* declaring that he was "one of the boys" and that he always had a friendly grin on his face. He graduated from the Naval Academy in 1939 and served on a couple of destroyers. Once the war started he attended Submarine School in New London, Connecticut, completing the program in March 1942. He was then assigned to *Gudgeon* just in time to take part in the Battle of Midway.

While sitting off the powerful island fortress at Truk, Strow wrote in his log that the radiomen had made a report back to ComSubPac in Hawaii describing the assumed destruction of the two Japanese ships and the intense depth charge attack. Strow noted that the radiomen received a response that was clearly from their hosts, the Japanese, because the transmitter sounded very odd. The keyed characters were "slurred," and they could not get the respondent to give them the proper "authenticator."[57] Stovall ordered that all communications cease, fearing that the Japanese would be able to DF (direction find) *Gudgeon* based upon the repeated transmissions. He ordered an all-day dive to keep the Japanese from locating the submarine.

The giddy Albert Strow wrote proudly, and inaccurately, that, "We have it all figured out—to date this boat has come very close to sinking 1% of the Jap merchant navy—so as soon as we get 100 boats out here, we will have done our part so this boat can return to the States for the duration. Good sound logic to me. Anything to get back. It cannot be too long though, for actually the old gal is getting brittle and she needs an extensive revamping in a good Navy yard before many more patrols."[58]

The next day Lieutenant Commander William S. Stovall Jr. received an order from higher up that he should terminate the patrol and head for Fremantle, Australia, because of the high pressure air leaks in the main ballast and negative tanks. The leaks were making acquisition of trim more and more difficult on the long dives that *Gudgeon* was making.

On August 19, 1942, Albert Strow turned in at 10:30 P.M. hoping to get some good rest. At midnight he was awoken from a deep sleep because two coded messages had just come in from ComSubPac. Strow, at the time a little groggy and highly irritated, indignantly told Shirley Stovall that the messages were sent in codes that he was not able to decipher. This angered Stovall who told Strow to call Honolulu back and give them hell for doing such a thing. Then, to Strow's surprise, he realized that he could indeed decipher the messages, doing so took him until 5:00 A.M. He found that the communiqués were quite important, containing "dope" that *Gudgeon* had been waiting for since the end of July.[59] After making sense of the messages he sheepishly approached Lieutenant Commander Stovall, telling him the whole story, expecting to be put "in hack" indefinitely.[60] Stovall took it in stride, telling Strow that he was forgiven. A short while later Stovall received congratulations from Admiral Chester Nimitz, who was now the Commander-in-Chief of the Pacific Fleet. Stovall also received praise from Admiral Robert English at ComSubPac. Lieutenant Albert Strow was sure that this was the first time a submarine commander had received congratulations from "both Big Boys" and concluded that the skipper had "made the varsity" and would surely get a Navy Cross.[61] The Navy Cross was the medal second in prestige to the Medal of Honor for Navy personnel and was awarded to officers and enlisted men who distinguished themselves by extraordinary heroism in military operations against an armed enemy.

By this time in his second patrol, newlywed Carl Finks had made quite a name for himself, and for understandable reasons he had almost been murdered. Shortly after he came aboard, he became well known as an excellent cook but even more so for being a practical joker. He was probably the kind of man who was loved by half the crew and hated by the others. George Seiler loved the guy. Finks would be doing his early morning duty, while many of the crew tried to sleep in their bunks. Finks would make his way to the boat's microphone system, which allowed him to reach all of the compartments on the submarine. Many times, just for the fun of it he would take out a toy that made rooster calls. So, at 2 or 3 A.M. the sleeping men would be awakened to "cockle-doodle-doo, cockle-doodle-doo."[62] Finks did this kind of thing all the time and kept many of the men very loose, laughing at his pranks. However, Finks went a little too far one night. He found poor old Moose Hornkohl deep asleep in his bunk. Hornkohl was flying an early morning flag, which was all too visible to the ornery Finks, who promptly tied it to the structure above the sleeping submariner. Then Finks yelled, "FIRE."[63] Hornkohl hurried out of his bunk, jumping over the side nearly dismembering himself in the process. Hornkohl was furious. He wanted to kill him. And, who could blame him? After some time the raging Moose Hornkohl was calmed. *Gudgeon* continued toward her safe harbor, this time in Australia. *Gudgeon* headed south toward her new base, on the southwestern end of Australia, at Fremantle, crossing the equator on the twenty-third.

With the submarine heading home, the temptation might have been for the men on board to relax, but as Strow wrote that would be a big mistake. There were still many roadblocks to be overcome. On the twenty-fourth he noted that for the past "two and a half days we have been running like the devil was chasing us—running the gauntlet of all these islands and passes through the Dutch East Indies."[64] Then to the displeasure of the men on board *Gudgeon*, a vital message was received that ordered, "ANY U.S. MAN OF WAR" that happened to be in the area of Ambon Bay to immediately head there.[65] Ambon Bay is located off the small Dutch East Indies Island of Ceram. *Gudgeon* was very close. Stovall ordered that the course should be changed and headed the boat toward Ambon Bay, seventy miles away. *Gudgeon* patrolled the area on the surface at thirteen knots until she was within twenty-one miles of the entrance to the Bay, then he ordered that *Gudgeon* dive to conduct a submerged patrol toward the entrance and across the western approaches off the bay for the rest of the day. Nothing was sighted. From there, it was on to Timor, then south, once again toward Fremantle, Australia. Strow estimated that the trip back would keep the men out of port for an additional five days, which was a crushing blow, the men having been on patrol already for forty-five days.

By this time in the patrol the *Gudgeon*'s official barber, George Seiler, had hacked his way through the seventy or so men on board several times. As time went on Seiler was "pretty sure" that his haircuts resembled "real" haircuts.[66] This was good because *Gudgeon*'s patrol was nearing an end, and Seiler had been the recipient of much scorn. In fact, golden-haired Alexander Sheffs had threatened to kill him if he did not do a satisfactory job on his locks. Seiler's improvement was obvious; the men on board were once again talking to him, and he had a pocket full of coins that would come in mighty handy once the boat reached shore.

Strow and the other men on board found their unwanted trip through the East Indies to be an incredible experience. By the twenty-fifth *Gudgeon* had been running through the islands for several days. The boat had not been out of sight of land the entire time. He guessed that there were a million of the tiny little islands. The only island whose name he could pronounce was "Timor." Dusty Dornin and Strow read the patrol reports from other submarines that had made the same passage and confirmed that they had gone through the area submerged because the Japanese were said to control the islands. *Gudgeon* did not do so. The *Gudgeon* officers figured that if the Japanese were to put ten men on each island, they would run out of men long before they had each island manned. Then the Japanese would have to keep the men on the strategically insignificant islands supplied. This would be an impossible and pointless task. Their reasoning proved to be sound. By the following day, Strow was excited to think that *Gudgeon* would be in the clear all the way to Australia. Except, of course, that the Army Air Force was patrolling the skies above *Gudgeon*'s path to safety. The men were hardly safe. He wrote, "They do not know the difference between a sub and a battleship and all ships are fair game—how we love our Army."[67]

On September 2, 1942, *Gudgeon*'s furious fourth war patrol was over after fifty-four days at sea. Albert Rupp, by this time a fifteen-year-old veteran of one war patrol, described entering port in his book, *Threshold of Hell*. In order to protect the privacy of the men he served with, one presumes, Rupp, uncertain whether he should use the actual name of ships, referred to *Gudgeon* as "*Rudderfish.*"

> The long low silhouette of Submarine Rudderfish lying just outside the nets at the gateway to the harbor was barely visible in the early morning darkness. A few short spheres of light pierced the darkness, and a signal of like kind returned. One more quick blink from shore, we were home.
>
> As the net tender started to part the nets, a launch pulled alongside Rudderfish. Hallelujah!, fresh milk, fruit, and the first mail in 67 days.
>
> Everything was quickly sent below and the hatch sealed. (Rudderfish was not yet in a safe harbor.) As the milk, fruit, and mail was passed out below, the Chief Quartermaster was busy tying a broom to number one periscope indicating a clean sweep of the patrol area. Spirits were high among the crew in anticipation of the impending shore leave which always followed a successful patrol run.
>
> The early light of dawn showed the nets were opened, bidding Rudderfish a warm welcome. The Skipper headed her into the channel, proudly displaying the broom firmly fixed to the periscope.
>
> All hands not on duty were mustered on deck, in uniform, as we slowly moved closer to the large gray ship about ⅔ of the way up the channel. It is the Submarine tender "Ryan," alongside which were three other submarines of the same classification and size as Rudderfish. As we prepared to come alongside the outboard submarine, a band started to play and the tender rails were lined with friends, happy at our safe return. Then lines were passed and as they were taken aboard, the haussers attached to the other end appeared, were taken in and looped around the davits, and at last we were secured and could relax.[68]

Rupp reported that the division commander then appeared at the gangway, boarded and congratulated Stovall and the rest of the sailors on board. There was a short formal ceremony with the Captain, Shirley Stovall, being temporarily relieved. Stovall, according to Navy custom, then relieved the officers and crew, happily turning *Gudgeon* over to the relief crew. It was a proud moment for the men on board *Gudgeon*. Her fourth patrol had been a highly successful one.

Shirley Stovall was certain that he had sunk four ships of about 35,000 tons, one of the better patrols as of that time in the war, and they were all alive to tell about it. Stovall said in his patrol report that the health of the crew was excellent. He felt that the boat had been very comfortable except for the time that the air conditioner was not functioning. *Gudgeon* had traveled seven thousand miles and expended around ninety thousand gallons of diesel fuel. The patrol ended with *Gudgeon* rolling into port with nine of her twenty-four torpedoes left and little fuel.

Stovall noted that the new technology, the SD radar, was used extensively for plane detection except when the submarine was within range of enemy bases, to avoid being DF'd. Stovall singled out the entire fire control party and especially Lieutenant Dornin for his brilliant work on the TDC. He noted the high percentage of hits—60 percent—and the successful attack on a screened double target on August 17, 1942. Lieutenant (jg) Webster Robinson, the diving officer, was also praised for his excellent depth control during approach and the subsequent depth charge attack on the seventeenth. He said that all officers and crew conducted themselves in a "highly commendable manner" during the major depth charge attack and every other encounter with the Japanese. Commendations were given.[69]

Lieutenant Commander Stovall added that the Japanese seemed to be employing small trawler-type ships for antisubmarine work. Their screws were very difficult to hear. They seemed to have echo ranging sound gear and depth charges. He theorized that they were also equipped with radar. This type of information would be of much interest to the other submarine commanders in the Pacific Theater, each of whom received copies of all war patrol reports. Stovall also reported that near the end of the patrol the submarine was not properly ballasted. At one time, *Gudgeon* had nine thousand pounds of stores, thirteen thousand gallons of fuel, extra torpedoes, too much fresh water, and other items which made it quite heavy and dangerous under certain wartime situations. Whenever there was a need to dive quickly, the excessive weight would make the dive more difficult to control. It is far better for a submarine to slowly glide down at a safe angle than sink like a stone because of the excessive weight. A final note by Stovall was of much importance. With the addition of SD radar to screen for airplanes, *Gudgeon* was able to stay on the surface the entire time, from Pearl Harbor to the assigned patrol area, except for diving drills and for ship contacts on July 23 and 24. The addition of radar meant that much more time could be spent searching for Japanese shipping. The radar had allowed *Gudgeon* to pick up planes as far away as 28 miles.

The Commander of Submarine Squadron Six, Commander Allan Mc-Cann, and the Commander of Submarines in the Southwest Pacific, Charles A. Lockwood Jr., were very satisfied with the patrol. McCann was particularly pleased with the vigor of the men on board noting that no health problems of any kind were experienced and that the morale of the crew was high. Stovall was praised for conducting contacts aggressively and for pressing home the attacks with vigor. McCann gave the officers and crew of the *Gudgeon* a well done and credit for having sunk four ships totaling 35,000 tons.

More importantly, Stovall's new boss, Admiral Lockwood, was equally impressed. He said that nine hits out of the fifteen torpedoes fired was a remarkably high percentage considering that all hits were obtained at distances over two-thousand five-hundred yards. He called the work of the men making up the torpedo control party, "A perfection that should be constantly striven for by all submarines."[70] *Gudgeon* was making quite a name for herself.

Lockwood agreed that *Gudgeon* should receive credit for having sunk four ships and awarded Lieutenant Commander William S. Stovall Jr. the Navy Cross. The citation, signed by Secretary of the Navy Frank Knox for President Franklin D. Roosevelt, said; "For extraordinary heroism as Commanding Officer of the USS *Gudgeon* during a highly successful and aggressive submarine war patrol in enemy controlled waters. After successfully locating enemy forces, Lieutenant Commander Stovall expertly maneuvered his boat into favorable attack position and boldly engaged the enemy with the result that the *Gudgeon* was enabled to sink four large Japanese vessels, three of which were closely convoyed by enemy destroyers. His outstanding leadership, aggressiveness and gallant devotion to duty reflect great credit upon Lieutenant Commander Stovall, his command and the United States Naval Service."[71]

However, things were not as rosy as they seemed. After the war, JANAC denied credit for all but one of *Gudgeon*'s sinkings, the sinking of the *Naniwa Maru*, a 5,000 ton cargo ship on August 3, 1942. The three *Gudgeon* torpedomen, Moose Hornkohl, George Seiler, and Ray Foster, who were all present during the attack stated vociferously that they got *all* of those ships on this patrol. No doubt about it. Strow agreed. In his log, written during the war patrol, he said that one of the ships the *Gudgeon* would eventually not receive official credit for having sunk "all but evaporated" and the another one was taking a "nosedive." [72] Perhaps the statements by Strow were inflated. After all, these were the first attacks he had been involved in, and he had shown signs of exaggeration in his writings. However, the three other men had seen plenty of action and have had more than fifty years to reflect on the attacks. Their adamant insistence that all three ships were sunk seems difficult to dismiss.

Of all the patrols that George Seiler would make during World War II, he said that *Gudgeon*'s fourth was the toughest, the most stressful of all. The same was surely true for the skipper, William Stovall. After Stovall angrily rebuked the *Gudgeon* officer—Dornin or Sherry—for having placed their hands on him, he became persona non grata to the crew and officers on board. The men would walk by Stovall, not say a word to him, nor even gaze his way, unless addressed by him. The men wondered what kind of a person the Old Man was, jumping all over somebody who had saved the boat. That he had seriously damaged his rapport with the crew would have been inescapable to Stovall, according to George Seiler. Despite the Navy Cross and the high praise, the burden of command, his damaging interaction, and the depth charge attacks had rattled him. In *Silent Victory*, Clay Blair reported that Admiral Charles Lockwood wrote in his diary at the time, "Very poor story. Skipper cracked up and asks to be relieved." [73] Despite the obvious stress-related problems that Blair reported, none of the *Gudgeon* sailors interviewed after the war said that they ever saw Stovall show any signs of fear or nervousness, and that he had no difficulty performing his duty. At the time, morale on board the submarine was quite good. The performance of all the men on board was exemplary. Regardless of what was going on inside of Lieutenant Commander William Shirley Stovall Jr., to the men on the USS *Gudgeon*, he was rock solid.

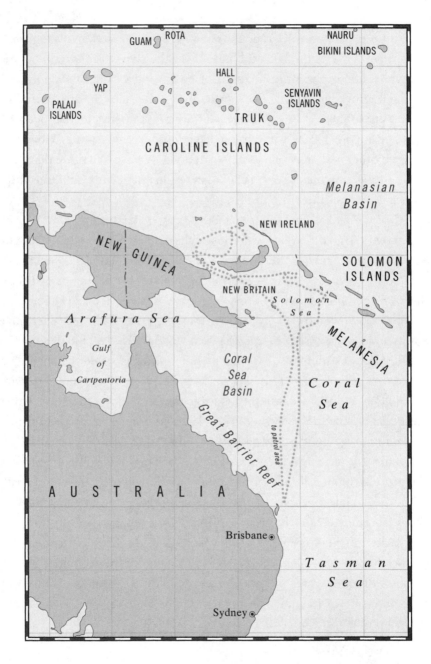

Fifth War Patrol • Approximate Course • Oct. 8–Dec. 1, 1942

▪ 5 ▪
Butchery in the Bismarck Sea

It's the wise man who stays home when he's drunk

Euripides ca. 425 B.C.

After the fourth patrol, *Gudgeon* arrived at the Allied submarine base at Fremantle, just south of Perth, Australia, on September 2, 1942. The establishment of a submarine base at Fremantle proved to be an important development because it allowed United States submarines to receive their maintenance and fuel closer to Japanese waters. A second base at Brisbane on the eastern side of Australia would serve *Gudgeon* later in the war. Most of the submarines based in Fremantle during the war were from the United States fleet, yet the number of submarines that would be sheltered in Fremantle would be less than a third of the American submarines that served in the Pacific theater. At this time, Fremantle was a temporary destination. Two-thirds of the *Gudgeon* crew disembarked to recuperate from the wild fourth patrol. Moose Hornkohl and George Seiler drew the short straws and had to ride *Gudgeon* farther south to Albany where the remainder of the crew departed on the fourth. They would have less time ashore than those who had disembarked earlier, but they intended to make the most of it. The submariners had been on the receiving end of the action far too often during the just completed patrol. They had taken around eighty-five depth charges in four different attacks, as well as having narrowly avoided catastrophe when one or two Japanese torpedoes slid just above the forward torpedo room.

George Seiler had been fighting a growing sense of personal disaster throughout the war. It seemed clear to him that his days were numbered; there was no way he was going to get out of this war alive. He was a nervous wreck. When *Gudgeon* came to a stop in Albany, he felt like the weight of the world had been lifted from his shoulders. He felt that he had to almost run off that boat before the purveyor of death discovered that Brother George had been forgotten. The split-second transition from feelings of intense dread to elation and freedom was striking. Before him lay the harbor at Albany, which to this day he says is the most beautiful one he has ever seen. "The entrance to the harbor is quite expansive. It narrows down to a couple of hundred yards, ideal to be netted off in wartime. Then it opens up to almost a mile across. There are mountains and high hills completely surrounding the harbor. As one progresses into the harbor, still on the starboard hand, one comes to the city, rather the village. I once recall a whale's tail coming right up in front of the bow. It was gigantic as it submerged."[1] The profound beauty of the place was so well timed that the war-weary George Seiler felt it deep inside his bones.

Seiler gladly grabbed his things and left *Gudgeon* accompanied by his pal, Moose. They could hardly get away fast enough and were determined to go someplace where they wouldn't be running into anyone who wore a uniform, preferably a place that offered booze and maybe, if they were lucky, women. As events unfolded, they reported that they found only alcohol—lots of it—and performed a humorous prank during their stay ashore that did the city of Mt. Barker a world of good.

Once ashore, the thirsty sailors crawled into a charcoal-burning taxi. Their main goal was to get as far as possible from the realities of war. Thousands of miles from home and for the first time on Australian soil, Seiler and Hornkohl looked forward to a great adventure. They instructed the driver to "just go."[2] Where, they did not care. They were leaving *Gudgeon* and all their responsibilities behind them. Wherever they ended up was better than being cramped up on that damned submarine for another week with no sun, its black holds, and the foul air.

There was not a soul in town wearing a military uniform. They paid the driver, probably with dollars that had been earned by Seiler from his job on *Gudgeon*. As they began to explore the little village and talk to the locals, it did not take the two friends and shipmates long to learn that the proprietors of the local hotels, a man and a woman, hated each other with a passion that had stood the test of time. The two hadn't spoken a word to each other in fifteen years, which was not a small feat, because Mt. Barker was a tiny village, not exactly a Melbourne. George settled in at Charley's place and quickly learned that the cellar was full of whiskey. Folks in these parts much preferred beer to whiskey so despite whatever wartime shortages may have existed, the stockpile had not been depleted by the locals.

George, ever the determined drinker, made it his personal mission to clean out the cellar of White Horse Scotch. As he recalled later, "I just drank the hell out of it."[3] It didn't take long, after George had generously reintroduced old Charley to the pleasures of White Horse Scotch, to learn of the Hatfield-McCoy-like feud that Charley had going with his business competitor, whose name has escaped the sailors after all these years. Since single Australian women or those who were perceived as being available were commonly referred to as "Sheila," she will be known as Sheila.

Moose and George began talking and, between drinks and laughs, decided that they were going to do their best to resolve the blood feud between Charley and Sheila. They developed a plan and set to work. The plan was simple. Get them both drunk and reintroduce them. The reintroduction, if successful, would not threaten headlines throughout the world like a Clark Gable affair, because old Charley was a man in his fifties, short and fat, jolly and bald. Sheila, a middle-aged woman, was not even appealing to the two love-starved submariners. George Seiler described her as most resembling Popeye's crow-voiced girlfriend, Olyve Oyl. George added that she was "tall and thin" and to say the least "hardly a ravishing beauty."[4]

Before long, George and White Horse and Charley had spent so much time together that Charley could hardly stand. Moose had gone up to the other hotel and undertaken his special mission, which was to accomplish the same with old Sheila, who by this time was far more than half skunked. After closing time, George led, or more accurately, carried, Charley to

Sheila's place, her love nest, and gently deposited the unconscious old gent in Sheila's bed.

Moose, dutifully fulfilling his part of the scheme, led the fully inebriated Sheila to her bedroom and laid her down next to her Casanova, Charley. Next was the challenge to make the scene more plausible. As a final touch, they left the two nearly comatose hotelkeepers in an embrace that would be completely convincing in its effect. Just enough clothing had been removed to satisfy the more skeptical of the two lovers. Laughing heartily the whole time, pouring down drink after drink of the White Horse Scotch, the dutiful submariners snuck out of the room and back to Charley's place to let the thing play out.

The following morning, as George would describe it a half-century later, doing his very best to speak in the Australian accent that he had learned during the war, as well as to suppress his laughter said, "Here came old Charley running down the street. It was only two or three blocks long, and he came running into the hotel and he said, 'By Christ. I'll never drink any more of that Horse.'"[5] Appalled at what had happened the night before, he continued, "The Horse took me up there and put me in bed with that woman."[6]

The two battle-weary sailors were delighted with Charley's reaction and bit their tongues, lest they give away the whole thing and spoil their efforts at making peace. They knew that they had been successful. They had gotten themselves as far as they could from that damned war, and they had performed a solid civic chore. As George said, "They had to [become friends], believing that they had been on such intimate terms the night before."[7] The tale of George and Sheila was perfected and retold a hundred times to the men on *Gudgeon*, each time drawing laughter and lightening the massive load on the shoulders of the submariners who were by this time doing the best they could to handle the profound stresses and strains of wartime submarine patrolling behind enemy waters.

While George and Moose were matchmaking and drinking their White Horse Scotch, the rest of the *Gudgeon* crew had finished their R & R in and around Albany and Fremantle. In the meantime, *Gudgeon*'s badly needed refit continued with the crew on the submarine tender USS *Pelias*. All too soon the rest and the wild times were over. The crew regrouped in Albany as ordered and boarded the submarine on September 25, 1942, with about twenty new submariners. Among those departing were teenager Albert J. Rupp and Chuck Ver Valin, who would eventually board the same submarine, the ill-fated *Grenadier*. Also departing was the jokester, Carl Finks, who had so cruelly pranked Moose Hornkohl. With his departure, the men on board would sleep much more soundly, but there would be no more wild, middle-of-the-night poultry calls—or worse—to wake the exhausted crew. Sadly, though, there would also be no more laughs inspired by Carl's hijinks. Another one of the men leaving *Gudgeon* was the hapless lookout Hershel Kiser, who had erred so grievously as lookout on the fourth patrol. Kiser felt that he had lost the confidence of his shipmates and transferred off.

On board for his first patrol was Edward Hammond of Sedalia, Missouri. Hammond enlisted in the Navy in June after graduation from high school. After struggling to earn his high school diploma, he saw no future in college. His inspiration to join the Navy came from the many movies of the day that glorified the Navy as a life of adventure and travel. He went to boot camp in Great Lakes, Illinois, and left as an apprentice seaman and then attended submarine school in New London. He was in New London when the Japanese attacked Pearl Harbor.

In September 1942, Hammond was on a relief crew aboard *Sailfish*. At the time, he was cleaning out a refrigerator on board when one of the relief crew chiefs passed through and told Hammond and another unrated seaman that *Gudgeon* needed two seamen for the next war patrol and that interviews were being held on the deck of the submarine tender. Hammond hurried up but had been beaten to the punch by other sailors trying to get aboard the well-known submarine. Luckily for Hammond, the seaman who was chosen for duty did not have enough dungarees in his seabag to be out of port for two months. Hammond was chosen in his place and proudly boarded *Gudgeon*.

Gudgeon traveled around the southern end of Australia to Brisbane on the eastern shore arriving on October 8. She pulled briefly alongside submarine tender USS *Griffin*. At 3:02 P.M., with Lieutenant Commander William S. Stovall Jr. and sixty-seven other men on board, *Gudgeon* slowly pulled away from *Griffin* and wove her way beyond the bay surrounding Brisbane. Moose Hornkohl, the *Oklahoma* orphan, remembered vividly what it was like watching the land slowly disappear behind him: "When we cut away from the tender and made that turn in the basin and were heading out from Fremantle or Brisbane, they were always playing "Waltzing Matilda." There was that echo when you were going out. It really wasn't an Australian anthem, but it was close to it. The bands never quit playing it. I always felt a kind of sadness. I really did. I felt like I was alone. You never knew what was out there. You could have an escort for two hundred miles, but you were still alone." [8]

With "Waltzing Matilda" eerily echoing in his head, Moose Hornkohl's mind was swimming, his heart heavy with fear and apprehension. He was aware that at the age of twenty-one this might be the last sight of land he would ever have. If so, how would it happen? Would it be fast, a result of a catastrophic explosion on board, or would Hornkohl die the hard way— wounded, covered with oil, burned and paddling desperately, barely able to keep his head above water as he viewed the wreckage of the once great *Gudgeon* and the burned and mangled bodies of his young friends and shipmates floating around him? Or perhaps even worse, would this be the patrol that ended up with his being taken prisoner and beaten to a pulp by the Japanese, as they were known to do whenever they got their hands on a submariner? The beatings, of course, were even more horrifying because they were a mere prelude to the beheading, which was sure to follow. *Gudgeon* moved slowly toward her new destination. A homesick Lieutenant Albert "Albie" Strow, now on his third patrol, could not avoid reminiscing about the leave just completed. Strow couldn't get away from the west coast of Australia fast enough, if for no other reason than the fact that the east coast of Australia was 2,000 miles closer to home. Nonetheless, young Strow was excited. It was rumored that *Gudgeon* would be patrolling in the area of the Solomons. Radio reports were rife with claims that many ships were in the area. Strow, now very proud of his service on the submarine, smugly noted the reports stating that the Army Air Force had been repeatedly bombing enemy ships but rarely sank one. Strow was sure that if *Gudgeon* hit one of them that it was going down "for keeps" and that once down, the enemy would no longer be able to aid the war effort because they would be "sitting on the bottom." [9] Strow surprised himself, noting that he was actually turning into an avid submariner. Strow was surprised at his transformation.

While ashore he was actually "stewing" to go back out on patrol.[10] He figured that if they sank a lot more ships, they would be pulled out for a breather. In his mind, he was sure that this was the way the Navy operated and was quite eager to obtain leave to visit home, as he was getting very homesick. A few days previously he had been angered when he saw the roster of officers in the squadron and learned that he had been credited with only one month in the Far East. As far as Strow was concerned he had been in the Far East six months because anything west of St. Louis *was* the Far East. Strow wrote in his log that three boats [most likely *Grampus*, *Grayback*, and *Gudgeon*] had been loaded up with enough spare parts to make a six-month patrol. Only the skippers of the boats, John Craig, Edward Stephan, and Shirley Stovall knew where they were headed. He was hoping that the skippers had been ordered to patrol as a wolf pack, just as the Germans had been doing.

Strow had been displeased with his leave for reasons other than the fact that Albany, Australia, was so far from home. When the men had arrived there, after turning the boat over to the *Pelias*'s relief crew, fellow officers Dusty Dornin, Webster R. Robinson, and "Tex" Penland had headed for Perth. The remaining officers settled into what Strow said could hardly be called a hotel, the Freemason in Albany. With Strow at the Freemason were Shirley Stovall and Sigmund A. Bobczynski. Strow was certain that if the Freemason was a hotel, he had been deluded all his life. He wrote that the temperature in the place never got above freezing at any time when the three young men were there. His room was slightly larger than those in previous hotels he had lived in, but much shabbier. When Strow had to use the toilet, he had to hurry down a flight of outside stairs to the next floor to use the community seat. Needless to say, the water was always very cold. Even the tough-minded Shirley Stovall could only take it a few days before he fled for Perth. Strow and Bobczynski lasted five days; then off they went to Perth, with "visions of a warm room and hot water."[11] Before leaving Albany, they made reservations at their destination and then expectantly hopped a train. Unfortunately, they had to share a compartment with two very drunk sailors. Strow and Bobczynski were not in any mood for this. They resorted to shouting and demanding that they be given a compartment by themselves. One can imagine the state they were in after having survived the intense fifty-three-day patrol in the tight confines of a submarine, followed by their severe discomfort in their quarters in Albany, then being stuck in yet another small compartment with two drunks.

Bobczynski and Strow would find that the nineteen hour, 350 mile trip was just a continuation of their misery, not relief from it. For one thing, there was no food on the train. Every time the train stopped the two officers had to hurry off for a sandwich and a cup of tea. The coffee was so horrid Strow could not drink it. Finally, after three stops the men felt well fed enough to try to sleep. Unfortunately, the berth in the train was even colder than the Freemason hotel, so they would have to sleep with all of their clothes on.

At about 2:00 A.M. Strow struggled to his feet realizing that he had been "frozen stiff and eaten to a hamburger state" by bedbugs and mites that had made the trip with them.[12] Finally, the tortuous train ride was over. Strow said that by the time the two young officers arrived they looked like the "wrath of the good Lord."[13] They scurried off the train excited with anticipation. Surely, now they would be able to really start their R & R. They hurried to their hotel, the Adelphi, dreaming of the pleasure of a hot bath and shave, heat, and a comfortable, clean bed free from mites.

When they arrived at the Adelphi they learned that the clerk had somehow mishandled their reservations. The two young officers had no place to stay. They erupted in anger and indignation, venting their frustration upon the unfortunate desk clerk. The two officers angrily confronted the manager; but the man would not budge. There were no rooms. The two disheveled and furiously angry officers trudged off; their clothes wrinkled, their skin itching, cold, and no doubt hungry by this time as well.

They hurried over to the Palace Hotel, which was nearby, and stole the room of two officers who had not yet shown up. Finally clean, fed, warm, and rested, they hurried back to the Adelphi to try to find their shipmates. Bobczynski and Strow learned that some *Gudgeon* officers (most likely, the trio of Penland, Dornin, and Robinson) were already quite well known at the hotel. It seemed that "the boys" had become well known to "ninety percent" of the residents of Perth.[14] The men had been partying hard every day until the wee hours of the night. The management had finally given up trying to control them. When the Adelphi's manager found out that Strow and Bobczynski were shipmates of the wild group of officers, all chances of their obtaining a room in the hotel were lost. They also discovered that the trio of riotous men had all but taken over the town's only nightclub and were as Strow wrote in his log, "practically running it." [15] Bobczynski and Strow harmlessly entertained some women their first night at The Palace and spent much of the rest of their time ashore trying to find some souvenirs. They could find nothing until the intellectual Bobczynski, an aficionado of fine poetry, happened onto some second-hand book dealers where he purchased several books of poetry.

Eventually the men ran into "Miss Fleming," one of the women they had entertained a few nights before, and went out to dinner. Over scones and tea, Miss Fleming, who claimed to be Operator #224 of the United States Secret Service, told wild stories about all the spies she had helped capture. At first neither Albie Strow nor Sigmund Bobczynski believed the stories of capers and arrests, but their ears perked up when she said that the women who ran the nightclub, now in the hands of the trio of *Gudgeon* officers, were suspected of being spies. The men were in very real danger of being compromised. Strow and Bobczynski speculated that the suspected Japanese agents wielded their femininity on the unsuspecting men, and then bled them for information about their boat and their patrols. After all, it was always done that way in the movies. After dinner, they hurried over to the club, where they found Dusty Dornin and passed on Miss Fleming's revelations. Dornin, now quite concerned, responded by saying he knew exactly to whom she was referring. Sigmund Bobczynski and Albert Strow left the rooting out of potential Japanese spies to Dornin. Just the same, Strow continued to doubt the story, surmising that a real agent would not reveal her cover.

Albie Strow loved Australia and said he would have even if it were the dead of winter. The Australian people were the friendliest he had ever known. He wrote that they went far out of their way to be kind to the American submariners. Of course, the fact that the strangers were officers and helping the Australians avert a Japanese invasion made a big difference. A few days later Strow and Bobczynski met a local family that invited them to dinner. Their cat was named Douglas MacArthur. The two young men had a great time drinking tea and chatting. The night ended with the friendly host giving the men a volume of poetry by Robert Burns and making them promise to visit if they ever stopped in Perth again.

Another subject Strow addressed in his diary was his amazement at how the hard-drinking sailors of *Gudgeon* kept at it all leave long and survived. He said that he had stayed sober the whole time and noted with irritation that he looked worse than the drinkers. Some of the men had been in Brisbane for four and a half days and never stopped carousing. He recalled that one evening, he and his friend Sigmund Bobczynski had gone ashore and visited a former shipmate who was in the hospital. They stayed too long to make it back to *Gudgeon* that night so they headed to a club that some of their shipmates had been known to frequent to see if they could find others from The Good Ole *Gudgeon*. Sure enough, the place was filled with men from the boat who were busy trying to get "tight" and get a "date."[16] One thing led to another, and before long Strow found himself and about every other submariner ashore at a party in the suburbs. It was a wild time for everyone there except Albie Strow. Because of his more conservative nature, before long, he found himself playing wet nurse to about twenty more or less "fried" civilians and submariners.[17] Because Strow was the only sober person present, it rested upon his shoulders to drive the revelers back to their homes. Before long, Strow found himself driving on the wrong side of the road in a strange world with eight drunks crammed into a small car built for four with lights that were so weak he could see only about thirty feet ahead. He started giving rides at 2:15 A.M. and had dropped off his last drunk by eight. He swore that he would never put himself into such a position again.

Two nights later *Gudgeon* had a ship's party. The officers had a cocktail party before the crew arrived. The get-together was a rousing success because of the extraordinary efforts of the friendly and popular junior officer from Texas, Lieutenant George Harvey "Tex" Penland. Before long the always-sober Strow found himself playing chauffeur again, this time from an apartment some of the officers had rented. Since the group of well-oiled men had not eaten anything, Strow volunteered to scramble the available twenty-seven eggs and make large quantities of coffee to help sober up the drunken men. By 4 A.M., with the last egg having been fried, Strow snuck away and once again resolved, "never again" would he be caught in such a situation.[18]

Back aboard *Gudgeon*, with the leave from hell behind them, Bob-czynski and Strow, along with the rest of the crew, had to readjust their attitudes for wartime submarining. With the all-business Lieutenant Commander William S. Storall Sr. having changed his mind about leaving *Gudgeon* at the helm barking orders, Strow, Moose Hornkohl and the others put aside whatever feelings of dread, homesickness, or wistfulness that lingered. The young men on board the high-scoring USS *Gudgeon* were among the finest the United States Navy had to offer, and once again it was time for the Japanese Empire to pay for making war on the United States.

As usual Ray Foster, Ralph H. H. Glaspey, and Ray J. McKenna—*Gudgeon*'s leading torpedomen—insisted that the torpedoes be serviced. The torpedoes of the day were complicated machines, comprising around three thousand parts and four sections tipped off with 640 pounds of TNT. Behind the TNT-tipped warhead was a chamber that held compressed air at 2,000 psi. Within the compressed-air chamber was a very small fuel tank that contained the multipurpose alcohol and croton oil. Next came the engine section of the torpedo that contained hundreds of small parts, each of which had to work properly for the torpedo to do its job.

Once launched, the jarring of the fish being thrust out into the ocean caused the compressed air to begin releasing. This, in turn, caused an injector valve to open and spray a mist of alcohol into a combustion pot. The alcohol was then lit by a pair of small, candle-like cartridges and burst into flame. Then a small water container was engaged and began spraying water into the intense flame, causing steam to be discharged, which created approximately 400 hp of thrust and held down the temperature to an acceptable level. All of this activity caused the propellers on the torpedo to spin at a tremendous 18,000 rpm, forcing compressed air out of the fish and causing two propellers to push the torpedo through the ocean. A gyroscope and other instruments, which were set by the men in the torpedo room, controlled depth, speed, and direction by steering two external rudders. The Mark 14 torpedo had been built with a magnetic exploder that is activated by a ship's hull and could be fired at two speeds, 46 knots for 4,500 yards, and 31½ knots for 9,000. The seldom-used lower speed was abandoned later in the war. The 24 foot long Mark 14 torpedoes weighed over 3,000 pounds. Their flaws, discovered as the war progressed, were many.

Robert Gannon in *Hellions of the Deep* describes the incredibly poor performance of the torpedoes. Nobody had more problems than the men on board the USS *Tinosa* (SS-283) experienced on July 24, 1943. *Tinosa* was lining up to shoot at the massive 19,000 ton *Tonan Maru III*, the largest of all the Japanese tankers in World War II. *Tinosa* fired six torpedoes at the maru with no results, then fired number seven which hit, but had no effect other than giving the Japanese a line of fire at the submarine's periscope for the massive maru's machine guns and 4-inch deck gun. Torpedoes number eight, nine, and ten all hit the target ship but did no damage to the fat and incredibly lucky tanker. By this time, the Japanese had obtained the added benefit of time, which allowed them to aim their guns a little ahead of the oncoming torpedoes as they headed toward their ship, to blow them up before they could strike the shipful of fuel. The Japanese were not successful, but they need not have fretted. Number eleven hit the port side of the maru but did not explode. What it *did* do was make a big splash, a right turn, and then jump clear out of the water "about one hundred feet from the stern of the tanker." [19] The determined submariners persisted with their attack. Unfortunately, torpedoes twelve, thirteen, fourteen, and fifteen also hit the tanker, dudded against the side of the ship and sank. With a destroyer bearing down on *Tinosa*, Commander Lawrence R. Daspit decided that it was not his day. He called off further offensive actions and began evasive maneuvers, saving one torpedo for the men at the base to look at. In all, nine torpedoes were reported to have hit their mark. None detonated.

Gudgeon didn't experience torpedo failures on the scale that *Tinosa* suffered. The surviving former torpedomen of *Gudgeon* insist that *Gudgeon*'s torpedo performance was much more reliable than that of most of the other submarines in the fleet, some saying that they had no torpedo failures. However, there were some instances where the facts seem to state otherwise. Oftentimes the torpedoes seemed to run deep; occasionally there were torpedoes that were "duds" and failed to explode. No amount of meticulous care by *Gudgeon*'s torpedo crew could cure all of the ills engineered into the flawed weaponry.

Once a week for three and a half years, the torpedomen on *Gudgeon* would examine the fish, which was easy to do when the torpedoes were on the racks. Those that had been loaded in the stern and bow tubes, however, had to be pulled out far enough for the men to have access to the aft end of the torpedo.

On October 11, *Gudgeon* went on a more alert status, having been tipped off by Squadron Six submarine *Trout* that an enemy submarine had been seen in the area. The alert did not materialize into anything of importance, and thus Lieutenant Albert Strow was able to muse in his log on the subject of the great, flamboyant and vain General Douglas MacArthur. Strow was once again thinking about his Australian leave, which by now must have seemed as if it was very long ago. He wrote that "Dugout Doug," as he called MacArthur, was holed up at the "swankiest" place in Brisbane, the Lennon Hotel, where MacArthur and his staff took up two floors so that the boss could "blow off steam writing communiqués."[20] With very clear shades of bitterness and anger in his words, Strow continued, noting that MacArthur was "fighting a tough war from there."[21] Strow reported that there were so many generals holed up with MacArthur that they had to have two generals per room, not what such men were used to. Strow did not understand why MacArthur was such a hero in the United States and considered such a "dud" in the war zone. He said that everybody, Americans or Aussies, Army or Navy, referred to MacArthur as "Dugout Doug." He remembered having lunch with an American aviator who had been in the Philippines when the war started, and that the man was "almost violent" when the subject of Douglas MacArthur came up. Strow understood that in the States, he was just "one junior to Christ." If anyone were to call him Dugout Doug there, he would have a fight on his hands.[22]

By the seventeenth, *Gudgeon* was in her patrol area south of New Hanover Island, which is part of the Bismarck Archipelago, slightly northeast of New Guinea. Stovall saw to it that *Gudgeon* was positioned to intercept any shipping proceeding south from the Gazelle Channel.

Cat and mouse games with Japanese ships of war continued until October 21 at 0850 when *Gudgeon*, still off New Hanover Island, sighted a convoy of five large merchant ships escorted by two destroyers. The convoy was fifteen miles away and smoking enough to attract the hungry *Gudgeon*. Stovall had *Gudgeon* in what appeared to be a near perfect position at about a right angle to the target vessel at periscope depth. The only thing that could make things better was for the destroyers to head in the other direction, turning *Gudgeon* loose on the convoy like a shark at a crowded beach. The lead destroyer, always on the lookout for American submarines, continued to guide the convoy from the left-hand side of the cluster of ships, with the second destroyer in position behind the convoy on the right-hand side and quite distant from *Gudgeon*. Because the sea was glassy-smooth, *Gudgeon*'s periscope could be easily seen. Stovall and Dornin decided to fire at the two ships nearest *Gudgeon*, from the starboard side of the target vessels. This plan would allow *Gudgeon* the greatest chance of escape.

The ships in this convoy were old and seemed to be badly in need of up-keep, which might have explained their very slow speed. The target ships appeared to be about 7,000 tons and were similar to the *Takatoyu Maru*. Each ship was about 450 feet long and decrepit enough that Lieutenant Commander Stovall was certain that one hit would be enough to sink them. To determine attack priorities and for post-action intelligence purposes, the submarine service used a reference known as the Japanese Merchant Ship Recognition Manual to match up the silhouette and size of the ship being evaluated for attack with one of the same class in the book.

At 1112, the attack began. With the men in the forward torpedo room rubbing the lucky brass Buddha and about ten-second intervals between fish, Lieutenant Commander Stovall roared, "FIRE ONE. FIRE TWO. FIRE THREE. FIRE FOUR. FIRE FIVE. FIRE SIX." [23] All six torpedoes, three aimed at each ship, were now in the water seeking their prey. The first target was thirteen-hundred yards away. Each torpedo was set to run at a slightly different angle, making it more likely that a hit would be obtained. For the second target, farther away, a less divergent angle was desired as the target was actually around 3,500 yards—two miles from the submarine. The torpedoes were set to run at 14 feet so they would actually run around 25 feet. Stovall observed that the ships seemed to be running high in the water as if they were not very heavily loaded. Timed hits were heard at 1113, 1114 and 1117, which suggested that the torpedoes blew up about when they were supposed to, and that two hits were made on the first ship, one on the second. Stovall noted that the third torpedo did not explode for a long time, possibly because the range to the target was underestimated by a thousand yards, or more likely because the second target was turning away when it was hit, thus increasing the distance between submarine and target ship.

The first hit was observed through the periscope and appeared to be amidships. Stovall saw a great deal of smoke and very little water geyser, causing him to feel confident of a desirable bottom explosion. By the time the second explosion was heard, Lieutenant Commander Stovall was wisely eyeing the two escorts, now angrily searching for *Gudgeon*. When the third torpedo exploded, *Gudgeon* was going deep and rigging for depth charges. Just three minutes after the last torpedo hit its mark, with both destroyers now steaming full speed toward *Gudgeon*, the expected depth charge attack started. Curiously, Stovall noticed that the depth charges were being thrown only one or two at a time rather than in massive barrages, like the ones in the bone-jarring, sixty-depth-charge attack of the fourth patrol. Stovall counted fifty-one explosions altogether, some of which sounded like ships breaking up as they went down. Only about eight had the characteristic sound of good close depth charges. After each attack ended, the destroyers would stop, listen, and use their sonar. While the attack was going on, Skipper Stovall had cleverly maneuvered *Gudgeon* close to and behind the second target ship, then between the two merchant ships toward the tail end of the convoy, using the noise of the enemy ships' screws and their wakes to confound the Japanese counterattack. It worked; *Gudgeon* sustained no damage.

Ray Foster remembered this escape very well. He said that *Gudgeon* "ducked in underneath the first ship. The boilers were blowing out, and we could hear debris hitting on our deck, and the destroyers were going around in circles dropping depth charges killing everybody that was in the water."[24] When Foster described the disintegration of the Japanese vessels and, in particular, the boilers blowing up, he is in effect stating that at least one of the ships went to the bottom. After two and a half hours of skillful maneuvering, *Gudgeon* rose to periscope depth and saw that one of the destroyers was still in the area of the attack, possibly still searching for the underwater hunter, or for survivors. The destroyer was not close to *Gudgeon*'s actual location. The Japanese merchant marine sailors endured an awful death. One minute they were traveling through the waters off the Bismarck Archipelago, and then suddenly, their ship was blown out from beneath them. Those still alive frantically searched for a lifeboat or wreckage to cling to; they were horrified to see one of their own destroyers approaching at full-speed, throwing huge explosives into the water. The sea was littered with shocked and wounded men, wreckage, and the screams and moans of dying men. Dusty Dornin recalled, "We saw considerable wreckage and life boats and one transport listing heavily to port and the survivors being taken off by the destroyer."[25]

A short while later a seaplane joined the search for *Gudgeon*. William Stovall decided that it would be wise to move on rather than remain and allow the seaplane time and opportunity to coordinate a fatal attack on his submarine. At 1946, *Gudgeon* surfaced far from the chaos she had created. By 2209 recovery from the attack was interrupted by another patrol vessel which smelled blood and was quickly closing on *Gudgeon*. Stovall ordered the crew to dive to 270 feet and rig for another depth charge attack. At this time in the war, the commonly held belief was that if the submarine went a couple of hundred feet down, she would be safe because the Japanese tended to set their depth charges to explode at a much shallower depth. This time, a depth charge attack did not occur because of Stovall's evasive maneuvers. The maneuvering must have been particularly skillful because at one time the little ship was actually rather close astern. *Gudgeon* would be given war time credit for having sunk an unknown seven-thousand ton cargo ship and JANAC credit for having sunk the 6,783 ton *Choko Maru*.

By this time in the war, the men on board *Gudgeon* had decided to keep track of their many successes by painting a battle flag on the wardroom bulkhead. Each time one of the men received a medal, his name went up on the wall: those winning the Navy Cross and Silver Star on the left, the Navy and Marine Corps Medal to the right. If the men had a particularly rough time ashore with women or the police, the encounter was humorously termed a battle. The first of these skirmishes was known as the Battle of Honolulu. The rough time that Strow and Bobczynski and the others had on R & R before the fifth patrol was memorialized on the flag as "The Battle of Perth." Each of these "battles" was recorded to the far right of the chart. Each sinking of a Japanese ship would be carefully drawn in. The rising sun flag meant that a Japanese ship had gone down by torpedo. A zero on a flag signified that a ship had been sunk as the result of a deck gun attack. *Gudgeon*'s escutcheon, in the upper middle of the battle flag, sported a lucky Buddha on red, a three leaf shamrock to the right on orange, and a kangaroo at the bottom surrounded by green above *Gudgeon*'s motto: "Find 'Em, Chase 'Em, Sink 'Em." The men who fought on *Gudgeon* wrote and spoke the motto with an emphasis on Find, Chase, and Sink to illustrate the aggressive nature of submarining on the SS-211. Finally, all bombings and depth charge attacks were recorded on the middle of the flag. The battle flag was good for morale. It served as a visual reminder of the boat's wartime accomplishments as well as the expectations for excellent performance of the crew boarding the submarine for the first time. It reminded all of the men on the submarine that they were there to serve their beloved *Queen Gudgeon* and to do their part in gutting the merchant marine of the Imperial Japanese Navy.

For the next several days, *Gudgeon* prowled back and forth attempting to find target vessels. But, submarining had once again become a monotonous affair. Even from the distance of so many years, George Seiler recalls vividly what those endless nights were like. The experience of being on watch, the dark silence enveloping the ship, and only *Gudgeon*'s diesel engines breaking up the stillness, all the time peering through a set of binoculars into the thick velvety night, "dead ahead and seeing a perfect wall of blackness. There's a sky with the stars above, then a perfect black line—a big black wall. Eerie you know. Really eerie." [26]

At this time the Japanese war planners had done very little to shore up defense of their convoys. To an extent one can understand why. The Allied submarine force as a whole had barely made a dent in the flow of Japanese soldiers or materiel. Japan had started the war with just over 6 million tons of merchant shipping of vessels weighing over 500 tons. It would take several more months, until December 1942, before the weight of available vessels dropped below the 6 million ton mark. Things were to change however. When interrogated shortly after the war on December 9–10, 1945, Vice Admiral Shigeru Fukudome stated that the United States submarine service was by far the greatest obstacle to the success of the Japanese Navy. He indicated that the Japanese made a very serious mistake at the outset of the war. They were certain that their submarines and personnel were far superior to the United States underwater fleet, which in turn contributed to their unwillingness to create an effective system for antisubmarine warfare throughout much of the war.

November 11, 1942, had been a rather ordinary one with *Gudgeon* passing between the Circular and Albert Reefs, again in the general area of New Hanover Island, until finally at 2310 smoke was sighted. Signalman Third Class Arthur C. Barlow had made the sighting. It took some time before the Officer of the Deck Lieutenant Harmon B. Sherry was convinced that there were ships out there. Eventually Stovall heard of Barlow's claims, and like a hunting dog on point, ordered that *Gudgeon* change course and head for the barely visible black smoke on this dark night. For Barlow the sighting would mean a much desired promotion and pay raise. They observed a convoy of five merchant-type ships of about 7,500 tons, escorted by the customary two destroyers. The destroyers were echo ranging as they plowed through the ocean. It did not take Stovall and his men long to set this one up. The mastery exhibited by Stovall and Dornin during the attack is nothing less than awe-inspiring. It was necessary for Stovall to plot a course of action that would allow firing from three different positions at three different ships.

Lieutenant Commander Stovall had *Gudgeon* remain on the surface for this attack. The first target was the second cargo ship in the convoy. It was traveling at eight knots, and was 2,200 yards distant. *Gudgeon* was converging on the convoy at 13½ knots. At 2327 *Gudgeon* lined up for a straight bow shot at cargo ship two. At 2347 Stovall opened fire. "FIRE ONE. FIRE TWO. FIRE THREE."[27] Three torpedoes from the bow tubes roared at intervals of ten seconds. One timed explosion occurred at 2351. Stovall was not sure whether it was the second or third cargo ship that was hit because they were nearly in line with each other. The men in the sound room reported that one of the two sets of screws that had been heard close together was now silent. The hits themselves were not observed because of the demands of the attack.

After firing, Stovall quickly swung *Gudgeon* left for a shot at another of the unfortunate merchant ships in the convoy. The vessel trailed the first ship that had been attacked and was also chugging along at eight knots and a range of one mile. Stovall set the torpedo to run at 1,560 yards and fired the last three fish in his bow tubes. Again the torpedoes were fired in quick succession exactly ten seconds apart at: 2352:30, 2352:40 and 2352:50. Each of them were set at ten feet. Three timed explosions were heard, two of them in perfect sync with the firing at: 2353:25, 2353:35, the third exploding a minute later.

Gudgeon once again swung left in a circular motion to line up her final shots on another cargo ship, this time on the rightfully worried men of cargo ship number five. From *Gudgeon*'s bridge, Lieutenant Commander Shirley Stovall observed two hits on cargo ship four. The ship was settling rapidly, the ship's screws had stopped; it was dead in the water.

Lieutenant Commander Stovall positioned *Gudgeon* so that the three stern tubes could be brought to bear on cargo vessel five, a hapless fellow who had foolishly veered toward *Gudgeon*. Stovall's complicated maneuvers had really confused the Japanese. With the final target heading roughly toward *Gudgeon* at eight knots and the range estimated to be about 2,500 yards, Stovall fired three more torpedoes. The torpedoes, fired at fifteen and ten second intervals, resulted in two timed hits. An explosion was observed on the ship from the eighth torpedo fired in the attack. The torpedo seemed to blow the vessel apart. The resulting concussion was so powerful that it was felt "severely" on the bridge of *Gudgeon*.[28] The underwater shock transmitted below decks was, as Stovall said, "a great deal more severe than that experienced from other hits."[29] This caused Dornin to surmise that the ship must have been loaded with ammunition for it "blew apart and lighted the area all up."[30] Stovall concurred. Art Barlow was sure that it was the lollygagging second destroyer that had been struck and was blown sky-high. To add to the confusion, the Officer of the Deck thought that it was the third cargo ship in the convoy that had dropped back after the attacks had begun and been struck. Stovall formed no firm conclusion, being too wrapped up in performing his duty—attempting to sink targets and keep *Gudgeon* afloat—to stop and evaluate the results, however satisfying the sight would have been. The momentary glows of phosphorescence alongside the targets indicated to him that they were side hits rather than bottom hits. Stovall had protected against the possibility of the torpedoes running too deep by setting the torpedoes at ten feet to make them run at twenty feet. Lieutenant Dusty Dornin was certain that the destroyers would catch *Gudgeon*, but Stovall bent on all four engines and was able to put a few miles of ocean between *Gudgeon* and the escorts. The first destroyer was now observed to be steaming toward the triumphant *Gudgeon*. *Gudgeon* successfully made her escape and, surprisingly, was not counterattacked. According to Dusty Dornin, Stovall was not done: *Gudgeon*'s aggressive skipper ordered that the torpedo tubes be reloaded for a follow-up attack. However, a sudden heavy tropical rainstorm formed quickly and saved the convoy from further devastation.

In light of concerns that would arise later in the war—that Stovall may have lost his desire to aggressively take the war to the Japanese—his desire to attack the convoy a second time is instructive. The convoy consisted of five cargo ships and escorts. As many as three or possibly four vessels had been hit. If three cargo ships had been struck, one of the destroyers might also have been damaged. If four cargo ships had been hit, *Gudgeon*'s final torpedo sneaking through and striking cargo ship number three as it slowed down, it meant that there were two undamaged destroyers still available to defend against *Gudgeon*'s advances. Stovall's designs on the convoy show that at this time in the war he was as full of an aggressive spirit as any commanding officer *Gudgeon* would ever have.

Gudgeon moved quickly away from the chaos she had created. The only noises heard were the roaring of *Gudgeon*'s engines, full bore, and the occasional explosions far behind the submarine, sounds that were believed to be the death throes of several stricken Japanese ships. Stovall noticed that a very strong odor of sulphur or burned powder had permeated the atmosphere prior to *Gudgeon* making her escape.

Lieutenant Commander William Shirley Stovall was confident about the outcome of this battle and felt quite pleased with the men on the submarine. *Gudgeon* had entered the convoy of seven ships, gotten off nine torpedoes in ten minutes, and her whereabouts was never discovered. It was an amazing piece of work for Dornin and Stovall and the rest of the men on board. It would seem that the ritualistic rubbing of the little Buddha had done its trick and that as many as three of Japan's cargo ships had found their way to the bottom. This was a very complicated, intricately timed succession of firing, movement, firing, movement, firing, and escape. Even the stoic, by-the-book Stovall must have shown his pleasure. Stovall was sure that he had sunk three vessels and damaged a fourth. Apparently the Japanese were so confused by *Gudgeon*'s masterful attack that they were unable to even attempt a counterattack, deciding instead to just pick up any survivors that could be found, lick their wounds, and get ready for whatever was to come their way. Had it not been for the storm it would have been the fierce USS *Gudgeon* that they would have had to contend with; again.

Perhaps the proudest man on board though was Art Barlow, for it was he who had sighted the convoy and was promoted. Navy records confirm that on December 1, 1942, Arthur Claude Barlow was promoted to signalman second class. *Gudgeon* would receive wartime credit for having sunk two 7,500 ton merchant ships and for having damaged a third. Despite the colorful and vivid descriptions of the attack by the eyewitnesses, JANAC would withdraw credit for all sinkings, based on a lack of unanimous agreement that the ships had been sunk. This means that *Gudgeon* was not allowed credit for the vessel that had exploded so stupendously that it caused the men on the submarine to conclude that it must have been an ammunition ship.

It was about this time in the war that George Seiler noticed that one of his fellow torpedomen was spending a lot of time scratching his crotch. Seiler ordered the young man to drop his shorts for a closer inspection, and indeed, the friendly young sailor had picked up a roaring case of crabs. Seiler raised hell, and sure enough, before long there in the hot moist environs of the *Gudgeon* much of the crew had similar visitations to their nether regions. The men wanted to kill the sailor, because all of those who were infected had to undergo treatment with an incredibly hot, thick brown ointment which not only burned unmercifully, but took off a layer of skin, in one piece, when it was removed.

By November 20, 1942, Albie Strow had about had it. The men on board the submarine had not seen the sun for forty days. During this time the submarine was submerged during the day and had only surfaced after dark. Lieutenant Strow, who was becoming increasingly homesick, figured that he had spent as much time submerged at sixty-two feet as he had spent with his beloved wife of seventeen months, Annmarie. In his log he wrote that *Gudgeon* was headed for home on the eleventh of the month, but added later that new orders had been received, *Gudgeon* was off to a new patrol area. The news was very disappointing to the men on board. Strow concluded that *Gudgeon* had been highly successful, sinking six ships, four of them in one attack. He figured that the ship's tonnage of sunken ships now exceeded one-hundred-thousand tons, an outstanding figure for that time in the war.

He recorded in his log that *Gudgeon* avoided a freak catastrophe when a Japanese submarine surfaced just under the *Gudgeon*'s stern. He noted, "It is just by the grace of the good Lord that we are still around to tell the story."[31] He said, "Why we did not shoot him is another story."[32] A story which will perhaps never be told. Strow did not elaborate in his log, and several surviving *Gudgeon* sailors recalled the near collision, but could offer no further details. Stovall's patrol report made no mention of the incident.

At about midnight on November 24, 1942, another small cluster of ships was sighted. Admiral R. W. Christie would say later that *Gudgeon* had found this convoy from information relayed from his office. There must have been two very valuable merchant ships present because the two ships were escorted by three destroyers, two ahead and one astern. Lieutenant Commander Shirley Stovall, probably drawing the same conclusion, did not let the prospect of taking on three destroyers hold him back. At 2037 with the bright moon putting the surfaced submarine in even greater peril, Stovall ordered that *Gudgeon* pull in from the starboard bow, remaining very low in the water with the deck awash, in order to stay out of the moon track. *Gudgeon* closed to about 6,000 yards and was preparing to dive when a flash from the right-hand lead destroyer was seen. With a three-gun salvo ringing in the distant night, *Gudgeon* dove deep and rigged for depth charges. The shots all missed, having been fired long. So long, in fact, that the men on the deck did not have any real idea where they had hit. With the Klaxon sounding dive and the men hurrying about, the destroyers fired no more shells from the deck guns. As the submarine passed ninety feet, a loud swishing noise was heard moving past the hull. The object had not been accompanied by the characteristic crack of a shell hitting the water. It was a torpedo passing dangerously close to the submarine.

Having avoided being sunk by the torpedo, the men on sound could now clearly tell that the three Japanese destroyers were bearing down on them at high speed. *Gudgeon* started evasive tactics utilizing radical course changes. *Gudgeon* was in mortal jeopardy. Three destroyers. One submarine. Frightening odds indeed. The Japanese knew about where *Gudgeon* was, a fact that had been made obvious by the torpedo—sounding very much like a truck—missing *Gudgeon* by the narrowest of margins. Only clever defensive maneuvers would save her, and lots of luck.

The destroyers would periodically make way at full speed and then stop abruptly, hoping to catch *Gudgeon* in movement so they could line up a fatal depth charging. At 2053 the attack began. The air conditioners were turned off and the heat was stifling. The men on board were silent, sweat streaming down their bodies onto the submarine's deck, their hearts pounding. Flight was impossible. The men were stuck in a 307-foot submarine with three enemy destroyers above them dropping massively potent depth charges. The patrol report indicates that thirteen charges were dropped at various intervals. The spacing was not regular because two destroyers were dropping their charges at the same time. To the men on the submarine, the lack of an expected rhythm made the attack even more unnerving.

Dusty Dornin would say later, "Upon reaching 180 feet, a barrage of approximately nine depth charges was dropped fairly close, within 100 yards. These three destroyers proceeded to work us over for one hour. Two departed and one remained in the area to keep us down and prevent us from making a further attack on this convoy. We were able to surface approximately four hours after these anti-submarine measures but we were never able to close the convoy again."[33]

At 2212 *Gudgeon* sustained another four-depth-charge barrage. BOOM. BOOM. BOOM. BOOM. With the destroyers heading east and *Gudgeon* making way southwest, the attack was soon over with neither the Japanese nor *Gudgeon* being much worse from the encounter. *Gudgeon* surfaced at around 0120 the next day about twelve miles from the place of the attack. No ships were in sight. One thing seems certain, if the torpedo had been fired a little more accurately, *Gudgeon* would have met her fate.

When asked later in the war whether or not he ever got accustomed to a depth charge attack such as the one he had just suffered through Dusty Dornin replied, "Well, I've read in our pre-war dope, it said that due to experience and training and discipline that you get accustomed to it. Personally, I don't think I will ever get accustomed to it. I don't like them, they scare me. I think they scare everybody. But after all, you just go ahead with your business; it just makes your heart pound a little more, that's all. I don't think I will ever get accustomed to depth charges."[34]

By the twenty-eighth an elated Lieutenant Albert Strow and crew finally saw the sun. Strow figured that he looked like either the "near dead" or the "actual dead."[35] Albie Strow had finally determined why he was fighting. "The forces of decency and justice," as offered by the radio commentary, he considered "tripe."[36] He said that he would bet that programs of that sort evoked more laughter from the sailors than any of the comedic efforts of the Charlie McCarthy program, which was so popular during the day. "War," he said, "is the most Godless thing on earth."[37] He continued, "Even the God-fearing get to a point where they are not as sure about it—while the Good Book says that there will always be wars, it does seem strange that enemies should pray to the same God to deliver the foe into their hands. Someone has to be let down."[38]

He added. "Fear is a funny thing."[39] He had come to some conclusions about the subject that were startling to him. He did not think anybody on board really feared death, just that they would be kept from doing all the things that they wanted to do. He knew that the men on board had faced death numerous times and said that no one gave it a second thought. "Every time we go into a scrap we have perhaps a little better than a 50-50 chance of getting out of it . . . "[40] He had decided that "mortal fear is little more than just a phrase."[41] Strow said that the only thing he feared was that someday his new bride might change her mind or that he would fail to make her happy. The lovesick, battle-weary Albie Strow wrote to his wife that, "The Power you hold in your hand is enormous—you have the power of making or breaking me for you are all that I live for. In my mind it is all perfectly clear."[42] The truth was that Albert Strow, the hard-working young officer from the hills of Kentucky, writing from deep in Japanese-held waters, was, when all was said and done, fighting so that he could return to the arms of his young wife.

Now traveling around 300 miles a day and burning up 3,000–4,000 gallons of diesel fuel, *Gudgeon* stormed toward her port at Brisbane, arriving on December 1, 1942. After forty-nine days at sea and more than her share of bad luck, mixed in with a little good fortune and several fierce battles, it was time for a rest.

At 0919 *Gudgeon* pulled alongside the submarine tender USS *Sperry* at the submarine base in Brisbane, Australia. In his post-action report, Stovall gave grudging praise to the Japanese for their efforts at protecting their shipping, noting that the escort patterns were with one destroyer escorting one to three ships and two destroyers escorting five ships.[43] He did not mention that on the last encounter with the enemy, three destroyers escorted two merchant vessels. He thought that it was odd that the destroyers were all using echo ranging in similar ranges and did not drop depth charges as often as did previous escorts. They seemed to try to locate the submarine with echo ranging, and then drop only one or two depth charges at a time. Perhaps even odder, Stovall said, they did not use depth charges at all during the attack on the eleventh, the skipper forgetting for a second that his fancy three-step attack was more than a little confounding to the Japanese escort vessels. Stovall surmised that the Japanese were using irregular patterning because it forced an attacking submarine to have to change position to fire a second set of torpedoes.

Gudgeon entered port with many mechanical problems. There were air leaks and problems with a trim pump, lube lines, injectors, and the ballasting system. Stovall praised the officers and crew for their "commendable manner" during all attacks and counterattacks.[44] He said that Lieutenant Dusty Dornin's performance on the TDC was "spectacular," especially so when firing at several different ships despite rapidly changing firing situations.[45] Stovall and *Gudgeon* had traveled only about 7,000 miles on this patrol because of the repeated patrolling in the area of New Guinea and the Bismarck Archipelago. Their philosophy was, if the enemy is there—just run around on the dinky and wait. Lieutenant Commander Stovall concluded that all torpedoes ran normally.

In his endorsement for the patrol, Admiral Christie, commanding Task Force Twenty-Two, wrote that it was "beyond doubt" that three vessels were sunk and one was damaged.[46] Christie even speculated that it was possible that one of the destroyers was damaged. After the war, JANAC reduced the total to one kill. Admiral Christie praised everybody on board for their excellent performance. He stressed the importance of confirming the damage to the enemy "whenever practicable," but acknowledged that the delivery of multiple attacks should take precedence.[47] He advised that the natural desire to go deep upon completion of the attacks should be avoided unless there was a threat of imminent counterattack. We must take into consideration the fact that this admonition was expressed by a man who was fighting his war from his office ashore. As of this time in the war, Shirley Stovall had been credited with seven ships and 57,000 tons, a total that would be reduced by JANAC to two ships and 11,683 tons.

With *Gudgeon* now far away from Pearl Harbor, she was under the administrative control of Admiral William F. "Bull" Halsey, Commander South Pacific Area and the South Pacific Force. Halsey was critical of Stovall for having expended too much fuel the first six days of the patrol and for having been detected prior to several attacks. The fact that many of the Japanese vessels had dropped into a zigzag pattern, repulsing *Gudgeon*'s advances, convinced him that this was so. He was not certain whether the air escorts had spotted the periscope or whether the target ships had done so, but, either way, he was sure that Stovall had been too free with the scope. He bemoaned the fact that *Gudgeon* had not yet been fitted with an SJ radar system, which would have greatly enhanced the offensive capabilities of the submarine. He indicated that if *Gudgeon* had had the new radar, it would have helped the men on board by allowing the submarine to submerge before the three destroyers picked her up on the twenty-fourth of November. He also pointed out that if *Gudgeon* had the new radar, "There is no telling how many targets would have been picked up by SJ during the many periods of reduced visibility due to heavy rains, the sound of which drowned out all other sounds and made the underwater listening equipment ineffective."[48] The SJ radar is capable of performing regardless of whether or not a storm is occurring and can pick up planes on cloudy days.

The SD radar that *Gudgeon* had used for the past several patrols was for the exclusive purpose of scanning the skies for aircraft and did not greatly increase a submarine's offensive capabilities, though it certainly complemented the efforts of the lookouts. The radar was not able to pinpoint the direction of an attacking plane in relation to the submarine; it showed that a plane was out there. The range was usually around six miles, which sounds like a lot until one remembers that a plane traveling at 300 mph can cover six miles in about a minute. Furthermore, SD radar is sometimes not functional because of stormy seas. Halsey finally lightened up. After all, *Gudgeon* had just sent 22,000 tons of Japanese shipping to the bottom: "The patrol in general was thoroughly satisfactory and the performance of the ship, its officers, and crew commendable throughout. The skill displayed in accomplishing the multiple-target attacks was outstanding. It is noted that Lieutenant Dornin is given credit for largely contributing to the successes attained." [49]

By this time in the war, *Gudgeon* was acquiring quite a name for herself, at least among those in the Silent Service. Public discussions of the feats of specific submarines were rare because of the Navy's desire to avoid publishing information that would be helpful to the enemy. But, an article about an unnamed submarine's war patrols was carried nationwide by AP. It concluded, "The submarine is still out there somewhere, slugging hard at the Japanese when the hunting is good, keeping station for lonely and monotonous weeks when the quarry is scarce." [50] The unnamed submarine in the article was the USS *Gudgeon*; a warrior that was doing an outstanding job yet was a virtual unknown to the general public.

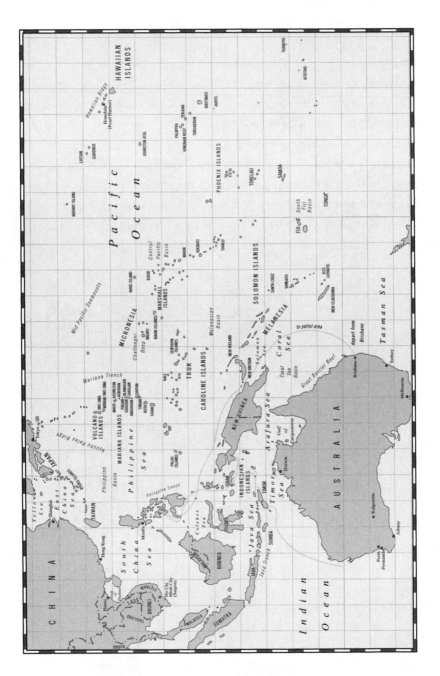

Sixth War Patrol • Approximate Course • Dec. 27, 1942–Feb. 18, 1943

▪ 6 ▪
Commando Operations

The drowning man is not troubled by rain.

Persian proverb

Before *Gudgeon* departed for Lieutenant Commander William Shirley Stovall Jr.'s third patrol as skipper, there was some wild activity between one of *Gudgeon*'s officers and Harry Nickel. Fireman First Class Harry Clark Nickel, a native of Hutchinson, Kansas, was the kind of guy you just plain couldn't help liking. A big strong man with a friendly smile and short-cropped hair, Nickel had boarded the veteran submarine on Shirley Stovall's first patrol, *Gudgeon*'s fourth. George Seiler and Moose Hornkohl remembered Nickel with special fondness because as Seiler said, "Everybody liked Harry. He had the broad shoulders of a logger and the naiveté of a nun." Seiler marveled at how his former shipmate, the lumbering Jayhawk, could avoid all his shipmates' nefarious activities.

One thing that George Seiler did not remember about Nickel was that in January 1942 he became engaged to a woman named Gladys. At the time of his engagement, he was a roughneck for Gulf Oil in the oil fields around Reed City, Michigan. After the war started, he enlisted and, on only a few hours notice, left to take his Navy training at Great Lakes, Illinois. Gladys, Nickel's former fiancée, George Seiler, and gunner's mate Ron Schooley all recall that Nickel neither smoked nor drank, which separated him from

most of the men on the submarine by a country mile. That is why it's surprising to learn that the solid-as-a-pillar-of-salt Harry Nickel beat up a
Gudgeon officer. There was one other thing about Harry Nickel, Schooley
explained. Harry Nickel was a former professional wrestler. As Schooley recalled the incident, Dusty Dornin, *Gudgeon*'s executive officer was very
angry with the crew about something; somebody had really messed up.
Dornin told the sailors that as a result of one sailor's shenanigans all of the
crew would be restricted to the boat unless one of them would go off the
boat with him and "take me to the Academy,"[1] meaning "fight him."
Dornin, a former All-American football player, always reminded the men
that he had also boxed at the Naval Academy. All-American or not, once he
was away from the boat, Dusty Dornin, like the men on his crew, was a bit
of a hell-raiser.

A few seconds passed, and the most unlikely of warriors stepped forward. Harry Nickel approached Dornin and said, "Mr. Dornin, I'm sorry,
I can't have you beating up on the crew,"[2] seeming almost apologetic for the
beating he would soon inflict upon *Gudgeon*'s executive officer. As Schooley recalled, the two men went topside and returned in less than ten minutes. Schooley reported that Harry Nickel had "whipped his [Dornin's] ass
good."[3] Harry Nickel was one tough hombre. Presumably, the saintly, hulking Nickel earned the praise and thanks of the crew who had earned back
their liberty ashore. It is not known what Harry Nickel did with his well-
earned time off the submarine, but it is certain that the local bartenders did
not make his acquaintance.

Another time, Dornin returned around 2 A.M., wanting to spar a few
rounds out on the dock with the former semi-pro boxer, George Seiler.
Once again, Dusty Dornin wanted to take a *Gudgeon* sailor to the Academy. Seiler, who had been restricted to the boat, was, for once, sober. He
understood that Dusty Dornin was a Naval Academy boxing champion and
respected Dornin greatly as an officer, but Dusty Dornin had never been
very friendly to him. Seiler didn't know the meaning of the word fear, and
he was game. Ray Foster, knowing his friend's affinity for fighting, told
Dornin, "Mr. Dornin, you are used to fighting gentlemen at the Academy,
but Seiler doesn't fight like a gentleman, so you had better go to your
quarters."[4] Dornin, perhaps seeking revenge for the routine scalpings that

Gudgeon's barber had been giving him, was in no condition to fight a brawler and thought better of it, wisely retiring for the night. George Seiler said that Dornin never spoke to him again except in the line of duty.

Thanks to Harry Nickel it was a great time for the hard-drinking men of *Gudgeon*, who just plain lived to run wild ashore, trying to get the most out of life before they "got theirs" somewhere out there in the great Pacific Ocean. As George Seiler put it, by this time in the war there was no doubt in his mind, or in the minds of most of the men on *Gudgeon*, that they were not going to make it through the war alive. The commonly held belief of the day was that by about the fifth war patrol a submariner had lived about as long as he could be expected to live. Anything more than five patrols was a fluke, a gift. So what chance did George Seiler or the others have of making it through the war, with neither Germany nor Japan anywhere near capitulation? That fatalistic way of thinking set the stage for the sailors to really let loose once they hit shore. What did they have to lose? What difference did it make what they did? What if they got into a fight ashore and were killed in the process? It made no difference; they were, after all, dead already.

The "dead by five war patrols" tenet was strongly held at this time; virtually all the submariners mentioned it when interviewed for this book. Who knows if facts to the contrary would have had any effect on the men? By the time *Gudgeon* departed for her sixth war patrol, twelve submarines from ports in Pearl Harbor, Manila, Java, Alaska, and Australia had gone down after about three-hundred sixty war patrols. If submarines were actually lost after every five patrols, about seventy-two submarines would have been lost by this time. In reality, a submarine had been lost approximately every thirty patrols, but with the world in flames and because they were so thoroughly outnumbered at sea, it surely must have seemed as if the end would be coming soon.

Ray Foster, the longtime *Gudgeon* submariner, put his newfound freedom ashore to good use. With a little booze in him to provide the boost he needed, Foster decided it was time to heist one of those Australian cop's motorcycles and take it for a joy ride. After all, what better way would there be to see Brisbane? Unfortunately, Foster's sightseeing pleasure tour did not last long. It ended early because Foster rode it on the *right* side of the road (which was the wrong side in Australia), crashed, and was then apprehended. A bobby with Foster in tow walked into a hotel bar where George Seiler and some others from *Gudgeon* were drinking. Foster, scraped up and a little tipsy, pointed to Seiler and said, "That's him. He told me it was his motorcycle."[5] No doubt, Foster hoped that Seiler would go along with it and the bobby would let him go. When the bobby asked Seiler if he knew Foster, Seiler responded, "Hell, no. I've never seen that drunken bastard in my whole life."[6] When the bobby explained what *Gudgeon*'s torpedoman had done, Seiler said only, "That guy's crazy. Throw his ass in jail."[7] Ray Foster was hauled off to jail only to be bailed out by one of the boat's cooks later that night.

Fifty-eight years after the event, Seiler, Moose Hornkohl, and Ray Foster erupt in laughter when they tell the story—Seiler and Hornkohl always laughing louder than Foster. Once Foster returned to the boat, he found himself restricted for the rest of the stand. However, he was, by all accounts, bulletproof when it came to discipline. Whenever he got himself into a jam on shore, which happened with some regularity, he would remind the skipper, whether it was Grenfell, Lyon, Stovall, or eventually Bill Post, that it would be a mistake to get rid of him because if he stayed, he would get them a Navy Cross. As a result, Foster would then be forgiven, and indeed Ray Foster would do his part in helping three of the four win one or more Navy Crosses. George Seiler said of Foster, "Ray Foster was as competent at being a first class torpedoman as any I ever knew, and I knew a lot of torpedomen. Ray was a slightly dumpy, congenial guy, about five feet six inches with a wonderful gift of gab. He was a leader who knew his job and made damned sure those under him knew theirs. He could find more damned ways of getting into trouble on the beach and getting out of it, without being disciplined, than anyone with whom I was ever acquainted."[8]

After a three-week overhaul alongside the submarine tender *Sperry*, Lieutenant Commander Stovall and the rest of the men on *Gudgeon* pulled away from Brisbane at 2:02 P.M. on December 22, 1942. The next morning, a crankcase in the number two main engine blew up. This was one of the engines just overhauled by the *Sperry* crew, so the explosion was doubly disappointing. Then the boat's first dive revealed numerous aggravating leaks that had not been fixed. Since the damage appeared to be rather serious, and Brisbane was only a hundred fifty or so miles away, Stovall turned *Gudgeon* around and headed back to the submarine base, arriving on the twenty-fourth. *Gudgeon* moored alongside *Gato*, then shifted berths and nestled between *Flying Fish* and the mother ship, *Sperry*. The freshly overhauled blown-out engine would be the first letdown in a largely nonproductive and highly controversial fifty-four day patrol.

On the twenty-fifth, while repairs continued on board, *Gudgeon* received about 2,000 pounds of special gear. Included was an eighteen-foot wooden boat. All of the gear, except for some gasoline that was brought on board, was placed below the floor plates in the forward torpedo room. The gasoline was carefully stowed in the forward escape trunk well, which effectively separated it from the rest of the submarine. To avoid sparking a catastrophe, each can was kept from touching another with an insulating material. After the repairs were completed and the materials were loaded on board, *Gudgeon* received even more cargo, six rough-looking Filipino soldiers headed by Major Jesus A. Villamor. Villamor had already proved his courage in encounters with the Japanese and their superior aircraft in the skies over Manila in the dark days following the attack at Pearl Harbor. He had also been awarded a much-deserved Distinguished Service Medal by General Douglas MacArthur. For a pilot in World War II, the Distinguished Service Medal was the third highest medal that could be earned. Villamor, after conversing with MacArthur, volunteered to lead an intelligence party on what would be one of the first commando parties to be sent to a Philippine island since the Japanese takeover. The plan was for Villamor to lead a small group of commandos to his homeland to establish an intelligence net and a secret service throughout the Philippines. For security purposes, when the commandos boarded *Gudgeon*, they were dressed in Navy dungarees and white hats. Disguised as submarine mess boys, they caused no outside comment or attention. This was vitally important because the Japanese had spies throughout Brisbane and would be very interested in knowing that an American submarine had stowed away a handful of Filipinos and their gear prior to leaving for a war patrol.

Villamor and his compatriots were bunked in the forward torpedo room. An additional meal was served on board to satisfy the increased numbers. The men blended in well with the submariners and did not cause too much disruption. Moose Hornkohl recalled that the six Filipinos were an impressive group of "fierce looking" fighters.[9] *Gudgeon* departed Brisbane on December 27, 1942. As usual, while heading out to the assigned area, quartermaster Art Barlow exchanged recognition signals with U.S. planes to keep them from harassing the submarine. At the same time the crew received extra training on the three-inch deck gun and the .50-caliber machine and Tommy guns, all the while checking for leaks and trying to improve the submarine's diving speed. On December 31 *Gudgeon* dove again after receiving a report that a Japanese submarine was in the area. Stovall and the crew did not wish to repeat the same mistake that the inattentive captain of the *I-73* had made eleven months earlier and end up on the ocean bottom.

Lieutenant Commander Stovall conferred with Jesus Villamor to perfect plans for landing. Stovall had been ordered to land the six men and their gear on the Philippine islands of Mindanao and Panay. The cautious Villamor changed the plan, though. For security purposes, he would have Stovall land all the men in one place rather than divide the group. He declined Stovall's offer of the wooden boat, preferring to use his own rubber boats, which the men already knew how to use. When Villamor declined use of the carefully stowed wooden boat, Shirley Stovall was angry because so much extra work had been required to haul the boat all the way from Australia, but he said nothing.

With the days cloudy and overcast, star sighting for navigation purposes was not easy, and by January 4, the weather was getting worse. With the heavy sea directly in front of *Gudgeon*, the struggling submarine was crawling along at about seven knots submerged. *Gudgeon* made her way along the east coast of Australia, heading north and through the hundreds of islands between the Solomons and New Guinea, past the Admiralty Islands and further northwest. The dreary weather did not let up. An almost constant downpour kept Stovall from being able to hug the islands in search of prey. By the time an absolute visual fix could be taken, *Gudgeon* was fourteen miles off course. Just south of Mindanao of the Philippine chain, the weather turned. On January 11, Stovall was able to close to 6,000 yards on a Japanese submarine running on the surface at around 12 knots but was forced to give up the chase because the target dove or was lost over the horizon.

It was now time to find a landing place for Major Villamor and his men. *Gudgeon* proceeded north on the surface toward Zamboango, a large southwestern Philippine island held by the Japanese. In so doing, they passed numerous small boats which did not seem to notice the submarine's periscope sticking out of the water. At 1859 on January 12, 1943, *Gudgeon* surfaced and manned her deck guns in case anybody on the little boats wanted to give them trouble. *Gudgeon* roared ahead on her four Fairbanks Morse diesel engines. On the evening of the thirteenth, she began her approach to the drop-off point. It must have seemed a little surreal to those on the deck as *Gudgeon* slowly moved forward, a warship surrounded by the apparently peaceful little fishing boats. There were so many natives fishing with lit torches that there appeared to be a solid string of lights along the beach. With that many people around, a landing would have been suicidal. Surely at least one of them was a Japanese sympathizer and would tell the enemy about the American submarine and the small group of men whom they had dropped off on the shore. Stovall and Villamor decided to cancel the landing.

In his book *They Never Surrendered*, an apprehensive Jesus Villamor described his memories of that day as he gazed toward his beloved but now occupied homeland. "In the thirteenth day of January 1943, submarine number 211 stood out on a straight course in the night-darkened waters of the Sulu Sea; her nose reared and plunged in the broken water and crests of white foam smacked impudently at her sides. She was USS *Gudgeon*, making twenty knots, and her diesels were throbbing with power. The surface of the sea was empty save for the waves and the night was silent. But through the semi-darkness I could see a coastline and then, in a moment, mountains emerge from where there had been no mountains. The cold stars above glimmered over the craggy hills and the land with the sky pouring starlight down on it looked like a vision of peace." [10]

Villamor recalled conversing with Shirley Stovall on the bridge as the men scanned the coast with their binoculars. Stovall was wearing his commander's cap with the gold trimmed bill. Villamor wrote, "The hard night wind was blowing biting salt spray into his face. He was in his mid-thirties, a wiry, handsome man of even features, with a mouth that found it easy to smile." [11] Villamor, already a war-hero in his home country, realized that he was so scared that his legs were shaking. The two men descended through the hatch, into the confines of the submarine as *Gudgeon* dove. Villamor, out of his element and on edge, said that he almost rode the skipper's shoulders down into the recesses of the war-tested USS *Gudgeon*.

Villamor, in the control room, looked on with great interest as Stovall surveyed the "Christmas tree," the panel of red and green lights that indicate when a submarine is sealed and safe for submersion. When the panel was completely green, Stovall ordered a dive. Villamor recalled the jarring sound of the diving alarm, the submarine heading down bow first, and the rush of water as the ballast tanks filled and dropped below the surface to the safety that the depths below offered.

Stuck on the submarine for another day, Villamor and his contingent of men were deeply disappointed that the landing had been postponed. As each moment passed the tension mounted. With Villamor were Rodolfo Ignacio, who he thought looked like the tough-guy American actor, Edward G. Robinson; Emilio Quinto, the old-timer of the group in his forties; Delfin YuHico; and Dominador Malic, who had already survived battle with the Japanese at sea. The fiery Patricio Jorge who was in his early twenties was not yet battle-tested and was the most excited of them all. The six men, who would be forever known as the Planet Party because of Villamor's idea to name all the Islands of the Philippine chain after a planet in the solar system, were forced to wait impatiently, trapped on *Gudgeon* as it lay off the coast of Negros, which was code named Neptune.

On board Chief Machinist Mate Eli Ernest Masse had many of the crew singing a simple tune, one of those little ditties that were silly but good for the spirits.

Oh the monkeys have no tails in Zamboango
Oh the monkeys have no tails
They were bitten off by whales
Oh the monkeys have no tails in Zamboango.[12]

That evening *Gudgeon* cooks made an extra effort, knowing that the Planet Party would be leaving the submarine the following day. One of the sailors jokingly referred to the bountiful meal as "The Last Supper." The food was good, the humor soothing to the nerves.

It is not known whether Villamor told the American submariners stories about his days before the war. Surprisingly, the talented Filipino ace had flunked his first attempt to get his solo pilot's license. After Villamor took his flight test, his examiner told him that his flying skills were so poor that it was a miracle that he was still alive. Villamor did not give up, though, and eventually earned his license. In 1936 he became one of the original seven cadets of the fledgling Philippine Air Corps. Villamor's difficulties learning how to fly a plane did not last long. He joined the Philippine Army Air Corps Flying School where he was so outstanding that he was sent to the United States for advanced flight training. One source stated that he was so skilled that he completed the course in three weeks rather than the customary four years. By 1938 Villamor regarded himself as a top pilot. By about 1939 he had been promoted to first lieutenant and was named the Director of Flight Training at the Philippine Air Corps Flying Station at Zablon Field on the outskirts of Manila.

It would not have made a very interesting story to the men on *Gudgeon* in 1943, but in the summer of 1939 Villamor was asked to train an unknown United States Army lieutenant colonel named Dwight D. Eisenhower. Eisenhower was on the staff of Douglas MacArthur, who was helping Philippine President Manuel Luis Quezon plan the nation's defense. Eisenhower had it easy in those days, spending weekends on the President's yacht playing bridge. He outranked Villamor, was a half foot taller, a quarter century older, and thirty or so pounds heavier, but that did not stop the little Philippine flier from ripping Eisenhower apart the day that he tried to impress Villamor with his skills as a pilot. Apparently, quite taken at the time with his own perceived status as a hotshot pilot, Villamor was very unkind to the future American legend. As Villamor recalled, it was a very windy day, a difficult day to fly. Eisenhower was training in a box of a plane, an old Stearman. He was doing his best, fighting a strong wind without much success. Villamor was in back speaking over the interphone, hammering away at the congenial future president of the United States, pecking at him with constant reminders of his many errors. Finally, an exasperated Villamor took over the controls and landed the biplane himself.

When the plane stopped, he jumped out, stared up into Dwight D. Eisenhower's face, and said, "Tell me Colonel, surely you don't expect the

plane to do things perfectly when you yourself don't follow the proper procedure. What the devil is wrong with you today? Don't you know what co-
ordination means? Can't your brains tell your muscles to work
together—at least while you are trying to fly an airplane?"[13] The dressing
down lasted three or four minutes. Eisenhower chose not to respond and
just stood there looking back at Villamor. Finally Villamor asked, "What
the hell is your excuse anyway?"[14] Eisenhower responded, "No excuse,
Lieutenant."[15] Eisenhower's humility stunned Villamor. In that moment,
Villamor realized that he had been very unfair to Eisenhower. The two
men, no doubt each feeling a little sheepish, departed. The ugly scene was
over. The American lieutenant colonel would eventually become the greatest United States military figure of World War II. The instructor, Jesus Villamor, was determined to defend his people and would become perhaps his
nation's greatest wartime hero.

Aboard *Gudgeon*, the evening's festivities over, Villamor and his men
waited off the coast of Negros. Villamor, unable to sleep, thought about
Gudgeon and the men on board. He had decided that the men on *Gudgeon*
were tuned up and ready to fight and were not used to playing the waiting
game. The camaraderie on the submarine had impressed him. He thought
that the morale of the men was high and that the men on board were quite
proud of their many achievements. Villamor was keenly aware that he was
"in the presence of men of incredible courage."[16]

He recalled a conversation with Executive Officer Dusty Dornin early
in the patrol, after the submarine was unable to close on a Japanese merchantman. Dornin was disgusted that the ship had escaped. Villamor, never
comfortable on the submarine, argued that it was not at all bad that they
had been unable to take on the ship and expose *Gudgeon* to danger. Jesus
Villamor admitted that he was scared. Dornin asked what he was scared of,
saying that the ship would not have had a chance if they had gotten close
enough to it. Villamor replied and, in so doing, rather closely and eerily described what would become known more than a half-century later about
the circumstances of *Gudgeon*'s mysterious loss: "Yeah, but don't forget
that before flashing sayonara it might have flashed a signal for help, and
before we'd have known it, planes might have been around, dropping little
things, little things that could have hurt us. Or don't you think that the

things planes drop can hurt subs?"[17] Dornin's response was perhaps even more prophetic, "Oh those things, yes, but the ones that get you are the ones you will never know about."[18]

Villamor and his group of men were not actually intent on fighting as commandos. The plan was to set up and coordinate guerilla activity ashore. Too many of the guerilla groups were fighting as independent units, some operating as nothing more than thieves, stealing from the people. Others were fighting bravely against the much larger Japanese forces. On January 14, 1943, Lieutenant Commander Stovall, with his boat now on the surface, reconnoitered up and down the coast looking for a good spot to land the Filipino contingent. Stovall finally found a favorable location at Catmon Point. An uninhabited sand beach beckoned. It was close to the little village of Jinobaan, an attractive feature to Villamor who wanted to make quick contact with the natives in order to set up his network.

Stovall surfaced with the island of Negros spread out before him. Negros is the fourth largest island of the Philippine chain at about 5,000 square miles. The men liked what they saw, a gentle sloping beach that appeared to be unoccupied. Shirley Stovall's voice broke the silence and called for the landing party to join him on deck. Villamor and his men hurried forward. As Jesus Villamor prepared to depart, he was trying to remember why he had volunteered for such a mission. With *Gudgeon* very low in the water to accommodate loading, and with the white ocean foam washing over the deck, Stovall, Dornin, and two lookouts were joined by many of the boat's crew to begin the loading process. Plywood stiffeners covered the floors of the rafts to provide support for the large cache of supplies to be taken ashore. Unfortunately, one of the boats would not hold air. Stovall suggested that they take the wooden boat that was still on board, but Villamor felt strongly that the boat, the "wherry" as he called it, would be too noisy and would ride so high in the water that it could be easily seen. Once ashore it would be easy to bury and hide the rafts, but he had no idea how to hide an eighteen foot boat made of wood. In declining the boat, Villamor made the tough decision to leave behind quinine and other drugs, insect repellant, token vitamins offered by Douglas MacArthur, and eight boxes of .30 caliber ammunition, which Stovall had provided directly from *Gudgeon*'s own stores.

The crew carefully loaded the two remaining rafts. There was just enough room for the men to fit alongside the arms, ammo, clothing, and canned rations, which had been carefully packed into the rafts. A box of gems worth 4,000 pesos and all the Philippine currency left in the Commonwealth Bank of Australia was to go ashore. Nothing like 350,000 pesos to make sure things went the way you wanted them to go in a country where money was not plentiful! In addition, Villamor and his contingent of men took batteries, generators, spare parts, gasoline, blasting caps for dynamite, and two small radio sets. Each box of supplies had been marked so that it could be put in an exact place in the raft. Loading had been practiced repeatedly. The crew held the rafts next to the submarine as Villamor crawled into the lead raft with Quinto and Malic, Thompson submachine gun in hand.

Ray Foster remembered clearly that the youngest of the men, presumably Patricio Jorge, became scared to death as he got ready to board his raft. As he crawled through the hatch, he stopped to pray loudly enough so that he could be heard by Foster and some of the others in the submarine stepping onto the deck. Once there, he continued to genuflect and pray before lowering himself into the raft. Before departing, a shaky Major Jesus Villamor told Foster and the others that he would entertain them at the Manila Hotel once the war was over. With the men of the Planet Party now in their rafts, they began the approach to shore. The landing party disembarked about 1,000 yards off shore at 1927. As he had agreed to do, Shirley Stovall swung *Gudgeon* around so that the submarine's guns could be brought to bear on the beach to protect the landing party should the Japanese be waiting for them. Soon the long dark hull of *Gudgeon* slowly disappeared to take a position further off-shore. The scene in many ways was one of great beauty, but the terror was overwhelming. The men in the two rafts landed safely ashore but were troubled to find that they had been observed by a fisherman on a small boat who was trying to speak to them in Visayan, a Filipino dialect not understood by the men comprising the intelligence party. Villamor was unable to ascertain whether the man was friend or foe before he disappeared into the stillness of the night.

In no time a group of surly guerillas operating on Negros captured one of the two groups of men. Villamor, Quinto, and Malic hid in the dense undergrowth. Villamor realized that *Gudgeon* was still on the surface and vulnerable should the Japanese send a bomber or patrol vessel to the area. Stovall and the others on board could be of no help to his men in their predicament so Villamor used his lamp to flash the letter "E" three times separated by three seconds, as prearranged. *Gudgeon* moved further out to sea, then dove. The following morning Villamor and the two men with him were captured. Villamor recalled that the guerillas who seized him were very menacing looking, their rifles always trained upon them as they marched through the thick jungle. At first the small group of guerillas was convinced that the members of the Planet Party were Japanese collaborators and considered killing them on the spot. While they were held at gunpoint, a slender older man, a schoolteacher in the prewar days, moved out from the dense undergrowth to inspect the prisoners.

One of the guerillas stepped up to Villamor, who was using a fictitious name, and ran his finger down a scar along the left side of Villamor's face. The schoolteacher talked quietly with his men. Soon the guerillas realized that it was Major Jesus A. Villamor whom they had captured. By this time in the war, Villamor's wartime actions were so well known that, even in this remote place, he had become a hero to his people, and, as a result, his life and the lives of the other five men were spared. The older man, apparently the leader of the group of guerillas, dramatically clicked his heels together and bowed slightly. He said that his name was Captain Jorge Madamba, and it was his privilege to welcome Major Jesus Villamor to the Philippines in their country's darkest hour. Greatly relieved, the men embraced each other, tears now running down their faces. Villamor said, "It's all over now, we are home among friends." [19] The members of the Planet Party were very lucky; Jorge, YuHico, and Ignacio had been captured and spent much of the night digging what was intended to be their own graves. Both groups of out-numbered men, emboldened by the presence of the other, blended slowly into the bush.

Jesus Villamor completed one dangerous wartime exploit after another beginning with the Japanese attack on the Philippines shortly after Pearl Harbor. Each time, when describing his actions, he acknowledged that he was quite frightened. He was not the kind of man who was able, as some men are, to push aside his fear and undertake dangerous tasks. Neither was he one to pretend he was fearless. In each situation he was all too aware of his real feelings. His legs actually shook as he stood on *Gudgeon* the day before the landing on Negros. Yet he still stepped forward and did his duty. Without hesitating, he clambered into a raft and paddled through the night to an island controlled by an overwhelming force of ruthless and cruel enemy soldiers.

Gudgeon, having seen the "E" signal, withdrew on two engines. The submarine was slowed by stormy weather, the currents were oftentimes unpredictable, the straits quite narrow. *Gudgeon* was covering a meager 100 nautical miles a day as she headed toward Cape San Augustin. By the seventeenth *Gudgeon* had reached her patrol areas southeast of the Cape. Despite being at sea for three weeks the crew sighted only a few ships. Life on a submarine at war in 1943 ranged from short periods of intense action to protracted times of boredom. The times of relative inactivity were necessary to conserve whatever oxygen was still in the submarine. The state of enforced suspension from any level of activity resulted in a nervous lethargy that could be difficult to endure. Luckily, those periods of malaise were followed by exhilarating times when *Gudgeon* ran on the surface with nary a threat in sight. The refreshing Pacific air, calming and smooth, and the relative freedom of movement did much to quell the psychic kinks in men experiencing uncomfortable physical conditions with too little to do and nowhere to go.

As Stovall positioned *Gudgeon* into what he hoped would be a busy merchant traffic lane on the southeastern tip of Mindanao, a small group of Allied commandos on Timor received a jarring bit of news. At 1700 on January 17, 1943, English Captain Douglas L. Broadhurst, Australian Lieutenant Frank Holland, and a small group of coast watchers and commandos with their native gun toters (creados) received word from a frantic native runner that the Japanese were engaged in an all-out search for the bands of men. Whenever Holland got a chance, he would write down the day's events on a piece of paper and stuff it into his gear, and as a result, the story of the men's flight is known. The complete story is told in a book about Holland's life, *El Tigre*.

Reportedly, the Japanese had the commandos virtually surrounded. As they pursued the hated commandos, the Japanese leveled a village known as Hide-Mumu which had stood at the foot of a mountain, with mortar and machine gun fire, then burned the village to the ground. A group of fleeing Portuguese, who were believed to be civilians and soldiers, had been camped there earlier in the morning before taking to the brush. The Japanese were heading directly toward Holland's group. Without delay, the commandos began a race for their lives traveling west across Timor. Before long it would be clear that if they were to go on living they would have to be extracted from the island. And fast. Their path and the path of the USS *Gudgeon* would, after a month's flight, cross on a beach at the mouth of the Dilor River.

The group of commandos headed out in an intense rain, passed through a thick jungle, and then had to climb up a slippery narrow track along a mountainside above the deep gorges below. At times, it was necessary to hang on to pieces of undergrowth in order to climb or descend safely. One of the native carriers handling the radio set fell very heavily, giving the case a severe jolt. The group eventually reached the village of Ahaubo, where Chief Dom Paulo de Frietas e Silva was camped. Broadhurst and the others laid down their gear, ate, and spent the night. As the men slept, many of the natives cleared out with the food they were carrying. In fact, one of Holland's own bodyguards fled; another ran and took with him the ammunition for Holland's Bren guns.

At 9:30 on January 18, another native runner told the men that two Japanese patrol groups were approaching the village. They had reached the old commando headquarters, and had, once again, subjected the area to mortar and machine gun fire and burned everything that was standing to the ground. Captain Broadhurst and some of the others decided to remain in the area with their radio. Holland and his men departed. After a few hours' trek, a group of Dom Paulo's armed natives, who had been out trying to locate the Japanese patrols, told the commandos that the Japanese were now pursuing them with horses and large dogs. They would have little difficulty catching the men unless the fleeing commandos were careful to cover their scents. As the rain once again descended upon them, Holland and the others found an abandoned native house where they spent the night.

At 0150 on the nineteenth, *Gudgeon* was patrolling on the surface for Japanese merchant vessels and sighted a 150 foot boat. The small vessel was suspected of being an escort for a larger ship, and so was of interest to

Gudgeon. The ship did not behave in a way that suggested she knew she was being followed. The vessel had a fairly high bridge structure and a stack roughly the same height, with two stick masts, the after mast being shorter than the foremast. Only one gun was visible. *Gudgeon* sped ahead of the boat using all four of her diesel engines, hoping that it was now on a course to meet a merchant ship somewhere ahead. Unfortunately for *Gudgeon*, the small vessel was lost due to poor visibility.

At the same time, on Timor, Captain Broadhurst sent word to Holland via a native runner that the Japanese had them surrounded. Holland's group was instructed to allow the runner to lead them to his [Broadhurst's] hideout. By 1600, Holland's group had joined up with Broadhurst's men and learned that the Japanese had burned Dom Paulo's camp to the ground and slaughtered the men, women, and children who had lingered in the area. Luckily, Dom Paulo had escaped. One of the men in his group had been captured and might soon be tortured, and possibly give up the location of the Allied commandos.

On January 20 the commando groups fled. The natives were starting to see that things on Timor were changing; soon it would be the Japanese alone on Timor ruling the island. As a consequence, the natives they encountered along the way wanted little to do with the commandos and provided very little information to them. An order was received from Australia. It was time to let the natives who were traveling with the commandos go. Some of the natives were told to scatter for their own safety and the safety of the commandos. Holland said, "I asked them to go back to their villages in Matabia and Calicai, hide their arms, keep quiet and at some later date we would be back and together chase the Japanese out of Timor forever."[20] Holland said that despite the flagging morale, none of the natives wanted to leave. "We were sorry indeed to see these faithful men leaving us."[21] Holland gave Domingos, his "head boy," fifteen patacas, and the others, six patacas each before sending them away.[22] He allowed those who were leaving to take their rifles and ammunition with them. All that remained in the camp were six Australians, eight Portuguese "half-casts," and around twenty natives.[23] The commandos still had Austen guns and other rifles, and some of the natives carried hand grenades. Food was now being strictly rationed.

The men traveled only two miles on the twenty-first, then stopped and huddled together for comfort in the pouring rain, remaining there the rest of the night. As Holland sat there huddled with the small band, he took some solace knowing that they would not be found in the heavy rain and that the Japanese also had to put up with the downpour. By the twenty-second, the group was once again completely surrounded. The tension was unbearable. The commandos headed off, this time with Dom Paulo's younger brother Francisco leading the way. They continued along a creek bed in order to leave no tracks for the pursuing Japanese. At 1000 hours a Japanese plane flew overhead causing the men to scurry into the underbrush. By 1630 the baying of dogs was heard. A fleeing native told them that the dogs the Japanese had with them had "big mouths and big ears."[24] Holland and his men cringed when they thought about the story of the man from the Netherlands who had been torn to shreds by just such dogs as Japanese soldiers stood by watching in amusement.

By the twenty-third the men were still running and eating whatever they could find on the land—coconuts one day and corn the next, but more than anything they were hungry. After another day's march they looked out on the 960 foot peak known as Bibeleu. All of the houses in the area were in flames, courtesy of the Japanese. The group came upon the Vei-Tuku River. It turned out that only 500 yards upstream a fire was burning at a camp inhabited by the Japanese soldiers who were pursuing them. Everyone that was wearing boots took them off so that no boot marks were left in the sand as they moved along the river. Realizing that they were much too close to the enemy, they marched barefoot until daylight, not even stopping for rest. As they fled, the men could think about the considerable damage they had inflicted upon the Japanese, as coast watchers radioing the whereabouts of the Japanese vessels they spotted, making these ships targets for any Allied submarines or aircraft in the area. They had also killed hundreds of Japanese soldiers and tied down thousands of others who could have been used to better advantage elsewhere.

Aboard *Gudgeon*, Shirley Stovall ordered that the submarine head southeast toward Ambon. On the twenty-fifth *Gudgeon* dove ninety feet to avoid being bombed by a Japanese patrol plane. Running through the area slowly at periscope depth, no targets could be seen. The frustrated skipper, now approaching day thirty of the patrol without having fired a shot, wrote that the submarine was not properly ballasted because of damage sustained on an earlier war patrol. The damage was supposed to have been corrected but inexplicably had been missed. With the humdrum twenty-fifth behind them *Gudgeon* found herself trolling for Japanese targets off the entrance to Ambon Bay, off the tiny island of Ambon, west of New Guinea. A scrawny patrol craft 75–100 feet in length was sighted. *Gudgeon* approached slowly as the little boat employed echo ranging to search the seas for enemy submarines. At 0735 Stovall set up for a torpedo attack from the stern tubes at 1,000 yards. A few minutes later, as Stovall eyed the Japanese vessel, her gun crew and lookouts in their khaki shorts were in turn scanning the seas with binoculars. Stovall decided that the little boat was too small for a torpedo attack and ordered *Gudgeon* to start moving away to avoid being detected.

It was then that the Japanese ship picked up *Gudgeon* by short-scale pinging. The Japanese fired up their engines and turned toward the submarine. As the patrol vessel turned, Stovall feared that his periscope had been seen and that the enemy knew exactly where *Gudgeon* was positioned. He was correct. The skipper later wrote in the war patrol report that only two feet of scope had been exposed for ten seconds. However, that is all that it takes sometimes, especially with the sea as flat and calm as it was on that day. The small ship was now speeding toward *Gudgeon*; within four minutes, she threw a cluster of four depth charges close astern to the underwater vessel causing what Stovall said was "considerable jar" but no serious damage.[25] Stovall started evasive tactics.

Even depth charge attacks that are not particularly close can be jarring to the nerves because sound travels best in dense hosts like salt water and steel. In an ocean at 59°F, for example, sound travels four times faster than above the surface. Because of the rapid speed, the human ear cannot discern which direction the sound is coming from since both eardrums are struck at the same time with equal intensity. When a depth charge blows up at a depth of 1,700 yards, the explosion is heard one second after the detonation. Because the sound is traveling so fast it gives the illusion that the depth charge is much closer than it actually is. The experienced submariner knows that the submarine is safe when the depth charge clicks before the deafening explosion. The clicking noise signals that the charge is surely some distance off. After the charge went off a shusssh sound could be heard through the boat. This was the sound of the water moving through the superstructure created by the explosion.

Despite Stovall's attempts to evade, a half hour later the little ship made a near-perfect run over *Gudgeon* from stern to bow. These anti-submariners were good. They had excellent sound gear and knew how to use it. The little ship was running almost parallel to *Gudgeon* from back to front. The men on board were certain that their luck had run out. All the enemy had to do now was drop the depth charges at the right depth and *Gudgeon* would be nothing more than a forgotten name in the war records. Sure enough, the Japanese skipper dropped four more depth charges which rocked *Gudgeon* like she had never been rocked before. Damage was especially severe in the after part of the boat. The charges were very close to the starboard side of the submarine and set to explode at approximately 250–330 feet. With *Gudgeon* at 315 feet, the Japanese had estimated the submarine's depth rather accurately and nearly sent the men to the bottom.

Stovall later wrote that the latter four depth charges caused the most severe shock ever felt on *Gudgeon*. Damage from the tiny ship with the accurate depth charges was considerable. In the forward torpedo room the emergency freshwater tanks were split and the QC sound head shafts were binding. The forward battery compartment, the control room, the conning tower, the pump room, the after battery, the engine room, the maneuvering room, the motor room, the after torpedo room, and topside also sustained damage. Leaks sprayed water and air all over, gauges broke, oil leaked, lightbulbs shattered, and the ship started to vibrate, mainly aft. In all, sixty-two damaged units were listed in the post-action report. Most sobering of all was the dished-in hull in the after torpedo room; this damage confirmed that the charge was at *Gudgeon*'s depth and close aboard, starboard of that compartment, and had all but ruptured the submarine's hull. Miraculously, electrician's mate John L. Cadman was the only man to have sustained a wound. He was cut on his knee by flying glass. Two other sailors sustained injuries when they were knocked out for awhile after being thrown against the bulkheads. Some of the men sported bruises for some time after the attack.

George Seiler was in the torpedo room at the time the side of the boat dished-in and vividly recalled the frightening encounter. He was certain that the depth charges were unusually large and said that they were being towed by the Japanese patrol vessel and were cut loose when the Japanese gauged that they were above *Gudgeon*. These bombs really ripped the submarine. Seiler said he actually saw the pressure hull of the submarine cave in like the plastic of a liter of Pepsi. He also had the sobering experience of having one of the manifolds come loose and fly across the torpedo room into his lap. "It happened so fast you didn't have time to get scared," he said of the experience.[26]

Seaman First Class Ron Schooley of Berkley, Michigan—on board for the second of what would be five runs on *Gudgeon*—recalled the attack and called it the most severe one that he ever experienced on a submarine. Schooley, a man of few words, offered a succinct and vivid description of what it was like to undergo a close depth charging. He said that the experience was something that you had to be there to "appreciate," and added that, "It's like putting yourself into a garbage can and having somebody beat the god-damned thing with a club."[27] By this time in the war, Ray Foster, known as "Guts," would show those around him the reason that he had acquired the nickname. His shipmates vividly recall him lying in his bunk during these attacks, eyes upward as if he was challenging the Japanese, yelling at them as if they could hear him, fist clenched as if ready to strike, "That's right, you bastards, use up all of your god-damned ammunition."[28]

In the midst of this brutal attack, the men on the submarine heard rain off in the distance. The clever Shirley Stovall seized the God-given opportunity and quickly headed toward the squall. Arthur Barlow recalled the evasive maneuvers used in silent running and the eventual escape made by *Gudgeon* at Ambon. "It's a combination of trying to be quiet and get out of there. So every once in awhile we would get a full blast from the screws to get running. In the distance we heard a squall. When rain hits hard on the surface of the water, it sounds like drums. So we headed for the squall. If you can imagine fifty to sixty drummers like the beating of a drum. We just maneuvered and got rid of them. We got rid of them through the squall."[29]

Barlow explained that it was very important to go deep because the deeper you went, the greater the water pressure. The water pressure would condense the size of the blast, meaning of course that to have an effect, the depth charge would have to be much closer to the boat. This also meant that the explosion would be magnified by the increased water pressure. The deeper water offered further protection for the same reason that it is harder to find a minnow in a river than a shallow creek. Finally, at 1000 hours, in the heavy rain, the distant echo ranging died out. The men on board could breathe a deep sigh of relief. *Gudgeon* had nearly been destroyed, but the tiny pest that packed such a huge wallop was gone. Repairs began immediately. After the attack, a crumpled piece of paper was found in the wastebasket in *Gudgeon*'s control room. On it someone had written, then tossed into the garbage can, "I wish to hell we had wings sometimes—sometimes!!!"[30]

Once again Shirley Stovall was proud of his veteran crew. Stovall commented that about "seventy-five percent of the gauges and lights throughout the ship were broken; the entire ship was pretty badly shaken around. However, the crew took it splendidly, it was nothing new to them, they had had close depth charging before and they had always stood up in an excellent fashion."[31]

With *Gudgeon* licking her wounds, the submarine moved slightly south. For several days *Gudgeon* patrolled far off Ambon Bay all the while working on repairs. Damage was severe throughout the submarine, quite a lot more severe aft than forward. Among the items that were broken or damaged were the emergency fresh water tanks, inclinometers, gyro, QC sound head shafts, depth gauges, and one of the propellers. There were air, hydraulic, oil, and water leaks. Various units on the *Gudgeon* shook and vibrated and did not work as they were supposed to. Only two of the submarine's ten torpedo tubes were functional.

For the commandos on Timor the twenty-fifth had been much less eventful than the near sinking of *Gudgeon*. Still in the area of the Vei-Tuku River, Holland, Broadhurst, and the rest of the fleeing commandos had heard nothing about the Japanese and chose to lay hidden all day. The area offered no shelter, and the desperate escapees once again had to tolerate a day's worth of heavy rain. The following day the commando group remained camped until late in the day and headed off southwest. An hour into the march they ran into a muddy swamp that swallowed their legs up to their knees. After a grueling struggle to get beyond the swamp, the commandos decided to rest on high ground where they were, as Holland said, "eaten alive with sand flies and mosquitoes."[32] The commandos were now in a part of Timor that nobody knew anything about. They were finally able to talk a reluctant native who lived in the area to lead them through the region, once Holland agreed to pay him handsomely. The guide led them through a particularly tough spot, the very long grass extending over everyone's head and sharply cutting everyone's faces as they walked. That evening, Dom Paulo, his wife, and a few natives somehow found the group of commandos and joined them, hoping also to be evacuated.

By January 27 the commando group reached Luca, where they hid to avoid a Japanese float plane that was searching for them. They met up with another group fleeing the Japanese, who Holland referred to as "the Portuguese group." He did not explain whether the group was primarily military or civilian. Perhaps, as a result of the accident on the mountain, the only available radio would transmit but no longer receive. This was a particularly serious setback because the commandos needed to coordinate their escape efforts with their command headquarters and the ship that would be sent to evacuate them. They asked that another radio set be dropped and that headquarters in Darwin monitor their frequency around the clock. The tired and hungry commandos and natives reached a deserted little village known as Uelolo where those that wanted to took a bath. Australian Sergeant Norm Smith and Holland had not bathed in two weeks and much enjoyed the experience. The men noticed that when they put their belts back on, they needed to be cinched up tighter than before. The commandos had not had one decent meal since they started their run across the jungles of Timor ten days earlier. No sooner had the men cinched up their belts closer to their dwindling, weakened bodies than Captain Broadhurst hurried over to them and told them that the Japanese were extremely close, having crossed the Luca River earlier in the day with 250 men. The commandos melted into the bush, and the drama continued as before. The commandos were being pursued unmercifully and ate whatever they could as they ran; the Japanese, with their vicious track dogs baying and plowing through the brush, continued forward in search.

While giving the entrances to the southern islands a thorough looking over on January 31, 1943, *Gudgeon* sighted an *Amagiri* or *Fubuki* class destroyer making high speed and heading in the opposite direction at 15,000 yards. It was not possible to close. The ship disappeared twenty-six minutes after being sighted. Later in the same day, after *Gudgeon*'s periscope had been exposed for a couple of minutes, a plane got in close and dropped "two heavy objects."[33] There was no explosion, just splashes. The men on board concluded that the depth bombs or depth charges were duds. Just how the plane had gotten in so close without being detected was not addressed in the war patrol report. *Gudgeon* moved further south, patrolling in the area of the Banda and Kai Islands.

On February 3, Holland's group decided to take a rest and were, to the extent possible, enjoying a meal of corn and sago, a hard white grain from the pith of a sago palm tree, when a terrified native rushed in and said that the Japanese had arrived. It turned out that the jumpy native was wrong. It was actually a second group of Australians that had also been fleeing the Japanese. The men were known as the Lancer commando group and were headed by another Australian officer, the coast watcher Harry Flood. By the wisdom of the old adage that there is strength in numbers, the two groups decided to join up and continue their dangerous journey across Timor. The Lancer group had also been chased across the island for the last several weeks, five of their men disappearing without a trace along the way. The Lancers had lost their only radio, so communication with anybody that could save them had been impossible.

By now the men's uniforms were in tatters and their boots were rotting on their feet. Attempts to get food and supplies dropped to them had been unsuccessful, greatly complicated by the malfunctioning radio. That evening a passing plane dropped parachutes into the nighttime brush. After several hours of search some of the chutes were located by the Lancer group. They found food and seven batteries, but the chute that had carried a fully functioning wireless radio to the ground could not be found.

By February 6, 1943, the situation on Timor took a turn for the better. None of the men had ended up on the working end of a Japanese bayonet, and they had successfully signaled a low-flying Hudson, which dropped supplies of food and two radios by chute. The food was divided up equally among the party, who rested for a while and sent messages to headquarters. Before the day was over the commandos were able to listen to the war news on the radio. By the seventh or eighth, Frank Holland was not sure which, the Japanese were once again hot on the trail of the commando group. At

1600 four more Lancers, presumably some of the men that had been lost, arrived at the camp.

Out at sea, the men on *Gudgeon* found themselves being pinged once again by a small patrol craft like the one off Ambon. The eerie déjà vu experience must have given Guts, Schooley, and the rest of the crew quite a start after the near-fatal attack of the twenty-sixth. The patrol craft was slowly moving about, trolling for submarines in the Wetar Passage of the Indonesian Islands. Nothing came of it. At 1200, *Gudgeon*, not having fired at a single ship the entire patrol, and having narrowly escaped being sunk, turned for home. Lieutenant Commander Stovall reported in his war patrol report that *Gudgeon* was experiencing extensive damage that could not be repaired. *Gudgeon* had nonfunctioning sound gear and propeller shaft damage that was causing an unsettling high noise level. The propellers and damaged items on the superstructure were making too much noise for the submarine to move stealthily in the water. *Gudgeon* would be vulnerable should she need to undertake deep evasion tactics. Noisy screws could be fatal under such circumstances. The deciding factor was that the submarine was almost eleven-thousand pounds heavier than she should have been at this time in the patrol. If an emergency dive became necessary, the excessive weight could cause a catastrophic dive.

On the ninth, the men on *Gudgeon* received word that when they passed the southern tip of Timor they were to evacuate a group of commandos. Ashore on Timor the going had been very rough for the commando group who had reached the Dilor River. For security reasons the ragged contingent camped in a mangrove swamp, without food, where it rained the last two days they were on Timor. When Holland heard the baying of dogs again, he laughed to himself, knowing that the Japanese would never find them in the swamp. Frank Holland described the evening: "The mangroves are a swamp forest. The trees are distributed in narrow belts along the seashore, throughout the tropical sea waters, and are very gloomy, they consist of large trees actually growing in the salt brackish water." He continued, " . . . a number of aerial roots extend downwards from the main branches of the trees. There is no under growth, as in the forest on the land. Because of the very extensive development of the root system, generally grow at sharp angles, from the main tree, it is very difficult to walk through, more so when the tide is in. Climbing among the roots, was very arduous and made one very weary, hanging on to whatever you can. The water is nearly up to our waist, which did not help our progress. The Captain [Broadhurst] called a halt, this would be far enough the open sea is just ahead, and much more daylight left. What a prospect of a miserable night, with hordes of mosquitoes to keep us company. But a lot better than being a prisoner of the Japanese. We look for some trees to stand up against or climb up into out of the water, and make our packs and wireless sets secure for the night. It is now high tide, so no worries of higher water. This we can tell by the marks on the trees, and fragments of seaweed left in the trees by other tides."[34]

The men found themselves surrounded by water but had nothing to drink, only a few emergency rations which had been dropped by a plane. Holland continued: "The night was a musical drama, mosquitoes singing, the waves lapping among the roots, and a plop now and again of a fish, or what ever it was in the water, men slapping, and swearing at the mossies. We sincerely hope, with all the bites we are taking, there are no disease carries [*sic*] among them. The night wears on, we talk, we sleep, when possible, it seems a never ending night, that will never be among our fondest memories of Portuguese Timor."[35]

Late on February 9, a message was received by the commandos from Australian headquarters indicating that they would be picked up the following day. Frank Holland, writing once again on a loose piece of paper, said the men were told that, "Arrangements were being made to evacuate you on the night of 10/11 Feb, or failing that, 11/12 Feb. Display white shirt clearly visible to the sea to assist in daylight reconnaissance by the craft."[36] That was not the only good news of the day. As luck would have it, a pig and some rice had been found, and the commandos had "a good feed" according to Holland.[37] The word was that the Japanese had not crossed the Luca River after all. Perhaps the evacuees were finally safe. The ensuing feast did much to raise the spirits of the ragged group of commandos.

The first problem for Frank Holland in the early morning hours of February tenth was to find a white shirt. There was nothing the Australians were dragging around with them that vaguely resembled a white shirt by this time. After some scrounging around among the natives' things a large white cloth was located and affixed between two bamboo poles which were placed on the beach in a little cleared area out among some small trees. The white cloth against the dark of the green brush would be easily observed by the rescue vessel. It was set up so that it could not be seen by the Japanese at Beaco, nor the others at Kicras to the southwest. A guard was placed nearby so it could be quickly removed if a plane approached. Due to the intensity of the hunt, the white signal cloth had to be taken down three times during the day.

Lieutenant Commander Stovall reconnoitered the island for several days prior to the extraction, looking for landmarks and searching for the Australians. By using fixes on distant mountain peaks and sighting man-made smoke, Stovall was able to determine roughly where the pickup would take place. On the tenth, the cautious Skipper eyed the white sheet to make certain that there would be Allied soldiers at the rendezvous, not the Japanese. For hours he scanned up and down the beach looking for any sign of life. The men manning the periscope noticed that the sheet was put up and down three times during the day. A decision was made to hang around the area and do the pickup after sundown the same day.

Feeling a little satisfied after the feast on the pig the night before, the tenth was looking like it was going to be the day that the worn-out commandos had been dreaming of each labored step of the way across rugged and dangerous Timor. Then a shot rang out. And, like a thousand times before, the commandos and their comrades grabbed their weapons and headed for the bush. It looked like they would have to take on those 250 Japanese soldiers and their big-mouthed dogs after all. They would just have to shoot their way off the beach. Everyone was overwhelmed with relief to find that the disturbance was made by one of the natives in the group who had fired at another wild pig and missed. With no pig in hand, the commando group had to settle for some more of that life-sustaining sago, no matter how distasteful and unsatisfying it was. As the men ate, they talked of the good meals they would be having when they reached Australia. They received a message from Darwin informing them that recognition signals from the craft to the commandos would be the letter "C." The commandos were then to flash "Z." Knowing that their lives depended upon them seeing the signal lamp, the commandos scanned the ocean constantly. The men organized a "sweepstake" as Frank Holland called it, with each man drawing one slip of paper from a hat that had one of the quarter hours after 1830 written on it.[38] The one that drew the time closest to the exact time that the vessel flashed the letter C to the men ashore would win.

Early in the evening, using their flashlights, the commandos exchanged signals with four Hudson bombers that flew overhead. Some time later after dark, supplies carried by two parachutes were dropped. Several of the chutes drifted out to sea and were lost. The men were able to retrieve bundles of rubber boats, lifebelts, and coils of rope with cork attached to keep them afloat when they hit the water. Unfortunately, only two of the boats were serviceable, an unsatisfactory situation considering that there were twenty-eight men to evacuate. The boats were quickly pumped full of air and the men hurriedly put their lifebelts on.

At 2015 the commandos first observed signals from *Gudgeon*. As a result, one of the new men from the Lancer group, Australian Private Harold "Lofty" Hubbard raked in whatever winnings he would derive from having had the good fortune of having had "2015" written on the slip of paper he had drawn from the hat. It is suspected that the winnings were paltry though; it is hard to conceive that the bedraggled men were carrying around very much cash with them as they cut through the brush only a half-step or so ahead of their Japanese tormenters. Whatever money Hubbard got from the lottery was ill-gained because *Gudgeon*'s special mission report indicates very clearly that they first exchanged recognition signals with the men on shore at 1907 hours. No doubt Holland's watch was an hour fast, the timepiece having taken the same beating as the commandos as they crossed the impossibly rugged Timor. *Gudgeon* came to rest a half-mile off the beach at 1945.

Arthur Barlow recalled that while Stovall was looking for the proper signal from the men ashore, a swimmer approaching *Gudgeon* was spotted. Barlow said that one of the starved, bedraggled, and war-weary Australians had jumped into the water to warn Stovall that *Gudgeon* was getting too close to an uncharted reef. The Australian ship that had delivered some of the men to the island many months before had become permanently attached to it. In contrast to Barlow's recollection, Stovall noted that at 2002 the "First group from beach came on board. It was discovered that they had only three serviceable two man rubber boats so it was decided to send in three seven man rubber boats which we had standing by and thus speed up their embarkation."[39]

Lieutenant Commander Stovall ordered Executive Officer Dusty Dornin to get a group of four sailors together to go ashore with three large rafts and pick up the remaining evacuees. It was then that a gung-ho Moose Hornkohl pulled a bit of chicanery in order to be one of those chosen. He approached Dornin and said, "Mr. Dornin, I'm probably the only one around here that's ever paddled a canoe."

Dornin wasn't so sure, asking pointedly, "You have Moose?"

Hornkohl responded, "Hell yes, I was raised in a canoe. Have you ever seen a half-breed Indian that didn't know how to paddle a canoe?"[40] Of course, as Hornkohl would admit later, it was a lie. It is true that he had some Native American blood in his veins, but he had never paddled a canoe or rubber boat in his life. Dornin relented, allowing Hornkohl, Guts Foster, Torpedoman William "Pappy" Low, and Chief Torpedoman Ray J. McKenna to go ashore for the exhausted contingent of men. A message was signaled to the men ashore. Due to the size of the rafts, *Gudgeon* would be able to take twenty-eight evacuees, not the twenty-three that they had indicated earlier. Frank Holland wrote that there would now be room for twenty-three Australians and English commandos, including "Senior" Pires, a lieutenant in the Portuguese infantry, and five native creados.

Moose Hornkohl recalled the dangerous events that followed. "Me and Pappy Low took off in the first boat. Right behind us was the second group of boats [three in total]. We could see the Australians flashing the light at us. They didn't flash them very long because the Japanese were searching for these guys. You could hear the surf roaring after awhile. I had never heard that, you know. We started in and the current picked us up, and heaved us in, and dumped us head-over-tea-kettle and we ended up with boats and everything ashore."[41] Before long Guts Foster and Ray J. McKenna also unceremoniously hit the shore, in the process ripping a hole in the raft on the rocks. Hornkohl was armed with a .45 and did not know whether it would work as wet as it was. Foster was armed with a Thompson submachine gun.

The situation ashore was tense and extremely dangerous. The Japanese had been in hot pursuit all the way. The native Timorese had been accompanied by their wives and children who were by this time crying and pleading with the men not to go. Moose Hornkohl said that the tiny "wide-eyed" natives slated for escape did not appear to be all that excited about the prospect of boarding the little boats and leaving the island.[42] It is easy to see why. The submarine must have seemed like it was from another world, and even more importantly, it was certainly unsettling news to the women and children to learn that their husbands would be departing, leaving them alone on the island with the Japanese. After all, they had only learned a few moments before that the men were leaving. Of the natives, those that were in most jeopardy were the male fighters. They would be the ones that the Japanese would most likely murder if they had the chance, but the Timorese fighters were worried about what might befall their women and children. There were so many factions and varied loyalties on Timor that it seemed almost certain that another native would tell the Japanese that it was their men who had been helping the Allies. Just what those left behind may have endured remains an unknown, but can be imagined with pity.

Guts Foster, Ray McKenna, and their two rafts made it to *Gudgeon* first. The *Gudgeon* crew on deck helped the exhausted and ill commandos out of the rafts onto the deck. Foster and McKenna once again headed for shore. Foster had left a signal light and his machine gun for the men on shore in case the Japanese arrived before the *Gudgeon* submariners could return to pick up the second group. The second trip to shore for both groups of submariners was a long tedious struggle against time, made more difficult by fatigued and sore muscles, and the knowledge that the angry Japanese were still out there behind the remaining commandos or on a plane heading toward the surfaced and vulnerable *Gudgeon*. Stroke by stroke they inched their way toward shore in the flimsy rafts with their small wooden paddles, taking so long that Broadhurst and the others had all but abandoned hope. Broadhurst said later: "We believed that the craft had been forced to leave. We began clearing the beach when to our joy a signal flashed out and shortly afterwards two of the large rubber boats came in [Foster and McKenna]. We set out through the surf and one boat capsized. Our natives could not swim and for a few moments we had great difficulty in getting them ashore and setting out again. This time we rode the surf successfully."[43]

Now, loaded once again with the thin, filthy, disease-ridden men, Ray Foster took one of his shoes off and showed the natives on board how to bail out the boat. Before long, "One bail and the shoe went over the side." [44] It was lost in the nighttime surf, never to be found again. The Timorese on Foster's raft just sat there. Foster paddled on toward *Gudgeon*, which by now was out of sight. From time to time a light was flashed from the boat. It was necessary to be looking directly at *Gudgeon* so that it could be seen as they bailed to prevent heading off in the wrong direction and being left behind. Looking back after a long life, Ray Foster recalled that it was "the greatest time of exhaustion in my life." [45]

Moose Hornkohl, having reached shore the second time for a load of evacuees, was regretting his bravado. He had loaded his canoe with many of the non-English-speaking natives even as the strong surf continued to push the raft toward shore. Hornkohl recalled being repelled by the breakers his first four or five attempts: "The damn surf would take us and pitch us over. So we had to fight and beat the surf, and we got the boat out far enough. Then we started pulling the natives out of the water and into the boat. I said, 'Bail. Bail. Bail.' and was showing them how to do it with their hands." [46] Hornkohl took his shoe off and showed the natives how to paddle with it. Hornkohl continued, "One of them took my shoe and started bailing water out of the canoe with it. And we kept paddling and paddling, and it started to get toward dawn and I thought we weren't going to make it." [47] Hornkohl pleaded for their help. The Japanese were out there somewhere searching for them. It was dark and Hornkohl, now off the coast of Timor in a slow raft armed with only a .45, felt quite vulnerable. Hornkohl and Low paddled away. In desperation, Hornkohl yelled sharply at the inactive natives telling them in words they did not understand that they "need to get this thing going or we are going to miss the trolley." [48]

At 2200, Moose Hornkohl and the men aboard his tiny craft were the only ones unaccounted for. By this time *Gudgeon*'s four engines were running in preparation for departure. Every moment on the surface meant added danger and greater risk of detection. Hornkohl said later that he wanted to yell at the men atop *Gudgeon*, but "with the Japanese around, you flat out don't do that." [49] George Seiler, aboard *Gudgeon* and worried that his friend might get left behind, recalled the episode differently, stating that he heard Hornkohl screaming, "Hey, you aren't going to leave without me. Hold the boat."[50] With Hornkohl paddling and the Australians bailing water out of the raft, they continued to make slow progress, but, as he added, "It was not exactly an outboard you know."[51] Finally at about 2225, Hornkohl's group made it aboard. They quickly deflated the rafts, shoved them down the hatches, and hurried down the hatch behind them. At 2229 the rescue was complete, and *Gudgeon* pulled away.

Having the unique opportunity to tell what it was like for a non-submariner to ride on a World War II submarine, Frank Holland did not disappoint. An exultant Holland wrote that when the men boarded the submarine, "We were given a royal welcome on board by all hands."[52] He continued, "In the darkness, this ship seemed enormous. We were told to get below as quickly as possible, and were shown the way through the conning tower, then down a small ladder into a little room, then through another small hole and down another ladder and into the control room. Here it was lit up with blue lights. I believe this is always so when the sub comes to the surface at night, but while submerged they use white lights. Here in the control room (found out later this was what this place was called) our rank and names were taken. Then the officers were taken to the forward part of the ship, given a towel, soap, and some clean clothes, and shown the shower, bath, and hot water. This bathroom was just enough for one man to stand in, but did we all have a wonderful bath. It had been a long time since any of us had a good wash, all of us had not taken our boots off for days, but we had left them on the beach when we got the signal from the sub."[53]

Holland knew that they had saved many lives and made it necessary for the Japanese to guard roads, bridges, oil dumps, and other sites, and thus kept those Japanese soldiers from fighting elsewhere, taking pressure off thousands of Allied soldiers in the area. Of the children of Timor, Holland wrote, "It is so sad to see children, black or white, the poor things do not know what it is all about and know only that their tummy is crying out for food. The little ones their mothers hug them to their breast, but there is no food there. They are dry through lack of food and ill health."[54] On board with Holland were the dangerously thin soldiers including English Captain Douglas Broadhurst, Australian Lieutenants William Thomas, John Cashman, Harry

Flood, John Grimson, and Portuguese Lieutenant Manoel de Yesus Pires. Also on board were the following Australian enlisted men: Norman Smith, Allen Wilkens, Robin Whelan, Alfred Ellwood, John Key, Harold Hubbard, James Ritchie, William Hayes, Jeffry Fraser, Stewart Duncan, Phillip Wynne, Thomas Miller, Eric Hansen, Trevor Finch, Arthur Jacobsen, and Robert Phillips. One of the Aussies claimed to be the heavyweight-boxing champion of Australia. According to George Seiler, the boxer had been reduced to a flyweight of around ninety-five pounds because of the lack of food, stress, and jungle illnesses. Ray Foster said of the men: "They were dirty. They had leeches on them. They were in terrible shape. Some of them had been tortured." [55]

Brothers Domingos de Freitas Soares and Chief Cosme de Freitas Soares had boarded the submarine with another set of brothers, Chief D. Paulo de Freitas e Silva and Francisco de Freitas e Silva, and with Sancho da Silva, a guide. Five of the group had malaria, two had diarrhea, and six had tropical ulcers. All twenty-eight had suffered minor cuts, abrasions, and fungus. One of the two chiefs was hysterical and suffering from seasickness and needed to be quieted down with some codeine.

Moose Hornkohl described the comical actions of the natives on board *Gudgeon*. "Not a one of them was over five foot tall. Them little suckers would run over the deck plates which were hot from the engines and they would just haul ass. We would try to give them shoes, but they'd take them off in ten minutes." [56] Before the rescue of the men on Timor, the crew was finding the food on the submarine monotonous. It was the same thing day after day, or so it seemed. The cooks were really given a hard time. The men seemed to do nothing but bitch. Then the twenty-eight evacuees came on board and absolutely ravaged whatever food they were offered. The half-starved men were comparing *Gudgeon*'s meals to the best Christmas dinners they had ever eaten.

Shortly after the rescue while the submarine was in a dive one of the natives disappeared. Arthur Barlow said that after a dive off the west coast of Australia, while in rough waters, one of the tough Timorese natives could not be found. The men on board began searching everywhere, even on the bridge, but the little warrior was apparently lost. To everyone's relief, he was located in the forward torpedo room head. The door to the head had swung shut on him, trapping him within, a victim of his world's lack of technological development. He did not know how to open the door.

The newcomers were amazed at the way that the submariners could walk around on board, coffee cup in hand, having no problems whatsoever with balance. The evacuees were so weak and exhausted they were having a hard time even standing up, let alone undertaking more complicated maneuvers such as balancing a cup of coffee. The hardships the commandos had endured helped the men aboard the boat put things in perspective; they understood more fully the sacrifices of others engaged in the fight against the Japanese. Serving on submarines had some distinct advantages. There were breaks between patrols, the food was the envy of the Navy, they had showers, changes of clean clothes, medical equipment, air conditioning, and, of course, there was extra pay for submarine duty.

The submarine was now packed with ninety two men, well over capacity. After forty-four days of breathing and rebreathing air that smelled like diesel fuel, stale and lit cigarettes, sweat, and all the other myriad and nauseating odors found in the small confines of the air-conditioned boat, *Gudgeon* once again headed for Fremantle. Exposure to men with jungle diseases was not desirable, but after taking one look at the forlorn souls, none of the *Gudgeon* sailors complained.

The weather turned for the worse. The sea swells were mainly from the west and were becoming more and more ominous looking. The waves heaved into watery skyscrapers overlooking the submarine and then disintegrated into tons of seawater that completely enveloped *Gudgeon* and the men on deck. A sea this tall was quite dangerous to anyone on top, exposing them to the risk of being swept overboard. By the sixteenth the wind was very strong, and the sea even heavier, now coming in from the south. On the surface *Gudgeon* was only able to make about nine knots on two of her engines.

It was a day such as this that Moose Hornkohl found himself on watch conversing with Lieutenant Sigmund Bobczynski, veteran of the boat's first six war patrols. As Hornkohl recalled, "Me and Mr. Bob were taking in some green sea when he called in two of the four lookouts, because the sea was so damn rough. I'm talking and we took a big green one, and I said, 'Boy, that was a rough one, wasn't it, Mr. Bob? Mr. Bob? Mr. Bob'."[57]

Bobczynski was nowhere to be seen. Now very worried about the missing young Lieutenant, Hornkohl continued to search the seas and yell. Bobczynski had been washed completely off the bridge and was hanging on a rail behind the cigarette deck, where the men on board would go to smoke on days much calmer than this one. As he was being carried out to sea, he grabbed onto the rail and thus avoided being washed into the ocean. Rescue would have been impossible. But, as luck would have it, it was not Sigmund A. Bobczynski's time to go.

The SS-211 reached port on February 18, 1943, and moored alongside the submarine tender *Pelias*. *Gudgeon*'s sixth war patrol was in the books. Once ashore, Lieutenant Frank Holland received a personal communiqué from General Douglas MacArthur thanking him for his work on Timor. Holland could not help but think of the Timorese, so vulnerable and still ashore under Japanese occupation. He was pleased that as the commandos were moving across the island for *Gudgeon* the villagers would oftentimes move into the bush only returning after the Allied soldiers left the area. The Timorese knew the soldiers were leaving the area and that soon it would be just the Japanese that they had to deal with. Why help the Allies, knowing that they could be punished later by the Japanese? Holland understood the actions of the natives, knowing that if they were found to have assisted the Allied commandos they could be beheaded, at best they would "only" have their crops and home destroyed. No matter how hungry the men were when they passed through the vacated villages, they refused to loot the empty homes for food and made certain that they left the areas as quickly as possible.

Shirley Stovall did not fare as well with his superiors as Frank Holland had done with General MacArthur. In his report, Lieutenant Commander Stovall noted that *Gudgeon* had seen only six ships in fifty-three days at sea, a disappointingly small number. What is even more surprising is that they were all naval vessels; there was not a merchant ship in the bunch. The enemy ships included a submarine, a destroyer, and four patrol vessels, including the tough little monster that had jumped *Gudgeon* off Ambon. Of the six, only two had been deemed potential targets. In his report, Shirley Stovall praised the small enemy craft, noting that the ships he ran into had excellent sound gear. He said he believed the would-be assassin of the twenty-sixth had, for unknown reasons, set his depth charges much deeper than usual 250–300 feet. The fact that the Japanese had bombed so deep must have sent a shudder throughout the ranks of the Silent Service because United States submarines of the day had been going deep and successfully avoiding Japanese depth charges the entire war. The enemy vessel nearly sank *Gudgeon* at this depth; the possibility that the Japanese had started routinely bombing deeper posed a serious threat to American submarines. Stovall said that he evaded attacks by using silent running and deep submergence. Once an attack was made, the lieutenant commander made radical turns at high speed using the confusion caused by the exploding depth charges as cover. He saved much praise for the officers and crew for their conduct during the poundings they had received: "This crew, after having had some 123 depth charges dropped on them, take it as routine and a thing to be expected."[58]

The *Gudgeon*'s commanding officer was very pleased with the performance of the SD radar, but only two plane contacts were made by radar, at eight and fourteen miles. The crew's health was not so good. One man had gonorrhea, while others suffered with German measles and fever as well as acute prostraititis and tonsillitis. Stovall and the men were rightly proud of the success of their two special missions. The bravery of the men who had twice gone ashore to rescue the commando groups could not be overstated. Stovall recommended Moose Hornkohl, Pappy Low, Guts Foster, and Ray McKenna for the Navy and Marine Corps Medal for their courageous rescue of the twenty-eight desperate men from Timor. The decorations were approved, and the four men's names were added to the fast-growing chart on the wardroom bulkhead. It would seem that Stovall should not be criticized for having not fired a torpedo, for, as he noted, he only sighted two potential targets, but this was not the perspective of his superiors.

While at Fremantle, the refit crew installed SJ radar and 20-mm guns forward and aft. Despite the heavy depth charging, examination of the underwater portion of the hull revealed no structural damage to the rudders and shafts. No derangements of the torpedo tube doors or shutters were noted. *Gudgeon* was re-ballasted. The crew on *Gudgeon* had used twenty-two sick days, which was noted by A. R. McCann, the Commander of Submarine Squadron Six to be "somewhat more than average."[59] McCann, in

Gudgeon's first endorsement of the sixth war patrol, indicated that the high number of illnesses might have been a reflection of the sagging morale on board, a consequence of the lack of contact with enemy ships. Twenty-two days off for the seventy plus on board over a period of fifty-four days, under the physical and psychological demands of war does not seem excessive, but it was for the tough young men of the Depression. McCann voiced no criticism of Stovall and was quite complimentary of the officers and crew for the success of the two special missions. McCann made note that the depth charges off Ambon were set to explode much deeper than usual and agreed that it was a matter of "especial interest as Japanese depth charges have been usually set to explode at considerably shallower depths than this in the past."[60]

A few months later, in June 1943, Congressman Andrew Jackson May, the sixty-eight-year-old Chairman of the House Military Affairs Committee, would return from a visit to Pearl Harbor where he had received many operational and intelligence briefings, then held a press conference at which time he reported that American submarines were surviving at such a high rate because the Japanese were setting their depth charges to explode at too shallow a depth. Amazingly enough, the press associations in the United States ran the story. An article was even printed in Honolulu of all places. Admiral Charles Lockwood was fighting mad. After May's breach of security, Lockwood said that the Japanese reset their charges to go deeper, and that, as a result, ten submarines and eight hundred men would be lost. This unfortunate incident, however, did not cause *Gudgeon* to be bombed at such a deep depth on the sixth war patrol. The patrol concluded in February 1943, three to four months *prior* to Congressman May's indiscretion. Indeed, the fact that *Gudgeon* was bombed so deeply before the blunder seems to suggest that the Japanese were already experimenting with greater depth settings.

By the time *Gudgeon* had reached Fremantle, Executive Officer Dusty Dornin and Shirley Stovall were at each other's throats. Dornin was of the opinion that Shirley Stovall had lost his fire and was quoted as saying, "Stovall won a couple of Navy Crosses and wanted to go home. I put him on report for not being aggressive enough. Al McCann who was serving as the temporary Commander of Task Force Fifty-One felt he should have penetrated Davao Gulf like Freddy Warder had done. So did I. We had not shot a single torpedo on this patrol, and we'd gotten hell knocked out of us. The upshot was, they relieved us both."[61]

A second endorsement, also by McCann, was critical of Shirley Stovall's performance. This endorsement was signed by McCann on February 27, 1943, five days after McCann's first endorsement. McCann said that, "The conduct of this patrol does not compare favorably with the aggressive standard set by this submarine during her two previous patrols."[62] Specifically, his criticisms were that Stovall failed to thoroughly patrol the Gulf of Davao, Talamo Wharf, and Davao City. McCann was certain that Stovall should also have reconnoitered and photographed the Kai and Tanimbar Islands as well as the north coast of Timor to determine the extent of enemy activity. McCann thought that Stovall had spent too much time in the area off Cape San Agustin.

A review of Stovall's war patrol report and other sources seems to justify some of the criticism. *Gudgeon* patrolled Cape San Agustin from January 17 through January 20. *Gudgeon* had headed to the area because an intelligence report indicated that a tanker was headed toward the Cape, but the tanker was never observed. On the twenty-first, Stovall penetrated the Davao Gulf where he remained for part of a day. He then took *Gudgeon* further to sea and patrolled outside the entrance to the gulf for two additional days. McCann felt that Stovall had *Gudgeon* too far off the entrance to have much chance of finding Japanese vessels in the area. On January 24, Lieutenant Commander Stovall headed the submarine toward Ambon where he patrolled until the twenty-sixth when *Gudgeon* was rocked severely by the small sub-chaser. After the four-hour encounter, *Gudgeon* patrolled off Ambon Bay until January 31 at around 1900 when Lieutenant Commander Stovall was ordered to head for the Banda Islands. McCann understood that due to the possibility of oil and air leaks, *Gudgeon* had rightfully headed to safe waters for repairs, but seemed to have an issue with the fact that *Gudgeon* patrolled forty miles off the entrance to Ambon Bay. Dusty Dornin said that late on January 31, *Gudgeon* was ordered to thoroughly explore the Banda Sea which contains the Kai and Tanimbar Islands and the north coast of Timor, locales that Stovall was criticized for not having explored extensively. The war patrol report indicates that late on February 1,

Stovall followed orders to proceed to Kai Island. *Gudgeon* remained in that area until February 4, when she was ordered to Saumlaki Bay off one of the Tanimbar Islands. *Gudgeon* was then ordered to patrol north of Timor on the sixth where she remained until the eighth when Stovall decided to terminate the patrol. Those plans were changed when *Gudgeon* was ordered to pick up the commandos off nearby Timor.

It is impossible to tell from the war patrol report exactly how close and thoroughly *Gudgeon* patrolled the areas that she was supposed to explore, but other than, perhaps, the Talomo Wharf and Davao City it appears that Lieutenant Commander Stovall took the submarine into the areas that he was later criticized for having not explored closely enough. Determining whether Stovall had thoroughly explored the areas was best done by Stovall, Dornin, and McCann, however. His patrolling must have been ineffective. Of patrolling in World War II many former shipmates of Shirley Stovall have said that if a commander really wants to find ships [to shoot at] he can. And, the fact remains that on *Gudgeon*'s sixth patrol the men on *Gudgeon* did not sight a single merchant vessel. However, none of the *Gudgeon* submariners interviewed for this book was aware of the tension between Dornin and Stovall at the end of the sixth patrol, nor should they have been. In fact, they were very surprised to hear of it. If they had known of the feud, the morale on the submarine would have been seriously compromised.

It seems nearly certain that Shirley Stovall was aware that the locales McCann wanted *Gudgeon* to thoroughly patrol were supposed to be rich with merchant shipping. Why did he not do so? Was Lieutenant Commander Stovall, who had asked to be relieved of command after the fourth patrol, losing his nerve? Were there any signs that the stoic All-Navy Stovall was experiencing overwhelming stress from the pounding of the depth charges *Gudgeon* had suffered since he stepped on board, as well as the other profound demands his command required of him? No, according to all of the *Gudgeon* submariners who were interviewed for this book, that is, except for Art Barlow. Barlow said he felt that Stovall was showing signs of either a physical disorder affecting his digestive system or perhaps a somatic disorder brought on by stress. He remembered the skipper standing on deck for very long periods belching in an attempt to relieve stomach upset and distress. Admiral Charles Lockwood's policy was to give submarine captains a rest after five war patrols. Stovall had completed three patrols, which was one more than any *Gudgeon* skipper had completed up until the time of his departure.

Perhaps Stovall was suffering from severe stress once again. Perhaps not. He kept *Gudgeon* from being sunk by the Japanese off Ambon, and made certain that she would live to fight another day. He then performed the difficult pickup of commandos on Timor. *Gudgeon* was awarded her sixth straight Battle Star signifying her satisfactory performance on the patrol. It is obvious that Navy brass did not have particularly serious concerns about Shirley Stovall as a submarine commander. After leaving *Gudgeon* he was sent back to the States where he was immediately named commanding officer of *Darter*, which was already under construction. In July he was promoted to the rank of commander.

Dusty Dornin was also transferred off *Gudgeon*. The reasons for his transfer seem rather clear. He had done six war patrols. It is likely that both men were overly tired and in need of rest. Another source said that it was *Gudgeon*'s new skipper, William S. Post Jr., that had Dornin transferred off the submarine, an action which angered the short-fused Dornin. Once ashore, Dornin's reputation as the Navy's top TDC operator would make him just the man to start a TDC school. Compared to the demands of a war patrol, Dusty Dornin probably greatly benefited from the relative calm of instructing young officers on shore and hated it immensely.

Of the stresses of war patrolling, Dusty Dornin commented " . . . depth charging has a great psychological effect on the crew and on the officers. For a period of a week, or even a month sometimes, any slight noise will upset you or make you jumpy, so to speak. The younger the man is the quicker he is able to throw this more or less condition off. The older he is, including officers and men, the longer he feels that—remembers the depth charge."[63] At the time of *Gudgeon*'s sixth patrol, Shirley Stovall was thirty-five years old.

It is not surprising that *Gudgeon*'s two senior officers were in need of a bit of time off; the strains of leadership under wartime conditions were tremendous. What is also not surprising is that both men were very quickly blended back into the active submarine service. Submariners as a group were very tough-minded individuals. After the war Admiral Thomas

Withers said that the Bureau of Medicine and Surgery had noted that submariners had only one-third of the number of mental health issues that the next best type of vessel experienced. He was certain that this was due to the careful selection process and high morale on most submarines.

After six war patrols *Gudgeon* had been credited with sinking eleven ships for 84,000 tons, two numbers that placed her at or near the top in both categories. Shirley Stovall returned home. To the folks in his hometown, Picayune, Mississippi, Shirley Stovall was a war hero. An article from Stovall's hometown newspaper proudly proclaimed that a hero had returned from war. A photo of Stovall landing at a local airport accompanied by his beautiful, raven-haired young wife Elizabeth, grabbing her hat to keep the wind from blowing it away, appeared in the paper. The local Rotary Club announced that because of Shirley Stovall, the men on the USS *Gudgeon* would be the recipient of a cash contribution.

The local paper was not the only one to notice the exploits of Lieutenant Commander Stovall. It is ironic that after not having fired a single torpedo on the ship's sixth run, a story ran nationwide entitled "10 Shots— 10 Japanese Hits."[64] In it, Lieutenant Commander William S. Stovall Jr., commander of an unnamed submarine, was highly praised for having fired ten torpedo shots, and achieving ten hits on Japanese ships. There was actually one miss, the author explained, which kept on traveling, finally hitting an unintended target. Of the ten hits, *Gudgeon* had sunk seven ships, damaged two, and probably sunk the tenth ship. Stovall was quoted as saying, "We had a team there, that's the principal reason for our success. The executive officer was particularly outstanding, and, for that matter, so were the diving officer and every other officer and man on the boat. They knew their jobs. The credit belongs to them, so please keep the 'I's' out of this story."[65] The article continued, discussing one of the attacks during the flurry of attacks: "Another attack came just at lunch time. Fifteen minutes later, Lieutenant Commander Stovall remembered that he had not eaten. He called down to the commissary officer and asked, 'How about some lunch?' To that, one of the men on the ship drawled, 'Looks like the 'Old Man' has to eat, whether he's going to sink or not'."[66] The "10 shot" story, which was known to be untrue by the Navy, made a good propaganda piece, however, and Stovall was considered to be one of the stand-outs of the submarine service. The actual firing statistics for *Gudgeon* during Stovall's first two patrols are identical. On the fourth and fifth patrols Stovall fired fifteen torpedoes each run, recording nine hits, for a total of thirty torpedoes fired and eighteen hits.

For the seventh patrol *Gudgeon* would have her fourth skipper, Lieutenant Commander William S. Post Jr. He had just been canned while serving as executive officer aboard the oversized and outdated *Argonaut* for having been insolent to his commanding officer, who had not been aggressive enough to suit Post. If the Navy was looking for a new man to rekindle the fighting spirit on *Gudgeon*, they had found the right one. The crew of *Gudgeon* would learn this very soon on the next patrol.

During *Gudgeon*'s sixth patrol an article in Webster City's local newspaper announced that Mary Clelland Ostlund, mother of William C. Ostlund, would be heading to Annapolis, Maryland, to attend the wedding of her son to Peggy Burrell of Indianapolis. The wedding took place on January 5, 1943, at the Naval Academy chapel on the same day as Bill's commissioning ceremony into the Navy.

Seventh War Patrol • Approximate Course • March 13–April 6, 1943

▪ 7 ▪

Wild Bill Wild Patrol

SEVENTH WAR PATROL: March 13, 1943–April 6, 1943

When an enemy thinks a design against him improbable,
he can always be surprised and attacked with great advantage.
It is true, I must run great risk;
but no gallant action was ever performed without danger.

John Paul Jones

After *Gudgeon*'s refitting was completed on March 4, Lieutenant Commander William S. Stovall Jr. and the other officers reported aboard, discharging the relief crew from their responsibilities. Bill Post boarded on March 6, 1943, and relieved Shirley Stovall. Also departing were Lieutenants Harmon B. Sherry and Sigmund Bobczynski. Bobczynski had reported for duty on *Gudgeon* before she was launched and had ably served on the submarine's first six patrols. Sherry had served for all of the Stovall patrols. Dusty Dornin had already been transferred, in a huff, on March 1.

It is not entirely clear why Dornin and the others were transferred off the *Gudgeon*. It may be that Dusty Dornin and Sigmund Bobczynski felt in need of a change after fifteen consecutive months of wartime service. The relief of Lieutenant Commander William Shirley Stovall Jr. on March 6 by Lieutenant Commander William Schuyler Post Jr. does not seem surprising in light of Stovall's just-completed "zero patrol." However, the fact that he had not sunk a ship by itself was not sufficient reason for him to have been relieved. At about the time that *Gudgeon* was on her sixth run, from October through December 1942, there were twenty-four war patrols run out of Brisbane, Australia, including *Gudgeon*'s fifth and sixth patrols. Of those twenty-four patrols, on only nine occasions did a skipper receive wartime credit for having sunk even a single ship. Sixty-two percent of the time the commanders returned with no sinkings. Of the fifteen times a submarine returned to base with no kills, on only three occasions was the skipper not in command on the subsequent patrol, Stovall (after *Gudgeon*'s sixth) being one of the three.

Therefore, it seems safe to conclude that Shirley Stovall did not leave *Gudgeon*—at least not solely, anyway—because he had not sunk a ship on his final patrol. This would seem especially certain because he had just run up some impressive numbers on the fourth and fifth patrols, winning the Navy Cross after the fourth and having been credited with three kills for the fifth. It seems that he would have earned plenty of cushion which would have allowed him to survive criticism for his goose egg on the sixth patrol.

So, the question is, "Why was Shirley Stovall relieved?" It seems likely that whatever stress-related problems Stovall had after the fourth patrol, at which time he asked to be relieved because he was "cracking up"—combined with the fact that *Gudgeon* had only *seen* six vessels on a fifty-three-day patrol, none of which were merchant ships, as well as the fact that *Gudgeon* had undergone a very close depth charging off Ambon, combined with Dusty Dornin's accusation that Shirley Stovall had not been aggressive enough, were *all* taken into account to "do Stovall in." In short, brass probably decided that Shirley Stovall needed a rest. It is easy to see why this was so, if it is true. It is understandable that Stovall's superior officers may have concluded that this was a necessary step, and that by insuring that Stovall was relieved from the stresses of war for a brief period of time, benefit might be gained for Stovall and for the war effort.

During Stovall's three war patrols *Gudgeon* had patrolled a whopping 160 days and had been on the receiving end of around 123 depth charges and bombs. If that would not make a skipper—burdened with all the pressures of command—a candidate for R & R, then nothing would.

Arriving with Bill Post for their first patrols aboard the USS *Gudgeon* were three Lieutenants, Maurice W. "Mike" Shea, who would serve as Executive Officer and Navigator, C. B. Pierce, and Donald R. Midgley, who would serve as the Assistant Engineer and Commissary officer. Staying aboard were the old faithfuls Lieutenant Albert Strow—now the Torpedo and Gunnery Officer—Tex Penland, Communications, and Webster R. Robinson, the Engineering Officer.

Bill Post was born in Los Angeles in 1908 in the area of town that is now known as Hollywood. He enlisted in the Navy in 1925, took the fleetwide exam, and did well enough to be admitted to the Academy at the age of eighteen, on August 14, 1926. It was not family connections that helped Bill Post be admitted into the Naval Academy. He got in strictly on merit.

While at the Academy, Post participated in many intramural activities, including football, crew, and boxing. He especially liked boxing, competing intercollegiately for two years. His affection for pugilism would surprise none of the men who would sail with the aggressive young officer on the *Gudgeon*. His senior-year bio in the Academy's yearbook, the *Lucky Bag*, described him as "gifted with an unusual amount of determination, which is a proper quality for a fighter. In the ring he gives and takes like the man that he is . . . ."[1]

Yet Bill Post was not just a scrapper. He would become a very well-liked, even idolized skipper to the men who served under him during the war. His *Bag* bio hinted at this, describing his demeanor at the Academy, " . . . his smiling face was gracing the halls of Bancroft, and it would require more than a hard battle with academics to erase this natural facial expression."[2]

He graduated from the United States Naval Academy in 1930 and then served on four surface vessels, until finally being sent to New London for submarine training in 1935. After graduating, he was assigned to his first submarine, the *R-11*. He next served on *Shark*. In May 1941, just prior to the outbreak of war, Post became Executive Officer of the *Argonaut* under the command of Lieutenant Commander Stephen G. Barchet, Class of '24. Post had military greatness in his genes, being the grandson of Philip Sydney Post, a Union general who won the Medal of Honor in 1864 at the Battle of Nashville. His father interrupted a promising Civil Engineering career to serve in World War I.

The circumstances were not favorable for the young aggressive officer from Los Angeles. The *Argonaut* was a huge, old submarine built for minelaying duties. In fact, the *SS-166* was the only submarine in United States history to be built primarily for the purpose of laying mines. The ship was

381 feet long and almost 34 feet on beam. The submarine's engines never worked as they were designed. They were designed to do 21 knots, but were only able to attain 15. Furthermore, the *Argonaut* dove slowly and was difficult to maneuver because of her great size.

To make matters worse for Post, Barchet, and the others on *Argonaut*, she was only equipped with four torpedo tubes on the bow and a complement of twelve torpedoes in all. *Argonaut* had no stern tubes. In short, the boat was ill-equipped to carry the war to the Japanese after the attack at Pearl Harbor.

When the attack occurred, Barchet, Post, and the *Argonaut* were patrolling off Midway Island with Mike Fenno's *Trout*. On the day of the attack, Barchet ordered *Argonaut* to approach what was believed to be an invasion force off Midway. Barchet was certain that the Japanese force would include escorts, which would sink *Argonaut* once the huge old minelayer let loose with her four tubes should he decide to attack the invaders.

However, the invasion force turned out to be a couple of destroyers that were inflicting significant damage on the island. Following the attack doctrine of the day, Barchet made a submerged sonar approach and failed to get close enough to the destroyers before they withdrew. The fact that an attack could not be set up was a huge letdown for the adventuresome Executive Officer, Bill Post, and the future Medal-of-Honor-winner, Dick O'Kane, or Ichabod O'Kane as he was known on *Argonaut*. O'Kane wrote after the war that all hands on *Argonaut* were faced with feelings of great disappointment because they had not been able to get a few licks in on the enemy on December 7. The fact that *Argonaut* was built to lay mines, not attack enemy vessels, created the circumstances for the discord that would develop between Bill Post and his commanding officer, Stephen Barchet. When Post heard of Barchet's decision not to attack, Post sarcastically asked, "Don't you think we ought to at least put up the periscope and take a look?"[3]

Barchet was infuriated by the taunt, and once ashore, sent a letter to brass recommending that Post be disqualified from submarines. He was not, instead being transferred to shore duty. It is unknown what effect the events had upon Bill Post. Given his nature, the transfer to Al McCann's staff at Submarine Squadron Six probably amounted to the equivalent of Chinese water torture. However, McCann must have been impressed with Post because before the year was up, Post would be sent back to sea as executive officer aboard *Seal*, and then as Exec for Lieutenant Commander "Moke" Millican on *Thresher*. Post would say later that he learned most of what he needed to know as a submarine skipper under the aggressive Millican.

Stephen Barchet was transferred also, but not before he received a Letter of Commendation on April 2, 1942, from Admiral Thomas Withers, who praised him for demonstrating a "keen sense of your responsibilities in maintaining the long and effective patrol. The *Argonaut* had returned from patrol without having suffered any injury or damage to personnel or materiel." He concluded, "The Commander Submarines, Pacific Fleet takes pleasure in congratulating you on your performance of duty as Commanding Officer of the *Argonaut* during your first war patrol."[4] In other words, Admiral Withers was going public with his endorsement of Barchet's actions off Midway Island, Bill Post notwithstanding. Barchet was then promoted to Commander and took over as commander of Submarine Division Thirty-Two.

Stephen Barchet's caution was validated when on her third war patrol on January 10, 1943, *Argonaut* intercepted a Japanese convoy returning to Rabaul and attacked. A United States bomber returning from a mission observed the attack. The encounter with the convoy would be the first and last time during the war that *Argonaut*—commanded by Lieutenant Commander Jack Pierce—would engage the Japanese in a torpedo attack. Pierce chose to attack one of the destroyer escorts, hitting it, and doing some damage. However, the destroyers counterattacked with depth charges and severely damaged the massive *Argonaut*. In desperation, the wounded submarine surfaced; the *Argonaut*'s bow broke through the water and hung high in the air at a steep angle. The Japanese showed no mercy, pumping shells into the defenseless boat, and she sank with the loss of all 105 men on board.

One would think that the sinking of *Argonaut* would have served as a sobering lesson for the gung-ho Bill Post, but if so, future events would prove that its effect was very slight. The recently promoted Lieutenant

Commander Bill Post who came aboard *Gudgeon* for the first time in March 1943 was a tiger that had not been tamed. In light of his aggressive nature, and his lineage as a descendant of a Medal of Honor winner, it is not surprising that on his very first patrol he would earn his first Navy Cross.

Lieutenant Maurice William "Mike" Shea, Class of '37, was a Cleveland native who lettered on the Navy's soccer team. His *Lucky Bag* bio was very complimentary of him, noting that he had spent two years in the Navy as an enlisted man before entering the Academy. He was described as a hard-working, sharp, "observant" man who was short in stature, but nonetheless "a big man."[5] They predicted that in twenty or thirty years he would be known as an efficient skipper, throughout the fleet. Little could the *Lucky Bag* writers have known that in only seven years, Shea would be commanding his own submarine, achieving some impressive numbers in a short career as a submarine commander at war.

What was ironic about the leadership that would be established on *Gudgeon* for the seventh patrol was that Mike Shea, the new executive officer, had been rejected just as Post had been. In contrast to Post, however, Shea was brought down by charges of *not* being aggressive enough. Shea was serving as third officer under Don McGregor of *Gar*. When *Gar* returned from her fourth patrol, McGregor was criticized for not having taken the fight to the Japanese. He did not use the five-inch gun and had only made two contacts with the enemy in thirty-nine days. Al McCann canned McGregor, Executive Officer John Fitzgerald, and Shea.

When Bill Post came aboard *Gudgeon*, George Seiler was less than thrilled. Post had served as judge at Seiler's court martial following an incident in Pearl Harbor. Seiler had been found guilty of the charges and placed on a year's probation. As soon as Post boarded, Seiler, believing that Post would have a grudge against him, put in his papers for transfer. Post called him into the wardroom and informed Seiler of his own history of having been "kicked off" *Argonaut* and stated that he himself was "no angel by any means."[6] He asked Seiler to make the seventh run with him and told him that if he wanted to get off the boat then he would allow it. He promised to never say anything about the fact that they had known each other previously. Seiler relented. The seventh patrol would go very well for George Seiler, well enough that at the end of it Post told him that he wanted to promote him. To which Seiler responded, "You can't. I'm on probation."[7] Touché.

By the time the patrol was over, Seiler had already acquired a deep respect and admiration for his new skipper: "I wouldn't have transferred off that boat for love or money, because that's the best man I ever saw."[8] In fact, Seiler said that he never knew of *any* sailor who tried to transfer off a boat skippered by Bill Post.

However, at the time, not knowing Post and having served three patrols for Lieutenant Commander Stovall, Seiler was not very hopeful for his prospects aboard the submarine as she was prepared for her seventh patrol. *Gudgeon*'s crew during the Stovall days was an experienced, proud, war-hardened group who knew their jobs and were confident of their abilities. They carried themselves as such, on board and ashore.

Yet, *Gudgeon* did not have a particularly happy crew. The skipper did not appreciate small talk, laughter, or joking, and as anybody who has ever worked in a strictly regimented, clearly hierarchical environment knows, the attitude and demeanor of the leader is infectious to those under him. In addition to Stovall's apparent lack of interest in establishing a sense of camaraderie with his men, George Seiler felt that Stovall had always wanted to be treated with more than his due share of deference. These factors combined to create uneasiness between the officers and crew.

The always-game George Seiler had enjoyed quite a break after the sixth patrol. He and several other *Gudgeon* sailors had decided to catch the diesel train out of Perth. The diesel-powered trains of the day were notoriously slow and lacking in power. When they reached a tall mountain peak, which took tremendous effort, they would often have to give up and roll back downhill again, only to work up a head of steam and try all over again.

Seiler and his shipmates decided to get off at Kalgoorlie, several hundred miles east of Perth. As George Seiler recalled, Kalgoorlie at that time had about six small hotels with pubs on the ground floor. None of the hotels was over three stories high. They were all compacted within a small, three-block area. The reason for the great number of hotels in the very small town was due to the presence nearby of many large gold mines. The area was known as "The Richest Mile in the World." George Seiler recalled that the miners around The Mile were hearty drinkers. When the miners were off-shift, they had some money in their pockets, and they needed a place to sleep and drink when they made it into town.

No sooner had the three submariners disembarked from the train than a friendly, middle-aged gentleman walked up to them and exclaimed, "Am I ever glad to see you guys. I haven't seen a Yank in a long time." [9] He proudly introduced himself as, Jack the Jew. The *pickpocket* Jack the Jew. The affable Jack continued, "I don't pick too many pockets any more." He invited the men to have a brew with him and promised them that he could get them anything that they needed; all they had to do was ask. [10]

The enterprising George Seiler, a former miner himself, no doubt feeling right at home in the busy little village, promptly put in a request for a case of his favorite—Jack Daniels. Later that day as *Gudgeon* men stood around the bar in one of the local pubs, Jack proceeded to successfully pick Seiler's pocket, repeatedly extracting money, watches, and anything else of interest found tucked into Seiler's tight uniform, each time returning the items with a chuckle. Nothing like an honest thief.

Later, Seiler watched him talking to the manager of one of the local gold mines. The slippery Jack stole the man's wallet and his watch, *with* the bob that had attached it to his vest. Before long Jack the Jew told the mine operator, a Mr. Thorn, that it was about time he bought the men a round of drinks. Thorn, by now used to Jack's thieving ways, quickly responded, "Christ, Jack, give me back my wallet." [11]

It turned out that Jack the Jew was a man of many talents. He obviously had connections in the black market trade so active in those days of wartime shortages and high demand. When Seiler woke up the next morning, there was a case of Jack Daniels waiting for him. Jack was an all right guy, so thought George Seiler and his drinking buddies.

All too soon, Seiler and his crewmates had consumed, sold, or bartered the whiskey away and found it was time to return to the boat. By this time, George Seiler had grown much attached to the good-natured thief. It had been a relationship that was good for both men: Seiler got the hard stuff he wanted, and Jack got the money he needed. Each enjoyed the other's company.

At the end of leave there were seventy-five men ready to board *Gudgeon*; twenty-eight had not been on board on the prior patrol. Perhaps this shakeup in personnel was prompted by Post, sensing the decline in morale on board and the fatigued state of the crew. Whatever prompted it, a full 37 percent of the crew that would ride *Gudgeon* on her seventh run had not been on board for Shirley Stovall's final patrol.

Gudgeon departed on March 13, 1943, for Bill Post's first war patrol as a submarine commander in World War II, first having to pass through a bombing restriction lane. Accidental attacks by Allied planes on U.S. submarines were a major problem by this time. Three new systems had been implemented to try to prevent an accidental—and tragic—disaster. First, the bombing restriction zone had been established and was much appreciated by submariners. They knew that for at least as long as they were within this restricted area they could proceed unharrassed on the surface without being forced to repeatedly submerge in attempts to evade their own planes. To further protect against accidental bombings of submarines, challenges were exchanged between pilot and submarines using passwords. Finally, pilots were forewarned when American submarines would be passing through the area.

However, the patrol had a rocky start. On the fourteenth there was a fire in the forward torpedo room, not a good location to have a fire. Luckily, it was contained by the use of four CO_2 fire extinguishers. With *Gudgeon* now well at sea, Lieutenant Commander Post ordered the crew of *Gudgeon* to undertake nearly constant drilling. They practiced both day and night surface approaches on an "enemy" ship, the *Isabel*. This was followed by more practice submerged day approaches, against a British ship, HMS *Van Galen*. Post felt that the crew was in need of much training to make the intermingled men work like a team, a team that would survive the patrol and take Japanese ships down in the process. Furthermore, this was Post's first command, and he had not worked with the men who would make up the firing party on *Gudgeon*. There was much work to do. A few seconds here or there might make the difference between getting a successful kill of an enemy ship or frantically diving below to escape a barrage of depth charges. Working under Operation Order S6-43, the Commander of Task Force 51.1 gave Post and his men the following orders:

When directed about March 13, 1943, proceed via BOMBING RESTRIC-
TION LANE to EXMOUTH GULF and fuel to capacity there. Thence
proceed via LOMBOK STRAIT to patrol approaches to SURABAYA.
Thence proceed vicinity BALIKPAPAN and patrol approaches BALIK-
PAPAN and shipping routes to as far north as MANGKHALIHAT.
Thence proceed to vicinity DAVAO GULF, reconnoitering MENADO
BAY and KEKA in northeastern CELEBES enroute. Patrol DAVAO
GULF area and thence proceed to vicinity TANAO PASS and patrol
approaches to PARACALE and PORT JOSE PANGANIBAN.

Depart TANAO PASS area at dark April 24, 1943 and return to FRE-
MANTLE via east coast of MINDANAO, MAKASSAR, and LOMBOK
STRAIT, exploiting likely shipping lanes enroute.

Conduct offensive patrol against all enemy ships encountered, making
every effort to ensure the complete destruction of same.[12]

On the morning of the sixteenth, *Gudgeon* moored next to a fuel barge at
Exmouth Bay and replaced the 8,000 gallons of diesel fuel that had already been expended. This extra fuel would allow *Gudgeon* to stay on
station longer. Post allowed the men to swim while the submarine was
being refueled, then drew them together and told them of their orders,
ending by giving the men what he referred to as a routine fight talk. Post
would say later that his talks were similar to those given by a football
coach at the beginning of a game. The purpose was to "increase their self-
confidence and get them into a fighting frame of mind."[13] Yet his pep talks
were not of the firebrand variety. He spoke concisely and calmly in one
tone. George Seiler recalled that his talks were effective because he was
confident and believable.

Post reminded the crew that the ship's motto on *Gudgeon*'s Battle Flag
was, "Find 'Em, Chase 'Em, Sink 'Em," and that each crew member had a
responsibility to reach the motto's goal. The responsibility of the lookout
was to find them, "the engineers and electricians to keep all the equipment
in first class condition" and give the boat the power needed to chase them,
then the "torpedomen and the firing control party to actually do the work
in firing the torpedoes and sink them."[14]

On St. Patrick's Day *Gudgeon* was running on the surface holding general drills, practicing day and night battle-surfacing, as well as target practices. The Navy's newly provided flashless ammunition didn't seem to be any less visible than the old powder. Indeed, Post thought it was far inferior to the flashless powder used by the Japanese: "When the Japanese used the stuff it looked as if they were 'flashing a signal or search light at us and the next thing we knew bullets were breezing over our heads." [15]

Unfortunately, on *Gudgeon*'s first dive, the three-inch telescopic deck gun sites flooded, rendering them useless. Gunnery Officer Albert Strow and Chief of the Boat Gunner Ogden took it upon themselves to do something about the problem, working well into the evening many nights in a row on the dark deck of *Gudgeon*, until they created a jury-rigged, wire gun site. According to war patrol reports from the first six patrols, the deck gun had never been used in the heat of battle, but Strow and Ogden wanted to play it safe and make certain that the gun at least had some kind of sight on it in case it was needed. Perhaps after meeting Bill Post, they could tell they would.

By this time in the war, George Seiler and the rest of the men on *Gudgeon* were growing weary of the kindly, gentle roughneck, Harry Nickel. Nickel had taken an interest in the poker games on board, but he didn't know how to play, and finally begged Seiler to teach him the rudiments of the game, which George, perhaps eyeing his friend Nickel as a potential sucker, gladly did. For the next few days, whenever there was time off, Seiler and Nickel would sit down and play.

Before long Nickel was actually joining in on the money games, and immediately the lucky Nickel was cleaning the crew out. Nickel's good fortune was not confined to poker games in the crew's mess. The *Gudgeon* crew would gamble on anything. They had ship's pools, betting on the exact minute the last line would be thrown off the cleat when the boat would leave port, or the exact minute when the first line was secured upon their return. Harry Nickel won them all, or so it seemed. He accrued quite a bankroll, which he kept locked in *Gudgeon*'s bank vault on board. Seiler came to strongly regret his tutoring of Harry.

On the eighteenth, after being out of Fremantle only five days, Post and the *Gudgeon* were in business. They had received Intelligence Serial

Forty-Six reporting that 85,000 tons of merchant shipping were somewhere around Surabaya. Post abandoned his original plans and proceeded via the most direct route toward Surabaya.

On March 19, while steaming toward the hot zone, the lookouts observed smoke. Post dove too close on a small craft about one-hundred-twenty feet in length, either an antisubmarine vessel or a Q-ship, not unlike the little devils that Stovall and Grenfell had encountered on earlier patrols. Post decided that there was too much "big game" in the area and declined to get tied up with this "small fry."[16] He surfaced and entered the Lombok Straits on a course past the islands of Java and north into the Java Sea south of Borneo.

It was around this time when Los Angeles High's Bill Post ran into an old high school classmate, Lieutenant Commander Barney Sieglaff, deep in the Japanese-held waters of the Java Sea. Sieglaff was skipper for *Tautog*'s sixth war patrol and had been the duty officer on *Tautog* when Pearl Harbor was attacked less than a year and a half prior. *Tautog* was the first U.S. submarine to draw blood from the Japanese when the machine gunners on deck of the moored ship knocked a Japanese plane from the sky near the submarine base.

On this day, Bill Post on *Gudgeon* and his former Los Angeles High classmate were talking on the surface, their submarines across from each other as they glided along. Sieglaff boasted of a few Japanese scalps from his just-completed patrol. Post, high atop the bridge of the USS *Gudgeon* used a megaphone, shouting to Sieglaff, "Nice going Barney; but you can't beat L.A. High."[17] The August 28, 1943, *New York Times* article which recounts the incident doesn't say how Sieglaff responded, but the exchange was one of the more unusual ones held in that part of the world on that day. It must have provided some relief; an illusion of safety to each of the war-weary skippers that even out there, in waters dominated by their ruthless foe, was an old pal from high school.

On the twenty-second the lookouts sighted a sea buoy off Surabaya. Hoping it would be a magnet for Japanese shipping, Post decided to remain close by the marker. It worked. At 0618 Post bellowed, "CLEAR THE BRIDGE. DIVE. DIVE."[18]

George Seiler described the process of a World War II submarine's submergence. "The lookouts and the OOD usually fell or jumped down the ladder into the conning tower. The men were then counted to make sure that nobody had been left outside. By this time *Gudgeon's* Klaxon would have already bellowed out the diving alarm for all aboard, '*Ah-oogah, Ah-oogah*'."[19]

He continued, "Many tasks were performed simultaneously. The man on the blow-and-vent manifold opened the flood valves to the ballast tanks. The engines were then shut down, with propulsion being transferred to the electric motors. The main induction valve supplying the engines with air when on the surface were quickly secured and locked. When the blow-and-vent operator saw that all outboard valves and openings had been closed, denoted on the lighted Christmas tree board, he reported to the diving officer, 'Green board, Sir.' At precisely the same time the man designated as the bow planesman reports, 'Bow planes rigged out, Sir.' If the Captain then wants the boat to be at periscope depth, just deep enough that the periscope will still ride above the waves, he will say, '60 feet.' If the submarine is under attack, the skipper may designate, 'Level off at 200 feet.' Logically, the speed of the boat at the time a dive was ordered will influence when the submarine reaches the desired depth. The diving officer can take steps to stop the descent. It is the job of the bow and stern planesmen to maintain an angle that will not allow the boat to get away from them. The watch officers are trained to be diving officers and are only put on their own when the commanding officer discerns they can handle the job. If the diving officer thinks the angle of descent is too sharp, he may lessen it by giving the command, 'Down angle 15 degrees' thereby lessening the angle by 5 degrees from the 20 degrees it was previously. The same command may come from the captain to the diving officer and thence to the planesmen. He may put an air bubble in the bow buoyancy tank to lessen the speed of descent. Approaching the desired depth he may put a bubble in the ballast tanks or 'blow negative tank.' The trim tanks, which are smaller tanks, allow a more refined trim of the boat for staying at a desired depth. The diving officer starts this procedure after the submarine has attained the desired depth."[20]

Gudgeon's first dive under battle circumstances ended without event after about an hour, but it had been a good opportunity to put the rigorous drilling into practice. On day ten of the seventh patrol Bill Post did what Shirley Stovall's unlucky group of submariners had not done in fifty-three days on the boat's previous patrol: They sighted a merchant ship. In fact, they sighted seven maru escorted by a destroyer and one corvette-type patrol vessel. Post decided to run an approach on the leading maru and shoot two torpedoes at each of the first three ships. The corvette-type boat was on the far side of the column. The destroyer was ahead of the column on the port side. The *Gudgeon* passed 800 yards astern of the destroyer to approach the convoy.

Like a boxer, Bill Post threw a left jab at the Japanese convoy, when at 1834, from a submerged position, latitude 6-31' S, 112-53' E, he fired his first two torpedoes as skipper of the uss *Gudgeon* at the leading maru. A minute later, came a straight right hand when two more torpedoes were fired at the second maru after explosions had been "heard and felt" coming from the first ship.[21] At 1836, while waiting for the setup on the third maru, Post observed a hit on number two. She was hit amidships and seemed to lift herself up out of the water a few feet, then sit her back down leaning toward one side. "Great billows" of black smoke and debris arose.[22] The unfortunate maru listed to the starboard side and started settling rapidly, indicating an explosion beneath the keel.

At 1837, Post sent two torpedoes toward the third maru. Post saw number two settling but could not see number one at all. The bad news was that he also saw a destroyer with "zero angle on the bow" and "a bone in her teeth" less than 1,000 yards away and heading right at *Gudgeon*.[23] Post wrote in his war patrol report that he decided that it was a lot better to forego the pleasure of taking a photo or watching the sinking boats, and just go ahead and go deep, rigging for the depth charge attack that this mad dog surely had planned for him. As *Gudgeon* began her escape, more explosions were heard, probably coming from the third merchant ship. Post was certain that two ships had gone down and perhaps all three with five hits.

Evasion would be difficult. Lieutenant Commander Shirley Stovall had proved himself to be a maestro at the art of evasion. Bill Post, on the other hand, was a conductor who had not yet directed his first symphony. Nobody knew how he would do, but it was his turn to perform, with the life of every man on board dependent on his skill. Much to Post's alarm, he discovered that he had been caught against a minefield in only 190 feet of water. *Gudgeon* was once again in a very dangerous spot. With a restricted amount of ocean to move laterally and a shallow pool to go deep in, *Gudgeon* was in a precarious situation.

Over the next three hours the destroyer and the corvette took turns pounding the silent, slithering submarine. Post spent his time quietly singing to himself, maneuvering and issuing commands. The depth charges that exploded around *Gudgeon* drowned out all noise on board the submarine, jarring the men, throwing them and everything that was loose on the boat.

Bill Post preferred to have only the helmsman who controlled the boat's movements, the TDC operator, and the two soundmen who could give him information about the whereabouts of the attacker—in the conning tower during an attack. The TDC operator slept in the conning tower when *Gudgeon* was on station. During a depth charge attack he would move one level below to the control room where he could work directly with the men controlling the movement of the submarine. Post would have one of the men get blankets, a cup of coffee, a vitamin pill, and a pack of cigarettes under such circumstances.

It was during these times of intense enemy activity that Post displayed a behavior that caused George Seiler, Moose Hornkohl, Edward Hammond, and Ron Schooley to recall it later with a chuckle. As they would pass through the control room during an attack or silent running, they were sure to see Post, moving back and forth between his charts and the periscope in the conning tower or conferring with his aides, humming the submariners' favorite, "Waltzing Matilda." Whenever Post was in the control room trying to avoid an avalanche of depth charges or when slowly approaching and sizing up his prey he sang—in a low, almost inaudible tone:

... up jumped the swagman, sprang into the billabong
You'll never catch me alive, said he.
And his ghost may be heard as you pass by that billabong
You'll come a-waltzing Matilda with me
Waltzing Matilda! Waltzing Matilda!

You'll come a-Waltzing Matilda with me

And his ghost may be heard as you pass by that billabong

You'll come a-waltzing Matilda with me.

George Seiler, manning one of the torpedo rooms, underwent many depth charge attacks while aboard *Gudgeon*. Many years after the fact it was clear that he was not all that impressed by the huge explosives: "They never bothered us to the point of panic, especially the old-timers. We were all scared but not to the point of not being able to function. We all knew when they were close. As a general rule, those that were awfully close, the explosions happened so fast you didn't have time to be scared. The hull on the boat was high tensile steel. If it didn't have so much give, we would all be gone. Of course, the frames [encasing the many compartments on board] were so close together they could withstand the impact."[24]

Post verified Seiler's comments, stating that even when the depth charges were exploding very close around them, the experienced seamen displayed an almost unnerving "nonchalance," as if they were merely in a drill.[25] George Seiler explained that the most vulnerable place on a submarine was the single hull above the waterline. Down below there were water ballast tanks that "absorbed a hell of a lot more than the single hull above."[26]

However, the depth charges did not need to be particularly close to wreak havoc. One submariner explained, "If they explode near you, they'll knock you off your feet; at fifty yards they'll knock the paint off your bulkhead."[27]

The barrage continued at a rate of approximately seven depth charges an hour for three hours. It was during an attack such as this one that Bill Post again behaved in a manner that was to leave a lifelong impression on George Seiler. While Seiler was passing through the control room, with the garbage-can-shaped explosives pounding all around them, the submarine rocking, the blasts absolutely deafening, the men laying or sitting quietly in the submarine in silent running, Bill Post looked over at Seiler. Perhaps noticing a look of concern on the veteran submariner's face, he asked, "What do you want to do, live forever?"[28] George Seiler never forgot the comment or the sheer bravery that it revealed. It was this looseness under attack that set Post apart from the other outstanding skippers that Seiler served under before and after his service on *Gudgeon*. At 2319, the barrage of twenty-one depth charges was over. *Gudgeon* was still afloat and undamaged. Bill Post ordered *Gudgeon* to surface free of her newfound "friends." A message was sent to ComSubPac telling of the sinkings and the presence of a Q-ship south of Lombok.

The forward torpedo room reloaded their tubes and prepared for further action. It was now about midnight. Bill Post realized that if a ship should be sighted, a night surface attack would be all but impossible due to the well-moonlit skies. Before long the lookouts spotted smoke on the horizon, and, using just two engines, *Gudgeon* started after the telltale discharge at 0140. Only two of the four engines were available to power the boat because the other two engines were needed to charge the batteries that controlled *Gudgeon*'s electric motors. By 0450 the batteries were fully charged, and *Gudgeon* was free to roar ahead at full power, leaving behind her own cloud of smoke in her wake.

At 0655 a target was picked up on radar. *Gudgeon* submerged to begin an attack on a second convoy in as many days. Post would eventually learn that this was a very large convoy of five cargo ships, two small tankers, and two or three corvettes. Water depth was once again a problem. *Gudgeon* could not close on the surface, and the convoy was a long way off, which precluded an underwater approach. *Gudgeon* would not be able to close effectively. Post hoped that a straggler or two would stumble into his area so that he could pick them off.

What he got, though, was trouble. The Japanese had quickly picked up the *Gudgeon*. In a few moments Bill Post and the men on board the embattled submarine were once again in a dangerously weak defensive position. With only about 100 feet of water to work in, Post began evasive tactics. Seven depth charges were sent *Gudgeon*'s way. BOOM. BOOM. BOOM. BOOM. BOOM. BOOM. BOOM. Post went deeper, actually hitting the ocean floor at 100 feet but fortunately sustaining no damage. She rose to 90 feet. With that little bit of water between their prey and the ocean's surface, the Japanese had a huge advantage. With two or three ships in on the attack, the chances of sinking the gallant USS *Gudgeon* were all too high. Either the Japanese were in too much of a hurry to get elsewhere and just wanted to subdue *Gudgeon* and move on, or they were really incompetent. With a shallow pool underneath and little more than 30 feet between the top of the periscope shears and the surface, *Gudgeon* slowly moved away from the Japanese. Whether it was sheer luck or one of the first displays of the "Bill Post touch," within four hours the corvettes and the convoy were gone, and *Gudgeon* was once again safely on the surface. Post reported the sightings, hoping that other U.S. vessels could pick up where he had been forced to leave off. Whatever force was in operation, Post's incredibly good fortune continued. Sometime after midnight the next night, the lookouts sighted another ship. It was as if Bill Post had conjured up this abundance of enemy targets with his siren call, "Waltzing Matilda." Post could point *Gudgeon* in any direction and practically bump into a Japanese vessel. He ordered that *Gudgeon* be flooded down low in the water to reduce her silhouette, making it more difficult to be sighted by the enemy, and roared ahead on four engines.

Torpedoman George Seiler was on deck at the time and recalled that the ship was thought to be a "converted yacht." [29] Seiler was on the bridge with the OOD, Lieutenant Mike Shea, and told Shea that he thought the yacht was actually a destroyer. Shea responded by saying, "No George, if it was a destroyer, he'd be firing at us." [30] At about that time the Old Man, Bill Post, came topside and concurred with Shea that it could not be a destroyer because it was not firing at *Gudgeon*.

Moose Hornkohl recalled that longtime *Gudgeon* submariner, Donald Stillson, veteran of every one of the submarine's first seven patrols, was also on deck. Stillson, Hornkohl said, "had the eyes of an eagle," and was giving Post information about the Japanese ship. [31]

Hornkohl continued, "The Old Man concluded that it was an ocean-going tug" and decided to sink it with the deck guns. [32] Post then devised a plan unlike those of any previous *Gudgeon* skipper. At 0318 he ordered that his three-inch deck gun and 20 mm machine guns be manned. His plan was to get as close as twelve-hundred yards, if possible, to "sweep the decks" of the enemy vessel with the 20 mm guns and then sink him with the deck gun. [33] If the Japanese skipper turned to ram, Post would simply turn to port and open up on him.

Gudgeon began its approach on the "tug" from the starboard side, still not having seen it very clearly due to the silhouette being so indistinct in the limited nighttime light. With *Gudgeon* in a hot and overly confident pursuit, and the poor little craft getting closer and closer to Surabaya and her treacherously shallow waters—the chase continued. The soundmen on *Gudgeon* were not taking soundings for ocean depth in order to avoid letting off a ping and giving away their pursuit of the tiny vessel. They were hoping that they had not been picked up.

Post, so certain that his prey was puny and toothless, was, in reality, it being as dangerous as a hungry shark, caught on a line and being reeled in. At 0355 the unidentified ship decimated *Gudgeon*'s confidence by turning sharply to starboard at nineteen-hundred yards. Seiler was so shocked, "I damn near dived in to the water when he swerved around."[34] As the ship turned, her silhouette revealed that it looked a whole lot like, in Post's words, a "young" destroyer.[35] To compound this dangerous new development, *Gudgeon* had been lured into dangerously shallow waters, now very close ashore.

If the ship was the youngest of destroyers as Post said, it may have been one of the 2,000 ton *Kagero* class destroyers, which possessed the overwhelming firepower of six 5-inch deck guns, two machine guns, depth charge throwers, and eight torpedo tubes. The destroyer's six big deck guns could easily punch devastating holes in *Gudgeon* before the submarine's puny three-inch gun was within range.

Luckily, the Japanese ship's skipper—who had been doing everything right until the moment of exposure—seemed undecided about what to do next. The quick-thinking Bill Post, never shy with an opinion or hesitant about an action—"took the bull by the horns" and ordered that *Gudgeon* turn to starboard to train his gun battery at the destroyer.[36] He could only hope that the young pup would make a mistake.

Post had every right to be alarmed at the revelation of the ship's actual identity, and alternately called the ship a destroyer and then a sub-chaser. *Gudgeon* was caught on the surface in a gun battle with a superior ship without water deep enough in which to dive. In fact, George Seiler would say years later that the *Gudgeon*'s chances of surviving a one-on-one battle with a destroyer, under such circumstances, were about "a hundred to one."[37] Bill Post and the men on *Gudgeon* were once again in mortal danger.

Each ship then simultaneously did a "ships right."[38] The destroyer started to give chase and was now bearing down on *Gudgeon*'s stern, the

Gudgeon intent on hightailing it. But, things got worse. A misunderstanding occurred between Post and the men controlling the submarine's escape. As George Seiler explained, "We had a system rigged up. Any change of speed on the annunciators was a message to the maneuvering room to get off the diesel engines because we were going to dive. So as soon as this destroyer made the fast turn, the Old Man said, 'All ahead flank,' and, of course, the helmsman had the annunciators right there before him and he was so shook up that he changed the speed that the Old Man had designated. Of course, in the maneuvering room they figured we were ready to dive and they cut off the [diesel] engines and put the [electric] motors on the line, and here we are trying to get away from this destroyer and we've lost all speed. The Old Man is yelling, 'WHO IN THE HELL CHANGED, GET THOSE ENGINES BACK ON LINE. GET THOSE ENGINES BACK ON LINE.'"[39]

At this time, Moose Hornkohl found himself on the ammunition train. The ammunition was stored in the dinette and was being passed from man to man, fireman-style, up the hatches to be loaded into the deck guns. Post gave the order to "CLEAR THE BRIDGE. CLEAR THE BRIDGE. STAND BY TO DIVE."[40] The men on deck started hurtling down the hatch as Hornkohl was trying to hand three-inch shells *up* the hatch. Seiler remembered Hornkohl "damn near shoved one of those shells up my butt."[41] Finally, Hornkohl, not sure what to do with "five guys practically climbing down" on top of him, laid the shell down and shouted, "Ah shit, what the hell is going on?"[42]

It was then that an alarmed OOD Mike Shea told Post that they could not dive because there was only 60 feet of water to work with. Hornkohl recalled that there was only 40 feet. Diving would assure *Gudgeon*'s demise. Running submerged would make certain that *Gudgeon* would travel very slowly and make herself a fat target just below the surface.

This was the only time that George Seiler ever saw Bill Post exhibit excitement. And, for good reason. *Gudgeon* was all but lost. Bill Post's career as skipper would end partway through his first patrol. Post was no doubt envisioning the prospect that he, along with every man on board, was about to go down in this submarine off the coast of Surabaya in the Java Sea. However, Bill Post was like a cornered badger. He had no intention of being killed by this Japanese destroyer or sub-chaser or whatever it was. He wrote in his post-action report that he lined up the stern torpedo tubes with the vessel, and at 0357 from a range of about 1,800 yards let loose with four torpedoes, by "seaman's eye." [43] All four missed.

Moose Hornkohl said years later that it did not actually happen this way. Hornkohl explained that the battle was like a "Laurel and Hardy movie." [44] George Seiler—on deck—remembered somebody yelling, "Where's the target? Where's the target?" [45] The response was, "We're the damn target. He's dead astern." [46]

At about that time, Hornkohl said, "Off went four torpedoes from the stern tubes." [47] He added that Torpedoman First Class Gilbert M. "Ducky" Drake, in the after torpedo room, was feeling certain that *Gudgeon* was going to be sunk and impulsively fired the four torpedoes without Post's verbal authority. The torpedo spread was already set, the numbers having been fed into the TDC. One of the torpedoes had a premature explosion, which scared the destroyer into turning away from the submarine, allowing *Gudgeon*'s gun batteries to bear on him, his broadside exposed instead of just his narrow bow. Post surmised that in so doing, *Gudgeon* had scared the Japanese destroyer as much as she scared *Gudgeon*. The men aboard were likely thinking, "God Bless those dud torpedoes." For once, the flawed Mark 14 torpedoes had played out to *Gudgeon*'s advantage.

With the destroyer closing but now subdued, and *Gudgeon* all but defenseless moving away very slowly, Post realized it was time to dance and jab. He knew that his only recourse was to get those diesels moving at top speed to keep the destroyer as far away as possible. By this time, Hornkohl and the others on the ammunition train had retrieved their shells and were once again trying to get them topside. It was complete bedlam. Despite the confusion, within fifteen minutes from the time that the destroyer had first turned, exposing herself, the *Gudgeon*'s gunner's mates opened up with her deck guns. The end result would be an almost three-hour deck gun battle between a submarine hightailing it for deeper water and a destroyer, "seeing red," in hot pursuit, firing all the while.

Lieutenant Commander Post, realizing that *Gudgeon* needed more speed than she had ever shown before, ordered Eli Masse and the others working the engines to "GIVE ME A FEW MORE TURNS. GIVE ME A

FEW MORE TURNS."[48] Masse yelled back that if they tried to get a few more turns out of the engines they would blow them, to which Post responded that if they did not get going faster it was not going to make any difference, anyway. So, Eli Masse fired up the boat's engines beyond their capacity in a frantic attempt to get *Gudgeon* away as quickly as possible to the safety of deeper water.

It was at 0410 that *Gudgeon* opened fire with the three-inch battery. The destroyer's 37 and 20 mm guns fired away in response to the firing of *Gudgeon*'s three-inch gun. Post said later that due to pure "luck" the *Gudgeon*'s fourth shot from the gun silenced the destroyer's after 37 mm twin-mount gun.[49] The odds were evening out a little.

Post wrote that the *Gudgeon*'s "gallant" gun crew and her "pitifully" primitive weapons were "magnificent."[50] Yet, he noted that out of sixty-seven shots, they were only able to hit their foe four times. This was because the open sights were no good at night, and the telescopic sights had been flooded ever since *Gudgeon*'s first dive of the seventh patrol. The gunnery officer had jury-rigged a gun sight with binoculars, but was never able to get it to work effectively so it was "next to useless."[51] Post said that if they had working sights, they "could, and would, have blown the sub-chaser out of the water with no strain."[52]

Bill Post did not give credit to the efforts of Lieutenant Albert Strow and COB (Chief of the Boat) James C. "Gunner" Ogden, but Moose Hornkohl and George Seiler did. They remain convinced that the roughed-out sights the men had made improved the gun's accuracy, thereby allowing for the four hits. They were also certain that if Ducky Drake had not panicked and fired the torpedoes, that *Gudgeon* would have been sunk on that March day in the southwest Pacific Ocean. The two sailors remembered clearly that Bill Post asked over the sound system, "Who fired those torpedoes?" Ducky Drake responded, "I did."[53]

Two and a half hours later, with *Gudgeon* on the surface making haste from the area, and the Japanese ship in hot pursuit, 8–9 miles to the rear, things seemed to be looking pretty good for *Gudgeon*. The speedy destroyer had been slowed considerably by the several shots the *Gudgeon* had put in to or near its engine room.

Just as *Gudgeon*'s crew was beginning to breathe a little easier, a two-engine Mitsubishi Type 97 bomber was sighted bearing directly at the *Gudgeon*. Post decided it was time to dive. He ordered that *Gudgeon* rig for depth charge and silent running. Eli Masse and the other motor machinists must have successfully gotten those few extra turns on the surface because when the submarine hit one-hundred feet submerged, they were still traveling at 11.5 knots.

Post then changed course 75 degrees to the port side and ran at standard speed for twenty minutes until the searching ship was heard. *Gudgeon* then slowed and began evasive tactics. These tactics were successful because after 2140, the ship and his bomber partner were never heard from again. The furious and at times almost-hopeless twenty-hour encounter with the destroyer and bomber was over. Post said later that the bomber pilot made a mistake when he hovered over the destroyer, giving away his presence, before starting his pursuit of *Gudgeon*. Bill Post and the USS *Gudgeon* would live to fight another day.

In his post-action report, Post did not make any mention of Ducky Drake having fired the torpedoes. Surely, it was impossible for Post to be angry with Drake. Post and the rest of the crew felt that the firing of the torpedoes and the premature explosion had saved the boat. Post said so in his war patrol report. The Skipper skirted the actual circumstances of the battle.

Seiler said that Post's report was typical of him. By making no mention of the unauthorized firing, he was protecting Drake. It was another reason that the crew would become very fond of Bill Post. Of course, Seiler added, Post probably had a more personal reason for not putting that information into the report. "He didn't want anybody thinking he was crazy enough to go one-on-one with a destroyer in shallow water."[54] The after torpedo room diary entry for the day seems to document that the torpedoes were fired by someone in the after torpedo room without authorization and reads as follows: "March 24 0130-Battle stations surface Hot pursuit of what turned out to be a Tin can. Manned 3″ gun. Four (4) fish fired aft. Two (2) by hand. We think we got at least one hit. We are the pursued now. (Are we fouled up.) Stand by for depth charges. 0905 Sighted plane. Dove. Hot as Hell."[55]

Reflecting upon the hair-raising encounter, Albert Strow wrote that "none of us went to bed for about a week and were awfully glad to get called back home."[56]

The legend of Bill Post was born by getting into a battle with a destroyer on the surface over shallow water, fighting it out furiously, and then having enough skill and good fortune to lead *Gudgeon* to safety. This guy was fierce, and just as importantly, he was bulletproof. Post could not be touched. The men felt great confidence in him. He took the Japanese on the way it should be done: Attack them at every turn. From this point on Bill Post would be known as "Wild Bill," and for good reason. Bill Post *was* wild. He was afraid of nothing. He was going to destroy every Japanese ship he saw or die trying. The men loved the attitude.

The next day, at 0612 on March 25, 1943, another Type 97 bomber was sighted five miles away at an altitude of 1,000 feet, far too close for safety. Going a couple of hundred miles an hour it would not take the bomber very long to be in a position to attack the *Gudgeon*. Once the order was given to dive, it would take about fifty seconds or so to get the submarine completely submerged, which in this circumstance would allow plenty of time for the plane to sight its target and release the bombs that were sure to follow. *Gudgeon* dove as the bomber dropped down low, beginning its approach on the submarine. Three minutes later a submerged *Gudgeon*, having rigged for such an attack, heard the first of four bombs estimated to be 500 pounders. BOOM. Then, BOOM, and BOOM again. The fourth and final bomb was heard to hit fourteen minutes after the first one. BOOM.

No significant physical damage was done, but a weary Bill Post decided that everybody was in need of some rest and that *Gudgeon* had worn out her welcome in this area, which greatly resembled the center of a jarred hornet's nest. *Gudgeon* headed for Balikpapan and a few days of rest en route. During times of relative inactivity the men on board tended to their duties but also focused on doing whatever they needed to do to get their nerves right, whether that meant resting quietly, gambling, or reading one of the books that was passed around the boat. One of the favorites of the day was the Mike Hammer detective series. Each time a sailor completed a book he handed it to the man whose name appeared next on the cover. Once a book had circulated through the entire crew, the process started all over again. The crew also listened to recorded radio shows and records.

The following day, while cruising on the surface, *Gudgeon* sighted the southbound USS *Gar*. The two submarines exchanged the usual signals with each other, each wishing the other "good luck." At about the time that *Gar* was out of sight, she signaled back wanting to know what "Patty's" phone number was. Patty was the sweetheart of *Gudgeon*'s sharp-eyed Chief Signalman Donald Stillson, who wisely decided not to share Patty's number with the men of *Gar* and instead told them to go to hell.

By the twenty-eighth *Gudgeon* had made its way to Balikpapan, her assigned area. At 1528 the top of a ship appeared. She was moving along very slowly, smoking heavily, estimated to be about 270 feet long with three seventy-five foot masts, one high stack, and a crow's nest on each of the two masts. Post decided that the ship was "too good to be true."[37] He speculated that the bombers that he had seen earlier that morning must have called in a Q-ship to try and sucker *Gudgeon* into a foolhardy attack. *Tautog* had reported seeing a Q-ship in the area. Post ordered that *Gudgeon* surface, ignoring the Japanese temptress, and head for Mangkalihat to patrol one of the routes to Balikpapan in the Indonesian islands.

By this time in the war, American submariners were growing hesitant to take on a Q-ship because they seemed to be virtually invulnerable to torpedo attack, being such shallow-draft vessels. A surface deck gun battle with them was also dangerous, because by their very nature, it was hard to determine what kind of firepower they had on deck, as the guns were kept under cover. Moreover, if the surface battle did not go well, the Q-ships had depth charge throwers. In short, they had many ways to kill you, while at the same time, making it extremely difficult for the submarine's safest tactic, the torpedo attack below the surface.

George Seiler recalled that Post once again promised the men on board a little rest. Surely they needed it. They had escaped catastrophe, and every man knew it. Such intense action takes a lot out of a man. But Lieutenant Commander William S. Post, ship magnet in hand, sighted yet *another* enemy ship in the early morning hours of the twenty-ninth. It appeared to be a huge tanker of the *Kukuyo Maru* class. With *Gudgeon* cruising toward her on the surface, the tanker opened fire with her two guns. The first salvo fell short about fifty yards, the second about fifty yards off the port beam. The *Gudgeon* continued forward, the men on the deck guns confident and fearless from their baptism under fire a few days prior.

At 0233, Post, with his bow torpedo tubes ready to go, about 2,000 yards from the 17,000 ton tanker growled: "FIRE ONE. FIRE TWO. FIRE THREE."[58] At the time of the attack the tanker was sitting on the equator, 118-18' E. Two hits were heard. The ship's screws grew silent. Post took a look and saw that the tanker was dead in the water and slowly settling by the stern, to port.

An hour passed with the tanker still afloat and continuing to fire at *Gudgeon*, using the torpedo wakes as a gun sight. Post was getting impatient. He took *Gudgeon* under the equator to the north latitudes and fired a fourth torpedo. The tanker was hit again, this time just forward of the bridge. Post dove and went "under the line" south, the Japanese firing north where the last wake had been seen.[59] He let loose with a fifth torpedo and saw a hit forward of the stack. The ship had now been hit with four torpedoes. This one would do the trick. Post said that he saw debris blowing 500 feet into the sky and the ship settling by the stern with a 45 degree angle to port.

In a gesture not reported as having been done by any previous skipper aboard *Gudgeon*, Post, ever-conscious about maintaining morale, allowed the crew to look through the periscope, one-by-one, at the sinking ship. He felt that the act "did them a world of good."[60] Post was surely not wholly satisfied at the expenditure of five torpedoes. It was a couple more than he would have liked. But Japanese tankers were important ships to sink. The fuel on board was now no longer available to power the Japanese tanks and other vehicles. Somewhere, the Japanese had been greatly weakened in their efforts at expansion. The efforts of the Marines and the Army were greatly enhanced. Lives would be saved.

At 0505 the men on the submarine watched the tanker sink to the bottom. The crew on deck were extremely pleased at the sight. The men throughout the submarine shouted their approval.

Within two hours smoke from another Japanese ship was seen. Wild Bill Post's luck was never-ending. He fired up two of his diesel engines and gave chase, foregoing a faster pursuit in order to get his batteries recharged.

Within four hours he was close enough to identify a tanker similar to the *Ogura Maru* of approximately 8,000 tons, heading south away from Mangkalihat, Borneo. At 1053, having positioned *Gudgeon* ahead of the tanker, the submarine once again submerged and began her approach. The tanker was now heading toward *Gudgeon*. At around noon *Gudgeon* was in good position to strike, and the first two torpedoes were fired. A few short minutes later the torpedoes hit the tanker, which started to sink by the stern with a 50 degree list to starboard.

By 1210 the boilers on the tanker exploded, and the crew was frantically abandoning the sinking hulk. When a boiler on a ship explodes, it is said to be a telltale sign that a ship is doomed. George Seiler described the sound as being like the rapping of a finger on a wooden desktop. The tanker was going down fast. The Japanese sailors were trying to make it into the boats that had been tossed into the water. As Post raised his periscope for a look at the sinking vessel, a large depth bomb was heard, the vibrations from its explosions felt immediately thereafter. A Japanese bomber had gotten in close on *Gudgeon*. Post ordered the submarine to go deep as five additional depth charges went off. Each having an accuracy termed "well above average," though no damage was done.[61]

It was during a pounding such as this one, with *Gudgeon* in great danger from explosions all around the boat and the men on board being thrown around like ragdolls, and very aware that the next bomb might be the one that would cause the submarine to implode, that Bill Post and George Seiler had another encounter that would be forever etched into Seiler's mind. Turning to Seiler who was passing through the control room, Bill Post winked, got a "big crazy grin" on his face, and said, "Fun, isn't it?"[62] *Gudgeon* continued its escape attempt, plunging to 250 feet.

On only the seventeenth day of this manically paced patrol, Bill Post had already fired seventeen of his available nineteen torpedoes. The remaining two were located in the unfavorable stern tubes. Post surfaced and headed toward Menado Bay to undertake task four of his operational order, to: " . . . proceed to vicinity DAVAO GULF, reconnoitering MENADO BAY and KEKA in northeastern CELEBES enroute."[63]

On the thirtieth, *Gudgeon*'s orders were changed, and *Gudgeon* was to return to Fremantle for a reload and short rest. The men on *Gudgeon* were jubilant over their flurry of sinkings. Morale was at a peak. Bill Post had made quite an impression on them. This guy was something else. And, unlike Lieutenant Commander Stovall, who was quite formal with the men, Bill Post had a way of interacting with them which made them feel like he cared about them. He had allowed them to view one of their kills through the periscope. He also had a practice of giving the men information about the goings on, announcing what was taking place on the surface over the submarine's sound system, which was another real boost to the crew's morale, making them feel that the skipper regarded them as an important part of the team. He was obviously able to find targets and seemed almost charmed. No matter how bad the predicaments were, Bill Post had gotten them out of it and sunk a host of ships in the process.

Gudgeon wove her way south through the many islands comprising the Dutch East Indies, through the Makassar and Lombok Straits, finally mooring up to a fuel barge at the Exmouth Gulf on April 3rd. Post once again allowed the crew to swim off the boat. He congratulated them for their outstanding performance and gave a brief talk ordering them to keep their lips tight once they reached Fremantle.

At 0730 April 6, 1943, the USS *Gudgeon* slowly pulled into Fremantle, Western Australia, and moored herself next to a submarine tender. This time, *Gudgeon* sported a broom strapped high to one of the periscope shears signifying that she had just made a clean sweep of Japanese shipping. A large three leaf shamrock signifying Post's good fortune adorned the starboard side of the conning tower. The furious first patrol of Wild Bill Post's career as skipper of the *Gudgeon* was over. In just twenty-two days he had seen eight ships worthy of attack. He had attacked three of them on March 22, one more on March 23, another on March 24, and two more on March 29. He claimed sinkings of three Japanese maru of 7,600, 10,500, and 8,300 tons on the twenty-second, a 17,000 ton tanker on the twenty-ninth, and an 11,000 ton tanker the same day. The boat had engaged in a deck-gun shootout with a killer-destroyer, had been depth charged with around thirty explosives, had encountered a Q-ship near the Lombok Straits and another near Balikpapan, and had encounters with Japanese bombers. It was a formidable challenge to the men and by all accounts a rousing success.

In his report, Bill Post said that all the attacks were made using the TDC, and that all torpedoes ran hot, straight, and normal, making no mention of the one that Ducky Drake fired which had exploded prematurely and scared the charging Japanese destroyer to slow down.

In his post-action report Post pointed out the defective gun sight on the small deck gun and said that it was useless, uncharacteristically discounting the fact that the crew had been profoundly brave and was able to get four valuable hits into the destroyer, slowing it down and allowing the *Gudgeon* to get away. By this time in the war, the *Gudgeon's* entire hull was vibrating. The periscopes, antenna mast, and SJ radar installation also vibrated excessively at any speed, whether submerged or on the surface. This made attack by periscope unnecessarily difficult because bearings other than "0" and "180" were quite hard to read. Somehow, Post and the others had been able to work around this. The radio and radar worked well throughout the patrol. Post noted that there were several thermal density layers at various depths throughout the area of the Makassar Straits, a vital bit of information that would be of interest to other submarine skippers charged with patrolling the area. The long battle with the destroyer around Surabaya would eventually become known by the men on *Gudgeon* as "The Second Battle of Makassar Strait." Years later, whenever any of the men wanted to get the "Old Man's" goat, they would mention the attack off Surabaya and remind Bill Post that he had forgotten to put some of the details of the encounter into his report. Such as, of course, that the ship was a destroyer, and that Ducky Drake had saved the boat by impulsively firing torpedoes at the charging Japanese vessel. Bill Post, it was said, would always get this "shit-eating grin" on his face and not say a word.[64]

Post could thank Shirley Stovall for the fact that *Gudgeon* had been so thoroughly re-ballasted before he took command. *Gudgeon* experienced no problems along those lines whatsoever. *Gudgeon* dove and maneuvered quite well during the entire patrol. On this patrol, in contrast to the previous one, only six sick days were taken, all of them by a sailor with an inflamed appendix.

Post also noted some minor difficulties, for one, an amorous sailor had picked up a case of gonorrhea while ashore. His medical status was now very apparent. For whatever reason, the reported problems with venereal disease on *Gudgeon* seemed to be relatively few compared to some of the other submarines of Squadron Six. One fellow submarine had 153 cases of venereal diseases only sixteen months after commissioning.

Post said that the food was excellent, ample in quantity and variety, was well prepared, and served "under sanitary conditions."[65] This was of no great surprise, of course, because the submarine service was well known for getting the best of the fresh fruits, vegetables, and meats. Furthermore, the boat had only been to sea for three-and-a-half weeks—too short a period of time for much of the submarine's food to spoil. In Post's first patrol report there is evidence of the leadership characteristics that would make him so beloved among the crew and officers. He repeatedly noted actions that he took to build morale and commented upon the men, their status, and their performance, thus giving evidence of his concern for the crew as people and his desire to build a submarine that was a well-functioning team of happy sailors.

Of morale he said: "Morale took care of itself on this patrol. The Commanding Officer feels that some form of recognition which enlisted men can 'show the folks back home' is essential to their continued high morale. This is particularly needed with the necessity for maintaining security of information. A little piece of ribbon would do the trick. We are making a serious mistake if we begrudge our men that small reward and then expect them to keep silent about their exploits."[66]

Lieutenant Commander Post had by this time really turned George Seiler around, from a man that almost wanted to run when he had learned that "the judge," Bill Post, was coming aboard as skipper of *Gudgeon*, to growing admiration about Post as a skipper and as a person. More than anything else, Seiler liked the fact that Post was aggressive. However, he also had a nice touch with the crew. Seiler also said, "Post knew submariners. He was so sure of himself that if he did not know something he would ask someone who did. He did not feel inferior for doing so. He was not afraid of delegating authority to someone below him. He was our leader, and he showed it. He could laugh, and he enjoyed his officers and men not only on the boat but also ashore. I never once saw anyone hesitate at one of his commands, let alone dispute it. If time allowed it, he would ask questions before he made a direct command. He was fearless, and he did not evade danger. He was the aggressor, and the crew was proud to serve under him. We loved him and had many a laugh over our drinks on the beach when we rehashed our exploits of the previous patrol."[67] Albie Strow, who admired Shirley Stovall so much that he was ready to travel through the Gates of Hell with him, was likewise becoming very impressed with the skipper from Hollywood, and referred to him after the war as "one of the finest officers I ever knew."[68]

It was not only the crew that was impressed by the unique skipper of *Gudgeon*. His initial performance played extremely well to brass. The Chief of Staff of Submarine Squadron Six, William Wakefield, noted that, "Full advantage was taken of all opportunities to attack." He recommended that *Gudgeon* be given credit for the sinking of three freighters on the twenty second of March, noting that it would be "most unusual" for the third freighter to be hit by two torpedoes and not sink. Post's running gun battle with the "sub-chaser" on the twenty-fourth showed "the commanding officer's determination to inflict damage on the enemy." Wakefield continued, noting in another attack, that despite the fact that shells from a tanker were landing around the submarine, *Gudgeon* remained on the surface, approached the ship, and opened fire, eventually sinking it. Similar praise was made for Post's marksmanship. Wakefield noted that of seventeen torpedoes fired, eleven were hits, which was a hit rate of 64.7 percent, and was considered to be, "unusually high."[69] He gave *Gudgeon* credit for five ships sunk at 35,261 tons and one damaged patrol craft.

A man can make the Hall of Fame by hitting a baseball 30 percent of the time. To hit ships one to two miles away under battle conditions, with a vibrating periscope, a rolling sea, under fire, in a life-threatening situation at a .647 clip is truly outstanding. The ratio of hits on this patrol was higher than the 60 percent attained by deadeyes Stovall and Dornin on the prior three patrols. Wakefield called it "excellent" and "highly commendable" and said that it was with great pleasure that he commended the commanding officer, officers, and crew of *Gudgeon* for an "outstanding" patrol.[70] *Gudgeon* was awarded her seventh straight battle star, signifying her outstanding performance in battle on the just completed patrol.

Admiral Ralph W. Christie, serving as commander of Task Force Seventy-One, had similar praise for Post and *Gudgeon*. Christie, who had been a defender of the flawed torpedoes, riding the tiger of criticism of the torpedoes' poor performance—which was becoming more and more well known—no doubt took great joy in noting the high percentage of hits. He added that four of the five torpedoes that missed were fired by "seamans eye." [71] He stressed the torpedoes' "excellent" performance. *Gudgeon* torpedomen still speak with pride about their work on *Gudgeon*. George Seiler commented, "Christie didn't realize we had the best torpedomen in the Navy. Torpedoes are only as good as the men who take care of them." [72]

Christie cautioned, "In any gun engagement the odds are usually against the submarine. These risks must always be accepted when they are justified by the expected gain." [73] However, Christie continued, "This surface attack was doubly risky due to the greater risks of danger incurred had the *Gudgeon* been forced to fight in shallow water." [74]

Christie continued, "The Commanding Officer, officers and crew of the *Gudgeon* have continued to exhibit that determined, aggressive fighting spirit which has been characteristic of that submarine since the war began." [75] He recommended that *Gudgeon* be given credit for having sunk four ships totaling 30,000 tons, with two additional ships damaged. He noted that *Gudgeon* had already sunk 78,400 tons and damaged 7,500 more.

Gudgeon would eventually be given wartime credit for having sunk two freighters on the twenty-second, and for having damaged a third. They would be given credit for having done damage to the patrol craft on the twenty-fourth that they hit with the "lucky" shots on the deck gun, and for having sunk a 10,027 ton tanker of the *Kokuyu Maru* class.

JANAC would later take away credit for the first sinking on the twenty-second. JANAC found enough evidence of the sinking of the stubborn tanker around the equator on the twenty-ninth. The 8,000 ton tanker attacked later that same day, which had been seen (through the periscope) to sink by the stern by the crew, was considered sunk during the war but was discredited by JANAC in later years.

The total officially credited on the patrol during the war was four ships for 29,000 tons sunk and another damaged, which was eventually reduced by JANAC to two ships for 15,000 tons. It was time once again for decorations. Lieutenant Albert Strow, with a Bronze Star already in tow, was awarded a Silver Star for "conspicuous gallantry and intrepidity as Torpedo

Data Computer Operator" for his role in sinking all of those Japanese ships.[76] Wild Bill Post would get his first Navy Cross for his work on the seventh war patrol. Post was praised for his "brilliant tactical knowledge and sound judgment" in maneuvering *Gudgeon* into attack positions and in sinking the Japanese vessels.[77]

The seventh patrol was considered by all involved to have been a complete success. The Silent Service had a budding star on its hands.

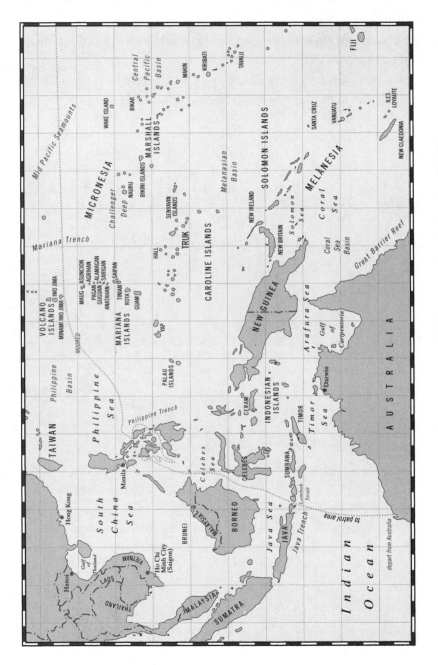

Eighth War Patrol • Approximate Course • April 15–May 25, 1943

■ 8 ■

Lieutenant Penland and the *Kamakura Maru*

Death does not blow a trumpet.

Danish proverb

Only six days after arriving at the submarine base in Fremantle for repairs, the crew of *Gudgeon* was hurried back aboard to test the repairs made by the men on the submarine tender. The seventh patrol had been so fast and furious it is likely that—even if the submarine had its full complement of twenty-four torpedoes, rather than the nineteen on board when *Gudgeon* left port—it still would not have lasted more than thirty days, well under the fifty-two day patrols of Grenfell and Stovall.

For the next run, *Gudgeon* was assigned a special mission to be undertaken at the beginning of the patrol. This mission may have explained the urgency in the preparation for the eighth patrol. There may also have been an element of, "Hey, these guys did a hell of a job on that last patrol; let's not break their hot streak." For whatever reason or combination of reasons, brass was pushing to get *Gudgeon* back to sea as quickly as possible.

The short break, however, did not keep George Seiler, now a veteran of five war patrols on *Gudgeon*, from enjoying himself. Once ashore, he trekked off to a little place in the mountains named Sawyer's Valley. As Seiler would explain later, "I loved to go to those places that are way off the beaten track because they're not acquainted with our maneuvers, you know."[1] Young George Seiler had a carefree attitude toward money, and never even bothered to learn the difference between shillings and florins. He remembered, "Hell, I just would spend the money. I didn't care. If they said it was ten shillings, I would give them a ten-shilling note. You didn't argue with them [the Australians]; you just trusted that they weren't going to fleece you."[2]

There were other reasons that Seiler didn't bother to learn the difference between a sixpence and a shilling. For one, he was certain that he wasn't going to live long enough to make the investment in time worth it. Who cares to know what a "zack" or a "deener" is, anyway, if you're going to be at the bottom of the Pacific Ocean tomorrow? In addition, he had been doing pretty well with money lately from his barbering business, and he was now a second-class torpedoman, a promotion that brought a pay raise.

One evening Seiler was quietly drinking at the local pub when Old Alf, the trustworthy man who owned the place, asked Seiler to tend bar for a while so he could run an errand. Seiler responded, "Sure, do you think I can?"[3] Alf may have considered it a rhetorical question, but it was actually a darn serious one. Since Seiler did not understand the value of local currency, there was a good chance that somebody was going to end up being short-changed. Alf, unworried, responded, "Yes, you can, they're all nice people, farmers from around here."[4] Alf probably thought George was just being shy.

The challenges for Seiler that night not only centered on his inability to comprehend the local currency. Though Australians speak English, language and cultural problems could be an issue. To give an idea of the potential difficulty: When Seiler took over the bar, he had been "drinking with the flies" (i.e., he was alone), but luckily he was "cunning as a Dunny rat" (clever). As bartender, Seiler undoubtedly feared he would appear to be a "drongo" (stupid person) and "make a blue" (mess up). He relented and told Alf "yes," knowing that before long the "cockies" (farmers) would drink so much "amber fluid" (beer) that they would be "off their face" (drunk) and "grinning like a short fox" (very happy). Nothing like a "hotel" (oftentimes only a pub) with a bunch of "cockies," "liquid laughing" or as it is also known showing the "Technicolor yawn" (vomiting), into the wee hours of the night while "going off" (having a lot of fun). As demonstrated, it sometimes took an interpreter.

At any rate, Alf, The Friendly Barkeep, hopped on a train and headed for nearby Perth. Before long the amiable farmers began to wander in, searching for an Emu, the favorite beer in the area. A gent would order a beer and then hand Seiler a ten-shilling note or two or three florins. Seiler—not knowing the difference, nor caring—would throw it in the cash register with a No Sale punched in for good measure. The cockie would say, "Boy Gee, I needs me change," to which Seiler nonchalantly responded, "You don't get any change around here, you just drink it up."[5]

Before long the place was crowded with the local characters and heavy drinkers. Smoke was everywhere, the place was getting noisier and noisier with the loud talk typically found in a drinking establishment, and beer was being purchased and drunk very quickly. Seiler remembered that the cash register sang a merry tune all night as he took each order, threw the money into the till, and never once made change. It was pure bedlam in that small Australian pub. George Seiler had no idea whether he was running a blue light special or robbing the kindly farmers of Western Australia.

Within four or five hours, Alf returned, and seeing all the cockies off their faces, and bills protruding from the cash register, shouted with amazement, "My Christ, Yank, what's going on?"[6] Seiler, having drunk his wages and being swamped all night with customers, had been as busy as "a cat burying shit," as they also say in Australia. He explained to Alf that at his bar, on this night, "You drink your change up."[7] Alf scurried over to the register, opened it, and said with glee, "By Christ, George, I haven't had this much money in the register in three years."[8] Seiler stayed in town the entire leave. The residents of the village explained to him later that it was good that he was a friend of theirs or there could have been some trouble due to the exorbitantly high rates they had paid for alcohol at the pub that night.

Years later, Ron Schooley also recalled an incident that he experienced while ashore between the seventh and eighth patrols, that was in some ways typical of that which occurred when an American sailor stopped in a foreign port during the war years. It also demonstrates the gratitude that the rescued commandos from the sixth patrol held for anybody associated with the USS *Gudgeon*. Schooley and six other *Gudgeon* submariners decided to go to a bar that the rescued Australians from the sixth patrol had claimed they frequented. They were well into the process of celebrating their status as still-living submariners when a large group of intoxicated Australian soldiers drinking close to them were heard to proclaim in loud voices their displeasure with the idea—perhaps not altogether delusional—that the American submariners in the pub had been "screwing our women." [9] The situation became more and more volatile, the Diggers making increasingly heated accusations and the Americans responding in ways appropriate to defend their collective honor. Eventually, as many of these bar confrontations do, the situation ended up with the Aussies challenging the men to a fight.

Schooley said that at just about the time the Aussies were going to come over and "whip our asses" another group of Diggers happened into the bar.[10] Luckily for the small group of men from the SS-211, this group of Aussies happened to be a cadre of the rugged and partially recuperated Australian commandos that Gudgeon had rescued from Timor in February 1943. This time it would be the outnumbered Americans that would be saved by the Australians. Schooley continued, "I've never seen such a beautiful thing. We walked into the bar and this one guy, in a thick Australian accent, said, 'Hey, Yanks, are you having any problems'?" [11] The no-longer-weak-and-decrepit-former commandoes from Timor attacked and seriously beat their compatriots for even suggesting that they were going to fight the American submariners. Then they sat down and drank some Emu with their old buddies from the USS Gudgeon.

Not only was this a very short period of rest for the Gudgeon crew but once the men reported back for duty to prepare Gudgeon for her eighth war patrol, a tragic accident would occur which would cost one of George Seiler's fellow torpedomen his life. George would be intimately involved in the incident. The death would be the first of the war for the men serving on Gudgeon. For torpedoman Seiler, it would mean another near catastrophe avoided, this time because of quick mind and reflexes.

Arthur Miller had been on Gudgeon for patrols five, six, and seven. He was by this time an experienced and valuable man to have on board. He was a young man who had proved himself to be competent even under the barrage of those horrible depth charge attacks. The accident occurred on April 13, 1943, at the submarine base in Brisbane. Seiler and Miller were in the process of loading torpedoes into the forward torpedo room at around 1 P.M. They found themselves in "the well," an area below the main deck where torpedoes were stored. Earlier in the day they had rigged for the storage of mines, the higher echelon later changing their mind and ordering that the mines be taken off the boat so that torpedoes could be taken aboard instead. The heavy, unwieldy 24 foot long fish were then hauled to *Gudgeon* on an ammunition truck. They were usually unloaded from the vehicle by attaching a cable with an O-shaped metal hook on the end around the nose of the torpedo; this time the torpedoes had been fitted with a C-shaped hook.

One of the torpedoes was hanging from a cable above the torpedo skid where it was to be placed so that it could be slowly and safely slid into the submarine. Tragically, the hook broke, causing the torpedo to be let loose. The men on deck screamed a warning. Seiler quickly dove between torpedo tubes one and two, under the lucky Buddha, and was safe. Miller was not as fast. The torpedo hurtled down the torpedo skid and pinned him to the deck, crushing his pelvis. The deck logs of *Gudgeon* indicate that Miller was transferred to the tender, the USS *Otus* for treatment of a crush injury of both thighs and shock. At first Seiler did not think the injuries were serious. When Miller started to bleed out of his penis, the extent of his internal injuries was more obvious. At 11:05 that evening, Torpedoman Third Class Arthur Howard Miller died.

After the tragic and sobering event, George Seiler, the hardened submariner, was really shaken up. The torpedo had crushed Miller's bones like a thousand-pound weight landing on a bag of ice. It was a horrible sight to see and an unnerving situation to live through. Seiler was reminded that his occupation was so dangerous that his end might not come at the end of a Japanese samurai sword or at sea. His end could come at any time, in any place—even in port loading torpedoes. When the torpedo was lifted off poor Miller and up the skid, Seiler noticed that the flesh on one of Miller's thighs had been ripped off to the bone. A half-century later the image still torments George Seiler. By this time Seiler had avoided death by losing a coin flip and avoiding the sea trials on the star-crossed *Squalus*. He had survived four war patrols and the perils those actions presented, and he had once again escaped death by diving out of the way of a runaway torpedo.

However, there was a war going on. The death of Arthur Miller, which so saddened his fellow crew members on the *Gudgeon*, had to be quickly pushed aside so that the war could be fought. Lieutenant Commander William S. Post Jr. had been ordered to direct the boat through the safe passage lanes of the Exmouth Gulf for refueling. After *Gudgeon* was fully loaded, she was ordered to first carry out another special mission—her third and final special mission of the war—and then proceed to certain assigned areas, working toward Pearl Harbor and making "every effort to assure complete destruction of all enemy ships encountered."[12]

Ten days later, Post's original orders were modified. After completion of the special mission *Gudgeon* was ordered to various points in the Philippine Islands area for patrol, to conduct a submerged reconnaissance at the east end of San Bernardino Strait, and, finally, on to the Royal Hawaiian for R & R to enjoy the spoils of war. On April 15, 1943, *Gudgeon* pulled away from *Otus* with sixteen fish, which was two-thirds of capacity. On board were four tough commandos provided by the U.S. Army, who had been chosen to carry out a special mission. They were Lieutenant Torribo Crespo, Sgt. Orlando Alfabeto, Pvt. Ali Lajahasan, and Pvt. Mangona Lajahasan. Also loaded on board were an extra six-thousand pounds of equipment. Once ashore the supplies would be the first that the Sixth Military District, the resistance on Panay, would receive from American submarines.

Making what would be his first and last patrol aboard *Gudgeon* was Lieutenant Commander Frank Lloyd Barrows, Class of '35, who had transferred to *Gudgeon* from *Gar*. He had taken over for Mike Shea who had been transferred off to board the newly constructed submarine *Raton*. Barrows, a Washington, D.C., native was nicknamed "Butch" at the Naval Academy. While a midshipman, he sang in the choir and was in "musical clubs." He was a better than average student, he liked to lift weights, and apparently liked the girls too because his friends said he liked to keep "one eye on the beach" in his free time.[13]

As usual, the tedium of slow travel to the assigned area was broken up by the necessary—but equally tedious—training and trim dives, in conjunction with other general drills and the daily chores of upkeep to the submarine that were needed in order to be fully ready for an engagement. Before long *Gudgeon* moored alongside a huge fuel barge to begin refueling at friendly Exmouth Bay. Once again, Lieutenant Commander Post allowed the men to swim beside the submarine. Among the sixty-nine young men swimming that day in 1943, smoking by the pier, laughing and clowning with their shipmates, were eleven who in just a year would be forever dispatched to waters elsewhere in the Pacific Ocean while on *Gudgeon*.

Under way on the twenty-first, things began to get interesting aboard the boat. At 1413 *Gudgeon* sighted Lombok Island, submerged, and awaited the darkness in order to slip through the powerful currents of the Lombok Strait under cover on the surface. There was no way that Post was going to attempt this passage while submerged. The currents were too strong and the Japanese patrol ships too plentiful. The men on board were ordered to keep a close eye out for the enemy. The Japanese were quite aware that American submarines preferred to run the strait on the surface during the evening hours. *Gudgeon* made it through the strait unchallenged that night, but the next night a Japanese patrol vessel sighted the submarine—once again on the surface—and challenged her with a searchlight. It is presumed that the vessel had been alerted to *Gudgeon*'s presence by a patrol plane that had sighted the submarine and attempted to close on her earlier in the day.

When *Gudgeon* did not reply to the Japanese challenge, the patrol vessel opened fire, sending four deck shots at the submarine. Post noted that the Japanese were now using the flashless gunpowder that he had heard so much about. He now knew that "It is *really* flashless." [14] Lieutenant Commander Post made no mention of it, but the torpedo crew in the after torpedo room wrote that *Gudgeon* fired five rounds from one of their deck guns, then made a "mad dash" on four diesel engines, eventually distancing herself adequately from the game little ship. [15]

By the twenty-second, Albie Strow found time to write in his personal log. Knowing that before long *Gudgeon* would be headed back to the States, things did not seem so bad to him those days. He wrote in his log that since coming aboard for the third patrol, *Gudgeon* had sunk fifteen Japanese ships, which made *Gudgeon* "the top sub in the U.S. Navy." [16] Strow also wrote of the challenges that the new officers on board were presented with when the change from Stovall to Post came about after the sixth patrol. Apparently Strow's father had expressed gloom and doom about *Gudgeon*'s chances for survival, having lost Stovall and Dusty Dornin. So much for the Silent Service. Strow wrote, "At the time we lost Dusty, we all thought and felt that at last our luck had run out on us. Cap'n Post and Mike Shea came aboard, and I became the TDC operator—the skipper was not yet qualified for command, had not fired a torpedo since he left sub school in '35. It was Mike's first time as exec or as a member of a fire control party and my first time on the TDC. Everyone on all the staffs did not give us more than a 50/50 chance of getting back from that one. But we fooled them and had the best patrol that has yet been run out of Perth and it took the least time—I guess that the 3 of us added up to one brain." [17]

Lieutenant Albie Strow was really excited about the prospect of seeing his beloved Annmarie next time he had a chance, but worried that he might be one of those chosen to stand watch on the submarine every few days once they hit port. If so, there would be no trip to the east coast to see Ann. Strow had missed getting several leaves because he had taken his break last so that others could go on R & R, only to have his leave cancelled. He was sure that "Cap'n Bill" would somehow make certain that he would get his month off "by hook or probably by crook." [18]

On the twenty-third *Gudgeon* found herself on the surface off the usually productive seas near Mangkalihat, an area that Post and the men had so enjoyed on their previous patrol. There would be no action until late on April 25. The target ship proved to be a cargo/passenger ship of about 9,000 tons. At almost midnight, Post fired a spread of three torpedoes hoping that two would hit their mark. It was then that the problem with the lousy ordinance would show itself again. Post reported that either the second or the third torpedo exploded prematurely, giving the men on the bridge quite a shower; nonetheless, one of the other torpedoes struck home. Five minutes later a loud explosion was heard, Post noted that it was not a depth charge being thrown *Gudgeon*'s way. As *Gudgeon* dove deep, he hoped the blast meant that the freighter had burst into a thousand pieces and had headed toward the bottom.

At exactly midnight, with the SJ radar poking above the surface of the sea, Post took a look. He was dismayed to see that the target ship was still afloat and underway. He ordered that three more fish be sent the freighter's way. While awaiting results of the second attack, another ship with much faster screws than the target ship was heard pounding angrily toward *Gudgeon*. Post concluded that this escort must have been on the far side of the target vessel and therefore not seen at the time of the attack. He began evasion, diving to 170 feet.

During the dive, Post heard two explosions which coincided roughly with the time that the ship should have been hit had all the calculations made before the attack been correct. Shortly thereafter the soundman reported

Gudgeon being christened on January 25, 1941 at Mare Island, California. (photo courtesy of Jane Duffey)

Gudgeon being launched at Mare Island, California on January 25, 1941.
(photo courtesy of Jane Duffey)

Gudgeon's officers at commissioning ceremony, April 1941. From left, Ensign Sigmund Bobczynski, Lt. jg Dusty Dornin, Skipper Joe Grenfell and Lt. Hylan B. Lyon. (photo courtesy of Jane Duffey)

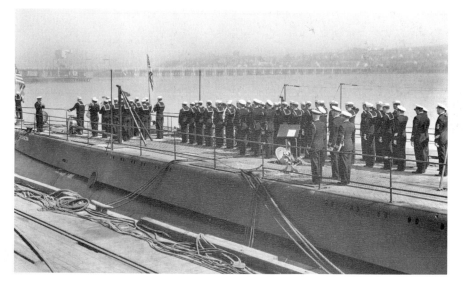

Gudgeon crew on deck of submarine at commissioning ceremony at Mare Island, California, April 1941. (photo courtesy of Jane Duffey)

Gudgeon skipper Joe Grenfell receiving the Navy Cross from Admiral Chester W. Nimitz at Pearl Harbor on April 18, 1942, for having sunk a freighter and the Japanese submarine I-73 on the submarine's first war patrol. (photo courtesy of Jane Duffey)

Pearl Harbor, October 1941. Submarine base is middle, left side of photo. (photo courtesy of National Archives)

Irvin W. "Moose" Hornkohl receiving Navy and Marine Corps Medal for rescue of Australians on *Gudgeon*'s 6th patrol. Ceremony took place on the deck of *Sealion* II, 1944. (photo courtesy of Irvin W. Hornkohl)

Gudgeon radioman John J. Sheridan on leave in July 1943. (photo courtesy of Kathleen Kimble)

1958 photo of *Gudgeon* signalman Arthur C. Barlow. (photo courtesy of Art Barlow)

Gudgeon torpedoman Ray Foster during World War era. (photo courtesy of Ray Foster)

(L to R) Lt. Webster Robinson, *Gudgeon* skipper Lt. Cmdr. Joe Grenfell and Lt. Dixie Farrell relax at Royal Hawaiian in Pearl Harbor between patrols. (photo courtesy of Jane Duffey)

Former *Gudgeon* captain, Vice Admiral Joe Grenfell conferring with President Kennedy. (photo courtesy of Jane Duffey)

Gudgeon's third skipper, William Shirley Stovall on deck of *Gudgeon* in 1943. (photo courtesy Shirley Thorup)

Gudgeon torpedoman George Seiler between enlistments at his hometown of Connellsville, Pennsylvania in 1940. Seiler fought on *Gudgeon* for patrols 3-8. (photo courtesy of George Seiler)

Australian Lieutenant Frank Holland, one of the commandos rescued by *Gudgeon* on Timor. (photo courtesy of John Holland)

Australian soldiers pose for picture after being rescued off Timor by Skipper Shirley Stovall's *Gudgeon* on 6th patrol. Only Norm Smith (front row left) is identified. (photo courtesy of John Holland)

USS Gudgeon in San Francisco Bay, California, August 7, 1943. (photo courtesy of National Archives)

Bill Ostlund before he boarded *Gudgeon*. (photo courtesy of Mike Ostlund)

Gudgeon officers relaxing on deck on a trip back to base during 7th run. (L to R) Albert Strow, Johnnie Kuehn, Don Midgley, Bill Post and Frank Barrows (front) Webster Robinson. (photo courtesy of Anna Laura Rosow)

Gudgeon crew enjoying a drink at sub's hang-out, The Irisher club, San Francisco, June 1943. (back L to R) William Low, Glenn Crandall, Ron Schooley, Dominick Corbisiere, Edward Hammond, George Curran. (front L to R) Charles E. Loveland with bartender. (photo courtesy of Ron Schooley)

Gudgeon Kill Book that crew used to keep track of their victories. (photo courtesy of Anna Laura Rosow)

Lt. George "Tex" Penland on deck
of *Gudgeon* before his death in gun
battle with Japanese, May 1943.
(photo courtesy of Shirley Thorup)

Bill and Peggy Ostlund before Bill
boarded *Gudgeon* in October 1943.
(photo courtesy of Linda Ostlund
Lipton)

Gudgeon commanding officer Bill Post being decorated by
Admiral Chester Nimitz. (photo courtesy of George Seiler)

Bill Ostlund's youngest brother John. Ostlund, an Eighth Air Force bombardier flew 35 missions over Europe during World War II. (photo courtesy of Beth Ostlund)

Milwaukee native, Lt.
Cmdr. Bob Bonin,
Gudgeon's skipper for the
12th patrol. (photo courtesy
of Regis Bonin)

Bill Ostlund's older brother Bob, early
in World War II. Captain Ostlund
served in Europe as a member of the
quartermaster corps. (photo courtesy
of John Ostlund)

3rd class Albert Everhart (middle) at sub school. Everhart was lost on
Gudgeon's 12th patrol. (photo courtesy of Joanna White)

Electrician's Mate Everett Dodson before his death on *Gudgeon's* final patrol. (photo courtesy of Marie Duncan)

Seaman John Piller before his death on *Gudgeon's* 12th patrol. (photo courtesy of Anthony Piller)

Torpedoman Lambert Hegerfeld (R) with unidentified *Gudgeon* submariner, was lost on *Gudgeon's* 12th patrol. (photo courtesy of Margaret Speers)

Former *Gudgeon* officer Dixie Farrell, photographed many years after the war. (photo courtesy of Dixie Farrell Submarine Force Museum)

Moose Hornkohl and George Seiler presenting Bill Post with a "Wild Bill Post" teddy bear at a submariner's convention in the mid 1990s. (L to R) Hornkohl, retired Rear Admiral Post, and Seiler. (photo courtesy of George Seiler)

Gudgeon officers pose for a photo at Presidential Unit Citation ceremony, Pear Harbor, Hawaii, December 27, 1942. From left: Lt. Burton Heyes, Lt. Addison Pinkley, Executive Officer Albert Strow, Lt. Cmdr. Bill Post, Lt. Donald Midgley, Lt. jg Bill Ostlund, Lt. Willie Floyd, and Lt. jg David McCorquodale. Heyes, Pinkley, Midgley, Ostlund and McCorquodale were lost on 12th patrol. (photo courtesy of Jane Duffey)

Lt. jg Bill Ostlund's memorial marker in Webster City, Iowa cemetery. (photo courtesy of Dave Ostlund)

hearing sounds of a ship breaking up. In total, the men on sound reported hearing twenty to thirty small, unidentifiable explosions. Post carefully checked to see whether others on the submarine had heard the same sounds. There was agreement from crew in each of the submarine's compartments that they had heard the many unidentified explosions.

Twenty-one minutes later, at 0025 hours, *Gudgeon* surfaced and sighted only the small, punchless patrol vessel. Post, desiring to clean up on the freighter if she was still afloat, followed the direction of the target's previous course for fifteen miles and saw neither of the ships on the surface, causing the confident captain to conclude that he was "positive that the target sank and the escort left vicinity." [19] *Gudgeon* would receive wartime credit for having damaged the freighter.

Gudgeon's problem with the prematurely exploding torpedoes was no small matter. It is certain that the flawed torpedoes resulted in fewer hits and kills of Japanese ships for the submarine fleet as a whole until the problems were corrected. The torpedo that had blown up prematurely might have been the one that sent this freighter to the bottom. Because it had exploded prematurely, probably at exactly the time when it had armed itself, spinning the requisite number of times, it was necessary for Post to expend three more torpedoes. Those additional three torpedoes were 19 percent of the sixteen fish on board *Gudgeon*. The shortage of torpedoes throughout the submarine fleet was by this time in the war a very serious one.

While such difficulties encountered by submarines of the Pacific fleet with their torpedoes clearly impacted the effectiveness of the force, for the men on board a submarine at war, it created an even greater problem. When the torpedo exploded prematurely, *Gudgeon* was forced to attack again—thus exposing herself once again to possible sinking by the enemy. These torpedoes not only lengthened the war by cutting down the effectiveness of the pre-October 1943 submarines, but they represented a serious danger to the brave submariners who had no choice but to use them. They deserved far better.

By this time in the war, *Grampus* and *Triton* had been lost, the first losses of the war for Squadron Six submarines. Both losses had been sustained within the previous two months. As *Gudgeon* patrolled her assigned area, there was no way for Post and the rest of the *Gudgeon* crew to know that a few days earlier on April 20, the USS *Grenadier* (SS-210), another Division

Sixty-Two submarine, had been sent to the ocean floor. Of the Division Sixty-Two submarines, only *Gudgeon, Gar, Grayling*, and *Grayback* were still afloat.

Grenadier was the submarine that George Seiler had been serving on when the war broke out. At the time of her sinking, she had been patrolling off the Malay Peninsula. The ship had been sizing up a couple of enemy merchant vessels when a Japanese bomber got too close. *Grenadier* dove in an attempt to elude. At 120 feet a Japanese depth bomb exploded near the boat. *Grenadier* was severely damaged but still afloat. No one had been killed. However, Lieutenant Commander J. A. Fitzgerald and the men aboard the veteran submarine were in deep trouble having lost their power and all of the lights on board.

The boat finally came to rest on the sea bottom at 270 feet. The men worked desperately in an attempt to get the burning and leaking submarine into running order. They were not successful. Fitzgerald finally gave the order to surface. The submarine would have to be destroyed to keep the Japanese from capturing her. *Grenadier* surfaced, the men abandoned ship, and scuttled the submarine, escaping before she sank. The entire crew of seventy-six men was taken prisoner by the Japanese and would receive exceptionally brutal treatment from the enemy. Submarine sailors were always treated especially inhumanely by their cruel and sadistic captors.

On board were Lieutenant Harmon B. Sherry, who patrolled with Shirley Stovall on *Gudgeon* for patrols four through six, as well as Charles H. Ver Valin who had served *Gudgeon* so ably for the first four patrols, and Albert J. Rupp, the fifteen-year-old boy who had drawn Lieutenant Commander Stovall's wrath by decorating the ocean with the milky white creosote solution on the fourth patrol. Ver Valin had left *Gudgeon* deeply disappointed that he had not become the boat's "fuel king." He had lost out to Alexander Sheffs. As Moose Hornkohl explained, Sheffs was the one person on board who was "responsible for putting every gallon of fuel in the submarine."[20] He was also responsible to "make sure that the tanks were all topped and that they have the lube oils for the engines and the fuel for the engines and anything that was not in stores."[21] Shirley Stovall had booted Rupp off the boat after he arrived late from leave one night as *Gudgeon* was preparing to depart for her fifth patrol. Little did the three men know that when they left *Gudgeon* their lives would take such an awful turn. Such were the fortunes of war. *Grenadier*'s loss was the fourteenth of what would eventually be fifty-two United States submarines lost in World War II. Later, when the crew of *Gudgeon* learned the fate of the *Grenadier* and crew, they were terribly saddened. It was yet another wartime case of "there, but for the grace of God, go I."

The next week would bring a series of events that created another of the submariners' experience of incredible highs followed by terrible lows. The boat would complete its third and final special mission of the war and follow it up with an ingenious but very dangerous maneuver ordered by the fearless Wild Bill Post. *Gudgeon* would also lose one of its most well-liked men.

The day of the twenty-seventh did not get off to a very noteworthy start. While patrolling off Pucio Point Panay, one of the larger Philippine Islands, *Gudgeon* spotted and attempted to close on a bulging 9,000 ton tanker. Unfortunately, no matter how hard Post tried, first running full speed submerged and then full speed on the surface, the tanker continued radically zigzagging and succeeded in staying out of firing range. Try as she might, *Gudgeon* was not able to close on the ship. The Japanese captain would not allow the determined Post the opportunity to get far enough ahead of him to permit *Gudgeon* to turn in and wait for the tanker so that Bill Post and the men on board could send their ship to the bottom. Furthermore, as a result of the frantic underwater full-speed pursuit, the boat's batteries had been expended in an hour and a half. Post decided to chase the ship on the surface using only two diesels, committing the other two to recharging the batteries. Before long it was obvious that even on the surface, they could not catch the ship.

A disappointed Bill Post finally gave up. The crew double-checked the torpedoes that had been loaded into the torpedo tubes. When the torpedoes were readied for firing, the outer doors on the torpedo tubes were opened, flooding the tubes to equalize the water pressure within the tube with that outside the boat. This prevented a large air bubble from escaping when a torpedo was fired, an air bubble which acted like a brightly-painted sea buoy showing an enemy exactly where a submarine was lying. The loaded torpedoes were inspected. This time, a closer look revealed flawed fish. After the day's extended chase, the *Gudgeon* torpedomen found that their torpedoes had been damaged by lying too long in the flooded tubes. Out of six torpedoes in the forward tubes, five had compromised after-bodies.

Three gyros and two exploders were flooded and needed to be drained off and dried.

The day would not prove to be a total bust. Spunky gunner's mate Ron Schooley was alert and doing his duty forty-five minutes before midnight on April 27, 1943. It was not a particularly easy night to do watch. Rainsqualls would come and go, and it was very dark. Torpedoman George Seiler was on the forward starboard watch, and Schooley was on the stern starboard watch. At around 2315, Schooley yelled out in excitement, "Oh my God, look at that big bastard."[22] In the split-second flash of light caused by a streak of heat lightning, Ron Schooley had sighted a very, very large ship. Seiler quickly turned around and with some difficulty could see the big monster coming out of a rainsquall heading roughly the same direction as *Gudgeon*. The ship was a little behind *Gudgeon* and off to starboard, heading slightly starboard-to-port. Luckily, the ship was still somewhat behind *Gudgeon*, which allowed enough time for word to be spread to the control room to ready the submarine for some hurried shots at the tail end of the large vessel. The men on *Gudgeon* realized very quickly that the ship must be a Japanese luxury liner, the 17,526 ton *Kamakura Maru*, known before the war as the *Chichibu Maru*. She was the pride of "Nippon Yusen Kaisha," otherwise known as the Japan Mail Steamship Company. At the time she was Japan's largest passenger vessel. Built in Yokohama, the *Kamakura Maru* had done prewar runs from Yokohama to a dock in San Francisco that was only a stone's throw from *Gudgeon*'s birthplace in Vallejo at Mare Island. Naval shipbuilders at prewar Mare Island could have almost stood on the not-yet-deadly *Gudgeon* and looked across and beyond San Pablo Bay at the grand *Chichibu Maru* as she steamed in and out of San Francisco Bay. This time it was Lieutenant Commander Bill Post who was standing on *Gudgeon*'s bridge eying the sleek white liner through a set of U.S. Navy binoculars and hoping to send it and her thousands of Japanese soldiers to the ocean floor in a tumult of confusion and death.

In his log, Lieutenant Albert Strow did not exaggerate when he called the *Kamakura Maru* "one of the swankiest that the sons of Nippon owned."[23] During the war the sleek white *Kamakura Maru* served many uses, including hauling large numbers of POWs to their places of captivity and serving as a hospital ship. In December 1942 she carried 2,213 POWs from Singapore to Nagasaki. On this day, though, the *Kamakura Maru* was loaded with

Japanese soldiers headed for war. The huge transport was clipping right along at 17.5 knots, zigzagging her way through the night. The Japanese were certain that her high speed made her all but invulnerable to any Allied submarines that she might encounter and thus chose not to send along escorts to protect the valuable cargo. Bill Post was shocked when he first viewed the ship at 584 feet long and 74 feet wide, it was so large that even at an obtuse angle, from almost two miles, the ship filled up more than half the "glass" on a set of 7/50 binoculars.

Post stormed ahead full speed on the surface trying to get ahead of the huge ship but to no avail. He decided on another tack. "We had quite a chase with this fellow and continued on April 28th which was the 14th day of our patrol. At 0104 having gotten in to a range of 2100 yards and 170 track was the best we could do. We fired a spread of four torpedoes. We were using a diversion spread of only twenty five yards."[24] Post fired the torpedoes at the stern of the ship, which he would gracefully call an "up the kilt" shot.[25] The torpedoes were the last ones available from the forward torpedo room. On this day the lucky Buddha must have really gotten a working over from the torpedomen because the little fella really did his job.

In what seemed like an interminable time later, but which was really only a couple of minutes, all hell broke loose on the massive ship as the torpedoes hit their mark. Gunner's Mate Ron Schooley was a little more uncouth than Post saying, "We fired two to hit, and two to go up its butt. It was loaded with five thousand troops."[26] The explosion was so massive it could only have been the ammo magazines on board exploding.

Post, who was anxiously watching the attack through the periscope, saw the ship crack near the stern—most likely from an internal explosion. To this day the surviving men on board *Gudgeon* that night talk with amazement about how fast the *Kamakura Maru* went down. Post wrote in his report that in just twelve minutes the big ship had gone to the bottom. He described it this way: "0116 *Kamakura Maru* sank. This happened so fast it was unbelievable. The target had been floating on an even keel and we believed we had only damaged him, and were swinging around to line up the stern tubes. The Commanding Officer was following the target through the periscope and just prior to sinking, flames were observed near the stern, apparently from an internal explosion. Target's bow suddenly rose into the air and it sank stern first in about the same time it takes to tell it. Just as he sank there was another terrific explosion."[27] The men on radar saw the sinking too. The pip slowly dwindled and finally disappeared altogether, the men began shouting with glee that the ship was gone. Another Japanese ship to the bottom, and this one a big troop ship loaded with soldiers.

Post added that the place of the sinking could be easily discerned. There were about a dozen lifeboats, floating debris, oil, and "swimming Japs" in a spread so massive that it covered several acres of ocean.[28] When *Gudgeon* surfaced, the sounds of the wounded and shocked Japanese were so horrific that Bill Post said it sounded like "Dante's Inferno."[29] Albert Strow added, "The liner had been full of troops—estimated at 3,000–4,000—and there were no more than a couple of hundred left. These devils were either wounded or shocked silly and were setting up the awfullest cry that can be imagined . . . it made one's flesh crawl, for we knew there was nothing we could do for them."[30]

After *Gudgeon* resurfaced, the original watch crew went back on top. This allowed George Seiler to observe the bedlam in the sea, the Japanese screaming and begging for help in complete agony surrounded on all sides by smoke, fire, death, and carnage. Seiler did not say how he felt about the scene, only reporting what he had observed. He did remember how the commando leader, Lieutenant Crespo, felt about the nearly hopeless plight of the Japanese in the water. Hearing the pathetic and desperate pleas for assistance, Crespo said, "Give me some hand grenades, and I'll give them all the help they need."[31]

Bill Post was a different breed from some of the others in the submarine service. He felt that enemy soldiers floating in water were off limits. He said, "When they were still aboard ship, they were the enemy; once they were in the water, they had become fellow mariners in distress."[32] He considered taking some of the survivors on board for either humanitarian or intelligence purposes but changed his mind, realizing that the boat was already overcrowded and that in taking survivors on board, the special mission would be jeopardized. With all that said—and Bill Post being urged by some to finish off the survivors in the water—he ordered that *Gudgeon* move on. There would be no massacre on Bill Post's watch even if they were Japanese soldiers.

In the cold reality of the day, knowing that if the soldiers in the water survived, they might eventually rearm and kill other Americans or our Allies it is easy to understand the attitudes of those that wanted to finish them off, as well as the horrific treatment the Allied prisoners of war received at the hands of those much like the wounded men in the ocean pleading for help. Those soldiers might just survive, and Bill Post knew it. Indeed, as it would turn out, some of them did survive to fight and kill American soldiers at another time, in another place. However, Wild Bill Post would not shoot unarmed, helpless men and, as it turned out, women in the water.

All of these years later, especially for those who have had no wartime service, it is easy to condemn the actions of the few U.S. submarine commanders who did not show mercy to the enemy in such situations. Yet it is also true that those who would be so ruthlessly machine gunned by others did not kill any more of Bill Post's countrymen. Those that were left floating in the water by the honorable Bill Post did. It is just another of the horrible conundrums of war.

For this venture, the Officer of the Deck Donald Midgley received the Navy and Marine Corps Medal. Ron Schooley, the first man to site the *Kamakura Maru* got the promotion he was already slated to get. Schooley recalls that Midgley, realizing this, told him, "The medal is half yours, but I'm wearing it."[33] Long-time *Gudgeon* radioman John Sheridan, on board for his eighth straight war patrol, drew the story of the *Kamakura Maru* to a close, "We watched it sink, and then went about our business."[34]

While the death of all those men was a horrible thing to watch, living on such a ship was no picnic either. It's true that the *Kamakura Maru* was huge, and perhaps the living conditions for the men on board were different from the conditions on other merchant ships that hauled Japanese troops, but it is doubtful. Author Mark Parillo, in his very thorough account of the Japanese merchantman, *The Japanese Merchant Marine in World War II*, succinctly described the living conditions aboard ships like the *Kamakura Maru*: "Life aboard the merchantmen was grim."[35] The men were so packed on board the steel-hulled ships that troops were placed anywhere they could be squeezed. Oftentimes, the men had to be stowed below decks where the temperature was as high or higher than 160 degrees. The moist heat allowed for the prolific breeding of rats and bedbugs. One soldier reported that during his voyage on such a ship there were eight men crammed into a six-foot square, and the voyage to their destination took a month. Another said that there were ten men crowded into a room about four feet by ten feet. Everybody was sweating profusely. The men were rarely able to bathe. Severe food and water shortages made the situation ripe for disease and severe morale difficulties. Then—just when things could not seem to get any worse—along would come a United States submarine.

Many miles from where the *Kamakura Maru* sank, former *Gudgeon* submariner Albert Rupp, by this time an ancient sixteen-year-old, was a week into his captivity but only at the beginning of the many years of torture and abuse that he and the other men from *Grenadier* would endure. Rupp's punishment for returning late from leave following his one and only patrol on *Gudgeon* hardly fit his offense. Had he reported on time, he may never have been assigned to *Grenadier* and been taken prisoner.

Shortly after being brought ashore (Rupp would spend most of his time as a POW in Japan), the men from *Grenadier* were led into a steamy one-story building and forced to stand at attention in front of Japanese guards for two straight days and nights. The only break from the torture were the few occasions that the men were allowed to go to the bathroom, at which time the men frantically drank from the toilet tank. During those forty-eight hours the *Grenadier* crew would be randomly beaten by the guards until they dropped unconscious from their stance at attention. The guards laughed during the beatings as the weakened submariners would start to crumble to the floor. It was apparent to Rupp and the others that if a man fell, he would be run through with a bayonet. Thus, with no food, little water, while standing in the tropical heat and totally exhausted from their ordeal, the submariners who remained standing would lean in tight on either side of a fallen shipmate, holding him up, saving his life until he could regain consciousness again, and come back to attention.

At one time, the submariners, still at attention, were told to turn around so they could see their skipper, John A. Fitzgerald, who was by this time tied up to a table outside the compound face up. The Japanese pried Fitzgerald's mouth open and poured a gallon of water down his throat. As Fitzgerald struggled to breathe, one of the Japanese guards jumped on his stomach, the water spewing out like a fountain. The Japanese guards once again laughed uncontrollably. The process was repeated once more before Fitzgerald was led off and the men were ordered to turn around and get back at attention. The *Grenadier* sailors were furiously angry but could say nothing.

A short while after Fitzgerald's torture, the submariners were released from their stances. But, angry and defiant, the captives refused to leave and continued to stand at attention for a third full day before finally being released to their pathetic quarters. At the time they were released it started to get really tough for the former *Gudgeon* submariners, Rupp, Sherry, and Ver Valin and their shipmates.

Meanwhile back aboard *Gudgeon*, following the sinking of the *Kamakura Maru*, a jubilant crew was allowed to take a fourteen-hour rest, while submerged. When the refreshed and rested *Gudgeon* crew was reawakened late at night, they set course for Pucio Point—and their third special mission. Once again they would insert commandoes on an island that was occupied by the enemy. A few days before sending the four commandos and their equipment ashore, one of the men, an anxious Lieutenant Crespo, asked Post, what should he do if he got his orders wet? The resourceful Lieutenant Tex Penland was present and had the solution to Crespo's problem. He stepped to the medical kit, found a rubber prophylactic, and handed it to Crespo. The men in the wardroom roared their approval.

What lay ahead of Crespo and the others must have been terrifying. Panay, while being the sixth largest of the Philippine Islands, is only seventy-five miles wide and ninety-five miles long. In the center of the island, north to south, there is a major river valley, flanked by mountains. There were plenty of places for the commandos to hide, but the island was very small. About 7,000 Filipinos originally defended Panay, but on April 16, 1942, the Japanese invaded with the Forty-First Infantry and declared the island secure four days later. *Gudgeon* spent much of April 29 off Pucio Point submerged and reconnoitering 1.5 miles off the coast. An advantageous point for an initial drop off was finally found 3.7 miles east of the point. Shortly after dark, the *Gudgeon* crew helped Lieutenant Crespo and Sergeant Alfabeto into a rubber boat so they could go ashore and make a more detailed reconnaissance of the area. This was a tense time, because the Japanese could be anywhere—possibly waiting ashore under cover with weapons in hand. Of course, the greatest danger as far as the men on *Gudgeon* were concerned was that the submarine would be spotted and that antisubmarine forces would be sent to the area. One did not know what lay ahead on that dark warm night.

The two soldiers were set adrift and were not seen again until dark had set in the following evening, when Crespo once again crawled back on the submarine. Once ashore Crespo and Alfabeto had made contact with Lieutenant Colonel Peralta's Volunteer Guards, spending the day at the organization's headquarters. When Crespo returned to *Gudgeon*, he made an oral report to Post which contained important intelligence information. Under the supervision of *Gudgeon*, Lieutenant H. J. Kuehn, the remaining men, and their supplies were carefully loaded onto the four seven-man rubber boats and two five-man rubber crafts. This time, the drop off of guerilla fighters on shore would be accomplished in one fell swoop—with, of course, the aid of Kuehn and seven unnamed *Gudgeon* sailors who were sent ashore to man the boats and help the commandos unload the equipment.

While the transfer procedure was proceeding, Lieutenant Crespo brought a Major Garcia and an unnamed Filipino captain on board. Garcia impressed Post as an exceptionally intelligent and capable officer. He indicated that the Japanese had been treating the Filipinos in the area quite well in order to restore normal trade conditions on Panay. He was very proud of his band of men, who he felt were fanatically in support of the resistance and had been very successful against the numerically superior Japanese invaders.

Major Garcia stated confidently that if he were provided 500,000 rounds of ammunition and 1,000 rifles, his small band of men could retake Panay. Post doubted the value of "taking" Panay, but he was so impressed by the Major and the reported exploits of his guerillas on the island that he would recommend that—since there was a torpedo shortage and hence extra room on submarines of the day—"every submarine bound for Philippine waters or the South China Sea [should] carry what men and equipment it can to these troops who are on the spot and capable of seriously harassing the enemy."[36]

Post also gathered intelligence about how to get Filipino resistance fighters into Japanese-occupied Manila without being detected. First, a Filipino must take a sailing boat into the harbor at outlying Batangas, posing as a merchant from a Japanese-occupied territory. Then he should proceed to the municipal building at Bauan and get a one-peso residence certificate from the Japanese. After being searched by the Japanese at the city limits, with certificate in hand, he could enter Manila. Some had done so by riding in the cab of a loaded truck. Strangely enough, the Japanese required no identification to get a residence certificate. The infiltrator only needed to let the Japanese authorities know that he was playing ball with them.

Post also obtained crucial information about troop strength and locations as well as data about the location of unescorted vessels in the area. Of especial interest to Post was confirmation by a coast watcher at Pucio Point that the submarine USS *Tambor* had indeed hit an unnamed maru on March 29, only to undergo an attack by an escort ship with about twenty depth charges. Even more important to Post was the confirmation that a ship answering to the description of the *Kamakura Maru*, stuffed with Japanese troops, had been observed heading south from Pucio Point. Those ashore confirmed that the *Kamakura Maru* had been carrying troops estimated to number in the thousands, as well as various government ministers and their administrative personnel who were traveling to remote posts in areas now under Japanese control. At the end of the briefing, Bill Post and the rest of the crew were invited to a big party on the beach by the mayor of Iloilo.

As if April 30 had not been exciting enough, late that evening under the fragile protection of the darkened skies, the men on board *Gudgeon* deep in Japanese-controlled waters began the very dangerous process of floating three torpedoes forward, the submarine lying in the harbor dead in the water, hatches open. Bill Post was uncomfortable with the fact that all of the torpedoes in the forward torpedo room had been fired. He had been emboldened to transfer the fish when the Filipinos assured him that there were no Japanese in the area. Post ordered the men to re-rig both the forward and after kingposts in preparation for a maneuver that perhaps nobody else in the submarine service *except* Wild Bill Post has ever attempted. But, by God they did it.

Post had three seven-man rubber rafts tied together with room enough for one torpedo to be laid on top. Each torpedo was pulled up out of the after torpedo room, through the after torpedo room hatch, then lifted over the side of the submarine and lowered carefully on to the rubber boats. The rafts were then slowly floated forward until they were in a position where the massive missile could be hoisted high above the forward torpedo room loading hatch, and slid down onto the cradle, which had been lined up to the skid that had been raised in the forward torpedo room. Each torpedo was lifted by two lines, not one, on the nosepiece—in order to avoid another catastrophe like the one that poor Arthur Miller had suffered. If one hook straightened out, the other would catch. The time–consuming and exhausting procedure would then be repeated twice more until three torpedoes had been moved to their new quarters, in the Buddha's forward torpedo room.

The delicate transfers took four hours. It may not sound like much of a feat, but torpedomen Edward Hammond and George Seiler stressed that it was a very dangerous time for the men on the submarine. *Gudgeon* lay protected by only a handful of lookouts manning their weapons on the deck. The nighttime transfer of the huge torpedoes was very hard work which required iron nerves and quick, efficient teamwork lest they be spotted and attacked by the Japanese on Panay or by Japanese patrol boats running through the area. Furthermore, detection would expose the landing and the presence of Crespo's group as well as the guerillas in the area.

Then the unexpected happened. A small Japanese patrol boat cruised slowly toward them. Art Barlow described the scene: "While the forward and after torpedo hatches were open and men were moving torpedoes, a Jap patrol boat moving along the coast came into sight. We were in sort of an exposed bay with the shore as our background so we couldn't be seen from seaward. The patrol boat was easy to see. All activity stopped, you could have heard a pin drop. After the patrol boat went behind the next point, we closed up all the hatches and put the boats away. The operation was over and the dance was cancelled." [37]

At the time, George Seiler and the men on board didn't give the transfer of torpedoes a second thought. But, having had more than a half-century to think about it, Seiler, who has revered Bill Post for all of those years, acknowledged for the first time that the maneuver "didn't exactly fit into something that I would term rational." [38] But he added, "Bill Post didn't earn the sobriquet 'Wild Bill' for nothing, and I loved him for it, as did every man on board." [39]

Gudgeon had been like a goldfish in a net while undergoing the transfer of torpedoes. Now she slowly pulled away from Panay into the evening's darkness, before finally easing herself beneath the waves to safety. The commandos ashore were on their own. The men on *Gudgeon* breathed deeply. They had escaped the patrol boat without a battle and made the transfers. *Gudgeon* was once again a shark, engaged in the primal search for the hated enemy.

It took a few days, but while patrolling submerged in the same area during daylight hours, *Gudgeon* attacked a small, armed trawler of about 1,500 tons with a spread of two torpedoes from *Gudgeon*'s stern torpedo tubes. The ship, which was described by the men in the after torpedo room as one of those pesky Q-ships but by Post as a small trawler, turned toward *Gudgeon* at just the wrong time causing the fish to miss on each side of the vessel. Knowing that the counterattack was coming next, Lieutenant Commander Post ordered the crew to rig for depth charge. *Gudgeon* smoothly and silently glided down to 250 feet.

The trawler skipper, seeking to punish *Gudgeon* for her affront, sent several waves of depth charges *Gudgeon*'s way. The charges blew up one after the other, twenty-three times in all. They were dropped singly and in groups of twos, threes, or fives, and luckily were not particularly close. Post estimated that they were set no deeper than 150 feet. The men in the after torpedo room were somewhat more impressed than the Old Man; this depth charge attack was close enough to the *Gudgeon* to worry them. As has been asserted, even depth charges set at 150 feet, exploding 100 feet above the submarine, were still close enough to shake you to the quick. Not wishing to expend any more torpedoes on the small ship, Post ordered that *Gudgeon* head south and west toward Naso Point.

On May 4, 1943, *Gudgeon* was reconnoitering the Nogas Islands area several hours before sunup in search of Japanese merchant shipping. On this day, *Gudgeon* would lose her second man within three weeks. At 0618 masts were sighted. *Gudgeon* turned to close on a ship that was identified as another small trawler of 500 tons and about 175 feet long. The boat was chugging along at a speed of 8 knots at a range of 12,000 yards.

It did not take long to close within about 2,400 yards where Bill Post initiated an attack with the *Gudgeon*'s three-inch deck gun and her machine guns. Post no doubt figured that this would be a difficult ship to hit with torpedoes because of its size and shallow draft, and he probably wanted to save the final four fish for bigger game. He hadn't had the men perform that dangerous transfer of torpedoes to be used on a 500 ton patrol vessel. As it would turn out though, after the surface battle Bill Post would likely have given his right arm to have used the torpedoes rather than the deck guns. However, if *Gudgeon* had been sent out with a full load of torpedoes in the first place, Bill Post would have had fourteen tin fish left and may have used a few of them on the small craft.

At 0759, with the trawler in range, the gunner's mates on board opened fire. Ninety-six rounds later the trawler was on fire and sinking. Unfortunately, only eleven minutes into the fierce battle, the Acting Battery Officer, Lieutenant George Harvey Penland of Dallas, Texas, was struck in the face by an ejected shell case from the three-inch deck gun. He was immediately knocked unconscious and fell overboard.

George Seiler and Albert Strow described the events leading to the death of the veteran of four war patrols. Seiler said that the deck gun was firing and *Gudgeon* was maneuvering to give the trawler a more difficult target; the submarine was running at great speed, "heeling" from one side to the other depending on the turn, left or right.[40] Penland was very close to the breech of the gun when *Gudgeon* turned sharply once again. Seiler said that Penland lost his balance and stumbled directly behind the breech as it opened up to eject a shell casing, each of which weighed around fifteen pounds, were extremely hot, and moving at a very high speed.

Strow was a little less certain why Penland had moved over to the rear of the gun but said that the shell hit Penland directly in the face and that he "folded over" and went down over the side, falling through the lifelines that bordered the deck of the boat. Two of *Gudgeon*'s gun crew dove, attempting to catch him before he fell overboard, but to no avail.[41]

Word was sent to Post who was on the bridge directing the attack, but it was too late. As *Gudgeon*'s screws sucked up water, Penland was surely pulled in through the huge propellers, his body no doubt horribly mangled in the process, then sent to rest at the bottom of the ocean. With the trawler smoking and aflame, Post broke off the engagement to search for Penland. Bill Post and the men on board the submarine moved slowly back and forth across the sea searching vainly for any sign of the man. On some level, the *Gudgeon* crew must have known all along they would not find him. Their only realistic hope was that Lieutenant Penland was unconscious at the time of his death and not aware of the events as they unfolded.

Twenty-nine-year-old Tex Penland had received a law degree from the University of Texas, then practiced law in the Dallas area, like his father who was chief counsel for a large railroad firm. Penland, who was known back home as "Harvey," could have served in a much less hazardous capacity in Naval Intelligence or JAG (Judge Advocate General) but decided against it. He wanted to fight the war and elected to become a submariner. His service was not in vain; Penland had already performed so admirably that he had won Bronze and Silver Stars before earning a Purple Heart when he dropped into the Sulu Sea just west of Negros. Finally, after an hour and a half of searching, back and forth across the area, with the tearful men on deck calling "Tex" over and over, a crestfallen Bill Post ordered that a rubber boat with provisions and water be dropped over the side just in case he had been missed—knowing all the while that he had not. Post then ordered *Gudgeon* to move on. It was time to get back in the war.

A few minutes later, in the area of the sunken trawler, Post moved past the Japanese survivors that were swimming in the water and picked up three Filipinos who claimed they had been forced on board the ship to work for the sixteen Japanese masters. The men identified the ship as the *Naku Maru* bound from Manila to either Iloilo or Davao. The boat was hauling a load of lube oil, ice, and fishhooks. Post must have been disgusted. Losing Tex Penland for fishhooks. Bill Post noted that when the ship was aflame, the lube oil made a particularly "beautiful fire." [42] Without going into detail when interviewed after the patrol, Post said that the Filipinos had some interesting information about the Japanese rule in Manila, no doubt having heard vivid stories about the sadistic treatment that their countrymen were suffering.

Wild Bill Post once again showed his humanity as he had when faced with the dilemma of what to do with the survivors of the sunken Japanese liner earlier in the patrol. Having just lost a truly beloved officer from his own ship, one would think that this could have simplified the situation for Post, who was as determined a killer as the submarine fleet had when the Japanese had weapons in their hands. There would be no vengeful slaughter of the Japanese troops bobbing up and down in the ocean that day. This time Post ordered that a rubber boat with provisions be dropped over the side for the Japanese survivors of the trawler. *Gudgeon* then glided on, once again in search of the ruthless enemy. It was time to find some more Japanese ships to send to the bottom.

The death of Penland was a major blow to the officers and crew on *Gudgeon*. As one sailor said, Tex Penland was one of those guys who always did his duty and had a "sunny disposition" while doing it.[43] Penland was well-liked by the crew, one reason being that he took advice from the more experienced men who were "below" him. As George Seiler put it, "There wasn't a dry eye in the place after Penland's death, including the Old Man's."[44] The Old Man, by now an "ancient" thirty-four-year-old, was crushed when he lost Penland. The men on a submarine are intimately dependent upon each other for survival. Each man has his own responsibilities, each of which, to an extent is equal to another in terms of the survival of the boat. If one man messes up, the result can be the loss of everybody on board. To have a young officer like Penland, who was such a positive force on the submarine, so willing to listen and learn from the crew, was very good for morale. He didn't pull rank, stubbornly insisting that it needed to be his way even if it was the wrong way. He listened and learned and performed, and became more and more of an asset to the submarine as the months proceeded.

Tex Penland was no neophyte. He was a veteran of all of Lieutenant Commander Stovall's patrols as well as Post's first two. To be certain, he knew that he should not have been behind that breech, so it has to be concluded that he had been thrown there by the sharp turn of the submarine, as George Seiler stated. Whatever the cause of the accident, he was gone. There would be no funeral service for Penland on board *Gudgeon* just as there was no service for Art Miller. Miller's was held at the naval hospital where he died. *Gudgeon* had no service for Penland because there was still the remotest chance that he was alive. Nobody wanted to jinx him by having a service, no matter how certain they were that he was gone.

After a few more sightings, some of which could not be developed properly for attack, and others Post seemed wise to avoid, on May 5, 1943, *Gudgeon* maneuvered in to attack a small coastal-type passenger freighter of about 1,600 tons. As if to seek revenge on the Japanese, *Gudgeon* rained fiery death on the small ship from the very gun that had claimed Tex Penland the day before. Within only ten minutes, after firing 104 shells, *Gudgeon* was able to pull away leaving the ship "burning fiercely" and sinking slowly about two miles off the beach fifteen miles west of Iloilo.[45] Post concluded that she had probably sunk or, if not, was surely a complete loss.

Lieutenant Commander Bill Post was pleased with the new binocular gun sights that had been placed on the larger gun by the relief crew of

Pelias. He said that the second shot fired at the burning ship hit squarely on the bridge and that his gunners were attaining hits on an amazing two-thirds of their shots. The stubborn ship was hit with around seventy shells and was still floating when *Gudgeon* pulled away. Post decided he would try and get a larger deck gun once the submarine reached shore. The three-incher did not pack the punch Post desired.

Later that day, *Gudgeon* tried to close on another ship with all four engines on line. As *Gudgeon* approached, the Japanese sailors threw something over the side. This worried the officers on *Gudgeon*. The objects could have been depth charges being towed behind the ship or set to drift. Post ordered *Gudgeon* to move slightly to the left to avoid whatever lay in the water. The target ship, now looking like a small tanker, changed course in an identical way as *Gudgeon*. *Gudgeon* was being stalked.

Knowing that he had been spotted, Post ordered a dive and continued ahead trying to set up for a good shooting angle on the tanker. Before long, the target started looking more and more like one of those damned Q-ships, now only 1,400 yards away and bearing down on *Gudgeon*. With Post softly singing "Waltzing Matilda" and trying desperately to get the stern torpedo tubes to bear, the Japanese man-of-war started throwing depth charges toward the submarine. Unfortunately *Gudgeon* had just one torpedo in the stern tubes.

The first depth charge was fairly close but as Post said, "not too close to stop our attack."[46] The second depth charge rocked the boat and was definitely "too close for comfort" breaking light bulbs in the after-part of the submarine.[47] Post, apparently deciding that the little tanker was definitely a wolf in sheep's clothing, ordered a dive to 250 feet as two more depth charges quite close to *Gudgeon* sent explosive shocks at the submarine and jarred the men on board. Strow said that the men did not know what kind of ship it was for certain, but that it was "seriously doing a good job of dropping them close."[48] Once again the men on board were in serious danger of losing their lives. These Japanese sailors knew what they were doing. Bill Post, certain that in this situation discretion was indeed the better part of valor, went deep and evaded. Before long he was able to put 16,000 yards between his submarine and the Q-ship. Post ordered *Gudgeon* to surface and hightailed it toward friendlier waters.

Seaman Edward Hammond remembered Bill Post and the many depth charge attacks *Gudgeon* suffered such as this. He considered Post to be a "sailor's skipper," describing him as "very cool" under such an attack.[49] Hammond was very open about his attitudes toward the hundreds of depth charges he had suffered at the hands of the Japanese. He hated each and every single one of them, and acknowledged that he was "scared to death." He added, "Anyone that wasn't was a damn fool."[50]

Lieutenant Commander Post decided that his crew had had enough war to last them a few days and ordered that the submarine run on the surface for a day to give the crew rest and fresh air. So, for the next day, with the crew enjoying the clean Pacific breezes and sky, *Gudgeon* ran toward Dumaguete. At 0342 on the eighth, day twenty-four of the patrol, *Gudgeon* inspected the approaches to Dumaguete on the southeast tip of the island of Negros. For a Bill Post patrol, things had actually been quiet for a day when suddenly a trawler-type patrol vessel burst out of the misty darkness at a range of almost a mile. The soundmen on board had missed the ship, and now another one of those undersized submarine killers was on the loose less than a mile away and headed toward *Gudgeon*. Post hurriedly fired one torpedo from the forward room, then turned the submarine around, and fired a second from the stern tubes. Post thought it was possible that a torpedo had "dudded" off the side of the ship, falling to the bottom after it bounced off the hull of the charging vessel. As a result of the torpedo's failure to explode, the aggressive foe was now counterattacking *Gudgeon*, which responded by diving to 200 feet. Once again, depth charges rained on *Gudgeon*. BOOM. BOOM. BOOM. BOOM. BOOM. BOOM. BOOM. BOOM. BOOM. BOOM. BOOM. Post counted eleven depth charges. An hour later, *Gudgeon* carefully rose to periscope depth. As the periscope broke the waves, the hunter set out again for *Gudgeon*, throwing five more depth charges toward her. BOOM. BOOM. BOOM. BOOM. BOOM. The men in the after torpedo room reported that five of the sixteen charges had really rocked the boat and were "good close ones."[51] Bill Post decided that this was enough and headed away. Half a day later *Gudgeon* surfaced and continued patrolling the area, then headed to Surigao Strait and on to San Bernardino Strait—heading generally northward toward Pearl Harbor all the way.

On the twelfth, with *Gudgeon* patrolling submerged in the San Bernardino Straits area, a ship similar to the *Manko Maru* appeared in the periscope sites. The ship was 4,400 tons and was moored north of Binorongan Point, Luzon. Post fired his fifteenth and sixteenth torpedoes at a range of 1,580 yards and a 50 yard spread. Both missed. Post must have found the misses a little humiliating. The firing crew had set the TDC correctly but not allowed for a two-knot current close to shore, which caused both torpedoes to miss astern, once again illustrating how difficult it was to hit ships with torpedoes in World War II. Even moored ships could be tricky. To make matters worse, Post was out of fish and ammunition for his three-inch deck gun and could not finish the job.

With all of the tin fish expended, Lieutenant Commander Bill Post, Frank Barrows, and the other men on board *Gudgeon* surfaced and headed for R & R at Pearl Harbor, certain, at least, that they had sunk three ships and damaged another, with only sixteen torpedoes. However, it was not to be an uneventful cruise home. The submarine was attacked on May 21 and May 22 by Type 96, Model 4 Mitsubishi "Nell" bombers. During World War II, the United States gave Japanese planes names like Nell and Zeke to ease communication. It was much easier to use the term Nell than to say that the plane was a Type 96 Mitsubishi GM3 twin-engine bomber.

The first attack occurred during the morning hours with *Gudgeon* storming on the surface toward Pearl Harbor. A radar contact picked up the bomber at ten miles as it closed rapidly to six miles. Post went into action: "CLEAR THE BRIDGE. DIVE. DIVE. DIVE."[52] Once again the familiar alarm, "Ah-oogah, ah-oogah" from the Klaxon was sounded, and the submarine headed for the safety of deeper water. This time *Gudgeon* could not reach safety before taking a bomb which was heard and felt while the submarine was on her way down. Once again *Gudgeon* luckily avoided catastrophe.

The following day, while approaching Midway Island, radar picked up another bomber at seventeen miles. The plane was sighted at three miles and dropped to about 1,000 feet. It could not yet be identified at a range of 1.5 miles and lackadaisically maneuvered in the direction of the sun, circled around on *Gudgeon*'s port side, and swept around the stern—eventually approaching from the starboard side of the submarine, at which time the rising sun was seen on the aircraft's wings and it was identified as another Nell bomber. Post acknowledged in an interview later in the war that his casual attitude toward the aircraft had been foolish. The plane's attack was not particularly aggressive, which caused the commander to conclude that there was another Japanese submarine nearby, and that the bomber was taking it easy.

Arthur C. Barlow, now a veteran of four patrols on *Gudgeon*, said later that when Post had let the Nell bomber get in too close on the twenty-second, he had been lulled to a level of excessive confidence because the air above them was supposed to have been controlled by the Allies. George Seiler added that Post had been overly confident because the United States had supposedly destroyed all of the Japanese planes at Wake Island, the only ones in the area that could do antisubmarine duty, and thus Post felt, incorrectly as it turned out, that *Gudgeon* was safe from enemy attack. Barlow had been called on deck to send signals to the plane in order to identify it as friend or foe. When the plane got in close enough that he knew the pilot could see the signals, Barlow flashed a recognition signal which was the day's three-letter code. The pilot, fearing that he was being fired at, then reared up, finally exposing the telltale red balls on the underside of the wings. It was then that he charged *Gudgeon* and dropped the bomb. George Seiler added that Post's theory about a Japanese submarine in the area had merit, because for many days previously *Gudgeon* had been trying to locate a Japanese submarine that was reported to be patrolling around Wake Island. The enemy submarine's mission was to replenish the Japanese soldiers on the tiny island.

Seiler remembered asking Bill Post what he was going to do if he had seen the Japanese submarine, since *Gudgeon* had no torpedoes or shells for the cannon. Post replied, "We're going to ram him." [53] To this day Seiler is not certain whether Post was serious. Seiler's uncertainty reveals a great deal about Wild Bill Post. All of these years later Seiler still thinks it's possible that Bill Post was sincere and that he planned on ramming the submarine. Seiler added that the bomber was close enough to *Gudgeon* with his bomb bay doors open that it was only due to a miracle that *Gudgeon* was not lost right there on May 22, 1943. That was the kind of mistake that could have cost the commanding officer his ship. A lucky or exceptionally well-placed bomb near the most vulnerable part of the submarine would have sunk it. How much longer could the men on *Gudgeon* continue to be so fortunate?

Gudgeon dove and arrived at Pearl Harbor on the surface on day forty-two of the patrol, May 25, 1943. It must have been quite a sight. The Navy band on shore was playing the customary military songs. Civilians and military personnel alike had hurriedly lined up to watch as the USS *Gudgeon* slowly crept forward, the chugging diesel engines competing with the band. The proud and relieved men on the deck handling the lines were haggard, sometimes unshaven and as white as a sheet. Brass eagerly waited on shore to jump on board and congratulate Bill Post and the others for the very fine patrol. On the way to the barn, Bill Post had approved of an addition to the submarine. One of the submariners, Edward Bland, had painted a kangaroo holding a torpedo on the forward side of the conning tower as *Gudgeon* headed home on the surface.

For George Seiler and the other men disembarking from *Gudgeon*—after having just served a wild forty-one-day patrol on a claustrophobia-inducing, smoky, smelly, diesel-oil-saturated submarine—to a brass band and fancy ceremony must have seemed surreal. They emerged from the bowels of their wartime submarine to a tropical paradise. A heaven, with the palm trees swaying in the gentle breeze, lovely warm sand, healing sunshine, soothing blue sky, beautiful women, and, of course, booze.

Since Moose Hornkohl and Guts Foster had transferred off the boat after the seventh patrol, the first chore for George Seiler and his new running mates would be to smuggle some of the torpedo juice off *Gudgeon* and hurry over to the submariners' paradise, the Royal Hawaiian to set up a still. So much for sunshine and blue skies. For George and his pals, setting up the stills would be the top priority. Long-gone were the well-stocked bars of Australia, Emu, and White Horse Scotch. In Hawaii, this otherwise heavenly locale, the best a sailor could do was get some of that bathtub gin, that ungodly tasting grain alcohol mixed with juniper which gave it a contrived flavor that is to real gin what toilet water is to fine red wine. But, before long the still was percolating happily, and the men from the *Gudgeon* torpedo room were partying wildly.

It had been another long patrol for the veteran submariner George Seiler, who had developed a whopping drinking problem long before he set foot on a U.S. submarine. Oddly, at sea, Seiler had no particular cravings. Performance of his duty and defeating the hated Japanese were paramount. While on board, all a sailor could drink was the so-called medicinal brandy that the pharmacist's mate, stored under lock and key. The skipper would occasionally order the "medicine" to be broken out to calm the nerves of the men after a particularly nasty depth charge attack or when there had been an unusually dangerous surface encounter. The skipper would hand out a tiny little airline-like bottle of brandy to each man. The men were expected to drink the stuff in the after battery room or in the control room while under supervision, so a sailor couldn't squirrel it away for later consumption. The amount of the "treatment" was so small, of course, that no man on board could possibly be impaired. By this time in the war, one would have to assume that the medicinal brandy had been broken out of the locked cupboards on many an occasion.

After a few days at Pearl, *Gudgeon* and the crew were underway for the west coast of the United States, arriving at the U.S. Naval Drydocks, Hunter's Point, San Francisco, California, on June 2, 1943. As *Gudgeon* pulled into the dock, she flew a red and white flag for every ship that she had sunk, by *Gudgeon*'s count: around twenty Japanese vessels in all. Homecoming was highly emotional. With the pride of a job well done and the knowledge that leave was ahead of them, the men of the *Gudgeon* were beside themselves with happiness.

In all, Post reported sighting twenty ships on the patrol. Of those vessels, he attacked seven with torpedoes, which expended *Gudgeon*'s small load very quickly. Two additional attacks were undertaken with machine guns and the larger deck gun. *Gudgeon* was wearing down. Her entire hull was vibrating, worse as time went on. This was particularly noticeable in the after torpedo room. Fogging and vibration on the periscope continued to make observations difficult. Post asked for a larger five-inch deck gun, noting that the barrel of the three-inch gun was so worn that the projectiles wobbled as they left the bore, like a dying quail—a sight that must have given the men little confidence. Furthermore, the breech mechanism did not close properly. Post said that the flaws seriously impaired the military effectiveness of the boat.

He claimed a sinking of the 9,000 ton trawler which was attacked on the twenty-fifth and twenty-sixth of April. He had heard breaking-up noises, and twenty or thirty small explosions, which were confirmed by men in every compartment on the boat. *Gudgeon* received no credit for this sinking in either the wartime or the official JANAC version after the war.

Nobody argued about the important sinking of the *Kamakura Maru*. The ship was of equal size to the *Nisshun Maru* No. 2, a huge tanker that had been sunk due to unknown reasons a few days earlier. The *Kamakura Maru* was one of only six merchant ships weighing more than 17,000 tons that postwar Japanese records positively confirmed were sunk during the war out of 2,346 merchant ships sunk. Had her thousands troops successfully reinforced one of the island garrisons prior to an Allied invasion, they would have inflicted many casualties on American soldiers. The *Kamakura Maru* had long been slated for conversion to an escort carrier, which would now never happen. Clark G. Reynolds in *War in the Pacific* noted that the *Kamakura Maru* carried not only troops and supplies but "1,000 civilian specialists bound for Singapore to try to hasten oil and rubber production in Malaya and the Indies."[54] Only twenty-eight survived the late night attack.

After the patrol, *Gudgeon* received credit for having sunk the 500 ton trawler during the gun action that resulted in Lieutenant Penland's death. As Post had reported at the time, it had taken ninety-six rounds of three-inch ammo to sink the ship. After the war, however, JANAC did not allow credit for the sinking, which was actually witnessed by many aboard *Gudgeon*. Much of the crew was topside, scanning the sea in search of Penland. The gun action that followed the next day, when *Gudgeon* expended her remaining one-hundred-four 3 inch rounds on the 1550 ton trawler, left it afire and "sinking," was credited to *Gudgeon* by Admiral Lockwood and others, but not JANAC.

Bill Post did not claim even a hit—much less a sinking—on the moored ship off Binorongan Point on May 12. None of his superiors in their letters of endorsement gave *Gudgeon* credit for having sunk the ship. Ironically, in 1947 when the JANAC report came out, *Gudgeon* was given credit for having sunk the *Sumatra Maru*, a cargo ship of 5,862 tons, which had been sunk at the exact location where Post had fired his last two torpedoes, missed, then given up because he was out of ammo. At the time Post reported that the two torpedoes missed astern and exploded on the beach. The explosions which had resulted in the sinking, must have been verified in Japanese records indicating that the ship had been sunk when *Gudgeon* had attacked it. It is difficult to explain how the men peering through the periscope could have been so mistaken. If JANAC erred in the direction of not allowing sinkings, it must be assumed that they could also err in the other direction.

In all, Lockwood gave *Gudgeon* wartime credit for having sunk three ships for 19,576 tons of shipping and for having damaged another 9,000 ton ship. Admiral Ralph W. Christie, Commander of Task Force Seventy-One, praised *Gudgeon*'s performance on the special mission. The dropping off of commandos and his men was "exceedingly well planned and expeditiously executed." Christie commended the officers and crew with a "well done" and noted that the recommendations made and the intelligence information provided would be "extremely valuable."[55] Lockwood praised the men aboard *Gudgeon* for their "aggressive and successful" patrol.[56] Post received particular praise for having sunk the *Kamakura Maru*, which he termed the "largest Japanese passenger liner listed."[57] Christie expressed deep "regret" about the loss of Lieutenant Penland, calling him an "excellent submarine officer and an outstanding leader among his men."[58]

He further noted that *Gudgeon* had now been credited with the outstanding record of having sunk 127,559 tons and having damaged 22,494 additional tons. The men on *Gudgeon* had undergone six different attacks by depth charges or aerial bombs over a forty-two day patrol. Though damage to the boat was not severe, damage to the nerves was considerable. It was time to rest and recuperate—submariner style. The overhaul would not be completed until the second week of August.

One wonders what damage Post and the men on the *Gudgeon* might have done had they had a full load of twenty-four torpedoes for each of Bill Post's first two war patrols. With only thirty-five of the forty-eight torpedoes that he might have had for the seventh and eighth war patrols, Post had been given wartime credit for having sunk seven ships. However, this was just the way it was for *Gudgeon* and for other submarines at this time in the war. There were not enough torpedoes, and those they had were undependable. It did not slow Post or *Gudgeon* down much, however. At this time in the war it was said that *Gudgeon* had sunk more tonnage than any other submarine in the service. Lockwood took no time in awarding Lieutenant Commander William S. Post Jr. another Navy Cross.

The old crew from *Gudgeon* scattered in every direction. Moose Hornkohl and Ray Foster were already long gone. Dusty Dornin had asked Foster if he wanted to go with him to board a newly constructed submarine. Foster agreed, having seven patrols under his belt. Moose Hornkohl had gotten into some trouble ashore after the seventh patrol and was restricted and not allowed to reboard *Gudgeon* for the eighth run. George Seiler would be transferred off the submarine after the eighth patrol. He had no desire to leave *Gudgeon* but was ordered to go to the States for new construction. His transfer would come, however, after more wild times on leave.

A local newspaper in Providence, Rhode Island, announced that *Gudgeon* sailor John J. Sheridan had, for the first time in eighteen months, touched United States soil when he and the other men on *Gudgeon* hit California. When he returned home to Providence a short while later, it was his first visit in over two years. Sheridan was one of the few of those incredible *Gudgeon* sailors who had served on board for all of her eight patrols. For Sheridan it would be time to return to the "real world." He would use his leave to get married in the local Church of the Blessed Sacrament to Margaret Walsh, an East Greenwich high school teacher. When interviewed for the local paper, he spoke of Douglas MacArthur, praising his style. Sheridan saw him once and decided that he was very classy in his appearance. In fact, Sheridan had by this time seen much of the world. Before the war started he only knew how to tune a ham radio. He had risen from the ranks of a lowly seaman to a radioman first class and by this time was planning a career in radio after the war, if only he could make it through alive.

Gudgeon would depart for her ninth patrol on September 1, 1943. This would give the men a lot of time to themselves, too much time for some, who would get themselves into serious trouble.

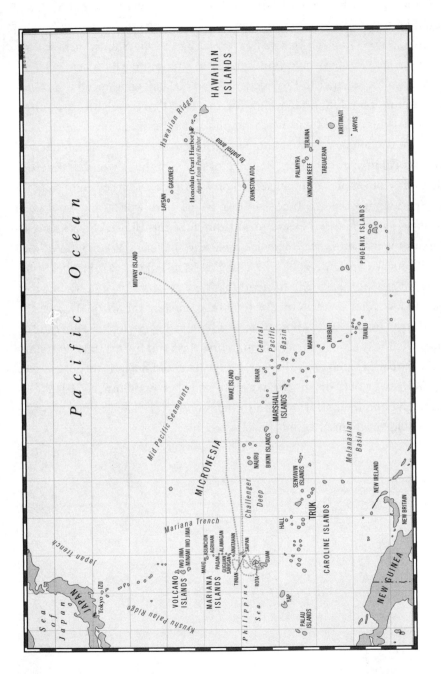

Ninth War Patrol • Approximate Course • Sept. 1–Oct. 6, 1943

▪ 9 ▪

The Irisher

When the cock is drunk, he forgets about the hawk.

Ashanti proverb

It took Lieutenant Commander William S. Post Jr. and the battle-weary men on board the USS *Gudgeon* five days to sail from Pearl Harbor to the U.S. Naval Drydocks at Hunter's Point, San Francisco, for the submarine's overhaul. By this time in the war, several submarines had done as many as nine or ten patrols, and most of the submarines of Squadron Six had completed seven or more. These early-war submarines were the workhorses of the first phase of the war, the darkest of times in the struggle against the Japanese. Clay Blair wrote that the fifty-four fleet boats that left for patrol from Pearl Harbor in 1942 accounted for 15 percent of submarine patrols, but that these submarines accounted for 45 percent of the Japanese ships sunk by submarines during that time. Credited by JANAC with seventy kills and far more wartime sinkings, Squadron Six had done its part in achieving this impressive ratio of success.

Some of the men spent their leave in San Francisco, while others headed to homes throughout the United States. The crew's hangout in San Francisco was The Irisher, a bar on Mason Street. Just why The Irisher became the preferred place for the crew of *Gudgeon* is an interesting story. By this time, with Moose Hornkohl and Guts Foster long gone, Foster having been married recently, torpedoman George Seiler was to an extent all alone and looking for action. It did not take long for Seiler and George Curran, another man from the torpedo room, to become fast friends. They had similar interests. Once *Gudgeon* had been safely moored at Hunter's Point for her overhaul, the two torpedomen went ashore. Their first stop was at a bar at Ellis and Market streets. The men wanted some liquor, but the barkeep there was following regulations of the day which prohibited sale of hard liquor until 4:00 P.M. The two sailors quickly drank their beers and then by chance stopped at The Irisher.

The bar had about fifteen stools and was murky black. It reeked of stale alcohol and cigarettes. The place was so small it did not even have tables. The two thirsty sailors sat down. The bar was empty, so it did not take long for the owner, Red Benson, to get to them. Benson asked them what they wanted, to which the sailors responded, "What we want, we can't get until 4."[1] Benson replied, "What the hell do you guys want? The hell with the regulation."[2] The men requested whiskey, explaining that they just got into port. Benson deftly poured a round of whiskey all the way to the top of three water glasses and quickly downed his. The two torpedomen were unable to match Benson's feat and nursed theirs, as Seiler recalled, for a full five minutes. When Seiler reached into his pocket to pay, Benson told him to keep his money. He explained to the two men that he was going bankrupt and that they might as well drink for free as have his creditors get their money. This gesture so impressed the men that they went out and found ten or fifteen of their shipmates, who drank a whole lot of booze and paid for it each time. Their actions over their leave, hardly heroic by war standards, nonetheless saved The Irisher. The bar became known as the submariner's hangout, and Red Benson—the once-beleaguered bar owner—became the *Gudgeon* crew's best friend.

The men would not have to board *Gudgeon* again until the end of June—two months off. One could almost predict that some of the young men unwinding from another stressful war patrol would get into some trouble, and the men from *Gudgeon* would not disappoint.

Machinists Mate Second Class Donald E. Smith got into the most trouble. Smith was a valuable crew member, having served under skippers Lyon, Stovall, and Bill Post. Each skipper approved of his work, or he would not have remained on board. By this time, Smith had survived countless attacks, bombings, and depth charges from both the Japanese and the United States.

Yet, on June 6, 1943, Smith would be shot—by of all people—one of San Francisco's "finest." The June 7, 1943, edition of the *San Francisco Chronicle* reported that the twenty-year-old Smith, accompanied by another *Gudgeon* sailor, John Wilkins Jr., a veteran of four war patrols on *Gudgeon*, had entered an unnamed hotel and caused a disturbance. A police officer named Dowd claimed that he had finished his evening dinner, stopped off at a bar where he had three glasses of "water," and was heading home out of uniform. Dowd walked by the hotel on Kearney Street where he saw Wilkins and Smith arguing with the landlady of the hotel. Dowd said he advised the men that they needed to quiet down, or he would turn them in to shore patrol. He searched them and left. A few minutes later Wilkins and Smith "accosted" Dowd as he would later claim, seeking five dollars that the submariners said was missing from Smith's pocket. Smith yelled, "Give me that five dollars you took off me."[3]

Dowd told Smith he was a police officer and retreated, bumping into a light pole. Dowd, by now feeling cornered by that big tall light pole, told Smith that he would shoot him if he were attacked, to which Smith replied, "Go ahead and shoot, we've seen plenty of bullets."[4] Indeed Smith had—and Dowd did. Twice. Smith slumped to the ground with a wound to his stomach. Another cop rushed to the area and observed that Dowd appeared to be "dazed," undoubtedly from the shock of the shooting or for having drunk too much of that strong Frisco water. Wilkins did admit that he and Smith had drunk several drinks earlier in the day.

George Seiler remembered the story much differently from the newspaper version. His version is a little more interesting and probably far more accurate. He said that Smitty and Wilkins were entering the hotel with Smith's fiancée, who had come out to visit him, when the tipsy Dowd approached them and inappropriately asked, "Where are you taking that whore?"[5] Smith took offense. The fight ensued, and Smitty, who was not armed, got shot.

George Seiler said that Bill Post was livid that one of his men on R & R had been shot by a policeman. Post called San Francisco's mayor, Roger Lapham, and raised hell, demanding that the cop be prosecuted "to the fullest extent of the law."[6] Things turned out pretty well for sailor Smith, who recovered from his wounds, but Donald E. Smith never made another war patrol on *Gudgeon*. Just what became of him is unknown. Getting shot in the gut may have been the luckiest thing that ever happened to Smith because he was not on board for *Gudgeon*'s twelfth patrol. The criminal case of Officer Dowd seems to have disappeared into oblivion. Neither the *Chronicle* nor the *San Francisco Examiner* covered the trial on the day the case was to be heard. For some time thereafter, neither paper contained an explanation about the status of the case. The way the case seems to have disappeared from the papers though, one has to suspect that the pull of the force was greater than Bill Post's influence. It was not long before Bill Post was back at sea, thousands of miles from San Francisco and off Lapham's back.

Drinking played a major role in the less serious difficulties the crew members pulled while in San Francisco as well. One night, with the submarine at Hunter's Point, Edward Wixted, a veteran of all eight of *Gudgeon*'s patrols, stole Post's jeep and drove it over to The Irisher. Wixted mistakenly thought that Post had retired for the evening and would not need his jeep any more. So Wixted "accidentally" as he would say later, stole Post's jeep. But Bill Post was not through for the night.[7] He trekked over to *Gudgeon* and noticed that many of the crew had left their posts guarding the submarine and was very angry. He decided to track down the rascals in his jeep but found that it, too, had disappeared. Before long, Post was able to locate a staff car and persuaded George Seiler to accompany him. Post, talking out loud to Seiler, tried to reason to himself where his jeep may be. He told Seiler that he had heard that the crew was frequenting a place called The Irisher and asked him if he knew anything about the place. Red Benson had probably placed a photo of Seiler above the bar, but Seiler, ever the loyal shipmate, responded slyly, but ever-so-transparently, "What's The Irisher club?"[8] Post snapped back at Seiler, telling him that he didn't want any of that "bullshit."[9] And, meekly Seiler led him to the bar.

Bill Post was right. Right there, parked in front of The Irisher, was his jeep. Post entered the smoke-filled bar and found the entire duty section—the men who were supposed to be guarding the submarine, in dungarees, not the whites that they were supposed to wear ashore. Post approached a sheepish Edward Wixted and asked him if he was supposed to be on watch, to which Wixted replied sheepishly, "Yeah, when Seiler is done."[10] Post knew exactly what was going on that night at The Irisher and informed the sailors that he was going to walk to the corner and come back. He said that if they were there when he returned, he would "own them" or something to that effect.[11] The tipsy sailors scampered out of the arms of their dancing partners and scattered like so many rats back to the *Gudgeon*.

On the ride home, Seiler asked Post how he knew that the crew had been hanging out at The Irisher. Post explained that some guy named Red Benson had once called wanting to throw a ship's party for the crew. Seiler said, "That's how much Red liked the *Gudgeon* crew. Of course, we kept him in business too."[12] Benson was particularly beloved by the men of *Gudgeon* and as it would turn out, the other submariners, because he let the men charge drinks and borrow money, knowing full well that many of the unfortunate young men would soon be dead and never be able to repay him for his kindness. George Seiler said that the story was typical of Post. Instead of getting "very military" and putting Wixted and the others on report, he took care of the problem and moved on.[13] It was an example of Post's touch with the crew that made him so beloved by the men.

Post, of course, was no fool. He wasn't about to throw the book at the *Gudgeon* crew because of their shore-time antics and make them unavailable for the next patrol. Post knew that the bumbling men ashore did not in any way resemble the talented submariners they were once they were back on board *Gudgeon*. The joy-riding Wixted was AWOL for twenty-nine hours later in the stand and was transferred off *Gudgeon* to Treasure Island Hospital for medical treatment. Nonetheless, other than the fatal twelfth patrol, the ninth patrol would be the low point in *Gudgeon*'s history. Post would, at the end of the patrol, term the affair an "amateur performance."[14] He would later pinpoint the turnover in crew and officers as the cause for the problems on the ninth patrol. Indeed, when one reviews the barely readable microfilm of the muster of the crew, it is easy to see his point. For the eighth patrol, he had Frank L. Barrows, another lieutenant commander, on board as executive officer. This was the only patrol in *Gudgeon*'s history on which there were two men on board that were ranked that highly. The outstanding veteran officer, Lieutenant Albie Strow, a veteran of five patrols under Lyon, Stovall, and Post, was also on board. Lieutenant Donald R. Midgley and Lieutenant W. R. Robinson, a veteran of the first seven war patrols, added a wealth of experience. George Penland, another experienced officer, served

Gudgeon well until his death. Lieutenant H. J. Kuehn was the only new-comer among the officers on the eighth patrol.

For unknown reasons, it is very difficult to find records that clearly state who the officers were for each patrol on *Gudgeon*. It is certain that Bill Post had Strow and Midgley aboard for the ninth patrol. Strow took over as executive officer after Barrows left to assume command of *Swordfish*. New to *Gudgeon* were at least three officers. They were Lieutenants Burton Heyes, Addison Pinkley, and Thomas Trent. If there were other officers than these men on board, it is unclear from the few existing records. But, according to the records, only Post and Strow had done more than one patrol.

It wasn't just the loss of experienced officers that would weaken *Gudgeon* on the ninth patrol. Iron-nerved veteran torpedoman Quent "George" Seiler as well as many others would be transferred off *Gudgeon* before the submarine left for patrol. In fact, about a third of the crew who boarded *Gudgeon* for the ninth patrol had not been on board for the prior patrol. This figure may be misleading because without question some of the newcomers had experience on other submarines. George Seiler is certain that this is so because many experienced men wanted to serve on *Gudgeon* because of her reputation as a "fighting submarine." [15]

Yet a significant change was taking place in the makeup of the crews on United States submarines. More and more inexperienced sailors were being sent to sea. There were fewer and fewer experienced submariners waiting ashore on relief crews. Greater numbers of submarines were being built. Each needed a core of experienced men to man her and to complete the training of the green crew and officers. Thus, the number of veterans on any submarine at this time was, out of necessity, far fewer than at the start of the war, when virtually all the men on the boats were naval regulars. George Seiler stated that by this time in the war, there were usually only about twelve to fifteen combat veterans on board a new submarine, usually the captain and exec, and one man in each compartment.

With the war in full gear, and the submarines being built as quickly as possible in many U.S. naval yards, submarine schools were rapidly cranking out submariners. Because of the necessities of war, they would not have time to serve, for example, aboard a surface craft prior to being assigned to a sub. They would get their submarine training and be sent directly to the submarine, then off to war. Their training at submarine school was much more narrow, focusing almost entirely on the trainees area of specialty. The new recruits would complete submarine training and report to boats with rates higher than those of the experienced, war-hardened submariners already onboard. The practice seems unfair as well as unwise. This was a very real source of irritation for the old salts. The green sailors would not only have better rates; they would also get more pay. Once on board they had to unlearn much of the sub school training they had received on the ancient pigboats and be retrained by their underlings, men who had been in the Navy for years, having served on many ships and proven themselves under the most demanding of times. The training boats were so different from the fleet submarines that the previous training in some ways hindered the performance of the men. The officers who moved quickly to submarine duty directly from training were known disparagingly as "90-day wonders." From here on out, *Gudgeon* would be getting her fair share.

Also among those departing after eight patrols was the Chief of the Boat, James C. (Gunner) Ogden. The loss of the experienced chief of chiefs was no small matter. Also gone were two other departmental heads, Chief Electrician's Mate Herman J. Fredette and Chief Machinist's Mate Harper A. Warner, in addition to Franklin B. Kohrs, a first class machinist's mate. Among the fourteen total crew transferring off the submarine was one of the heroes of *Gudgeon*'s seventh war patrol, Gilbert M. "Ducky" Drake, who had impetuously—but fortuitously—fired torpedoes at the charging destroyer in March 1943.

Since the last patrol, the men on *Gudgeon* had experienced a very long break. After arriving at the dry docks at Hunter's Point, there was no official duty until July 28 when the crew returned to *Gudgeon* to test the submarine's readiness for sea. They fired dummy torpedoes, conducted sound and deep submergence exercises, fired the new five-inch deck gun, and loaded provisions and torpedoes. Bill Post was probably just itching to get that big gun into action, anticipating its superior firepower and the damage it could wreak. His thinking was probably that with a bigger gun, torpedoes could be saved for prime targets, and the result would be more enemy ships sunk. *Gudgeon* also had a new look. The conning tower had been altered, the submarine's profile cut down from the boxier look she had prior to the war to look like the sleek *Trigger*.

On August 9 it was time to leave the west coast behind, conduct trim dives, general drills, and fire control en route to Pearl. Much to Post's dismay, he found that continued overhaul during transit was needed because the boat was not ready for wartime patrolling. A new policy had been implemented. Submarines were sent to sea with their overhauls not yet finished. The policy to finish overhaul items en route to Pearl Harbor was a new one, designed to get the submarines into the water more quickly. These tasks were added to the drills undertaken while en route.

George Seiler, still on board *Gudgeon*, recalled, "After leaving Hunter's Point the *Gudgeon* pointed her bow toward Pearl Harbor, and we went through the routine diving exercises throughout the day, not only for the benefit of the new people aboard, but to get the old hands sharpened because of the long layoff. We went through so many battle surface ascents that it became a routine procedure, and fast. Our crash dives got faster until we could get under in a time that we had never experienced before. Wild Bill Post had the bit in his mouth and was ready for the run."[17]

Gudgeon transported a passenger to Pearl Harbor, a Commander Leon Blair, formerly the skipper of *Stingray*, whom George Seiler had served under and, in fact, despised. The feeling was mutual. Seiler said that the none-too-popular Blair had been known as "Captain Bligh" on *Stingray*. Some time earlier, before the war, Blair had been constantly giving some of the torpedomen on *Stingray* hell because of their incessant swearing while doing their duty. As luck would have it, shortly thereafter Blair ordered Seiler and some of his shipmates to his home to do some work around the house. The work lasted into the evening, so the four sailors ate dinner with the Blair family. One of the many Blair children, a young boy, was miffed, knowing that there was only so much food to go around, and that because of the presence of the sailors his piece of pie was bound to be much smaller than he would have gotten, or worse, he would not get a piece at all. Greatly irritated, he repeatedly asked his dad if he could have his pie. The upright Blair told him each time that he would have to wait until everybody was done with their main courses. Finally, Blair told his son to go ahead and take a piece of pie, to which the exasperated little boy responded, "Jesus Christ, it's about damn time I get my pie." George Seiler almost spit out his mouthful of food across the room trying to suppress his laughter. He could not wait to get back to the boat to tell the torpedomen what had transpired. Before long, every time Blair would traverse the *Stingray*, he would hear his crew wisecracking as he disappeared into the next compartment, something along the lines of, "Damn, I wish I could have a piece of pie now," or, "Do you want a piece of pie, Skipper?" Blair hated Seiler for his betrayal; the embarrassment and lack of respect shown him by his crew was infuriating.[18]

As luck would have it, very early on in *Gudgeon*'s cruise to Pearl Harbor, Blair was standing atop the deck with Bill Post when he sighted his archenemy, George Seiler, at the time a veteran of six war patrols, and asked, "What are you doing here?"[19] Seiler responded, "I'm fighting the war, what are you doing?"[20] Post looked at Seiler bewildered, never having seen Seiler show such disrespect for a senior officer. A short while later, Post took Seiler aside and asked, "George, what in hell is wrong with you? Do you know Commander Blair?"[21] Seiler told Post all of the reasons for his disregard for Commander Blair, to which Post explained that Blair had never done a war patrol and had been assigned to Admiral Nimitz's staff at Pearl Harbor. The day after arriving at Pearl Harbor a few days later, George Seiler was transferred off *Gudgeon* for reasons he did not understand until a half-century later. Bill Post had not requested the transfer, George Seiler hadn't asked for it, and no correspondence had been received notifying Post that Seiler was to be transferred. In retrospect, Seiler is certain that "Captain Bligh," wanting to "get" Seiler, had him transferred off *Gudgeon*, a move which had always confused and angered him until he realized that Blair's revenge may have saved his life.[22] George Seiler was not on *Gudgeon* for the upcoming fatal twelfth run.

On September 1, 1943, Lieutenant Commander Post learned that he had been promoted to commander. And, even better, that *Gudgeon*, for the first time under Post, would be loaded with a full supply of torpedoes. She pulled away from Pearl Harbor accompanied by *Trigger*, which was heading out for her sixth patrol under the command of former *Gudgeon* executive officer Dusty Dornin, who had taken over for Roy Benson. The two submarines set course for Johnston Island, southwest of Pearl Harbor, where they would stop for refueling. *Gudgeon* and *Trigger* reached Johnston Island on September 3, where they dropped off what might just as well have been gold bricks. Twenty sacks of mail were left on the island for distribution to the troops. *Gudgeon* also received provisions, topped off the tanks with fuel and water, and even arranged to get some help from the Seabees who worked on the number one main motor. Some of the crew swam and happily took on a good burn. Best of all was the fact that there was plenty of beer on shore. By 1810 *Gudgeon* was once again heading off, this time to an area designated as "Area 14," south down by the Marianas Islands.

By the eighth, a man in the after torpedo room had already written in the after torpedo room workbook of the patrol—which was becoming tedious—"Underway as before-Same bullshit." [23] On the eleventh, the same writer wrote in the workbook that *Gudgeon* had some bad luck because the boat had lost her hydraulic power because of "Hunter's Point efficiency." [24] The men aboard the boat were obviously angry. The submarine had been laid up for all that time between the eighth and ninth patrols, and then something as serious as this had happened because of the incompetence of the mechanics in San Francisco. The problem was obviously fixed or worked around because *Gudgeon* was on-station and approaching Japanese-held Saipan by the following day. After observing another couple of Nell bombers—and probably being spotted—Post ordered *Gudgeon* to head for Guam. He had not found any ships worth stalking in Balau Bay, Saipan.

For a short while the air conditioner had gone out. The boat was once again like a steam oven. Indeed, the workers at Hunter's Point had done a poor job on *Gudgeon*. So, armed with a relatively green crew and officers, missing key individuals from *Gudgeon*'s previous highly successful patrols, it seemed things couldn't get worse. That is, until the fancy new SJ radar went out and was determined to be unfixable.

Then what surely must have been Post's biggest frustration as *Gudgeon*'s skipper occurred. After avoiding a couple of patrol boats, at noon on September 16, Commander Post fired a spread of four bow torpedoes at a maru anchored off a place known as Luminao Reef. As far as could be determined, none of the torpedoes exploded. Post said later that the visibility was quite poor for a submerged periscope attack. The target was completely obscured because of a heavy sea swell. Post swung around for a stern shot and fired four more torpedoes. The men waited silently for the sound of explosions, but, once again, there was only an eerie silence. Apparently the torpedoes were running normally; and all eight torpedoes had missed their target. Post was livid.

The only saving grace was that the torpedoes had made no discernible noise; they attracted no antisubmarine forces. *Gudgeon* retired to review the situation. The men took observations from three different positions, and by this time the visibility had improved considerably. The observation of the target before the first eight torpedoes were fired had been very unsatisfactory. Post discovered that the ship was not a small tanker, but a large freighter anchored in Apra Harbor, not moored at Luminao Reef. The visibility had been so poor for the first two attacks that Bill Post could not tell for certain what the ship was or even where it was stationed. At 1330 Post made an approach by navigation intending to fire across Calalan Bank and sink the ship there at anchor. At 1351 *Gudgeon* let loose with four more torpedoes set at low speed and a depth of ten feet. This time at least three of the torpedoes exploded. Post reported seeing geysers of clear water containing no debris, in line with the target. In fact, for a time, the target was completely obscured by a wall of water followed by another wall of smoke. When the scene cleared, the freighter was observed sitting placidly in the water, unharmed. Post was unsure what had happened but concluded that some of the torpedoes may have gone beyond the target while others must have gone under the ship and hit the beach. He thought that the fish may have run too deep. Who knows? All Post knew was that the target sustained no damage beyond a "good shaking and wetting." [25] Now, certain to have attracted attention, Post started evasive tactics. The Japanese counterattack was weak, however, with one half-hearted depth charge being flung and landing far off the port quarter of the submarine.

Gudgeon, tail between her legs, having launched twelve unsuccessful torpedoes at a docked ship, moved on, this time towards Rota Island. The diving officer that day wrote in *Gudgeon*'s diving book, "Fired 12 at maru anchored inside reef. All missed, but blasted hell out of reef protecting harbor." [26] This must have been a bitter disappointment for Bill Post, having been so productive on his first two war patrols, while fighting the war with a partially loaded ship. Now, with a full load of torpedoes he had expended half of them on a vessel that continued to lie unharmed at her mooring. It is obvious that Post carried out the attack under very difficult conditions. The first two sets of four torpedoes had been fired at long ranges—between 3,700 and 4,500 yards. The frustration of the men on board was perhaps best expressed by the after torpedo room writer who wrote that the only hits had been on the "Reaf [sic], God damn it." [27]

At 0535, in the early morning hours of September 17, 1943, Post and the rest of the men on board had a chance to work off their severe disappointment of the day before. *Gudgeon* sighted and charged new quarry, a patrol vessel. With all four diesel engines roaring, Wild Bill Post tried to decide whether he could take care of the ship with his new deck gun. Post was surely dying to give the big gun a try. Before long the vessel flashed the letters AA with her searchlights, hoping that the approaching submarine was friendly. The range was 6,000 yards. The men on *Gudgeon*, still smarting from the prior humiliation, chose not to talk with anything but their new five-inch cannon, which bellowed and rocked the submarine as its first projectile sailed toward the friendly Japanese ship. The little guy responded with a steady dash, still hoping, one would assume, that *Gudgeon*'s shot was a clumsy letter and that the two ships could converse rather than fight. Unfortunately, with the SJ radar out and the five-inch gun causing so much vibration when it was fired, Post was forced to give up using his high-power periscope and sight by seaman's eye.

Executive Officer Albert Strow remembered this battle clearly. In the dual role of navigator and executive officer, Strow had done his morning fix and was having breakfast when word was sent through the submarine that a ship had been sighted. Post suggested to Strow that he come up and take a look at her. He told Strow that he was going to attack it with the deck gun, and that since Strow had never been on the deck during a gun action on the surface, he should come up and stay for the show. After all, Post continued, he would be commanding his own boat one of these days, and he ought to see how Post carried out such an attack. No sooner had Strow hit the deck when the Japanese opened fire. Strow said, "He was spraying us with bullets for heaven's sake, and I was standing up on the bridge with nothing to do. I'm not that kind of hero so I was going to get behind anything to protect myself." [28] It was the only time that Strow—as an individual—was shot at during the war. He did not like it one bit.

The little 600 ton vessel played it coy with his bow pointed directly at the submarine giving the gunner's mates the smallest possible target. As the ship approached *Gudgeon*, she kept popping away with a small forward deck gun and .50 caliber machine guns. These Japanese gunners could shoot. Bullets zinged off the armor plating on the bridge where Post and Strow stood. It was pure luck that none of the shots hit one of the *Gudgeon*'s officers. By this time it was readily apparent that the new five-inch gun was unsatisfactory. Post had speculated that getting the larger guns would enable the submarine to inflict a great deal of damage before *Gudgeon* was even in torpedo-firing range. This was not to be; the gun sights designed by the crew on the *Pelias* for the previous patrol came out of bore sight on the very first salvo the *Gudgeon* fired. With both ships gamely charging each other at around 4,000 yards, *Gudgeon* finally scored a couple of hits, one near the waterline at the front of the ship, the other behind the stack on the superstructure of the vessel.

The bravado of the men on the Japanese patrol ship was more easily understood when fourteen minutes into the attack a second ship was seen coming over the horizon. The time was now 0550 with dawn slowly breaking. After eighty-five shots and only two hits, a once-again-disappointed Post ordered that *Gudgeon* turn away. By this time, the patrol vessel was listing to starboard and smoking heavily with tongues of flames "adding color to the smoke." [29] A plane joined the action and was circling over the stricken vessel. The second ship pulled aside the damaged patrol ship, and ignored *Gudgeon*, which suggested to Post that the vessel was severely damaged and going down fast. The pilot of the plane apparently felt that it was more important to give aid than chase the hunter. With the patrol ship "dead in the water," Post, perhaps anticipating the perennial problem of gaining credit for a job well done, noted finally that, "The ship was never seen again in the area." [30] As *Gudgeon* approached, then patrolled clockwise around Guam, a total of eight distant explosions were heard.

Lieutenant Strow continued with his recollections of what happened after the battle: "I was sitting in the wardroom having a cup of coffee trying to get my shattered nerves back together and the Captain came in and said, 'How was your birthday present?' I said, 'Not worth a damn, why?' Post replied with a grin, 'I've been trying to scare you for three years and I finally did it. Ho Ho Ho." [31]

On the eighteenth, with *Gudgeon* returning to the sight of her prior humiliation, Post sighted the same ship at anchor that had somehow survived *Gudgeon*'s recent twelve-torpedo salvo. This time, realizing that twelve torpedoes were more than the target merited, *Gudgeon* rolled on. On the nineteenth, the lookouts spotted six twin-engine Nell bombers bearing directly at *Gudgeon*. *Gudgeon* wisely submerged for several hours. On the twentieth a cluster of four small sampans was sighted, escorted by a sub-chaser and a small converted yacht. Post considered attacking, but with the seas high and periscope observations very difficult, *Gudgeon* went deep to allow the "motley armada" of ships to pass by without incident.[32]

The waters in the area surrounding Japanese-held strongholds were teeming with patrol planes: Nells, Hiros, and twin-engined flying boats called Aichi A1s. The hunting and diving and surfacing and searching continued until the twenty-fifth, when *Gudgeon* found herself eyeballing two Kamikaze class destroyers about 8,000 yards away. Post was hardly afraid of a couple of destroyers, though the two of them had *Gudgeon* greatly outgunned. *Gudgeon* moved forward, starting her approach on the two killer ships. Probably by coincidence they zigged away and withdrew out of range and sight. Later that evening another Kamikaze class destroyer materialized out of a rain-squall at a range of just less than one mile. It was a surprised Bill Post who ordered that *Gudgeon* quickly dive. The men on watch scurried down the hatches to their battle stations. *Gudgeon* smoothly slipped beneath the waves and out of sight. However, the destroyer had sighted *Gudgeon* before the dive and turned to stalk her. One of the sailors in the after torpedo room correctly predicted what would happen next when he wrote in his log that *Gudgeon* was "about to receive a present from our little brown brothers."[33] When *Gudgeon* reached 40 feet, the first of nine depth charges exploded, causing him to comment that the bombing reminded them of "another dude we met on one of our vacation layovers under the name of *Truk Is*."[34]

It was depth charge number two that did the most damage, breaking some light bulbs and causing damage throughout the boat. Perhaps most severe of all, at least to the submarine's habitability, was the loss of Freon from the number one air conditioner unit. Luckily, the mechanical whizzes on *Gudgeon* were able to get it up and running in two hours.

With Bill Post working his way through "Waltzing Matilda," *Gudgeon* continued to glide deeper and deeper under the waves, finally entering the security of a density layer where the *Gudgeon* out-sat the Japanese destroyer. A density layer is a layer of water with a different temperature. Some of these layers were so dense that when a submarine went under them, the layer muted or confused the sonar pinging, which made it difficult for sub-chasers to locate the sub. Diving officer Lt. jg Burton Heyes wrote, "Tried to pick up our date (DD) [destroyer] but when we saw her at 800 yds, decided to 'stand her up'. She got sore and decided to slap us 9 time. One hurt."[35]

Gudgeon was now patrolling the critically important Saipan-to-Japan shipping lanes. On September 27, Post found himself eyeballing an unescorted maru standing out of Tanapag Harbor, Saipan. Two destroyers were in the area. This time, the visibility was quite acceptable, and the ship was about 1,800 yards away. Post explained the difficulty in firing at the ship: "It was just after sunset and we did our best to make the attack before dark as our SJ radar was out of commission, and we were unable to obtain a QC range. However, darkness beat us, and since our last five set-ups checked perfectly with the TDC we fired on a generated bearing when the range had closed to 1,200 yards. Sound followed the torpedoes on their run and reported them running hot, straight, and normal long after they should have hit. Nothing was 'seen, heard, or felt'."[36] *Gudgeon* was now an unprecedented zero for sixteen on torpedo shots fired on the patrol. The men on *Gudgeon* were deeply frustrated. Lt. Midgley wrote, "At sunset started after a fat one. Black as hell out. No results. 4 more-sixteen to zero-damn!!"[37]

But as basketball players always say: "The best way to get yourself out of a shooting slump is to just keep on shooting." So, on the twenty-eighth, Bill Post and his inexperienced crew did exactly that. This time a 7,000 ton maru similar to the *Matunoto Maru* was the target. During *Gudgeon's* approach the tanker was zigzagging so radically that all four sides of the ship were observed. With no torpedoes in the stern tubes it was all that the men on *Gudgeon* could do to keep the bow of the submarine pointed at the target, the vessel's maneuvers were so effective. Post described the maneuvers that were necessary to hit a ship in World War II, this time a gyrating one. "As we were about to fire on a forty starboard track, range about 1,500 yards, target zigged radically to right presenting a ten degree port angle on the bow. Range was now under 1000 yards, gyro angle 30 left, increasing rapidly. Decided better to twist in a hurry and shoot him 'up the kilts' at greater range with zero gyro angle than accept large parallax shot at uncertain short range with large gyro, QC ranges being still unreliable."[38] Shortly thereafter, Post fired four torpedoes, two of which were seen to hit the doomed vessel. The boat quickly squatted by the stern and listed to starboard. The Japanese hurriedly threw lifeboats into the water. An escort vessel was observed hurrying to the rescue.

As usual Post ordered the submarine to prepare for Japanese retaliation. This time seventeen of the large barrel-like devices exploded around *Gudgeon*. BOOM. BOOM. BOOM. BOOM. BOOM. BOOM. BOOM. BOOM. BOOM. BOOM. BOOM. BOOM. BOOM. BOOM. BOOM. BOOM. BOOM. Each explosion was deafening, but not so close that they damaged the submarine. Post took an observation with ten feet of periscope and sighted a total of six or more lifeboats and other patrol vessels "milling" around the site of the sinking and snapped a picture.[39]

This would be the only ship that *Gudgeon* would receive JANAC credit for having sunk on the ninth run. The vessel was eventually identified as the *Taian Maru*, a passenger-cargo ship of 3,158 tons. A few minutes later, as *Gudgeon* was leaving the area submerged, a plane snuck in and surprised the submerged submariners. Even during these days in the war, when the Japanese had not made major efforts to battle the American submarines by air, they had proven over and over that they could get close enough to *Gudgeon* to bomb her. Luckily their aim and their estimation of *Gudgeon*'s depth were inaccurate. However, the troubling fact remains that planes were by this time in the war far too consistently getting far too close. On this patrol, the lack of functioning SJ radar played a major role.

The following day found Post and Executive Officer Albie Strow on duty, off the northeast tip of Saipan. At 0534, *Gudgeon* ignored two smaller patrol vessels in the area and lined up for shots on two maru that were quite difficult to see clearly, but seemed to be similar to 7,950 and 8,610 ton maru that had been located in the *Japanese Merchant Ship Recognition Manual*. Post fired two torpedoes at each ship, which were estimated to be about 1,400 yards away. Given the timing of the explosions and the distance to the targets, it was likely that one torpedo had hit each of the ships. By the time Post could take a look at the stricken vessels, he was shocked to see that one of the two Kamikaze class destroyers seen earlier but ignored was bearing in on *Gudgeon*. This was usually the fate of the World War II submariner. Fire your fish at the enemy then prepare to get the hell pounded out of you, and if you were lucky, you would live to tell about it.

As Post described it later, "We ducked for our chastening," once again making speed for the relative safety of the density layer at around 180 feet to hide the submarine's whereabouts.[40] It did not keep the destroyer from initiating another thundering depth charge attack. BOOM. Twenty-six depth charges rained down on *Gudgeon* over the next couple of hours. None was close enough to do damage, but as usual, the deafening explosions and the violent pressure of the ocean against the submarine created a terrifying and unique experience for the submariners on board, especially those that had never done a war patrol. The attack no doubt not only scared them to their core, but also likely urged them to reacquaint themselves with God.

Gudgeon finally found sanctuary under the density layer, which made the 307 foot submarine all but invisible. The pursuit of *Gudgeon* by the Japanese was none too impressive, Post reported at the time. The patrol vessels and destroyers were, by this time, close to one of the stricken maru, which was now listing to port and down by the stern. They all seemed to be "getting in each other's way."[41] A visual search several hours after the attack with twelve feet of periscope stuck far above the waves did not yield a clue as to the fate of the first target. It was never seen again. As *Gudgeon* churned slowly away through the once-again peaceful depths of the Pacific Ocean, explosions continued to ring out from the direction of the stricken Japanese maru.

Traveling on the surface, heading for the safety of Midway, *Gudgeon* was now approached by the forty-fourth enemy plane sighted on this patrol. This time, the single plane turned out to be another of those menacing Nell bombers. Originally picked up by radar at fourteen miles, the plane closed rapidly on the submarine. *Gudgeon* dove deep, suffering attack from two more small depth bombs on the way down. The bombs were set to explode at preset depths in hopes that the ensuing explosion would match the depth of the submarine and sink it. Once again the enemy had no luck. When Post raised his periscope to look for the bomber, the plane dove and started firing machine guns at the scope. Because the pilot was out of bombs, the bomber now had the ferocity of a charging Chihuahua.

Gudgeon soon arrived for a rest at Midway Island. This had been a frustrating, disappointing, thirty-seven day patrol during which *Gudgeon* had undergone six separate attacks by depth bomb or depth charge, comprising a total of fifty-six individual bombs of one kind or the other. On the patrol *Gudgeon* had traveled 7,845 miles expending 81,000 gallons of diesel fuel.

In his post-action report Post described the Japanese antisubmarine activity in the area as intensive but "non-persistent and ineffective." [42] The Japanese were throwing everything at the Allied submarine service that they could—bombers, sampans, trawlers, armed patrol vessels, and destroyers. Post doubted that most of the ships had any sound gear and said that if any was present it was usually of poor quality. The soundmen aboard *Gudgeon* could detect the high-speed screws of Japanese propellers at 206–340 rpms at ranges of 6–10,000 yards, but *Gudgeon* remained undetected at ranges as low as 200 yards. On the other hand, the men on *Gudgeon* had grown very aware of the almost complete "air umbrella" over Saipan. [43]

To be fair, it was not just that *Gudgeon* had lost so many of her experienced crew that caused her problems on this patrol. When explaining his firing crew's lack of success, Post noted that *Gudgeon* was without SJ radar for virtually the entire patrol. Even when it worked, it was deemed extremely unreliable. Its absence made the *Gudgeon*'s attacks more primitive and obviously less effective. Fortunately the older SD radar worked well at picking up planes as far away as 26 miles. To complicate matters, the JK sound gear used to monitor the ocean around the submarine was useless after September 10, when it broke down. The QC sound gear required constant upkeep but performed reasonably well when it was running.

Skipper Post sang the praises of the various density layers that were found repeatedly when *Gudgeon* was in jeopardy from the attacking Japanese ships. The layer was found surrounding Saipan and Guam and 15 miles southwest of Agrinan Island, always at 180 feet. This was critical information to pass on to the other submarines in the service. Post discussed the folly of the Navy's policy of hurrying submarines out of port before they were mechanically ready for patrol. In the past, submarine skippers had been able to count on a period of time after their submarine left the dock to be used to prepare the new crew for war by drilling, practicing dives, gunnery practice, and other activities critical to the survival of the submarine. This time the men on *Gudgeon* were expected to finish the overhaul that had not been completed after a period of almost two months at dry dock. After leaving San Francisco, there was so much mechanical work to do on board that by the time they reached Pearl Harbor the crew was exhausted. They were so fatigued that Post considered that the demands upon the men had "seriously hampered the battle effectiveness of the crew." [44]

With overpowering understatement dripping from his words, Post concluded, "The Commanding Officer feels that it cannot be stressed too strongly that it is far better to overhaul a submarine in a navy yard than in enemy patrolled waters." [45] One gets the impression from reading these words that the frustrated Post wanted to wring someone's neck for the sub-par performance of *Gudgeon* on her ninth patrol.

Post said that the patrol was an "amateur performance" when compared to his prior tours de force aboard *Gudgeon*. [46] Despite the less-than-polished performance of the crew, Post said that with the occasional "rare exceptions" the conduct of all hands left "nothing to be desired." [47]

Post was, as usual, pleased with the food. The submarine had once again received the lion's share of fresh meat and fruits. Unfortunately, 1,200 pounds of meat was spoiled before being loaded on board. The endorsements of *Gudgeon*'s work on the patrol were as expected: Lukewarm. The Commander Submarine Division Twenty-Two, Commander Joseph Anthony Connolly agreed that the lack of SJ radar had hindered *Gudgeon*'s success. The torpedo-firing party was criticized for the failure of the attack on September 16, when twelve torpedoes had missed their mark.

Admiral Lockwood was kinder than his underlings. He praised the crew for their "good area coverage" and "close surveillance" of all harbors encountered. [48] He said that, as usual, the patrol was "aggressive in spirit." [49] He judged that organization difficulties due to the turnover in officers and enlisted personnel were eventually largely overcome and "effective" damage to the enemy was accomplished. [50] He considered the patrol to be successful, which meant that for the ninth straight patrol, *Gudgeon* had passed muster and been awarded a Battle Star. Decorations would once again reflect that level of success. Lockwood congratulated Post and the other officers and men on board for the patrol, and credited *Gudgeon* with having sunk two maru totaling 15,008 tons and for damaging two others at 9,214 tons. On the next patrol, *Gudgeon* would welcome two young ensigns. One was from Orange, Texas, the other from Webster City, Iowa.

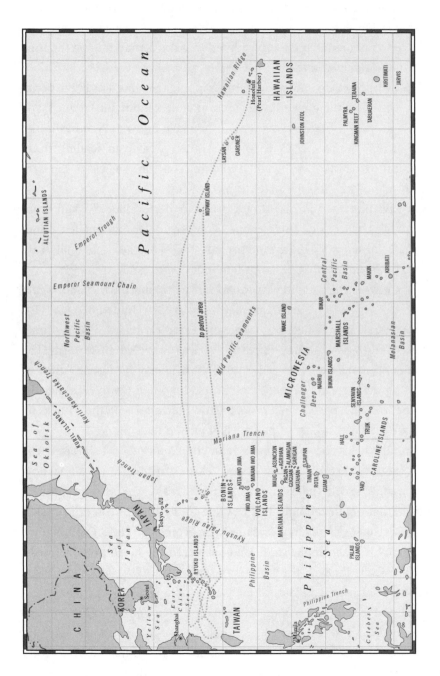

Tenth War Patrol • Approximate Course • Oct. 31–Dec. 11, 1943

▪ 10 ▪
Reporting for Duty

The test of any man lies in action.

Pindar 5th century BC

On October 22, 1943, William Conrad Ostlund of Hamilton County, Iowa reported aboard *Gudgeon*. Bill Ostlund had honorably answered his country's call to arms. However, for the twenty-five-year-old ensign this would be a fateful as well as honorable day. He was recently married and full of promise and hope. He had everything to live for, but fate and destiny would have their way.

Three days prior to reporting, on October 19, 1943, Bill Ostlund of Submarine Division 102, San Francisco, California, wrote his maternal Uncle, Jack Clelland and his Aunt Blanche of Chicago:

Dear Aunt Blanche and Uncle Jack,

Have meant to write you for some time, and though I have no good excuse for not doing so sooner, I just never have been able to get around to it.

I sure appreciate your both coming down to the station when Peggy and I were in Chicago. I was anxious to have you meet her. It's unfortunate that we couldn't have had a better visit but that can be overlooked in the rush and high-tension conditions of living at the present time.

In Mother's last letter she mentioned that you had been there on your vacation. I'll bet you hardly recognized what formerly was the '833 Boone Street Clubhouse'. Mother certainly has a nice place now. I can't help but think back on the terrific beating the three of us 'brats' gave the old house—broken windows, pictures pasted on the walls, athletic gear thrown thru and all around the place, and tons of tracked in dirt. Must be some relief for her not to have to put up with that now.

Naturally, I can't tell you much about anything out this way. I'm feeling fine despite being pretty lonesome and homesick every once in awhile. My work is quite interesting and keeps me busy enough to stay out of trouble at least. The food's good and there's no place to spend any money so I guess I could be in far worse shape.

Thanks again for coming to the station and I hope when this whole thing is over you'll both have a chance to become well acquainted with Peggy. I'm sure you'll like her. Sometimes I wonder how she puts up with me but she doesn't seem to mind so I certainly can't complain.

Very sincerely,
Bill

Ensign W.C. Ostlund
USNR Sub. Division 102
c/o Fleet Post Office
San Francisco, Calif.

By 1943, Mary Ostlund's three sons were all in the service far from home. Lieutenant John Ostlund was a bombardier in the Eighth Air Force, flying missions over Europe. Bob was a lieutenant in the Quartermaster Corps and would be deployed in Europe on Omaha Beach, six days after the invasion. Both Bob and John survived the war; Bob died in 1999. John, the third of three boys born to Newet and Mary Ostlund, does not speak much of their childhood. Times were tough. The family owned and operated the first farm implement business in the county, on the main street of Webster City. Shortly after the start of the Great Depression, Newet died of pneumonia. Mary was left to raise the boys and run the store. Bill was twelve years old, Bob eleven, and little John only six.

Years later, Bob would recall waking in the middle of the night after his father's death and hearing his mother crying. He remembers trying to comfort her, and despite her policy of not worrying her sons with adult matters, in her despair she blurted out that their implement store had only taken in eleven cents that day. Still, Bob remembered, there was always a freshly baked chocolate cake sitting on the kitchen counter or a jar full of homemade cookies on the shelf for the boys and their friends to enjoy when they got hungry. The townspeople, as well, did what they could to help out the young widow by dropping off a chicken or some produce, always saying that they had extra so as not to embarrass the young woman with the charity.

John remembers a childhood spent with his two older brothers and friends in the small town filled with Boy Scouts, church events, family get-togethers, and sports—basketball, baseball, football, swimming. The Ostlund boys would be involved in anything that a boy could do with a ball. They had a club composed of their best pals, and one summer built an ingenious fort down by the creek that had underground rooms and a treehouse annex. For years after they were grown and gone, the spot was still marked by a huge boulder that they had used to cover the secret entrance from discovery by other clubs in town.

Bill, being the oldest, was expected to help mind his younger brothers. They attended the Lutheran church every Sunday without fail, and Mary sang in the choir at the front of the church behind the pastor's lectern. One Sunday the boys were sitting together in the front pew—clean, shiny, and dressed in their depression-era best. Bob and John were trying not to fidget, but it was summer, and the church was hot, the sermon long. Finally the sermon ended, and a woman began a solo. Unfortunately, the music was well outside her vocal range. As she strove to hit the high notes, the two younger Ostlund boys began to react. First John would start shaking silently, doing his best to keep his face expressionless, but Bob, sitting next to him, could feel the mirth through his younger brother's shaking body. Bob tried to hold his breath to keep from laughing. Bill, charged with the younger boys' good behavior, looked sternly in silence at them. Then the vocalist hit an especially difficult passage, Bob blew out his breath and dissolved into giggles, John, his face red and sweating from the effort to control himself, finally dissolved into snickers, and Bill, horrified, glared at his two brothers. The entire church was now aware that the Ostlund boys were out of control. Mary, sitting in dignified and powerless silence behind the soloist, could do nothing but watch as her boys became less and less in control of themselves. She looked beseechingly at Bill, silently begging him to get the two younger boys under control. Bill caught her look and turned once more to his brothers, prepared to deliver an angry but whispered order to "get yourselves under control." As he looked at his brother's red faces, wreathed in grins and wet from tears of laughter, the soloist hit a particularly ugly high note, and Bill, too, could no longer contain himself. He guffawed loudly, and the three boys, all in a row, quickly lowered their faces into their laps and silently shook with laughter for the remainder of the service. Mary remained mortified in the choir loft, embarrassed beyond words. Brother Bob recalled years later, "It was just one of those situations where the more you know you aren't supposed to find something funny, the funnier it becomes. As soon as one of us lost it, it was only a matter of time until the other two fell apart as well. We were the Three Musketeers, and even though Bill was supposed to be the older brother he was still just a kid, like John and I were."[1] The memory of that Sunday was important to Bob because it represented to him the closeness of the boys, the dearness of their devout mother trying so hard to do the right thing by them, and the camaraderie the three brothers felt from childhood on, a camaraderie that eventually won out over anything else, even if it manifested at the very "worst" of times.

During the summers, Bill had to drive to nearby Fort Dodge, twenty miles away, to pick up and drop off parts for the implement business. Bill would take his little brother John with him for the trip. Fort Dodge, with about twenty-one thousand residents, was considered to be a big city and was quite a treat for a little boy. Bill and John would always stop at their favorite little shop for malted milks. The next stop would be to see Uncle Bob Clelland, who ran the local Pepsi bottling plant. Uncle Bob was always good for a free bottle of Pepsi, and the boys were always made to feel special by the uncle who was trying as best he could to step into the shoes of their dead father.

Bill was very well-liked in high school and a member of the National Honor Society. He took part in the class play his senior year, but sports were his love. He was by all accounts a good athlete. Bill was captain of the baseball team and also played football and basketball, and ran track. His best sport was basketball. His promise was captured in a description of him in the class yearbook *Torch* his senior year, 1936, which read, "His excellent characteristics make him outstanding."[2] Bill's accomplishments as a basketball player got him a place on the basketball team his freshman year at Iowa State College, now known as Iowa State University. He started on the freshman team but decided to leave after his first year at the college. Bill had acquired a severe case of poison ivy while attending Iowa State. He had missed many classes, fell behind in his coursework, and soured on the school. Bill had his sights on a smaller setting. That summer, a disappointed Louis Menze, the head basketball coach at Iowa State, accompanied by a former Iowa State College All-American basketball player, stopped by the Ostlund house in Webster City and tried to talk Bill into returning to Ames. According to Ostlund family lore, Bill was promised a starting position as a sophomore.

In the fall, he was off to Butler College in Indianapolis, Indiana. He joined the Phi Delta Theta fraternity and made good. A cursory review of a year or so of the *Butler Collegian*, the college newspaper, revealed that Bill thrived at Butler. At one time or another he was Class President, President of his fraternity, Editor of the Yearbook, was twice voted a Big Man on Campus, and also one of the ten most outstanding men on campus. According to the accounts of everyone who knew him, he was an extremely bright, handsome young man, who was not given to bragging or bad behavior. To this day, when people talk about him, they use a special tone of voice that speaks volumes about his character and popularity. In his senior year, he was named to the Who's Who Among Students in American Universities and Colleges for the second time and was voted the "Best Looking Man on Campus."[3] He was quite a golfer too; a small paragraph in the *Collegian* announced that he was determined to beat a double eagle that he had scored the year before.

While at Butler, he participated in four sports at one time or another, lettering in at least two. His senior year he sparkled so brightly as quarterback on his fraternity's intramural football team that he was recruited by Butler legend Tony Hinkle, Butler's football coach, halfway through the season to play halfback for the varsity. It was a mixed bag for the Butler

Bulldogs that year. Purdue thrashed them 28–0, but they finished 4–4–1 and won the Indiana Intercollegiate Conference for the second straight year. All that is known about Bill's varsity career is that he carried the ball twice late in a blowout win over DePauw for sixteen yards before suffering a shoulder injury in a practice a few weeks later. In a pattern that would repeat itself with tragic consequences, Bill Ostlund's football career would end before its time.

Attending Butler during those days was not just fun and games, however. The newspapers of the day were full of stories about the German and Japanese aggression. The day Bill received one of his awards, an article in the same issue of the *Collegian* stated prophetically: "Japan warned today that attempts to 'stifle' her in the South Pacific would have most grave results and said that efforts are being made to assure that the Phillippines [sic] 'will not endanger Japan in the future.'"[4] Bill and younger brother Bob, who followed Bill to Butler, worked their way through school as busboys at a campus sorority. Along with having many new "sisters" and having a great time, they also were teased quite a bit. It was just too easy to make the two young Iowans blush, and the sorority girls were unable to resist. The busboys were supposed to serve the table silently and efficiently. But, as in church when they were younger, if one of the sorority girls could tease a grin out of either brother, it wasn't very long before both of the young men would be fighting back chuckles as they continued to bring in bowls of vegetables or clear empty plates from the long dinner table.

While at Butler, Bill met his future wife, Peggy Burrell, of Indianapolis. He left Peggy and returned home to Webster City after graduating from Butler in 1941 with a degree in Business Administration. He was needed to help run the family business. Two months after the attack at Pearl Harbor, Bill felt that as much as he was needed at home to help his mother, he was needed more elsewhere, and enlisted in the United States Naval Reserves. On February 26, 1942, two days after his enlistment, an article ran in the local paper featuring a picture of Bill sitting at the family dining room table, his head bent over a math textbook. Bill was studying math nine to twelve hours a day in an attempt to make up for the fact that he had not taken enough math at Butler to be accepted into the Naval Reserve Officers' Training Corps. The serious-minded young man was quoted as saying, "I hope the younger kids just now finishing high school and entering high school and entering college have learned what I didn't—that all military work is based upon mathematics. If they expect Uncle Sam to give them a better-than-average position in his armed forces, they'll have to learn all they can about math now."[5]

Bill had already covered a full semester's college algebra course in two and a half weeks by cramming his days full of study. He had begun a second course, trigonometry, which he was hoping to complete in ten days, thereby meeting the requirements for admission to NROTC. Just to make sure that he was adequately prepared, he was going to take a few more math courses prior to reporting. When discussing his future, he said, "After four months' training the fellows are commissioned. Then it's hard to tell where they'll send a fellow. He might be in command of a small destroyer or a mosquito boat, and, of course, somebody has to supervise the naval recruiting stations, but I hope I can draw something more exciting than that." Bill continued, "While in training the fellows get $75 a month plus room, board, and clothing. After they are commissioned, they get $1,650 a year base pay besides meals and an allowance of $250 a year for uniforms. The training prepares you for good jobs in civilian life later on. It looks like a good opportunity, and I hope more fellows will become interested."[6] Bill was called up in October, accepting appointment as a Midshipman in the Reserves and was sent to Annapolis for training. On January 5, 1943, he was commissioned as an ensign, then married Peggy at a chapel at Annapolis later that same day. Somewhere along the way Bill decided that he wanted to go into the submarine service. He knew that the silent service was very prestigious and that it would impress people after the war, already having decided he wanted to run for political office once things settled down. And it was a whole lot more interesting than supervising a recruiting station. He was ordered to Submarine Division Twelve and reported to the Submarine Base at New London, Connecticut, for training in March 1943. He trained on the old submarine *R-13* and was fiftieth in a class of 103 students. He graduated in about ninety days and was then off to Submarine Division 102 and duty on relief crews.

On October 22, 1943, Bill, with his seabag over his shoulder, boarded *Gudgeon*. A handwritten note on the deck log signed by Executive Officer

Lieutenant Albert J. Strow summarized the event: "Ensign William Conrad Ostlund E-V (E) USNR reported aboard for duty. Auth: Comsub for Pacflt. Subord Command, Orders Serial 126 dated 10-22-43."[7] Also boarding the submarine as one of *Gudgeon*'s new officers was Ensign David Mc-Corquodale. Departing was Thomas Trent, who served the *Gudgeon* on only her ninth patrol.

David Bennett McCorquodale was from Orange, Texas. McCorquodale, like Bill Ostlund, was a high achiever. He had finished high school at the age of fifteen. He was also an Eagle Scout and one of Orange's "superior all-around athletes."[8] After high school, he attended Lamar College in Beaumont, finishing his college work at Texas A & M, eventually earning a degree in Petroleum Engineering. McCorquodale was twenty-eight years old when he joined the Navy. Prior to enlisting, he had worked briefly as a Petroleum Engineer.

For this patrol, Ostlund and McCorquodale, the "Georges" as they were called, or lowest ranking officers on the submarine, would join a full contingent of other officers, all of whom had at least one patrol on *Gudgeon*. In addition to a more experienced group of officers, as well as the fact that Albie Strow had a patrol under his belt as executive officer, *Gudgeon* had only lost sixteen of the crew after her last patrol, retaining fifty-eight men with experience on the submarine. As a result of this improved situation, the spirits of Albie Strow and Bill Post were no doubt high, their expectations even higher. She pulled out after a two-week refit followed by a rather intensive nine-day training period. This time the men on *Gudgeon* would not disappoint either Post or the Navy brass ashore.

Gudgeon departed Midway Island on October 31, 1943. By November 8, she had traveled to Chichi Shima, known more commonly these days as Chichi Jima. Chichi Shima is one of the four island groups making up the Ogasawaras. Another of the island groups, the Volcano Islands, is best known for Iwo Jima, the site of the fierce World War II battle. The refit by the Submarine Division 44 relief crew had gone well. For the next ten days, the men on board the submarine would undergo extensive training. Post had the men practice general drills, deep dives, and fire the five-inch gun as well as the smaller caliber weapons. They practiced periscope and radar approaches and fired three exercise torpedoes. The training period must have been exciting for Ensign Bill Ostlund. This submarine was light-years beyond the rusty old *R-13*. It is likely that the crew became tired of all the drilling. So when *Gudgeon* slowly pulled away from Midway Island on Halloween Day 1943, the men on board bristled with excitement.

The mood on the USS *Gudgeon*, a veteran submarine of nine war patrols, shot sky high on November ninth when a Japanese aircraft carrier was sighted. Unfortunately, it was twelve miles away. A desperate race began with Post firing up all four of *Gudgeon*'s diesel engines, the *Gudgeon* in frantic pursuit of the most prized of all targets, a Japanese flat top. Post figured that the large unidentified vessel was one of the *Ryuju* class escort carriers. Just which one it may have been is unclear, but it was not the *Ryuju* herself because she had been sunk in the Battle of the Solomons in August 1942. Escort carriers are much smaller than the full-sized flat tops, and the *Ryuju* class carriers displaced only about 13,000 tons with a crew of six-hundred, and fifty or sixty planes. Post was pretty sure the ship was headed for Tokyo Bay. Post and the men on *Gudgeon* were determined to get this vessel. Her sinking would have been nice revenge for the attack on Pearl Harbor and for all of the damage the Japanese had done since. When you sink carriers, you know you have really done something special for the war effort. Post felt that he had to get this ship.

In the mid-afternoon, four hours into the chase, with *Gudgeon* running on the surface in frantic pursuit of this fat plum, a small trawler or patrol craft appeared. This vessel was on a course that *Gudgeon* must cross if the submarine was to catch the carrier. As a result Post could not maintain the chase on the surface. The Japanese ship would send out word of the sighting, and *Gudgeon*'s chances to stealthily approach and sink the carrier would be gone. Post had no choice. He submerged, and lost two and a half hours because he had to stay out of sight of the trawler. Worse yet, the men on *Gudgeon*'s radio had been trying unsuccessfully to get someone to respond to their message notifying the Navy of the location and approximate course of the carrier. In frustration, they finally sent the message blind to the Naval Base at Pearl Harbor. The lack of receipt meant that nobody else would have a chance at the carrier, and *Gudgeon*'s sighting would be a complete loss if she did not catch the small birdcage. The following day the chase continued in very high seas. The submarine would surface for a while, then promptly get radar contact of a plane in the area, and be forced to dive again. With each dive the distance between *Gudgeon* and the flat top increased. After a day's frustrating chase, Post was forced to give up, and *Gudgeon* headed for the southeast corner of her originally assigned patrol area.

Most likely in a deep funk after the loss of the carrier, Albert Strow wrote on the eleventh that all he had done since leaving port was to "hold school" for the new crew.[9] He criticized those ashore for their practice of giving sailors a rest after three patrols, thereby leaving a submarine like *Gudgeon* with many inexperienced officers. He estimated that out of all the new crew that *Gudgeon* had welcomed in the past six months, only five were graduates of sub school. Even those who had completed submarine school had trained on such ancient boats that once aboard their assigned submarine, one had to "unteach" them everything they learned on the obsolete pigboats and then re-instruct them on how things were done on a "real" submarine.[10] Strow wrote, "It is tough enough fighting this war with trained personnel but with a crew that does not know the bow from the stern it is even harder."[11]

Of the two new ensigns, Bill Ostlund and David McCorquodale, Strow added, "All in all we did better this last time than ever before because both of them were sub school graduates though they had never been to sea before."[12] Because of their inexperience, Strow noted that the new officers could not be trusted to supervise watch alone since it was uncertain how they would react in an emergency. If he put one of them on watch too soon and the Old Man found out, he would get up and "be about," getting more fatigued and "growling" a lot.[13] Not knowing whether the men assigned to do watch were competent made it tough to sleep. An error could mean that *Gudgeon* would be sent to the ocean floor.

Albie Strow was not above having a little fun at the expense of Ensigns McCorquodale and Ostlund. He wrote in his log that since they could not stand watches on the deck alone he had allowed himself to be put back on the watch list. In his diary, he confided to himself that he was not standing enough watches to hurt him but wrote that this gave him [Strow] a "big weapon" over them: "if they are not good little boys I will stop standing watches and that will make it come much more often."[14] One suspects that

Albie Strow ate many extra desserts on *Gudgeon*'s tenth war patrol given to him by the green new officers, Bill Ostlund and David McCorquodale. Strow regretted missing the carrier, writing that every submariner dreams of sinking a "bird house."[15] "Birds," possibly from such a bird house, had forced *Gudgeon* to dive five times the day before. Strow said that they were tempted to "do a German submarine trick—surface, man our guns, and shoot it out."[16] However, cooler heads prevailed, and *Gudgeon* continued to go deep each time an airplane appeared. Albie Strow was getting plenty frustrated with *Gudgeon*'s "foul luck."[17] About all the *Gudgeon* lookouts had seen were fishing vessels and "flying machines."[18] Strow could not understand how the "simple Japs" could hope to bring in all their conquered wealth if they did not use their ships to do it.[19]

By the thirteenth, *Gudgeon* was patrolling in her assigned area, northwest of Amami O Shima of the Ryukyu Islands, roughly halfway between Tokyo and Formosa. At 0630 *Gudgeon* went to battle stations after a ship was spotted in one of the harbors on the island. Bill Post must have shuddered when he realized that the ship was moored, remembering the humiliating attacks off Luminao Reef on the prior patrol. This time he fired four torpedoes from the bow tubes. All missed behind the ship and were seen to explode on the cliffs; *Gudgeon* reversed engines and turned the stern tubes toward the target vessel. At 0716 the men in the after torpedo room let loose with four torpedoes. Post roared, "FIRE SEVEN. FIRE EIGHT. FIRE NINE. FIRE TEN."[20] One of the latter four torpedoes was seen to blow up in a submarine net about fifty yards away from the ship directly between the maru and *Gudgeon*. The others missed ahead and astern. By this time the men on the Japanese ship were firing small arms toward the submerged *Gudgeon*. The counterattack by the Japanese was a waste of ammunition. Post fumed. A few minutes later, the perplexed Skipper ordered that *Gudgeon* pull away from the harbor. The withdrawal was accompanied by many unidentified explosions of moderate intensity.

Post would explain that there were many challenges which made the attack difficult. Their charts of the harbor were old and unreliable, and he did not know if there were mines in the waters, and if so, where they were. He knew nothing about the currents in the harbor, just that the water was shallow and he was not able to double-check the ship's position before firing. Aware of the challenges he would have hitting the ship, he went ahead and attacked, realizing if he succeeded he would effectively jam up the entrance to this principal port.

Post shouldered the blame for the missed opportunity. After all was said and done, he concluded that he should have more carefully studied the area before attacking, and closed the distance to 2,500 yards so that he would have been successful. George Seiler defended his former skipper, adding, "A moored target is the most difficult of all shots, because nobody has had any training on how to do it."[21] To make matters worse, Post noted that the ship bore a "strange resemblance" to the moored ship that had been attacked in the San Bernardino Straits during the eighth patrol.[22] It is hard for the non-submariner to conceive that hitting a stationary vessel with a torpedo is the "most difficult of all shots."[23] Setting up trajectories at such a target was a "learn as you go" experience for submariners targeting a nonmoving target.[24]

All that *Gudgeon* had accomplished was to anger the Japanese, who responded by sending patrol boats and planes in search of the underwater raider. At 1010 *Gudgeon* skillfully evaded a sub-chaser. At 1058 a mast on the horizon was seen. *Gudgeon* moved to battle stations. As *Gudgeon* approached the ship, identified as a merchantman, the target seemed to morph into a cluster of three patrol crafts. Post told the men to rig for depth charge and ordered that the submarine go deep once the ships had closed to about a mile. Strow wrote that *Gudgeon* had no sooner finished her unsuccessful attempt on the moored ship than the Japanese "called in four patrol vessels to chastise us." Strow continued, "By the time we saw them they were right on top of us and why they never picked us up I will never know. They came right over our heads and we were all standing around with our fingers in our ears waiting for the bangs to begin."[25] This time the Japanese, although seeming to be in a perfect attack position, did not fire a shot. *Gudgeon* moved on silently below the surface to get as much distance as possible from the formidable antisubmarine force above.

Albie Strow had found the day to be one of the longest he had ever lived. The men had maintained battle stations most of the day from 0630 on. He regretted not having sunk the moored maru but was pleased that they did succeed in "scaring the goodie out of all the Japs for miles" around.[26] The process of surfacing, diving, then surfacing once again only to dive and evade took its toll, but that was nothing compared to what it might have been like had the Japanese started throwing depth charges *Gudgeon*'s way. Strow was able to write approvingly of his submarine, the "*Queen*" *Gudgeon* as the men called her, saying, "It is the most amazing thing—I think the old gal is just about half human. When we are out fooling around she takes her time in going under, is never in trim, and the engines smoke something terrible. But, just as soon as things get hot the engines stop smoking, she dives like a harpooned whale, and is in perfect trim. It is uncanny."[27] However, as Strow would note in his log, the day's action was not over. After avoiding the cluster of patrol vessels and running submerged, *Gudgeon* surfaced. After two minutes the lookouts sighted smoke. Strow was convinced that it was a patrol boat and told Post they ought to "lay off."[28] However, Bill Post could do nothing but be Bill Post. He remained on the surface to get a good look and make certain that it was a patrol vessel. Strow was correct. Soon the lone ship was joined by three others. *Gudgeon* dove to evade. The four ships were entirely different ones than those encountered earlier in the day. Strow was certain that the Japanese called in these other ships to rid the ocean of the uss *Gudgeon*.

Fortunately, the slippery Post and his men in the control room were able to shed the Japanese rather easily. The day had really worn Strow out. He wrote that night that the men on board now called *Gudgeon* the "thrill a minute boat."[29] The officers on board celebrated late that night combining two birthdays and the wedding anniversary of one of the officers. The men ate a tremendous amount of chocolate cake and washed it down with bicarbonate of soda. Lieutenant Willie Floyd announced that he was now twenty-one years old, and that he could not wait for a new officer to arrive on board who was younger than he was, so that the others would stop calling him Junior of the eight officers celebrating that night—Bill Post, Albert Strow, Donald Midgley, Addison Pinkley, David McCorquodale, Burton Heyes, Bill Ostlund, and Willie Floyd, three survived the war.

The day following the party was a day of rest on board. Albie Strow was sure he had never slept so hard in his life. His deep sleep followed a day of intense action and felt something like a drug-induced coma. He said the ship could have burned and sunk, and he would not have known it. Strow was pleased that they had been able to put the two new ensigns on watch that day. He anticipated the day when they would be completely trustworthy and he could just "sit back and enjoy life."[30]

Strow explained why he had found himself so exhausted. He was not only the executive officer for the patrol but also the navigator. He wrote, "We spend all our days dodging airplanes and all our nights dodging islands. Since they get me up for either one, I am beginning to think I am not getting any proper rest. Whenever I am wanted on the bridge, one of the troops rushes breathlessly into the room and yells, 'Navigator to the bridge.' It is terrifying—I do not know if we have sighted a ship or if we are just before piling up on a bunch of rocks. Try as I may, I cannot get any information from them and have to tear up to the bridge in my skivvies to see what's cooking. Worst of all—it has always been an island—never a ship."[31]

Gudgeon was now two weeks into the tenth patrol. Strow said it seemed like it had been a month and that he was getting "blood-thirsty."[32] By this time in the war, Strow and Donald Midgley were becoming good friends. So good, in fact, that Midgley, who was not married, wrote Strow's wife and requested recipes for chocolate cake, rhubarb pie, spaghetti and meatballs, chocolate ice cream, and Brussels sprouts. He asked Anna to knit him a red stocking cap that was big enough to pull down over his ears for his times on deck, and that she inscribe a small label with, "Stolen from Midgley."[33] Albert Strow could not believe that Midgley would request anything having to do with Brussels sprouts. Midgley had asked one of the cooks why he never had Brussels sprouts on board. The cooks decided to help Midgley out by serving Brussels sprouts three times a day for a week, and, Strow continued, "No one here can bear them," except Midgley, of course. Strow was certain that *Gudgeon* had "half the world's supply" on board.[34]

On November 15, 1943, Volume One, Number One of *The Gudgeonian* appeared. In all, five copies were printed and distributed. The paper was edited by Lieutenant Willie Floyd. Assistant Editor was Lieutenant William C. Ostlund. E. L. Bland served as copy boy and publisher. The paper was typed neatly on yellow onionskin-thin legal-sized paper. Because two of the five sections of the paper contained secret information, the editors stressed the importance of destroying every copy of the newspaper so that it never left the ship. Luckily, before Bill Post would disembark *Gudgeon* the last time, he took one of the copies off the submarine with him, the only copy which survives to this day. Typical fare from the World News section of the paper was an article, with dateline Madong or Macong, New Guinea, which one could not be determined because some of the letters had been typed over: "The slant-eyes woke up the other day (Nov. 15) to find the place in ruins. According to our informant (usually a reliable source) this was the heaviest raid yet launched in New Guinea, our planes dropping over 223 tons of bombs. According to our 'fly-fly boys' the Nippers had a heavy concentration of anti-aircraft around the place, and sent up a heavy barrage of fire. . . . " [35]

Ostlund and Floyd took advantage of every opportunity they had to take a jab at their "yellow" enemy. From Tokyo it was reported: "In a recent speech to the people of Japan 'ol Tojo' [General Hideki Tojo] admitted a serious shortage in transportation, and urged all workers to exert every effort toward Japan's winning of the conflict. The 'guy' said (and we quote), 'Things is tough' (unquote)." [36] In another article, the Navy Department announced that American submarines in the Pacific and Far East had sunk a total of 496 ships. It was noted that two of the ships that were sunk were "two medium freighters." The editors added, "We know who done that deed." [37] Then a humorous addition was inserted about the wild times *Gudgeon* sailors had ashore before *Gudgeon*'s tenth patrol: "In a further communiqué the Navy Department stated, 'It is earnestly hoped that the USS *Gudgeon* will cause as much damage to the Japanese fleet on their present patrol as they did during their last re-fit period, to installations and morale, on a certain unnamed island'." [38]

The men on the *Gudgeon* were well aware of their success relative to the rest of the submarine fleet. In the "Submarine News" section of *The Gudgeonian*, the successes of several other submarines like *Haddock*, *Trigger*, *Seahorse*, *Sargo*, and *Scorpion* were listed, with the exhortation, "At the present time we have over thirty submarines at sea 'clinking' the enemy at every opportunity. Get in there and pitch, you look-outs, and the 'ol Gud' will still lead the league at the end of this run." [39] The "Ship News" section reported that one of the *Gudgeon* chiefs had been engaged in a graffiti duel with an unknown sailor. Apparently the chief had really slammed the anonymous writer but wanted to let his foe know that he had enough of the fight and did not want to continue the mess-hall bulkhead graffiti war. Volume one ended with a couple of short poems. The first was:

> I'm glad I am an American
> I'm glad that I am free,
> I wish I were a little pup
> And Hitler were a tree.

The second poem was written by an unnamed *Gudgeon* sailor about his lost love, or perhaps more accurately about a relationship that never progressed beyond first base:

> Here lie the bones of Mary Hyde
> For her life held no terrors.
> A virgin born, a virgin died,
> No runs, no hits, no errors.[40]

The paper served an important function on board, sharing news about the war and strengthening camaraderie with jabs at the Japanese as well as fellow shipmates.

The patrol continued with *Gudgeon* carrying on her pattern of careful dodging and surfacing and diving until the seventeenth when Post decided to do something about a junk that for inexplicable reasons was closing on *Gudgeon*. Many common fishing boats were equipped with radios and sometimes even depth charges, supplied, of course, by the Japanese. Consequently, one could not be too cavalier about these small craft. Post went down to the wardroom and told Albert Strow to assemble a boarding party. Word quickly spread from compartment to compartment, and when Strow appointed the boarding party, he angered nearly every sailor on board who was not chosen. Post had his gunners fire a shot across the ship's bow, and the Chinese vessel stopped immediately. Or as Strow wrote, "We closed to about 400 yards and told him to 'heave to' in the international language of putting a shot across his bow. Never in my life have

I seen sails furled so quickly as he did—one instant they were up and the next they were down."[41]

Bill Post then sent the boarding party, led by Lieutenant Donald R. Midgley, onto the little craft. The crew found that the men on the junk were all Chinese and that the cargo consisted wholly of bowls and rice paper, samples of which were obtained in exchange for food, cigarettes, and clothing. No ship's papers or radio equipment was on board. This junk was clean. Strow described the incident, "We could easily see that they were Chinese and not our buck-toothed friends."[42] Strow continued the interesting tale, "We tied them up alongside and everyone came up to see if they could talk to them. Someone tried the old gag of asking if they were on Tojo's or Chiang Kai-Shek's side and they did not want to speak either name."[43] The men on board tried to communicate with the Chinese sailors by using Pidgin English, seeking intelligence information. But, their efforts were point less, the Chinese did not understand a word they said.

The occasion was very unusual for the men on board. Many of the submariners came up on deck and yelled and pointed at the Chinese and took their pictures. By this time, the Chinese skipper and Post understood who the "boss fellows," as Strow called them, of each vessel were.[44] Post wrote that both he and the Chinese captain spent much time bowing to each other. The sailors broke out some bread, candy, canned goods, and cigarettes and tried to give these items to the Chinese who would not accept them until they found something to give back to the Americans. The Chinese offered the submariners Joss sticks, chow-chow bowls, and reams of rice paper. Art Barlow recalled the incident and said that Bill Post would not allow the men to accept the Joss sticks, because they were a religious symbol to the Chinese. Strow continued with the story, showing the kindness of the American submariner in wartime situations. "All the troops felt badly at the Chinese' bare feet and patched clothes, so they all tore below and brought up enough clothes to equip a small army."[45]

Post wrote that the crosscultural communication consisted "principally of a bowing competition between the two skippers. The junk's captain won 'hands down' when we 'flooded down' to take back our boarding party."[46] *Gudgeon* lowered herself in the water to make it easier for the boarding party to return to the submarine. The escaping air from the ballast tanks was then vented out so that water could be taken *in* to lower the submarine, thus scaring the Chinese captain severely and causing him to bow repeatedly. Strow added that the Chinese thought their end had come and "they all started to crossing themselves and if Midge had not been there [on their ship] I honestly think a couple of them would have jumped over the side."[47] Strow thought the encounter did the Americans a lot of good because it gave the men something to talk about "instead of all this shipping we ain't seeing." Strow continued, "Still *I* would like to see a couple of fat marus."[48]

Albert Strow's gloomy mood was evident. The weather had been bad, and he was having difficulty getting star fixes. The storms were so severe, the seas so rough that the men had to tie themselves into their bunks when they slept lest they be pitched from them and severely injured. One time, after tying himself into his bunk, Albie Strow was called to the bridge because land had been sighted. By the time he got himself disentangled and made it to the bridge, a rainsquall had set in, and the land could no longer be seen. The whole thing was repeated a few minutes later, with the land again out of sight by the time he made it topside. The pattern was followed throughout the night until land was again sighted around dawn. *Gudgeon* was twenty miles from where she was assumed to be. Strow finally got some sleep and concluded that navigating was about "10% skill" and the rest just "plain guess work."[49] Strow admitted that he had been showing signs of stress recently. His friends on board were calling him "Laughing Boy–the Great Thundercloud" because of frequent mood changes.[50] He had been "cracking the whip" at everyone who crossed his path, including Midgley, about three times a day.[51] The navigator was likely suffering from sleep deprivation.

Luckily for all, by now the second *Gudgeonian* was making its rounds on the submarine. The editors were careful to point out good news emanating from London, Honolulu, and Italy. In the Southwest Pacific, more "hot dope" was printed about U.S. light bombers attacking "slant-eye" installations in the Northern New Guinea area.[52] Editor Willie Floyd, once again assisted by William Ostlund, added, "Representatives of forty-four United Nations met to discuss post-war reconstruction plans. Editors Note: We are all for reconstruction, but we believe a little destruction will be necessary before we start building again; what do you think?"[53]

The paper announced that Motor Machinist Irvin "Bucko" Moss was collecting money to try to purchase hair restorer for Gunner's Mate Frank "Hair" Turner. Another sailor, Seaman Abe Morrison, was kidded about his good luck with the women. Morrison, who was referred to in the paper as, "A certain Mexican greaser," responded by saying, "I don't think I'm good looking, but 50,000,000 people can't be wrong."[54] Someone even wrote a short poem, another one of those little gems that brought a chuckle to war-stressed submariners. This one was a word to the wise about *Gudgeon*'s heads:

After answering nature's call
Do not be reluctant to pump or blow
Less thy head on thy shoulders
Be likened to the deposit left below.[55]

By November 21, plane contacts from Japanese aircraft continued because *Gudgeon* was now approaching the Chinese coast. Post played it a little risky, not diving quite as fast as he normally would because of his desire to put *Gudgeon* in a fertile shipping lane as quickly as possible. He noted that his reluctance to dive resulted in five depth bombs from Japanese patrol planes, but that the submarine received no damage. *Gudgeon* dove to 420 feet to avoid the bombing.

On the twenty-second, *Gudgeon* made a dive to avoid aerial bombing. *Gudgeon* was in a precarious position with eighty feet of water above her shears and thirty below. No damage was sustained. Bill Post remained quite unhesitant to patrol in shallow water. The following day, while patrolling in the dark on the surface, the lookouts sighted a very promising convoy about 7,000 yards away. There were three large ships—a freighter, a tanker, and a transport—each estimated to be around 10,000 tons, with only one escort present, a modern-looking destroyer. Post sized things up. As he went to work setting up the attack, he softly sang "Waltzing Matilda." Post masterfully maneuvered the submarine into a position which would present the smallest silhouette possible to any target that cared to return fire. Light conditions were favorable; only a thin quarter moon subdued by a mostly overcast sky prevented the attack from taking place in total darkness. Post, now back in his element, decided to fire two torpedoes at each of the three merchant ships. At 0332 Commander Bill Post bellowed, "FIRE ONE. FIRE TWO. FIRE THREE. FIRE FOUR. FIRE FIVE. FIRE SIX."[56] The air pressure that pushed each torpedo out of the tubes vented back into the submarine, which made a "shussssh" sound each time a fish shot out of the boat. If it were allowed to vent into the ocean, the bubble would give away the submarine's position. The boat vibrated slightly as the sea rushed into the torpedo tube, replacing the weight of the just-departed torpedo, which kept the submarine in trim and enabled the submarine to be ready to fire again. When Post determined that the last torpedo was running toward the target, he swung the stern of the submarine around to get a shot at the destroyer, certain that the Japanese killer would make a run at *Gudgeon*. The maneuver was not needed because the destroyer, which would be identified later as the *Wakamiya*, a light cruiser, inadvertently intercepted one of the torpedoes intended for the troop transport. Post watched in amazement as the *Wakamiya* broke in two and sank "in a V" in about a minute.[57] The freighter in the group moved on undamaged. The tanker absorbed two hits, and there were clouds of dense black smoke a thousand feet above the crippled ship, but the tanker limped on away from the *Gudgeon*. The troop transport had taken one hit also. Bill Post called the scene "a good show with excellent illumination, furnished by the disintegrating destroyer."[58] This situation had turned into a submarine captain's dream, and *Gudgeon* prepared to move in for the kill. While the forward tubes were being reloaded, the men from the after torpedo room finally got into the action. At 0347 *Gudgeon* fired two torpedoes from the stern tubes obtaining one more hit on the troop transport. By this time, the transport had stopped and was slowly settling. *Gudgeon* surfaced and at flank speed on four engines pursued the stricken freighter and tanker. The two ships were quickly out of sight, heading for land and what they hoped would be the safety of shallow water of about eight fathoms, or forty-eight feet. The Japanese captains knew that American submariners avoided such shallow depths.

These facts did not seem to bother Bill Post in the least. His job was to sink ships. He knew that in order to do that you sometimes had to take risks, which Wild Bill did unflinchingly. As the men in the control room were developing their attack strategy, and with *Gudgeon* moving forward at full speed after the two fleeing merchant ships, the men manning the radar watched the tanker—now almost five miles away—disappear from the radar screen. She was never seen again. Post had watched the cruiser go down, was certain that the troop transport was sinking, and had been told that the tanker had disappeared from the radar screen. The logical conclusion was that the tanker had sunk. He had only the freighter to worry about. She was headed as fast as she could move toward the beach. If *Gudgeon* chose to give chase, the submarine would be in only fifty feet of water off the coast of China.

This time, Post chose discretion and the sure target offered by the crippled transport. Once sunk, many hundreds or thousands of Japanese soldiers would no longer be around to kill Americans, making the transport an especially attractive target. *Gudgeon* changed course. Within twenty minutes, Post and the men on the bridge were eyeballing the transport. At 0437 with *Gudgeon* about 1,400 yards away, Bill Post fired a spread of three torpedoes from the bow tubes. Post was in a hurry to finish off the transport so he could turn and take a run after the freighter—making haste in the opposite direction—but still a potential target. The attack was so hurried that Post accepted firing the torpedoes at an unfavorable angle, "down the throat," meaning bow to bow. All missed.[59]

This transport was hard to sink. At 0439 with the lighting having improved considerably for the Japanese, the men on the deck of the transport impressed Post greatly by their courageous deck gun attack on *Gudgeon*, which was still on the surface. The three bow fish having missed, Post swung the boat around and fired two more torpedoes from the stern tubes. The target was now much farther away, and the situation was more serious because the torpedoes that had just been fired were the last torpedoes from the after torpedo room. The hurtling fish missed, and the transport was on the move again away from the submarine. With the moon now dangerously bright and the submarine in danger because of the valiant efforts of the Japanese, their shells peppering the ocean around *Gudgeon*, Post ordered a dive. *Gudgeon* descended to forty feet and proceeded forward slowly in pursuit of the transport.

Within ten minutes *Gudgeon* had closed to 1,400 yards and then fired three torpedoes at 900 yards. With the Japanese troopship a nightmarish vision of death and destruction, so full of water that she was almost awash, debris and bodies floating everywhere, and the transport burning brightly, three more torpedoes from *Gudgeon* hit their mark. BOOM. BOOM. BOOM. At 0521 Bill Post watched the transport list heavily to starboard and drop below the surface. In a little over two hours Bill Post and the men on *Gudgeon* had ravaged a four-ship convoy. Certain that three of the ships were at the bottom, *Gudgeon* surfaced and slowly crept in the direction of the sunken troop transport. The ocean was littered with debris and a thick coat of oil. Lifeboats and rafts of all sizes were in the water. *Gudgeon* crashed into the main mast of the sunken vessel but sustained no damage. *Gudgeon* slowly churned on, the submarine making little wake, her diesels chugging noisily. Lieutenant Midgley wrote, "A few more Nips were helped in the Hari-Kari racket—fired 16 pickles. Sunk three (including one dirty DD) and sent one other to the beach on unexpected liberty."[60]

In this incredible savaging of a Japanese convoy, *Gudgeon* had fired sixteen torpedoes from tubes fore and aft, scoring eight hits and three apparent sinkings: the transport, the escort, and the tanker. The crew watched the cruiser and the troop transport sink, the tanker had disappeared from the radar screen. Post decided that it might be worth a try to see if they could take one of the Japanese soldiers on board as a prisoner for intelligence purposes. It was not an easy process. In such situations the Japanese usually did everything they could to avoid being picked up, fully aware that in so doing they were assuring themselves of a slow death at sea. After much work, Albert Strow and some other men were able to get a Japanese seaman aboard. Strow described how they had done so in his war diary: "The Japanese sailor we picked up surely did not want to be saved—every time we came close enough to him to pick him up he would go under. Finally we flooded down to where the deck was just awash and with two sailors hanging on to my feet I was able to grab on to him and the 2 of us were dragged on board."[61] The soldier, fanatical and suicidal, had been saved at the insistence of Bill Post and because of the persistence of Albie Strow. Though he did not like it at the time, he would live to tell the story of his time aboard a United States submarine at war. What an amazing story it would prove to be. Once again Bill Post defied requests from some of his men to finish off the other Japanese sailors in the water. These refusals to shoot the defenseless Japanese would differentiate him from a few of the other submarine commanders of the day.

Not often discussed and not mentioned in the classic texts about submarine warfare in World War II were the actions of USS *Gar's* commander P. D. Quirk, who took the fellow Division Sixty-Two submarine out on patrols five through eight. Crew often described Quirk using the same glowing terms that the *Gudgeon* crew used to describe Post. Quirk, like Post, was not a bit afraid of the Japanese, nor was he hesitant to battle them on the surface. However, there were major differences between Wild Bill Post and Lieutenant Commander Quirk. Quirk ordered the machine-gunning of Japanese sailors as well as natives in the Japanese employ on several occasions. Navy brass, not aware of the actions, decorated Quirk with a Navy Cross. When Admiral Christie learned of the slaughter and that the crew had taken pictures of the sordid affairs, which were then printed in an Australian newspaper, he took back the Navy Cross and disqualified Quirk from submarines. Quirk, apparently a fearless and effective submarine skipper, has disappeared from the more well-known books describing World War II submarining.

One would be tempted to conclude that the cruel treatment *Gar* and a few other submarines gave the Japanese survivors in the water accounted for the unusual hatred the Japanese felt toward United States submariners, a hatred that resulted in unspeakable atrocities and cruelty inflicted on American submariners when they were taken prisoner. One might surmise that some of the machine-gunned Japanese left for dead in the ocean made it to shore and reported what some of the American submarine captains were up to. This does not appear to be so. The Japanese inflicted horrors upon conquered people long before the start of World War II.

It appears that the practice of slaughtering Japanese after they abandoned ship was not a common practice for American submariners. Or maybe such actions were fairly common but were hushed up by the Navy. Or perhaps skippers like Mush Morton and Quirk, who were known to have performed such actions, were the exception. It is certainly telling that Christie took such decisive action against the men on *Gar* and their skipper. But the question arises: was the disciplinary action against *Gar* taken because the acts were prohibited or because the photos were published? After all, the legendary Mush Morton was not relieved of command. Then again, Mush Morton was the most prolific maru killer in the American submarine service during World War II.

The Japanese sailor picked up by Post and the men on *Gudgeon* was, indeed, fortunate although at first he had his doubts. There would be no arbitrary torture or beheadings on board *Gudgeon*. Strow recounted the interesting and humorous tale of the only Japanese POW taken by any *Gudgeon* skipper during the war. "By the time we finally picked him up he was in pretty rough shape from exhaustion, fear, and a stomach full of sea water and fuel oil. When we passed him down the hatch into the crew's mess, he passed out. Our pharmacist's mate came to examine him and the first thing he wanted to do was to get the sailor out of his wet and oily clothes. To do this he laid the Jap out on one of the mess tables and started cutting his clothes off with a rather large knife. He was just about down to bare skin when the Jap came to. He awakened to see a bunch of American sailors watching another sailor stand over him with a large knife. With a yell that could have been heard in Tokyo, he grabbed his privates and passed out again." [62] With the terrified Japanese sailor nicknamed "Tojo" now on board, *Gudgeon* roared off on four engines. Destination: Tokuno Shima.

Torpedoman Edward Hammond continued the story adding that the sailor, who claimed he was from Formosa, was chained to one of the torpedo skids in the forward torpedo room under twenty-four hour guard. Before long, after learning that the submarine was close to some Japanese-held territory, he came out with the "request of the year—the $64 question" as Albie Strow wrote later, and indeed it was a bold one.[63] He asked to be put adrift in a boat so he could row ashore. Strow said there was no way this was going to happen, "After the job I had dragging him aboard it would be over my dead body that he went ashore." [64] He wrote in his log that "Tojo" then went on a hunger strike because he was not given his freedom.

Hammond and Strow continued with the story. The crew assigned to guard the prisoner hated the job. It was painfully boring sitting there staring at the POW chained to the torpedo racks. Within only a few days of his being captured, the men came up with an idea that would ease the load in the kitchen and relieve themselves of the responsibility of having to watch

Tojo all the time. Post liked the idea. The Japanese prisoner was assigned to the kitchen washing dishes, cleaning tables, and pouring coffee. It was then that he acquired the name by which he would be forever remembered by the men on the submarine. He was called "Jamoke" which was slang for coffee. Once freed from the handcuffs, Jamoke brightened up considerably and learned to like his duties, even donning navy dungarees and a white hat. He acclimated so quickly to his new status that he was commonly seen napping in the crew's dining area with his head leaning against the shoulder of one of *Gudgeon*'s crew.

On the twenty-third, the eighth edition of *The Gudgeonian* reported that Albie Strow had announced that *Gudgeon* was heading home and would arrive at Midway Island by December 7. Bill Post was exultant and wrote up a congratulatory message to the crew that was printed in *The Gudgeonian*:

Congratulations to all hands on your splendid performance. You have carried on the fine tradition established by this great ship early in the war. During this patrol you have kept the ship in excellent material condition, trained hard, and been good shipmates. As a result of your efforts we have covered our area thoroughly, obtained valuable information for future operations, and destroyed the following enemy ships:

One tanker 10,000 tons
One transport 11,000 tons
One destroyer 1,500 tons

As Gudgeon sailors, fully aware of her past and present achievements, we may all wear, with pride, the ribbon of the 'Presidential Unit Citation,' which will be presented shortly after our arrival in Pearl Harbor about December 15.[65]

Gudgeon radioed ahead so that any submarines in the area could be sent to the productive area where the convoy had been found. Fearing that the Japanese would determine his approximate position from the communication, Post considered not sending the message but sent the report anyway, certain that there was a greater good that justified the risk. On the very next day, November 24, 1943, Post learned that in so doing *Gudgeon* was placed in some danger. The Japanese had determined where *Gudgeon* was and had sent a ship to jump her. *Gudgeon* was on the surface, heading for port, when the alert men on watch sighted a Japanese submarine in the haze in front of Tokuno Shima, which was said to provide a picturesque backdrop. The Japanese submarine was trying to do to *Gudgeon* what Jumping Joe Grenfell had done to the I-73. Of the prospect of going to war against a Japanese submarine, Albert Strow wrote, "Sub against sub is too much like cannibalism to suit me—but then they did not ask me what I wanted them to send out after us. But that is just like the damn Japs—they never do anything properly."[66] However, *Gudgeon* dove and easily evaded before surfacing again and moving forward on four diesels. *Gudgeon* was out of torpedoes.

The men on board had much to be thankful for, not the least of which was that they were still alive, despite the countless battles the men on *Gudgeon* had experienced. On Thanksgiving Day, November 24, 1943, Post, Strow, and the others on board sat down for a Thanksgiving meal. Post said, "Since this is Thanksgiving and I think we have a lot to be thankful for, I think we should have the blessing before we begin. Booth will you do the honors?"[67] This touched and surprised Strow who was called "Booth" by Bill Post. Strow concluded from the experience that it just goes to prove the old saying that "the exec's job is indeed a jack of all trades job."[68]

Home for *Gudgeon* this time was Midway Island. No doubt the men were in a celebratory mood, possibly breaking out into one of their favorite tunes, which was called "Rig to Depth Charge," this one poking fun at Lieutenant Donald R. Midgley and sung to the tune of "Clementine."

Rig for depth charge, Rig for depth charge
Take her down to 90 feet
Watch your angle Mr. Midgley
Cause the water ain't so deep.

Hard rise, Mr. Midgley
Bring her up to 60 feet
We will take a look around
But do not secure the sound.

Target sighted, target sighted
Sighted on the starboard bow
Tell the Cap't we are ready
to go up and show them how.

All clear Cap't, cried the soundman
ease your Rise, don't let her broach
Forward room stand by your tubes
We are starting the approach.

Ready forward, ready forward
We are waiting for the word
To fire all our Pickles
And get away undisturbed.

Fire one, fire two,
Fire three, and fire four
We don't need #5
So secure the outer door.

There goes one, there goes two
Three and four are on the way
We have sunk the yellow Bastard
So our work is done for today.

Call the Cap't, call the capt.
Tell him we have sighted smoke
We will surface and follow
Till we sink the bloody bloke.

Battle surface, battle surface
Quickly man the 5-inch gun
We will battle all the night through
Till we sink the rising suns.

As *Gudgeon* steamed on for safety, Albie Strow was pleased that *Gudgeon* was finally able to pick up a radio station other than Tokyo Rose's broadcasts. It appeared to him that the war in the Pacific was going to really heat up soon, none too quickly as far as he was concerned. Strow was growing weary of his "school of navigation," which he was holding for about half of the officers who never had done any navigating.[69] "Navigating would be a big task even if I were a good instructor, but I am not one by any manner of speaking."[70] He concluded that the only good thing was that while the weather had been too bad to give the men much opportunity to practice, it had recently improved and gave the greenhorns the opportunity to give it a try. The amount of learning required of a new officer on board a submarine was incredible. Because of the inexperience and extremely fast training the new men had received, they did not have anything close to the broad experience of the old hands.

By this time, it was apparent to Quartermaster Arthur Barlow that Jamoke's life was in mortal danger. Ambrosio Fernandez, a third class mess attendant, who hailed from Zamboango City of the Philippines, hated Jamoke profoundly and for understandable reasons. Fernandez and his family had run into the conquering Japanese when the Philippines fell. The invaders had beheaded his uncle, raped his aunt, and put him into forced labor on a small ship. Fernandez was continually and cruelly supervised to make certain that he and the other prisoners did their jobs. The Japanese considered themselves to be vastly superior to the Filipinos. As a result, the Japanese treated Fernandez and the other prisoners with incredible savagery. The ship that Fernandez had been on eventually sank, and Fernandez was rescued, winding up in Fremantle with a hatred for the Japanese that held no boundaries. The men on *Gudgeon* had heard that he almost preferred to drown rather than board the Allied vessel for fear that it was the hated Japanese who were attempting to rescue him. Once ashore he signed up for the United States submarine service to go to war and get revenge against his detested enemy, and ended up on *Gudgeon* for the seventh patrol. Barlow said that the crew had to be careful to keep Jamoke and Fernandez apart because Fernandez wanted to really hurt him and might have killed him if given the chance.

On the twenty-seventh as *Gudgeon* continued toward Midway. Strow wrote that on November 27 at 0800 he and Lieutenant Donald Midgley, or "Midge" as he was called, were on the bridge arguing about their current location. What was first thought to be an island turned out to be smoke.

The men hoped that they could close on the smoke and that it would turn out to be an unescorted maru. *Gudgeon*—out of torpedoes—would have to go after it with her large deck gun. *Gudgeon* changed course and headed for the ship. It would be the perfect ending for the patrol. Post, quite enthralled with his new five-inch gun, was very pleased at the prospects. Strow wrote that as far as the exec was concerned, Wild Bill was a little too excited because what they had hoped was a single maru turned out to be a maru with three escorts. This contrasted with Post's identification of the convoy in his patrol report. He stated there were two maru, two sub-chasers, and one unidentified escort vessel. It was a dangerous proposition either way. Bill Post wanted to charge the entire cluster of ships, five-inch deck gun roaring. The other officers were astonished that Post wanted to go after the convoy with only a five-inch deck gun. A heated argument ensued with the contingent of men in the control room eventually talking their bold skipper out of the attack, which Wild Bill wanted to undertake in the very worst way.

By 1311 the two sub-chasers had been joined by a low-flying plane. The escorts had spotted *Gudgeon* on the surface in broad daylight while she tracked the convoy. Strow wrote that he could just see the Japanese "rubbing their hands with glee over the prospect of laying a lot of eggs on us." [71] Post ordered that the gunners fire the first of six shells over their bows at a range of around five miles with the large deck gun. Strow said of the strategy, "This pistol we have back aft is one that will make most anyone sit up and take notice. And these two fellows did just that—they reminded me of a Mickey Mouse cartoon in which Goofy skids for a half a block when trying to stop." [72] Indeed, the big gun had a sobering effect on the little sub-chasers just as Post had expected. They "spun on their tails" retreating all the way back to a rather useless and non-protective stance on the far side of the maru. [73] Goofy was now hiding behind Minnie Mouse.

In a strange turn of events that must have seemed odd indeed, regardless of which uniform you were wearing, for a while *Gudgeon*—enjoying the spoils of her newfound respect—and the small convoy sped on courses parallel to each other, one not bothering the other in any way. Strow felt badly about his heated argument with Post, the second disagreement the two had experienced on the patrol, but wrote that he was sure that his insistence had been well-founded because all of the others had agreed with him. He felt worse that the submarine had not been able to "slip a pickle into them."[74] Strow and the rest of the submariners chuckled at Jamoke for his actions during the incident. The frightened Japanese sailor stuck cotton in his ears and buried his head in a pillow. Every time the diving alarm sounded, he "jumped about three feet."[75] His response to the general alarm was even more dramatic.

As the submarine continued toward Pearl Harbor, there arose serious worry that the submarine would run out of diesel fuel. At one point in the patrol, one of the fuel tanks went dry long before it was supposed to. Strow noted that they all wanted to go after Midge's scalp because he had the responsibility to see that this would not happen. A submarine out of fuel would eventually have to surface and would be the most helpless of targets. Strow was still confident that they would make it but worried that they would eventually have to break out the oars or an "egg beater" to do it.[76] Also of concern to Executive Officer Strow was that the officers' card games were going poorly. Midgley had been consistently beating him at poker. Strow even quit one game in a huff. Midgley had everyone's money. Albie Strow enjoyed it thoroughly when a pot grew very large and Willie Floyd was sitting pretty with four aces. Strow wrote that much of Midgley's "blood" was spilled in the hand.[77] Apparently a kind-hearted Floyd was feeling remorseful after he "bled" Midgley white, having raised the stakes over and over again and then showed the unsuspecting Midgley his four bullets [aces].[78] Midgley got an odd look on his face, threw down his cards, pushed out the rest of his chips swearing that he would never play the game again. Strow and the others, having no sympathy for Midgley, heartily congratulated the submarine's new hero, Lieutenant William Floyd.

With the fighting over and *Gudgeon* usually on the surface still storming for Midway Island, the submarine's kangaroo court went into session. The judge, "Neptunus Rex," called one sailor after another into the court room to consider contrived charges against the crew. One of the sailors had made the statement that he was twenty years old, a fact that the men on the boat did not believe. They also did not believe that he had once crossed the equator on another ship. One of the older *Gudgeon* sailors had him arrested and brought before the judge to hear the case. Not surprisingly, he was found to be guilty as charged and was ordered to get an "Indian haircut" since he claimed to be of Native American descent.[79] However, the kindly judge felt sorry for the sailor, telling him that if he wore a blanket around his shoulders from that point until the end of the patrol, the prescribed punishment would be suspended. If he was seen without the blanket around him, he was to be given the scalping immediately. Strow was sure that the sailor had no chance of making it to Pearl Harbor with his hair intact because he would either be seen without the blanket or someone would say he had been seen without it. The men howled in laughter as the young sailor moved through the submarine with the blanket over his shoulders whether going to duty or just passing through.

Very shortly word spread that the water supply on board had become quite low. The much-abused Donald Midgley was being approached repeatedly by men desiring to take a quick shower who needed his permission. Midgley would always respond that they needed to wait a few days and by then "we will have plenty" of water.[80] But there was not plenty of water, and Midgley would never give permission. Finally the men, tired of their own odor, defied Midgley and showered. It was worth the abuse they got from Midgley to get the war patrol's grime off their tired bodies.

Good old Jamoke, having taken to his chores and become very relaxed around the men, continued to entertain them—although his value in this regard was surely secondary to having watched the massacre of Lieutenant Donald Midgley at the card table and the dastardly "lying" sailor's perambulations around the submarine with his blanket around his back.[81] The crew taught Jamoke to play all of the games that the men were playing. He had been steadfastly refusing to take a bath because he did not want to open up a cut on his foot. Finally, the sailors could take his odor no longer and threw him into a shower. He was already miffed that when he had received a haircut, the barber had not shaved his head as he had requested with hand gestures. Now in the shower, against his will, the sailors told him that being a prisoner of war produced many hardships. He had to take a bath and eat fried chicken whether he wanted to or not.

Finally, on the fifth, *Gudgeon* entered the friendly port at Midway Island. Word quickly spread on shore that *Gudgeon* had taken a prisoner of war.

Soldiers came on board to see the prisoner and walked slowly by Jamoke as he was fulfilling his duties. After all, he looked just like the other sailors, dressed in his United States Navy dungarees. As the disappointed men left the submarine, they would invariably conclude that the rumors were false. There was no Japanese POW on *Gudgeon.*

Long after the war, Albert Strow would say that not all the men who came aboard to view the POW on *Gudgeon* were there just for "sight-seeing." [82] As Strow tells of the events, a small group of Marines who had yet to see action got all "beered up" and decided they wanted to get the "Jap" on *Gudgeon.*[83] They hurried over to the submarine fully intending to kill Jamoke. When the men from *Gudgeon* heard what was about to transpire, they jumped off the boat and defended Jamoke against their countrymen, the Marines. Strow said that there arose "the biggest melee you ever saw."[84] The *Gudgeon* sailors won out of course, because when *Gudgeon* sailed for Pearl Harbor, Jamoke was on board and fit as a fiddle.

The day before departing for Pearl Harbor *Gudgeon* received mail. Strow was exulting at the thought of playing "Paducah" for Midge, a recording that was supposed to have been sent to him some time ago. Robbie (Lieutenant Webster Robinson), who had been playing "Pistol Packing Momma" over and over on his record player, had driven everybody on board almost mad. The men had even received their rightful ration of beer. The problem was that the beer had something like formaldehyde added to it and almost everyone who drank it was sick. By this time in the patrol, Jamoke had apparently concluded that he was now a member of the crew. Strow said that Jamoke had taken to his job with such enthusiasm that he wanted to enlist in the American Navy. He would get quite a surprise at Pearl Harbor. On December 11, the men on the submarine received an invigorating patriotic welcome. The Navy band was blaring, people ashore were watching eagerly, waving and cheering, a broom was hanging high on the periscope shears, countless Japanese flags fluttered colorfully in the breeze. As *Gudgeon* moved slowly toward the submarine dock, the crew must have felt a sense of accomplishment and relief. Once again they had fooled the Grim Reaper.

Bill Post, having become attached to his adopted shipmate and perhaps no longer seeing him as the enemy, brought Jamoke up through the hatch without anything over his head and turned him over to security. The officer in charge of the detail, having an entirely different attitude toward the prisoner, let Post have it for not having a bag over his head. The obviously scared Jamoke was last seen being led away by a contingent of Marines with tears in his eyes. Many of the battle-tested, war-hardened sailors from one of the top ship killers in the United States submarine service, the USS *Gudgeon* stood there watching their prisoner walk away, tears rolling down their faces. Jamoke, whose actual name was not known, was never seen or heard from—or about—again. The men on *Gudgeon* did not treat the Japanese sailor kindly because they were trying to soften him up for questioning, but radioman John Sheridan said that he heard that the friendly and talkative sailor had sung like a songbird to his interrogators and provided much useful information to naval intelligence.

So in a surreal ending to another action-packed war patrol, a purportedly insanely cruel and fanatical Japanese sailor was led away as the men aboard the USS *Gudgeon*—sworn to kill him and everyone of his ilk at every opportunity—cried silently to themselves, devastated to see him go. To be sure, war is hell, but war is also crazy.

On December 11, 1943, two years to the day since *Gudgeon* had slid out of Pearl Harbor on her first war patrol, the men of *Gudgeon* completed the submarine's tenth run. Forty-one days at sea. 9,714 miles traversed. Twenty-four torpedoes fired. Eight hits. Three apparent kills, including *Gudgeon*'s second sinking of a Japanese warship, the first such kill since the I-73 went down in January 1942. *Gudgeon* was out of torpedoes and was virtually out of diesel fuel when she reached Midway Island.

Japanese records translated after the war indicated that when the *Wakamiya* went under, 157 of the 161 crew went down with her. The troop transport was eventually identified as the *Nekka Maru*. She was hit in a coalbunker on the port side by a dud torpedo, thus calling into question the commonly held belief that any submarine that left port in October–November 1943 or later had well-functioning torpedoes. Perhaps *Gudgeon*, the boat that had carried out the first war patrol, had also experienced the last dud torpedo of the war. The other torpedoes—which were not duds—hit amidships on the starboard side, amidships in number four and five holds, and her engine room. She was carrying 253 Navy men of the First Sasebo

Landing Force, 157 men of the Iwakuni Naval Air Force, and 985 other passengers. Of the torpedo-attack victims, 308 were passengers, seventy-nine were from the crew. Records indicate that the third and fourth ships in the convoy escaped. The tanker, whose radar pip had disappeared, apparently had outrun the radar screen and was not sunk.

Despite the dud torpedo, Commander Post noted that the performance of the Mark 14 torpedoes was conclusive proof of the effectiveness of the latest modifications to the Mark 16 exploder. At the time, two years into the war, submarines like *Gudgeon* were using torpedoes that were mostly unflawed. The Japanese report of a dud hit was, of course, not known to Post at the time he wrote the patrol report. After Commander Post's extreme disappointment over the performance of the crew on the ninth patrol, the men who had served on the tenth received much praise. The training of the crew was greatly improved. He wrote in his war patrol report that their performance of duty under combat conditions "left nothing to be desired."[85] Post pleaded for a radar officer and a radio technician.

He noted that the just-completed patrol was the first for five third-class petty officers, who had received their ratings at training schools or elsewhere ashore. He condemned the practice of promoting men ashore to the rank of petty officer, then bringing them aboard and having them receive their training from lower-rated men, veterans of wartime patrols. The veteran sailors had proven that under wartime conditions they were capable of performing their duty. The presence of the green petty officers on *Gudgeon* was regarded as a "serious" problem in morale, training, and discipline.[86] Post added, "The rating of enlisted graduates of training schools ashore before they have had an opportunity to demonstrate their leadership and ability at sea is believed to be a serious mistake."[87] It eroded the morale of the men who had to earn their rates "the hard way." The standards for petty officers throughout the Navy were thus lowered; the quality of the World War II submariner was slowly degrading because of the great number of new submarines and the need for so many men to man them. It is impossible to argue with Post on this point, it would seem obvious that the chiefs should have been developed from the experienced wartime veterans on board the submarines and that the men just coming aboard would be rated lower and shown the ropes by the veterans.

Post, in an apparent attempt to hang onto the men who had performed so admirably, noted that the recent war patrols were less strenuous than the early ones had been; the need to transfer experienced crew off the boat for rest, less urgent. He said that there were officers on board who had served for eight patrols with no apparent ill effects, referring, of course, to Albert Strow who had served on *Gudgeon* since the Midway Patrol, *Gudgeon*'s third.

Post pleaded for the addition of a single barrel "wet type" 40 mm machine gun, which could be used as a hard-hitting, rapid-fire weapon to "cool the ardor of all the Japanese fishing boats which carry depth charges."[88] Post thought that in so doing, some of the convoy escorts would have to be diverted to the boats to protect them from marauding submarines like *Gudgeon*, thus making the convoys more vulnerable.

By this time in the war, the officers' decorations were really stacking up. For the tenth war patrol, Albert Strow received a Gold Star in lieu of his third Bronze Star for meritorious service on the just completed run. If it were not for Bill Post's comments on his post-action patrol report, it would be impossible to know sixty years after the fact how the young Ensign, William C. Ostlund, had fared on his first patrol. Luckily Post singled out his two ensigns for praise. Of them he said, "This was the first war patrol for two reserve ensigns. They had received their previous training at the Reserve Midshipman's School USNA, Submarine Division 12, Submarine School New London, and Submarine Division 102. Their natural ability and excellent previous training enabled them to qualify for top watches shortly after our arrival in the area, and to become real assets to the ship."[89]

Bill Ostlund must have been very pleased as he left the submarine for R & R. No doubt Commander Post had let him and his cohort David McCorquodale know how satisfied he was with their performance. There would be no quick transfer off *Gudgeon* for Bill Ostlund. He had done it. He had proven himself under war conditions. It had been a long trip from Webster City, Iowa, home of some of the most fertile earth on the planet to the depths of the East China Sea for a young man who, before December 1941, had never even thought of joining the Navy.

His age-yellowed letter of December 18, 1943, typed on onionskin-thin USS *Gudgeon* stationery exists to this day. In it, he is obviously confident and homesick for his pretty young wife, Peggy, and none too kind to his "yellow-bellied" adversaries. Just who Bill was writing is uncertain. He wrote as follows:

Dear Folks,

When I got back in off patrol about a week ago I found both your letter and Christmas Box waiting for me. I sure thank you for both of them.

Censorship only allows me to say that we had a successful run and I certainly feel none the worse for it. At the conclusion of each patrol all submarine crews are given a two weeks rest period and after that we spend another ten days in getting ready for the next run. So I won't be going out again until after New Years. I'm staying at a rest and recuperation center which is a hotel that has been taken over by the Navy. My room rented for sixteen smackers per night pre-Tojo but I pay a dollar a day which includes all meals so you can understand why I feel like a big shot. The submarine base also furnishes us with a car each day filled with gas so bit by bit I have seen most of the sights. However, you can bet your neck I'd trade it all in for a place around Mother's Christmas dinner table.

In recent letters from both Peggy and Mother they have mentioned arranging for a week-end together in Chicago. I hope they were able to do so for that would give you another opportunity to see my Peggy. For a guy whose [sic] only been away from his wife for five months now I'm sure a sad apple. However, in this particular branch of the service I have a pretty fair opportunity to take it out on the yellow-bellies for every day they keep me from her.

I hope this finds the two of you in the best of health. And even though it is a bit late for holiday greetings I do wish you the best of everything in this new year to come. Things are looking good out this way and perhaps another year might see the job done. That's more a hope than an Uncle Bob prediction so don't put me on a predictor's limb if it doesn't work out that way.

Thanks again for the letter and the gift.

As always,
Bill

Ensign W.C. Ostlund USNR
U.S.S. Gudgeon
c/o Fleet Post Office
San Francisco, California

With so much to live for, the young ensign would be forever dispatched to the sea in just 118 days.

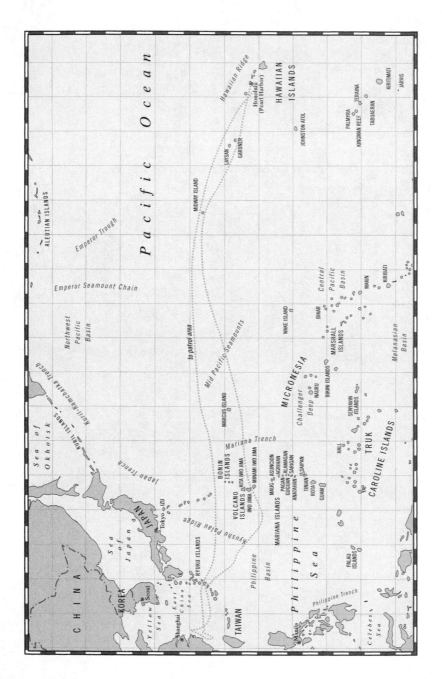

Eleventh War Patrol • Approximate Course • Jan. 16–March 5, 1944

▪ 11 ▪
Down the Throat

ELEVENTH WAR PATROL: January 16, 1944–March 5, 1944

The paths of glory lead but to the Grave.

Thomas Gray, 18th century

A s the relief crew of the USS *Griffin* refitted *Gudgeon* for action, Post received his marks from his superiors. The reviews were not entirely complimentary. Captain Frederick "Freddy" B. Warder, Commander Submarine Division 122, who had patrolled on *Seawolf*, was critical of the fact that only 33 percent of the torpedoes had hit their mark, a number far below that attained by the Stovall-Dornin team on patrols four and five, and below the previous low of 36 percent established by the Grenfell-Lyon-Dornin team on the second patrol.

It would seem that Freddie Warder might have been slightly more understanding about the low percentage of hits achieved by the firing control party, which was due in part to the failure to hit a moored target with four torpedoes. When the war was young, Warder—on *Seawolf*—had bravely penetrated a Japanese harbor and fired eight torpedoes at a Japanese seaplane tender at anchor. All missed. The similarities between Warder and Bill Post do not end there. Like Post, he was beloved by his crew, once risking his career and going toe-to-toe with an admiral who wanted to discipline one of Warders submariners—unfairly, in Warder's estimation. On another occasion, he penetrated very shallow waters off Bali to force an attack, almost losing *Seawolf* in the process when the Japanese dropped forty-three depth charges very close to the submarine.

Like Bill Post, Warder's audaciously bold nature earned him a nickname. Warder was called "Fearless Freddy" by his crew. Over and over, Bill Post's division commander had courageously taken on the Japanese, even interrupting invasions by attacking Japanese warships. Anything that could be done to sink Japanese vessels, Warder did without hesitation. He must have loved having a skipper like Bill Post in his command. Therefore, when Warder also stated that the tenth patrol "was entirely in keeping with the splendid reputation of this fighting ship; attacks being pushed home with great persistence in shallow waters,"[1] nobody was surprised.

In another evaluation, the Acting Commander Submarine Force of the Pacific Fleet (Class of 1914) John H. "Babe" Brown reminded Bill Post of the line between recklessness and appropriate aggression, stating that the use of deck guns is sound for sampans, lightly armed minor patrol vessels, and some shore targets, or in finishing off badly damaged unarmed vessels of a greater size. He continued, "It must be continuously born in mind by all commanding officers, however, that the execution of such gun fights must be carried out only after careful consideration of the value of the target and risk involved."[2] He recognized that such fights were good for morale but also that such encounters "must not jeopardize the ultimate mission of the submarine on war patrol by allowing one's vessel to be damaged."[3] The comments are in marked contrast in tone and content to Warder's.

Brown did not say so, but it is likely that when he heard of Post's plans to attack a convoy of one or two maru and three escorts with a five-inch gun and machine guns on November 27, 1943, he thought Wild Bill Post needed a few words of caution. Albert Strow and some of the others on board had experienced the same concern, finally persuading their skipper to back off. Brown's statements were, in a way, similar to the shaking Dusty Dornin had given Lieutenant Commander Stovall, who was concentrating only on the ships he was trying to sink and not paying any attention to the two charging Japanese destroyers bearing down on *Gudgeon* on an earlier patrol. The men on board received congratulations for "one more excellent contribution towards the destruction of the enemy."[4] After all, *Gudgeon* had sunk the *Wakamiya*, the transport, and the freighter, totaling 13,728 tons, and damaged a 10,052 ton tanker. Post's strong words of criticism in the war patrol report after *Gudgeon*'s tenth run regarding the Navy's policy of promoting untested newly trained submariners received strong support from Warder but no comment from Brown.

By the time *Gudgeon* was ready for the eleventh patrol, she had received a new PPI radar system. By use of the PPI scope, the layout of an attack situation appeared on a screen with *Gudgeon* in the middle, the enemy ships appearing as small lights or pips which corresponded to the ships' actual positions relative to the submarine. Post had *Gudgeon*'s bridge altered to match the style of Dusty Dornin's *Trigger*, deck guns were exchanged with *Tuna*, and the scraped hull got a coat of light grey camouflage paint. While practicing training dives, *Gudgeon* dropped below the surface to periscope depth in forty-nine seconds. *Gudgeon* was ready to go.

The men of the *Gudgeon* received the highest unit award that a Navy vessel could be given in a ceremony at Pearl Harbor on December 27, 1943. Fleet Admiral Chester W. Nimitz presented Bill Post and the men of the USS *Gudgeon* the Presidential Unit Citation (PUC) for *Gudgeon*'s accomplishments on her first eight war patrols. The PUC is awarded to a unit when their actions are equivalent to those of an individual winner of the Navy Cross. *Gudgeon* was one of thirty-four submarines to receive the award during the war. The citation read[5]:

For outstanding performance in combat during eight aggressive and brilliantly executed war patrols in enemy controlled waters since December 7, 1941. Although opposed by severe depth-charge attacks, aerial bombing and gunfire, and frequently operating in shallow and hazardous waters, the GUDGEON boldly struck at the enemy. Fighting with remarkable prowess and daring, she achieved an illustrious combat record in the sinking of 19 Japanese ships, including one submarine, which totaled 133,957 tons, and in damaging 3 more ships totaling 13,944 tons. The superb efficiency and readiness for battle which enabled the *Gudgeon* to fulfill these vital missions with only slight damage reflect great credit upon her gallant officers and men and the United States Naval Service.

For the President,

Frank Knox
Secretary of the Navy

A picture of the officers decked out in their formal Navy whites on that memorable evening shows Commander Bill Post in the center, his hat tilted cockily to the left, as well as a rightly proud Ensign William C. Ostlund in the back row. Also in the photo were Executive Officer Lieutenant Albert J. Strow, Lieutenant Burton L. Heyes, Lieutenant jg Addison B. Pinkley, Lieutenant Donald R. Midgley, Lieutenant William Floyd, and Ensign David B. McCorquodale. Before the next year was over, most of these men would be lost on *Gudgeon*.

For the eleventh patrol all eight officers who had served on the prior patrol would remain. Twenty-four out of the seventy-three crew, or 33 percent were either new to the submarine service or were on *Gudgeon* for the first time. Part of the reason for the very high turnover of crew, the second highest of the war for *Gudgeon*, was the fact that cooks Seymour Feit and Jack Edward Wood had deserted. Arthur C. Barlow described the events leading to the men's desertion. Barlow said that as *Gudgeon* was prepared for patrol, storage space on the submarine was at a premium. Boxes were placed everywhere, including in the crew's shower. After working on board one day, Feit and Wood asked if they could go ashore to shower before *Gudgeon* pulled out for patrol. They never returned. A notation in the January 16, 1944, ship's log stated tersely that in accordance with Bupers Manual Article D-8002 (2) the men were declared deserters. Arthur Barlow, an eight-patrol veteran of *Gudgeon*, recalls that Post was terribly angry that the two men had deserted. He told everyone on board that he did not want to hear the names Wood and Feit ever again. The two deserters had served on the boat for the two prior patrols. It is not known why they had not returned to *Gudgeon*, nor is it known what happened to them. Their desertion probably resulted in their surviving the war. How or whether they coped with the knowledge that their desertion led directly to the death of the cooks who replaced them is unknown.

On January 6, 1944, *Gudgeon* pulled away from the Submarine Base at Pearl Harbor and headed toward Midway Island accompanied by the high-scoring submarines *Flasher* and *Snook*, before turning around and returning to Hawaii for repairs to a badly bent and noisy propeller. By the sixteenth, repairs had been completed, and *Gudgeon*, accompanied by Thomas B. Dykers' submarine *Jack*, again headed slowly out of Pearl Harbor. Dykers and Post took turns diving and exposing their periscopes so that the new crew would know what one looked like at a range of 2,000 yards. They also practiced radar-tracking drills. The weather was so bad on the twentieth that *Gudgeon* and *Jack* dared not enter Midway for fear of damaging their submarines. On the twenty-first *Gudgeon* was ordered to head for her patrol area without refueling at Midway but not before Post sent word to Midway Island that they needed two ship's cooks to replace Wood and Feit. Two men stepped forward. They were Edgar Russell Kramer, ship's cook third class and Herbert Patriquin, ship's cook second class. Arthur C. Barlow, who had so bravely performed his signaling duties high atop the submarine base tower at Pearl Harbor while the attack played out at his feet, had recently received his honorable discharge from the Navy. He promptly reenlisted and received a promotion to first class. Barlow remembered Herbert Patriquin quite well because, as Barlow said, Patriquin was far too old to be serving on a submarine at war. Patriquin had lied about his age to get on the boat. Patriquin was forty-four years old when he enlisted in the Naval Reserves in late 1941. He was forty-six years old when *Gudgeon* pulled away from Midway Island for the eleventh patrol. Barlow said that Patriquin was a patriotic man who jumped at the chance to serve aboard *Gudgeon*, just desiring to do his part for the war effort.

As *Gudgeon* headed for her patrol area, the usual pesky antisubmarine vessels and patrol planes appeared. *Gudgeon* played the jumping jack game all across the Pacific Ocean, diving and surfacing over and over again as the submarine approached her newly assigned patrol area on the East China Sea. The tedium was interrupted on February 1, 1944, when two floatplanes dropped four depth bombs, which, fortunately, did no damage.

On February 2, just off Lot's Wife, *Gudgeon* once again sighted a small Japanese escort carrier. One can imagine Bill Post's reaction when he laid eyes on the prized target. After the war, the carrier would be identified as *Unyo*. Preserving the stricken carrier was of utmost importance to the Japanese. She was damaged, moving slowly, and escorted by at least three destroyers. A fourth ship that looked like a destroyer was close to the flat top and may have been towing it. Despite being greatly outnumbered and outgunned, Wild Bill Post was seeing red. Post was going to go after the carrier; of that there was no doubt. The only question was how to do it most expeditiously. The carrier was zigzagging. Her escorts were moving back and forth with her, like honeybees protecting their queen. Carriers in World War II were submarine magnets, and Bill Post had no intention of trying to withstand the pull of this one, even if she was being protected by as many as four destroyers.

Inexplicably, at 0753 with *Gudgeon* still sizing up her prey, two distant depth charges rocked the ocean. Post continued to observe and maneuver the submarine until 1008 when *Gudgeon* began an approach on a 1,400 ton *Hatsuharu* class destroyer that was charging at two-thousand yards. Post stared unflinchingly directly at the charging warship until she was about 900 yards away then let loose with four fish right "down his throat," as Post would say later, all the while keeping an ear out for the depth charges the submarine killer was throwing *Gudgeon*'s way.[6] All the torpedoes missed the narrow bow of the destroyer, which was still heading full steam at *Gudgeon*. The situation was very dangerous. *Gudgeon* went deep and rigged for counterattack. Within moments depth charges started raining down. BOOM. BOOM. BOOM. BOOM. One explosion after the other rocked the ocean around *Gudgeon*. BOOM. BOOM. BOOM. BOOM. Two additional destroyers joined in the attack. BOOM. BOOM. BOOM. Depth charges continued to fall around *Gudgeon* for two hours. BOOM.

Gudgeon was now outnumbered three to one but managed to survive the barrage of thundering depth charges. Post had *Gudgeon* rise to periscope depth for a look. None of the charges had done any damage, but the convoy had left the area. The destroyers had done their jobs well, successfully tying up the underwater assassin while the carrier moved out of sight. All of the action attracted another U.S. submarine, the *Saury*, which was engaged on her ninth war patrol. Post sighted *Saury* on the surface, fired recognition smoke signals, and surfaced. Lieutenant Commander Tony Dropp on *Saury* was not quite sure what to make of the situation and submerged before deciding that all was well, resurfacing to converse by megaphone with Post. The two captains decided to attack the convoy together, *Gudgeon* from the east, *Saury* from the west.

At 1527 *Gudgeon* dove and attempted to close on the convoy of warships, Post watched carefully through the periscope. By 1535 it seemed obvious that *Gudgeon*'s scope had been seen. The carrier had launched a plane to search for the submarine, just as another angry destroyer started another depth charge attack while charging *Gudgeon*. BOOM. BOOM. BOOM. The destroyer was fortunate because the men in *Gudgeon*'s firing party could not maneuver the submarine into a favorable firing position, though the destroyer was looking fat at a range of only 700 yards. BOOM. BOOM. Once again Post ordered *Gudgeon* to go deep, rig for charges, and evade. BOOM. BOOM. BOOM. BOOM. Two of the explosives really rocked the submarine and were described as "moderately severe" though no serious damage was sustained.[7] Post continued to evade as the men on *Gudgeon* engaged passively in that Godawful silent running, sweat pouring down their faces. The crew heard distant explosions, but they did not sound like depth charges. Post and the men on board hoped that Tony Dropp and *Saury* were having better luck than they were. But as it would be known later, Dropp had been forced deep by one of the destroyers and had lost contact with *Unyo*. Of the encounter, Post would say later that he didn't mind this barrage of depth charges nearly as much as missing the chance at a carrier.

More than an hour later, *Gudgeon* surfaced and opened her hatches. The first men to the deck were shocked to see a twin float monoplane, perhaps a Jake directly overhead only five-hundred feet up. But, Bill Post's luck prevailed once again. *Gudgeon* submerged quickly, and the plane did not attack. Perhaps the Jake had no bombs, but it had *Gudgeon* dead to rights. The earliest stage of surfaces, before the radar can be deployed, the periscope raised, and the lookouts sent topside, was a very vulnerable time for a World War II submarine. In effect, Bill Post and the rest of the men on board were surfacing "blind," entrusting their survival to the twists of fate. Would there be a plane waiting for them with bombs? Would the bomber attack? It was a crapshoot. This time *Gudgeon* came out of it all right.

At 1708 the encounter with Japanese sea vessels and aircraft continued with *Gudgeon* once again trying to surface. For the first time this day, the SD radar was used. It picked up another plane, this one was almost overhead. Submariners would say later that on some occasions later in the war, commanders were so confident that they would not use the technology that they had at their disposal. Perhaps that is why Post had not deployed the radar an hour earlier when they had discovered the passive Jake. Patrolling on a submarine had become more dangerous for submarines, because by February 1944 the Japanese had designated an air unit to do nothing but antisubmarine warfare, though it seems probable that the planes were from the carrier. This could have been determined if the plane had been sighted, rather than been picked up by radar. Once again the Japanese plane dropped no bombs. This plane was the same punchless Jake that had flown harmlessly above *Gudgeon* earlier. A few minutes later the soundman picked up screws. Post took a look and saw another destroyer, the third charging destroyer of the day which had probably been tipped off by the plane and was heading straight for *Gudgeon*. Post swung the ship's stern tubes around as the destroyer quickly descended upon *Gudgeon*. At an average range of only 800 yards, Post ordered, "FIRE SEVEN. FIRE EIGHT. FIRE NINE."[8] As planned, the men waited for the destroyer to begin evasive maneuvers before they fired the final torpedo hoping for a knockout at a close range. The setup looked perfect. When the destroyer came to within 700 yards, the final torpedo whooshed out of stern torpedo tube number ten. *Gudgeon* dove. Post was confident that the destroyer would soon disintegrate as the *Wakamiya* had, thus clearing a path for *Gudgeon* to approach the carrier, but in about forty-five seconds the destroyer had advanced to where *Gudgeon* had fired. BOOM. BOOM. BOOM. BOOM. The ocean around *Gudgeon* began filling with the devastatingly powerful depth charges once again. BOOM. BOOM. BOOM. BOOM. BOOM. BOOM. BOOM. BOOM. Twelve depth charges exploded around

Gudgeon, one of which went off dangerously close and knocked out the submarine's gyro and damaged the SJ radar. This barrage of depth charges was so close that it "made the birdies sing,"[9] Post jokingly referring to what happens to a cartoon character after it has taken a severe blow on the head. The unusually skilled destroyer skipper—Post really respected this guy—had again maneuvered skillfully, avoiding the four fish so confidently sent her way.

Post would state in his post-action report that he had many times wondered what would happen if he missed on a down-the-throat shot at a destroyer. He wrote in his patrol report, "Today we found out twice. Glad to be able to report that it's not much worse than a routine working over."[10] Like Freddy Warder, the fearless Wild Bill Post had entered into dangerous waters by twice taking on destroyers head-on within a few hours of each other and living to tell about it. Even with the damage *Gudgeon* had sustained and the birdies singing, Bill Post's enthusiasm had not been dampened.

Post, becoming bolder and perhaps more desperate as the battle raged, surfaced *Gudgeon* at 1840 and stormed forward for an attack on one of the destroyers. *Gudgeon*, high atop the waves traveling at full speed, the night's darkness partially shielding her from the enemy ships, turned in for the attack. When *Gudgeon* got within 9,000 yards, she was picked up by the destroyer which started firing large projectiles from her deck guns at the submarine as she continued to travel swiftly through the waves, the ocean curling off her bow. *Gudgeon* plunged ahead in pursuit of a third encounter with a Japanese destroyer on the same day. After an hour and a half, Post ordered that *Gudgeon* submerge and begin another approach on the destroyer.

With Commander Post sizing up another down-the-throat shot, a resistor in the banged-up SJ radar unit burned out, and one of the torpedoes in the after tubes slipped past the "stop bolt." The depth charge attack had caused more damage than was first realized. In order to keep the torpedo from arming itself, Post reluctantly called off the attack and ordered that the men in the after torpedo room try to recover the torpedo. It was eventually fired with the propeller lock on, which precluded the fish's screws from being able to spin the requisite number of times to arm it. The torpedo sank harmlessly to the bottom. The foul-up cost Post his last chance at the carrier. *Gudgeon* had little difficulty evading the destroyer, but by now, the convoy was a long way off.

Five hours after the disappointing conclusion to the battle, *Gudgeon* surfaced and moved ahead on one of her diesel engines, the three others being assigned to the weakened batteries for a charge. Lieutenant Midgley summarized the day's events: "Sighted a 'bird-house' but the b____d really s____ on us! 54 times!"[11]

Post continued chasing the phantom convoy all of the next day (the third) until on February 4, 1944, the lookouts sighted columns of smoke. At 1642, believing that the carrier convoy had been found east of the Ryuku Islands, *Post* put all four engines on line and attempted to close. As they approached the convoy Post observed a periscope at 2,500 yards and veered away to get out of the submarine's track. This time, the Japanese were very clever. Knowing that an unusually aggressive submarine commander was chasing an aircraft carrier, they sent out decoys, dropped a submarine to periscope depth and waited. Luckily, the *Gudgeon* men on watch were alert, much more alert than the Japanese who seemed to not even see the American submarine speeding for the convoy, because it did not give chase. The hunter had been, for a short time, the hunted. Post considered that he was fortunate to have been traveling so fast, and a fast-moving submarine is much more difficult to hit than a slow one. By nightfall, *Gudgeon* had been unable to reestablish contact with the prize carrier. Post's flirtation with the 20,000 ton *Unyo* was over. The carrier would make it to dry dock to receive much needed repairs but was destined to meet her end in September 1944 at the hands of the USS *Barb*.

Ambrosio Fernandez had the men of *Gudgeon* in stitches. Since being rescued from the sunken Japanese vessel, he had slowly and none-too-masterfully picked up English and continued to help with the duties in the kitchen. Fernandez was a friendly, short, black-haired man in his early to mid-thirties who had gone ashore a few days prior with the same expectations as the rest of the crew on *Gudgeon*. The crew delighted in teaching him swear words combined with necessary naval terms so that the phrase was sure to be stated in front of the old man. The crew roared watching Wild Bill Post teach Fernandez to take, "ah shit" or worse out of his vocabulary. But, as George Seiler recalled, Fernandez was most entertaining when he returned from R & R. He would invariably strike out with women ashore. When asked how he had made out with the ladies, Fernandez would respond in his broken English, "No way fer shit, much money no GG [girls]." [12]

It was now time for *Gudgeon* to return to her assigned area near Anami O Shima. Getting there took a few days. On the seventh, *Gudgeon* sighted a properly lit hospital ship speeding by, ignored it, and continued her submerged patrol. Of course, there could have been Japanese troops, arms, or American POWs on that hospital ship, but Post chose not to attack. *Gudgeon* continued to sail toward the Chinese coast. Along the way, Post worked to avoid countless Chinese junks, *Gudgeon* sometimes being surrounded by as many as eighty of the rickety vessels.

At 2107 on February 11, 1944, *Gudgeon* zeroed in on a ship located by radar at twelve miles, heading toward *Gudgeon*. Post ordered a dive to forty feet and began a submerged approach on the vessel because of the moon and light conditions. Before long *Gudgeon* was once again engaged in battle with the Japanese. It had been determined that there were more than one ship approaching them. Post identified one of the targets as a troop transport, the other, a destroyer. At a range of 2,200 yards Post fired six torpedoes from the forward tubes, three at the transport and the others at the escort. Post observed one or more hits and a burst of "murky smoke" from the transport. A faint explosion was heard by men in several compartments. A few minutes later they heard the distant explosion of a torpedo striking the beach. The three fired at the escort had missed. Post presumed that the torpedoes were set too deep because the ship which was first thought to be a destroyer turned out to be much smaller, and was likely a sub-chaser. The vessel was riding quite a lot higher in the water. BOOM. BOOM. BOOM. BOOM. BOOM. BOOM. BOOM. BOOM. BOOM. BOOM. BOOM. BOOM. BOOM. BOOM. BOOM. BOOM. *Gudgeon* dove to 75 feet and began maneuvers to avoid the depth charges that were now being fired toward the submarine, which caused minor damage to the SJ radar system and were so powerful that they rang all four bells on a telegraph machine in the engine room. BOOM. BOOM. BOOM. BOOM. BOOM. The depth charges rained down around *Gudgeon*.

Gudgeon was deep and in silent running; the men were doing their best to remain completely quiet for fear that the Japanese on their sound gear might pick a noise up. By now their hearts were pounding out of their chests, the adrenaline pulsing through their veins, their brains in survival mode, not a thing to be done, nowhere to go. The hardest job of all was sometimes forcing oneself to do nothing. For Bill Ostlund, it was a long way from quiet Webster City, Iowa, a place with no water around at all except for a very few small bodies of water where he used to catch crawdaddys. Just a year or so ago, he was at home minding the family's farm implement store. Now, here he was, a landlubbing midwesterner who, prior to attending submarine school, had never been on a boat of any kind, except perhaps for the tiny homemade rafts that he and his friends used to "sail" down the Boone River. With the pounding he had been taking since stepping aboard *Gudgeon*, it was entirely possible that if he didn't get it this day, his day would come.

Bill Post defiantly thrust the periscope into the darkness above the surface and saw that the Japanese had been firing at the junks in the area, sending them to the bottom, the entire time they were depth-charging *Gudgeon*. What reason there was for this action is hard to comprehend. Perhaps it was just another opportunity to kill the Chinese. Or possibly, the Japanese skipper wanted to illuminate the area, to more easily observe any torpedoes fired her way. Art Barlow recalls that as *Gudgeon* made her escape, they could see ten or twelve fishing junks on fire, the dark horizon silhouetting the burning ships off *Gudgeon*'s stern.

A little before midnight, February 11, 1944, *Gudgeon* rose again to periscope depth in the same area. Post saw a large troop transport, heading north at 8 knots. One *Gudgeon* submariner described the response of the crew when a Bill Post–commanded *Gudgeon* made such a sighting and moved in for the attack: "I can't imagine any greater thrill than the melodic sound of the battle stations alarm. Then the whoops of joy when the Captain got on the loudspeaker to describe the target or targets. The Captain would always convey to the crew what we were attacking. There was too much activity to dwell on anything but the present moment and the thrill of the hunt. Then the word came from the conning tower, if we were submerged, to make ready all tubes. The silence was only broken by the lead torpedoman opening the air pressure to the WRT (water round torpedo tank) to blow up water to fill the torpedo tube. The vent valve to the tube was opened at the same time so that we would know by the overflow that the tube was filled. If the outer doors were opened without the water filling the tubes, then the air present in the tubes would be forced out by the seawater rushing in, and create a huge bubble on the surface that would perhaps give away our presence. Gyro settings came from the TDC in the conning tower. Depth settings would also be transmitted by voice from the conning tower, and the silence would be broken by the voice in the headphones giving his, 'depth settings at eight feet.' 'Aye aye.' Then would come, 'Firing order, eight, nine, ten at the target.' Maneuvering into a firing position, the Captain would order the outer doors to be opened, and we would wait anxiously for the order to 'Fire eight.' Eight seconds would elapse, 'Fire nine.' Nine seconds later, 'Fire ten.' The soundman would convey, 'All torpedoes are running hot, straight and normal, Captain.' The quartermaster would tend the helm during the attack. About this time the torpedoes fired at the vessel would have reached their target, and when they contacted, the sound would be very much like the tip of your finger sharply striking a bare table. Then a second and a third. If there was a third hit it would be superfluous. Then there would be joy abounding."[13]

The transport, seen late this day, was probably the same one that had been attacked earlier. She had her engine amidships, one large straight funnel, double deck superstructure, main deck flush, and a slightly raked bow. She was a big one. Very inviting. Post swung *Gudgeon* around to line up her stern tubes and rose to forty feet. Radar indicated the vessel was only a couple of thousand yards away and had graciously slowed to 6.5 knots. Post let loose with three fish at 2327. Three minutes later, with midnight fast approaching, the crew heard an explosion, then another forty-five seconds later, and finally, a third just twenty-five seconds after the second.

The apparent torpedo hits were followed by many internal explosions and the distinct breaking-up noises of the underwater explosions of a doomed ship going to the bottom. Post watched the ship sink by the bow. The stern was high in the air at an angle of about thirty degrees. Men in every compartment of the submarine reported more "muffled" noises and breaking-up noises for some time. Three more explosions boomed in the distance as the men in the forward torpedo room loaded their tubes. Apparently good old Buddha had once again done his job. The Japanese troops were engaged in a desperate struggle for survival, the transport having been blown away below them, the men being thrown from the ship or diving into the water. The smoke and fire and instinctual screams and moans created a deathly scene. *Gudgeon* made way on two engines at the surface when the escort began firing her deck guns. This time the Japanese were not using flashless powder, and their intent could be easily observed. Luckily, Post noted, their shooting was "rotten" but "sincere enough" for Post to order that *Gudgeon* move ahead at flank speed on all four diesel engines.[14] *Gudgeon* maneuvered through a large fleet of junks, circled, and eventually lost the escort at 0125 on the morning of February 12.

Lookouts sighted the wreckage of one of the ships *Gudgeon* thought she had sunk on the prior patrol the next day just off the Chinese coast. Now in the area of Saddle Island, many small craft and mine sweepers were conducting a systematic search of the area. Post speculated that the recent attacks in the area by *Gudgeon* during the current patrol were considered peculiar enough—having been brazenly conducted in shallow water—that the Japanese had probably concluded that *Gudgeon* had laid mines. This is an indication of the uniqueness of Bill Post as commander of *Gudgeon*. The Japanese were unwilling to believe that *Gudgeon* was patrolling for ships that close to the Chinese coast in such shallow water.

On the seventeenth, Post noted that with the seas so heavy, *Gudgeon* approached a couple of very small sampans of about fifty tons. Certain that the ships were being used militarily by the Japanese, Post ordered an attack. At 600 yards one of the ships was sunk with a 5-inch shell. The other sampan was tracked down and sprayed with 20-mm and .50-caliber fire before being lost in the dark. The skipper gave up the pursuit to avoid the chance of collision. Art Barlow remembered the encounter with the small vessels. At one time during the attack, one of the sampans appeared as if it was trying to ram *Gudgeon*, though Barlow believes that everyone on deck or in the wheelhouse was probably dead at the time. He found it to be kind of spooky, like *Gudgeon* was being attacked by ghosts doing a kamikaze charge.

On the twenty-second, just off Iwo Jima, *Gudgeon* made four separate plane contacts. The waters from the Marianas to Japan were rich with merchant ships and thus teeming with enemy patrol planes. Sighting another hospital ship, Ensign Bill Ostlund wrote, "Calling Dr. Kildare and have him get rid of the G___ D___ hospital ships." [15]

In December 1943, the Japanese had set up the 901 Kokutai to do anti-submarine work. The 901st was under the command of the Grand Escort Headquarters and was the first air unit to do only antisubmarine work. None of the four planes spotted *Gudgeon*. *Gudgeon* once again headed for home. On the twenty-eighth Bill Ostlund, hoping to get a break from the war once he hit shore, wrote that the submarine's name was "USS *Transfer*," and that the ship's location was "new construction." [16] Just what was meant by the comments are not known, but it may be that Bill Ostlund desired a transfer off the *Gudgeon* prior to the next patrol.

On March 1, *Gudgeon* moored at Midway Island where the stark-white crew loaded fuel, water, and other provisions. In a few hours *Gudgeon* headed home toward Pearl Harbor, from which she had departed for her initial war patrol. *Gudgeon* arrived on March 5, 1944. For the forty-nine day patrol, *Gudgeon* had traveled a whopping 10,963 miles and expended 123,000 gallons of diesel fuel. *Gudgeon* had fired only seventeen torpedoes, expelled one harmlessly into the ocean, and returned with six. The patrol was terminated because *Gudgeon* was down to 5,352 gallons of fuel, which, at the rate fuel was being burned on this patrol, meant that she had better get home and let the Oil King fill her up. The crew on *Gudgeon* would learn later that her running mate, *Saury*, had avoided near disaster on her way home following the encounter with *Unyo*. The submarine had "pooped," taking in tons of water, and had been stranded helplessly on the surface for a day while repairs were frantically being made to non functioning machinery. Luckily the repairs were completed before she was spotted and sent to the bottom by a passing Japanese bomber.

Post noted in the eleventh war patrol report that the Japanese sound gear seemed to be improving. *Gudgeon* had been picked up at 4,000 yards. The carrier escort began throwing depth charges at a range of 1,500 yards, confirming in Post's mind that "even their first team, in the absence of a satisfactory method of depth charge control, merely employs embarrassing barrages, from which only an occasional lucky drop comes close." [17] The *Gudgeon* commander noted that evasion in shallow water of fourteen fathoms presented no unusual difficulties. Post ran at 75 feet during these attacks. He concluded that such patrolling is "no picnic" but that the danger of doing so is exaggerated in training.[18] While deep in Japanese-controlled seas, *Gudgeon* had sent radio messages, but only one was received. Thus if *Gudgeon* or any other submarine with similar equipment got into trouble, they knew that the chances of receiving help were slim. These submarines by and large remained lone wolves hunting in very dangerous places.

Albie Strow, *Gudgeon's* iron man officer had just finished his ninth straight war patrol despite the supposed policy of transferring officers back to newly constructed ships or other noncombatant duties after five patrols or so. Strow must have been an extraordinarily capable officer with immense interpersonal skills. He had boarded *Gudgeon* for the third patrol serving under Pop Lyon, had been able to adapt and continue to serve under the command of Lieutenant Commander William S. Stovall for three patrols and two special missions, followed by five more patrols and a special mission under Bill Post. In that time even such fine officers as Dixie Farrell, Mike Shea, Dusty Dornin, and Frank L. Barrows had come and gone, taking command of their own boats. In fact, of all the executive officers Post had during the war, each of whom, he said, were outstanding, he considered Albie Strow the best of them all. Very high praise indeed. Long gone by this time, of course, were men like George Seiler, Moose Hornkohl, Ray Foster, Ron Schooley, and Edward Hammond, all Navy regulars, having significant pre-war experience at sea and long training and indoctrination periods. Also no longer on board by the end of the eleventh patrol were longtime *Gudgeon* sailors Norris F. Cain, Vernon A. Rhodes, John J. Sheridan Jr., and Donald L. Stillson, who had the distinction of being *Gudgeon's* longest-serving sailors of the war—each man having served for ten war patrols.

At the start of the eleventh patrol, *Gudgeon* had thirty-six qualified submariners. An additional nineteen qualified before the patrol was completed. Seventeen of the men on board during the eleventh patrol were experiencing their first war patrol. During the patrol Bill Ostlund had received the good news that he had been promoted to lieutenant junior grade.

In the first endorsement of the just-completed patrol, the division commander, W. V. O'Kegan, said that he regretted that Post's persistent and aggressive approaches on the carrier were not better rewarded. He noted that when *Gudgeon* took off after the aircraft carrier she had to first fire two down-the-throat salvos at destroyer escorts within seven hours of each other, then bear up well under a rain of depth charges, once again showing "to the highest degree the fighting spirit of the *Gudgeon*."[19]

In the second endorsement, Charles B. "Swede" Momsen, now the squadron commander, praised the commanding officer, officers, and crew of *Gudgeon* for another fine patrol. He also noted the unfortunate outcome of the encounter with the destroyer escorts, praising the skills exhibited by the men on the destroyer, but pointing out that "their ardor was considerably dampened by the *Gudgeon*'s offensive action."[20] ComSubPac head Charles Lockwood concurred saying, "Two of the attacks made resulted in down-the-throat, close range shots at destroyers and were particularly outstanding for their daring."[21] If anyone hesitates to understand the utter bravery of William S. Post Jr., all he needs to do is visualize the situation facing Post that day—*Gudgeon*, greatly outnumbered and outgunned by Japanese ships of war in waters completely dominated by the Imperial Navy, going at it face-to-face with two Japanese destroyers. *Gudgeon* was credited with having sunk the 10,000 ton transport and a 50 ton sampan. JANAC would later discount the ear and eyewitness accounts of the transport breaking up, the bow observed to be below the waves, and the stern high in the air at a thirty degree angle. *Gudgeon* was awarded her eleventh Battle Star.

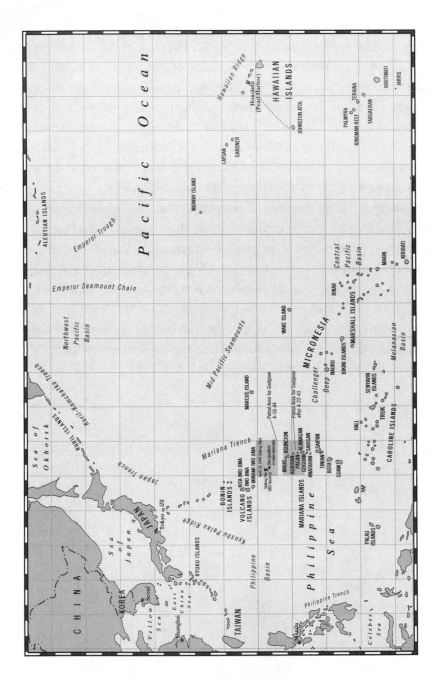

Twelfth War Patrol • Approximate Course • Departed April 4, 1944

· 12 ·
Missing—Presumed Lost

TWELFTH WAR PATROL: Departed Pearl Harbor—April 4, 1944
Lost Due to Unknown Circumstances

Our life is made by the death of others.

Leonardo Da Vinci, ca. 1500

By this time in the war the uss *Gudgeon* had made eleven war patrols. Even the two patrols on which *Gudgeon* did not fire a shot were hardly uneventful. On the third patrol, *Gudgeon* was engaged in the most decisive battle of the Pacific War, the Battle of Midway. *Gudgeon* and other submarines had fanned out in search of the Japanese flect. The Japanese were routed, and the balance of naval power was back closer to the Pearl Harbor configuration. On *Gudgeon*'s sixth patrol, she had barely survived the most extensive depth charge attack of the war. One-hundred twenty-three times the massive underwater explosives rocked *Gudgeon* and the men on board. Nonetheless, Lieutenant Commander Stovall and the others on board landed six intelligence men on Negros and then rescued twenty-eight worn-out commandos from the Japanese-dominated island of Timor. The twelfth patrol promised nothing less.

At the time *Gudgeon* departed for her final patrol, she was regarded as a lethal boat. According to Admiral Charles Lockwood, *Gudgeon* had sunk twenty-four ships weighing 166,818 tons, each total placing *Gudgeon* near the top of the entire American submarine fleet.

Very little is known about the thirty-day layover in Pearl Harbor between patrols. What had happened to *Gudgeon* during those thirty days? Had the submarine received the necessary repairs? Or had *Gudgeon* been forced to return to the war zone with equipment that broke down frequently, as was the case far too often on past runs? Equipment that was not working properly could have set up the men on *Gudgeon* for the twelfth patrol disaster. *Gudgeon* had experienced problems with the all-important radar as recently as the ninth and eleventh patrols. Post wrote in his patrol report following the ninth patrol that the SJ radar had gone out shortly after *Gudgeon* left Johnston Island and "defied" all attempts to repair it.[1] Following the eleventh patrol, Commander Post said in his patrol report that the SD radar had become virtually useless because the enemy could Direction Find (DF) the submarine when it was being used. For the eleventh patrol, a new SJ high-powered PPI unit had been installed. The "Plan Position Indicator" was an important technological advancement because the submarine's position could be seen on a screen similar to a television, showing *Gudgeon*'s position relative to planes or ships. If it did not work though, it was useless to the men on board. On the eleventh patrol, the SJ radar had worked at times and not at others. So it is possible that at the time the men on the submarine needed functioning radar most critically, the SD unit was collecting dust, and the SJ unit was again out of commission. The radars were not the only items that were functioning poorly during *Gudgeon*'s eleventh patrol. The many sets of binoculars kept flooding, a torpedo stop bolt didn't do the job, and there were several problems with the 5-inch gun and the auxiliary engine, the dinky. Of much potential significance, though, were problems with the trim pump, which is used to move water from one trim tank to another to get and keep the trim of the boat and maintain a designated depth. Post noted that during the eleventh run, "on going deep we never knew if it was going to pump when needed or not."[2] He pleaded for a reliable new pump with a larger capacity. Was one provided? Surely it was, but who knows. Did it work properly? If *Gudgeon* was stuck with the same old malfunctioning pump when she needed to dive deep faster than at any other time in her service, all could have been lost. If the new pump was provided, as it almost certainly was, did it work properly?

Besides the possible malfunctioning of the trim pump and the new SJ radar, another potentially critical flaw on *Gudgeon* that could have contributed to her loss had to do with the personnel on board for the final patrol. After the eleventh patrol, Bill Post wrote in his report that "The addition of inexperienced personnel beyond the saturation point is beginning to show its effects. During the calendar year 1943 twelve new officers reported for duty, representing a turnover of 150% of the complement of 8. During the same period 98 new enlisted men reported on board representing a turnover of 148% of the complement of 66." He concluded saying that "State of training was good, this patrol [*Gudgeon*'s eleventh] was ideal from the standpoint of training. However, the continued dilution of experienced officers and men as during the past year will eventually result in a serious detriment to fighting efficiency."[3] It's almost as if Post predicted *Gudgeon*'s loss. And that was before *Gudgeon*'s manpower situation was diluted even more seriously when both he and Executive Officer Albert Strow were transferred off *Gudgeon* before the twelfth patrol. The Navy essentially ignored Post. How else can one explain the dilution of the crew *followed* by the transfer of Post and Strow? *Gudgeon* was further weakened when Art Barlow took his eight patrols' worth of experience with him to a relief crew. Also lost were Torpedoman Second Class Douglas Tellier with eight patrols of experience. Edgar Kramer, the ship's cook who had answered Bill Post's call for cooks at Midway Island after Feit and Wood deserted, also departed. Herbert Patriquin, the middle-aged patriot, was not so lucky. He boarded *Gudgeon* for the final patrol, as did seventy-eight other men.

Most likely, many or most of the twelve men who transferred to *Gudgeon* were green. It is not known exactly what kind of experience and talents the men brought, but in all likelihood, the submarine experience of the men boarding was less than that of those departing. That was just the way it was on World War II submarines at the time. There were a lot more 90-day wonders around than war-hardened submariners. The exigencies of war dictated that skippers keep some experienced men around in each area of the submarine, and then hope that the rookies would be competent and composed enough to perform under fire. None of the new crew members for the twelfth patrol had any experience on *Gudgeon*. That is certain. Eight of the twelve new men who boarded *Gudgeon* were either third class in their area of specialty or they were seamen. Still on board *Gudgeon* was the popular but reluctant gladiator, Harry Nickel. Sailors who left *Gudgeon* prior to the final patrol recall that Nickel had been saving thousands of dollars in winnings from the submarine pools and card games, in of all places *Gudgeon*'s on board vault. He had let it be known that when the war was over, he was going to pull his savings out and buy a farm.

On Tuesday April 4, 1944, *Gudgeon* departed Hawaiian waters from the same location she had started the submarine offensive against the Japanese twenty-eight months earlier. The only man alive known to have witnessed *Gudgeon*'s departure that day is Art Barlow. Barlow explained that, as was customary, he and several other men who had been transferred off *Gudgeon* went down to the pier, took in *Gudgeon*'s mooring lines, and sent her off. Art Barlow has never forgotten what happened next. He was talking with his friend Radioman First Class Bill Remaley prior to *Gudgeon*'s departure. Remaley looked at him with the seriousness of a man on the gallows and said, "We're not going to come back."[4] He did not explain why he thought that this was so, but he was sure of it. Barlow tried to talk him out of it, assuring him that he would be seeing him again in a few months. Remaley would have none of it. Sixty years later the memory of Remaley's premonition and what was to follow still haunts him.

Gudgeon's period of calm was over. One month had passed before the war-tested veteran submarine moved slowly around Ford Island and through the East Loch. Having moved out of the harbor and past the submarine nets, she gained speed and was soon in the open sea, heading toward her destiny. Bill Remaley and the rest of the men on *Gudgeon* were heading for Johnston Atoll, code named Jackknife, 720 miles southwest of Pearl Harbor. Throughout the war, the United States had greatly expanded the island's size, creating enough land for a landing strip, a submarine base, and oil storage to top off submarines en route to their patrol destinations.

There is disagreement about the circumstances surrounding *Gudgeon*'s change in command. In an interview in 1982, Bill Post said that Lieutenant Commander Robert Alexander Bonin had come on board *Gudgeon* at Midway Island when she stopped off on her way back to Pearl Harbor after the eleventh patrol. The author of the article indicated that it was Bill Post's decision as to whether or not he would turn *Gudgeon* over to Bonin. Post was impressed with Bonin and said of him, "He was a real corker, very knowledgeable, very courageous, and very prudent at the same time. I had full confidence in him. I felt comfortable turning over command of the ship I loved."[5] Yet, when interviewed long after the war, Mary Post, Bill's wife, said, "I know when he gave up command he was real upset about it. He wasn't quite sure. I know he had a little fight about that, about giving it up."[6] Is Mary Post's memory accurate? Had Bill Post "fought" to stay on *Gudgeon*? Or perhaps Post's fight was the tortured anguish of a survivor, whose feelings ate at him for the rest of his life after *Gudgeon* had disappeared—anguish that Mary Post knew all too well.

When interviewed before his death, Albie Strow spoke with regret that the Navy had decided to replace him with a new executive officer after the decision by or about Post had been made. Strow's presence on nine straight war patrols made him a good candidate for a break. Yet he had received a break of over three months between *Gudgeon*'s eighth and ninth patrols when the submarine was being overhauled. Strow always said that his departure from *Gudgeon*, which was involuntary and done in less than half an hour before the boat left on the twelfth patrol, should not have occurred. With the crystal clear vision that a half-century of hindsight allows, Lieutenant Albert J. Strow was perhaps correct. *Gudgeon* was lost on the twelfth run, and maybe, just maybe, having Albie Strow on board in the number two position could have made a difference.

Gudgeon's new skipper was Robert A. Bonin, the son of a city of Milwaukee truck driver who graduated from the local Boys Trade and Technical High School, then attended Marquette where he planned a career as a civil engineer, only to be appointed to the Naval Academy after one year of study in Milwaukee. At the Academy, he was regarded as an expert in professional subjects; in particular, he knew all about the ships in the Navy. While he was in Annapolis, Bonin was quite active, participating in intramural cross country, and the Rifle Club. The *Lucky Bag* biographer said that Bonin would make a "fine addition to any ship's wardroom" but also made a jab at Bonin, adding that "as a wife Bob is always obliging and anxious to help out in any way possible."[7] Just what is meant by the wisecrack is unclear. Famed author and World War II submariner, the late Edward L. Beach, an underclassman, remembered Bonin well from his Academy days.

He did not find Bonin very "wifely." Beach and Bonin lived on the same floor early on in Beach's time in Annapolis. Bonin was at the time a first class midshipman, whom Beach regarded as "a tough son of a bitch."[8] Beach continued, "We were all scared to death of him. He would report us, or dress us down, or chew us up. I don't think Bonin was vindictive, but I think he was better at playing mad."[9] Beach said that the growling Milwaukeean did not make a lot of friends at the Academy, at least among the younger men.

Bonin graduated in 1936 and served aboard *Grayling* for her first seven patrols, eventually being promoted to executive officer. He earned a Silver Star on *Grayling* before departing to command *Gudgeon* for her twelfth patrol. The well-liked but much maligned Lieutenant Donald Midgley was promoted to serve as the ship's exec, his first time in that position, though he too had significant experience, having served on *Gudgeon* for five patrols prior to the twelfth.

Midgley was a Naval Academy graduate, class of 1941, from Hopedale, Massachusetts. In his photo in the *Lucky Bag* in his final year at the Academy, Midgley looks so sad-eyed you almost wonder if he anticipated his end on *Gudgeon*. While at the Naval Academy, Midgley ran track, and being an east coast boy was a member of the Boat Club. The author of his biography described the young man as being full of "optimism" and "humor."[10] Attempting to be humorous, the writer described Midgley as kind of a common, friendly sort. With hindsight, however, the write-up had a melancholy tone as the author wrote: "Ten years from now, I want to remember Midge sitting in the room with a skag in his hand, oversized feet propped on the desk, green eyeshade hanging dismally over his eyes, and steel-rimmed glasses riding precariously on the end of his nose. There he sits, running his hand through his slowly disappearing hair, his long, gangling figure sagging in the chair, and a far-away look in his bright blue eyes. Maybe he's thinking of all those wonderful days of leave spent in the Massachusetts woods, or of his home and family in the thriving metropolis of Hopedale. Or perhaps he's thinking of the future and the plans he's made for it."[11]

Lieutenants Burton Heyes of Portland, Oregon, and Addison B. Pinkley of Tucson, Arizona, were on board for their fourth patrol, as were newly-promoted Lieutenants Bill Ostlund and David McCorquodale for their third. Two new officers arrived for the twelfth patrol. They were Lieutenant

James Sylvester Coghlan from San Francisco and Lieutenant Robert Cope Collins from Philadelphia. The twelfth patrol was to have been an exciting one for Ben Dickenson. He had served *Gudgeon* since the fifth patrol, most recently as a first class electrician's mate, but had been promoted to ensign for the twelfth. The promotion meant more money, more stature, and a dramatic change in roles on board the submarine—all of which would prove to be short-lived.

With *Gudgeon* at sea for two days, Mary Clelland Ostlund, Bill's proud mother, opened up the Thursday April 6, 1944, edition of Webster City's paper, *The Freeman Journal*. She was pleased to learn that the three-column article she knew would be running one day had finally made the paper. The article discussed the military service of her three sons. Each was pictured in uniform. The article at least did something to assuage the daily feelings of dread and fear that each day brought. Three sons in the service. How many of them would make it home alive? The article was titled, "3 Brothers Officers," and told about her boys' prewar lives as well their careers as officers. The article described nineteen-year-old Second Lieutenant John Ostlund, who was in the Air Force as a military "triple threat" because he had been schooled in gunnery, navigation, and bombing. Of course, he had also been trained as a pilot. Bob, the middle son, had received his initial training at Camp Warren, Cheyenne, Wyoming, and then his officers' training at Camp Lee, Virginia. Prior to being deployed in Europe, he had been involved preparing troops for overseas action. Later, the author of the article referred to the three brothers as a "triple threat."[12]

With a dangerously depleted crew, a new skipper and exec, a number of questionable but vital systems on board, and a group of rather inexperienced junior officers, Lieutenant William C. Ostlund and the other seventy-eight men on *Gudgeon* topped off *Gudgeon*'s fuel tanks and departed from Johnston Island. The date was Friday April 7, 1944. *Gudgeon* was headed for an area northwest of the Marianas. The Japanese were frantically trying to reinforce Saipan, Truk, and Palau with convoys of troops and munitions. The skies were full of aircraft searching for the submarines that could keep the precious cargoes from reaching the areas preparing for battle. The dangerous waters that *Gudgeon* entered in April 1944 was known as the Valley of the Shadow.

Much like the premonition of death that Bill Remaley had prior to *Gudgeon* leaving Pearl Harbor, Bill Post, hundreds of miles from his beloved boat and crew, became overwhelmed with an awareness that *Gudgeon* had been lost. He would explain later, "Authentic instances in the folklore of the sea show that sailors have experienced extrasensory perceptions about ships and crew they have become a part of. On the presumed time of *Gudgeon*'s loss in April 1944, I clearly received such premonitions." [13]

When his feelings were confirmed, Commander Bill Post was grief-stricken for the loss of his shipmates and for the grief of their loved ones. He said, "I know damn well she went down fighting." [14] On June 7, 1944, shortly after noon, Regis Bonin received the dreaded Western Union telegram from Washington, D.C., at her home at 156 Colonial Drive in Milwaukee, Wisconsin complete with numerous misspellings. It stated, [15]

THE NAVY DEPARTMENT DEEPLY REGRETS TO INFORM YOU THAT YOUR HUSBAND LIEUTENANT COMMANDER ROBERT ALEXANDER BONIN USN IS MISSING FOLLOWING ACTION IN THE PERFORMANCE OF HIS DUTY AND IN THE SERVICE OF HIS COUNTRY. THE DEPARTMENT APPRECIATS YOUR GREAT ANIETY BUT DETAILS NOT NOW AVAILABLE AND DELY IN RECEIPT THEREOF MUST NECESSARILY BE EXPECTED. TO PREVENT POSSIBLE AID TO OUR ENEMIES AND TO SAFEGUARD THE LIVES OF OTHER PERSONNEL PLEASE DO NOT DIVULGE THE NAME OF THE SHIP OR STATION OR DISCUSS PUBLICLY THE FACT THAT HE IS MISSING.

VICE ADMIRAL RANDALL JACOBS CHIEF OF NAVAL PERSONNEL.

As far as the Navy was concerned, after topping off with fuel on Friday April 7, 1944, *Gudgeon* was never seen or heard from again. Until recently her loss has remained a mystery.

Part II

· · · · · ·

Finding Uncle Bill

· 13 ·

The Mysterious Yuoh Island

TWELFTH WAR PATROL—THE THEORY:
April 4, 1944–April 18, 1944

This is courage in a man,
to bear unflinchingly what heaven sends.

Euripides, ca. 422 BC

Part Two contains the more personal side of the story, the story of my search to find out what had happened to my uncle, Lieutenant William C. Ostlund and his shipmates. One day in mid-2001 while casually reading about *Gudgeon*, I decided to follow up on a hunch to see if I could resolve what seemed to be a translation error made shortly after the war by the Navy, and in so doing, solve the mystery of the loss of *Gudgeon*. The Navy has long discounted the claims of a Japanese pilot who said that he had sunk a U.S. submarine off a nonexistent island named Yuoh Island at about the time that *Gudgeon* and *Gudgeon* alone disappeared from the United States submarine fleet. I've always had a sense that if Yuoh Island could be "found," *Gudgeon* would be found. And, as luck would have it, my intuition was correct.

This is how it happened.

The story of *Gudgeon*'s disappearance began when *Gudgeon*, a proud veteran of twelve war patrols, pulled away from Pearl Harbor for her patrol on Tuesday April 4, 1944. She stopped at Johnston Island to load up with fuel on the seventh, and then made her way toward her patrol area, which was a rectangle, approximately 180 by 230 nautical miles, from longitude 21 to 24° N by latitude 143 to 147° E. If she arrived on station after April 22, *Gudgeon* was to patrol farther south, 17 to 21° N, and 143° to 147° E, closer to Maug Island of the northern Marianas.

For almost sixty years, this was the end of *Gudgeon*'s story, at least as far as what was known with any certainty. As far as the Ostlund family was concerned, it was all anyone would know about Bill's death until about 1996. Prior to that time, Uncle Bill's two brothers and their families had known only that *Gudgeon* had disappeared in April 1944. Bill's death was as mysterious to us as the disappearance of Amelia Earhardt.

During my early childhood, in the early to mid-1960s, the mysterious disappearance of Uncle Bill on board *Gudgeon* was a fairly common item of discussion. Early on, when my father would bring up the subject, his grief was so obvious that even as a boy of nine or ten, I felt a need to try to cheer him up, once telling him that it was possible that Bill had been shipwrecked and had gone ashore on some remote Pacific island. I told him that one day he would be found alive and return to his family where he could live the life that had been awaiting him prior to the outset of the war. I thought the story of Robinson Crusoe gave credibility to the theory. My dad was unimpressed and said nothing.

My older brother Dave also recalled being a very little boy and listening to our father tell how Uncle Bill had been in a submarine that had been lost somewhere in the Pacific. In the guileless way of an innocent child, Dave asked, "You mean poor Uncle Bill is still floating around somewhere out in the sea?"[1] He was horrified when Dad broke down into uncontrollable sobbing.

As I got older, the discussion of Bill's death took on a more adult tone. My dad talked about the war very infrequently. On one of those occasions, he told my older sister Linda that he was in Europe with the Army when he received word that Bill, the idolized older brother, was missing at sea. He said that he collapsed into a foxhole where he lay sobbing for a day. The devastating news had brought him down more efficiently than anything that the Germans had thrown at his Forty-Seventh Quartermaster Group.

Year after year Uncle John, Aunt Bev, mom, and dad snuck off to a corner for some Christmas Eve "adult-talk." No kids allowed. As they sat there in the subdued light, the Christmas tree glistening with the thin strands of silver icicles, the flashing of the richly colored red, green, blue, and yellow lights punctuating the conversation, the talk would invariably return to the subject of the family's greatest grief—the brother who did not return from the war. One year, curious about this "Uncle Bill," this guy who had died so tragically, I crept up close enough to hear. For some reason I have always remembered that the consensus of the group was that if the experienced skipper, some guy named "Bill Post," had only been on board, then *Gudgeon* would not have been lost, and Bill would be here with us.

The adults reasoned that *Gudgeon*'s loss occurred because she had a new skipper when she left for her final patrol. The new man had made mistakes. Searching for answers, groping for theories that made any sense at all is, of course, the unending burden for those who have survived a loved one's mysterious death. In time, as facts would unfold, the unintended rap on veteran submariner, skipper Bob Bonin, would completely unravel.

I was born eight years after the war. World War II was still all-too-fresh for the veterans approaching middle age when I started to become aware of the catastrophic dimensions of the conflict in the early 1960s. I was very disappointed to find out that my father had brought home a trunk full of war memorabilia, including German and Japanese flags, a Lugar, and things like that, which had been destroyed in a flooded basement shortly after the war. Dad still had his old Eisenhower officer's jacket and his captain's cap. One day, while rummaging through the attic, I took "the Eisenhower" off its hanger where it had been for twenty years and put it on. I went through each pocket and discovered fifteen tiny browned snapshots which had been taken at one of the concentration camps. The pictures were all too easy for Dad to forget that he had. Several of the pictures showed the capos, the Jewish assistants, with their long metal poles in hand, standing beside the dead bodies laid out on a rack just before they were pushed into the ovens. Others showed stacks of rail-thin dead people, one on top of another, genitals exposed, mouths open, their faces frozen in grotesque grimaces, their skin stretched tightly over their gruesomely starved bodies. "My God," I thought, "these stacks are thirty feet high." I was too old to not really understand that the Holocaust had taken place, but the pictures inspired haunting questions nonetheless. "How did this happen? Did this really happen on this planet?" It was as if the horror occurred on another world.

Yet, I knew, it was so. Who could have done this? Hitler, I knew. "My God. Nobody could have been this cruel." But he was. I knew that those awful photos were related to the death of Uncle Bill. Those responsible for the mass murder of all of those helpless people were in cahoots with the Japanese who had killed Bill. The photos galvanized my developing interest in the war but did nothing to help me make sense of it.

As I grew older, anything having to do with World War II drew my interest, especially submarine movies. I never passed up the opportunity to watch one. Each time the awareness that long-lost Uncle Bill had been on a submarine, very much like the one on the screen, was with me. Each movie told me a little more about submarines, about what it must have been like for Bill.

More recently the History Channel has become available. It has covered much of World War II and submarine warfare. One day, several years ago, I recorded a documentary about American submarines in the war. For years I had been trying to capture *Gudgeon* or even better, Uncle Bill, on the screen. I was convinced that if I kept watching and kept the VCR running, I would eventually find them both. After watching the tape, I hurriedly sent it off to Webster City. I thought I had seen Bill on a submarine and wanted my dad and Uncle John to tell me whether or not I was correct. Sure enough, after both the men watched the tape, I received a phone call. Indeed, it was Bill standing there on *Gudgeon*, wearing a light officer's jacket, not moving, standing below the bridge as the submarine returned to port. Both men were sure of it. Bill just stood there silently, staring vaguely toward the camera, a small, contented smile on his face, his features so faint on the old black-and-white footage that he almost appeared to be a ghost.

Nonetheless, for all my interest, nothing new was known about Bill or his disappearance until about 1996 when my identical twin brother, Chris, called me one day very excited about what he had found. He had come across a book about World War II submarine warfare at a garage sale. He had gladly paid a quarter for it after he read an account describing what may have been the circumstances of *Gudgeon*'s unexplained disappearance. The author said that after the war a Japanese pilot claimed to have sunk a United States submarine on April 18, 1944. The pilot reported that he dropped two bombs on a submarine that *may* have been *Gudgeon*. The first bomb hit the bow of the submarine, the second hit the bridge. The center of the submarine burst, with pillars of oil shooting high into the sky. But, the author continued, the attack took place near an island the Japanese pilot said was called "Yuoh Island." There was no island in the Pacific named Yuoh Island, nor one that sounds like the word "Yuoh." Therefore, the Navy has long discounted the pilot's claim.

Word spread quickly throughout the Ostlund family. The desire to satisfy John and Dad with the knowledge of what actually happened to their brother was very strong. The confusion about Yuoh Island, compared to having no information at all about Bill's death, did not totally dampen the excitement of the news. It did not take much effort to find a few other books at the University of Iowa Main Library that described in greater detail the attack that was referred to in Chris's book. What the other authors said about that attack was critically important. One text reported that the attack occurred "166 miles 13° T" (i.e., true north) off Yuoh Island, while each of the handful of others that reported the attack said it had occurred "166 miles 132° T" off the mysterious island. The location would have placed the sinking either northeast of the island (i.e., 13° T) or southeast of the island, at 132° T. The sinking locations were a concern. How could they be so different? But even more confusing. Where in the world is Yuoh Island?

I sent for *Gudgeon*'s war patrol reports and muster rolls through the National Archives, and asked Uncle John to gather what was left of Bill's Navy records. I purchased photos of *Gudgeon* and acquired dusty old wartime interviews of former *Gudgeon* officers. I tried to get my hands on anything that had the word *Gudgeon* on it. Why? I did not really have a goal in mind. My pursuit was surely driven by the same old questions I had always had about Bill. Who was he? What was he like? What happened to him? Early on I had no illusions that I would ever have the answer to his fate.

One day, as more and more material came in, I joked with my son Aaron's nurse Jude that I would not be happy until I found an autographed picture of Bill Ostlund in his Navy whites. Then, to my utter amazement and great delight, Jane Duffey, the daughter of deceased Admiral Joe Grenfell, kindly sent me the picture of Bill and the other officers on *Gudgeon* after the tenth war patrol that had been sent to her father years ago by Commander Bill Post. In the back row, there was Bill Ostlund looking sharp in his best Navy whites. The picture contained the autograph of every officer in the photo, Bill's read: "W. C. Ostlund."

What was learned after continued reading about *Gudgeon*'s loss was puzzling. Not only was there a report of a submarine sunk near a nonexistent island on April 18, 1944, but there was another theoretical account of *Gudgeon*'s sinking. By this time I was becoming convinced that the mystery of *Gudgeon*'s loss could be solved, thoughts which I kept to myself, lest my family think I had gone off the deep end. The emergence of the second attack that may explain her loss was not exactly great news. It seemed to only complicate things.

Other books about World War II submarining explained that on May 12, 1944, while stationed near Saipan, quite a ways south of *Gudgeon*'s assigned patrol area at the time, men on American submarines *Sandlance*, *Tunny*, and *Silversides* reported that they had heard a long depth charge attack about ten miles away. As it turns out, just like the Yuoh Island attack, if a United States submarine had been attacked, it had to have been *Gudgeon* because no other American submarine was lost at that time, nor had any submarine reported an attack. Yet, the attack on May 12 could have been a Japanese attack on a Japanese submarine, just like the many attacks *Gudgeon* had sustained during the war from American bombers. Or perhaps a Japanese surface vessel had mistakenly attacked a submarine that was not actually there. Finally, as has been discussed, the Japanese were known to throw depth charges into the water as a means of scaring away U.S. submarines from the area.

By May 12, *Gudgeon* would long have been incommunicado. In fact, *Gudgeon* had not been heard from since April 7. It seems unlikely that Bob Bonin would have been out of contact for more than a month, but it is not out of the question. Radio problems or the need to maintain radio silence while *Gudgeon* lay in Japanese waters could have explained *Gudgeon*'s lack of communications with ComSubPac. Bonin was sent a message on May 11, 1944, ordering him to leave his area to undertake a lifeguard mission for downed aviators; U.S. bomber crews that had not made it back to their bases after dropping their loads on the Japanese. The Navy required a response from *Gudgeon*. Since acknowledgment of the order was not received, it is strongly suggestive that *Gudgeon* was lost before the depth charge attack off Saipan the following day. The following day she was once again asked to acknowledge receipt of the assignment. If it was *Gudgeon* that had been attacked on May 12 off Saipan, she would have been quite a ways from her assigned patrol area for the day. The third possible cause of *Gudgeon*'s loss is that *Gudgeon* was sunk in an unrecorded attack and that as a result her loss will always remain a "mystery of the sea."

In *Undersea Victory*, W. J. Holmes described the anxiety that *Gudgeon*'s disappearance caused at Admiral Lockwood's Operations Room. Each morning after *Gudgeon*'s failure to check in, Lockwood would enter the room and glance at *Gudgeon*'s marker on a wall chart. He would look through all of the incoming dispatches for news of the submarine's whereabouts, knowing full well that he would have been awakened if news about Lieutenant Commander Bonin and the other seventy-eight submariners had been received.

On May 14, Lockwood radioed Bonin to immediately bring *Gudgeon* into Midway Island rather than allow her an extra few days to finish her patrol, relieving Bonin of any criticism for having terminated his patrol early. In addition, the suspense was becoming increasingly uncomfortable for Lockwood and Operations Officer Richard Voge. He did not want to wait those extra few days. Day after day *Gudgeon*'s marker was moved an average day's travel along her assigned track toward Midway Island. By May 23, *Gudgeon* should have reached the 500 mile circle around the island. Lockwood and Voge knew that a critical time had arrived. Standard practice dictated that when a submarine approached the circle, she would report her presence to avoid being mistaken for a Japanese submarine. When Bonin did not report, things became all too clear. Even so, Lockwood sent out special search planes to see if a damaged and hobbling *Gudgeon* was slowly making her way home. As time went by, it was obvious that *Gudgeon* was gone. On June 7, 1944, she was officially reported "overdue and presumed lost." The following morning when Voge was alone in the operations room, he quietly removed *Gudgeon*'s marker from the chart, and from that moment on *Gudgeon* existed only in the hearts and memories of the men who had known her. Undated serial number 00627 prepared by Admiral Lockwood contained *Gudgeon*'s totals as of the time of her loss. The Navy figured that *Gudgeon* had sunk or damaged 208,628 tons of Japanese shipping. Lockwood said of *Gudgeon*, "On her eleven previous war patrols

Gudgeon firmly established herself as being one of the most outstanding submarines of this Force." He added later, "Her loss will be keenly felt by this Submarine Force and the entire Navy."[2]

Armed with the ambiguity of *Gudgeon*'s possible loss on April 18 and the less likely sinking off Saipan, my quest was on. The April 18 account seemed more credible. I learned that the Pacific Ocean is 64,000,000 square miles in size, and that the Japanese bombing of an American submarine took place at the exact time that *Gudgeon* was to be positioned in a small area of ocean between Iwo Jima and Maug Island southeast of Japan.

I sensed that if Yuoh Island could be found, the mystery could be solved. Where was it? Did it even exist? Did the American officer err when he recorded the island's name as "Yuoh"? What was a Yuoh? Had a secretary hurried through the interview and typed the wrong name of the island down? If Yuoh Island could be found, where was *Gudgeon* supposed to be in relation to it on April 18, 1944? Were there any enemy bombers in the area which could have carried out such a mission? What do the Japanese say about this now? As it would turn out, every question pointed in only one direction.

Year after year, summer after summer, I acquired more information. The search for "the answer" was not precisely formulated and remained more of a nagging question that occasionally came to the fore. I sensed that the key would be to find Yuoh Island, but the method that I was using to solve the mystery was to increase the amount of data that I had acquired about *Gudgeon* and submarine warfare in World War II. The more data, the greater the chances that the answer might just fly off one of those yellowed pages into my lap. It did not take long for me to decide that despite all of *Gudgeon*'s achievements, she had been all but forgotten by historians. By 2001, I was zeroing in on the cryptic "Yuoh Island." Many times I had picked up a map of the Pacific Ocean and scoured it, pronouncing the names of island after island, then following it with "Yuoh." It did not take long to discover that Iwo Jima and Yuoh Jima were quite similar and that Jima is a word for "island" in Japanese. I could not believe how much they sounded alike, astounded that only a few years after the invasion of Iwo Jima, the Navy did not notice the same thing, concluding that no island in the Pacific sounds like Yuoh Island.

The study of Iwo Jima had not proceeded too much further when the solution was found. I learned that Iwo Jima was one of the Volcano Islands and, in fact, had been formed from two cones of a volcano, the most well known being Suribachi. Iwo Jima was the island that United States Marines struggled so valiantly to capture, then to raise their flag, later splendidly immortalized in bronze. I learned that the island smelled of sulphur, the sulphur pits still boiled, giving off a noxious and unpleasant odor that is noticed immediately after a person has stepped foot on the island. Iwo Jima *means* "Sulphur Island."

In June 2001, I decided to search the University of Iowa's libraries for Japanese-English/English-Japanese dictionaries hoping to find some information which might shed light on the word "Yuoh." The University had many such dictionaries, all but one of which were gibberish to me. It was *Brinkley's* Japanese-English Dictionary, printed by the University of Michigan Press in 1963, which contained the answer. By using a process known as transliteration to look up the actual meanings of words as they sound in Japanese, I thought it would be possible to find out what "Yuoh" meant. Hesitant to look up Yuoh, because I feared it would not be there, and needing to confirm that this dictionary could be used the way I thought it could, I looked up "Iwo." Sure enough on page 443, I learned that Iwo meant, "1. Sulphur. 2. Sulphur matches." I hurried on to page 1660 for "Yuoh," and there it was as plain as day. The term "Yuoh" was listed as: "*Yuo, n.* sulphur."[3]

The significance of the find was obvious to me after reading it. The discovery sparked pangs of strong emotion. Part of me wanted to scream, "That's it! I found it!" I wanted to tell everybody around me that it seemed that I had stumbled across this absolutely amazing thing about my uncle, and his heroic shipmates who had died so long ago. But, as I looked around, seeing the college-aged students studying quietly, I knew that none of them would care and that I had a lot of work to do. Nevertheless, it was now clear. Yuoh Island means Sulphur Island. Both Yuoh Island and Iwo Jima are names for Sulphur Island. It seemed to be quite possible that Uncle Bill and the other men on *Gudgeon* were lying there 166 nautical miles off Iwo Jima. I thought to myself, "I think I've found Uncle Bill."

Word spread quickly through the family. By this time, my dad was dead, but Bill's brother John was excited to hear what seemed to be rather persuasive information that could explain his long-lost older brother's death. It had bothered him for more than half a century. "The Navy knew where they were trying to go, but not what happened to them. That's probably bothered me more than anything all these years," John would say later.[4]

By this time, research about *Gudgeon* had become my principal summer pursuit and, for that matter, a major pursuit during the school year. The research had become serious. It was time to get some answers. Things proceeded quickly from that point. I had previously written a letter to Harry Holmes, the author of the book, *The Last Patrol*, which told the stories of each of the fifty-two United States submarines lost in the war. The effort resulted in no new information coming my way. Holmes said that *Gudgeon* was one of his favorite topics but that there was nothing new and that her loss would be one of those that forever remained a mystery. However, he did provide me the name of a retired Japanese Navy captain in Tokyo who had been known to help American researchers.

The Captain's name was Noritaka Kitazawa of the National Institute for Defense Studies located in Tokyo. By this time I had only seen one book that stated that the submarine sunk on the eighteenth was "13° T". One book, said that it was a bomber from the 901 Kokutai that had made the attack on April 18. I asked Captain Kitazawa for the war diary of the antisubmarine warfare unit, the 901 Kokutai, which I had learned had a base at Iwo Jima in April 1944. Captain Kitazawa graciously assisted. How ironic it was that this former officer, who I understood was an adversary of the United States during the war, was now assisting the nephew of a man who had been killed by his countrymen. Indeed, time heals all wounds. Captain Kitazawa sent several photocopied hand-written pages from the war diary of the "Chichi-Jima Houmen Advanced Base Group" for the time around April 18. Chichi Jima is an island just north of Iwo Jima. The term "Houmen" suggests that the Chichi Jima base was administratively responsible for those that surrounded it, including of course, Iwo Jima.

Captain Kitazawa translated the material and paraphrased it for me. In his letter dated August 30, 2001, Captain Kitazawa wrote, "War diaries of the 901st Kokutai in this archive has no records concerning this case, but War Diary of the Chichi-Jima Houmen Advanced Base Group contains some records of this attack. According to the War Diary of the Chichi-Jima Houmen Advanced Base Group, No. 1 aircraft of Iwo-Jima dispached [sic] team from 901st Kokutai reported 0845 JST (Japanese Standard Time) 18th April that Bombed Enemy Sub. 132° Iwo-Jima 166 Nautical miles, Sunk certainly 0630."[5] He continued, "And according to the same War Diary, at 1815 JST from Commanding officer of Iwo Jima dispached team was reported that No. 3 aircraft of No. 1 subdivision which took off 0500 from Iwo-Jima, at 0630, on 132° Iwo-Jima 166 Nautical miles. Bombed an Enemy Sub. Just after his submergence, with two 250 kg bombs. And 1st bomb hit sub's head and 2nd bomb hit sub's bridge straight, and the aircraft sighted on the center of hull to spring big yellow-green explosion, and to spring up tall oil piller [sic] and enlarged thick crude oil circle about 150 meters in diameter, so this target evaluated sinking."[6] The Japanese records confirmed that the attack was 166 miles, at 132° T off Iwo Jima. The 250-kilogram bombs that had been used in the attack were massive, each weighing 600 pounds. A second letter was received a few weeks later. Captain Kitazawa explained that he had reread the material and concluded that only one aircraft was involved in the attack. He had misunderstood the old diaries. He could find no additional information nor the names of the crew involved in the attack.

I wondered whether *Gudgeon* could have arrived at the point of the attack by April 18. I made further contacts with an expert, Rick Dunn, on Japanese aircraft during the war who would later find that a dispatch from the 901 Kokutai for April 20 that gave the specific location for the attack on the eighteenth. The dispatch stated that the attack took place at 22-45° N, 143-40°E. The distance from Johnston Island located at 16.45° N, 169.31° W to this proposed sinking site is around 2,700 nautical miles. There is no way of knowing *Gudgeon*'s speed on her way from Johnston Island to the point of the attack. After all, there was no radio contact, and all the men who were on board, along with their records, lie at the bottom of the Pacific. Assumptions about *Gudgeon*'s speed after departing Johnston Island sixty years after the fact amount to conjecture, yet it is certain that *Gudgeon* could have been there off Yuoh Island on April 18, 1944. More important than any personal calculations is the fact that the Office of the Chief of Naval Operations (in

United States Submarine Losses World War II) indicated that *Gudgeon* would have been in her assigned patrol area as early as April 16 if nothing unusual had been encountered enroute.

So in the vast expanses of the Pacific Ocean, the question is, "Where is the proposed sinking site (the Dunn site) in relation to where *Gudgeon* was supposed to be on the eighteenth?" According to *United States Submarine Losses World War II*, *Gudgeon* was to patrol 21-24° N by 143-147° E. The area envelops the site of the attack as reported in Dunn's Japanese radio intercept.

Former Navy skipper John Ackerman sent me a detailed map of the area and plotted the 132° T sinking site 166 miles off Yuoh Island (Iwo Jima), indicating that it was very close to the Dunn site. Using the rougher estimation of the sinking site, the Japanese were indicating that the sinking location was 22-52.5°N, 143-32°E, which is seven nautical miles southeast of Dunn's site. Ackerman's site falls well within Gudgeon's assigned patrol area for the 18th.

I had previously called a naval historian, thinking that the Navy would be interested in what I had learned. The historian was not interested. He asked, "What do you expect the Navy to do, go and search for an 'ordinary' submarine like the *Gudgeon*?"[7] He added that the Navy did not have any manpower committed to keeping track of new information about old boats. Certain that he must not have known much about *Gudgeon*, I tried to point out a few of her accomplishments and said that she had been the first United States submarine to sink a warship from another country. He disagreed, telling me about United States submarine L-2, which he said had been credited with having sunk a German submarine in July 1918 during World War I. I would learn later about the bizarre circumstances of L-2's very dubious sinking. Despite the fact that the L-2 had not even fired a shot, the British gave the L-2 credit for a sinking. I would learn later that almost everyone on this side of the ocean knows that the Germans sank their own submarine and that the L-2 had not fired a shot. I was dumbstruck. That was the end of my discussions with the Navy.

Because of the unpleasant encounter, I attempted no subsequent contacts with the Navy. I was flabbergasted that the historian had referred to *Gudgeon* as an ordinary submarine. I knew that the men who sailed on

Gudgeon had not been riding an ordinary submarine. My conviction that *Gudgeon* had been lost to history was now certain. I decided upon another strategy to get the word out about my findings. After all, there were seventy-eight other families who had lost a son or a brother on *Gudgeon* and many others who had fought on the submarine and survived, as well as those interested in submarines and World War II history, who would like to know what I had learned. I submitted an article to *The Submarine Review*, a quarterly for naval professionals, explaining my research and findings in detail. I was excited to learn that they would print the article in their October 2001 edition, as well as a follow-up in April 2002. The article was entitled, "Finding Uncle Bill." I heard from many who had read the article, but as far as I knew, the other families of deceased crew members were not aware of the new findings. It seems likely that none of the families of the lost men subscribed to the periodical. I am certain that if they had read the article, they would have contacted me for further information.

I was determined to continue to gather more information about *Gudgeon*'s sinking but had no intention of writing a book until our friend Jude asked me one day, "Why don't you write a book about the *Gudgeon*?" [8] I laughed at the ridiculous suggestion and responded, "Me write a book? That's the last thing I'm going to do." [9] But the idea ate at me for a few days. By this time, I had acquired quite a lot of information about *Gudgeon*, I knew of her storied history, and the fact that nobody had written a book telling it bothered me. The men on *Gudgeon* had fought so gallantly and accomplished so much. I felt that this was a disservice to the men who had served, and I decided that it would be worthwhile to write a book and give the men credit for what they had done. And one thing I knew for certain: *Gudgeon* was not just *another* submarine. The men who fought on *Gudgeon* had fought valiantly and honorably and many had died doing so. Very simply it came down to this: I would write a book because the *Gudgeon* submariners, living and dead, deserved one.

Some of the information which follows is speculative because I do not have the resources to do a more detailed search of U.S. and Japanese records and I do not speak or read Japanese. Japanese antisubmarine efforts had been virtually nonexistent until April 1942 when they created two convoy escort groups consisting of twenty-four ships each. The vessels were mostly old destroyers that were expected to cover impossibly large areas of sea off the coast of Asia and around Truk. By November 1943, the Japanese merchant shipping losses were staggeringly high. Thus, belatedly, the Grand Escort Command Headquarters was created with the all-but-hopeless responsibility of protecting Japanese shipping from the air. In December 1943 the 901 Air Group (i.e., Kokutai) was organized at Tateyama for the sole purpose of escorting convoys. The 901 Kokutai had a variety of planes in service to achieve the task, including the Mitsubishi G3M Type 96 land attack bomber which was known to the Allies as "Nell." The Nell land-based, long-range, two-engine bombers had a wingspan of 82 feet, were 52 feet long and about twelve feet high. They could carry as many as 800 kilograms (1,746 pounds) of bombs externally and flew around 240 mph. They were capable of reaching heights of 33,730 feet and had a range of almost 4,000 miles. The Nell bombers were first flown in 1935 and were considered to be obsolete by the beginning of the war. Calling the bombers obsolete is rather inaccurate in view of the plane's surprising performance during the war, which included the sinking of Great Britain's two big battle cruisers, HMS *Prince of Wales* and *Repulse*.

The men comprising the 901 Kokutai were hurried into service before they were adequately trained. Because of the heavy losses of merchant shipping, they were forced into service in January 1944 and had to learn "on the fly." The force was originally equipped with only forty-eight land-based planes that were shifted from base to base according to the number of Allied submarines known to be in each area. The sea around the Bonin Islands, just north of Iwo Jima, the other Volcano Islands, and the Marianas, were monitored by radar stations spread throughout the islands as well as by patrol planes and ships.

Japanese antisubmarine planners were certain that they had turned the corner on the Allied submarine threat a few months after the 901 Kokutai was formed. In March/April 1944, merchant shipping losses were noticeably reduced. The Japanese were not aware that a large number of United States submarines had been diverted to lifeguard duty during the time. This meant that there were fewer submarines to attack Japanese shipping, which might account for the decrease in merchant shipping losses. Before long though, the American efforts were once again focused upon the merchant fleet.

Losses mounted. Sometime thereafter the chain of radar installations on islands outlying Japan were destroyed along with the hope that the Japanese could save their merchant marine. By the fall of 1944, the Japanese antisubmarine warfare program had failed beyond salvation.

Despite all of the Japanese shortcomings in their antisubmarine warfare program, they did develop an ingenious Airborne Magnetic Detecting device (aka "MAD"), which was carried on planes from the 901 Kokutai and was able to detect submarines below the surface. By using MAD, the planes could follow and track American submarines. The units were deployed sporadically shortly before *Gudgeon* was lost. It is possible, therefore, that *Gudgeon* achieved another first, that she may have been the first United States submarine lost to MAD technology. When using MAD, a pilot flying between ten and 50 meters above the ocean could detect submarines under the surface as deep as 250 meters. The planes were allowed to attack once a submarine had been sighted and were usually equipped with 250 kg. bombs, just like the bombs used by the bomber which reported sinking a submarine off Yuoh. The Japanese claimed four sinkings in the "Japan area" by MAD-equipped planes and aircraft alone during the war.

MAD-equipped airplanes were allowed to follow a submarine contact for several days before abandoning it. Once an attack had taken place, they would systematically drop pieces of aluminum where the submarine had been to show surface vessels which would follow where the attack had taken place. Mad-equipped planes usually attacked in twos and never or rarely at nighttime. Captain Kitazawa was pretty certain that only one plane bombed the submarine on April 18, 1944.

More than a year went by before I could translate the faint diary pages from the Chichi Jima Houmen group. Captain Kitazawa's paraphrase of the information was undoubtedly correct, but I decided that the records could contain additional information which he had not mentioned. Indeed, portions of the diary pages (pages 79–82) translated by Captain Kitazawa had not been completely paraphrased in his correspondence to me. So, in a roundabout way, I contacted distinguished Japanese biologist Dr. Ken-Ichi Manaka for help. The translation was not perfect, Dr. Manaka explained, because of the faint print and the multiple possible meanings for some terms. He attempted to translate all of the material in the diary, but some

Japanese will not translate word-for-word. Another difficulty was that some of the words and ideographic figures were from a much earlier time than World War II but were still in use by the military, making translation in 2003 even more challenging.

A potentially important diary entry from April 17 at 2118 stated: "There was found the enemy submarine at 38 nautical miles of the south of ? island. Watch the bay out strictly." [10] Unfortunately the name of the island eluded Dr. Manaka. Whether the submarine that was referred to having been found was the same submarine that was attacked the next day off Yuoh Island (i.e., *Gudgeon*) or another submarine in the area is unclear. But, if it was *Gudgeon*, it would be consistent with *Gudgeon* having been sunk by MAD technology. The submarine could have been found at night, followed all night, then attacked by the bombers Kitazawa referred to.

The next dispatch dated April 17, at 2200 stated only: "It was almost assured that the enemy submarine was found at N 26' 01", E 142' 14" at 1700 on 17th." [11] The submarine referred to in the dispatch was almost certainly the same one that attacked a Japanese vessel at this exact location earlier in the day at 1729. And, very possibly, the one referred to in the 2118 reference. The location of the attack appears to be directly north of Haha Jima, which is north of the *Gudgeon* sinking site the following day. Other dispatches in the diary make it clear that a ship known as the *Nosiro Maru* #2 was certainly sunk. One would like to think that *Gudgeon* took down the *Nosiro Maru* #2 the night before she was lost, then headed south to meet her fate southeast of Iwo Jima. Some historians give *Searaven* credit for the sinking, others *Haddock*. *Gudgeon* is not even mentioned in such discussions. The last few words of another entry appeared at the top of page 79 of the diary and state: "leave in the dawn to attack submarine." [12] An entry in that position in the war diary means that it was made on April 17, 1944; the day before *Gudgeon* was sunk. The entry is consistent with the attack the following day on *Gudgeon*. If the entry refers to *Gudgeon* when it says that an attack was to be made on a submarine at dawn, it is another finding that is consistent with *Gudgeon* having been spotted by a pilot using MAD technology, then followed during the nighttime hours for an attack at first light. This procedure is consistent with MAD attack doctrine. The pilots were free to attack whenever they liked during daylight hours, as soon as the pilot deemed that he could do damage to a submarine. This would also explain why there was a bomber right there waiting for *Gudgeon* when Bob Bonin surfaced.

The attack on the submarine believed to have been *Gudgeon* first appears in the diary on the eighteenth when it is stated that the "No. 1 plane" of the 901 Air of "Io-Jima" (island) reported to the 901 Air dispatcher of Iwo-Jima (Army) (CJBCO) that "I attacked an enemy submarine at 132 degree bearing by 166 nautical miles. It is sure the submarine has been foundered at 06:30 AM."[13] Later in the same day, at 1815, the 901 Air dispatcher from Iwo Jima sent a secret telegraph to the 901 Air (Kanku) (CJBCO), which gave more details of the attack. It read: "No. 7 Flight Report of No. 901-Air dispatcher of Iwo-Jima (18th April): The third plane of a platoon left at 05:00 AM bombed an enemy submarine just going undersea at the point of 132 degree, 166 nautical miles from Iwo-Jima at 06:30 AM. Using 1 a 3h I type bombs, the first hit the bow and the second hit the bridge. Big yellow-green explosion was seen in the center of the boat. The big oil pillar was spouted, momentarily the heavy oil was spread to 150 m wide, then the boat was foundered."[14] Another source said that the submarine sustained a direct hit on the bridge creating a gaping hole in the center of the ship visible to the Japanese bombers.

The only way to confirm the Japanese report of a bombing on April 18, 1944, is for someone to find *Gudgeon*. I made contact with Wayne Sampey, Projects Director of the National Underwater and Marine Agency (NUMA) in Australia. Dr. Clive Cussler, the best-selling author, is NUMA's chairman. In his *Sea Hunter* books, Cussler tells the story of the countless ships that NUMA has located throughout the world. Knowing this, I wrote Mr. Sampey telling him of my theory. He was quite interested in my research about *Gudgeon* and eventually agreed to search for her. It so happens that Sampey and his associates were already planning what they called The South China Sea Project. NUMA, a nonprofit organization dedicated to the preservation of maritime heritage, through the discovery, archeological survey, and conservation of shipwreck artifacts, was planning a search off the east coast of Asia to look for sunken U.S. submarines from World War II as well as vessels from Japan and one from Russia. He readily agreed to include *Gudgeon* in his search, realizing that if *Gudgeon* were located, a significant naval mystery would be resolved.

The South China Sea Project was to take place during the summer of 2002 with a search for U.S. submarines *Wahoo, Tang, Albacore, Gudgeon,* and *Cisco*, along with Japanese vessels *Kongo, Junyo,* and *Urakaze* as well as the Russian submarine *L-9*. Because of the need for additional planning, the project was put off until the summers of 2003, 2004 and once again in 2005, but never did take place. Sampey continues to work to set up a search for *Gudgeon* and the other vessels, now with his organization called Ocean Wilderness Group out of Australia.

Recently, even more information has arisen that supports the Yuoh Island theory of *Gudgeon*'s loss. Part of a book printed and distributed in Japan, *Teki Sensuikan Kogeki*, which means "Enemy Submarine Attack" in English, written by Jiro Kimata, contained additional information that confirmed the Yuoh Island theory. Kimata describes *Gudgeon*'s passage toward Japanese waters after leaving Johnston Island on April 7, 1944. The author added that at about that time the Japanese sent a fleet called the "Toomatsu Higashimats" (another source referred to the convoy as "Higashi Matsu") south toward the Marianas Islands, a fleet carrying many soldiers who were being sent to enforce the defenses around the Marianas. Kimata said, "Therefore Japanese Air Force (i.e., 901 Kokutai) was being very cautious." [15]

The broken translation continues with the fleet referred to as "Higashimats 4." It was said to contain twenty-six merchant ships, six marine destroyers, and four additional ships. Also on board the vessels were an unknown number of Type 97 tanks. Kimata continued, saying of the 901 Kokutai, which was made up of Type 96 land-based bombers and Type 97 airplanes: "They stationed a couple planes of force in Manilla, Saigon, *Yuoh Island* (italics added), East Port in Taiwan, Shooroku in Okinawa and Domura Village in Kyushu Japan." [16] Of much significance and pleasure was the fact that Jiro Kimata had casually used the term Yuoh Island. He added, "This type 96 land based bomber that was sent to Iwo Jima found enemy submarine surfacing April 18. They found this 166 miles southeast of Iwo Jima. The American submarine tried to submerge, but the Japanese bombed it. The first bomb hit the main part of the submarine, the second bomb hit the bridge. The American submarine broke open and heavy oil pillars arose." [17] He continued, thus buttressing the Yuoh Island theory of the sinking[18]:

However, when this document was submitted to the United States right after World War II finished, the Japanese translator translated the name of Yuoh Island incorrectly. The Americans ignored this information because they said that there was no island called Yuoh Jima. Of course, this refers to Iwo Jima. According to the record, this American submarine immediately after it sunk had big explosion and they sunk. This was the last moment of Gudgeon and Captain Robert A. Bonin and other 78 crew. All Died.

It is important to point out that this is the only Japanese book that I have had translated. It speaks very matter-of-factly about the translation error, which caused the United States Navy to wrongly conclude that the attack took place at an island that did not exist. All of this is quite powerful and seems to, when combined with all that came earlier, resolve the mystery of *Gudgeon*'s loss, though the matter cannot be incontrovertibly settled until somebody finds *Gudgeon* off Sulphur Island. The proposed sinking site is adjacent to the Marianas Trench, in the direct area, ironically enough, of a deep underwater ditch known as the Bonin Trough. According to very detailed charts of the area, *Gudgeon* very likely lies in water as deep as 4,000 meters, which is two-to-three miles down, *deeper* perhaps than the waters that contain *Titanic*. Certain types of underwater terrain can obscure the existence of even very large vessels, though there have been many technological advances. But, the wreckage may not be there. It is possible that the Japanese pilot gave the wrong location for the attack and that *Gudgeon* lays elsewhere, far enough away that the submarine that was sunk will not be found. Clive Cussler once said that sunken ships are rarely found where they are supposed to be.

This analysis stands by itself, each source of information supporting the other. This research does not prove anything for certain. Others have speculated that *Gudgeon* was sunk in that April morning attack. Since World War II, most sources have stated that nobody would ever know whether *Gudgeon*'s demise occurred during the April 18, or May 12, 1944, attacks, or in some other way. Now, with the knowledge that Iwo Jima and Yuoh Island are one and the same, and the fact that the Japanese identify this attack matter-of-factly as the sinking of *Gudgeon*, there appears to be little reason to doubt that *Gudgeon* was sunk on the eighteenth.

This conclusion is partially based upon the premise that the Japanese were telling the truth about having sunk a submarine on April 18, 1944. Yet, the truth is that the Japanese, like the other warring nations, were known to exaggerate their claims of success, and the 901 Kokutai was no exception. The 901 Kokutai made exorbitant claims of sinkings, claims which were proven to be exaggerated. The question arises then: what, if anything is it about this claim by the 901 Kokutai that separates it from the others which were known to be untrue?

When interviewed shortly before his death on December 1, 2002, Captain Edward L. Beach said that he had heard of the reported attack on a U.S. submarine on April 18, 1944, years before. He said he heard that this submarine "opened like a flower" after it was bombed the second time.[19] When I asked him about the possibility that the Japanese had fabricated the whole story about the sinking on this day, because they had been known to do so, he said that he doubted that this was the case, reasoning that, "a lot of that stuff that the Japanese lied about could easily be disproved later," this one was an exception.[20] The interview with Beach occurred before parts of Jiro Kimata's book had been translated. Yet Beach said that it was quite possible that this attack accounted for the loss of *Gudgeon*, because as I have stated earlier, all of the data is consistent with the fact that *Gudgeon* was sunk on April 18, 1944. There is not a single piece of information that is known by this writer to be inconsistent with this theory.

Beach also said that *Gudgeon*, in comparison to submarines that were built later and benefited from technological and shipbuilding advances, was more vulnerable to such a bombing. He explained that *Gudgeon*'s test depth was only 270 feet and that she had one big engine room with all four engines in it. *Trigger*, only one class more advanced than *Tambor* class submarines like *Gudgeon*, had her four engines in two separate engine rooms. The extra compartment offered significant protection from bombing. The later submarines were a little longer and could thus go deeper to safer waters. Of the fact that *Gudgeon* was bombed on the surface, when radar may have been available for protection, Beach added, "You know we got more and more self-confident. We would not dive before we saw the plane heading for us. We knew we could get out of there before she could get us."[21]

It therefore appears that *Gudgeon* was patrolling the Saipan to Tokyo traffic lane when, early in the morning on the eighteenth, Bonin decided to surface. George Seiler explained that when a submarine was surfacing, it was a most vulnerable time because there would be no lookouts, and for a while, when surfacing, the radar would not be deployed. But, as has been shown, *Gudgeon* skippers did not always deploy the radar anyway, even if it could have been deployed. Bill Post dodged death on earlier patrols when planes were sighted directly over *Gudgeon* after a surface. Or, Seiler continued, the radar could have been warming up and not been functional. World War II radar required a significant warm-up time. Another possibility is that since the SJ type radar broke down frequently, it may have been inoperable. SD radar was not even being used in *Gudgeon*'s later patrols because the Japanese used it to direction find the submarine, and it caused more danger than benefits.

Or perhaps, as Art Barlow suggested, *Gudgeon* may have done a quick sweep with the low-power periscope to make certain that the enemy was not close, then a little slower sweep with the high-power scope, and then surfaced. The Japanese bomber may have been closing between the time that the sweeps were done and the time *Gudgeon* cracked the surface and the lookouts climbed out to their watch locations. Or, as Barlow explained, "It would have been easy to miss the bomber on either sweep." [22]

Jiro Kimata added an important element, stating that *Gudgeon* was bombed just *after* she had surfaced, then attempted to submerge. It seems to suggest that *Gudgeon* was surfacing and that shortly before *Gudgeon* hit the surface or perhaps shortly afterwards, she may have deployed the radar and picked up the olive green–skinned Japanese bomber overhead, her KEA marking indicating that she was an antisubmarine bomber from the 901 Kokutai, or perhaps one of the men opened a hatch and saw a bomber. *Gudgeon* then made a desperate dive. This time, not even the lucky Buddha piece could save *Gudgeon*. It was then that they were hit with the first bomb on the bow, the second on the bridge. A 250 kg depth charge needed to be within 40–50 feet to inflict damage. Early in the war, in order to sink a submarine they would have needed to explode within twenty feet. Though later in the war, perhaps by April 1944, the Japanese doubled the explosive charge on the depth charges, making them far more potent.

Seiler concluded that the sinking was a fluke, "Five minutes later, or ten minutes sooner, and it would not have happened."[23] It seems likely that it would have made no difference who was commanding *Gudgeon*. The Japanese caught Bonin and *Gudgeon* at an extremely opportune time. Of course, if the Japanese had been using MAD technology, the odds against Bonin or even the wily Bill Post, had he been in command, were really stacked against them.

Through newspaper articles printed in central and eastern Iowa, these revelations have comforted a few of the families of the lost *Gudgeon* sailors. *Gudgeon*'s mysterious loss continues to touch a large number of people. After feature articles were run in the *Des Moines Register* and the *Cedar Rapids Gazette* in March 2003, I received phone calls from the sisters of Lambert Hegerfeld of South Dakota and Albert Everhart, formerly of Pleasant Plain, Iowa, both of whom died on *Gudgeon*. Both of their sisters currently live in Iowa, one a half hour north and the other a half hour south of my home in Iowa City. A third person who contacted me after reading one of the articles was a cousin of Bob Bonin who lives a few blocks from my home. I received a fourth phone call from the nephew of Bob Bonin, who lives in Davenport about 60 miles away. Another was from the brother of James Carney of Dubuque, Iowa, who also died on the twelfth patrol. And still another call from a sister of Everett Dodson from Joy, Illinois.

The relatives were relieved to learn that the men's deaths were likely instantaneous. Joanna White of Washington, a white-haired woman in her late seventies, was perhaps the most relieved of them all. Fifty-eight years after the fact, she was able to finally put to sleep her deepest fear, that her brother, Albert Everhart, had been taken prisoner by the Japanese and tortured to death with nobody even knowing that it had happened.

The Associated Press picked up the story from the area papers and ran with it, but it was not carried in the states where the information could have been the most meaningful. Ten men from California and six from New York state died on *Gudgeon*. The families of those sixteen men, as well as the fifty-six or so other families, probably do not know about these findings. Getting this information to the families of these sailors is another of the more compelling reasons for writing this book. It may bring them relief.

The enormity of World War II was never made clearer to me than when I scoured Kendall Young Library in Webster City, Bill Ostlund's hometown, for information about Bill. In all, from a city of 6,800 in 1940, around 1,300 men served in the armed forces at some time during World War II. This seems like an incredibly high number. After all, how many men of fighting age were there in Webster City, Iowa, during the war years? Growing up, I knew of course that my father, John, and Bill and a few others fought in the war. Everyone in Webster City was aware of the old shell-shocked veteran who deep into the 1960s was still diving to the ground whenever he heard an automobile backfire. And, I recall that when I was very young my dad repeatedly told me the story of one of his friends who was killed in the war. He said that his friend was fighting the Germans in Africa and that he lost his composure when one of his buddies was shot and killed, and just like you see in the movies, he stood up and yelled something like, "You can't do that to my buddy!" The Germans mowed him down with four well-placed shots to the chest. In retrospect, my father obviously needed to repeatedly tell me of the young man's death in order for the events to lose their hold over him. The records at the local library and elsewhere are incomplete and ambiguous, but it appears that at least seventy-seven Webster City men died in World War II. But, there's a catch. The only official list I was able to find does not contain the name of Bill Ostlund, so it is strongly suspected that the number is low, perhaps very low. It seems highly unlikely that by coincidence, only Bill was missed on the official casualty list. Similarly, one source said that 7,183 Iowans were killed in action during the war. Another listed 8,398 such deaths.

It is doubtful that most of the young people today are able to comprehend the sacrifices of the generation that fought the war. From Bill Ostlund's Lincoln High School, Class of 1936, of the fifty-nine pictured males in the yearbook, around thirty-four were known to have served in the armed forces during the war. I could find information indicating that five of them were killed in action. Fifty-eight percent of the boys in that class alone served. Eight percent died. Yet, these numbers from Webster City are probably not unusually high. They are likely typical of the sacrifices that were made by young men in every city in the country. When the involvement of men in every locale throughout the United States in similar proportions is considered, the selfless valor of an entire generation is astonishing. When one considers the sacrifices of those at home, the efforts of the women and others who filled the shoes of the departed soldiers, the achievements of "The Greatest Generation" are truly humbling.

Harry Nickel, the former Michigan oil worker, hailed from Hutchinson, Kansas. He had been quite lucky while on *Gudgeon* and had taken the crew for thousands of dollars during the war. His luck ran out on the twelfth run when he perished along with his money stash, which was stored in *Gudgeon* ship's safe. Neither his family nor his fiancée ever knew about his winnings aboard the ship. Nickel probably wanted to surprise them with his good fortune after the war. His fiancée was quite surprised to hear of this when she was interviewed.

The old cook, Herbert Patriquin, who boarded *Gudgeon* at the request of Bill Post after two other cooks had deserted, hailed from Norton, Massachusetts. He enlisted when he was in his mid-forties and had served previously on the submarine *Seahorse* before Post coaxed him on to his submarine at Midway Island. Patriquin was a former highway department maintenance man whose sons were serving in the Army at the time of his death. The 46-year-old Patriquin had no business being on a submarine at war. He was too old. Art Barlow said that he was a patriotic guy though, and *made* it his business to be on one, lying about his age to get on board and then losing his life. The memory of the patriotic old cook still touched Barlow well into the twenty-first century.

Executive Officer Lieutenant Don Midgley was twenty-three years old when he was lost on *Gudgeon*. He was president of Hopedale, Massachusetts's graduating class of thirty-two students in 1935. After graduating from the Naval Academy, he was assigned to the cruiser *Astoria*. He then received training as a gunnery officer as well as his submarine training in New London. He had done a fine job on *Gudgeon*, serving patrols seven–twelve, moving his way up to executive officer on the final patrol. When he died, he was the tenth Hopedale resident to lose his life in the war.

What should one conclude from all of the findings about *Gudgeon*'s loss? As has been stated, until this time opinions about *Gudgeon*'s loss have varied. Many historians have theorized that *Gudgeon* was lost April 18, others believe it was lost in the depth charge attack off Saipan on May 12, and others are convinced that nobody will ever know. In the early 1960s the authors of *United States Submarine Losses World War II* played it safe, no matter how inaccurate they were when they drew their conclusions. On a chart at the front of the book they indicate that *Gudgeon* was lost in a surface craft attack with depth charges *and* by aircraft. They combined the April 18 and May 12 attacks into one incident and led readers to believe that *Gudgeon* was sunk by surface vessels and aircraft. As a result, many subsequent books on World War II submarine warfare state matter-of-factly that *Gudgeon* was lost in an attack by both vessel-directed depth charges and aerial bombs. The *Dictionary of American Fighting Ships* put out by the Navy in 1968 concluded that Japanese records "shed no light on the mystery." In *Gudgeon The Official Chronology of the U.S. Navy in World War II*, Robert Cressman wrote that *Gudgeon* may have been sunk on April 18, 1944, off Iwo Jima but concluded that the attack occurred *southwest* of the island. Just why he feels that the attack took place southwest of Iwo Jima is not known. Clearly, the record of *Gudgeon*'s loss southeast of Iwo Jima is information that needs to work its way into the books that are printed so that the record on *Gudgeon* is complete.

Throughout all of this I have in effect been trying to learn what I can about Bill Ostlund. What *was* he like? Who was he? My relatives do not say much about him other than that "He was a great guy." Perhaps after all these years, it is still difficult to think much about a 26-year-old who died long before his time. From having met and befriended three former *Gudgeon* submariners, and from getting to know several others over the phone, I have learned what he was like. Bill was just like they were. He was brimming with courage, patriotism, and a sense of duty. He was willing to fight for his shipmates, for his loved ones, and for his country. Perhaps on April 18 when that first bomb hit *Gudgeon*, he may have briefly foreseen his death. But in those few moments of life that he had left, I am certain that he was still fighting to do everything he could to assure *Gudgeon*'s survival and to do what he could do for his shipmates. In fact, I am sure that they were all doing whatever they could do for the submarine, because that is what Foster, Barlow, Hornkohl, Seiler, Post, Stovall, Lyon, Schooley, Grenfell, and the others would have done.

Bill Ostlund was a capable person and a talented submariner. He did so well on *Gudgeon* that he and Lieutenant McCorquodale had been praised by "Wild Bill" Post after their first patrol. He was bright enough to earn his submarine dolphins and make it through exclusive and difficult submarine training and, like the other *Gudgeon* submariners, Bill was humble. Of that I have no doubt. Had he survived he would have lived his life quietly, allowing those around him to believe that it had been very ordinary.

On February 10, 1946, almost two years after Bill's death, his family and friends held a memorial service at the local English Lutheran Church for him. His obituary contains the usual information about his accomplishments, his marriage to Peggy, his bachelor's degree from Butler in Business Administration, and all the awards he had received in his short life. The article indicated that he had served aboard *Gudgeon* for four patrols. The actual records from *Gudgeon* indicate clearly that he boarded just prior to the tenth patrol and that he had died on his third patrol. His memorial service was held before a church filled to capacity. The local American Legion presented an American flag to the young widow, Peggy Ostlund. Bill's empty grave in Webster City has long supported a small granite marker that says simply, "In Memory of William C. Ostlund 1918–1944 Lieutenant U.S. Navy U.S.S. *Gudgeon*."

In 1951 a group of advanced submarines was launched in memory of some of the most accomplished submarines in service during World War II. Among them were the *Tang*, *Trigger*, *Wahoo*, *Trout*, *Harder*, and a second *Gudgeon*, the USS *Gudgeon* (SS-567). A smiling Mrs. Robert A. (Regis) Bonin, Lieutenant Commander Bonin's widow, christened the second *Gudgeon*. Bob Bonin's only daughter Jean, who had celebrated her third birthday on the very day her mother learned that her husband was missing, served as Maid of Honor.

▪ Afterword ▪
After the *Gudgeon*

Grieve not: though the journey of life be bitter,
and the end unseen,
there is no road which does not lead to an end

Hafiz Ghazals, 14th century

Before we follow up on the men who fought on *Gudgeon* during the war and survived, as well as those whose lives were touched by *Gudgeon*, let's take a look at the odd experiences that the nephew of one of the men who died on *Gudgeon* experienced. Keith Dodson, a nephew of electrician's mate third class Everett Dodson, who was lost on *Gudgeon*'s twelfth patrol, grew up not even knowing that he had an uncle who served on World War II submarines. The way he learned about the death of his long-lost uncle is an eerie but fascinating tale. His father had been born in 1940 and had never really known his brother and never saw a need to tell his son Keith about Everett. Keith Dodson graduated from high school in 1984 and on a whim dropped out of college. For reasons not really very clear to himself, he joined the Navy and reported to boot camp in Great Lakes, Illinois. He was chosen for the Navy's nuclear power program and was designated an electrician's mate. He was then asked if he wanted to serve on submarines, aircraft carriers, or destroyers. For no particular reason Dodson volunteered for submarines. He became an EM3/SS (Electrician's Mate 3rd Class Submarines).

While receiving training in San Diego, he and a friend decided to tour the city. While visiting Old Town San Diego, the men saw a sign announcing a psychic fair. Knowing nothing about psychics but always having been curious about them, he went from booth to booth in a large gymnasium until he found a "normal" looking grandmotherly woman.[1] Neither Dodson nor his old high school friend was in uniform nor did they disclose their military status to the woman. Dodson was a skeptic and felt as if he was pouring his money down a rat hole, but went along with the kindly old woman who by now had her eyes closed and was holding his hands. He sat silently as instructed. The elderly psychic told him that he had two male spirits that followed and guided him. One was a young boy, perhaps a relative or a close friend. (Dodson's best friend had died when they were twelve years old.) The other spirit she claimed had carried "tools of engineering" and helped Keith Dodson professionally. She believed that he was the spirit of a man who had died in "the war."[2] She thought he was related to his father's side of the family.

Dodson was confused and unimpressed. He had no relative on his father's side of the family who had died during any war. The woman was full of it. Several months later Dodson attended his cousin's wedding in Illinois. Dodson, in uniform, was talking with his paternal aunt, Marie Dodson Duncan, who quizzed him about his naval duties. It was then that she told Dodson about her brother Everett who had served on and died aboard *Gudgeon* during World War II. And for the first time Keith Dodson knew of his uncle, Everett Dodson. Like Keith Dodson, his uncle Everett Dodson was EM3/SS Dodson (Electrician's Mate 3rd class-Submarines). The strange events had profound meaning to Keith Dodson. He has since received several newspaper clippings and photos of his long-lost uncle who died so long ago. He has placed the items on his mantle at home and says at times that he feels certain that he is living the life that Everett Dodson was not able to live, a life cut short by a Japanese bomber in April 1944 off Iwo Jima.

What became of the men who served on *Gudgeon* after they left the submarine? What of their families? What of those associated with *Gudgeon*? As can be expected, many died later during the war, a period lasting a year and a half after *Gudgeon* disappeared. Many stayed in the service and established long careers in the military or were associated with the national defense in some related way. Some reached the upper echelons of the Navy. Most were not so fortunate. George Seiler, for instance, descended into the depths of Skid Row and then, showing the grit and determination that it took to get through the Depression and World War II, righted himself, his life a testament to the indomitable spirit and innate toughness that some people are blessed with. In each of the lives, the effects of war and strife can be seen. The paths of those who survived led in many directions.

Old Submarine Squadron Six fought proudly during the war but ended up with an extraordinarily high number of lost submarines, especially *Gudgeon*'s Division Sixty-Two. Of the six G-boats that started the war, only *Gar* survived the war's last shot. Lost in addition to *Gudgeon* were *Grampus*, *Grayling*, *Grayback*, and *Grenadier*. Of the Division Sixty-One submarines, *Triton* and *Trout* were lost. *Tambor*, *Tautog*, *Thresher*, and *Tuna* survived the war. Squadron Six lost 58 percent of their submarines and around 555 submariners. The submarine fleet as a whole lost 18 percent of the submarines that patrolled during the war. Squadron Six got their licks in though. Of the seven lost submarines, all of them did at least six war patrols. Of those that were lost, *Gudgeon* survived the longest. By JANAC count, the squadron sank 111 Japanese vessels, accounting for 420,000 tons.

Out of 16,000 or so men who served on submarines in the war, 3,506 were lost. Twenty-two percent of the men who served in submarines died in combat; the Silent Service ended up with the highest mortality rate of any branch in the service during World War II. But the submarine service had performed very well indeed. Submariners accounted for only 1.6 percent of men in the Navy but according to JANAC, submarines sank 55 percent of the Japanese ships that were sunk in the war. According to *wartime* figures, the numbers are even higher. If the figures were known for the number of Japanese soldiers and merchant marine sailors lost as well as the losses of oil, rubber, food, coal, and munitions carried on those thousands of ships sunk by submarines, a more precise appraisal of the cost to the Japanese could be made.

Plunger (SS-179) and *Pollack* (SS-180), the two submarines that followed *Gudgeon* out of Pearl Harbor a few days after she left port on December 11, 1941, saw their wars end at about the time that *Gudgeon* was lost. *Plunger* completed twelve war patrols and was credited by JANAC with twelve kills for 48,000 tons. *Plunger* did her final patrol during the summer of 1944 and was sent to New London to assist in training submariners. She was stricken from the Naval Vessel Register in 1956 and sold for scrap in 1957. *Pollack* did eleven war patrols and received credit for having sunk 30,000 tons. She met with an inglorious fate similar to *Plunger* when she was sent to New London in January 1945, then scrapped in February 1947.

It may not be surprising to learn that Kentucky Congressman Andrew Jackson May, the man who had drawn the wrath of American submariners for having announced to the world that the Japanese weren't setting their depth charges deep enough to sink United States submarines, went on to perform patently criminal acts during the war. The type of man who would make such an offhand remark to the press without giving a thought to the lives of those he was dooming is the same kind of person who would try to make himself rich off the service of those same men. And he did.

The former Chairman of the House Military Affairs Committee was convicted of taking payoffs, of steering munitions contracts to companies that he chaired, then building faulty explosives which killed or wounded over a hundred American soldiers. For all of his crimes he was sentenced to a federal prison where he served nine months before President Harry Truman pardoned him.

It is not known whether the aggressive Lieutenant Crespo or any of the other three United States commandos who were landed on Panay in April 1943 survived the war. Of the twenty-eight men rescued from Timor on *Gudgeon*'s sixth war patrol, some things are known. Captain John Edward Grimson of the Z Special Unit was killed in action on August 22, 1944. Corporal Alfred Ellwood and Leftenant John Cashman were taken prisoners of war but survived. Corporal John Rivers Key also survived the war. Key had lied about his young age so that he could join the armored tank division in the Australian Army that eventually became the 2/4 Independent Company posted in Japanese-occupied East Timor. After landing in Timor, Key established a lookout post in the hills east of Dili to keep an eye on Japanese troop movements. Before long, things had become very hot around Dili. Key and the men he was with had to melt into the mountainous terrain from which they continued the fight. Key had the opportunity to leave the island later in the war but, wishing to continue to serve, decided against it.

After leaving Timor, Key joined up with the Z Special Unit, an elite multi-services band of commandos. He was an accomplished sailor/navigator and a skilled linguist and was put in charge of a ship called *The Black Snake*. While aboard *The Black Snake*, which was made to look like a Chinese junk, he was charged with the very dangerous responsibility of traveling up and down the coastlines and estuaries of Borneo and Sumatra to provision and support the small intelligence units working ashore. At the war's end, Key had a harrowing experience, one that was triumphant and tragic all at once. Key and his tiny crew from *The Black Snake* were the Allies closest to Sandaken, Borneo, and were ordered into Sandaken Harbor to take the Japanese surrender. Outnumbered by 1,100 war-hardened Japanese soldiers, the tension was overwhelming. Key, the highest ranking of the men on board the ship, was a tall thin man. He was dressed only in boxer shorts as he met the Japanese commanding officer in a tin shed at the end of a jetty. The Japanese commander was humiliated to be surrendering to such a young officer, dressed in his underwear and escorted by his ragged shipmates. Nonetheless, he turned over the command's Japanese flag and his personal dagger to John Rivers Key in the strained ceremony that followed. Shortly thereafter, Key and the others learned that a large number of Australian POWs that they hoped to free had been murdered or died on the Sandaken Death March several months earlier. There were virtually no POWs still alive in the area.

After the war Key sought a peaceful and remote existence fishing for crayfish and building beautiful boats. Key was considered an outsider in the crayfish industry. The Tasmanian Cray fishermen were a brawling, hard drinking lot, and Key was an educated, articulate man who was as much at ease in dinner clothes as he was in fishing gear. Once retired, Key lived a simple, almost monastic life. He listened to music, swam for fitness, and did wood-working in his shop. He died in the summer of 2003, sixty years after Shirley Stovall and the four volunteers from the crew of *Gudgeon* rescued him.

In written correspondence, Robert O. Phillips, a member of the 2/4 Australian Independent Company, recalled his adventures on Timor before being rescued by Shirley Stovall and *Gudgeon* early in 1943. Phillips said that the Japanese who were pursuing his group were the least of his worries. He was more anxious about the effect that malaria, exhaustion, and lack of food would have on him. After being picked up by *Gudgeon*, he recalled that the rescued commandos were spread out all over the submarine, his bunk a blanket spread out over the hollow between two torpedoes in the forward torpedo room. His relief at being aboard the submarine and feeling safe "took a dive" when he learned that the submarine was going to patrol Koepang Harbour for enemy shipping. He said, "We thought shit 'out of the frying pan into the fire'."[3] Of *Gudgeon*'s loss Phillips said, "The submarine experience is something I will never forget and our boys looked on *Gudgeon* as 'our sub.' Knowledge of its loss years later caused us great sadness."[4]

Lieutenant Frank Holland, who provided such vivid descriptions of his escape from Timor at the end of *Gudgeon*'s sixth war patrol, then of his experiences on the submarine, survived the war. He was designated an MBE, Member of the British Empire after the war, for his meritorious service. After the war Holland returned to the jungle, this time volunteering to lead a small rifle company, the Papau and New Guinea Volunteer Rifles. After taking command on September 20, 1951, Holland took the men into the jungle and taught them the survival skills he had learned during his service in the war.

For the next several years, he helped develop the area primarily by building roads. In March 1958, Holland left the bush for Australia and then returned to England, his place of birth. After docking at Southampton on May 12, 1958, he hurried ashore to search for his mother whom he had not seen for thirty-four years. Frank Holland, the 46-year-old former commando, eventually found her. Holland's only son John witnessed the reunion and reported, "I am able to tell you there was not a dry eye to be seen in this group of people."[5] Frank Holland retired in July 1973. Over the years, many honors and ceremonies would be bestowed on Holland, commemorating his heroic service during the war. An unusual event occurred in September 1984. On the eighth, Frank Holland opened a mysterious package that had arrived from the United States. In it was a submarine combat insignia which he was told he had qualified for by riding *Gudgeon* for eight days in February 1943. At the age of 90, Frank Holland succumbed to old age, passing three months prior to his sixtieth wedding anniversary. Frank Holland's story is not complete until the touching tale of the little eight-year-old girl he met in Timor is told. Holland met the youngster while helping evacuate the area of Lai-Sora-Lai before the Japanese arrived early in World War II. The story follows just as Holland wrote it:

". . . a little Timorese girl about eight years old came up to me very shyly handed me a small Boneca, a black doll made from the horn of the buffalo. She was with the nuns, and some said she was Dom Paulo's [Dom Paulo de Frietas de Silva was rescued by Gudgeon] daughter Angela.

"I was more than fully occupied assisting to move the refugees under great stress and agitation, just ahead of the Japanese, and I said a brief 'thank you' and dropped the doll into my pocket. I treasured this article for the thought behind it of a little girl who could not express her feelings in my language, and I cherished it through the years. In the following years of peace an ever increasing regard for this small black figure, seven inches high, crept into my heart and attached itself to my affections. Some intuition told me I should meet again its donor, and as a precaution against damage I never let my children play with it, nor later their children.

"Years later, at Christmas 1975, my wife Mabel and I booked our passage to Timor, just before the trouble broke out. Having spent Christmas 1942 in the mountains of Timor with 'Z' Special Unit, my sentimental journey was again prevented by war. As we watched T.V. one evening, I saw refugee nuns arriving in Darwin [Australia] from Timor, and my mind flashed back thirty-four years. Could some of these sisters be among those that we had helped to evacuate in 1942, and being refugees once again? The news report indicated that the sisters were to be flown to Brisbane, and taken to Canossa Hospital at Oxley. A phone call to my daughter Ann in Brisbane, who rang the Mother Superior at the Canossa Hospital, revealed that four sisters we had helped to evacuate were in the group.

"I was thrilled and excited by this news and decided to fly to Brisbane. Ann on my arrival drove me out to Oxley. I took the little black doll along hoping one of the sisters would be able to remember the donor, and what had become of her. I explained my mission to the Mother, who was delighted and sent for the sisters.

"A joyous reunion took place. I met Sister Rita Casaste, who recognized me, also a young woman who was a baby in arms at the time. I was unable to meet Sister Giovana Aita, who had spent forty-eight years in Timor and Sister Lauigina Critte with fifty years, as both were not very well after their ordeal. The Mother Superior presented a smiling middle-aged sister as Angela Frietas, Dom Paulo's daughter, who was a small child at the time of the evacuation, during the Japanese occupation of Timor, and later became a nun joining the Canossa Order.

"As I shook hands with a mature woman now in a nun's habit, her face caused me to recall a bare legged shy little girl. I looked closely and met with a scrutinising gaze. Sister Angela spoke in Timorese. I put my hand into my pocket, and withdrew the black doll and placed it in her hands. Slowly the bewilderment in her eyes changes to recognition and a startled gasp and a flashing smile of joy swept her dusty countenance. With the doll clasped to her, and with excited gestures she conveyed the message that she remembered me and the black doll, the occasion of her self as a little girl shyly bestowing a doll upon a rescuing soldier so many years before. She was not alone with misty eyes, as with excited interpretation we recalled some of the events of that enduring march. The Mother Superior summed up quietly saying, 'it is the will of God that Dom Paulo's daughter should meet you again so many years later and so far away'."[6]

Sadly enough for the little girl, it was not long after her father Chief Dom Paulo de Freitas e Silva was rescued by *Gudgeon* that he was reinserted into Timor, captured, brutally tortured, and then murdered by the Japanese for the assistance he gave Frank Holland and the other members of the Z Special Unit on Timor.

Unfortunately, it was not just the eighty-one *Gudgeon* submariners who were lost during the war. Ship's cook James E. Westmoreland transferred off *Gudgeon* after the pioneering first patrol, eventually landing on *Flier* for her second war patrol in August 1944. *Flier* was patrolling off the Philippine Islands when, on August 13, the submarine suffered a huge explosion. Some of the men on board who survived the devastating explosion reported later that when the ship blew up they noted "a strong smell of fuel, a terrific venting of air, and the flooding and screaming of men below."[7] One of those screaming men was likely James E. Westmoreland because he was one of the unfortunates who had been overwhelmed by the onrushing ocean and the devastation. Westmoreland was not able to make his escape and is entombed with his shipmates off the Philippines. As submariners say, James E. Westmoreland remains on Eternal Patrol.

Hugh French served ably on *Gudgeon* for ten patrols before transferring off the submarine and ending up on *Kete*, which disappeared without a trace in March 1945. When *Kete* went down, she also took Abraham J. Katz, who had served on *Gudgeon* for patrols eight through eleven, as well as eighty-five others. The cause of her sinking remains unknown. Franklin B. Kohrs was another longtime *Gudgeon* sailor who did not make it through the war. Kohrs boarded *Barbel* for the fourth patrol when she was most likely sunk by an air attack. One of the bombs hit the bridge, and *Barbel* exploded into a massive fireball, not unlike the sinking of *Gudgeon*. *Barbel* dropped to the bottom, taking Kohrs and all the other men on board with him.

Grant M. Fuller, who had also served on board *Gudgeon* and had worked himself up to the rank of Chief Motor Machinist, went down on *Bonefish* in June 1945 as the result of a depth charge attack. All that was left of *Bonefish* after the attack was the oil and wood chips that floated to the surface.

Motor machinist John O'Connell Jr. was lost on *Escolar*. O'Connell's skipper was Commander W. J. "Moke" Millican, the aggressive former skipper of *Thresher* whom Bill Post says taught him everything he knew about commanding a submarine. It has been speculated that the bold Millican was aware his submarine was approaching a minefield but he nonetheless led *Escolar* into the area, where it disappeared.

Former *Gudgeon* submariner Chief Gunner's Mate Frank Turner didn't seem to have a chance. No matter which way he turned he was doomed. He served on *Gudgeon* for patrols seven through eleven before being transferred off *Gudgeon* prior to the fateful twelfth patrol. But his good fortune turned on him when he found himself in the Gulf of Siam on *Lagarto* undergoing an attack by a Japanese minelayer in shallow water late in the war. *Lagarto* was lost. The last *Gudgeon* submariner who was known to have died during the war was Quartermaster Dee E. Gambrell who went down on *Swordfish*.

Edward L. Bland Jr., who is believed to have been the artist who did the painting of the kangaroo and shamrock on the *Gudgeon*'s bridge as well as the chart on the bulkhead of *Gudgeon* in the wardroom was *truly* lucky, however. Twice. He rode *Wahoo* for her first two war patrols before boarding

Gudgeon for the sixth patrol. Had he stayed on *Wahoo*, he would have met his death with Mush Morton and the other men when the submarine was lost off the Russian coast. He served as radioman on *Gudgeon* until the eleventh patrol after which he transferred off the submarine. He avoided death on *Gudgeon* and *Wahoo* and, as far as is known, survived the war.

Old "eagle eye" Donald Stillson, the man who refused to give up the phone number of his girlfriend to submariners on *Gar* while patrolling deep in the Pacific, did an impressive ten war patrols on *Gudgeon*, transferred off and did two more on *Jallao* before the war ended. He continued to serve on many additional ships until he retired in 1962. He married but had no children.

Chuck Ver Valin survived the first four war patrols on *Gudgeon*, then lost the battle with Alexander Sheffs to see which of the men would become *Gudgeon*'s Fuel King. When Sheffs prevailed, Ver Valin transferred to *Grenadier* where he was taken prisoner and tortured for several years by the Japanese. Moose Hornkohl knew Ver Valin well and until recently saw him frequently at annual World War II submariners' conventions. Hornkohl recalled the following about Ver Valin's captivity: "Because Ver Valin was big, he was about six feet something, the Japanese put him in charge of issuing the rice kernels. He said that because they were so damn hungry, they practically had to count the kernels. They were down to eating rats and mice if they could catch any. The men would start trading their meal tomorrow for extra food today, they were so damn hungry. Sometimes they would be three or four rations in the hole. It didn't take [missing] many rations and they were practically ready to go. Ver Valin told me that."[8] It is believed that Albert J. Rupp was referring to Ver Valin in his book *Threshold to Hell* when he said that the Japanese especially liked picking on a man named Chuck because he was so big. The Japanese guards achieved more twisted pleasure seeing a large defenseless man beaten to the ground than a man of smaller stature. All that is known about Chuck Ver Valin's life after the war is that he moved to the west coast and worked as a dogcatcher before retiring.

Gudgeon's Fuel King would go on to greater heights. Alexander Sheffs served aboard *Gudgeon* for her first six war patrols, transferred and made one patrol on *Scabbardfish*, then three more on *Shad* before retiring from active service as a chief in 1946. He served in the merchant marine, then returned to college and worked as an aerospace engineer. He married and had one child, Alexander Sheffs Jr.; the elder Sheffs died several years ago.

Mess Attendant Eugene N. Mosley Jr. was in the brig on shore when the Japanese attacked Pearl Harbor in December 1941. For Mosley, in an odd way, the attack had a silver lining. He had gotten himself into hot water and was spending his days in the brig. When the Japanese attack began, the jailers let Mosley go. Serving ably on several submarines during the war, Mosley made the most of his freedom. After the war, he acknowledged that in the midst of a depth charge attack on his first patrol aboard *Gudgeon* because he was so frightened, he had been reduced to tears. He served aboard *Gudgeon* for five war patrols and then did four patrols on other submarines during the war. He went on to earn a Bronze Star. After the war, he married and raised a family.

Albert J. Rupp, the underage sailor who boarded *Gudgeon* early on and drew Lieutenant Commander Stovall's wrath when he did too thorough a job cleaning *Gudgeon*'s head, causing a long white trail of creosote to mark *Gudgeon*'s whereabouts, eventually landed on *Grenadier*. When *Grenadier* was lost, he was taken prisoner by the Japanese, was horribly tortured for years, but survived his captivity and had a family, and wrote two books. Albert J. Rupp died within the last several years.

Charles E. "Jim" Loveland boarded *Gudgeon* as a radioman. He rode the submarine for the first nine war patrols and left as chief. He would go on and marry his sweetheart Janet and raise a family on the east coast. In all of the years they were married, Janet Loveland said that he only talked about the war one time, describing the circumstances of how he won the Bronze Star. He told her that he was passing *Gudgeon*'s sonar room one day and heard "sonar noises." He scurried up to *Gudgeon*'s skipper and told him what he had heard. *Gudgeon* dove and apparently avoided being sunk. Sadly enough, by the time Mrs. Loveland was contacted in 2001, Jim was in a nursing home suffering from Alzheimer's and Parkinson's disease. The longtime submariner who had served his country so ably sending and receiving vital messages for Joe Grenfell, Pop Lyon, Shirley Stovall, and Bill Post had ironically been reduced to speaking with words that made no sense to anyone.

Edward F. Wixted, another great friend of *Gudgeon*'s torpedomen and a torpedoman himself, served on *Gudgeon* for eight patrols and survived the war. Wixted was the man who drew Bill Post's wrath when he stole Bill

Post's jeep and drove it to the submariner's haven, The Irisher in San Francisco. He is one of those men who did not adjust well, despite having served admirably. His friends understand that one day years after the war he was walking beside a busy highway after a day of drinking and was hit by a car and killed. To this day, his friends from *Gudgeon* grieve his death.

Cecil "Carl" Finks, the wisecracking sailor who became well known on *Gudgeon* for his pranks, including rooster calls on the intercom in the middle of the morning, went on to serve on several other submarines before he was overcome by stress on *Scabbardfish*. In one of the *Scabbardfish*'s war patrol reports, he was said to be suffering from "extreme nervousness" and "mental depression." The *Scabbardfish* skipper said he was saved from killing himself when a crewman prevented him from cutting his own throat. Earlier on in the patrol he had requested Phenobarbital and sodium amatol to calm his nerves. A note he had written was found in his pocket, requesting disqualification from submarines. That is the official version. The actual facts surrounding the incident are a little different. George Seiler produced a letter written to him by Al Sheffs in April 1986. In it Sheffs refuted the claim that Finks had "lost it" aboard *Scabbardfish*. Shortly after boarding the "Scab," Finks told Sheffs, who was also on board, that this would be his final patrol and that he would soon be sent back to the States. When Sheffs asked Finks how he was going to pull this off, all Finks would say was "You'll see," thereby convincing Al Sheffs that he [Finks] was going to manipulate his way off the submarine. Al Sheffs was sure Carl Finks's suicide scene was faked. But, Carl Finks's final submarine "prank" had taken on serious overtones. Though his act was obviously designed to get him off submarines, it displayed for all to see that he had run out of jokes, and he was desperate to get off submarines. It was time to get off. As one former Gudgeon submariner said about Finks, "Cecil Finks was a good shipmate who did not have all his oars in the water."[9]

John J. Sheridan was the *Gudgeon* radioman who received the "URGENT" message announcing that Pearl Harbor was under attack on that fateful December 7. He served on board the submarine through the tenth patrol. After the war, Sheridan raised a family and served in the Navy as an electronics technician in various places, then as the Attendant Officer in

Charge of the transmitter station at Kodiak, which was part of the U.S. early warning system, and later still as an instructor at an electronics school. He was eventually hired on in private business as an electronics engineer and worked as a member of a Minuteman missile team, then moved on to Raytheon doing similar work before retiring in 1984. He wrote several books, including many adventure novels. The old submariner died in 2004.

Torpedoman Edward Hammond left the Navy after twenty-seven years of service. He worked in the Electric Boat Division at General Dynamics in Groton helping build, test, and deliver missile boats to the Navy. He had one child, a daughter, who he says knows very little about his days aboard *Gudgeon*. As far as is known he is alive and well on the east coast.

Art Barlow, the signalman who bravely performed his duty on the submarine base tower as Pearl Harbor was laid to ruin below him, left *Gudgeon* after eight war patrols. He then did four runs on *Boarfish* before the war ended. When he boarded *Boarfish* late in the war, there were only eight experienced submariners on board. By that time the Japanese merchant marine was in such shambles that target ships were rarely even seen. Barlow is rightfully proud of his time in the Navy, having made an admirable twelve war patrols before being promoted to chief on *Boarfish*. He retired as a chief warrant officer and then worked for the City of San Diego before retiring once again. He is alive and well in San Diego.

Gunner's Mate Ron Schooley, the man who sighted the "big bastard" of a ship the *Kamakura Maru* on *Gudgeon*'s eighth patrol, left *Gudgeon* after her ninth run. He made two war patrols on *Steelhead* before she was overhauled. He put the submarine out of commission after the war in 1946 and then left the Navy. Years later, after having trouble adjusting to civilian life, he reenlisted and finished off a 22-year career. Having interviewed him so many times over the phone, I was hoping to meet Schooley at a national submarine convention in late 2003. A few months before the convention, I learned that Schooley had died in May 2003 but not before he entrusted me with the after torpedo room workbook of the USS *Gudgeon*, signed by Dusty Dornin and filled out in pencil by the men manning the stern tubes. He also gave me his section of the "Homeward Bound Pennant" that Bill Post had cut into pieces for every man on board as *Gudgeon* headed home from a patrol.

Torpedoman Ray "Guts" Foster, who stood on deck as *Gudgeon* pulled out of Pearl Harbor after the devastating Japanese attack, eventually transferred to *Sandlance*. For many years Navy and submarine historians have speculated whether or not *Gudgeon* had been sunk in a depth charge attack on May 12, 1944. *Sandlance* was one of several submarines that heard the exploding depth charges several miles off Saipan. If the attack was actually the sinking of *Gudgeon*, then Ray Foster may have unknowingly listened to her demise. The bold, sharp-tongued ace torpedoman of *Gudgeon* must have mellowed somewhat as he got older because he retired from the Navy at the rank of lieutenant. At the time of his retirement after a fine 30-year career, he said he was doing the best work he had ever done, and was nonetheless informed that officers in his category were typically retired to make way for the development of younger officers. The Navy had to push the Gung-Ho Guts Foster from its ranks. At the age of 86, Ray Foster gets up early every day and swims. A few times a month he takes the ferry from Vallejo, California, where he once worked as Superintendent of Ships for the shipyard that overhauled submarines, to San Francisco's Fisherman's Wharf where he serves as a tour guide on the old World War II submarine, *Pampanito*. One of his four daughters reports that her father has no trouble handling any of the questions that are thrown his way. It is clear that the stout-hearted Guts Foster has changed little over the years. All his life, Guts Foster has been irritated with Jumping Joe Grenfell, because in Foster's estimation he ended *Gudgeon*'s first two war patrols before it was necessary. After the terrorist attacks in September 2001, Foster, in his early to mid-eighties, wrote the Secretary of the Navy and volunteered his service, stating that he would go anywhere and do anything that he could do to serve, explaining that he was completely expendable at his age and that he wanted to serve his country.

Maurice William "Mike" Shea, who served as Bill Post's executive officer on *Gudgeon*'s wild seventh patrol, left *Gudgeon* and boarded the newly constructed *Raton*, taking over as skipper for the submarine's fifth patrol during the summer of 1944. Shea and *Raton* sank seven ships weighing 18,000 tons during his three patrols in command before the war ended.

The time for command would finally arrive for Frank Lloyd Barrows also. Barrows was Bill Post's executive officer on *Gudgeon*'s eighth patrol.

Barrows had already served on *Gar* and *Gudgeon* before taking command of the war-hardened but brittle *Swordfish* for her ninth patrol, this one to Empire waters. Clay Blair (in *Silent Victory*) said that Barrows brought *Swordfish* in early with no kills because the submarine was so banged up that it was noisy and hence dangerous. Then, fearing that he had erred, Barrows insisted that he be relieved as commanding officer. His executive officer thought otherwise, stating that he had done a very fine job as the ship's skipper. Barrows was sent back to the States to pick up a newly constructed submarine, but the war ended before he could get in on any more action. Later in the year, *Swordfish* was lost on her thirteenth war patrol.

Elton W. "Jumping Joe" Grenfell, the high energy path-finding skipper of *Gudgeon*, who took the submarine out for patrols one and two, had a most distinguished career in the Navy. This was despite the fact that, according to his widow Martha, he could barely get up and down in a submarine after his plane crash early in 1942. The crash did not keep Grenfell out of submarines though. He was certain he could do the job and convinced his superiors that he should be given command after he recuperated. He commissioned the USS *Tunny* (SS-282) and hoped to take her out for her first war patrol, but the realization set in that he was too banged up to command the new submarine. He gave way to John Scott who took over for Grenfell after he departed. Grenfell was then assigned to the staff of the Commander of Submarines of the Pacific Fleet to serve as Strategic Planning Officer. From there he served as Commander of Submarine Division 44 and Submarine Squadron 34. During the latter assignment he was awarded a Gold Star in lieu of a second Legion of Merit. Grenfell was eventually promoted to vice admiral and served in many important positions in the Navy including Commander of the Pacific Submarine Fleet. In 1960 he was named Commander of the Atlantic Submarine Fleet. He was the first man to command both the Atlantic and Pacific fleets, a feat which has rarely been repeated. While in command after the war Grenfell was very popular with the enlisted men and became known as the "enlisted man's admiral."

Joe Grenfell never lost his amazing gift for memorizing names. Ray Foster was serving on a submarine tender as a weapons officer many years after the war and had been invited to attend a luncheon at an officer's club. As he was going through the receiving line he found himself face-to-face with his former skipper. Grenfell, who had no way of knowing that he would be seeing Ray Foster and his wife on that day, greeted him warmly and then said "Hello" to Foster's wife using her first name. Joe Grenfell still remembered the name of Foster's wife a good twenty years after having memorized it when Foster was on board *Gudgeon*. Grenfell's second wife Martha explained how he did it. Every time he wanted to remember something he would spin a ring on his hand in order to make a sensory memory at the same time as a cognitive one.

Joe Grenfell's second marriage, this one to Martha Lindsay, widow of Lieutenant Commander Eugene Lindsey, worked. They had several children. One of his sons, Steven, is said to be the spitting image of his father. Steven Grenfell said his family life under the watchful eye of the Admiral was very structured. He recalled preparing his bed to Navy standards before falling asleep and sleeping on the floor next to it when he knew his work would have to pass inspection from his dad, the admiral, in the morning. As Commander of Submarines Atlantic, he was administratively in charge when the USS *Thresher* (SS-593) went down in April 1963. Long before the tragedy occurred, while Joe Grenfell was in the Naval Academy, he had talked one of his teammates on the track team into volunteering for submarine duty. When *Thresher* disappeared during a test dive, Grenfell's old friend was lost in the forward part of the boat. His family recalled that until the end of Joe Grenfell's life he would occasionally become distraught at the memory of the death of the friend he had talked into the submarine service.

Slade Cutter, the former All-American football player for Navy who became a submarine skipper of almost unequalled regard during World War II, said of Joe Grenfell before he died, "He was a very good submarine skipper. He was the old school. He didn't have anybody to show him. We had the advantage watching how they did. We avoided their mistakes and fought the war much more aggressively." [10] A photo from the *Baltimore Sun* dated September 2, 1964 shows a haggard, exhausted-looking Grenfell, face down, as the Undersecretary of the Navy pinned a Distinguished Service Medal on his chest. After thirty-eight years, it was time for the old war-horse, Vice Admiral Elton W. "Jumping Joe" Grenfell to call it quits. Grenfell was felled by a combination of strokes and other medical problems before he died in 1980. His family remembers that until the end, he was a wisecracking sports nut, especially when it came to Navy sports teams, which he followed with much enthusiasm.

Hylan B. Lyon, *Gudgeon*'s second skipper, who took command of *Gudgeon* right before the Battle of Midway before vision problems forced his disqualification, went on to serve as navigator of the carrier USS *Independence*. The ship was torpedoed at Tarawa later in the war. He then served as executive officer of the USS *Missouri* and was present for the surrender ceremonies which were held on *Missouri*'s deck in Tokyo Bay. He was a signatory to the surrender document. His last command was of the USS *President Jackson* in 1953. At one time he served as the Director of Procurement for the Bureau of Weapons. He retired with a Silver Star for his service on *Gudgeon*. Pop Lyon raised a family and is recalled as a loving grandfather. But, life after the war was not always easy for him. His son, Hylan B. Lyon Jr. remembers visiting him when he was the executive director of NROTC at the University of Minnesota shortly after the war. The older Lyon was showing a training movie to cadets that depicted a depth charge attack and was so psychologically triggered by the celluloid explosions that he panicked and ran out of the building into a field surrounding the campus. His son ran after him and finally caught up with him and helped him back inside the building. Lyon was shaking, reliving the horror that he had endured so valiantly when the shells were flying.

Hylan B. Lyon, who braved three war patrols on *Gudgeon*, the torpedoing of his carrier the *Independence*, and countless other attacks, was a victim of his times. He, like thousands of other World War II vets, carried huge amounts of war-induced stress. So many of these tough-minded, courageous men had their wartime trauma compounded by the fact that their post-war days were in the 1940s when little was known about treating post-traumatic stress disorder. To make things worse, World War II submariners had the pledge of silence, of the Silent Service, drilled into them and, as a result, rarely felt at ease to talk about their experiences. These veterans of World War II coped the best they could with what was available at the time.

The long military history in the Lyon family was carried on by Pop Lyon's namesake, Hylan B. Lyon Jr., who recalls his first exposure to the armed forces being the surreptitious trips that he took with his dad on the old *Gudgeon*, the SS-211. During the war in Vietnam, he spent his days as an Air Force pilot as he said, "chasing Russian submarines." [11] Lyon was on his way to promotion to Captain at a very young age when he soured on military life and left the Air Force, thereby severing the family tradition that had endured since the days of the Green Mountain Boys and the Revolutionary War. For as long as he lived, the elder Lyon did not speak a word to his son about his experiences at war. Pop Lyon, who was promoted to rear admiral before he retired from the Navy in 1958, was in his early nineties at the time of his death a few years ago.

William Shirley Stovall Jr., *Gudgeon*'s third skipper, was known as an outstanding approach officer and marksman. Indeed, the combination of Stovall and Dornin achieved a very high percentage of hits during their patrols on the fourth and fifth runs. The by-the-book commander had requested to be relieved after the fiery fourth patrol, then changed his mind and had a successful fifth patrol, followed by a final patrol which was highlighted by two special assignments. *Gudgeon* did not fire a shot at the enemy on the sixth patrol, angering Dusty Dornin. Perhaps, as has been published elsewhere, it was as Dornin said, Shirley Stovall had won a couple of Navy Crosses and wanted to go home. If so, it is reasonable to assume that the extraordinarily heavy depth-charge poundings that *Gudgeon* took on his patrols may have finally convinced the fierce *Gudgeon* commander to make this decision. What is known for certain is that when the handful of sailors who served under Stovall on *Gudgeon* were interviewed many years later, not a one of them remembers ever seeing a hint of nervousness or fear in the cold stare of William S. Stovall Jr. In fact, they were greatly surprised when they learned of the Dornin-Stovall conflict which had resulted in the transfer of both officers in favor of Bill Post and Mike Shea.

George Seiler thought Stovall was "not very congenial" but was "one hell of a submariner." [12] Moose Hornkohl said that Stovall was "very professional," a "good skipper," a "smart one" whose ability to outmaneuver the Japanese under silent running was "probably the main reason that a lot of us are here today." [13] Art Barlow recalled that Stovall was "cool and calm" in command and that "if it was possible to sink a ship he would do it." [14] The one thing that is certain about Shirley Stovall is that his performance on the sixth patrol did not greatly alter the Navy's view of him as a commander of submarines. After leaving *Gudgeon*, he was assigned to the spanking-new *Darter*, taking her out for her first two patrols and receiving credit for the sinking of an additional Japanese vessel.

According to John P. Mansfield in *Cruises for Breakfast*, Stovall had an interesting encounter with General Douglas MacArthur when he was commander of *Darter*. While readying for *Darter*'s second run, Stovall was ordered to Finschhafen on the north coast of New Guinea where he learned he had been assigned a special mission to drop off Army personnel as coast watchers. As commanding officer of *Gudgeon* on her sixth patrol, Stovall had dropped off Jesus Villamor and five other men comprising the Planet Party. Stovall was very well versed in such operations and practiced the landing for three days. When he thought his men were ready to go, he sent a message to headquarters providing his route so that a bombing restriction lane could be established. General MacArthur responded to Stovall telling him that he would have to take his chances; there would be no bombing restriction lane for *Darter*. Stovall was furious and defiant and ordered the coast watchers off his submarine. They got their gear and hurried ashore. And, Stovall and *Darter* were off for patrol.

Despite a sinking on *Darter*'s second patrol, Lieutenant Commander Stovall received criticism reminiscent of that made of him after his final patrol on *Gudgeon*. Several sources hint that he was relieved of command before the boat's third patrol because he had been overly cautious during *Darter*'s approaches. Others say he was relieved because he was ill. Who knows? But Shirley Stovall's career as a submarine commander during the war was over after five war patrols. For the war, Stovall won a couple of Navy Crosses and two Bronze Stars, among other decorations. For his two special operations on *Gudgeon*'s sixth patrol he was awarded the Philippine Republic Presidential Citation. Stovall would go on to command submarine squadrons and serve in many important administrative positions in the Navy before retiring in 1959, when he received promotion to rear admiral. Stovall and his wife raised a family. Of the conflict between Dusty Dornin and Shirley Stovall, Admiral Stovall's daughter, Shirley, said that her father was always very fond of Dusty Dornin and that historians have made too much of their disagreement. She said that their conflict did not affect the cordial relationship between the two men.

Like many veterans, the former skipper had some difficulty dealing with the war-induced stresses that he experienced. Stovall's daughter Shirley said that years later he still "heard those bombs." [15] Like Shirley Stovall's career on *Gudgeon* and *Darter*, his death at the age of 58 was enigmatic. Did William S. Stovall Jr. give in to the stresses caused by the war or had he accidentally overdosed on Secobarbital when he was found dead in 1965? The coroner in San Diego could not decide. The real reasons surrounding William Shirley Stovall's death remain a mystery. What is not a mystery is that Stovall served his country heroically during the war. The United States Submarine Service was greater for having had Shirley Stovall of Picayune, Mississippi, as a skipper during World War II.

Lieutenant Sigmund Bobczynski served under Grenfell, Lyon, and Stovall on *Gudgeon*. Bobczynski, along with his pal Lieutenant Albert Strow, went on an unforgettable train trip in Australia early in the war. After leaving *Gudgeon*, Bobczynski served on *Archerfish* under Joe Enright. Together, with Bobczynski serving as executive officer and assistant approach officer, they sank the *Shinano*, a Japanese aircraft carrier of 59,000 tons. *Shinano* is the largest ship ever sunk by a submarine in *any* war by any nation. Bobczynski went on to raise a large family and is deceased.

All of the men who landed with Jesus Villamor on Negros during Shirley Stovall's third patrol as skipper of *Gudgeon* survived the war. As did Villamor. His fame and fate were well-documented in many books about the plight of the Filipinos during the war. After leaving *Gudgeon*, wherever the Planet Party traveled on Negros, Major Villamor was recognized. As a result, for security reasons, he hid out in a retreat far away from the common Filipino, directing his intelligence net. He is oftentimes regarded as the best and most daring of all the commandos who served on the Philippines. The Japanese knew all about his presence and did everything they could to catch him, without success.

The U.S. Army is certain that Villamor had established one of the most active and best-connected intelligence groups in the Philippines during the war. At the time, despite the best efforts of the Planet Party, his group received very little support or attention from the Allies and was withdrawn from the Islands in November 1943. The Allies eventually sent in their own men, who built their own intelligence net from scratch. After the war the

United States acknowledged that it had been a mistake to not take advantage of Villamor and his men—who were regarded as quite intelligent and capable. As time went on Villamor became more and more angry with the Allies. He felt especially betrayed by the Americans. He was sure that certain American elements had sabotaged messages that he had sent to General MacArthur and that some of his American counterparts were racists who regarded the Filipinos as inferiors and treated them accordingly. His memoirs written after the war have a strong anti-American slant. His anger is easy to understand. Villamor and his men took great risks and made tremendous sacrifices. It is commonly held that his complaints were valid. As the years passed, Villamor's anti-American attitudes grew. He blamed the United States for many of the problems on the Asian continent and in 1966 correctly predicted that the United States would not win the war in Vietnam.

Jesus Villamor retired in 1971 but not before he was awarded a United States Distinguished Service Cross, the Legion of Merit, the Philippine Medal for Valor, and many other decorations. As a final tribute to Villamor, the Philippine Air Force's principal facility in Manila was renamed the "Colonel Jesus Villamor Air Base." Villamor's efforts should make him a hero beyond the Philippines. His exploits are examples of courage and heroism for oppressed peoples everywhere. To this day a marker sits at Catmon Point where Jesus Villamor, dropped off by *Gudgeon*, stepped ashore on January 14, 1943. Villamor died of cancer at the age of 56.

Dusty Dornin, Shirley Stovall's executive officer on *Gudgeon*, also left the submarine after her sixth run. Despite what he repeatedly told the crew on *Gudgeon*, he did not box at the Naval Academy. One suspects that he said he was a boxer to the men on *Gudgeon* for effect, in order to enhance his position of authority. On *Gudgeon* he was a man who liked to party and on occasion engage in fisticuffs. As time would show, Dusty Dornin did not need subterfuge to lead men.

After leaving *Gudgeon*, Dornin took *Trigger* out for her sixth patrol and was credited with downing four ships. On *Trigger*'s seventh patrol he got four more, followed by a couple more on the eighth run. His executive officer on *Trigger* was Edward L. (Ned) Beach, who said of Dornin when interviewed for this book, "He was a fighter from the beginning. They used to say he had eyes in the back of his head. He was a good football player. Being a big football player you have to have eyes in the back of your head. He would get uptight and hot. He was a feisty skipper, first class. He commanded a submarine in a way that I'd never seen it done. Better than any I ever saw. He taught me a lot about submarining, and I don't mind admitting it. He was terrific." [16] Out of the hundreds of men who served as commanders of submarines in World War II, Beach regarded Dusty Dornin and Bill Post along with Gene Fluckey, Slade Cutter, and George Street as five of the top ten submarine skippers of World War II.

Slade Cutter said of his old teammate on the Navy offensive line: "Dusty was courageous, and he was smart. He was a hell-of-a-lot-smarter than the rest of us [at the Academy]. He worked awfully hard, and he stood high in the class." [17] Dornin was promoted to commander late in the war and retired at the rank of captain. During the war he was awarded two Navy Crosses, four Silver Stars, and two Presidential Unit Citations for his service on *Gudgeon* and *Trigger*. He went on to command several other ships before retiring in 1965 because of an unnamed physical disability. He and his wife Eleanore had several children. He died in 1982 at the age of 69.

Lieutenant Richard "Dixie" Farrell served on board *Gudgeon* for patrols one, two, and three and then became executive officer of *Hake*. After several patrols on *Hake* he took command of *Gato* for three war patrols and sank several ships. He was awarded a Silver Star on each of the three submarines where he served as well as countless other commendations and awards. He worked in many other capacities in the Navy before retiring after a 30-year career in 1960. He and his wife Eleanor raised two children. After he left the Navy, Farrell worked at Lockheed Missiles and Space until 1975. Slade Cutter recalls that Dixie Farrell was a "quiet man," not the type to "rough-house." [18] He was a good friend and a "good submarine skipper." [19] Farrell died of a stroke at the age of 83 in 1995. When interviewed, Eleanor Farrell said that she and Dixie had a great life together but he never talked about the war. She remembered that at all times he felt that he should maintain the secrecy that he had been sworn to keep. Submarining was a "very secret club." Eleanor Farrell regards World War II as, "that very terrible time in their lives." When the topic of the war was broached, she said Dixie would just say, "Let's have another drink. I think that's what service people did, they just had another drink."[20]

It has been a major disappointment not to have been able to interview *Gudgeon*'s longtime officer, Lieutenant Albert J. Strow, before his death. Like Bill Post, Albie Strow served with Bill Ostlund for two patrols before leaving *Gudgeon*. Strow referred to Bill Ostlund several times in his log. Strow was *Gudgeon*'s longest serving officer of the war, serving on patrols three through eleven. After he left *Gudgeon* he had a little time away from submarines before being assigned to *Tench*. Toward the end of the war Strow was named commanding officer of *Haddock*, taking the submarine out for two war patrols. By this time, thanks primarily to the Silent Service, the pickings were slim. Consequently, *Haddock* had no sinkings but did a creditable job at lifeguard patrol, picking up numerous downed aviators. In recorded interviews he made for his family and others, he described the circumstances when he learned that the Japanese had surrendered. He got the good word before *Haddock* pulled into Midway Island en route to Hawaii after his second patrol. Within a few minutes the partying started. He said that he remembered drinking a lot and for once, being "really hung over" the next day. The man who had served as the designated driver in Australia for the many drunken men and women at the parties ashore finally decided to hang one on. And for good reason. It was done. He had survived. Strow was indeed a very lucky man. He had survived nine war patrols aboard *Gudgeon* and left a few minutes before she went out on her final run. Then, when the war was over, he was back in the states only a few days after the Japanese surrender.

Lieutenant Commander Albert Strow was another highly decorated *Gudgeon* officer. He ended the war with a Silver Star and two Bronze Stars. After the war he served in a variety of capacities, including commanding officer of several ships. He left the Navy in 1959 after twenty years service. He went on to work for Raytheon, where he eventually retired. He remained married to Annmarie, the woman who kept him going during the war. Together they raised a daughter, Anna Laura, who said, like a lot of the men who fought against the Japanese during the war, her father had a strong war-induced prejudice against "them" until the day of his death a few years ago.

Gudgeon's fourth skipper, William S. Post Jr. left *Gudgeon* after five highly successful patrols, finally giving way to Robert A. Bonin as commander for *Gudgeon*'s twelfth patrol. He took a short break and then took *Spot* out for her first two runs. Some of the men who served under Post on *Spot* were interviewed at the 2001 United States Submarine Veterans of World War II convention. One remembered that before *Spot*'s first patrol, which was shortly after *Gudgeon* had been lost, Post lined the entire crew up on deck and said, "I can't tell you where we're going to go—but we're going to go out and get these sons of bitches." [21] Another remembered Post saying that leaving *Gudgeon* and then having it sunk without him was the worst thing that ever happened to him. The nearly unanimous opinion of the former submariners who were interviewed for this book and had served with Post on *Gudgeon* was that he was the best of a bevy of fine skippers whom they had served under. Most of the sailors who served with Post on *Spot* had identical sentiments. One of the men who was interviewed said that Post was a "fantastic skipper, great guy, nobody could be better." [22] Another agreed and added, "I never was around a man who would take the chances he did with the confidence that he would get us back. And he did. He was a wonderful guy." [23]

Despite *Gudgeon*'s sinking, Bill Post was hardly a changed man on *Spot*. The crew understood very early on why he had been nicknamed Wild Bill. Post took his new submarine *Spot* out in early January 1945 for her first patrol. He could hardly wait to get his big deck gun into action. He attacked and sank two small trawlers with the gun shortly after beginning the patrol. Four days later *Spot* destroyed a small freighter, then sank several more trawlers with his favorite, the five-inch gun, in the next few weeks. Post torpedoed a few more ships using all of his fish up rather quickly. Next, Post attacked a small boat that was trying to ram him. After finishing off the Japanese sailors on board, he sent over a boarding party to attempt recovery of intelligence information. The men boarded the boat but had to quickly leave because the vessel was listing severely to port and was about to sink. *Spot* received wartime credit for having sunk four ships on her first patrol. But, as is almost to be expected, none of the ships were recognized by JANAC, a fact that continues to anger Post's shipmates from *Spot*.

On Post's second patrol aboard *Spot*, he ventured to the East China Sea. On the second night out, *Spot* expended all of her available torpedoes on a Japanese convoy, sinking a ship and damaging another. The all-out attack on the convoy and the gun action and chase which followed were all very familiar to Post, who had successfully outrun a Japanese destroyer when a *Gudgeon* torpedoman impulsively scared the pursuer off by firing a burst of torpedoes at it. Just as before, the fact that *Spot* was in dangerously shallow water had not scared off Wild Bill Post. However, this time *Spot* had the additional challenge of carrying out the attack in stormy weather with unusually high seas. After the stunning flurry of torpedo attacks on the convoy, *Spot* surfaced and headed for deeper water, all the while being chased, this time by a Japanese minelayer that had opened fire on her.

The men from *Spot* manned their guns and returned fire. The heavy sea continually washed over the deck making defensive firing very difficult. There was no way that Post was going to order a dive because it would slow *Spot* down and the submarine would be extremely vulnerable in such shallow water. So *Spot* remained on the surface, a ripe target for the charging Japanese vessel. With *Spot* at flank speed and the huge waves washing over her, the submarine's gunners opened fire. After the gunners fired the first shot, a heavy wave washed over the submarine and knocked all the men down. Luckily none were lost. The gunners scurried back to their weapon and were able to hit the base of the enemy's forward gun, silencing it. A short while later, with the Japanese firing round after round at *Spot*, another huge wave scattered the gun crew along the deck. Now fearing for the lives of the men, and the Japanese blasting away and closing, Post ordered the five-inch deck gun secured. *Spot*'s defensive firing with the after 40 mm gun on the bridge continued until another huge wave washed over the cigarette deck and jammed its loading mechanism. By now the Japanese were very close, only a mile and a quarter away. Just as he had done on March 24, 1943, when the destroyer was closing in on *Gudgeon*, Post swung *Spot* around so that his forward 40 mm gun could bear on the minelayer. This time the Japanese skipper accepted the challenge and kept driving forward through the storm at top speed, intent upon ramming *Spot*. Fearing for the lives of the remaining gun crew, Post ordered that the gun be secured and ordered the men below. Wild Bill Post, however, remained on the bridge as the enemy's machine gun bullets ricocheted wildly off *Spot*. The charging vessel was getting closer and closer, and Bill Post remained topside. It seems all but certain that Bill Post yelled the words to "Waltzing Matilda" into the storm to calm his nerves and steel himself for whatever was to follow. Post standing alone, shells flying around him, eyes staring intently at the Japanese vessel, was trying to force the Japanese skipper into retreat by the power of his own will. Within a short time the minelayer was little more than a football field away. And, Bill Post, out of torpedoes and deck gun crews down below, continued to stand there, one hand poised above the diving alarm, the other above the collision alarm before deciding what he would do. Incredible as it may seem, Bill Post was playing chicken with a charging, fully armed Japanese minelayer. Then, only a football field away, the Japanese commander lost his nerve and called off the charge, swinging his ship to the left and far beyond the range of Bill Post's wild stare. By this time the minelayer had sustained considerable damage from *Spot*'s water-soaked gunners. With what must have been great relief, Bill Post sounded the diving alarm, and *Spot* went below, now safe from the threat of the Japanese vessel. Wild Bill Post had done it again. Post's incredible courage allowed his submarine to rule the day and escape to fight another day. This time *Spot* received *wartime* credit for having sunk two ships on what would be Post's final patrol as a commanding officer of a submarine at war. The claim was later downgraded by JANAC to one and a half vessels.

At the end of the war, according to JANAC, Post ranked thirty-fourth in terms of ships sunk with eight and a half. The 54,213 tons he was credited with ranked him among the top twenty skippers in the war in tonnage. For Bill Post, obviously these numbers do not tell the whole story. For his service in World War II, he earned three Navy Crosses, two Silver Stars, and a couple of Legion of Merit medals as well as countless other decorations throughout his career. From *Spot*, Post went on to command a submarine squadron and serve in significant administrative positions. He served in the Korean War as commander of the attack transport *Cavalier*. He commanded the heavy cruiser *Newport News* before becoming the Deputy Director for Intelligence on the Joint Chiefs of Staff after being promoted to rear admiral. Admiral Post retired from the Navy in 1965, then served as Executive Vice President of the Alaska Steamship Company. Bill Post and his wife Mary had two sons, one named Philip Sidney after the Civil War general and the other William Schuyler Post III. Post had a severe stroke four years before his death in December 2001. But even following the devastating stroke, Wild Bill Post was not finished. He hung on for four long years, dying at the age of 93. His wife Mary said that the sinking of *Gudgeon* "broke his heart" more than anything else that ever happened to him in his lifetime.

Before his death, not knowing of the severity of his health problems, I wrote Post a letter summarizing the main points of the early "Yuoh Island" theory. When Mrs. Post read the most important parts to him, she reported that he clearly gestured for her to read the pertinent parts of the letter again. It is satisfying to think that this great submarine commander got some solace from his grief before his death, knowing what had likely happened to his beloved USS *Gudgeon* and the men he had commanded. It was disappointing to me that Bill Post and I could not have talked. If he were able to do so, he could have told me many stories of his days as the skipper of his junior officer, Lieutenant William C. Ostlund. For awhile, an aged Mary Post and Slade Cutter resided in the same retirement home in Annapolis. But the former submarine ace, Slade Cutter, died recently. Of Bill Post, his old friend, he said light-heartedly, "He was a great one. He was a good man. His wife, I see every day. She's a delightful person. She's a lovely person. The complete opposite of that husband of hers."[24]

Sadly, the man who Post had warred with, Stephen G. Barchet, Post's skipper on *Argonaut*, died at the age of 53. There were traces of bitterness held toward Bill Post by some of the members of the Barchet family for quite some time after the war. This is unfortunate, because like Bill Post, Stephen Barchet had a distinguished Navy career, rising to the rank of rear admiral, then raising a son of the same name who retired at the same rank.

Irvin "Moose" Hornkohl, the *Oklahoma* sailor who had fired eye-to-eye at the Japanese marauders just overhead as they attacked the fleet at Pearl Harbor, survived the war and went on to fight in several more. By the end of *Gudgeon*'s seventh run, Hornkohl had no desire to leave a Bill Post–commanded submarine, but he got into some trouble and was not allowed to board. When *Gudgeon* arrived in Australia, each man was given a "chit," a small chip which could be turned in at the beer mess in exchange for a case of beer. Hornkohl was tired and thirsty after the intense seventh patrol and realized that he had left his chit on his bunk on board *Gudgeon*. He was in no mood to bow down to some shore-bound officer who was fighting his war behind a stack of beer cans and angrily pointed at the list of men from *Gudgeon* lying before the lieutenant. He screamed, "That's me. You can see my name, now I want my beer."²⁵ The argument got very heated. It was a fight which Moose Hornkohl should have known he could not win. Before long the furiously angry Hornkohl was hauled away by shore patrol and put on report. Because of the altercation, Moose Hornkohl lost his entire leave and was restricted to the base for a couple of months. His days of patrolling with Bill Post and George Seiler on *Gudgeon* were over.

Hornkohl was assigned to a relief crew in Australia. Several weeks later, at about the time that Hornkohl determined that his restriction was over, he ran into two former *Gudgeon* shipmates, Campy Campana and Leroy Loudon. They had been assigned to *Grayling*. The three old shipmates laughed and joked about how great it would be to be on the same boat again. Moose Hornkohl decided that he wanted to sail with his two buddies. The men marched up to *Grayling*'s wardroom and talked to Executive Officer Lieutenant H.W. Criswell Jr. to see if Hornkohl was needed on the next patrol. Sure enough, *Grayling* needed a torpedoman. Hornkohl was told to get his seabag. An excited Moose Hornkohl ran to the submarine tender and grabbed his gear. He had been very unhappy ashore and was itching to go to sea again. By the time he returned to *Grayling*, Lieutenant Criswell had discovered that Hornkohl had another week to go on his restriction. Hornkohl was rejected and crestfallen. *Grayling* went out on her seventh run without him and was lost, taking Lieutenant Criswell and Hornkohl's two former shipmates from the *Gudgeon* with her to the bottom. Hornkohl eventually boarded *Gar* and did two more war patrols, the submarine's ninth and tenth runs. From there he was granted leave and went home to see his family for the first time in three years, a grizzled veteran.

After his leave, he reported for duty on *Sealion II*, commanded by Eli Reich, where he remained until the war was almost over. While on his first run, *Sealion* sank *Kongo*, a large Japanese battleship, and a destroyer later in the day. From *Sealion* he went back to the states. Hornkohl decided that he had had enough wartime submarining and headed to New London to teach young submariners the tricks of the torpedo trade. He was assigned to the ancient R-5 which he described as "a leaking old tub."[26] He said, "When they pulled the plug on that sucker, you almost needed an umbrella. If that sucker got in over forty feet you got worried."[27] But, before long it was back to the war. He was assigned to *Cubera* very late in the war under the command of Roger Paine. By this time, Hornkohl had completed eleven war patrols. At one time or another he had served under George Street, who won a Medal of Honor, George Grider, and Ned Beach, in addition to Bill Post, Roger Paine, Shirley Stovall, Joe Grenfell, Hylan B. Lyon, and Eli Reich—some of the most well-known World War II submarine skippers of the war. Yet, as far as he was concerned, Bill Post was the best of the lot, though he had great respect for all of them in one way or another. While serving on *Cubera* Hornkohl heard "scuttlebutt" that the war was over. He hurried topside. Men were standing around expectantly as if they were waiting to hear whether their pregnant wife had delivered a boy or a girl. Before long word got out that it was official; the Japanese had surrendered. The place went crazy. Moose Hornkohl was elated. Everybody was elated. He said that all of the men got two days off and as he recalled, "There was plenty of room for quite a few beers."[28]

Hornkohl left the Navy as a first class torpedoman in 1951 having also served during the Korean War. Yet that was not the end of his days at war. Years later, after finding civilian life unappealing, Hornkohl signed up for the Seabees, the Navy's land-based engineering corps, and ended up in Vietnam in 1967. The war-toughened veteran found himself in very odd circumstances. During this war he would be building bridges on land. Hornkohl found himself in Saigon when the Tet Offensive got underway. In the middle of Tet, Chief Hornkohl had a very strange experience. He was scurrying around, ducking in and out of buildings because the city was under very heavy attack. Explosions were going off all around him. People were dying. Buildings were being leveled. Not particularly impressed by the efforts of the enemy, Hornkohl had turned a corner and decided that he would rather grab a cup of coffee than seek shelter. Lo and behold just standing there was old Howard "Hurdy Gurdy" George, his former *Gudgeon* shipmate. George was a big guy whom Hornkohl had not known very well during the war. Each man stopped in his tracks and stared at the other, by their expressions confirming to the other that they had served together almost a quarter of a century earlier on *Gudgeon*'s second patrol. The two men talked for a while, and then Hornkohl went his way to have a cup of coffee.

A few days later Hornkohl was busy repairing a bridge that had been blown up by the Viet Cong. Hornkohl and a steel worker were on the bridge when a secondary charge exploded. Moose Hornkohl and a mass of concrete landed in the mud alongside the bridge. He vividly recalled the experience of being thrown high into the air because at the time he was still conscious. A civilian steel worker was also seriously wounded by the blast. The other man "came to" faster than Hornkohl and carefully picked mud from Hornkohl's mouth because Hornkohl was unconscious by the time he hit the ground. He dragged Hornkohl out from under the bridge, carefully handling one of Hornkohl's arms, which was broken in two places. When Hornkohl awoke, the two men gingerly climbed into a nearby vehicle and drove off seeking immediate medical care, Hornkohl in the passenger's seat, the steel worker doing the driving. Before long the driver, bleeding severely, passed out behind the wheel. Luckily Hornkohl was sharp enough to reach over with his foot and stop the jeep. With one arm he painfully lifted the man and pulled him over to the passenger's seat, called ahead for an ambulance and drove off using his good arm to do the steering. The pain was excruciating. Before long an ambulance arrived and the men were taken to a nearby air base.

A huge cast was placed on Hornkohl's shattered arm. Hornkohl was in excruciating pain from the wounds. The only relief he could find was lying absolutely motionless on one of the carts in the makeshift hospital tent. That evening the base came under fire. The medical personnel told Hornkohl, "We're going to have to move you, Chief." [29] Hornkohl almost shouted back, "No you don't; leave my ass here. I hurt all over." [30] Hearing none of it, they rolled Hornkohl onto a stretcher and carried him to a mortar pit, a dug-out opening in the earth.

Hornkohl did two tours in Vietnam. After the second one, he was sent to Cambodia where, as he says, "We were fighting the Khmer Rouge." [31] While in Cambodia, Hornkohl was assigned to the embassy as security. He was given the responsibility of putting armor coating on two of Cambodian president Len Noll's cars. He found the experience to be complete hell. The country was in tremendous turmoil at the time, and Noll's men trusted nobody, not even Hornkohl. Noll's guards stood over him staring menacingly the entire time he worked on the limousines. To make matters worse, every three or four days the President's grounds would undergo a rocket attack from nearby rebels. But Moose Hornkohl, who had survived one battle after another on several World War II submarines, had survived the war in Korea, the Tet Offensive, and being bombed by the Viet Cong, would also survive the shelling of Len Noll's grounds by the insurgents.

After twenty-eight war-torn years Irvin Hornkohl decided that he had finally had enough. He retired from the service and is doing well. Hornkohl and his wife Eunice recently moved to Idaho to clear out some land and live on a rather primitive ranch, far away from civilization. And wars. The charming Hornkohl—like so many or perhaps most of his former shipmates—had a rough go of it for some time after the war but is doing well these days. Reflecting on his experiences in four wars, Hornkohl said, "I'm sure the war did a lot psychologically to me. There was once when I couldn't sleep a whole night. You'd get so used to those engines shutting down [the submarine's diesel engines]. The minute them engines shut down you knew you were going to dive. When you dove you knew that something was wrong, so you'd wake up and look and listen. It was more psychological. It made a wreck out of me. It wasn't so much that you were sitting in fear. You weren't scared. You were more worried what was going to happen next, where you were going to go. A lot of the time it was very normal to catch a couple of bombs, 'whammm,' while you were going down. I don't say it scared the crap out of me but it worked on you." [32]

When discussing the adjustment of fellow submariners, Hornkohl said he never knew anyone who didn't have some issues with excessive drinking. He knew of one officer he served with who "practically killed himself with alcohol." [33] He added, "It was our way of dealing with it." [34] Hornkohl found the experience of being interviewed for this book to be very trying. He is a friendly man who admitted that the process was tough on him because he had spent so many years trying to forget his wartime experiences. Yet he was eventually able to enjoy rehashing old memories just as he enjoys seeing his old shipmates at submarine conventions every year. Every year, the few that are still alive. The old *Gudgeon* submariners are truly a band of brothers. The men who served on *Gudgeon* were a closed society of elite submariners who worked together to win the war and to stay alive. Hornkohl and his former shipmates made it very clear that anybody they served with on *Gudgeon is* their brother. And the men are certain that all of the others feel the same way. The last time he saw Admiral Post, as Hornkohl respectfully calls his old commander, was at dinner a few years before Post's severe stroke. To show his gratitude and appreciation to Bill Post for what he had meant to him as a skipper, a mentor, and eventually a dear friend after the war, Hornkohl gave him his prized Navajo ring. Hornkohl said, "There wasn't anybody other than him that I would have given something like that to." [35]

As for George Seiler, he too left *Gudgeon* after the eighth patrol. Seiler's battles after the war were perhaps greater than those during it because once he was out of the service he did not have the structured life of the Navy to prop him up. But, during George Seiler's life, he overcame his enemies admirably, if not heroically. His departure from *Gudgeon* was a surprise to him because he was still on board when *Gudgeon* returned to Pearl Harbor after her long layover for overhaul at Hunter's Point, California, after the eighth patrol. After a run-in with his former skipper Commander Blair, the surprised and disappointed Seiler was temporarily assigned to a relief crew working on *Sculpin*'s torpedo tubes. Before long the submarine's commanding officer, Fred Connaway, asked Seiler to board *Sculpin* for the upcoming patrol. Seiler felt uneasy about the prospect and refused. *Sculpin* went out without him and was lost. Captain John Cromwell, who was on board to take command of a wolf pack, became a legend in the process. Cromwell chose to go down with the ship rather than try to escape *Sculpin* and risk being taken prisoner and giving away vital information to the Japanese. For this act, he was posthumously awarded the Medal of Honor. George Seiler had once again made the right choice, avoiding likely death on *Sculpin*.

By this time Seiler had married his sweetheart from Hawaii, then returned to the States for a newly constructed submarine.

When his leave ran out, he reported to the Submarine Base at New London and was assigned to the crew of *Escolar*, then under construction at Cramp Shipyard in Philadelphia. The shipyard crew had continuous problems completing the submarine, which allowed Seiler and a motor machinist from Alabama a full two months to engage in a continuous drunk ashore while the submarine was being made ready for the crew to board. Seiler, whose instincts for survival were impeccable, was dubious about all the delays on *Escolar* and received permission from his squadron commander to travel to Philadelphia to take a look at his new submarine. When he returned a few days later he told his buddies that he was getting off that boat as fast as possible. As the crew continued to await *Escolar*'s completion, a young man named Tommy Sarko, also from Seiler's hometown of Connellsville, Pennsylvania, reported for his first submarine duty and was assigned to *Escolar*.

Seiler and Sarko knew each other from the many fistfights they had when they were growing up. Seiler approached his new shipmate with a different agenda this time, telling Sarko, "Tommy, you and I fought all our lives, from the time we were in the fourth grade through high school. I'd hate like hell to see you die because of a pile of shit that's supposed to be a submarine. You'd better get off with me."[36] Sarko, who was rightfully impressed by Seiler's wartime experiences on submarines, was convinced that *Escolar* was a submarine that he wanted nothing to do with. But Sarko, not being the experienced veteran Seiler was, did not want to make waves with his superiors. He did not know how to get off the submarine. Seiler assured him that he'd take care of it and told Sarko that he didn't have to say a word. Seiler and Sarko headed off to the squadron commander's office where George Seiler asked that the two men be transferred to other ships because they desired to get into the war. Seiler was so certain that *Escolar* was a death trap that he chose to go to war to be safe. Seiler's ploy worked. Tommy Sarko was reassigned to the shipbuilding yard at Manitowoc, Wisconsin, and survived the war. Seiler was assigned to *Barbero*, built at the Electric Boat Company in Groton, Connecticut. *Escolar*, with Moke Millican in command, went out and was lost on her first patrol.

Seiler, now on *Barbero*, was used to being around experienced submariners and was horrified with conditions on his new boat. Although *Barbero*'s first patrol was uneventful in terms of fighting the war, Seiler found that serving on the submarine was a dangerous and nerve-wracking experience. By this time, George Seiler was a torpedoman first class and had been assigned to the after torpedo room. He had seven torpedomen under him, all of whom were rated. One of them was a chief torpedoman. He has never forgotten going down bow-first on the submarine's first dive and having "everything loose on board skating back at me." [37] Seiler told the Old Man that he was in more danger on this boat than he had been when he was fighting the war.

George Seiler's enlistment ran out on January 31, 1945, but he was held over for the duration of the war. He frequently reminded officers that he was a civilian, and it was against the Geneva Convention for any member country to hold a civilian against his will to fight a war. The officers always gave Seiler a good laugh for his comments, but the joke drew anger from the new draftees, who were probably feeling a little bit like prisoners themselves. Soon Seiler was transferred and rejoined his old friend Moose Hornkohl on *Sealion II*.

In Brisbane one day, George Seiler sauntered into a pub. He was standing behind a horseshoe-shaped bar when a huge Australian soldier walked in accompanied by a bunch of his mates. He approached Seiler and asked very threateningly with his strong Australian accent, "Are you an American submariner?" [38] Seiler told him that he was. The brute then said, "I think I'll beat the living hell out of you." [39] Seiler, no shrinking violet, took a quick gulp and squared off in anticipation. "Well hell, at that stage you'd fight at the drop of a hat because hell, you didn't give a damn one way or the other which way you went. But anyway this guy came around the bar but instead of swinging at me he grabbed a hold of me in a great big bear hug and said, 'George, don't you remember me?' It was the former Australian heavyweight boxing champion [whom Seiler and the others on *Gudgeon* rescued off Timor]. It was a wonderful feeling." [40] Indeed, as he told the story over a half-century later, there were obvious tinges of emotion in his voice as he recalled the feeble Australian soldier who had boarded *Gudgeon* in February 1943 along with twenty-seven other emaciated men. The man was in such sad shape at the time that there was no chance that Seiler would recognize him later in full health and vigor.

It was July 1944 when George Seiler heard that *Gudgeon* was missing on her twelfth patrol. He was devastated. But all he would say about the grim news was, "A hell of a lot of tears were shed when I heard that." [41] After his runs aboard *Sealion II*, the submarine headed back to the Bethlehem Steel

Navy Yard in San Francisco. It was at about that time that the United States had dropped the second atomic bomb on Japan. *Sealion* pulled into the dock and standing right there, as if he was there to greet his old *Gudgeon* shipmate, was George "Swede" Janson. Seiler and Janson had patrolled on *Gudgeon*'s fifth and sixth runs. They were together, there on the dock when they heard the news that the war was over. It was at that time that George Seiler, veteran of nine war patrols on three different submarines, came to the shocking realization that somehow he had survived the war. Of his survival he said, "I was the most amazed guy in the world that I was still alive." [42]

Once George Seiler's feet hit shore in San Francisco, an old foe would become unmanageable. He passed a very challenging test, which provided him a second mate license, and allowed him to navigate any ship on any ocean in the world. Seiler was quickly hired on to navigate a tanker to South America. The ship's captain asked Seiler if he had ever been on a tanker. Seiler responded, "No, but I've helped sink a hell of a lot of them." [43] Seiler, a highly capable man when sober, successfully guided the ship from Hoboken, New Jersey, to Cartegna and back.

He moved on to other things. Finding that his drinking was dominating his life, he sought the structure of the service and enlisted in the Air Force during the Korean War era. He was assigned to operate a crash boat in Houston. Unfortunately, the job had mostly downtime, and Seiler spent most of his time fishing and drinking at a nearby bar. His drinking progressed into the chronic alcoholism phase. He left the Air Force in 1956. Over the course of thirteen years he jumped from job to job, first as the man in charge of the picket boats at Cape Canaveral, where he picked up testing missile remnants; then as an oil rig roughneck in Louisiana; lumberjack in Idaho; irrigator at an apple orchard in Washington; and, finally, as an elevator operator in Chicago. His severe addiction to alcohol had reduced this courageous wartime torpedoman, trained to navigate ships anywhere in the world, to the role of elevator operator, which he found he could not handle, and was fired. Seiler continued to bounce around from skid row to skid row, riding trains as a bum, inevitably ending up in one of hundreds of jails throughout the country where, each time, he was forced to go through cold-turkey withdrawal until his release. George Seiler was gone. In his place was a tough drunk known as Blackey. Seiler remembered, "I became known as somebody to stay away from if I didn't like your company. Freight trains were my mode of travel so cross-country drunks were commonplace."[44]

George Seiler had gone full circle. First, he was a Connellsville teenager making a transcontinental freight train ride to Lodi, California, and the beet fields where he worked long hours, returning home on the train with a pocket full of money to help his destitute family during the Depression. Seiler went to war and returned, and now he was losing a war against his most powerful foe, the bottle, and riding freight trains. In fact, trains were his home, drinking his occupation. For years George Seiler, a "bum," continued to ride trains, and where they went he did not know nor care. All he needed was some booze, anything that would satisfy his over-whelming cravings, and enough food to keep him alive. Finally, in the spring of 1969, George Seiler found himself in Seattle. There was no reason for him to be there, but everybody has to be somewhere, even a bum. Seiler was being presented to a judge, having been charged with one thing or another. The difference between this judge and all the others was that this judge had access to a treatment center and an inclination to get alcoholics into treatment. A representative of the Seattle-based alcoholism treatment center known as Cedar Hills confronted Seiler and another couple of drunks, saying: "Jesus Christ. How much more of this fun can you stupid assholes take? You look just like a monkey that has *screwed* a skunk. You smell as bad, and I'm damned sure you act worse."[45] The former boxer George Seiler was furious and wanted to kill the man, but he was too malnourished and weak to stand, let alone throw a punch. Many years ago he would have, without a second thought, taken on a former boxing champion from Australia, and now George Seiler could not even stand. Seiler volunteered to go to treatment. He was placed in a holding cell, where, for eleven days, he was racked with severe DTs. He had to go through DTs before his transfer to the treatment center. "First, came the uncontrollable shakes, then the sweats with the insatiable thirst which water could not quench. Each time I drank, I vomited, then started the convulsions. I could not keep food down. Then came the diarrhea, then the delirium tremens, a literal Hell of horrible illusions, hallucinations, and the most frightening delusions of horrible creatures each trying to kill me, crawling over my body and believing that it was real. Screaming didn't help because I was so frightened that my vocal cords were incapacitated."[46] On Good Friday, 1969, the battle with the Japanese long over and the DTs now finally conquered, Seiler started a successful treatment program. Blackey was dead, once and for all. Seiler was hired on as a counselor, then worked for the rest of his career as the supervisor of counseling. "It took me forty-seven years to accumulate the necessary twenty to get a retirement. I had already met my wonderful wife, LuCyle. We moved from the Seattle area to Mesa, Arizona, where we live currently. It has two golf courses and easy access to a lot of AA meetings."[47]

When reflecting upon his days as a wartime submariner, Seiler spoke of his attitude toward the enemy during the war: "I remember one boat that had this big banner that would fly from its antenna that said 'Kill the Bastards.' That was one that made me laugh. That's exactly what it was all about. You kill them before they kill you. You know when people say, 'Didn't you regret all of the people that you killed?' I would say, 'No, as a matter of fact I considered it a great privilege to kill those bastards.'"[48] He continued, this time talking about Bill Post: "I remember Wild Bill Post was our leader. He was the most wonderful guy that I've ever known in my life, but I never saw him flinch one time. That's something, with all the stuff we went through. I don't believe anybody else saw him flinch either."[49]

For his time in the submarine service Quent Seiler acquired no extraordinary recognition. There were no Navy Crosses, no Silver Stars, no Bronze Stars for him. He had been approached by an officer on one occasion about being put in for one but scoffed at the suggestion saying, "I was just doing my duty."[50] The old submariner does not consider himself a hero for the same reason. He added, "I've never known of any submariner that wanted any glorification. Hell, we had a job, we loved our country, and we loved our people, and we were going to make damn sure that nobody came in and took away what our ancestors had fought for. I saw so much of what would be called bravery now that we thought was commonplace. You did what had to be done. That wasn't bravery—that was just doing your job. I've known of a dozen men, close friends, who were on the boat in our squadron who kept going back until they were forced to return to the States for new construction or died on the boat."[51]

At a different time Seiler commented on the *Gudgeon* submariners whom he never knew, including Bill Ostlund, saying, "Remember we're talking about the war, and this includes your Uncle. We had a hell of a lot of durability and a hell of a lot of guts. You had to work, and you had to connive and use all the ingenuity that you could to survive in those days of the Depression. These are the guys that fought World War II. This is the breed of cat that we were, that your uncle was."[52]

George Seiler would heartily disagree with the premise that when the submariners were fighting the war, under profound pressure, the threat of death always hovering above them, fighting for the well-being of the men on board and those at home, giving their survival hardly a second thought—that that was the *purest* form of heroism. It seems that Seiler and the other World War II submariners, as well as so many of the other old veterans, were brave so routinely that they are not even aware of the awe that the *attentive* noncombatant has for the men who performed so valiantly. Facing danger was so much a part of their everyday lives as young men that they have lost all perspective of the normal experiences of men or women who have not been in uniform during a war. In short, they are too close to their experiences to see themselves for what they really are. They are a rare breed in America these days. They were profoundly brave men. They are *true* heroes. Like all of the sailors from *Gudgeon* who were interviewed, George Seiler is amazingly humble. These men have never asked for anything. Neither Quent Seiler nor Irvin Hornkohl nor any of the other sailors who were interviewed for this book ever sought publicity or fame for their selfless gallantry during World War II. It was I who found them.

George Seiler, like the other *Gudgeon* submariners who were interviewed for this book, would not have traded his experiences during the war for anything. Seiler said, "The submarine experience made us the men we are today. I am glad to have served. The people in the country today will never know the proud feeling that we had to be an American during those days. I believe the war and how we tolerated it during the formative years and what we learned about ourselves, tolerance, perseverance, faith over fear, trust in ourselves and in others, endured for our entire lifetime. Without equivocation I loved my shipmates and the *Gudgeon*. They are closer to me than are my brothers and sisters."[53]

George gave me a large metal Mare Island, USS *Gudgeon* ash tray with "USS *Gudgeon* SS-211" cut into it. Bill Post had taken it off the submarine when he hurried off *Gudgeon* before the fatal twelfth patrol. After Post's incapacitation, Mary Post gave it to Seiler, who gave it to me, knowing that I would take proper care of it. It is one of the few items that exist that were once part of the USS *Gudgeon*. Seiler and Moose Hornkohl also had their World War II medals and insignias melted down into belt buckles that say, "WW II Sub Vet USS *Gudgeon* SS-211" and "WW II Subs—Courage Runs Deep." Centered in the middle of each, with a dark blue background, is a small metal World War II submarine riding high above the waves. Seiler designated that his should be given to my disabled fifteen-year-old son Aaron in order to give him courage and to remind him of the ability of the individual to overcome the overwhelming challenges that life presents.

Bill Post and two brothers, John and Bob, survived the war and raised large families. Bob served in Europe from June 1944 into late 1946 before being discharged. He died in 1999. John is another of those forgotten heroes. He completed his thirty-fifth and final mission over Europe shortly after Bill boarded *Gudgeon* in October 1943. He had been involved in some of the most harrowing and well-known bombing raids of World War II. His 385th Heavy Bomber Group had hit targets at Munster, Brest, Stuttgart, Nuremburg, and Manheim. He had watched bombers around him get hit and blow up leaving nothing but a cloud of smoke. He had bombed an oil refinery in Czechoslovakia and Hamburg, the marshalling yards at Cologne, the Messerschmitt airplane factories at Regensburg, the ball bearing works at Schweinfurt, and harbor targets at Bremen. He had hit Munich and even had the pleasure of bombing Berlin several times and decorating Adolf Hitler's neighborhood with cascades of fire and fury. When striking the oil refineries at Merseburg, he had his roughest experience of the war. All four engines on his B-17 Flying Fortress had been hit, and the plane barely made it across the channel to the base in England where he landed safely. John is like all the *Gudgeon* submariners I've come to know. One would never know that he was a war hero. In fact, I suspect that Uncle John would prefer that others not know about his service in the war. Neither John nor my father was wounded during the war, but, if asked, Uncle John will show others the piece of German flak that lodged itself in his B-17, about a foot from his head. Only John is still alive, still living in Webster City, a few blocks from the home in which the three brothers grew up.

Peggy Burrell Reid, Bill's widow after only fifteen months of marriage, was only a name and a face on a picture standing next to long-lost Uncle Bill as I was growing up. Nobody in our family knew what happened to Peggy, the beautiful young bride who disappeared from the family shortly after the war, determined to put her life with Bill behind her. When I realized that after all these years Bill's death could possibly be explained, I knew that I needed to try to find her, hoping that the knowledge would ease some of the long-ignored remaining grief she might still have. I found her in mid-2001. The phone call was very difficult for me because I did not know how she would react to an inquiry about her late husband. The last thing I wanted to do was upset the poor woman. Of course she did not even know I existed and was no doubt shocked to hear from anybody with the last name of "Ostlund." Peggy has lived an entire lifetime since Bill's death. She had been widowed a second time but is currently married happily to Robert Reid, also a World War II veteran, and resides in Florida. It had been over fifty years since any Ostlund had talked to her. She apologetically told me that she had tossed everything that she owned that had to do with Bill a long time ago, including all of his Navy items. She chose not to be involved for any extensive interviews. The memories may have been strong enough that the experience would be unpleasant. She was helpful in other ways, however, and said, "I will always be interested in whatever happened to the *Gudgeon*. It will always be a part of my life. Bill was a fine person and you have every right to be proud of him."[54]

The time spent researching the service of *Gudgeon* during the war, of tracking down those involved and interviewing them by phone or in person, and the time spent writing this book have been priceless to me. These men let me into the lives they led during the war, into the time that was both most meaningful and important but also so horribly sad. They helped me understand what it was actually like to fight a war on a United States submarine. For some, this was a time of their lives that had been locked up as tightly. Their stories and their adventures were as George Seiler put it, "in danger of being tossed into a garbage can" and forgotten when they passed on.[55] The knowledge that their exploits will live on in a book pleases them.

I have met many brave and honorable men and have learned about many others—men who have done far more for their country and the people of this country in it, of whatever age, than most of us can ever know. They fought the enemy without hesitating, they were eager to serve, and, in far too many instances, they lost their lives in that pursuit. They kept fighting despite the death of so many shipmates, friends, and loved ones. They persevered so that the world was saved from domination by men who would have shaped it in grotesque ways. All of these men were changed by the war, some for the worse, some for the better. Their service to their country molded them into the men they are today and, in some instances, into the friends they are today. I am honored to know George and Moose and Ray Foster and to count them as my friends despite our great age differences. After talking with them so many times, I have in a sense gotten to know Edward Hammond, Art Barlow, and Ron Schooley. Because of the record that they left, I feel I know Bill Post and Albie Strow and Shirley Stovall and Dusty Dornin and Jack Camp and John J. Sheridan and, in a sense, all of the men who served on *Gudgeon*.

I did not expect that such a strong bond would develop between Moose and George and me. Why is it that we are so close? I was not even alive during the war. I never set foot on *Gudgeon*, nor have I fought in *any* war. I have never done anything as heroic as these men have done. But they've accepted me as one of theirs. I believe it is because they feel I "get" it. I understand. I would like to believe that I understand and appreciate their service as well as any person who did not actually live those experiences is able to. Their experiences live through me and give them hope that their story will be told to others and remembered—not for their personal glory but so that others will understand what has been done to maintain this democracy and so that others will value America's strengths.

I was honored and touched when Moose Hornkohl declared at the United States Submarine Veterans convention in 2003 that he and George would be my uncles since I had never known Bill. It was touching to watch Moose as he prepared to leave the convention to drive back some 500 miles to his ranch to save his calves from the predators that gotten out of hand only a few hours after he had arrived at the convention. Here was this kind old man, a veteran of four wars and untold horrors, who at 80 years old was visibly tortured at the thought that wolves were killing his calves. Apologizing for leaving so quickly he explained, "You ought to see them, Mike. It's just awful to see what they do to those little things."[56]

As Moose Hornkohl prepared to leave, accompanied by George Seiler, Billy Mansfield, John Adams, and Joe Bell (three former shipmates of the two *Gudgeon* sailors from *Sealion II*), Moose Hornkohl stopped in front of each of the men. Tears were visible in his eyes as he told each of them he loved them. Moose and the others know darn well that each time they see each other it may be the last time. Each man hugged the other. Then in the blink of an eye Moose stopped in front of George Seiler, his running mate from *Gudgeon*, and they broke into a satirical version of "Waltzing Matilda," the version that they had come up with during World War II which had been written as a jab at one of their *Gudgeon* shipmates who was big, menacing, and smelled very bad. Moose explained that the humorous song was always sung when the hulking submariner was elsewhere on the boat for fear he would do them great bodily harm. In an instant the melancholy, emotional scene of repeated farewells between aged shipmates had vanished as completely as a submarine disappearing beneath the waves. George Seiler and Moose Hornkohl erupted into laughter, singing with absolute certainty and strength as if they were once more with their shipmates on the USS *Gudgeon*, surrounded by the darkness and stillness of the Pacific Ocean. For a minute they were young again. They were back on board the old SS-211. They had escaped their slowly-fading bodies, and they were as in the past, young virile submariners, strong enough and tough enough to fight and win a world war.

This whole endeavor, learning the story of *Gudgeon*, of my uncle who died before his time and of the men who served her, has been one of the greatest learning experiences of my life. How often does a person get to mingle with *truly* heroic men? These men lived a life that is incomprehensible for most Americans, myself included. How can one who has never lived through the Great Depression understand what those men went through? How can one who did not ride *Gudgeon* even "touch" those experiences? What was it *really* like when *Gudgeon* moved slowly past the sunken fleet in Pearl Harbor toward Japan to finally settle alone, deep in the waters off Japan? How can anyone who was not present understand what it was *actually* like to have undergone the soul-shaking depth charge attack off Ambon? Can anyone really know what it was like to have your submarine, considered to be a loved being by those who served on her, sunk, taking countless former friends and loyal shipmates with her to the bottom, somewhere, somehow in the spring of 1944? How can one comprehend how difficult it was to once again pick one's self up and continue serving knowing full well that any day it could be your turn to go? Will we ever know what it was like to be 19, 20, or even 15 years old standing tall on the deck of a World War II submarine as the shells of Japanese gunners are flying past your head? Can we comprehend the exhilaration of sinking one of the submarines that helped carry out the attack at Pearl Harbor or the rather gruesome thrill of sending thousands of your sworn enemy to the bottom as compensation for the horrors they had inflicted upon your countrymen? It is impossible to know. It can only be sought, and if lucky touched, so that in some way, while it is being acknowledged at the thinking level it is also being felt in the heart.

If you can get close to their experiences, you might be able to understand the sincerity of longtime *Gudgeon* submariner John J. Sheridan who had first received word of the attack at Pearl Harbor on *Gudgeon*'s radio on that profoundly dark day in December 1941, who sixty years later, lying in his nursing home bed, a physical wreck of a man said, "If I had to do it all over again, I would, as would we all."[57] He meant it. Every single one of those men who fought on the USS *Gudgeon* would do it all over again.

Even Uncle Bill.

▪ Acknowledgments ▪

It would be a big mistake if I did not first thank my wife Kerry who believed in me enough to allow me to take on a second "full-time job" for five years so that I could get *Gudgeon*'s story in print. She stepped aside and took over far more than her fair share of everything else while I set out on this romp. Next in line are Nathan and Aaron who have had to do without their dad far more than they would have liked. Nathan deserves a special thanks for being my Number One cheerleader. Next comes twin brother Chris, who found the book that lit the spark of inquisitiveness in me ("Where in the heck is Yuoh Island?") and then drove to the sub convention in St. Louis to help me do the first interviews of our new friends: George, Moose, and Guts. Then comes Jude, who told me I ought to write a book. Next in line are my siblings, but especially Beth and Chris (again), who advised me, consoled me, inspired me, and sold me on the fact that I could actually do it, actually research and tell the story of Uncle Bill's old *Gudgeon*. And again to Beth who did the first edit, the toughest edit of the 600-page manuscript, and to Philip Post, who plowed through and did a second edit, shortening the text by many thousands of words and encouraging me whenever I needed it. Then there was Dr. Tom Walz, my old college professor, who gave me sound advice and an outsider's opinion that *Gudgeon*'s story would be put in print. And, Cheeni Rao, for a few leads resulting in the hiring of my agent, Deborah Grosvenor. The other essential people were the *Gudgeon* "crew" without whose history the *Gudgeon* story would have remained forgotten. These men and the *Gudgeon* "families" in almost all instances helped me with every request I made. George has spent hundreds of hours telling me *Gudgeon*'s story e-mailing me with answers to my questions and repeatedly reviewing my manuscript to make certain that it was as true to *Gudgeon*'s story and to World War II submarining as possible. For that matter, Moose and Art Barlow studied the manuscript and then made certain that whatever needed to be changed was changed. A special thanks to Ray Foster and Art (again), who reside in California; Edward Hammond on the East Coast; and to Ron Schooley and John Sheridan (who have since passed), each of whom allowed me access to the stories of their days as submariners on the USS *Gudgeon*. What would I have done without the contributions of the former *Gudgeon* submariners, who made sure that they told their story on paper or tape before they died. They are Albert Strow, Joe Grenfell, Jack Camp, Albert J. Rupp, and a special shipmate, the commando Frank Holland. And, to the other indispensables, Uncle John and my father, who kept Bill alive by talking about him during my childhood; Anna Laura Rosow (Strow); Eleanor Dornin; Shirley Thorup (Stovall); Mary Post; Eleanor Farrell; Hylan B. Lyon Jr. ; Kathleen Kimble; Peggy Reid and Robert; Jane Duffey (Grenfell); Stephen Grenfell; Annmarie Strow; Martha Grenfell; Regis Bonin; Jane Kelso; Ken-Ichi Manaka; Paul Kelso; John Ackerman, John D. Alden; Wayne Sampey; Noritaka Kitazawa; Mary Ann Rupp; John and Mabel Holland and Peter Stone; Harry Holmes; Rick Dunn; Gladys Harkins; Stephen Barchet; Robert O. Phillips; Betty McCorquodale; and Geri Bennett, whose future book about the G-boats will tell the whole story of *Gar*, mentioned briefly in this book; and to Janet Loveland on the East Coast; and the legends who have since passed, Slade Cutter and Ned Beach. Finally: Al Ford, Roger Mansell, Rusty Dornin, John Schaffner (Bonin), Lu Cyle and Mrs Moose, Margaret and Linden Speers (Hegerfeld), Joanna and Myron White, Clarence Carney; the Kendall Young Library, John McMurray, Marie Duncan and Keith Dodson, C. J. Karamargin, Dick Farrell; Jean Bonin; Hollis Duel; John Morris; Patrick Gilliacus; Claude Pilcher; Dick Cotton; Joe Bell; John Adams; Billy Mansfield; Vernon Miller; Jim Broshot; James Langdale; Larry DeZeng; Al Sheffs; Jack Sheridan; Ben Bastura; Raylene Thompson; the National Archives; *The Submarine Review*; Dawn Graham; Craig Fuller; Kim Lestina; and to the rest of Pop Lyon's family, Linda Lipton, Lezlie Hall and the ICPL, and UIH libraries.

To those that I've neglected to formally mention, please accept my sincere apology. Your contribution has not been forgotten by me, it has momentarily slipped my mind.

▪ Appendix 1 ▪
List of Officers and Crew for the USS *Gudgeon*

Abbot, Oscar A.   9, 10, 11, 12†
Acosta, Joseph F.   7, 8, 9
Andrick, Grant E.   1, 3, 4, 5, 6, 7, 8, 9, 10
Ankeny, William   12†
Arzonico, Louis H. 3rd   1, 2, 3, 4
Ashworth, Laurel C.   3, 4
Aubrey, Walter R   7, 8, 9, 10
Ball, James R.   10, 11, 12†
Barlow, Arthur C.   4, 5, 6, 7, 8, 9, 10, 11
Barrett, Milton P.   12†
Barrett, Walter E.   1
Barrows*, Frank L.   8
Becker, Robert Clayton   5, 6, 7, 8
Berry, Rodney   2
Birchfield, Paul H.   11, 12†
Bland, Edward L. Jr.   6, 7, 8, 9, 10
Blessing, James H.   11, 12†
Bobczynski*, Sigmund A.   1, 2, 3, 4, 5, 6
Bonin*, Robert A.   12†
Bossong, John G.   11, 12†
Britt, Thomas B.   1, 2

Brock, Emerson W.   1, 2, 3, 4, 5, 6
Brown, Walter L.   1, 2, 3, 4
Butts, Eugene J. Jr.   1
Byers, William N.   1, 2, 3, 4, 5, 6, 7, 8, 9
Cadman, John Lester   5, 6
Cain, Norris F.   1, 2, 3, 4, 5, 6, 7, 8, 9, 10
Cain, Ray E.1,   2, 3, 4, 6, 7, 8, 9, 10
Callejo, Alejandro   10, 11
Camp Jack E.   1, 2
Campana, Carmine J.   7
Carney, James R.   10, 11, 12†
Cates, John T.   3, 4, 5, 6
Christian, Richard O.   9, 10, 11, 12†
Clairmont, Loyd Benedict   7, 8, 9
Clock*, Richard L.   1, 2, 3, 4, 5, 6
Coghlan*, James W.   12†
Collins, Robert C.   12*†
Comstock, Roland W.   3
Copeland, Charles B.   9, 10, 11, 12†
Corbisiere, Dominick   7, 8, 9
Crabb, Hugh A.   7
Crandall, Glenn E.   7, 8, 9, 10, 11, 12†

Curran, George J. 7, 8, 9, 10

De Carlo, Eugene 2, 3, 4, 5, 6, 7, 8, 9

De Julis, Edward 3

Dean Roy L. 1, 2, 3, 4, 5, 6

Della Torre, John A. 1

Dickenson*, Ben 5, 6, 7, 8, 9, 10, 11, 12†

Dickson, Thomas J.1, 2

Dillard, William Lee 9, 10

Dodson, Everett H. 10, 11, 12†

Donovan, Jeremiah P. 11, 12†

Dornin*, Robert E. 1, 2, 3, 4, 5, 6

Drake, Gilbert M. 2, 5, 6, 7, 8

Eckersley, Benjamin B. Jr. 1, 2, 3, 4, 5, 6, 7, 8, 9

Egan, John W. 5, 6, 7, 8, 9

Estabrook, Robert L. 7, 8, 9, 10

Evans, John W. 11, 12†

Evans, Melton 1 2, 3, 4, 5, 6

Everhart, Albert R. 9,10,11,12†

Fairchild, George 5, 6

Farrell*, Dixie P. 1, 2, 3

Feikert, Wayne Edward 7, 8, 9, 10, 11, 12†

Feit, Seymour 9, 10

Fernandez, Ambrosio 7, 8, 9, 10, 11, 12†

Finks, Cecil 3, 4

Fink, Wilmer G. 5, 6, 7, 8, 9, 10

Floyd*, William 10, 11

Foster, Raymond F. 1, 2, 3, 4, 5, 6, 7

Fournier, Jack A. 9, 10, 11, 12†

Francis, Ira A. 1, 2, 3

Fredette, Herman J. 1, 2, 3, 4, 5, 6, 8

French, Hugh 1, 2, 3, 4, 5, 6, 7, 8, 9, 10

Fuller, Grant M. 3, 4, 5, 6

Gambrill, Dee E. Jr. 3, 4, 5

Garrett, Howard O 9, 10, 11, 12†

Gaughan, Edward C. 9, 10, 11, 12†

George, Howard E. 1, 2

Glaspey, Ralph H. H. 1, 2, 3, 4, 5, 6

Goldhammer, Harlan Karl
    (Listed as passenger) 11

Gonsalves, Joe M. 7

Goodhue, Theodore L. 7, 8, 9, 10

Grady, James N. 5, 6, 7, 8, 9

Granum, Peder 10

Grenfell*, Elton W. 1, 2

Gumeringer, Martin 2, 3, 4

Hall, Verl E. 7, 8, 9, 10, 11

Hammond, Edward E. 5, 6, 7, 8, 9, 10

Hammond, Karl L. 10, 11, 12†

Harger, John 1

Hegerfeld, Lambert G. 10, 11, 12†

Hemmer, Wallace Proctor 10

Henderson, William H. 1

Henry, William R. 10, 11, 12†

Hensley, Elijah C. 12†

Heyes*, Burton L. 9, 10, 11, 12†

Hitt, Riley M. 7, 8, 9, 10, 11, 12†

Hodge, John T. 1

Hofer, William R. 2, 3, 4, 5, 6

Holder, Aubrey F. Jr. 9

Hollingsworth, Charles F. 1, 2, 3, 4

Hornkohl, Irvin W. 2, 3, 4, 5, 6, 7

Hubbard, Lawrence F. 1

Hudgins, James L. 1, 2

Hughart, Robert E. 8, 9, 10, 11, 12†

Jacobsen, Carl O. 3, 4

Janson, George T. 5, 6

Jeffcoat, Clifford E. 5, 6

Jochim, Bernard J. 1, 2, 3, 4, 5, 6

Johnson, Warren E. 1, 2, 3, 4, 5, 6, 7, 8, 9

Jones, Bonner R. 1, 2, 3, 4

Kansir, Wallace 3

Katz, Abraham J. 8, 9, 10

Keller, Donald C. 12†

Keller, Norman C. 9, 10, 11, 12†

Kirkpatrick, John F. 1

Kiser, Hershel 2, 3, 4

Kohrs, Franklin B. Jr. 1, 2, 3, 4, 5, 6, 7, 8

Kohut, Steven 12†

Kramer, E. R. 11

Krueger, Kenneth P. 10, 11, 12†

Smith, Donald E. 3, 4, 5, 6, 7, 8
Sorenson*, Vernon F. 1, 2, 3
Sponheimer, William H. 11, 12†
Stillson, Donald L. 1, 2, 3, 4, 5, 6, 7,
  8, 9, 10
Stovall*, William S. Jr. 4, 5, 6
Strow*, Albert 3, 4, 5, 6, 7, 8, 9, 10, 11
Sullivan, Owen J. 3, 4, 5, 6, 7, 8, 9,
  10, 11, 12†
Suoja, John 8
Super, Walter 6, 7, 8, 9, 10
Swinson, Paul W. 12†
Tashby, Samuel 9
Taylor, Robert H. 11, 12†
Taylor, Samuel H. 11, 12†
Tellier, Douglas E. 5, 6, 7, 8, 9, 10,
  11, 12
Tellier, Norman L. 7
Thomas, Clarence F. 11, 12†
Thompson, Charles E. 1, 2, 3, 4
Thurman, Delmar W. 4, 5, 6
Tillo, Bernardo 7, 8, 9
Trent*, Thomas 9
Turner, Frank D. 7, 8, 9, 10, 11
Uken, Joseph L. 5, 6, 7, 8, 9
Updike, Harold E. 12†

Vance, Norman 12†
Van Norden, Frederick E. 10, 11, 12†
Vaughn, George F. Jr. 2, 3, 4
Ver Valin, Charles H. 1, 2, 3, 4
Walker, Bernard E. 2
Walker, Joel McGee Jr. 7, 8, 9, 10,
  11, 12†
Walker, Joseph W. 5, 6
Warner, George E. 8, 9
Warner, Harper A. 1, 2, 3, 4, 5, 6,
  7, 8
Waters, Harold A. 10, 11, 12†
Watson, George J. 10, 11, 12†
Webster, Earle A. Jr. 11, 12†
Webster, Raymond E. 5
Westmoreland, James E. 1
White, Thomas J. 11, 12†
Whitelow, Joseph 9, 10, 11, 12†
Wilkins, John Jr. 3, 4, 7, 8
Wixted, Edward F. 1, 2, 3, 4, 5, 6, 7, 8
Wood, Jack E. 9, 10
Worthington, Wesley W. Jr. 9, 10,
  11, 12†
Wortman, Ralph 3, 4, 5, 6
Wyers, Ralph L. 1, 2, 3, 4, 5, 6, 7, 8, 9
Zimmerman, Charles A. 12†

* Officer
† Died while serving on *Gudgeon*. Lt. G. H. Penland and Arthur Miller died prior
  to the 12th patrol.

▪ Appendix 2 ▪
The *Gudgeon*–A Retrospective

Where knowledge decreaseth, honor ceaseth.

Unknown Author

Excluding *Gudgeon*'s final moments, her war patrol reports reveal that the submarine was attacked by planes nine times, enduring twenty-four bombs by both Japanese and Allied bombers. *Gudgeon* is known to have been narrowly missed by torpedoes from Japanese ships on two occasions. The *Gudgeon* was depth charged by antisubmarine vessels twenty-three times, absorbing the massive explosions of 300 depth charges, before she was sunk taking seventy-nine sailors to the bottom.

Despite the pounding that the Japanese laid on *Gudgeon* and the other American submarines, fifty-two of which were sunk, it is clear that the submarine fleet won the battle of the Pacific. The Joint Army-Navy Assessment Committee was appointed in 1943 by order of the heads of the Navy and Army to assess Japanese merchant and military shipping losses during the war. Representatives from the Navy, the Army, and the Army Air Force were ordered to undertake the impossible task of determining which of the thousands of Japanese ships had been sunk, when they were sunk, where they were lost, and who should get credit for the sinking. The committee was comprised of four representatives from the Navy and three from the Army. The members met from time to time to consider the losses of all naval vessels of the Imperial Japanese Navy as well as the loss of all Japanese merchant ships greater than 500 tons.

According to JANAC, the United States Silent Service accounted for the destruction of over 5.3 million gross tons of merchant and naval shipping. The submarine fleet downed 201 naval vessels at 540,000 tons, and an additional 1,113 merchant vessels and 4.8 million tons, which was 55% of the total shipping destroyed. Of the remaining Allies, the submarine fleet of Great Britain had the second highest total with 43 sinkings totaling 91,436 tons. By comparison, the American surface fleet sank 123 ships weighing 321,166 tons.

At the time *Gudgeon* was lost she had received wartime credit for twenty-four sinkings and 166,000 tons which made her one of the top submarines in the United States fleet. At the time of *Gudgeon*'s disappearance, the more conservative JANAC group placed *Gudgeon* fourth in tonnage sunk with 71,047. *Trigger*, with 72,247 tons, led the way. While the men on *Gudgeon* still patrolled, their achievements in terms of shipping sunk were at or near the top regardless of which figures were used, JANAC or the wartime numbers. As legendary submarine commander Slade Cutter stated shortly before his death, "*Gudgeon* was up there in the top."

When the JANAC report was released, listing all of the Japanese ships that were known to have been sunk, as well as which unit had been credited with sinking them, it received high praise from many circles. As time went on, though, many vociferously disputed the committee totals, believing that the submarine fleet should have been credited with far greater numbers of ship sinkings. If the men who were actually there, who reported seeing ships sink, who heard keels break up or boilers explode are correct, the JANAC group did a major disservice to countless submariners.

More recently, due to the availability of hundreds of Ultra intercepts and recently translated Japanese documents, retired submariner and author Commander John D. Alden has updated the sinking attributions he made in his book *U.S. Submarine Attacks During World War II*. His most up-to-date conclusions regarding the *Gudgeon* are reflected in the third column of Appendix 2.

Alden's totals suggest that *Gudgeon* sank 13½ enemy ships, "probably" or "possibly" downed 3 others, and damaged or "probably" damaged 9 more.

The total, perhaps not coincidentally, is almost identical to the number of ships that *Gudgeon* received wartime credit for having sunk. The no-holds-barred way that Bill Post fought the war is reflected in the Alden numbers. According to Alden, in five patrols Post sank 10½ ships, "probably" sank 2 more, and likely damaged an additional 6 vessels.

▪ Appendix 3 ▪
Attacks of the USS *Gudgeon* During WWII

DESCRIPTION OF ATTACKS:
Claimed Results from War Patrol Report

#	First War Patrol – Elton W. Grenfell, skipper
1	**1-4-42**: 32-11' N, 131-52' E Fired 2 torpedoes at 1,500 ton coastal freighter. Both missed.
2	**1-9-42 to 1-10-42**: 31-56' N, 132-15' E Fired 3 torpedoes at large freighter. CO reported a "shock" & saw it sink. TM heard 2 thuds. Believes 2 hits. Explosive reverberations heard.
3	**1-27-42**: 28-24' N, 178-35' E Fired 3 torpedoes at I-68 class sub. CO believes "2 hit." Two thuds felt.

#	Second War Patrol – Elton W. Grenfell, skipper
4	**3-13-42**: 31-14' N, 128-06.5' E Fired 2 torpedoes at Q-ship. 2 misses. One torpedo went under ship.
5	**3-26-42**: 32-31.5' N, 127-10.5' E. Fired 3 torpedoes at freighter. 2 hits. Ship started down by stern and turned over.
6	**3-27-42**: 33-53' N, 127-33.5' E Fired 3 torpedoes at large cargo-passenger ship. 2 hits. Lifeboats in water, ship sinking by bow.

#	Wartime Credit	JANAC Credit	Alden
1	No credit given.	No credit given.	Did not list attacks if damage was not claimed.
2	SUNK Unknown merchant vessel 5,000 tons.	No credit given.	Possible dud hit.
3	SUNK 1,400 t. submarine.	SUNK "I-173" (actually *I-73*)	SUNK sub *I-73*

#	Wartime Credit		
4	No credit given.	No credit given.	
5	SUNK Unknown freighter 5,000 tons.	SUNK Unknown maru 4,000 tons.	Unknown maru possibly sunk.
6	SUNK Unknown cargo-passenger vessel 10,000 tons.	SUNK Unknown maru 4,000 tons.	Probable damage to *Nissho Maru*

7   **3-28-42**: 31-49' N, 127-13' E
Fired 3 torpedoes at Q-ship (same one missed 3-13-42). One passed under ship. 12–14 DC dropped, damage sustained.

#	**Third War Patrol – Hylan B. Lyon,** skipper

Battle of Midway

#	**Fourth War Patrol – William S. Stovall Jr.,** skipper

8   **7-23-42**: 9-49' N, 154-42' E
Fired 3 torpedoes at Q-ship. 3 missed. 1 passed under target.
7 DC dropped.

9   **7-31-42**: 7-37' N, 150-10' E
Fired 3 torpedoes at ship similar to 8,500 ton *Ginyo Maru*.
2 timed hits. Target disappeared. Assumed sunk. 6 DC dropped.

10   **8-3-42**: 7-37' N, 150-17' E
Fired 3 torpedoes at 9,500 ton ship similar to *Africa Maru*.
2 hits. Ship sank in 5 minutes

11   **8-17-42**: 7-43.4' N, 151-13.5' E
Fired 3 torpedoes at 8,500 t. freighter-transport. 3 timed hits. 2 observed through periscope. Ship took heavy port list. No screw noises.

12   **8-17-42:** Same location as above.
Fired 3 torpedoes at 8,500 ton freighter-transport. 2 timed hits reported. 1 hit observed through periscope. Screw noises stopped. Believed ship sank. 60 depth charges. Damage sustained.

#	**Fifth War Patrol – William S. Stovall Jr.,** skipper

13   **10-21-42:** 3-30.2' S, 150-30.6' E
Fired 3 torpedoes at 7,000 ton merchantman similar to *Takatoyu Maru*. 2 timed hits reported. 1 hit observed amidships, lots of smoke, little geyser indicating bottom explosion. 43 explosions heard.

14   **10-21-42:** Same location as above.
Fired 3 torpedoes at 7,000 ton merchantman similar to *Takatoyu Maru*. 1 timed hit reported. 8 depth charges.

15   **11-11-42:** 3-31.5' S, 148-13.8' E
3 torpedoes at 7,500 ton merchantman. 1 timed hit reported though uncertain which of 3 ships were hit.

16   **11-11-42:** Same location as above.
3 torpedoes fired at a 7,500 ton merchantman. 1st and 2nd torpedoes were seen to hit target. Ship seemed to be settling rapidly. Screws stopped. 3rd torpedo may have been hit on another ship.

7	No credit given.	No credit given.	No credit given

#	Wartime Credit	JANAC Credit	Alden
	None.	None.	None.

#	Wartime Credit	JANAC Credit	Alden
8	No credit given.	No credit given.	
9	SUNK Unknown freighter 8,500 tons.	No credit given.	Miss.
10	SUNK Unknown freighter 9,500 tons.	SUNK *Naniwa Maru* 4,858 tons.	SUNK *Naniwa Maru* 4,858 tons.
11	This ship or second ship attacked on this date credited as sunk.	No credit given.	Probable light damage to *Shinkoku Maru* 10,020 tons.
12	One of two ships attacked on this date credited as sunk.	No credit given.	Probable light damage to *Nichiei Maru* 10,020 tons.

#	Wartime Credit	JANAC Credit	Alden
13	Credit for sinking given for this 7,000 ton cargo ship	SUNK *Choko Maru* 6,783 tons.	SUNK *Choko Maru* 6,733 tons.
14	No credit given.	No credit given.	Attack not listed in book. In pvt. Letter. "miss" on *Tajima Maru* reported.
15	No credit given.	No credit given.	Miss.
16	Sunk 7,500 ton merchant ship.	No credit given.	Miss. Possible premature explosion.

17 **11-11-42:** Same location as above.
Fired 3 torpedoes at 7,500 ton merchantman. 2 timed explosions reported. Tremendous explosion seemed to blow it apart. Concussion felt "severely" on the bridge. Shock felt below decks more severe than felt from prior attacks. Smoke seen. 1 of 2 hits could have been on another ship. Strong odor of sulphur reported.

 # Sixth War Patrol – William S. Stovall Jr., skipper

None. Gudgeon was attacked on several occasions. Completed two special missions.

 # Seventh War Patrol – William S. Post Jr., skipper

18 **3-22-43:** 6-31' S, 112-53' E
Fired 2 torpedoes at maru similar to *Syoto Maru*. Two explosions heard and felt. First maru disappeared.

19 **3-22-43:** Same location as above.
Fired 2 torpedoes at 10,500 ton ship similar to *Taketoyu Maru*. 1 torpedo hit amidships and seemed to lift the ship up a few feet and set it to one side. Great billows of black smoke and debris arose. Heavy list to starboard. Settling.

20 **3-22-43:** Same location as above.
Fired 2 torpedoes at ship similar to 8,300 ton *Yuki Maru*. Heard 2 hits. Went deep because destroyer charging *Gudgeon*. Believe 2 of 3 ships attacked on this date were sunk, possibly all 3.

21 **3-24-43:** 6-25' S, 113-48' E
Charging 1,900 ton sub-chaser. *Gudgeon* in grave peril. Fired 4 torpedoes. Fired 67 times with 3" guns. Torpedoes missed but likely saved the *Gudgeon* by turning sub-chaser. 4 hits by 3" deck gun.

22 **3-29-43:** 00-00', 118-18' E
Fired 5 torpedoes at tanker of *Kukuyo Maru* class. Heard 2 hits, screws stopped. Settling by stern to port. Then saw hit forward of bridge. Heard another hit forward of the stack. Debris blown 500' into air. 40–50° list to port. Crew allowed to observe sinking.

23 **3-29-43:** 00-54' N, 119-01' E
In a different attack on this date *Gudgeon* attacked a second tanker with 2 torpedoes. 11,000 ton tanker similar to *Ogura Maru*. Saw and heard 2 hits. Seen to sink by stern, with list to starboard. Boilers exploded. Boats in water. Crew abandoning ship which was seen to be going down fast. Received 6 bombs.

| 17 | Sunk 7,500 ton merchantman. | No credit given. | Miss. |

#	Wartime Credit	JANAC Credit	Alden
	None.	None.	None.

#	Wartime Credit	JANAC Credit	Alden
18	Sunk *Syoto Maru* class freighter of 5,254 tons.	No credit given.	Miss.
19	Sunk 6,965 ton freighter similar to *Taketoyu Maru*.	SUNK *Meigen Maru* 5,434 tons.	SUNK *Meigen Maru* 5,434 tons.
20	Damage to *Yuki Maru* class freighter.	No credit given.	Miss.
21	Damage to 290 ton patrol craft.	No credit given.	Probable damage to unidentified vessel.
22	Sunk 10,027 ton tanker of *Kokuyu Maru* class.	SUNK 9,997 ton *Toho Maru*.	SUNK 9,997 ton *Toho Maru*.
23	Sunk *Ogura Maru* class tanker of 7,311 tons.	No credit given.	Probable damage to *Kyoei Maru* #2, 1192 tons.

#	Eighth War Patrol – William S. Post Jr., skipper
24	**4-25-43–4-26-43**: 01-48' N, 119-11' E Fired 3 torpedoes at freighter. Premature explosion heard. A timed hit then a loud explosion was heard by CO. Target still afloat. Fired 3 more torpedoes. *Gudgeon* was charged by patrol craft, went deep and heard 2 explosions that sounded like torpedoes on target. Heard sounds like a ship breaking up. 20–30 small explosions.
25	**4-28-43**: 10-17' N, 121-44' E Fired 4 torpedoes at ship identified as the *Kamakura Maru* a 17,526 ton passenger vessel. Heard explosions. Ship sank so fast it was unbelievable. Internal explosion on magazine possibly. Bow rose into air and sank stern first.
26	**5-2-43**: 10-33' N, 121-51' E Fired 2 torpedoes at 1500 ton trawler. Missed. 23 DCs.
27	**5-4-43**: 10-10' N, 121-42' E Opened fire with 3"/50 deck gun on small trawler. Fired 96 rounds and 20 mm. guns. Saw trawler sink. Lost Lieutenant Penland.
28	**5-5-43**: 10-02' N, 121-46' E Fired 104 rounds of 3"/50 deck gun at small coastal-type passenger-freighter. Ran out of ammunition. Fired 20 mm guns. Left ship burning fiercely and slowly sinking near Iloilo.
29	**5-8-43**: 9-29' N, 123-29' E Attacked trawler-type patrol vessel with 2 torpedoes. Missed first one. May have had dud hit on second one. Attacked by 16 depth charges and deck guns.
30	**5-12-43**: 12-43' N, 124-08' E Fired last 2 torpedoes at ship similar to *Manko Maru*. Both missed and exploded on beach. *Gudgeon* out of 3"/50 ammunition. Claimed no damage to ship.

#	Ninth War Patrol – William S. Post Jr., skipper
31	**9-16-43**: 13-30' N, 144-34.5' E Fired 12 torpedoes by fours at ship similar to *Akagi Maru*. Visibility very poor. No explosions noted for first 8 torpedoes. "Heard, felt, and saw" 3 hits on 3rd group. Torpedo may have run under ship. Received 1 depth charge.

#	Wartime Credit	JANAC Credit	Alden
24	Damage to freighter of 9,000 tons.	No credit given.	Miss.
25	Sunk 17,526 ton *Kamakura Maru*.	SUNK *Kamakura Maru* 17,526 liner.	SUNK *Kamakura Maru* 17,526 ton liner.
26	None.	None.	
27	SUNK 500 ton trawler of *Naku Maru* class.	No credit given.	No credit given in book. In pvt. Letter, gives credit for sinking *Noku Maru.*
28	SUNK *Murasaki* class passenger freighter of 1,550 tons.	No credit given.	Probable sinking of 667 ton *Hanazo Maru.*
29	None.	None.	
30	None.	Despite *Gudgeon* claiming no hits, JANAC gave *Gudgeon* credit for having SUNK 5,862 ton cargo ship *Sumatra Maru* at exact location of *Gudgeon*'s reported attack.	TOTAL LOSS *Sumatra Maru.*
#	Wartime Credit	JANAC Credit	Alden
31	None.	None.	

32	**9-17-43**: 13-51' N, 145-02' E
	Charged Japanese patrol vessel which was signaling *Gudgeon*. Bullets were bouncing off the submarine's conning tower. *Gudgeon* answered with 5" shells. 85 shots, 2 hits. Ship listing to starboard, smoking heavily with "tongues of flame." Many distant explosions as *Gudgeon* withdrew.
33	**9-27-43**: 15-12' N, 145-40' E
	Attacked ship similar to *Akagi Maru* with 4 torpedoes. Missed.
34	**9-28-43**: 15-21' N, 145-37' E
	Attacked ship similar to *Matunoto Maru*, 7,061 tons with 4 torpedoes. Heard and saw 2 timed hits. Target squatted by stern and listed to starboard. Lifeboats in water. Ship gone. Took picture. 18 depth charges/bombs thrown *Gudgeon*.
35	**9-29-43**: 15-37.5' N, 145-52' E
	Attacked freighter with 2 torpedoes. Heard 1 timed hit. First target disappeared. Explosions heard. *Gudgeon* attacked by destroyer and patrol vessels.
36	**9-29-43**: Same location as above.
	Attacked second freighter with 2 torpedoes. 1 timed hit. Target listing to port and down by stern. Explosions heard. Received 26 depth charges. Evaded.

#	Tenth War Patrol – William S. Post Jr., skipper
37	**11-13-43**: 28-29' N, 129-29' E
	Fired 4 torpedoes, then 4 more. First 4 observed to have missed. One of second group blew up in torpedo net. Others missed.
38	**11-23-43**: 28-49' N, 122-11' E
	Attacked 10,000 ton freighter with 2 torpedoes. Freighter appeared undamaged.
39	**11-23-43**: Same location as above.
	Attacked 10,000 transport with 2 torpedoes. Crippled transport with 1 hit. Then fired 2 more torpedoes at transport. 1 more hit. Transport slowly settling and stopped. Fired 3 more torpedoes. 0 hits. Fired 2 more torpedoes. 0 hits. Fired 3 more torpedoes. Ship took on a starboard list and was observed to sink.
40	**11-23-43**: Same location as above.
	Attacked 10,000 ton tanker with 2 torpedoes. Absorbed 2 hits but kept going. PIP disappeared.
41	**11-23-43**: Same location as above.
	One of torpedoes intended for transport struck destroyer. Destroyer broke in two and sank in a vee in about a minute.

#	Wartime Credit	JANAC Credit	Alden
32	Damaged 600 ton patrol vessel.	No credit given.	Damage to *Fumi Maru* #2 Identity questionable. 304 ton mine-layer.
33	None.	None.	
34	SUNK *Matumoto Maru* type vessel of 7,061 tons.	SUNK *Taian Maru* a passenger cargo ship of 3,158 tons.	SUNK *Taian Maru* 3,158 tons.
35	Damaged *Attuta Maru* of 7,950 tons.	No credit given.	Miss
36	Damage to *Kansei Maru* type vessel of 8,610 tons.	No credit given.	Damage to *Santo Maru* a 3,266 converted gunboat.

#	Wartime Credit	JANAC Credit	Alden
37	None.	None.	SUNK *Tango Maru* 6893 ton cargo vessel.
38	SUNK 992 ton freighter of *Bunsyu Maru* class.	No credit given.	Miss.
39	SUNK 10,936 transport of *Husimi Maru* class.	SUNK *Nekka Maru* a 6,784 ton transport.	SUNK *Nekka Maru* an army transport.
40	Damaged 10,052 ton tanker of *Kyokuto Maru* class.	No credit given.	SUNK *Goyo Maru* 8,469 Tons.
41	SUNK 1,800 ton light cruiser of *Wakamiya* class.	SUNK *Wakamiya* a frigate of 860 tons.	SUNK *Wakamiya* which was an 870 ton frigate.

42	**11-27-43**: Originally sighted at 29-32' N, 140-28' E, attack 5 hours later. Exact location not known. Fired some 5" shells at subchaser from 9,000 yds. Missed.
43	**11-27-43**: Same location as above. Fired 5" shells at second sub-chaser. Sub-chaser withdrew.

 # Eleventh War Patrol – William S. Post Jr., skipper

44	**2-2-44**: 28-50' N, 138-07' E Charged destroyer. Fired 4 torpedoes "down his throat." *Gudgeon* dove. All torpedoes missed. 42 depth charges.
45	**2-2-44**: Same location as above. Fired 4 more "down the throat" at second destroyer. Went deep. 12 depth charges. All shots missed.
46	**2-11-44**: 27-38' N, 121-15' E Attacked large transport with 3 torpedoes. Murky smoke appeared after one or more hits. A faint explosion was heard.
47	**2-11-44**: Same location as above. Fired 3 torpedoes at small torpedo boat. Believe torpedoes ran underneath escort. 25 depth charges.
48	**2-11-44**: 27-38' N, 121-15' E Attacked same transport as earlier on this date with 3 torpedoes. Heard many explosions. Internal cracking up noises. Believe ship was hit twice. Ship was seen to be sinking with the bow resting on the bottom and the stern high in the air at a 30° angle. Distant explosions heard as Gudgeon departed.
49	**2-17-44**: 28-01' N, 123-23' E Attacked wooden diesel sampan of 50 tons with deck guns, including 20 mm and 5" deck guns. 52 rounds of 5" shells sank ship.
50	**2-17-44**: Same location as above. Attacked wooden diesel sampan of 50 tons with 20 mm deck gun and .50 caliber fire. Damaged ship before losing him in dark.

 # Twelfth War Patrol – Robert A. Bonin, skipper

Gudgeon lost. No attacks are known to have been made before *Gudgeon*'s sinking.

Note: John D. Alden's material originates from his book, *U.S. Submarine Attacks During World War II* and a privately printed updated version.

42	None.	None.	

43	None.	None.	

#	Wartime Credit	JANAC Credit	Alden
44	None.	None.	

45	None.	None.	

46	No credit given.	No credit given	

47	None.	None.	

48	SUNK large transport of unknown class and 10,000 tons.	No credit given.	½ sinking of 3,091 ton *Satsuma Maru.*

49	SUNK 50 ton sampan.	JANAC did not usually include ships this small in its report.	Probable sinking of unidentified ship.
50	Damaged 50 ton sampan.	JANAC did not usually include ships this small in its report.	Probable damage to unidentified ship.

#	Wartime Credit	JANAC Credit	Alden
	Unknown.	Unknown.	Unknown.

▪ Selected Bibliography ▪

Most books and articles that were referenced in order to research and write this book are listed below. With only a few exceptions author interviews, personal communications, and official military documents are only included with the Notes, when appropriate.

Alden, John Doughty. *The Fleet Submarine in the U.S. Navy: A Design and Construction History.* Annapolis, MD: Naval Institute Press, 1979.

————. *The Fleet Submarine in the U.S. Navy: A Design and Construction History.* Annapolis, MD: Naval Institute Press, 1985.

————. *U.S. Submarine Attacks During World War II: Including Allied Submarine Attacks in the Pacific Theater.* Annapolis, MD: Naval Institute Press, 1989.

Anti-Submarine Training and Equipment, Interrogation No. 63. Edited by the United States Strategic Bombing Survey. Vol. 1, *Interrogations of Japanese Officials.* Washington, D.C.: Government Printing Office, Naval Analysis Division, 1946.

Anti-Submarine Warfare, Interrogation No. 74. Edited by the United States Strategic Bombing Survey. Vol. 2, *Interrogations of Japanese Officials.* Washington D.C.: Government Printing Office, Naval Division, 1946.

"Artful Dodger." *Time,* December 5, 1949.

Austin, Aleine. *Matthew Lyon, "New Man" of the Democratic Revolution, 1749–1822.* University Park, PA: Pennsylvania State University Press, 1981.

Bagnasco, Erminio. *Submarines of World War Two.* Annapolis, MD: Naval Institute Press, 1977.

Blair, Clay. *Silent Victory: The U.S. Submarine War against Japan.* Annapolis, MD: Naval Institute Press, 2001.

Boyd, Carl, and Akihiko Yoshida. *The Japanese Submarine Force and World War II.* Annapolis, MD; Naval Institute Press, 1995.

Breuer, William B. *Retaking the Philippines: America's Return to Corregidor and Bataan, October 1944–March 1945.* New York: St. Martin's, 1986.

"Bulldogs Frown after a Look at Record, Written in Red." *The Butler Collegian,* October 30, 1940.

Bueschel, Richard M. *Mitsubishi/Nakajima G3m1/2/3 96 Rikko L3y1/2: In Japanese Naval Air Service, Schiffer Military/Aviation History*. Atglen, PA: Schiffer, 1997.

Campbell, N.J.M. *Naval Weapons of World War Two*. Annapolis, MD: Naval Institute Press, 1985.

Carpenter, Dorr, and Norman Polmar. *Submarines of the Imperial Japanese Navy*. Annapolis, MD: Naval Institute Press, 1986.

Chinard, Gibler. *Honest John Adams*. Boston: Little, Brown, 1933.

Coffin, Tris. "Washington Peep Show." *The Nation*, August 3, 1946.

Collins, Lewis, and Richard H. Collins. *Collins' Historical Sketches of Kentucky: History of Kentucky*. Covington, KY: Collins, 1882.

"The Cop Who Shot a Sailor: Court Continues Case Awaiting Boy's Recovery." *San Francisco Chronicle*, June 8, 1943.

"The Cop Who Shot a Sailor: More about Charge against S.F. Officer." *San Francisco Chronicle*, June 7, 1943.

"The Cop Who Shot a Sailor: S.F. Officer Is Charged with Intent to Kill." *San Francisco Chronicle,* June 7, 1943.

Cope, Harley Francis. *Serpent of the Seas, the Submarine*. New York and London: Funk & Wagnalls, 1942.

Cree, David. *Operations of the Fremantle Submarine Base 1942–1945*. Garden Island, N.S.W.: Naval Historical Society of Australia, 1976.

Dauer, Manning Julian. *The Adams Federalist*. Baltimore: Johns Hopkins Press, 1953.

Delaplane, Stanton. "Sub Commander Tells of Raid on Jap Shipping." *Buffalo Evening News Magazine*, July 18, 1942.

Detwiler, Donald S., and Charles Burton Burdick. *War in Asia and the Pacific, 1937–1949: A Fifteen Volume Collection*. New York: Garland, 1980.

Enright, Joseph F., and James W. Ryan. *Shinano!: The Sinking of Japan's Supership*. New York: St. Martin's Press, 1988.

Friedman, Norman. *U.S. Submarines through 1945: An Illustrated Design History*. Annapolis, MD; Naval Institute Press, 1995.

Gannon, Robert. *Hellions of the Deep: The Development of American Torpedoes in World War II*. University Park, PA: Pennsylvania State University Press, 1996.

"Garssons Get It." Newsweek, July 14, 1947.

Grenfell, Captain E.W. "A Japanese Q-Ship." *United States Naval Institute Proceedings* 79, no. 8 (1953): 899–900.

"Gudgeon Crew Cited." *New York Times*, October 1, 1943.

Guingona, Tito. *The Gallant Filipino*. Pasig, Metro Manila: Anvil Publishing, 1991.

Gunston, Bill. *An Illustrated Guide to Bombers of World War II.* New York: Prentice Hall Press, 1986.

"Handy Andy." *Time*, June 9, 1947.

Hart, B. H. Liddell. *History of the Second World War.* New York: G.P. Putnam's Sons, 1970.

Hashimoto, Mochitsura. *Sunk: the Story of the Japanese Submarine Fleet, 1941–1945.* New York: Holt, 1954.

Holmes, W.J. *Undersea Victory: The Influence of Submarine Operations on the War in the Pacific.* Garden City, NY: Doubleday, 1966.

Hoyt, Edwin Palmer. *Submarines at War: The History of the American Silent Service.* New York: Stein and Day, 1983.

Hunt, Ray C., and Bernard Norling. *Behind Japanese Lines: An American Guerilla in the Philippines.* Lexington, KY: University Press of Kentucky, 1986.

"In Shooting Case." *San Francisco Examiner*, June 8, 1943.

Ireland, Bernard, and Jane's Information Group. *Jane's Naval History of World War II*, New York: Harper Collins, 1998.

Japanese Airborne Magnetic Detector, Interrogation No 48. Edited by the United States Strategic Bombing Survey. Vol. 1, *Interrogations of Japanese Officials*. Washington D.C.: Government Printing Office: Naval Analysis Division, 1946.

The Japanese Air Forces in World War II: The Organization of the Japanese Army & Naval Air Forces. London: Arms and Armour Press, 1945.

Jentschura, Hansgeorg, Dieter Jung, and Peter Mickel. *Warships of the Imperial Japanese Navy, 1869–1945.* Annapolis, MD: Naval Institute Press, 1977.

Kamide, S. "Anti-Submarine Warfare," edited by Naval Analysis Division, 309–12. United States Strategic Bombing Survey, 1946.

Karamargin, Constantine. "USS Gudgeon 'Ship of Firsts'." *The Dolphin*, January 22, 1982.

Kaufman, Yogi, and Paul Stillwell. *Sharks of Steel.* Annapolis, MD: Naval Institute Press, 1993.

Kentucky Historical Society, and Bayless E. Hardin. "The Register of the Kentucky Historical Society." Frankfort, KY: Kentucky Historical Society, n.d.

Kentucky: A History of the State-Lyon Co. 3rd ed: Battle, Perrin & Kniffin, 1986.

Kerrigan, Evans E. *American War Medals and Decorations*, rev. ed. New York: Viking, 1971.

Kimmet, Larry, and Margaret Rogis. *U.S. Submarines in World War II: An Illustrated History.* Seattle: Navigator, 1996.

Koyama, Tadashi, "Japanese Capture of Wake Island." *Interrogation No. 95.* Edited by Naval Analysis Division, 370–73. United States Strategic Bombing Survey, 1946.

Lapham, Robert, and Bernard Norling. *Lapham's Raiders: Guerrillas in the Philippines, 1942–1945*. Lexington, KY: University Press of Kentucky, 1996.

"Largest School Vote Names Ten Outstanding Men." *The Butler Collegian*, February 18, 1941.

Launer, Jay. *The Enemies' Fighting Ships*. New York: Sheridan House, 1944.

Lockwood, Charles A. *Sink 'Em All: Submarine Warfare in the Pacific*. New York: Dutton, 1951.

Lott, Arnold S. *A Long Line of Ships: Mare Island's Century of Naval Activity in California*. Annapolis, MD: United States Naval Institute, 1954.

"Lt. Comdr. Strow to Be Decorated at Philadelphia." *Paducah Courier Journal*, October 29, 1945.

Mansfield, John, Jr. *Cruisers for Breakfast: War Patrols of the USS. Darter and USS. Dace*. Tacoma, WA: Media Center Publishing, 1997.

"Math Will Get Bill into Naval Reserve." *Daily Freeman Journal*, February 26, 1942.

"May Not." *Newsweek*, August 5, 1946.

McLaughlin, James Fairfax. *Matthew Lyon, the Hampden of Congress, a Biography*. New York: Wynkoop Gallenbeck Crawford, 1900.

Michno, Gregory. *USS Pampanito: Killer-Angel*. Norman, OK: University of Oklahoma Press, 2000.

Miller, David. *The Illustrated Directory of Submarines of the World*. London: Salamander, 2002.

Miller, Vernon J. *Japanese Submarine Losses to Allied Submarines*. Bennington, VT: Merrian Press, 1999.

"Mississippi Hero Orders Lunch during Fury of Jap Bomb Attack." *New Orleans Times-Picayune*, n.d.

Mitchell, Joseph B., and James Otis. *The Badge of Gallantry: Recollections of Civil War Congressional Medal of Honor Winners*. New York: Macmillan, 1968.

Mooney, James L., United States Naval History Division, and Naval Historical Center *Dictionary of American Naval Fighting Ships*. 8 vols. Washington D.C.: Navy Department, Office of the Chief of Naval Operations, 1959.

Mooney, James L., and Naval Historical Center (U.S.). *Dictionary of American Naval Fighting Ships*. Washington D.C.: Naval Historical Center, Government Printing Office, 1991.

Morison, Samuel Eliot. *The Two-Ocean War: A Short History of the United States Navy in the Second World War*. Boston: Little, 1963.

"New Charges Against Cop." *San Francisco Examiner*, June 15, 1943.

"Nineteen Are Listed in College Book of 'Who's Who'." *The Butler Collegian*, April 22, 1944.

"Obituary William C. Ostlund." *Daily Freeman Journal*, February 13, 1946.

Oi, Atushi. "Why Japan's Anti-Submarine Warfare Failed." *United States Naval Institute Proceedings*, 78, No. 6 (1952): 587–601.

Okamoto, T. "Japanese Airborne Magnetic Detector," edited by the Naval Analysis Division, 197–200: *United States Strategic Bombing Survey*, 1946.

Ostlund, Mike. "Corrections to Finding Uncle Bill." *The Submarine Review* (2002): 136–37.

———. "Finding Uncle Bill: Surprising New Information Uncovered about USS *Gudgeon*'s Loss in 1944." *The Submarine Review* (2001): 142–48.

Padfield, Peter. *War beneath the Sea: Submarine Conflict, 1939–1945*. London: John Murray, 1995.

Parillo, Mark. *The Japanese Merchant Marine in World War II*. Annapolis, MD: NavalInstitute Press.

Perrin, William Henry, J. H. Battle, and G. C. Kniffin. *Kentucky. A History of the State, Embracing a Concise Account of the Origin and Development of the Virginia Colony; Its Expansion Westward, and the Settlement of the Frontier Beyond the Alleghanies; the Erection of Kentucky as an Independent State, and Its Subsequent Development*. Louisville, KY and Chicago: F.A. Battey, 1886.

Poolman, Kenneth. *Allied Submarines of World War Two*. London: Arms and Armour Press, 1990.

"Portrait." *Newsweek*, August 4, 1947.

Professional Association of Diving Instructors. *The Encyclopedia of Recreational Diving*, 2nd ed. Santa Ana, CA: PADI, 1996.

Randall-Hinkle, David, Harry H. Caldwell, Arne C. Johnson, and Naval Submarine League (U.S.). *United States Submarines*. Annandale, VA: Naval Submarine League, 2002.

Reynolds, Clark C. *War in the Pacific*. New York: Military Press, 1990.

"Richard Marvin 'Dixie' Farrell." *Saratoga News*, December 6, 1995.

"Rites Set for Robert Dornin, Former NTC Commander." *San Diego Tribune*, September 1, 1982.

Robles, Philip K. *United States Military Medals and Ribbons*. Rutland, VT: C.E. Tuttle, 1971.

Roscoe, Theodore, and Richard G. Voge. *United States Submarine Operations in World War II*. Annapolis, MD: Naval Institute Press, 1949.

Rottman, Gordon L. *World War II Pacific Island Guide: A Geo-Military Study*. Westport, CT: Greenwood Press, 2002.

Rupp, Albert. *Beyond the Threshold*. Long Beach, CA: Almar Press, 1983.

———. *Threshold of Hell*. Long Beach, CA: Almar Press, 1983.

"Sailor on Sub Dreams of Wings." *The New York Sun*, May 13, 1943.

"Services Slated Monday for Rear Admiral W.S. Stovall." *The San Diego Union*, January 1, 1966.

Smith, Page. *John Adams*. Garden City, NY: Doubleday, 1962.

Smith, William Ward. *Midway: Turning Point of the Pacific*. New York: Crowell, 1966.

"Snap, Crackle, Pop." *Time*, August 5, 1946.

Stone, Peter, Mabel Holland, John Holland, and Frank Holland. *El Tigre: Frank Holland, M.B.E.—Commando, Coastwatcher.* Yarram, Vic., Australia: Oceans Enterprises, 1999.

"Submarine Gudgeon Gets Unit Citation." *New York Times*, December 28, 1943.

"Submarine Operations." *United States Naval Institute Proceedings*, 69, no. 5 (1942): 719–20.

"Submarines Neutralized Jap Base at Truk to Speed Advance on Tokyo." *The Courier-Journal*, June 1, 1945.

Submarine Veterans of World War II: A History of the Veterans of the United States Naval Submarine Fleet. Dallas, TX: Taylor Publishing, 1986.

Supreme Commander for the Allied Powers, and Douglas Macarthur. *Reports of General Macarthur*. Washington, D.C.: Superintendent of Documents, Government Printing Office, 1966.

"Suspend Cop in Shooting." *San Francisco Examiner*, June 7, 1943.

Sweeney, James B. *A Pictorial History of Oceanographic Submersibles*. New York: Crown Publishers, 1970.

"Thirty-nine Hinklemen Complete 40 Grid Season with View of Good, Bad; Lucky, Unlucky." *The Butler Collegian*, September 10, 1940.

Thorpe, Donald W. *Japanese Naval Air Force Camouflage and Markings, World War II*. Fallbrook, CA: Aero Publishers, 1977.

"Three Brothers Officers." *Daily Freeman Journal*, April 5, 1944.

"Trial: The Cumberland Job." *Newsweek*, May 19, 1947.

"Two Day Poll of 1,500 Will Confer 'BMOC'." *The Butler Collegian*, February 12, 1941.

United States Submarine Veterans of World War II. Taylor Publishing Company, 1986.

"U.S. Skippers Tell Submarine Sagas." *New York Times*, August 28, 1943.

U. S. Congress. House. Committee of Privileges. *Report of the Committee of Privileges, to Whom Was Referred, on the Sixteenth Instant, a Motion for the Expulsion of Roger Griswold and Matthew Lyon, Members of This House, for Riotous and Disorderly Behaviour, Committed in the House, 20th February, 1798, Ordered to Lie on the Table*. 5th Cong., 2d sess., 1797–1798. Committee Print.

U.S. Congress. Senate. Committee on Veterans' Affairs. *Medal of Honor Recipients, 1863–1978: "In the Name of the Congress of the United States."* Washington, D.C.: Government Printing Office, 1979.

U.S. Joint Army-Navy Assessment Committee. *Japanese Naval and Merchant Shipping Losses During World War II by All Causes.* Washington, D.C.: Government Printing Office, 1947.

U.S. Navy Pacific Fleet. Submarine Force. *U.S. Submarine Losses, World War II.* Washington D.C.: Government Printing Office, 1949.

U.S. Office of the Chief of Naval Operations. *United States Naval Chronology, World War II.* Washington D.C.: Government Printing Office, 1955.

U.S. Office of the Chief of Naval Operations, and Ernest Joseph King. *U.S. Navy at War, 1941–1945: Official Reports to the Secretary of the Navy.* Washington, D.C.: U.S. Navy Department, 1946.

"USS Gudgeon (SS 211)." *Polaris*, April 1977.

Van der Vat, Dan. *The Pacific Campaign: World War II, the U.S.–Japanese Naval War, 1941–1945.* New York: Simon & Schuster, 1991.

Villamor, Jesus A., and Gerald S. Snyder. *They Never Surrendered: A True Story of Resistance in World War II.* Quezon City, Philippines: Vera-Reyes, 1982.

Watts, Anthony John. *Allied Submarines.* New York. Arco, 1977.

Wheeler, Keith. *War Under the Pacific,* vol. 23, *World War II.* Alexandria, VA: Time-Life Books, 1980.

Wheeler, Richard. *Iwo.* New York: Lippincott & Crowell, 1980.

Willoughby, Charles Andrew. *The Guerrilla Resistance Movement in the Philippines, 1941–1945.* New York: Vantage, 1972.

Withers, Rear Admiral Thomas. "Preparation of Submarines Pacific for War." *U.S. Naval Institute Proceedings*, 76, no. 4 (1950): 387–93.

▪ Notes ▪

Chapter 1

1. Irvin Hornkohl, author interviews by telephone or in person.
2. Ibid.
3. Ibid.
4. Arthur Barlow, author interviews by telephone.
5. Ibid.
6. Ibid.
7. Ibid.
8. After torpedo room workbook, USS *Gudgeon*.
9. Eleanor Farrell, author interviews by telephone.
10. Ibid.
11. Ibid.
12. Ibid.
13. John Ostlund, author interviews by telephone or in person.
14. From records contained at Kendall Young Library, Webster City, Iowa.
15. Elton W. Grenfell, Rough Outline of Rear Admiral Grenfell's Early Tour in the USS *Gudgeon* (SS211), unpublished document, 2.
16. Robert E. Dornin, "Narrative by Robert E. Dornin, *USN*," Office of Naval Records and Library, 1943, 19.
17. Jack Camp, "Diary of Jack E. Camp, EM1," National Archives.
18. Ibid.
19. Grenfell, Outline, 2.
20. Ibid, 2.
21. Theodore Roscoe, *United States Submarine Operations in World War II*, (Annapolis: Naval Institute Press, 1949), 12.
22. B. H. Liddell Hart, *History of the Second World War* (New York: G. P. Putnam's Sons, 1970), 682.
23. Camp, Diary.
24. Ibid.
25. Ibid.
26. Ray Foster, author interviews by telephone or in person.
27. Wilfrid J. Holmes, *Undersea Victory: The Influence of Submarine Operations on the War in the Pacific* (New York: Doubleday & Company, Inc., 1966), 3.
28. Grenfell, Outline, 2.

29. Martha Grenfell, author interviews by telephone.
30. Thomas Withers, "Preparation of Submarines Pacific for War," *US Naval Institute Proceedings*, April, 1950, 76, no. 4, 393.
31. *Lucky Bag*, 1926, 525.
32. Ibid., 525.
33. Elton W. Grenfell, "Vice Admiral Elton W. Grenfell, U.S. Navy Retired," biography, Navy Office of Information, 1.
34. *Lucky Bag*, n.p., n.d.
35. *Lucky Bag*, 1939(?), n.p.
36. Grenfell, Outline, 3.
37. Quent Seiler, author interviews by telephone or in person.
38. Camp, Diary.
39. [Elton W. Grenfell?], "Sub Commander Tells of Raid on Jap Shipping," *Buffalo Evening News Magazine*, July 18, 1942, 1.
40. Elton W. Grenfell, "War Diary," unpublished document may be obtained at Hoover Institution, Stanford University, Stanford, California.
41. Camp, Diary.
42. Grenfell, Outline, 4–5.
43. Dornin, Narrative, 11.
44. Ray Foster, author interviews by telephone or in person.
45. Ibid.
46. USS *Gudgeon* First War Patrol Report, 3.
47. Grenfell, Diary.
48. Dornin, Narrative, 1.
49. Camp, Diary.
50. Ibid.
51. Foster interviews.
52. Ibid.
53. Wendell Webb, "U. S. Commander Says Napping Sub Soon 'Wasn't There,'" source unknown, n.d.
54. Holmes, *Victory*, 16.
55. [Grenfell?], *Raid*, 1.
56. Grenfell, Outline, 5.
57. Ibid, 5.
58. Ibid, 6.
59. Foster interviews.
60. Camp, Diary.
61. Dornin, Narrative, 16.
62. Ibid, 17.
63. Ibid, 1.
64. Constantine Karamargin, "USS *Gudgeon* 'Ship of Firsts,'" *The Dolphin*, January 22, 1982, 12.

65. Forrest M. O'Leary to ComSubPac, memorandum, Endorsement for First War Patrol of USS *Gudgeon*, February 3, 1942.
66. Allan. R. McCann to ComSubPac, memorandum, Endorsement for First War Patrol of the USS *Gudgeon*, February 3, 1942.
67. Foster interviews.
68. Norman S. Ives to ComSubPac, memorandum, Endorsement for First War Patrol of the USS *Pollack*, February 6, 1942.
69. Foster interviews.

Chapter 2
1. Jack Camp, "Diary of Jack E. Camp, EM1," National Archives.
2. Ibid.
3. Ibid.
4. Irvin Hornkohl, author interviews by telephone or in person.
5. Ibid.
6. Ibid.
7. Ibid.
8. Ray Foster, author interviews by telephone or in person.
9. Camp, Diary.
10. Ibid.
11. Captain E.W. Grenfell, "A Japanese Q-Ship," *US Naval Institute Proceedings*, 1953, 79, no. 8, 899.
12. Grenfell, Q-Ship, 899.
13. Hornkohl interviews.
14. Camp Diary.
15.–18. Ibid.
19. Hornkohl interviews.
20. Ibid.
21. Ibid.
22. Ibid.
23. Grenfell, Q-Ship, 899.
24. Foster interviews.
25. Robert E. Dornin, "Narrative by Robert E. Dornin, USN," Office of Naval Records and Library, 1943, 15.
26. Camp Diary.
27. Foster interviews.
28. Ibid.
29. Ibid.
30. Hornkohl interviews.
31. Ibid.
32. Camp Diary.
33. Ibid.

34. Foster interviews.
35. Ibid.
36. Ibid.
37. Elton W. Grenfell, personal log of the second war patrol of the USS *Gudgeon*, [in possession of author].
38. Camp log.
39. USS *Gudgeon* Second War Patrol Report, 14.
40. Dornin, Narrative, 2.
41. Richard M. Farrell, "Officer Biography Sheet," Navy Office of Information, 1958.
42. *Gudgeon*, Second Report, 19.
43. Forrest M. O'Leary to ComSubPac, memorandum, Endorsement for Second War Patrol of the USS *Gudgeon*, April 16, 1942.
44. Allan R. McCann to ComSubPac, memorandum, Endorsement for Second War Patrol of the USS *Gudgeon*, April 17, 1942.
45. Ibid.

Chapter 3
1. Clay Blair, *Silent Victory: The US Submarine War Against Japan* (Annapolis: Naval Institute Press, 1975), 212.
2. US Congress, *Report of the Committee of Privileges* (Washington: House of Representatives, 1798), 4.
3. John Wood, *The Suppressed History of the Administration of John Adams: From 1797 to 1801* (Philadelphia, 1846), 111.
4. *Report of the Committee of Privileges [For the expulsion of Roger Griswold and Matthew Lyon]* [Washington?], 1798.
5. Page Smith, *John Adams* (Westport, CT: Greenwood Press Publishers, 1963), 950.
6. Kentucky Historical Society, *The Register of the Kentucky Historical Society* (Frankfurt, KY: Kentucky Historical Society, 1964), 194.
7. *Lucky Bag*, 1931(?), n.p.
8. Forrest M. O'Leary to ComSubPac, memorandum, Endorsement for Third War Patrol of the USS *Gudgeon*, June 16, 1942.
9. Quent Seiler, author interviews by telephone or in person.
10.–17. Ibid.
18. USS *Gudgeon* Third War Patrol Report, 3.
19. Ibid. 4.
20. Ray Foster, author interviews by telephone or in person.
21. *Gudgeon*, Third Report, 7.
22. Foster interviews.
23. Blair, *Silent Victory*, 242.
24. Robert E. Dornin, "Narrative by Robert E. Dornin, USN," Office of Naval Records and Library, 1943, 3.

Chapter 4

1. Quent Seiler, author interviews by telephone or in person.
2. Ibid.
3. Ibid.
4. *Lucky Bag*, 1929(?), n.p.
5. Albert Rupp, *Threshold of Hell* (Long Beach: Almar Press, 1985), 3.
6. Rupp, *Threshold*, 3.
7. Seiler interviews.
8. Ibid.
9. Ibid.
10. Ibid.
11. Ibid.
12. Irvin Hornkohl, author interviews by telephone or in person.
13. Albert Strow, wartime personal log.
14. Ibid.
15. Ibid.
16. Ibid.
17. Ibid.
18. USS *Gudgeon* Fourth War Patrol Report, 4.
19. Ray Foster, author interviews by telephone or in person.
20. Ibid.
21. Ibid.
22. Ibid.
23. Seiler interviews.
24. Foster interviews.
25. Hornkohl interviews.
26. Strow log.
27. Ibid.
28. William Shirley Stovall Jr., "Narrative by Commander W. Shirley Stovall, Jr.," Office of Naval Records and Library, 1943, 15.
29. Hornkohl interviews.
30. Seiler interviews.
31. Ibid.
32. Hornkohl interviews.
33. Foster interviews.
34. Stovall, Narrative, 13.
35. Ibid., 14.
36. Seiler interviews.
37. Strow log.
38. Ibid.
39. Ibid.
40. Stovall, Narrative, 14.
41. Foster interviews.

42. *Gudgeon*, Fourth Report, 10.
43. Seiler interviews.
44. Hornkohl interviews.
45. Rupp, *Threshold*, 5.
46. Ibid, 5.
47. Hornkohl interviews.
48. Ibid.
49. Strow log.
50.–61. Ibid.
62. Seiler interviews.
63. Ibid.
64. Strow log.
65. *Gudgeon*, Fourth report, 13.
66. Seiler interviews.
67. Strow log.
68. Rupp, *Threshold*, 6.
69. *Gudgeon*, Fourth Report. n.p.
70. Charles A. Lockwood, Jr. to ComSubPac, memorandum, Endorsement for Fourth War Patrol of the USS *Gudgeon*, September 14, 1942.
71. Frank Knox, Award of Navy Cross to Lt. Cmdr. William S. Stovall Jr.
72. Strow log.
73. Clay Blair, *Silent Victory: The US Submarine War Against Japan* (Annapolis: Naval Institute Press, 1975), 312.

Chapter 5
1. Quent Seiler, author interviews by telephone or in person.
2.–7. Ibid.
8. Irvin Hornkohl, author interviews by telephone or in person.
9. Strow log.
10.–18. Ibid.
19. Robert Gannon, *Hellions of the Deep* (University Park, PA: The Pennsylvania State University Press, 1996), 91.
20. Strow log.
21. Ibid.
22. Ibid.
23. Edward Hammond, author interviews by telephone.
24. Ray Foster author, author interviews by telephone or in person.
25. Robert E. Dornin, "Narrative by Robert E. Dornin, USN," Office of Naval Records and Library, 1943, 4.
26. Seiler interviews.
27. Arthur Barlow, author interviews by telephone.
28. USS *Gudgeon* Fifth War Patrol Report, 29.
29. Ibid.

30. Dornin, Narrative, 5.
31. Strow log.
32. Ibid.
33. Dornin, Narrative, 6.
34. Dornin, Narrative, 11.
35. Strow log.
36.–42. Ibid.
43. *Gudgeon*, Fifth Report, 49.
44. Ibid., 51.
45. Ibid.
46. Ralph W. Christie to The Commander-in-Chief US Fleet, Endorsement for Fifth War Patrol of the USS *Gudgeon*, December 4, 1942.
47. Ibid.
48. William F. Halsey to The Commander-in-Chief, US Fleet, Endorsement for Fifth War Patrol of the USS *Gudgeon*, December 4, 1942.
49. Ibid.
50. "10-Shots—10 Japanese Hits," newspaper article, source unknown, n.d.

Chapter 6

1. Quent Seiler, author interviews by telephone or in person.
2. Ray Foster, author interviews by telephone or in person.
3. Ron Schooley, author interviews by telephone.
4. Foster interviews.
5. Seiler interviews.
6. Ibid.
7. Ibid.
8. Ibid.
9. Irvin Hornkohl, author interviews by telephone or in person.
10. Jesus A. Villamor, *They Never Surrendered* (Quezon City, PI: Vera-Reyes, Inc., 1982), 1.
11. Ibid., 1
12. Hornkohl interviews.
13. Villamor, *Surrendered*, 29.
14. Ibid., 29.
15. Ibid., 29.
16. Ibid., 7.
17. Ibid., 5.
18. Ibid., 5.
19. Ibid., 19.
20. Frank Holland M.B.E., *El Tigre*, (Yarram, AU: Oceans Enterprises, 1999) 134.
21. Ibid., 134.
22. Ibid., 134.
23. Ibid., 134.

24. Ibid., 135.
25. USS *Gudgeon* Sixth War Patrol Report, 21.
26. Seiler interviews.
27. Schooley interviews.
28. Hornkohl interviews.
29. Arthur Barlow, author interviews by telephone.
30. "Sailor on Sub Dreams of Wings," *New York Sun*, May 13, 1943. n.p.
31. Narrative by Commander W. Shirley Stovall, jr., 1943, 9.
32. Holland, *Tigre*, 136.
33. *Gudgeon*, Sixth Report, 27.
34. Frank Holland, unpublished manuscript.
35. Ibid.
36. Holland, *Tigre*, 145.
37. Ibid., 145.
38. Ibid.
39. William S. Stovall Jr., Evacuation of a Party of Twenty-Eight Men from the Island of Timor, report of, February 15, 1943, 3.
40. Hornkohl interviews.
41. Ibid.
42. Ibid.
43. G. B. Courtney, *Silent Feet: The History of 'Z' Special Operations 1942–1945* (McCrae, VIC: R. J. & S. P. Austin, 1993), 203.
44. Foster interviews.
45. Ibid.
46. Hornkohl interviews.
47.–51. Ibid.
52. Frank Holland unpublished document.
53. Holland, *Tigre*, 148.
54. Holland, *Tigre*, 152.
55. Foster interviews.
56. Hornkohl interviews.
57. Hornkohl interviews.
58. *Gudgeon*, Sixth Report, 39.
59. Allan R. McCann to Commander Task Force Fifty-One, Endorsement for Sixth War Patrol of the USS *Gudgeon*, February 22, 1943.
60. Ibid.
61. Clay Blair, *Silent Victory: The US Submarine War Against Japan*, 357.
62. McCann, sixth patrol letter.
63. Robert E. Dornin, "Narrative by Robert E. Dornin," USN, Office of Naval Records and Library, 1943, 10.
64. "10-Shots—10 Japanese Hits", newspaper article, source unknown, n.d.
65. Ibid.
66. Ibid.

Chapter 7

1. *Lucky Bag*, 1930, n.p.
2. Ibid.
3. Edwin P. Hoyt, *Submarines at War* (New York: Stein and Day, 1983), 93.
4. Thomas P. Withers, Letter of Commendation, April 2, 1942.
5. *Lucky Bag*, 1937, n.p.
6. Quent Seiler, author interviews by telephone or in person.
7.–11. Ibid.
12. USS *Gudgeon* Seventh War Patrol Report, 1.
13. William S. Post Jr., "Narrative by Lieutenant Commander W. S. Post, USN," 1943, 6.
14. Ibid., 6.
15. Ibid., 6.
16. Ibid., 7.
17. Robert Trumbull, "US Skippers Tell Submarine Sagas," *New York Times*, August 28, 1943, n.p
18. Ron Schooley, author interviews by telephone.
19. Seiler interviews.
20. Ibid.
21. *Gudgeon*, Seventh Report, 5.
22. Ibid., 6.
23. Ibid., 6.
24. Seiler interviews.
25. Post, *Narrative*, 10.
26. Seiler interviews.
27. "Submarine Operations," *US Naval Institute Proceedings*, May 1942, 720.
28. Seiler interviews.
29. Ibid.
30. Ibid.
31. Irvin Hornkohl, author interviews by telephone or in person.
32. Ibid.
33. Seiler interviews.
34. Ibid.
35. *Gudgeon*, Seventh Report, 8.
36. *Gudgeon*, Seventh Report, 8.
37. Seiler interviews.
38. Hornkohl interviews.
39. Seiler interviews.
40. Hornkohl interviews.
41. Seiler interviews.
42. Ibid.
43. *Gudgeon*, Seventh Report, 8.
44. Hornkohl interviews.

45. Seiler interviews.
46. Ibid.
47. Hornkohl interviews.
48. Ray Foster, author interviews by telephone or in person.
49. Gudgeon, Seventh Report, 8.
50. *Gudgeon*, Seventh Report, 8.
51. Ibid., 8.
52. Ibid., 8.
53. Seiler interviews.
54. Ibid.
55. After torpedo room workbook USS *Gudgeon*.
56. Albert Strow, wartime personal log.
57. *Gudgeon*, Seventh Report, 11.
58. Edward Hammond author interviews by telephone.
59. *Gudgeon*, Seventh Report, 12.
60. Ibid., 12.
61. Ibid., 13.
62. Seiler interviews.
63. *Gudgeon*, Seventh Report, 1.
64. Seiler interviews.
65. *Gudgeon*, Seventh Report, 27.
66. *Gudgeon*, Seventh Report, n.p.
67. Seiler interviews
68. Strow log.
69. William Wakefield to Commander Task Force Seventy-One, memorandum, Endorsement for War Patrol Seven of the USS *Gudgeon*, April 7, 1943.
70. Ibid.
71. Ralph W. Christie to Commander-in-Chief US Fleet, memorandum, Endorsement for Seventh War Patrol of the USS *Gudgeon*, April 11, 1943.
72. Seiler interviews.
73. Christie, Seventh Patrol Endorsement.
74. Ibid.
75. Ibid.
76. Frank Knox, Award of Silver Star to Lt. Albert R. Strow.
77. Frank Knox, Award of Navy Cross to Lt. Cmdr. William S. Post Jr.

Chapter 8
1. Quent Seiler, author interviews by telephone or in person.
2.–8. Ibid.
9. Ron Schooley, author interviews by telephone.
10. Ibid.
11. Ibid.
12. USS *Gudgeon* Eighth War Patrol Report, 1.
13. *Lucky Bag*, n.p.

14. USS *Gudgeon* Eighth Report, 3.
15. After torpedo room workbook USS *Gudgeon*.
16. Albert Strow, wartime personal log.
17. Ibid.
18. Ibid.
19. *Gudgeon*, Eighth Report, 5.
20. Irvin Hornkohl, author interviews by telephone or in person.
21. Ibid.
22. Schooley interviews.
23. Strow log.
24. William S. Post Jr., "Narrative by Lieutenant Commander W. S. Post," USN, Office of Naval Records and Library, 1943, 27.
25. Seiler interviews.
26. Schooley interviews.
27. *Gudgeon*, Eighth Report, 7.
28. Ibid., 7
29. Ibid., 7
30. Strow log.
31. Seiler interviews.
32. Navy Combat Art Collection, Kn-21777.
33. Schooley interviews.
34. John Sheridan family interview.
35. Mark P. Parillo, *The Japanese Merchant Marine in World War II* (Annapolis: Naval Institute Press, 1993), 146.
36. William S. Post Jr., Report of Special Mission, May 25, 1943, 3.
37. Arthur Barlow, author interviews by telephone.
38. Seiler interviews.
39. Ibid.
40. Ibid.
41. Strow log.
42. William S. Post Jr., "Narrative by Lieutenant Commander W. S. Post, USN," Office of Naval Records and Library, 1943, 30.
43. Seiler interviews.
44. Ibid.
45. *Gudgeon*, Eighth Report, 11.
46. Ibid.
47. Ibid., 12.
48. Ibid., 12.
49. Edward Hammond, author interviews by telephone.
50. Ibid.
51. Torpedo room workbook.
52. Hammond interviews.
53. Seiler interviews.
54. Clark G. Reynolds, *War in the Pacific* (New York: Military Press, 1990), 60.

55. Ralph W. Christie to Commander Seventh Fleet, memorandum, Endorsement for the Special Mission-USS *Gudgeon*, June 19, 1943.
56. Charles A. Lockwood, Jr. to Submarine Force Pacific Fleet, memorandum, Endorsement for the Eighth War Patrol of the USS *Gudgeon*, May 29, 1943.
57. Ibid.
58. Ibid.

Chapter 9
1. Quent Seiler, author interviews by telephone or in person.
2. Seiler interviews.
3. "The Cop Who Shot a Sailor," *San Francisco Chronicle*, June 7, 1943, n.p.
4. Ibid.
5. Seiler interviews.
6.–22. Ibid.
23. After torpedo room workbook USS *Gudgeon*.
24. Ibid.
25. USS *Gudgeon* Ninth War Patrol Report, 22.
26. Dive workbook USS *Gudgeon*.
27. Torpedo room workbook.
28. Albert Strow audio recording, n.d.
29. *Gudgeon* Ninth Report, 28.
30. Ibid.
31. Strow log.
32. USS Gudgeon Ninth War Patrol Report, 7.
33. Torpedo room workbook.
34. Ibid.
35. Dive workbook.
36. *Gudgeon*, Ninth Report, 28.
37. Dive workbook.
38. *Gudgeon*, Ninth Report, 30.
39. Ibid., 11.
40. Ibid., 32.
41. Ibid., 12.
42. Ibid., 34.
43. Ibid., 34.
44. Ibid., 36.
45. Ibid., 47.
46. Ibid., 36.
47. Ibid., 36.
48. Charles A. Lockwood Jr. to The Commander-in-Chief US Fleet, memorandum, Endorsement for the Ninth War Patrol of the USS *Gudgeon*, October 14, 1943.
49. Ibid.
50. Ibid.

Chapter 10

1. Bob Ostlund comment to author.
2. *Torch.* 1936, n.p.
3. "Seniors Pick Two Likely to Succeed," *The Butler Collegian*, n.d., n.p.
4. "Japs Give Warning," *The Butler Collegian*, Feb. 18, 1941, n.p.
5. "Math Will Get Bill Into Naval Reserve," Feb. 26, 1942. *Daily Freeman Journal*, 1.
6. Ibid.
7. Deck Log USS *Gudgeon*, October 22, 1943.
8. Article from unknown newspaper, 9-15-44.
9. Albert Strow, wartime personal log.
10.–19. Ibid.
20. Strow log.
21. Quent Seiler, author interviews by telephone or in person.
22. USS *Gudgeon* Tenth War Patrol Report, 20.
23. Seiler interviews.
24. Irvin Hornkohl, author interviews by telephone or in person.
25. Strow log.
26.–34. Ibid.
35. *The Gudgeonian*, Volume One, Number One.
36.–40. Ibid.
41. Strow log.
42. Ibid.
43. Ibid.
44. Ibid.
45. Ibid.
46. *Gudgeon*, Tenth Report, 7.
47. Strow log.
48.–51. Ibid.
52. *The Gudgeonian*, Volume One, Number 2.
53. Ibid.
54. Ibid.
55. Ibid.
56. Strow log.
57. *Gudgeon*, Tenth Report, 9.
58. Ibid.
59. Ibid, 25.
60. Dive Workbook USS *Gudgeon*.
61. Strow log.
62. Ibid.
63. Ibid.
64. Ibid.
65. *The Gudgeonian*, Volume 1, Number 8.
66. Strow log.

67.–84. Ibid.

85. *Gudgeon,* Tenth Report, 33.

86. Ibid., 33.

87. Ibid., 33.

88. Ibid., 40.

89. Ibid, 33.

Chapter 11

1. Frederick B. Warder to The Commander-in-Chief US Fleet, memorandum, Endorsement for the Tenth War Patrol of the USS *Gudgeon*, December 16, 1943.

2. John H. Brown to The Commander-in-Chief United States Fleet, memorandum, Endorsement for the Tenth War Patrol of the USS *Gudgeon*, December 21, 1943.

3. Ibid.

4. Warder, Tenth Patrol Letter, 1943.

5. Frank Knox, Award of Presidential Unit Citation to the USS *Gudgeon*, 1943.

6. USS *Gudgeon* Eleventh War Patrol Report, 4.

7. USS *Gudgeon* Eleventh Report, 4.

8. Albert Strow, wartime personal log.

9. *Gudgeon*, Eleventh Report, 23.

10. *Gudgeon*, Eleventh Report, 5.

11. Dive workbook USS *Gudgeon*.

12. Quent Seiler, author interviews by telephone or in person.

13. Ibid.

14. *Gudgeon*, Eleventh Report, 9.

15. Dive workbook USS *Gudgeon*.

16. Ibid.

17. *Gudgeon* Eleventh Report, 30.

18. *Gudgeon* Eleventh Report, 30.

19. W. V. O'Kegan to The Commander-in-Chief US Fleet, memorandum, Endorsement for Eleventh War Patrol of the USS *Gudgeon*, March 8, 1944.

20. Charles Momsen to The Commander-in-Chief US Fleet, memorandum, Endorsement for the Eleventh War Patrol of the USS *Gudgeon*, March 11, 1944.

21. Charles A. Lockwood Jr. to The Commander-in-Chief US Fleet, Endorsement for Eleventh War Patrol of the USS *Gudgeon*, March 19, 1944.

Chapter 12

1. USS *Gudgeon* Ninth War Patrol Report, 34.

2. USS *Gudgeon* Eleventh War Patrol Report, 31.

3. *Gudgeon*, Eleventh Report, 35.

4. Arthur Barlow, author phone interviews.

5. Constantine Karamargin, "USS Gudgeon 'Ship of Firsts'," *The Dolphin*, January 22, 1982.
6. Mary Post, author phone interview, August 5, 2001.
7. *Lucky Bag*, 1936(?), n.p.
8. Edward L. Beach, author phone interview, May 12, 2002.
9. Ibid.
10. *Lucky Bag*, 1941, 249.
11. Ibid. 249.
12. "3 Brothers Officers," *Daily Freeman Journal*, April 6, 1944, n.p.
13. "USS *Gudgeon* ships of firsts," *The Dolphin*, January 22, 1982.
14. Ibid.
15. Vice Admiral Randall Jacobs to Regis Bonin, telegram, June 7, 1944.

Chapter 13

1. Conversation with Bob Ostlund.
2. Charles A. Lockwood, Jr., "USS *Gudgeon* (SS211) Loss of," n.d.
3. *Brinkley's Japanese-English Dictionary* (The University of Michigan Press: Ann Arbor, MI),1963, 1660.
4. "Nephew Discovers Clues to WWII Sub Mystery," *The Des Moines Register*, February 13, 2003, 3b.
5. Noritika Kitazawa to Mike Ostlund, August 30, 2001.
6. Ibid.
7. Conversation with a historian, by telephone, June 2001.
8. Conversation with author.
9. Comment by author.
10. War records of the Chichi Jima-Houmen base (901 Kokutai), April 1944.
11.–14. Ibid.
15. Jiro Kimata, *Teki Sensuikan Kogeki*, Asahi Sonoroma, 1982, n.p.
16. Ibid.
17. Ibid.
18. Ibid.
19. Edward L. Beach author phone interview, May 12, 2002.
20. Ibid.
21. Ibid.
22. Arthur Barlow, author phone interviews.
23. Quent Seiler, author personal or phone interview.

Afterword

1. Keith Dodson to Mike Ostlund, email, March 23, 2003.
2. Ibid.
3. Robert O. Phillips to Mike Ostlund, May 20, 2002.
4. Ibid.
5. Frank Holland, *El Tigre* (Yarram, AU: Oceans Enterprises), 188.

6. Ibid., 118–119.
7. Clay Blair, *Silent Victory: The US Submarine War Against Japan*, p. 714.
8. Irvin Hornkohl, author interviews by telephone or in person.
9. Alexander Sheffs to George Seiler, April, 1986.
10. Slade Cutter, author interview by telephone.
11. Hylan B. Lyon Jr. author interview, April 2002.
12. Quent Seiler, author interviews by telephone or in person.
13. Hornkohl interviews.
14. Arthur Barlow, author interviews by telephone.
15. Shirley Thorup, author interview by telephone, May 2002.
16. Edward L. Beach, author interview by telephone, May 12, 2002.
17. Cutter interview.
18. Ibid.
19. Ibid.
20. Eleanor Farrell, author interviews by telephone.
21. Dick Cotton, author interview, St. Louis, August 2001.
22. Patrick Cilliacus, author interview, St. Louis, August 2001.
23. Claude Pilcher, author interview, St. Louis, August 2001.
24. Cutter interview.
25. Hornkohl interviews.
26.–35. Ibid.
36. Seiler interviews.
37.–53. Ibid.
54. Peggy Reid, author interview by telephone.
55. Seiler interviews.
56. Hornkohl interviews.
57. John Sheridan, interviewed by family.

▪ Index ▪

and depth charges, 166–67,
168–69, 183
description of submergence, 203
and dolphin insignia, 19
first in US, 15
Japanese, 32
liquor on, 253–54
lost in WWII, 151, 373
maneuvering to targets, 23–24
minority sailors on, 37
names of, 15–16
number of patrols, 259
overhauls on, 266
and phosphorescent wakes, 20
sinking merchant ships, 12
squadrons of, 16
Tambor class, 14
and "torpedo juice," 88
venereal disease on, 219–20
war patrols from Brisbane, 191–92
wartime patrol experience of,
25–26
Submarine Squadron Six, 36, 50–51, 259
lost submarines of, 373
at Midway Island, 81

T
Taian Maru, 274
Tambor class submarines, 14
Teki Sensuikan Kogeki "Enemy Submarine
Attack" (Kimata), 362
Tellier, Douglas, 337
They Never Surrendered (Villamor), 155
Thomas, William, 179–80
Threshold of Hell (Rupp), 93, 380
Timor, Allied commandoes in, 162–65,
169–70, 171–73
evacuation of, 173–81
Tonan Maru III, 132
Torpedo Data Computer (TDC), 24
Torpedoes
cost of, 18
improvements of, 312
Mark 14, 38–39, 64
problems with, 24, 39–40, 98, 132
shortage of, 23, 41, 233
specifications of, 131
"Torpedo juice," 88
Trent, Thomas, 264, 286
Truk Island, 96
Truman, Harry, 374
Turner, Frank, 297, 379

U
Undersea Victory (Holmes), 351
United States
first submarines of, 15
protocol on merchant shipping, 12
United States Silent Service. *See* Submarines
*United States Submarine Losses World War
II*, 356, 369
Unyo, 322, 326
U.S. Navy. *See also* specific personnel,
submarines in
and *Gudgeon's* disappearance, 356, 369
and torpedo juice, 88–89
U.S. Submarine Attacks During World War II
(Alden), 422
USS *Albacore*, 362
USS *Archerfish*, 390
USS *Argonaut*, 22, 193–94, 195
USS *Arizona*, 2
USS *Barbel*, 379
USS *Barbero*, 403–4
USS *Blackhawk*, 30
USS *Boarfish*, 383
USS *Bonefish*, 379
USS *Cachalot*, 79
USS *California*, 91
USS *Cisco*, 362
USS *Cuttlefish*, 79
USS *Darter*, 389
USS *Dolphin*, 79
USS *Escolar*, 379
USS *Excolar*, 402–3
USS *Flier*, 378
USS *Flying Fish*, 79
USS *Gar*, 14, 233–34, 373, 398
patrols of, 50, 196, 215
treatment of Japanese, 301–2
USS *Gato*, 79, 392
USS *Grampus*, 373
loss of, 233
patrols of, 50, 51
USS *Grayback*, 14, 233–34, 373
patrol of, 50
USS *Grayling*, 14, 233–34, 373, 398
at Midway, 79
patrols of, 96
USS *Grenadier*, xv, 14, 373
captivity of crew, 234–35, 240, 380
loss of, 233–34
at Midway, 79
patrols of, 50, 51, 96
USS *Grouper*, 79